What Every Special Educator Must Know and Be Able to Do

3.2 Beginning special education professionals understand and use general and specialized content knowledge for teaching across curricular content areas to individualize learning for individuals with exceptionalities.

3.3 Beginning special education professionals modify general and specialized curricula to make them accessible to individuals with exceptionalities.

Standard 4 Assessment

Beginning special education professionals use multiple methods of assessment and data sources in making educational decisions.

4.1 Beginning special education professionals select and use technically sound formal and informal assessments that minimize bias.

4.2 Beginning special education professionals use knowledge of measurement principles and practices to interpret assessment results and guide educational decisions for individuals with exceptionalities.

4.3 Beginning special education professionals, in collaboration with colleagues and families, use multiple types of assessment information in making decisions about individuals with exceptionalities.

4.4 Beginning special education professionals engage individuals with exceptionalities to work toward quality learning and performance and provide feedback to guide them.

Standard 5 Instructional Planning and Strategies

Beginning special education professionals select, adapt, and use a repertoire of evidence-based instructional strategies to advance learning of individuals with exceptionalities.

5.1 Beginning special education professionals consider an individual's abilities, interests, learning environments, and cultural and linguistic factors in the selection, development, and adaptation of learning experiences for individual with exceptionalities.

5.2 Beginning special education professionals use technologies to support instructional assessment, planning, and delivery for individuals with exceptionalities.

5.3 Beginning special education professionals are familiar with augmentative and alternative communication systems and a variety of assistive technologies to support the communication and learning of individuals with exceptionalities.

5.4 Beginning special education professionals use strategies to enhance the language development and communication skills of individuals with exceptionalities.

5.5 Beginning special education professionals develop and implement a variety of education and transition plans for individuals with exceptionalities across a wide range of settings and different learning experiences in collaboration with individuals, families, and teams.

5.6 Beginning special education professionals teach to mastery and promote generalization of learning.

5.7 Beginning special education professionals teach cross-disciplinary knowledge and skills such as critical thinking and problem solving to individuals with exceptionalities.

(Standards continued on back endsheet)

CENGAGE Learning

***Educating Exceptional Children,* Fourteenth Edition**
Samuel Kirk, James Gallagher, Mary Ruth Coleman

Product Manager: Mark Kerr
Content Developer: Kate Scheinman
Content Coordinator: Sean M Cronin
Product Assistant: Julia Catalano
Associate Media Developer: Renee C. Schaaf
Marketing Manager: Kara Kindstrom
Art and Cover Direction: Carolyn Deacy, MPS Limited
Production Management and Composition: Naman Mahisauria, MPS Limited
Manufacturing Planner: Douglas Bertke
Photo Researcher: PMG/Sree Meenakshi R
Text Researcher: PMG/Nandhini Lakshmi Srinivasagopalan
Text and Cover Designer: Lisa Buckley
Cover Image: © Michael Pole/CORBIS

Library of Congress Control Number: 2013957653

ISBN-13: 978-1-285-45134-3

ISBN-10: 1-285-45134-1

Cengage Learning
200 First Stamford Place, 4th Floor
Stamford, CT 06902
USA

Cengage Learning is a leading provider of customized learning solutions with office locations around the globe, including Singapore, the United Kingdom, Australia, Mexico, Brazil, and Japan. Locate your local office at **www.cengage.com/global**.

Cengage Learning products are represented in Canada by Nelson Education, Ltd.

To learn more about Cengage Learning Solutions, visit **www.cengage.com**

Purchase any of our products at your local college store or at our preferred online store **www.cengagebrain.com**

Printed in the United States of America
2 3 4 5 6 7 18 17 16 15 14

14th EDITION

Educating Exceptional Children

Samuel Kirk
Late of University of Arizona

James Gallagher
University of North Carolina at Chapel Hill

Mary Ruth Coleman
University of North Carolina at Chapel Hill

CENGAGE Learning

Australia • Brazil • Japan • Korea • Mexico • Singapore • Spain • United Kingdom • United States

Honoring the Memory and Celebrating the Life of James J. Gallagher

FPG Child Development Institute

Dr. James J. Gallagher, senior author of *Educating Exceptional Children,* died on Friday, January 17, 2014 at the age of 87 in Chapel Hill, NC. Dr. Gallagher made numerous vital contributions to educational policy on state, national, and international levels. From 1967 to 1970, he served as the U.S. Associate Commissioner for Education and was the first Chief of the Bureau of Education for the Handicapped in the U.S. Office of Education. In that capacity he outlined the components of the first Handicapped Children's Early Education Assistance Act, beginning a national program of model projects that changed the nature of special education for young children with disabilities. He subsequently served as the Deputy Assistant Secretary for Planning, Research, and Evaluation for the Department of Health, Education, and Welfare (HEW).

He contributed to groundbreaking efforts to establish federal policy for gifted and talented students, including *The Marland Report* and *National Excellence: A Case for Developing America's Talent.* During his career, Dr. Gallagher served as president of the Council for Exceptional Children, the National Association for Gifted Children, and the World Council for Gifted and Talented Children.

Dr. Gallagher was a pragmatic visionary. He saw what could be, what should be. He saw the vision of educational excellence for all children, and he devoted his life to making this a reality.

- He realized that the complex needs of a child with disabilities would require a unique educational response and the IEP (Individualized Education Plan) was born.
- He understood that a prepared workforce of teachers would be critical to students' success and he wrote textbooks and created model demonstration sites.
- He knew that families were key to supporting child development and he advocated family friendly practices.
- He believed that gifts and talents existed across all cultural and economic groups and he advanced appropriate policies for identification and services.
- He saw that a strong infrastructure was critical for sustaining positive changes and he developed a technical assistance model of support.

From 1970 to 1987, Dr. Gallagher served as the Director of the Frank Porter Graham Child Development Institute at the University of North Carolina at Chapel Hill, one of the leading institutes dedicated to research in early childhood education. He was

FPG Child Development Institute

a researcher on the Abecedarian Project, one of the first scientific studies to demonstrate important long-lasting benefits in academic performance in a cohort of children from lower socioeconomic circumstances. During his tenure, he served as Director of the Carolina Institute for Child and Family Policy.

Dr. Gallagher published over 200 journal articles and 39 books. He has been the recipient of numerous national and international awards, including the *Gold Medal of the American Psychological Association for Psychology in the Public Interest*, the *John Fogarty Award for Distinguished Government Service*, and the *Old North State Award* (the premier award for public service bestowed by the state of North Carolina). Other awards include the *Distinguished Scholar* and *Distinguished Service* Awards from the National Association for Gifted Children, the *J. E. Wallace Wallin Award for Contributions to Special Education* from the Council on Exceptional Children, the *North Carolina Department of Education Lifetime Award for Exceptional Service,* and the *Peabody Award* from the University of North Carolina School of Education.

Special and gifted education exist as we know them today to a large extent because of Dr. Gallagher.

Brief Contents

Contents

2 Children with Exceptionalities and Social Institutions: Government, Courts and Schools 31

MR Bob Daemmrich/The Image Works

PART TWO High-Incidence Exceptionalities 64

3 Early Intervention Supports and Services 65

nandana de silva/Alamy

4 Children with Intellectual and Developmental Disabilities 105

© dotshock/Shutterstock.com

Flossie & the Fox

9 Children with Communication, Language, and Speech Disorders 283

Elizabeth Crews/The Image Works

10 Children Who Have Special Gifts and Talents 317

Bob Daemmrich/The Image Works

Ellen B. Senisi/The Image Works

12 Children with Visual Impairments 387

Mitch Wojnarowicz/The Image Works

13 Children with Physical Disabilities, Health Impairments, and Multiple Disabilities 419

Dedication

We dedicate this 14th edition of *Educating Exceptional Children* to the memory of Dr. Nicholas Anastasiow, a colleague, a mentor, and a friend.

Dr. Anastasiow was a dedicated teacher and scholar who worked for more than 50 years in the service of children with a focus on early childhood and development. He began his work as an elementary school teacher and also served as a principal. The senior author of this text met Nick Anastasiow when they were both at Stanford University in 1960, and he was impressed by Nick's intelligence, commitment to education, and good humor. Nick received his Ph.D. from Stanford University in 1963 and served as the Director of the Institute of Child Study at the University of Indiana from 1967–79. He was on the faculty of the University of Colorado Medical School and was named the Thomas Hunter Professor of Education at Hunter College in New York City and professor of educational psychology at the Graduate Center of the City University of New York (CUNY). Nick retired from Hunter College in 1992.

Dr. Anastasiow was an influential member of the Division for Early Childhood of the Council for Exceptional Children, and he served as its president in 1976. He was devoted to his students, encouraging them in the same curiosity and integrity that marked his own professional career.

Dr. Anastasiow was a widely respected researcher and prolific writer, publishing both theoretical works and practical curriculum designs, and was an author of more than 200 articles and books, including *Languages and Reading Strategies for Poverty Children, The At-Risk Infant,* and *Development and Disabilities*.

Nick was coauthor of this textbook, *Educating Exceptional Children,* from the eighth edition in 1998 through the 13th. Nick passed away in 2013. As we prepared this 14th edition, we have missed his insights, guidance, and kind words of support.

James J. Gallagher & Mary Ruth Coleman

Preface

More than fifty years ago, Sam Kirk, a brilliant scientist and educator, penned the first edition of *Educating Exceptional Children*. Since then monumental changes have taken place in our knowledge of these special children and in the educational strategies needed to help them achieve and prosper.

When the first edition of this text was published in the 1960s, the future for children with exceptional learning needs was just beginning to change. Still a decade ahead was the key legislation that promised children with disabilities a "free and appropriate public education" (FAPE). Still further ahead were the numerous court decisions that solidified the educational rights of these children with exceptionalities.

In the first edition of this book, there was no mention of "inclusion" or "positive behavior supports" or "common core state standards" or "mirror neurons" or "DNA." The brain, so central a concern of ours today, was treated as a black box where stimuli went in and responses came out. We had little understanding of what went on inside. The predominant educational strategy for children with serious losses in hearing, vision, or intellect was to isolate them in large residential institutions far away from family and ordinary schools.

We have learned a great deal since that time. As we learn more, we write new editions of this textbook that reflect the most current theory and research about special education, the increased sophistication of our educational strategies, and the most recent changes in public policies for exceptional students.

What's New in the 14th Edition?

As our knowledge about children with exceptionalities, their families, and their schooling expands, we add new emphases to each new edition of the text. In this 14th edition, we have updated each chapter with current research and best practices.

The Council for Exceptional Children's professional standards for new teachers are addressed within each chapter. You will see a note at the beginning of each chapter with the CEC icon that reminds you to check the standards that appear on the inside book covers.

CEC

We have incorporated new information from the recently released *Diagnostic and Statistical Manual of Mental Disorders (DSM-5)*, and we emphasize access for *all* students to common core standards. Throughout each chapter we follow four themes:

- The Earlier, the Better
- Intensity and Duration
- Teaching to Strengths
- Education is a Team Game.

These themes are discussed in the Introduction section that follows this preface. Specifically, we address several areas worthy of additional consideration due to the progress that has been made in these special fields.

The Common Core State Standards

The Common Core State Standards (CCSS) were assembled at the request of the National Governors Association and the Council of Chief State School Officers so that students would have a common set of standards throughout the country in K-12 language arts and mathematics. These standards were largely drawn from existing standards in individual states. The standards form a guide for the curriculum and instruction of each student. In this text we explore the impact of these standards on children with exceptionalities. We explore the challenges of honoring the child's IEP while ensuring that he or she has the opportunity to learn the common core. We discuss the importance of ensuring that, while accessing the CCSS, students continue to receive support in the expanded curriculum areas when needed (e.g., learning Braille, mobility skills, and/or functional life skills). We look at the special needs of children with severe disabilities and the role of the team in designing alternative learning standards that are aligned with the CCSS. In Chapters 3–13, we include a section showing how Universal Design for Learning strategies can be used to give students with exceptionalities access to the CCSS. These sections are highlighted with a special icon to call attention to their importance. There are concerns voiced in individual states about the standards but it appears that some version of these standards will be implemented by the majority of the states.

Text Coverage of Diversity Issues and Disproportionate Representation

Disproportionate representation of culturally and linguistically different, and economically disadvantaged, children within special and gifted education is a complex and persistent challenge. Within special education we see an overrepresentation of African American, Hispanic, and American Indian children. This pattern is reversed within gifted education, where these children are markedly underrepresented. Poverty, while certainly contributing to these patterns, does not fully explain them. In other words, ethnicity, language, culture, and gender all make unique contributions to the patterns of disproportionate representation that poverty alone cannot account for.

While we must make sure that all children who need supports and services receive them, we also must be sure that childrens' strengths and needs are appropriately identified. Throughout this text, we have examined these developmental patterns across areas of exceptionality. Within each chapter, we address the specific issues related to appropriate identification and services to address children's needs. We discuss the social as well as educational consequences of policies and practices. We also explore the role of culturally inclusive curriculum and family-centered approaches to create culturally responsive services for all children. Because we have integrated this content within each chapter, throughout the book we have placed a special icon showing where this important information is located within each chapter.

- Chapters 1 and 2 look at families and the social impact of culture, language, and poverty.
- Chapter 3 examines family-centered interventions and culturally resonant practice in early intervention.
- Chapter 4 explores the social implication of identification for children with intellectual and developmental disabilities, along with a discussion of the use of measurement data in decision making.
- Chapter 5 discusses the dramatic increase of identification of children with autism in our society. We also note gender differences—four times as many boys are identified with autism spectrum disorder as compared with girls.
- Chapter 6 explores the increasing identification of Latino youth as learning disabled and raises questions about the impact of language differences on identification.

- Chapter 7 examines the differences in identification and treatment for children of color and poverty within ADHD, looking at the disparity in access to medical interventions.
- Chapter 8 examines the role of cultural perspectives in defining emotional and behavioral disorders, and the importance of cultural competence for appropriate identification and support.
- In Chapter 9, we discuss the critical importance of understanding a child's cultural and linguistic background in assessing communication, language, and speech disorders, along with typical language development patterns for bilingual children.
- Chapter 10 addresses the disproportionate underrepresentation of children of color and poverty in services for gifted learners, and offers examples of programs that have addressed these challenges.
- Chapter 11 explores the impact of Deaf culture on children and families, and the need for bilingual/bicultural approaches to understanding the needs of children with hearing impairments.
- Chapter 12 addresses the multicultural needs of children with visual impairments and their families.
- In Chapter 13, we focus on honoring differences, while recognizing the shared nature of humanity, as we address the needs of children with physical, health-related, and multiple or severe disabilities.

Throughout the text, we also focus on the RtI approach to addressing students' needs. We believe that this multitiered model holds promise for providing early supports to address children's diverse strengths and needs, and that through early intervention we can place all children on pathways for success.

New Chapter on Attention Deficit/ Hyperactive Disorders (ADHD)

The 14th edition includes a new chapter (7) focused on children with attention deficit hyperactive disorders (ADHD). We have chosen to add this chapter to highlight the specific needs of children who can be found in significant numbers within our schools. Supports and services for children with ADHD often include medical interventions, and in this chapter the role of the multidisciplinary team is discussed in detail. Since ADHD is a neurological condition that can and does appear with a variety of other exceptionalities (such as learning disabilities, autism, behavior disorders, and intellectual disabilities), we also address these *comorbidities* and the difficulty this can create in identification. ADHD also affects a child's ability to effectively process information; we offer several educational strategies to help students learn. We are excited about this new chapter!

The Information Processing Model

In this 14th edition, we continue to emphasize the information processing model (IPM) as it relates to the education of exceptional children. Our IPM visually illustrates how each area of exceptionality impacts an individual's ability to learn. In each chapter, the information processing model graphically outlines the key elements of information reception (input), thinking (central processing), and expression (output), as well as showing how the executive function interacts with each of these—all within the context of emotion. Understanding how a child processes information allows educators to adapt learning environments, teaching strategies, and curriculum to address the child's strengths and needs. Further, the IPM describes how decision making takes place through what we call the executive function. The executive function determines what we attend to, what mental processes are used to solve problems, and which of the many ways we have of acting on information. Finally, the IPM includes an emotional context that influences how we take in information, think about it, and act on it. For more detailed information about the IPM, please see the introduction that follows this preface, and note the appearance of the IPM in each chapter of the text.

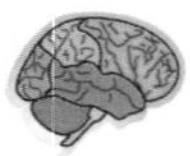

Special Coverage of Neurology and Genetics

Two rapidly developing scientific fields, neurology and genetics, are dramatically changing our understanding of the development of children with special needs. Tools such as magnetic resonance imaging (MRI) and the results of the Human Genome Project have allowed us to peer into the brain's function and begin to understand the very building blocks of life: our genes and chromosomes. There have probably been more discoveries regarding brain function in the past two decades than in all previous history put together. We no longer think it unusual to ask the neurologist what is going on in the brain when a child solves the simple problem 2 + 2 = 4 or when a child imitates an adult bouncing a ball or mimics her mother in saying "ma-ma."

For many children and families, it is more important to understand what is happening neurologically when the child is *unable* to imitate the behaviors of others easily, as is the case for some children with autism. Our understanding of neurology can help us learn how we can counteract these difficulties. A special section in each chapter will bring readers up to date on current neurological findings related to children with exceptionalities. This section will be highlighted with an icon to mark its importance.

Great advances have also been made in the science of genetics. While we have long been aware of how children physically resemble their parents, now we can begin to develop a portrait of their genetic similarities. Looking at the relationship of genetics to exceptionalities, we can see the impact of genetic differences, and we can counsel parents regarding potential risk factors.

While we know that genetics does not predetermine the future of children and adults, we are nevertheless aware that genes can influence a child's development in various ways. Genetics can influence tendencies toward aggressiveness, hyperactivity, or social isolation. The progressive and sequential interactions between genetic traits and the environmental envelope surrounding the child remain a rich field to explore. In each chapter, we summarize key genetic information for each of the various exceptionalities under discussion.

Focus on Early Childhood and Early Intervention

In the not-too-distant past, we became aware of special developmental problems in children only when children appeared at the schoolhouse door at age five or six. While this age may seem young to us, it is, in fact, quite late in children's development if we wish to enhance their chances for optimal educational success. Early intervention and support, beginning at birth, can significantly improve the success of a child with special needs. Conversely, a failure to respond in the early years can prolong major difficulties—as when a child with serious hearing problems has difficulty in language development or a child with special learning disabilities is prevented from learning the phonics necessary for her to read.

The early years are so important to the development of exceptional children that we have not only devoted a full chapter to early intervention (Chapter 3), we also discuss this in each chapter; looking at the years from birth onward that are so crucial because if we intervene with appropriate supports and services we increase the child's chances for success.

Coverage of Inclusion in Every Chapter

One of the consistent themes of modern special education is the desire to address the needs of children with exceptionalities within the general education classroom and school. Inclusion rests on the firm belief that children with exceptionalities should be *a part of,* not *apart from,* the general population. This issue has been underscored with the adoption of the common core curriculum and the requirement that *all* students participate to the greatest extent possible in both the learning of and assessments for these standards. A discussion of strategies needed for full inclusion of children with exceptionalities is now part of each chapter. We also realize that for some children, the least restrictive environment means that a different therapeutic approach may be needed, and so we also discuss the continuum of supports and services that must be in place to ensure that all students can meet with success.

Continued Emphasis on the RtI Model

RtI

One educational strategy that integrates both general and special education, providing a framework for inclusion, is the response to intervention (RtI) model. The illusion of two separate groups of children ("regular" and "special") has been created by laws designed to aid children with exceptionalities. One unintended consequence of these laws has been an overemphasis on eligibility for special education rather than a focus on meeting children's individual needs through educational problem solving. Many children who do not qualify for special education have trouble learning in school and need additional support to meet with success. Many children who are not eligible for gifted education have strengths that should be enhanced and nurtured. RtI, a multitier approach to supports and services, addresses the strengths and needs of the children who fall between general and special or gifted education. RtI plays a major role in our discussions throughout this text. We believe that this approach, if implemented well, may help address the challenges of disproportionate representation across exceptionalities that we discussed earlier. A special introduction to the RtI model appears in the introduction following this preface, so that students can begin to understand the model and see how it is changing the way we meet the needs of children with exceptionalities.

Increased Coverage of Assistive Technology

Human beings are toolmakers. Whenever there is a particular need (e.g., to create a means of transportation, prepare meals, or educate the young, for example), we devise special tools to make the tasks easier. The education of children with exceptionalities presents special challenges, and these challenges have brought forth a variety of tools. Cochlear implants and monoculars, for example, are two tools that help to minimize the impact of sensory disabilities.

The major tools of recent decades, however, have been computers and alternative/augmentative communication devices. A range of assistive technologies to support children with exceptionalities is discussed in each chapter; showing how, with appropriate support, the challenges of learning and life can be made a bit easier.

Reorganization of the Educational Response Sections

In this 14th edition, we have reorganized the educational responses portion of Chapters 3–13 into two primary sections:

- Organizational structures to support students (with each exceptionality)
- Curriculum and instruction for students (with each exceptionality)

In the organizational structures section we discuss how a continuum of services can be delivered and include examples of the RtI approach using mutitier services. Within the curriculum and instruction section we include an expanded discussion of the use of Universal Design for Learning (UDL) to give students with exceptionalities access to the CCSS.

Each Chapter (3–13) includes a table showing UDL strategies that can be used to modify the curriculum for students. We also cover specific strategies to address the strengths and needs of each population. For example, we address disruptive behaviors through functional behavior assessment and positive behavior supports, and we address ways to enhance learning through the use of problem-based curriculum. The educational responses are highlighted by special shaded pages toward the end of these chapters. They provide a useful overview for preservice educators, clinicians, and individuals already practicing in the field.

Organization of the 14th Edition

This book is divided into three major sections. Part One provides the history and foundations of special education. Part Two deals with high-incidence exceptionalities (those experienced by more than 1 percent of the population). Part Three addresses low-incidence exceptionalities—those experienced by students who make up less than 1 percent of the general population. Although they will appear more rarely in the general classroom, their needs may be even more pressing and demanding of the attention of school personnel. Please refer to the detailed table of contents for more information about text and chapter organization.

Student Learning Features

In each chapter of the 14th edition, we have included evidence-based pedagogical features that are designed to help students master course content. It is our hope that these special text features will also enhance student learning:

- **Chapter-opening focus questions,** numbered and correlated to the main sections in each chapter, provide an overview of the key issues within each chapter. These questions guide readers as they work their way through the chapter. If students can give thoughtful answers to the focus questions, they are well on their way to understanding the needs of children with exceptionalities and their families.
- **Exceptional Lives, Exceptional Stories** boxes offer first-person pieces about exceptional children and their families. These special stories share the insights, perceptions, and wisdom of individuals with exceptionalities and their families, capturing the joys and sometimes the frustrations faced in everyday life.
- **TeachSource Video Connection boxes** feature footage from the classroom to help students relate key chapter content to real-life scenarios. Critical-thinking questions help the student reflect on the content in the video.

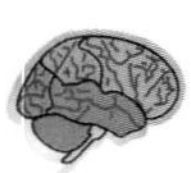

- **Neurology and Brain Development sections** describe how the brain is impacted by the exceptionalities discussed in each chapter. These sections spotlight recent scientific research findings that help us understand the neurological implications for children's learning.

TeachSource Digital Download

- **Digital Downloads** include practical tools appearing in the textbook plus expanded coverage of RtI and UDL materials, for students to access online, often customize, and use to review key concepts and in the classroom! Look for the Digital Download label that identifies these items.

- **Marginal features** such as websites and icons alert the reader to special information throughout the chapter.
- **Educational Responses sections** (located within Chapters 3 through 13) offer practical guidance for future teachers and multidisciplinary teams. These sections address organizational structures for service delivery and teaching and learning strategies across grade levels for each area of exceptionality.
- **Assistive Technology sections** provide information on technologies that can be used to support exceptional individuals with learning and daily life skills. Relevant websites are often included in these boxes because the area of assistive technology is ever emerging!
- **Moral Dilemma boxes** at the very end of each chapter's narrative are brief case studies that offer students a chance to reflect on their own values and beliefs and explore how these will influence them in their work with exceptional children and their families.
- **Chapter-ending summaries** are provided to highlight key themes addressed within the chapter. These summaries should help the reader anchor learning by recapping the major points covered in each chapter.
- **Future Challenges sections,** now also available as digital downloads, discuss the areas we are still wrestling with as the field of special education continues to evolve. These are areas that students may wish to follow up on in future work as they grow professionally. They can also be used by professors for classroom discussion.
- **Relevant Resources** (such as journals, books, and websites) are provided at the end of each chapter to support further learning, and to help students who wish to pursue an area of interest in more depth.

Specific Chapter Revisions in the 14th Edition

We have revised and updated each of the chapters in this 14th edition. Here are the highlights of these chapters:

Chapter 1: Children with Exceptionalities and Their Families

Explored in this chapter are the definition of exceptionalities and the influence of family and siblings on the child with exceptionalities. We also discuss the information processing model, which describes the effect of the exceptionality on the child's learning and adaptation potential, as well as the RtI model, which is a key response of the schools to students with special needs.

Chapter 2: Children with Exceptionalities and Social Institutions: Government, Schools, and the Courts

This chapter presents the social and cultural influences on children with exceptionalities. The predominant influences from society come from the institutions of government, the courts, and the schools. Legislation such as No Child Left Behind is analyzed for its influence on children with exceptionalities, and the latest actions of the courts are noted as well. The influence of schools, and the rules and standards they set, are described so that the reader can gain a perspective on the impact these entities have on children with exceptionalities. We introduce the common core state standards and explore what these mean for children with exceptionalities.

Chapter 3: Early Intervention Supports and Services

Early intervention has seen the rapid development of preschool programs for both exceptional children and children of typical development. The importance of early intervention is now widely accepted by both professionals and the general public. This chapter addresses how early intervention supports and services can meet the needs of young children and their families. Early childhood mental health, inclusion within an RtI framework, and family-centered approaches are focus areas for the chapter.

Chapter 4: Children with Intellectual and Developmental Disabilities (IDD)

This chapter explores the special needs of students in the intellectual and adaptive behavior domains. It also explains reasons for changing the terminology from *mental retardation* to *intellectual and developmental disabilities*. Attention is given to how RtI can be used to cope with the educational and social challenges these students face, strategies for accessing the common core, and a special emphasis on the transition stage from school to community.

Chapter 5: Children with Autism Spectrum Disorders

Autism is the fastest growing disorder in the population of children with special needs. This chapter presents the social and communicative needs of these children. It also details the many recent advances in diagnosis (including the new *DSM-5*) and the array of methods designed to cope with the special social, motor, and learning challenges faced by these students. The reasons for the rapid increase in prevalence are noted together with a major emphasis on early intervention approaches. Specific strategies to support the social and educational success for children with ASD are presented.

Chapter 6: Children with Learning Disabilities

The largest group of children in special education consists of those with learning disabilities. The distinctive nature of the individual's needs creates educational challenges for the teacher. The RtI model stressed in this text emerged out of concern for children with learning disabilities and the shortcomings of historical definitions. An expanded section addresses strategies to support students with learning disabilities in accessing the common core standards successfully.

Chapter 7: Children with Attention Deficit Hyperactive Disorders

This new chapter features a discussion of students with ADHD and the role of the multidisciplinary team in designing and implementing educational and/or medical interventions. We examine the comorbidity of ADHD with other disabilities and discuss the dilemmas presented with identification of strengths and needs. Strategies for learning and coping with ADHD are given. This chapter also addresses the use of UDL to access the common core standards.

Chapter 8: Children with Emotional and Behavior Disorders

Children with pervasive interpersonal challenges and children with deep anxieties and depression are described separately with regard to their identification and treatments. The roles played by positive behavior supports and functional behavioral assessments are emphasized. The information processing and RtI models are presented to show the developmental areas of special concern. We discuss UDL strategies for accessing the common core and explore strategies to help students cope with their challenges.

Chapter 9: Children with Communication, Language, and Speech Disorders

This chapter addresses the needs of children who have communication, language, and speech disorders. In it we examine how the needs of children can be addressed through collaboration within an RtI framework. Special emphasis is given to children with language differences and to children who are bilingual. We also address UDL strategies for supporting students as they access the common core curriculum.

Chapter 10: Children Who Have Special Gifts and Talents

The reasons why these students have substantially been ignored in the educational system are laid out in the debate between equity and excellence as educational goals. The major societal contributions that some of these students make in adulthood are discussed, along with the difficulty and importance of finding students with gifts and talents from culturally and linguistically diverse and/or economically disadvantaged families. A variety of methods, such as educational acceleration and special curriculum interventions (e.g., the International Baccalaureate) are analyzed, and strategies to enhance the common core curriculum standards are given.

Chapter 11: Children Who Are Deaf or Hard of Hearing

The challenges of early language development are discussed together with the need for intense support for communication with young children who are deaf or hard of hearing. New medical and technological advances with cochlear implants are presented along with the need for multiple supports and services. Attention is also devoted to the Deaf culture, bilingual approaches to sign language, and to the need for family support in decision making regarding communication systems. Best practices for supporting academic development and reading have been expanded along with UDL strategies for accessing the common core curriculum.

Chapter 12: Children with Visual Impairments

Students with visual impairments include individuals who can use visual enhancement techniques to learn and individuals who require an expanded core curriculum (including Braille, mobility training, and specially trained teachers) for success. Given the low incidence of students who are blind, the challenges of providing services that are intensive and sustained enough to make a difference are discussed. The Universal Design for Learning is presented along with the advanced technology to give students access to the common core curriculum. The RtI model is part of a full continuum of services.

Chapter 13: Children with Physical Disabilities, Health Impairments, and Multiple or Severe Disabilities

This chapter provides students with an opportunity to reflect on all they have learned about other areas of disability as they focus on students with some of the most intense challenges. Addressing the needs of children with physical, health-related, and multiple or severe disabilities requires a multidisciplinary team; how this team works collaboratively is the focus of much of the chapter. An expanded discussion of the challenges and supports needed for accessing the common core learning and assessments has been included. A new section explores the role of chronic sorrow in the family's journey to cope with their child's disabilities.

Supplemental Materials to Aid Teaching and Learning

This edition offers an expanded and enhanced package of support material for students and instructors:

Student Ancillaries

Cengage Learning's Education CourseMate brings course concepts to life with interactive learning, study, and exam preparation tools that support the printed textbook. Access the eBook, Did You Get It? quizzes, Digital Downloads, TeachSource Videos, flashcards, and more in your Education CourseMate. Go to CengageBrain.com to register or purchase access.

TeachSource Videos

The TeachSource Videos feature footage from the classroom to help students relate key chapter content to real-life scenarios. Critical-thinking questions provide opportunities for in-class or online discussion and reflection.

Instructor Ancillaries

Cengage Learning's Education CourseMate brings course concepts to life with interactive learning, study, and exam preparation tools that support the printed textbook. CourseMate includes the eBook, quizzes, Digital Downloads, TeachSource Videos, flashcards, and more—as well as EngagementTracker, a first-of-its-kind tool that monitors student engagement in the course. The accompanying instructor website, available through login.cengage.com, offers access to password-protected resources such as PowerPoint® lecture slides and the online Instructor's Manual with Test Bank. CourseMate can be bundled with the student text. Contact your Cengage sales representative for information on getting access to CourseMate.

Online Instructor's Manual with Test Bank

An online Instructor's Manual accompanies this book. It contains information to assist the instructor in designing the course, including sample syllabi, discussion questions, teaching and learning activities, field experiences, learning objectives, and additional online resources. For assessment support, the updated test bank includes true/false, multiple-choice, matching, short-answer, and essay questions for each chapter.

PowerPoint® Lecture Slides

These vibrant Microsoft® PowerPoint lecture slides for each chapter assist you with your lecture by providing concept coverage using images, figures, and tables directly from the textbook!

Cengage Learning Testing Powered by Cognero

- Author, edit, and manage test bank content from multiple Cengage Learning solutions.
- Create multiple test versions in an instant.
- Deliver tests from your LMS, your classroom, or wherever you want.

Acknowledgments

The authors would like to acknowledge the following individuals for their support with this work.

First, we would like to thank our spouses, Rani Gallagher and Phil Coleman, for their strong support and willingness to endure our absences and the neglect they have suffered because of our focus on this work.

Second, we thank the team here at FPG. Thanks to Sam Odom, director of the Frank Porter Graham Child Development Institute, whose generous allotments of time, facilities, and space made the production of this edition possible. Thanks to Meredith Sinclair and Dede Addy for their constant attention to detail and steady focus on getting things right. Meredith and Dede kept the project moving forward, taking on the role of assistant editor to help us with all aspects of the work from the smallest to the largest. We owe them a huge debt of gratitude!

We thank Kate Scheinman, development editor, for her dedicated editing of the many drafts and her feedback, which was thoughtful, insightful, and supportive. We appreciate all that you brought to the ideas as they developed.

We also wish to thank the entire Cengage book team Mark Kerr, Sean M Cronin, Kara Kindstrom, Renee C. Schaaf, Jeremy Judson, and Matt Ballantyne—for all of their care and attention to this book and for their patience with us as authors. The strong commitment to excellence that this team showed was a joy to see, and the personal support you offered us was very helpful. We thank the strong editorial team under Naman Mahisauria at MPS Limited who helped to polish the chapters into final form.

We also wish to express special appreciation for the dedicated work of Meredith Sinclair, for her careful work in shaping the ancillary materials that accompany this text. Her attention to detail and dedication to supporting learning are very much appreciated. Special thank you also to Emily King, whose contributions to our new chapter on ADHD helped bring the content to life. Emily, we so appreciate your insights and wisdom!

We owe a special debt to the individuals who provided in-depth reviews for each of the chapters. These outstanding professionals gave of their time, their ideas, and their expertise to help shape the revision and bring the content up to date. Much of what you see in this 14th edition was shaped by their feedback and wisdom. Any errors that you find, however, are the sole responsibility of the authors. We thank our colleagues:

Don Deshler, University of Kansas
Tom Farmer, Penn State University
Veronica Pamparo Fleury, University of North Carolina
Susan Fowler, University of Illinois

Juliet Hart, Arizona State University
Sheldon Horowitz, National Center for Learning Disabilities
Darcy Mitchell, Colby Sawyer College
Nicole Myers, University of Mary Washington
Arnold Nyarambi, East Tennessee State University
Sandra Owen, Cincinnati State University
Diane Plunkett, Fort Hays State University
Ariane Schratter, Maryville College

Finally, we would like to acknowledge the senior author of this text, Dr. Samuel A. Kirk. His vision for this book and for the field of special education continues to guide us. Sam was a true giant in the field of education. He was a scholar, teacher, writer, mentor, policy maker, colleague, and friend. Thousands of children and families who never knew his name have benefited from his work.

In this text, we attempt to capture the changing views of the child with exceptionalities, our changing bodies of knowledge, and the changing education scene. We welcome your comments as this text continues to grow along with the field.

James J. Gallagher
Mary Ruth Coleman

Introduction

The 14th edition of *Educating Exceptional Children* contains several themes and models that are addressed in each of the context chapters (3–13) of this text. We describe them briefly here so that you can familiarize yourself with them and recognize them when they reappear in the chapters.

Themes

- The Earlier, the Better
- Intensity and Duration
- Teaching to Student Strengths
- Education is a Team Game

Models

- Information Processing Model (IPM)
- Response to Intervention (RtI)

As you read each chapter you will see how these themes and models play out; helping us understand children with exceptionalities, their families, and the educators who work to meet their needs.

Themes

The Earlier, The Better

In the early years of special education we adopted a "Wait to Fail" approach and most children had to fail in their general education program before we would attempt to modify it to help them meet with success. When students showed that they were unable to learn under "normal" circumstances they would be referred for assessment and placed in special education—if they qualified. Attempts would then be made to remediate the learning problems of the student. By the time special education services kicked in, many students would have experienced a couple of years of school failure, compounding their original learning challenges and solidifying their learning behaviors into patterns that were difficult to modify.

Since then, a mountain of research has been building on how important the early years are for the development of every child, so the approach we now take in special education has changed. We actively attempt to find youngsters who are in need of supports as early as possible; beginning our interventions in the preschool years or earlier. The result is that many children with early challenges can enter school with the positive attitude and skills they need to meet with success. Early intervention with the needed supports and services will not always "cure" the difficulties, but it will almost always lead to more positive outcomes.

We believe this approach in the early years is so important that we have devoted an entire chapter just to early intervention, or the attempt to find and developmentally enhance the skills of young children with exceptionalities. The public schools are also recognizing the importance of the early years and many have introduced preschool programs, like Head Start. These public preschools allow children to enter school at age four, and sometimes even three; giving them extra years of support prior to kindergarten. When we see a hesitancy to do this in some geographic areas, this reluctance has more to do with economic barriers (how do we pay for this?) than with disagreements about the positive impact of early intervention.

The "earlier the better" principle also comes into play for older students, where we know that if we can recognize and address emerging difficulties we can often prevent secondary problems. If we can, for example, provide early intervention support for a child who is experiencing difficulties with learning to read, we can prevent secondary problems with self-esteem, patterns of acting out, and perhaps dropping out of school. You will see the theme of the "earlier the better" in each chapter and learn how critical early intervention is to helping students with exceptionalities achieve positive outcomes.

Intensity and Duration

The second theme that we follow throughout the chapters is that the intensity and duration of support must be sufficient to address the needs of each student. With each student, the question is "how intense and how long (duration) must the special adaptations be to have a positive impact?" How much effort must we apply to get the growth we want, over what period of time? We know intuitively that five days a week is likely to be better than once a week, and that six weeks is likely better than one week. We know that having one teacher to work with a small group of students will likely have more impact than one teacher for a group of 30. We know these things generally, but how to decide the specific duration and intensity needed for Maria or for Marcus? These decisions must also be made in the context of the limited resources we have available (funds, special personnel, time) to address each student's needs.

There is always the temptation to hold back and use as few resources as possible because of the economics of education. But we have learned that when too few resources are applied, we run the risk of getting no meaningful response at all.

In each chapter we have described programs that have been successful in adapting the program for individual students. In almost every case the successful interventions have been of high intensity and have been delivered over an extended period of time. We realize that we are in the business of trying to modify behavioral patterns that have been established over years and that it takes a major and extended effort to change them, regardless of the nature of the intervention we apply. This is naturally bad news for the administrator trying to apply the scarce resources available to meet seemingly unlimited needs, but it is a fact that we ignore at the peril of the exceptional individuals we serve. If we do not provide supports of a sufficient intensity and duration, our goals for children with exceptionalities cannot be reached. So *intensity* and *duration* are key parts of effective special education programs and we will see how this works for the children we meet across the chapters.

Teaching to Strengths

One increasing trend over the past two decades has been to use the strengths of the child and family as the basis for making progress. This is in direct contrast to the older idea of trying to "repair the child's deficit." This may mean, for example, helping children with hearing losses to find alternative means of communication that use their capabilities (using sign language) and strengths with visual arts, as well as supporting their speech deficiencies and difficulties. It may mean focusing on constructive strategies of learning to read and concentrating on building successful school experiences instead of simply punishing the child who acts out with hostile and aggressive language when he is frustrated with school.

The use of the relatively stronger abilities of the child instead of focusing on the deficient reverses the medical model we have used in the past—that of attacking the illness directly. It is in line with the positive psychology championed by Martin Seligman and others. Positive psychology stresses positive experiences, relationships, and institutions. This philosophy does not aim to replace an emphasis of seeking and eliminating the causes of various disorders, but rather to take advantage of the strengths present in the child and family to build toward success.

This positive approach also recognizes the emotional attitude of the child involved. If we focus on what children have great difficulty doing, we are pointing out their negative aspects and may unintentionally reinforce the children's sense that they are failures and not as worthy as their peers. When that is combined with possible negative comments from peers, the result can be depression and undermine children's willingness to attack the tasks in front of them.

The positive approach recognizes that how children feel about themselves will contribute a great deal to the eventual goal of independence and self-management. Once they feel good about themselves, their motivation to learn new skills and knowledge increases. There are suggestions for teaching to strengths of the child and family in each of the chapters.

Education Is a Team Game

Much of the literature about education has dealt with the teacher-student relationship, of how one person can influence and shape the lives of young people for the better. Such stories are often inspiring and true, but give an incomplete picture of modern education. If we still have that image of that dedicated teacher, let us remind ourselves that we are now asking that teacher:

- to have mastery of curriculum at the level of his or her students
- to assess students' progress in meeting academic goals
- to diagnose learning problems
- to remediate those students who fall behind
- to understand problem behavior and emotional problems and control misbehavior when it occurs
- to plan for tiered assignments to deal with individual differences
- to understand and work well with differences in cultural backgrounds
- to be a good counselor and communicator to parents
- to fit into the bureaucracy of the school faculty and administration.

We can go on, but the impossibility of one human being carrying out these goals should be obvious, particularly when faced with a student body that is diverse in ability, motivation, interests, and backgrounds. What is called for is a *team approach* by professionals, in partnership with families, each of whom brings to the table some unique skills to apply to this impressive collection of responsibilities.

The legally mandated individualized education program (IEP) requires team planning for the exceptional child with a minimum group of a special education teacher, general education teacher, parent, psychologist, principal, and others as needed. This recognizes the need for a team of individuals who can use their special knowledge and skills to devise and carry out the necessary adaptations for the child with exceptionalities. The medical profession has recognized the importance of a team approach to deal with complex problems. Education needs to do the same and organize for collaboration to be an expected part of the special education program (Coleman, Gallagher, & Job, 2012).

COMMON CORE STATE STANDARDS

Common Core State Standards

The adoption of CCSS by 45 states has been a significant recent school reforms. These standards guide the curriculum for *all* students, including students with disabilities. The implementation of a single set of standards is not without challenges as we look at the range of strengths and needs of today's students. In each chapter of the text we explore the impact that the standards are having. We look at how Universal Design for Learning principles can be applied to give students access to the standards. For students with significant cognitive delays, we discuss the tension that can exist between the students' IEP goals for functional living skills and state standards. We reflect on the role of alternative standards for students with severe challenges and how these alternative learning goals should be assessed. In the chapter for students with gifts and talents we include a discussion of how standards can be enhanced to address advanced learners. For students with sensory and mobility challenges we consider the difficulties of addressing extended core curriculum needs (such as Braille, mobility, assistive technology) while still addressing the common core standards. There are no simple answers to many of these issues, so throughout the text we examine the standards and offer suggestions for their use in the education of children with exceptionalities.

Models

The two models used throughout this text are designed to help us keep the complex nature of the learner and the learner's environment in mind. The information processing model (IPM) helps us see the nature of the difficulties the child is experiencing and how these can impact learning. Response to Intervention (RtI) offers a structured approach to address the needs of the child with collaborative supports and services. Both models, discussed below, are used to anchor our understandings of the child and how we can support the child's success.

Information Processing Model (IPM)

Human beings have a complicated system that helps us react effectively to our environment and the necessary tasks within it. When one element of the system experiences difficulties it influences other parts of the system, causing even more difficulties. As we have discovered more about how children learn, how they processes information, we become more impressed with how complex these processes are and how many factors go into making the process work well. In order to capture the complexity of these processes and enable us to keep the whole system in mind, we present an information processing model (IPM) for each area of exceptionality. The IPM within each chapter shows a likely pattern of challenges and strengths for the children with each exceptionality, and more importantly, it also shows us the direction we can take to support the child's success. The major parts of the IPM are shown in Figure 1 and are discussed below.

- INPUT—These are the variety of environmental stimuli that impact on the student. If the means for absorbing these stimuli are blocked or are not functioning (e.g., think about vision being absent) then this will influence all of the other parts of the system.

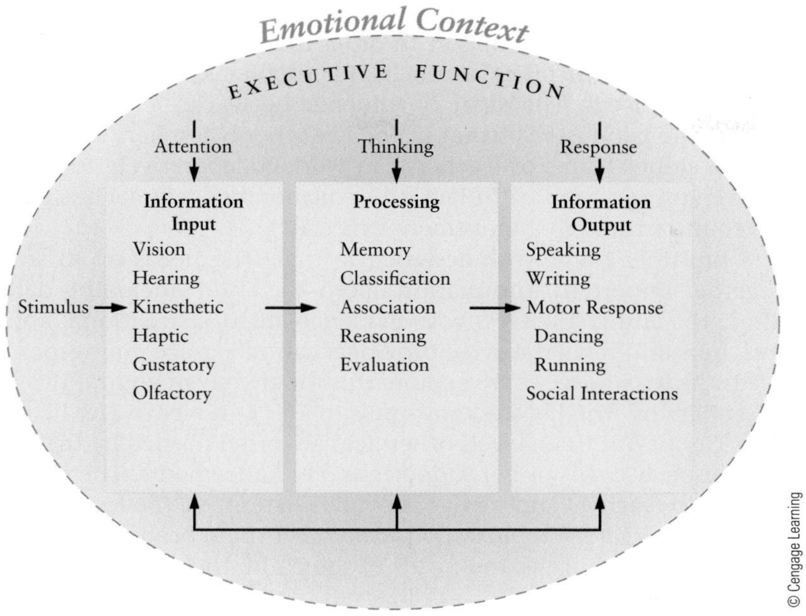

Figure 1 The Information Processing Model

- PROCESSING—These are the elements that allow the student to take new information and transform it for personal use through reasoning, evaluation, or combining with already existing knowledge in their memory. We often call this "thinking."
- OUTPUT—The student then responds to the information in a variety of ways, such as speaking, writing, and participating in social interactions. Again, if any of these processes are impaired the student will experience difficulties.
- EXECUTIVE FUNCTIONING—This is the part of the model that determines what alternatives the student acts upon with the information, it is the *decision-making* part of the model. It determines what we pay attention to, what thinking processes we use and what responses we will make to the information. The inability to make proper use of executive function can be very challenging for students.
- EMOTIONAL CONTEXT—How well we use the rest of the model is dependent in part on the emotional context with which the information is received. Is the student angry or depressed, or worried about family or peer relations? If so it will color all the rest of the model.

Differing parts of the IPM will be shaded to represent the areas of special impact. For example, social interactions will be difficult for children with autism, executive function for children with intellectual and development disabilities, and so forth. These will represent special areas that need to be attended to in planning a program for groups of students, or for the individual student. The rest of the model will also represent strengths that can be responded to. The IPM represents a model to be used in designing the legally mandated individualized education program (IEP), described further in Chapter 2.

The Response to Intervention Model (RtI)

One of the major challenges teachers face in schools today is meeting the wide range of student needs. In any given classroom, teachers will have students who struggle to learn sitting beside students who learn easily. Most classes will have students who have been formally diagnosed with disabilities, and other students who just seem to need more support in order to achieve success. Some students will have emotional difficulties and behavior problems, while others may have social adjustment needs. The range of students' needs can feel overwhelming to a teacher. But the good news is that in today's schools teachers are not expected to do the job alone! Teams of teachers can work collaboratively to address their students' strengths and needs. In fact, this collaborative approach is catching on across the country through a movement called **RtI**.

RtI is a multitier framework designed to meet the needs of all students. It brings together important information about the child (including data on the child's strengths and challenges) with evidence-based instructional approaches, so that teachers and related service providers can recognize and respond to students' needs. As we will see as we explore this for any given child, RtI is not a linear set of services by which a student begins in Tier I, moves to Tier II, and finally is served in Tier III. All three levels of services are often needed by the same child for different aspects of his or her supports and enhancements. The three tiers are designed to help teachers and service providers determine the level of the child's needs in order to organize their responses to meet these needs. Again, remember that the greater the strengths and needs of the child, the more intensive the services must be.

RtI is the approach used throughout this text to describe supports and services for children with exceptionalities. We have chosen RtI as the anchor for this text because it reflects our belief in the collaborative approach needed to meet the needs of today's students. RtI approaches are being implemented in a variety of ways in school districts across the country. While we believe that RtI holds promise for the future, we know that it must continue to evolve through further research and experience in the coming years, and we look forward to this evolution.

RtI Coverage within This Text

RtI

Through this text, when RtI is discussed, you will find a small RtI triangle icon in the margin.

When you see this icon, you may wish to refer back to this introduction to remind yourself what RtI is and to refresh your understanding of the key components of the RtI approach.

Why RtI?

In the past we often created two groups of children, the "regular education children" and the "special education children." This is an artificial dichotomy. There are not two groups of children, there are just children, and many of the children we teach will have special needs. Two major difficulties are created when we divide children into distinct groups:

- Teachers get assigned to one or the other group and often do not pool their expertise to meet the needs of all children.
- The children who are struggling with some aspect of learning, *but who do not meet the eligibility criteria for special education,* often fall through the cracks. getting very little extra help to be successful. Conversely, children who are advanced but do not qualify for gifted education services often get little help address their strengths.

We need a structure that allows us to work together, collaboratively combining resources and expertise to meet the needs of children. The tiered approach to services that RtI offers (see below) provides the structure needed to support the collaboration between general and special education. Tiered supports and services provide a framework for addressing the strengths and needs of children. Using this framework we can provide extra support for children who do not need the intense and full services we provide through special education. We can also provide additional enhancements for children who need them. Tiered supports and services allow us to match the child's strengths and needs with appropriate interventions.

We believe that RtI represents an educational approach that moves us toward a better future, a future where children's needs are addressed by *multidisciplinary teams* (professionals from various domains such as special education, speech pathology, and occupational therapy) working collaboratively to address children's special needs. Resources are focused on meeting children's needs, and families work in partnership with professionals, consistent with the "education is a team game" theme.

Key Components of RtI

RtI can be implemented in many ways, but all RtI approaches share some key components:

- A tiered hierarchy of supports and services
- Comprehensive assessments and progress monitoring used to make informed decisions about a child's strengths and needs
- Standard protocols, drawn from evidence-based practices, for intervention when children need more support
- Problem-solving approaches that include parents to plan supports and services.

Explaining the RtI Model

Figure 2 shows the relationships between each of the key components in the response to intervention (RtI) model. As you look at the RtI triangle carefully, you will see that the shading deepens as you move from the bottom to the top. This shading indicates that the supports and services offered at each tier increase in intensity and duration—with Tier III being the most intense level of service. *The RtI triangle shows that as the intensity of the child's strengths and needs increase, our response to these strengths and needs also increases in intensity.*

- Tier I: Universal supports and services are typically provided in a general education setting for all children. This tier incorporates universal screening to detect if children need any additional support or enhancement to meet with success, and progress monitoring to ensure that the support being provided is appropriate for the child. Progress monitoring is critical because it allows educators to see very quickly when a child needs additional supports and

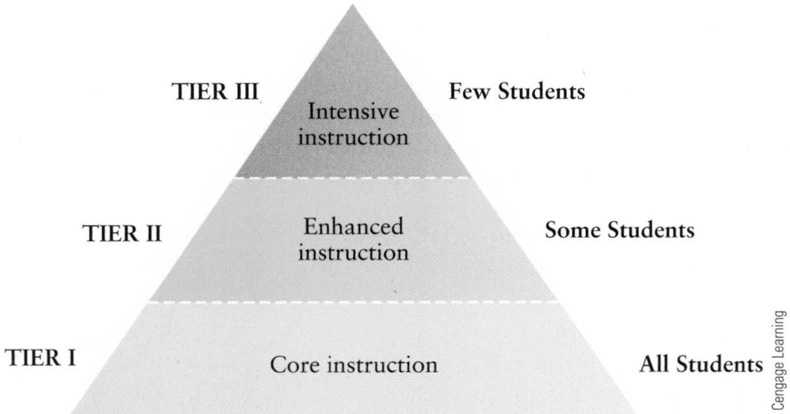

Figure 2 Visual Representation of the RtI Model

enhancements to achieve success. For children who need more support, we can move to Tier II.

- Tier II: Targeted supports and services are provided collaboratively, drawing on general and special educational resources, and additional personnel when needed. A full implementation of Tier II will likely require additional personnel. In Tier II, the supports and enhancements become more targeted and they are based on the documented strengths and needs of the children. These services may include more intensive and explicit instruction or more rigorous and challenging curriculum provided in smaller groups, and will often involve more frequent progress monitoring to make sure that learning stays on track. Some children will need even more intensive supports and/or enhancements to meet with success. For these children, Tier III should be considered.
- Tier III: Intensive supports and services are provided to address specific student strengths and needs. These supports and services may include the formal identification of students for special and/or gifted education. Supports and services provided at Tier III are tailored specifically to the child's strengths and needs and typically require individualized educational programming. Most of the children you will meet in this text will receive supports and services at the Tier III level.

You may also notice, as you examine the RtI triangle, that there are dashed lines between each tier. The dashed lines are important because as children develop and as their strengths and needs change, our educational services should also change. You will meet several children in this text and learn through them that our educational supports and services must remain flexible. It is important to note that children with intense needs may be referred for the services provided at Tier III at any time from the other tiers.

The use of a collaborative planning process must also be part of an RtI approach, because this allows a multidisciplinary team to work together to address the child's needs (usually through his IEP). This team should include teachers, related service providers, and parents. Throughout the text, the importance of the multidisciplinary team will be discussed. The importance of the parents or caregivers as members of the multidisciplinary team, described as the family-centered approach, is a cornerstone of special education and is critical to RtI.

Major innovations like the RtI model always bring with them a series of questions in the school system's attempt to implement them. How will the RtI program be administered, and who will be responsible for hiring staff and monitoring the program? This is especially true of Tier II, which is an addition to existing operations. Also, who will pay for the costs of the RtI model, which will likely go beyond existing funding? There are many hardworking educators who are addressing this issue right now, and some form of collaboration between general education and special education is expected. The recognition of the need for such a model to assist students with exceptionalities is almost universal, and we expect the next decade to be one of expanding the existing RtI services.

Taken as a whole, the RtI approach attempts to bring together the best of general and special education to create a bright future for children with exceptionalities.

About the Authors

Samuel Kirk, Ph.D., is the founding author of *Educating Exceptional Children*. He earned his doctorate in clinical psychology from the University of Michigan in 1935, which led to 60 years of work and research. He developed the term "learning disabilities" in the 1960s after years of observation during work with teenagers with IDD in Chicago and a training school in Ann Arbor. President Kennedy named him as the director of the Federal Office of Education's Division of Handicapped Children, and Dr. Kirk was instrumental in convincing the government to provide funding for training teachers to work with students with special needs. He was also the founding director of the Institute for Research on Exceptional Children at the University of Illinois. He ended his career at the University of Arizona.

James J. Gallagher, Ph.D., is a senior scientist emeritus and former director of FPG Child Development Institute, which he has been affiliated with since 1970. Dr. Gallagher served on Governor James B. Hunt's planning team to develop the North Carolina School for Science and Mathematics. Prior to joining FPG, Dr. Gallagher was the first Chief of the Bureau of Education for the Handicapped in the U.S. Office of Education. He oversaw a wide range of new legislation representing the first major thrust by the federal government to help children with disabilities. The Bureau was the leader in helping to implement laws that provided funds for research, personnel preparation, technical assistance, regional resource centers, centers for media development, and state grants to help with the education of children with disabilities. He was promoted to Deputy Assistant Secretary for Planning, Research, and Evaluation during the tenure of Commissioner Jim Allen. Dr. Gallagher also served as the assistant director of the Institute for Research on Exceptional Children at the University of Illinois at Champaign-Urbana. Dr. Gallagher has produced over 200 articles in a wide range of professional journals. He has also authored and edited a number of book chapters and books.

Mary Ruth Coleman, Ph.D., is a senior scientist at the FPG Child Development Institute at the University of North Carolina at Chapel Hill and a research associate professor in the School of Education. She directed Project U-STARS~PLUS (Using Science, Talents, and Abilities to Recognize Students~Promoting Learning in Under-served Students), and Project ACCESS (Achievement in Content and Curriculum for Every Student's Success). She was the coprincipal investigator for the Early Learning Disabilities Initiative sponsored by the Emily Hall Tremaine Foundation. She has served three terms on the board of directors for the Association for the Gifted (TAG), one of which she was president; three terms on the board of the National Association for Gifted Children (NAGC); and two terms on the board of directors for the Council for Exceptional Children (CEC). She was president of the Council in 2007.

PART 1

Introduction, History, and Social Forces in Special Education

CHAPTER

1

Children with Exceptionalities and Their Families

Standards Addressed in This Chapter

CEC

All of the CEC Standards are addressed in this chapter. Please see the inside book covers for the complete list of the standards.

FOCUS QUESTIONS

1-1 Who is the child with exceptionalities?

1-2 Why is early identification of children with exceptionalities so important?

1-3 What are some of the major causes of exceptionalities?

1-4 How many children with exceptionalities are there?

1-5 How does the child with exceptionalities affect the immediate family—the parents and the siblings?

1-6 How do cultural differences in families affect children with exceptionalities?

1-7 What challenges do students with exceptionalities face as they transition to life beyond school?

The main goal of this book is to introduce you to children with exceptional educational needs. Throughout the chapters, you will come to know and understand many children, learning the most effective ways to support and educate them. Whether you plan to teach in general education, teach in special education, or specialize in speech pathology, school psychology, or educational administration, you will meet children with exceptionalities every day.

In this first section, we begin with a look at who **children with exceptionalities** are. We will review the rich history of special education over the past five decades, and we will learn about the social forces that have played a significant role in establishing special education in the schools. In Chapter 1, we focus on children with exceptionalities, their families, and the social environments that surround them. In Chapter 2, we explore the impact of three major social institutions on children with exceptionalities: the government, the courts, and the public schools.

It's not easy being different. We have all felt the sting of not belonging, of not feeling a part of the group. We have all felt overwhelmed when asked to do things beyond our skills and capabilities, and bored when asked to do simple things that do not challenge us. Of course, being different is not always negative: It is what makes us interesting people.

But it also means we may have to adapt to social expectations that are often designed for the person who is "typical." When being different means that a child is not able to receive information through the normal senses; is not able to express thoughts, needs, and feelings; or processes information differently, special adaptations in the education program are necessary. All children need and deserve an educational environment where they belong and where their differences are addressed and honored. This book will provide you with important information about how schools and communities can support individuals with special needs across a variety of environments to ensure that being different does not mean being left out!

1-1 The Child with Exceptionalities: An Overview

Who is the child with exceptionalities? The term *exceptional* is generally used to include both the child with developmental disabilities and the child with gifts or talents. Here we define a child with exceptionalities as a child who differs from the typical child in (1) mental characteristics, (2) sensory abilities, (3) communication abilities, (4) behavior and emotional development, and/or (5) physical characteristics (these areas of difference are fully explained in Table 1.1). In exceptional children, these differences occur to such an extent that they require either a modification of school practices or special educational services to develop their unique capabilities.

Of course, this definition is general and raises several questions. What do we mean by "the *typical* child"? How extensive must the differences be for the child to require a special education? What is special education? What role does the environment play in supporting the child? We ask these questions in different forms throughout this text as we discuss each group or category of children with exceptionalities.

Individuals with exceptionalities help us better understand human development. Variation is a natural part of human development; by studying and teaching children who are remarkably different from the norm, we learn about the many ways in which children develop and learn. Through this knowledge, we inform ourselves more thoroughly about the developmental processes of all children. In this way, we develop our teaching skills and strategies for all students. Throughout this book we will meet many children and their families, and we will glimpse a small part of the life they lead. We also come to understand that while an area of difference makes the child unique, the child with exceptionalities is a child first and so shares the same needs as all children.

1-1a Educational Areas of Exceptionalities

If we define a child with exceptionalities as one who differs in some way from a group norm, then many children are exceptional. A child with red hair is "exceptional" if all the other children in the class have black, brown, or blond hair. A child who is a foot taller than his or her peers is "exceptional." But these differences, though interesting to a geneticist, are of little concern to the teacher. Educationally

TABLE 1.1 Disability Categories under IDEA (2004)

The definitions of the specific disability categories are below. These are federal terms and definitions.

1. Autism	A developmental disability significantly affecting verbal and nonverbal communication and social interaction, generally evident before age three, that adversely affects a child's educational performance.
2. Deafness	A hearing impairment so severe that a child is impaired in processing linguistic information through hearing, with or without amplification, that adversely affects a child's educational performance.
3. Emotional Disturbance	A condition exhibiting one or more of the following characteristics over a long period of time and to a marked degree that adversely affects a child's educational performance: **a.** An inability to learn that cannot be explained by intellectual, sensory, or health factors. **b.** An inability to build or maintain satisfactory interpersonal relationships with peers and teachers. **c.** Inappropriate types of behavior or feelings under normal circumstances. **d.** A general pervasive mood of unhappiness or depression. **e.** A tendency to develop physical symptoms or fears associated with personal or school problems. The term includes schizophrenia. The term does not apply to children who are socially maladjusted, unless it is determined that they have an emotional disturbance.
4. Hearing Impairment	An impairment in hearing, whether permanent or fluctuating, that adversely affects a child's educational performance but is not included under the definition of *deafness*.
5. Intellectual and Developmental Disability (formerly known as Mental Retardation)	Significantly subaverage general intellectual functioning, existing concurrently [at the same time] with deficits in adaptive behavior and manifested during the developmental period, that adversely affects a child's educational performance.
6. Multiple Disabilities	Concomitant [simultaneous] impairments (such as intellectual disability–blindness, intellectual disability–orthopedic impairment, etc.), the combination of which causes such severe educational needs that they cannot be accommodated in a special education program solely for one of the impairments. The term does not include deafblindness.
7. Orthopedic Impairment	A severe skeletal impairment that adversely affects a child's educational performance. The term includes impairments caused by a congenital anomaly, impairments caused by disease (e.g., poliomyelitis, bone tuberculosis), and impairments from other causes (e.g., cerebral palsy, amputations, and fractures or burns that cause contractures).
8. Other Health Impairment	Having limited strength, vitality, or alertness, including a heightened alertness to environmental stimuli, that results in limited alertness with respect to the educational environment: **a.** due to chronic or acute health problems such as asthma, attention-deficit disorder or attention-deficit hyperactivity disorder, diabetes, epilepsy, a heart condition, hemophilia, lead poisoning, leukemia, nephritis, rheumatic fever, sickle cell anemia, and Tourette syndrome; and **b.** adversely affecting a child's educational performance
9. Specific Learning Disability	A disorder in one or more of the basic psychological processes involved in understanding or in using language, spoken or written, that may manifest itself in the imperfect ability to listen, think, speak, read, write, spell, or do mathematical calculations.

(Continued)

TABLE 1.1 Disability Categories under IDEA (2004) (*Continued*)

10. Speech or Language Impairment	A communication disorder such as stuttering, impaired articulation, a language impairment, or a voice impairment that adversely affects a child's educational performance.
11. Traumatic Brain Injury	An acquired injury to the brain caused by an external physical force, resulting in total or partial functional disability or psychosocial impairment, or both, that adversely affects a child's education performance. The term does not apply to brain injuries that are congenital or degenerative, or to brain injuries induced by birth trauma.
12. Visual Impairment Including Blindness	An impairment in vision that, even with correction, adversely affects a child's educational performance. The term includes both partial sight and blindness.

SOURCE: Individuals with Disabilities Education Improvement Act of 2004, Public Law 108–446, U.S. Department of Education, Washington, D.C.

TeachSource Digital Download Access online

speaking, students are not considered "exceptional" unless the educational program needs to be modified to help them be successful. If a child's exceptionalities mean he needs additional support to read or to master learning, or if he is so far ahead that he is bored by what is being taught, or he is unable to adjust to the social needs of the classroom, then special educational methods become necessary.

Kali Nine LLC/E+/Getty Images

There are children with exceptionalities in almost every classroom in the country.

A child with disabilities can be eligible for special education services in thirteen different legal categories, as shown in Table 1.1. These categories are outlined in the Individuals with Disabilities Education Improvement Act (IDEA) of 2004, an important piece of federal legislation (discussed in detail in Chapter 2). The definitions in the table are given in technical language, but they are the best descriptors that we have of these areas of exceptionalities. Through case studies and vignettes in the chapters ahead, we will meet students who live with these disabilities. We will also come to see how we can support each child's success.

You may have noticed that children with special gifts and talents are not included in Table 1.1. This is because federal legislation, which generated this list, does not address children with special gifts and talents. These children do, however, have special needs. They need to escape from boredom with the typical curriculum and be motivated to use their talents to the fullest. Every child has the right to reach his or her potential; for children with special gifts and talents, it is also important to society that we support their unique contributions.

You may also note that attention-deficit hyperactivity disorder (ADHD) is included under Other Health Impairment instead of having a category of its own; Chapter 7 will go into detail explaining this oddity.

1-1b Interindividual and Intraindividual Differences

Children with exceptionalities are different in some ways from other children of the same life age. These differences between children are called **interindividual differences**, and they can present educators with many challenges. What sometimes goes unnoticed is that some students also show substantial intraindividual differences. **Intraindividual differences** are differences that occur within a single child. These differences must be taken into account when planning for the child. For example, Jason, who is 9, has the intelligence of an 11-year-old but the social behavior of a 6-year-old, and so both interindividual and intraindividual differences must be addressed.

It is just as important for teachers to know the child's unique pattern of strengths and challenges as it is to know how the child compares with other children. Understanding a child's intraindividual differences can help us develop individualized approaches to instruction. These approaches are tailored to the strengths and needs of the individual child. One reason for the development of the **individualized education program (IEP)**—we will discuss IEPs throughout the text—is that these intraindividual differences can pose unique patterns of needs that educators must address.

1-1c The Story of Max: A Historical Case Study

Let us now gain some historical perspective about society's treatment of children with special needs. Consider the story of Max, a short, stocky 8-year-old boy who has been diagnosed with autism, a condition that seriously affects his ability to communicate and form relationships with others. He is receiving special services to strengthen his social skills and build his academic achievement. An interesting question, though, is this: What would have happened to Max if he had been born in 1850 or 1900 or 1925 or 1950 or 1975?

In 1850, only a smattering of physicians were interested in children like Max. Two doctors, Jean-Marc Itard and Edouard Seguin, were the first known individuals who tried to teach children with intellectual and developmental delays (which is likely how Max would have been viewed). In all likelihood, Max would have dropped out of school early, if he had had any schooling at all. At this same point in history, several individuals were interested in helping children who were deaf. Thomas Gallaudet and others were experimenting with various models of communication for children with hearing loss. However, this would not have been much help to Max.

In 1900, there were some isolated stirrings within urban communities focused on starting classes for children with disabilities. These, however, would have been unlikely to help Max, who would probably have been called "mentally deficient" if he had received any attention at all.

In 1922, the Council for Exceptional Children (CEC) was founded in order to organize teachers who were working to help children with exceptionalities. A few classes had begun in urban settings, but these still would not have been much help to Max.

In 1950, the post–World War II era saw the beginnings of special programs for children with exceptionalities (in states such as California and Illinois). If Max had been in the right place, he might have received some help in one of these special classrooms.

By 1975, Congress had enacted legislation designed to provide real help for children like Max. The courts were validating parents' claims to a free and appropriate education for their exceptional child. Still, autism was not a well-known disorder, and

Courtesy of the University of Illinois Archives

Dr. Sam Kirk—a key figure in the beginnings and organization of special education, original author of this text, and director of the Institute for Research on Exceptional Children at the University of Illinois, 1948–1966.

TeachSource Video Connection

Watch the video, "Inclusion: Grouping Strategies for the Classroom." In this case, you will see a fifth-grade classroom where a teacher uses small groups to provide appropriate learning opportunities for typical children and for children with special needs. The teacher collaborates with specialists to individualize the lessons focused on a shared topic.

As you watch this video, what do you notice about the collaboration between these teachers? How is the lesson enhanced by having specialists involved?

Watch online

any well-meaning efforts might not have been sufficient for Max's needs.

Today, there is a greater likelihood that Max would be seen by a multidisciplinary team of specialists (neurologists, psychologists, speech pathologists, etc.) who would be aware of his condition and the special adaptations needed to maximize Max's strengths and abilities. The good news is that today Max's opportunities to meet with educational success have greatly increased.

This brief historical overview featuring Max reveals, however, that intentional, organized, and multidisciplinary efforts are a relatively new development for children with disabilities. For good reasons, the medical profession was the first to become interested in children with exceptionalities. Many children with exceptionalities had physical and health problems that brought them to the attention of physicians. The early terminology relating to these exceptionalities was dominated by medical labels, such as *phenylketonuria, Down syndrome, mental deficiency, blindness,* and *deafness.*

The medical community is still deeply involved in the prevention and discovery of causes related to exceptionality. However, even though a disability might have a medical cause, we in education have gradually realized that we are the key professionals who must address the needs created by the unusual and atypical development of children with exceptionalities. Teachers work with and spend the most time with the child every day. Further, enhancing developmental patterns is usually the province of educators, social scientists, and therapists rather than of medical practitioners. For these reasons, education has become the key profession responsible for supporting the child with exceptionalities.

The field of special education received a good amount of attention at the beginning of the twenty-first century. This is due to the fact that during the 1970s, a strong state and federal legislative base for special education was established. A history of favorable court decisions supporting a "free and appropriate public education" (FAPE) for all students also resulted in the establishment of special education practices (see Chapter 2 for more details about FAPE). This interest of the government, the courts, and schools in children with exceptionalities is a clear indication of the general support of the larger society. This support is critical as programs for children with exceptionalities continue to evolve.

RtI

In public education today, a new approach used by teams of school professionals is the **Response to Intervention (RtI)**. As noted in the introduction of this book, the RtI model has three layers or tiers of intervention. Tier I includes classroom-wide changes to incorporate children with exceptionalities into regular programs (with adaptations within the classroom). Tier II provides for targeted intervention for small groups of students requiring special instruction (such as special reading groups). Tier III represents individualized programming for children with special needs and even a totally different school environment. RtI provides educational environments for special education to collaborate with general education to meet the needs of children who need help but who sometimes may not need special education services. Each chapter of this text will spotlight different aspects of the RtI model.

When children have learning problems, the chances are that something has gone wrong with their processing of information. Box 1.1 provides a model for that system, to be used throughout the text, which is used to pinpoint the problem.

BOX 1.1 The Information Processing Model

One way to think about the complex way children learn is by using an **information processing model (IPM).** We will be using an IPM (Figure 1.1) throughout this text to explore the various components of information processing that are impacted by the presence of a disability or exceptionality. Information processing explains how students interact with and respond to the world around them and describes the learning process. First, children receive information from their senses through input (visual, auditory, etc.). Next, they process this information through memory, classification, reasoning, and evaluation abilities. Finally, they respond to information through output, such as speaking, writing, or acting. Students are aided in this processing of information by their *executive function,* or a decision-making ability to choose how to interpret the information and which option to use in response. Information processing takes place within an overall *emotional context* that influences every aspect of the system: input, processing, output, and executive function.

For example, Gloria may hear from her teacher (hearing) about an assignment of a report due on Friday. The assignment is also written on the teacher's handout (seeing). Gloria remembers (memory) what happened the last time she missed an assignment and decides to use her *reasoning* and *evaluative* abilities to create a report. She will go to the library (motor) and prepare to give an oral report (speaking). Finishing the report tends to reduce Gloria's anxiety about her school performance (emotional context).

Special education is often required when a student is unable to process information effectively. The problems of a student may be in the *input* of information (visual, auditory, or other) or the internal *processing* of that information (using memory, reasoning, or evaluation) or in the *output* or response to the information. The *executive function* is the decision-making aspect of the model that helps the student attend to the input by choosing what thinking processes he or she should call upon and deciding how to react. Imagine what happens when the executive function doesn't respond well.

All of this information processing is done within an *emotional context,* which can help or scramble the other components of the model under conditions of stress, anxiety, or lack of self-confidence. In each of the following chapters, we will present the information processing model and show which elements may be impacted by the exceptionality under discussion.

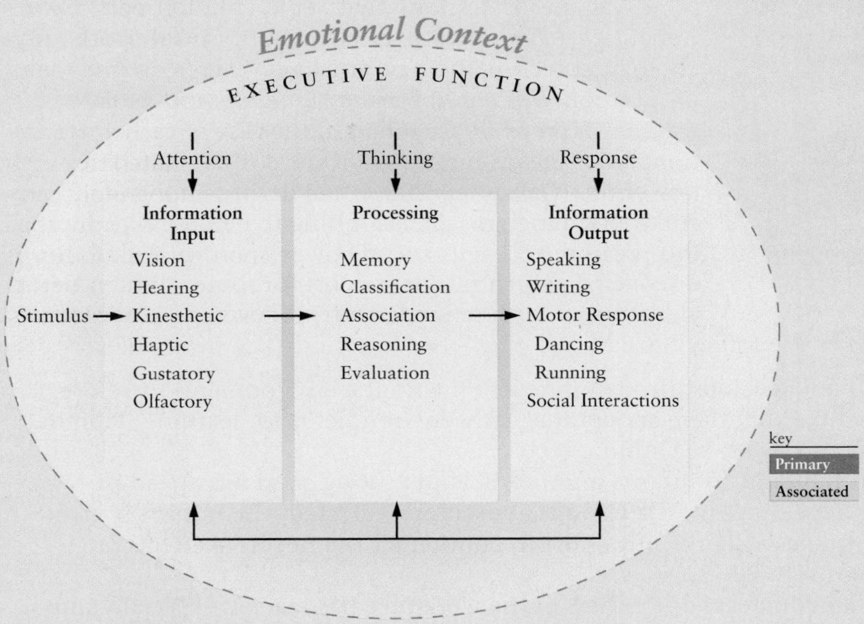

Figure 1.1 Information Processing Model

TeachSource Digital Download Access online

1-2 Early Identification of Children with Exceptionalities

Educators take identification of students with exceptionalities (defined in Table 1.1) quite seriously, because this identification is often the first step to successful interventions. Appropriate identification is important so that we can match supports and services, or interventions, to the child's specific needs. If we know, for example, that a child has a learning disability in reading, we know what interventions should be put in place to support the child. There is also an economic reason for appropriate identification. Children who are formally identified as having disabilities (as defined in Table 1.1) can receive support from specialized personnel. These supports and services are provided through funds from the federal and state governments. Because of this, identification becomes a policy and economic issue—as well as an educational issue.

Until recently, the American public school system was not involved with the education and care of young, preschool-age children. Given their extensive K–12 responsibilities, there was some resistance to public schools taking on the additional responsibilities of prekindergarten programs. Because of this, the needs of the child with special needs from birth to 5 years have historically been in the hands of a wide variety of persons representing a variety of disciplines. Early childhood programs have taken many forms including family day care, center-based care, Head Start, and Title I (Improving the Academic Achievement of the Disadvantaged). Many of these entities can offer early intervention programs to help families who have young children with special developmental problems or disabilities (Cryer & Clifford, 2003).

A disability is not always easily observed by teachers or peers

All of the professions that serve children with exceptionalities (e.g., medicine, education, social work, psychology, speech pathology, and so on) agree on one major proposition: *The earlier the intervention in the developmental sequence of the child, the better.* In the case of early intervention, *better* means more significant positive outcomes with less effort (Gallagher, 2006). Public preschools and early childhood programs are beginning to emerge with increasing pressure to begin treatment as soon as a disability is discovered, which means support for some children begins at birth—well before kindergarten or even prekindergarten.

We know the following:

1. The brain develops through interaction with the environment; therefore, it is essential that there are optimal early environments for learning (Plomin, Defries, Craig, & McGuffin, 2003).
2. What happens to infants and toddlers casts long shadows ahead in their development; if a child is abused or neglected, the impact is great and it takes a significant effort to counteract the negative effects later (Thompson, 2005).
3. The rapid increase of mothers in the workforce has made it especially important to have positive early child care (Haskins, 2007).

Chapter 3 in this text is devoted to young children with exceptionalities, and we will also comment in each chapter on the special issues that involve the preschool child with specific disabilities because we, too, believe that the earlier the intervention begins, the better!

1-3 Causation of Exceptionalities

Each succeeding chapter devotes some space to the many potential causes of the exceptionality discussed. The role of *neurology* and *genetics* is so important to the discussion of causation that it will have a special section within each of the chapters. A discussion of the roles of heredity and environment is central to understanding causation of various kinds of exceptionality.

1-3a The Interaction of Heredity and Environment

Few topics stimulate more fascination than the question of how we become who and what we are. What forces shape our development and sequentially build a confident and complex adult from an apparently helpless infant?

For many decades, we have been aware of the effects that both heredity and environment have on the developing child. Because it is the role of educators to change the environment of the child through instruction, we have often ignored the role of heredity.

But the recent dramatic progress in the field of genetics makes heredity impossible to ignore. Historically, we have been through three major stages in our belief systems about the relative influence of heredity and environment, and each stage has had a profound effect on how we have behaved as educators. Up until about 1960, it was strongly believed that heredity drove and determined various conditions related to intelligence, such as *mild* intellectual disability, giftedness, or mental illness. Our beliefs about the potency of heredity led us to consider it more or less impossible to change a child's condition, and the role of educators was seen as helping individuals adapt as well as possible to their hereditary roll of the dice (Plomin & Petrill, 1997).

Starting around 1960, there was a major movement to stress the important role played by *environment,* recognizing that many exceptionalities can be created or intensified by various environmental conditions. Researchers reasoned that mild developmental disabilities could be caused by lack of early stimulation or that special gifts and talents emerged only because the environment for some children was incredibly favorable. Educators were encouraged to try to find ways to reverse unfavorable environmental effects and to accentuate favorable outcomes through education.

Around 1990, a similar shift in the view of the relative roles of heredity and environment took place. The emphasis was placed on the progressive *interaction of heredity and environment* and the resulting effects of those interactions. Gottlieb (1997) proposed that by changing the environmental conditions of early childhood, we can activate different patterns of genes, which then can result in behavioral changes.

The growing sophistication of genetic research has made it clear that many conditions that lead to exceptionality are linked to an intertwining of genetics and environment. Conditions such as fragile X syndrome, intellectual and developmental disabilities (IDD), attention-deficit hyperactivity disorder (ADHD), and dyslexia all seem to have strong genetic components (McGuffin, Riley, & Plomin, 2001), yet all can be positively influenced by favorable environments.

One of the most dramatic scientific breakthroughs has been made by the Human Genome Project (see ▶ Figure 1.2). The goals of this international project were to determine the complete sequence of the three billion DNA subunits (bases) and to identify all human genes and make them accessible for further biological study (Tartaglia, Hansen, & Hagerman, 2007). The U.S. Department of Energy and the National Institutes of Health were the U.S. sponsors. The initial goals of determining the entire Human Genome were reached in 2003. The many research projects fanning out from these basic discoveries include a number that relate to children with exceptionalities.

Human Genome Project
www.ornl.gov/hgm

As our ability to identify genes has increased, we have become interested in gene-environment interaction. Some of the earlier questions have been oversimplified (such as which gene causes which condition), but we now have a better view of reality reflected in the following understandings:

a. Genes do not control behavior directly.
b. Almost all behavioral traits emerge from complex interactions between multiple genes and environments.
c. The causes of personality and ability are found across complex neural networks—not in a single location in the brain (with the exception of extreme causes of focal brain lesions) (Beauchaine et al., 2008).

In short, we cannot say that genes cause depression or ADHD, but rather that the complex mix of environments and multiple genes can result in some unfavorable

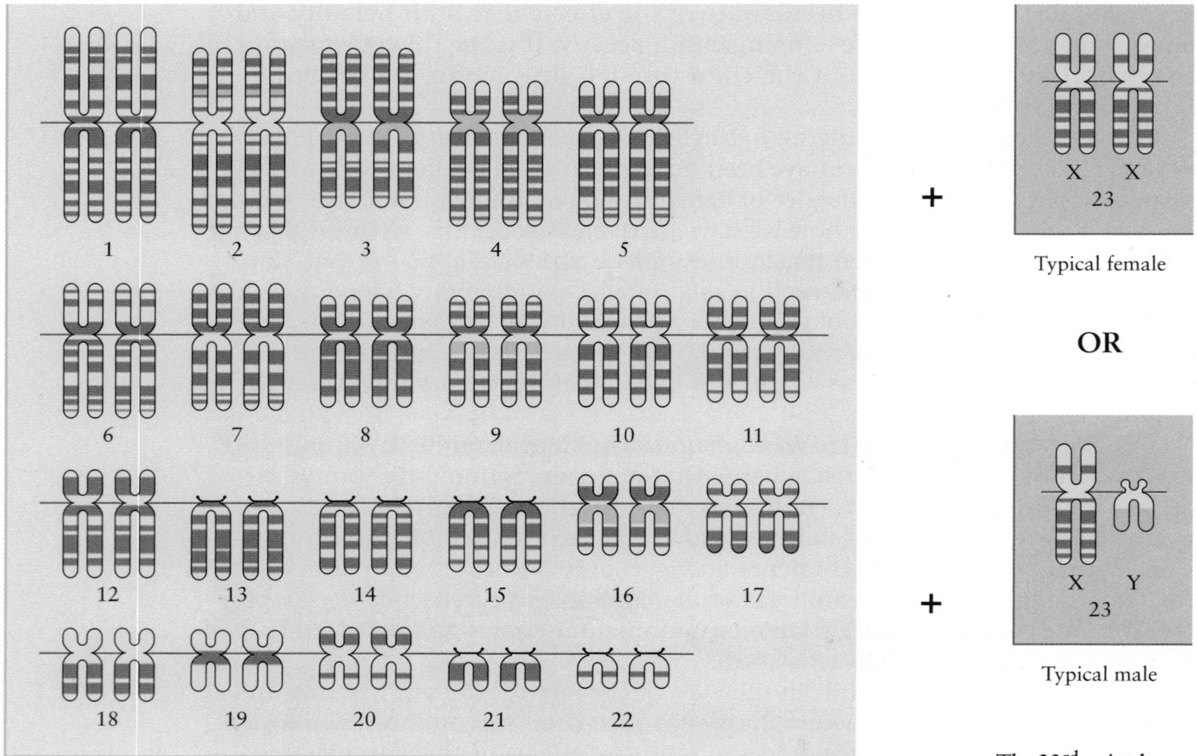

Typical human females and males have 22 chromosome pairs in common.

The 23rd pair, the sex chromosomes, differentiates between females and males.

Figure 1.2 The Human Genome
Source: From FREBERG. Discovering Biological Psychology, 2E. © 2010 Cengage Learning.

outcomes. Since we can do little about the genes, we continue to concentrate on intervening within the environment to improve educational and social outcomes for children (Rutter, 2007).

1-4 Prevalence: How Many Children with Exceptionalities Are There?

There are many persons interested in the answer to this question, including public decision makers, legislators, and even budget analysts. Once we know how many children are in this classification, we will know approximately what the extra cost will be for educating them. What we are not able quantify are the benefits, both human and financial, that will be obtained by providing them opportunities that were denied to past generations of exceptional children.

RtI

The general public appears to look on these categories of exceptional children as "present" or "absent." One either has the condition (autism or learning disability or emotional disturbance) or one does not. In reality, things are not that simple. For example, why do some professionals say that 1 percent of the school population has emotional disturbances while others say that actually 20 percent of the population does? This is a difference of thousands of children (Cullinan, 2004). The answer is that there is a gradual shading (as the colors of the rainbow blend into one another) within every category of exceptionality. The category itself has been formed by establishing an arbitrary cutoff point determined by medical, educational, and psychological professionals who diagnose children with exceptionalities. The children on either side of this arbitrary cutoff point, however, are very similar to one another. This is one important reason for using the RtI approach (described in the Preface) that recognizes that some children falling just outside the line demarcating the need for special education services still need additional supports to perform successfully in academic settings. The tiered approach to supports and services used in RtI can address the needs of children who miss the cut-off points for formal identification but who still need some supports.

A reasonable estimate is that more than six million children in the United States can be classified across the categories of exceptionality (OSEP, 2011). This estimate is obtained by aggregating the reports from the fifty states. This means that approximately one out of about every ten children is *exceptional* (using the definitions in Table 1.1). This is one reason for the extensive attention given to children with exceptionality in our school systems today. Such figures must be considered only estimates. While IDEA 2004 requires educating every identified student, they cannot account for those who have not been identified.

Children with disabilities are not distributed equally across the defined categories—far from it. Figure 1.3 gives a breakdown of the six high-incidence categories of disabilities. The term **high-incidence disabilities** include the categories of disability that are most prevalent—composing at least 1 percent of the school population. The prevalence of children in the gifted category is not included here because special gifts and talents are not included in the federal legislation from which these figures are derived.

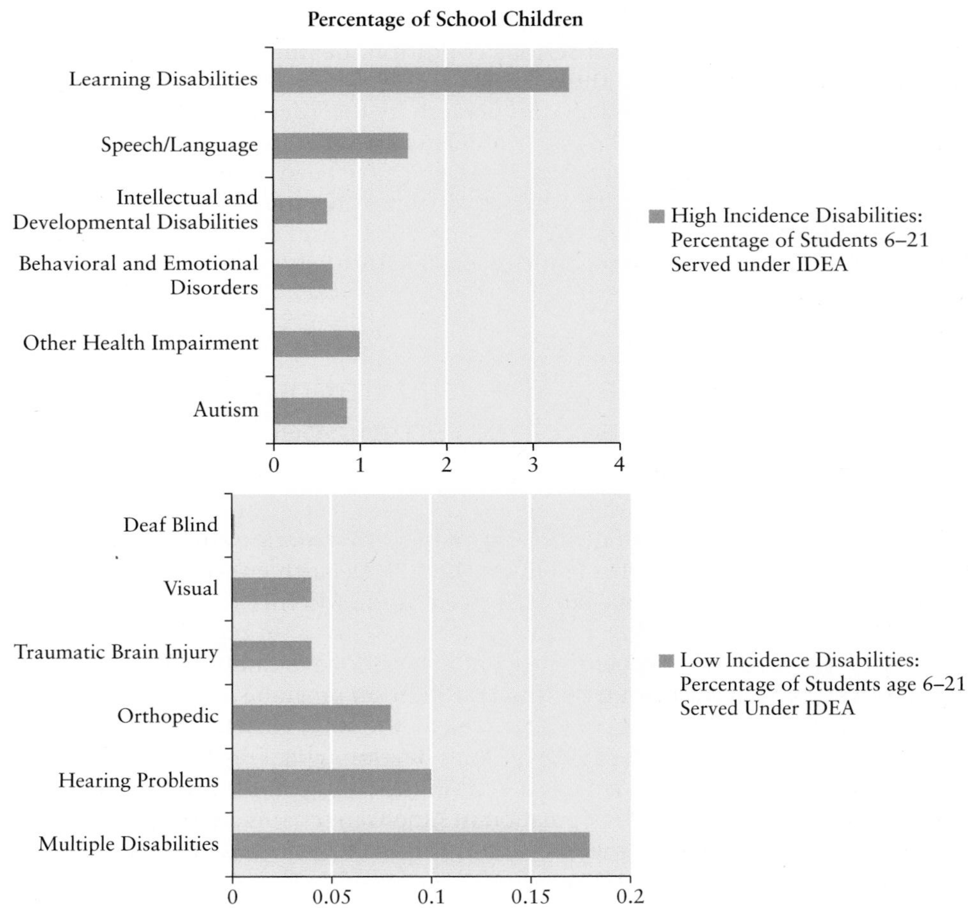

Figure 1.3 Prevalence of High and Low Incidence Disabilities
Source: Data Accountability Center. (2013). *Part B child count (2011)* [data set]. Retrieved from https://www.ideadata.org/arc_toc13.asp#partbLRE

Figure 1.3 represents the number of children reported who are served by the U.S. Department of Education, drawing on reports from the fifty states (Data Accountability Center, 2013). Note that these are the numbers of children *receiving service*—not necessarily *all* of the children in each specific category. There are a number of children with disabilities who are undiagnosed. By far the largest category is that of learning disabilities—3.4 percent, a smaller percentage than in previous years. (Chapter 4 will discuss these figures and their implications.)

About 1.6 percent of children are found in the Speech/Language category, while close to 0.6 percent of children are either identified as having an intellectual or developmental disorder (IDD) or a behavioral and emotional disorder (EBD). The data point that has changed over the years is autism. The actual figure as of 2012 is closer to 1 percent, an increase of three to four times that was assumed ten years ago. This increase in autism spectrum disorder diagnoses has received substantial media attention, and it will be discussed in greater detail in Chapter 5.

Figure 1.3 also provides estimates of prevalence of **low-incidence disabilities**. These are categories that make up less than 1 percent of the school population. Children with these exceptionalities show up only rarely in the general education classroom. Multiple Disabilities is the largest of these categories. The reason for the small percentage (less than 0.5 percent) for visual problems is that although many children wear glasses, this figure only includes children with "uncorrected" vision problems that can interfere with learning. The traumatic brain injury category makes up only about one-half of 1 percent of children. Furthermore, while it is a serious condition, deafblindness in children is extremely rare (only one in a thousand).

The category of attention-deficit hyperactivity disorder (ADHD) has received much attention recently and is now included as a separate chapter (Chapter 7) in this text. The prevalence numbers for ADHD have been included in the Other Health Impaired category in the statistical reporting here. The link between ADHD and learning disabilities and between ADHD and emotional and behavior disorders has been well known; this makes it difficult to provide definitive numbers for this condition.

1-4a Disproportionate Representation of Culturally/Linguistically Diverse Children in Special Education

One specific way in which culture interacts with educational decisions is the overrepresentation of some culturally and linguistically diverse students assigned to special education. The issue of disproportionate representation came to the attention of the Office of Civil Rights (OCR) in the U.S. Department of Education, and OCR mounted a major national survey to determine whether these patterns were valid (Donovan & Cross, 2002).

Figure 1.4 shows the risk percentage or the likelihood of finding a child of a particular racial or ethnic background in special education programs. For example, black students may be twice as likely as white students to find themselves identified for a program serving students with intellectual and developmental disabilities. Note that there are still likely to be more white students in these programs than black students, because the base figures of each population in American schools are so different.

Similarly, Asian students may be one-third as likely to find themselves in a learning disabilities program as black students, as seen in Figure 1.4. And Hispanic students would have about half the chance of being identified for a program serving students who are emotionally disturbed as white students. These risk figures are upsetting to many observers who see racial discrimination at work. While discrimination undoubtedly does occur, an alternative explanation stems from the

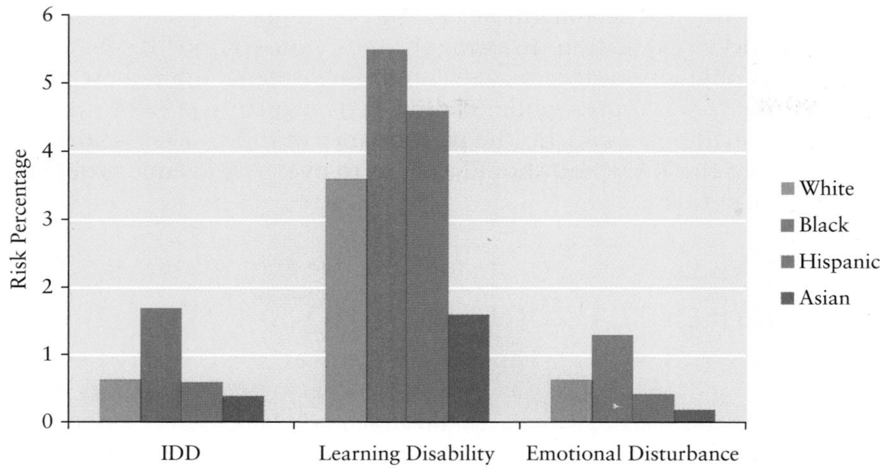

Figure 1.4 National Special Education Risk Percentages by Race/Ethnicity
Source: Reschley, D. (2009). Minority special education disproportionality findings and misconceptions. *Minorities in Special Education.* U.S. Commission on Civil Rights.

data presented in Figure 1.5, showing the results of fourth-grade students' reading proficiency on the National Assessment for Educational Progress (NAEP).

One of the reliable indicators of achievement in our country, the NAEP covers many content areas, is administered across the country, and provides a general picture of student attainment. Figure 1.5 provides a portrait by racial/ethnic background of fourth-grade reading.

- A basic score represents the minimum acceptable score.
- Proficient represents a highly acceptable score for the grade level.
- Advanced denotes clearly superior performance.
- Below basic represents less than adequate performance.

As you can see, the findings are disturbing. While 20 percent of the white population falls below basic, about 50 percent of both the black and Hispanic samples fall below the minimum acceptable performance. Given these figures,

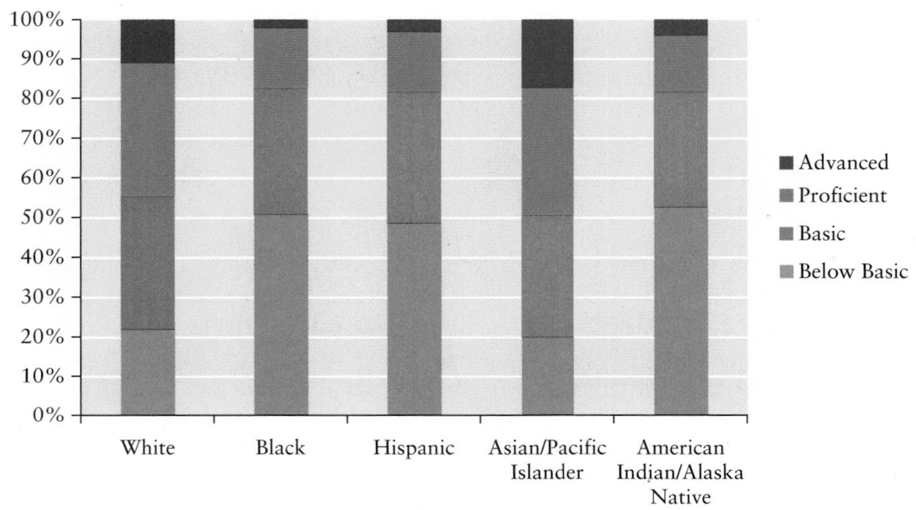

Figure 1.5 Fourth-Grade Reading Proficiency by Race/Ethnicity
Source: U.S. Department of Education, Institute of Education Sciences, National Center for Education Statistics, National Assessment of Educational Progress (NAEP), 2011 Reading Assessment.

it is easy to see why teachers might be referring a number of black and Hispanic children for special education assessment and consideration. It also explains why the Asian population does not get similar treatment, since they are equal or slightly superior in fourth-grade reading performance relative to the white population. These findings mirror the performance of these racial/ethnic groups on other parts of the NAEP and should alert us to overall academic problems for some groups of students.

1-5 The Family System and Exceptional Children

In this section, we will discuss both the positive and challenging components of the family's role for children with exceptionalities.

1-5a Ecology and Exceptional Children

With the recognition of the role of the environment in development, the field moved from a medical model of exceptionality, which assumes that a physical condition or disease exists within a patient, to an ecological model, in which we see the child with exceptionalities in complex interaction with many environmental forces.

The ecological approach tries not only to modify the exceptional child's learning and behavior but also to improve the environment surrounding the child, including the family and the neighborhood—the entire context of the child's life. This ecological approach became the strategy of Head Start and other programs targeted at children from economically disadvantaged families. Head Start pays much attention to the family, in addition to the child (Zigler & Styfco, 2004). The ecological model also helps us understand what we can realistically expect to accomplish through intervention programs.

Increasingly, the approach that educators use to support the child who has milder forms of exceptionalities is to try to aid the child's adjustment by modifying the life circles around the child (see Figure 1.6), in addition to directly addressing the child's developmental delays and other exceptionalities (Gallagher, 2006).

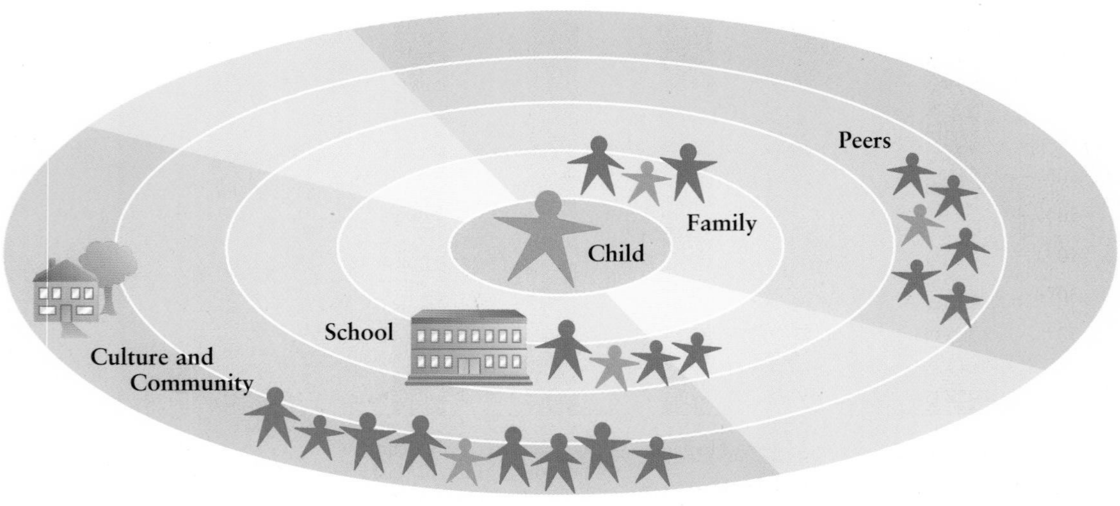

Figure 1.6 The Context/Ecology of the Exceptional Child
Source: U.S. Department of Education (2003). *Twenty-fourth Annual Report to Congress.* Washington, DC: Offi ce of Special Education Programs.

1-5b Role of Families

Just as our views of children with disabilities have changed over time and with experience, so has our perspective on the role of families and their cultural backgrounds. Although we easily accept the statement today that "special education is inevitably a family affair" (Singer, Maul, Wang, & Ethridge, 2011, p. 637), such was not always the case.

The earlier work of Farber (1959), a sociologist who pioneered research into families with children with disabilities, showed that the family well-being was improved and less stressful after institutionalizing children with intellectual and developmental disabilities (IDD). Of course, as Blacher & Hatton (2007) have pointed out, this research was done prior to the 1970s in the United States, a time when parents had limited access to publically funded educational services for their children with IDD. There were few types of family support and no federal regulations ensuring rights for persons with IDD.

The focus of research on the family was so narrow that we had to be reminded that "families are more than mothers" since most of the studies focused on the impact on the mother rather than on families as social systems with fathers and siblings. There was also an incomplete understanding that the family is embedded in a larger sociocultural setting and that many important values and practices reflect a cultural history that needs to be understood for effective planning and parental interaction.

For example, the goal of independence in adulthood so valued in American society may take second place to loyalty to family values and ethnic heritage in families that do not necessarily see acculturation (adopting practices of the majority culture) as positive. Teachers and educators who ignore these cultural differences may well be puzzled at the lack of response to their efforts.

Turnbull et al. (2007) point out that not only should such cultural values be part of the teacher's preparation but teachers also need to be self-aware of the effect of their own cultural background on their attitudes and the standards they expect of their students.

One of the major forces that influences the child with exceptionalities, as with any child, is the family system. Because the family is a system, we expect that anything that happens to one member of that family will have an impact on all the other members of the family (Cox & Paley, 1997). If we expect to be effective in special education, we need to interact with the members of the family in which the child lives—not just with the child.

The trend toward early intervention (before the age of 5) increases the importance of the family. Much of the intervention with young children is directed toward supporting the family environment and preparing the parent(s) or caretakers to care for and teach children with disabilities. At the very least, intervention tries to support constructive parent–child interactions. (Chapter 3 focuses specifically on early childhood intervention from a variety of perspectives.) Years of experience and study have led to the following principles regarding the family:

1. Children and families are inextricably intertwined. Intentional or not, intervention with children almost invariably influences families; likewise, intervention and support with families almost invariably influence children.
2. Involving and supporting families is likely to be a more powerful intervention than one that focuses exclusively on the children.
3. Family members should be able to choose their level of involvement in program planning, decision making, and service delivery.
4. Professionals should attend to family priorities for goals and services, even when those priorities differ substantially from professional priorities (Turnbull & Turnbull, 2004).

Families of exceptional children play an important role in early intervention. Parents can teach their children some of the skills and learning tools that will later be reinforced in a school setting.

BOX 1.2 EXCEPTIONAL LIVES • EXCEPTIONAL STORIES

A Day in the Life of Roger's Family

The responsibilities of two-parent working families are difficult enough without adding the special needs of a child with disabilities. Roger is a five-year-old boy with cerebral palsy and developmental delay. Roger's father and mother are awakened at 6:30 a.m. by the cries of Roger's younger sister, Anna. Roger has to be washed and dressed, a task of considerable difficulty because of his cerebral palsy. Meanwhile, Roger's mother is setting out breakfast and beginning to think about her own workday as a teacher at a local school.

Roger's father gets Roger washed and dressed and down to the breakfast table and then begins to think about a shower and shave before going to the construction company where he works. Before work, he takes Roger to the developmental day-care program, where he is in an integrated program with his same-age peers. The family is fortunate in that Roger's sister goes to the school where her mother teaches, so one transportation problem is solved.

Breakfast is often a chaotic affair with no one sitting down at the same time. Roger needs extra help eating because he has difficulty directing the spoon full of cereal and milk to his mouth. Mom puts the breakfast dishes in the dishwasher, and Dad is off with Roger while Mom helps Anna find her bookbag so they can also head off.

In the late afternoon and evening, the same procedure is reversed. This time Mom picks up Roger because Dad is at a construction site on the other side of town. She is delayed by the teacher, who describes an incident that involved Roger's conflict with another child over possession of some toy. There is still dinner to prepare, baths to be given, and stories to read before the children are tucked in. Is it any wonder that the parents are weary at the end of the day? Tomorrow will be even more challenging because Roger has a medical checkup in addition to the normal daily activities, and the parents haven't decided who will take him to the doctor.

When both parents share responsibility for the family tasks, there is *family harmony*. The important factor in family harmony is that parents understand the roles and responsibilities that each will fulfill to meet the family's needs so that each parent feels supported.

Imagine what would happen if the parents cannot agree about responsibilities or if there are tensions between them regarding discipline, finances, or expectations for the children. It is easy to see that the family relationships are key to a positive context for the exceptional child.

When considering basic family responsibilities, it is important to realize the enormous diversity of families. There has been a substantial increase in the number of single-parent families. Because many single mothers live in poverty, their children are less likely to receive good prenatal and postnatal care, and this increases the chances of a child having physical, academic, and emotional problems. It is difficult to imagine the added stress single mothers face in meeting the needs of their children.

There are many stresses in the lives of families who have children with disabilities, but their lives also can be filled with joy, laughter, and fun. Children can light up parents' hearts with a smile, and parents of children with disabilities, just like other parents, have their favorite stories of their child's adventures and antics. As a parent, your child is always your child first, and his or her exceptionality comes second.

Box 1.2 shows the typical stresses and pressures on a family in caring for a child with a handicapping condition.

1-5c Family Response to a Child with a Disability

The response to the information that they, the parents, have a child with disabilities is remarkably varied and personal. The family response is critical because it may well determine the success of intervention and school programming for the exceptional child. In the family that is attentive and optimistic, the child can respond positively to educational stimulation. If parents are "in denial" about their child's learning or developmental challenges, the child may not receive important early interventions that are critical for his or her future success (Blacher & Hatton, 2007).

When their child is first diagnosed as having a serious disability, most parents feel shock and then denial, guilt, anger, and sadness before they finally adjust. A few parents react with severe depression. Support groups composed of parents of children with similar disabilities can be quite effective in helping new parents by sharing ways in which they have faced similar challenges in their own families.

A crisis that many parents of a child with exceptionalities face is the problem of providing daily care for the child. A child who has cerebral palsy or is emotionally disturbed is often difficult to feed, dress, and put to bed. It is the continual, day-to-day responsibilities and care that often exhaust families. The realization that their child may not go through a normal developmental process and may never gain independence as an adult often causes parents to worry about their child's future. Parents and family members therefore require support and empathic professional attention.

1-5d Family-Professional Relationships

Over the past few decades, the relationship between professionals and families in the field of exceptional children has changed. Originally, the professional's role was to explain the special needs of the child to the parents and give them directions and training for the proper care and treatment of the child. The mother was the traditional contact, and other family members played a lesser role. Today all family members are encouraged to play a significant role in the life of the child with disabilities, and supports are provided to help families meet the needs of their child. Professionals work in partnership with families, and interventions are centered on the families' needs.

Turnbull and Turnbull (2002) describe the **family-centered model** in this way:

> First, the family-centered model primarily attempted to honor family choice by changing the power relationship between professionals and families.
>
> Second, the family-centered model abandoned a pathology orientation and adopted a strengths orientation.
>
> Third, the entire family has become the unit of support—not just the child with a disability and the child's mother (p. 92).

These three principles center the relationship between the family and professional on family needs, motivating special educators to look for the strengths in the child and family rather than focusing on the deficits. The purpose of this family-focused (or family-centered) approach is to help parents become autonomous and confident in their abilities to meet the needs of their child.

The change from an almost exclusive emphasis on the child to an emphasis on the family has placed a lot of professionals in unfamiliar territory. Many teachers, psychologists, occupational therapists, and others are more accustomed to the old "treat the child" model. But the family-focused approach is essential to establishing the supports needed for the well-being of the child.

1-5e Emotional Development and the Family

The emotional repertoire of the child is not only the natural manifestation of his or her constitutional makeup, but it is also socially constructed through learning and experience (Shonkoff & Phillips, 2000). When a child is not able to understand and interpret the behaviors and communications of others, there are long-term social consequences (Flavell & Miller, 1998). The emotional repertoire of the child is, in part, socially constructed, so then it can be socially modified. Helping the child develop a healthy social and emotional repertoire is one of the major objectives of special education.

1-5f Siblings of Children with Exceptionalities

We now know enough about the family environment to dismiss the proposition that two children experience the *same* environment when they are growing up—merely because they live in the same household. Obviously the home environment is not the same for a child with disabilities as it is for his or her nondisabled sibling, or for an older daughter as it is for a younger son.

Assumptions are often made about families with a child with a disability—that the nondisabled sibling is inevitably neglected because the parents must pay so much

BOX 1.3 Concerns of Siblings of a Child with Disabilities

- Why does he behave so strangely?
- Can she grow out of this?
- Will other brothers and sisters also have disabilities?
- Will he ever be able to live on his own?
- Will I be expected to take care of her as an adult?
- Am I loved as much as my brother?
- How can I tell my best friends about my sister?
- What am I supposed to do when other children tease my brother?
- Will my own children be more likely to have a disability?

TeachSource Digital Download Access online

attention to the child with disabilities and that, as a result, the sibling becomes resentful of the child with disabilities. It is now clear that although this set of events may happen, it certainly does not have to happen, particularly when the parents are sensitive to natural sibling rivalry and the needs for equivalent attention to each child.

Siblings of the child with a disability can spend at least the same amount of time with their mother and receive the same type of discipline that their brother or sister with disabilities receives. Siblings may perform a greater amount of household tasks. Older siblings may be vulnerable to special adjustment problems if the parents have given them additional child-care responsibilities. As in other family situations, it is not so much the actions of the parents that count as how the sibling interprets those actions. If the sibling is sure of being loved and cared for by the parent, then being given additional responsibilities for the child with disabilities does not seem to cause a negative reaction (Gallagher, Powell, & Rhodes, 2006).

It is important that siblings understand the special challenges of their brother or sister with disabilities

Still, however, parents often worry about the effect that the child with disabilities has on his or her siblings. Will they grow resentful of the child with special needs or of the attention that the parents inevitably have to spend on him or her? When the parents grow old and are no longer able to take care of the child (then an adult) with disabilities, will the siblings pitch in and help meet their brother or sister's needs? Although each situation is different, there does not seem to be any evidence that the siblings of children with disabilities are more stressed or face greater adjustment problems than siblings of children without disabilities. The goal of most American parents is for their child with disabilities to become an independent and self-sufficient adult living away from home, and many siblings appear willing to assume the role of protector if that is necessary (Krauss, Seltzer, Gordon, & Friedman, 1996).

Answering the siblings' questions to help them understand their brother or sister's needs is an important part of the parents' responsibilities. For example, consider the questions in Box 1.3, which are examples of concerns a sibling may have but feel uncomfortable sharing.

The fact that siblings may not verbalize fears and questions does not mean that they are not thinking about them. It is the parents' responsibility to try to answer even unverbalized questions and anxieties that the brother or sister may have about the sibling with disabilities and the family.

The number of questions that siblings have does not diminish over time. The concerns evident in the questions will reflect developmental changes. For example, an illness or the death of one of the parents may heighten the siblings' concern about their own responsibilities. If the parents are gone or are no longer able to care for the child with disabilities, will they be expected to share in the care of their sibling throughout his or her lifetime? Each family has to answer these questions in its own way, but the answers must be clear and unambiguous for all family members. You may want to think about the kinds of questions you would have if your brother or sister had a disability.

A resource available to siblings of exceptional children is Sibshops, which are designed as workshops for siblings of children with special needs (Meyer & Vadasy, 2007). These Sibshops have been conducted in over 200 communities and eight countries, an indication of their popularity and usefulness. Originally designed by Don Meyer for children ages 8 to 13 who have siblings with special needs, these workshops are presented as having goals such as learning "how others handle situations commonly experienced by siblings with special needs" (Sibling Support Project, 2010).

These Sibshops are commonly facilitated by a team of service providers who have been trained in the process of Sibshops—such as social workers, special education teachers, and psychologists. Comments from participants are positive, but no formal evaluation has been done on the effectiveness of these workshops.

Sibling Support Project
www.siblingsupport.org

1-5g Assessment of Families

There has been a need for some way to measure family status and reaction to having a child with disabilities. Ann and Rod Turnbull at the University of Kansas developed the Family Quality of Life Scale (see Table 1.2), which provides a measure of family status and resilience in each of five major dimensions of family life (Park et al., 2003).

For each of the 25 items in the scale, the person responds on a five-point scale where 1 = very dissatisfied, 3 = neither satisfied nor dissatisfied, and 5 = very satisfied. This scale helps to answer questions such as does having a child with disabilities influence family status? It does seem to elevate family stress, with autistic children causing more family stress than other disabilities (Singer et al., 2011). The results in the five dimensions of the scale can point to areas where additional family support may be needed.

Because the social and emotional well-being of the child is closely tied to the quality of family life, researchers have begun to look at these issues. By defining and measuring a family's quality of life, we can see how and where additional supports would be helpful. This scale can be used to reflect the current quality of the family's life, to document progress as a result of family support programs, and to inform planning for particular families of children with exceptionalities. The scale includes the emotional well-being of the family and the key elements of parenting, and captures the degree of help provided to support the child with disabilities.

Assessment of family interactions is important in planning with families

TABLE 1.2 Family Quality of Life Scale

Category	Sample Item
Family Interaction	My family solves problems together.
Parenting	My family members teach the children how to get along with others.
Emotional Well-being	My family has the support we need to relieve stress.
Physical Well-being	My family has a way to take care of our expenses.
Disability-Related Support	My family member with special needs has support to make progress at school or work.

SOURCE: Beach Center on Disabilities. (2006). Family Quality of Life Scale. Beach Center on Disabilities, Lawrence, KS.

1-6 Culturally and Linguistically Diverse Families

Families are unique and complex. Each family has its own perspectives, but families who share cultural orientations often have similar values and beliefs. These values and beliefs influence child-rearing practices. Respect for the breadwinner, religious beliefs, child disciplinary practices, and even attitudes toward professional support may reflect the values of the family's cultural group. Because cultural values play a crucial role in shaping the child's world, it is critical that these are understood and honored by professionals working with the child and family.

Here are some examples of how cultural values might affect the child with special needs: If a family's culture emphasizes a dominant masculine role, how will the father of a child with disabilities respond to a female professional working with his child? Will he reject her advice and suggestions in order to maintain a strong masculine self-image? And what does he feel about his son who has disabilities so serious that he despairs of the boy ever being able to fulfill a masculine role? These issues of core values are not easy to discuss, but they can rest at the heart of parental concerns over time.

One of the first challenges educators face is how to correctly identify children with exceptionalities from culturally and linguistically diverse families. Clearly, giving a child who does not speak English an IQ test in English is a bad idea. But the issue is more complicated than that. For children who are bilingual, language develops differently (see the full discussion in Chapter 7). This makes it difficult to determine if a child has a learning disability or just a normal delay as he masters two language systems. All too often, culturally/linguistically diverse children are inappropriately referred to special education services when, in fact, they need a very different set of experiences to support their success.

One of the most difficult tasks facing the schools is how to correctly assess students with different ethnic and linguistic backgrounds. This is particularly true for students with a Hispanic background. Guiberson (2009) has suggested the use of instructional support teams (composed of teachers, special education personnel, psychologists, etc.) that would provide targeted intervention to meet the individual student's needs. This approach would represent Tier II in the RtI model. If the student fails to respond to this approach, then a referral to special education is called for.

Guiberson cautions that such a team should have access to staff who have special knowledge of bilingual and English language development and should present a consistent and intense treatment plan. Half-hearted interventions would result in little or no difference. This supports this text's view that unless interventions are intense and over a substantial period of time, they will not get the results intended.

RtI

This again is where the RtI model is helpful. Because the needs of many children from culturally and linguistically diverse families fall in between the general education and the special education services, RtI offers a collaborative level of support (Harry, 2007). It is in Tier II, targeted support, where many students' needs will be addressed, because while they may not need special education services, they may well need some type of supplementary supports in order to meet with success in the education system.

The needs of children from culturally and linguistically diverse families may be further impacted by issues related to poverty. The overlap of race and poverty of children with disabilities have led many to wonder if overrepresentation is related to two separate categories of special education students. The first involves neurological and biological problems (for example, children with Down syndrome, cerebral palsy, autism, and so forth). The second involves socially constructed conditions or outcomes such as mild intellectual and developmental disabilities (IDD), emotional disturbance, and learning disabilities that may come as a result of environmental factors such as poverty. As Harry (2007) points out, special education should reconceptualize struggling learners on a continuum of instruction rather than requiring that they be defined as "disabled." We believe that the RtI approach may help us by focusing on the child's needs rather than the program options.

1-6a Alternative Families

Once upon a time the word *family* evoked an image of a mother, a father, and two or more children. Today's families, however, are more varied. In fact, the National Institute of Mental Health defines "family" as merely "a network of mutual commitment" (2010). Today many families are headed by a single parent. One of the clear consequences of the single-parent family is reduced economic circumstances. Many families exist at or near the poverty line, a circumstance that makes expensive care for children with special needs extremely difficult. This may mean that during the early developmental period when children need special help, they are less likely to receive it. The public policy movement toward welfare reform (Haskins, 2007) has forced many mothers into the workforce again, but it does not provide an answer for children with special needs. Often, policy reform designed to address one issue creates unintended consequences.

However, positive forces in the larger society are trying to cope with these problems. The establishment of prekindergarten programs in public schools allows children with special needs to be identified at age 3 or 4 and to receive important care earlier. Also, a wide variety of child-care and day-care options have been established to try to meet the needs of children whose parents work outside the home. It is important that these programs are of high quality so that children with disabilities can be appropriately cared for. Some current evidence shows that all too often the quality of child care in the United States is not high enough (Early et al., 2007). The result of uneven care for young children is that too many children enter kindergarten unprepared for the experience, and the consequences for increased school failure become predictable (Lee & Burkam, 2002). An investment in early childhood education and support for families of young children may be one of our society's greatest policy needs.

1-6b Technical Assistance for Parents

The Office of Special Education Programs (OSEP) in the U.S. Department of Education has funded the *Technical Assistance Alliance for Parent Centers*, which is an innovative partnership of one national and six regional parent technical assistance centers. This nationwide system of centers in turn provides help for over 100 Parent Training and Information Centers (PTIs) and Community Parent Resource Centers (OSEP, 2009).

This alliance provides up-to-date information for parents in addition to high-quality resources and materials, holds national conferences and institutes, and provides management expertise. The parent centers provide training and information to parents of infants, toddlers, children, and youth with disabilities and to the professionals who work with them. Many of these centers are staffed by parents of children with disabilities or by adults who have disabilities themselves, making them uniquely qualified to provide counsel and advice for parents.

1-6c Family as Advocate: The Power of Parents

The recognition that society and the community at large, as well as schools, have a responsibility for caring for exceptional children stemmed in large measure from the activities of parents. Years ago, parents who were unable to get help for their children from local governments created their own programs in church basements, vacant stores, or any place that would house them. These informal groups, loosely formed around the common needs of the children, often provided important information to new parents struggling to find help for their children with disabilities. They were also a source of emotional support for parents—a means of sharing and solving the problems of accepting and living with exceptional children.

These parent groups quickly realized that fundamental changes were needed in the allocation of educational resources at local, state, and federal levels. A casual, haphazard approach was not going to provide the kind of help or support that parents or their children with exceptionalities needed. Accordingly, large parents' groups, such as the National Association of Retarded Children (now the Association of Retarded Citizens, ARC); the United Cerebral Palsy Association in the 1940s and 1950s; and the Association for Children with Learning Disabilities in the 1960s (now the Learning Disabilities Association of America, LDA) began to form. Parents of children with Down syndrome, autism (Autism Society of America), and other specific conditions have also formed groups to advocate for their children's special needs. These parent organizations have successfully stimulated legislation at the state and federal levels that has provided additional trained personnel, research, and equipment. To a large extent we can thank parents for the gains we have made as a society in the inclusion of individuals with disabilities in education settings.

Organized parents' groups for children with special gifts and talents have not yet had the same political influence as the national organizations for children with disabilities. Still, these groups are helping the parents of children who are gifted cope with the problems of precocious development (Gallagher, 2002).

1-6d Assessment of Family Programs

Although concern for the families of children with special needs has been around for decades, there are still limited formal evaluations of the effectiveness of interventions with the family. The task is made more difficult because the interventions take so many different forms in content, length, and intensity.

The authors of a review of twenty-six different articles (Friend, Summers, & Turnbull, 2009) tried to draw some generalizations from the diverse attempts to help families:

> Intervention research suggests that parent training programs improved parenting skills and relieved parental stress. ... General family-centered practice offering an array of support, improved family cohesion and parental well-being... respite care has short term effects on reducing parent stress. (p. 468)

In short, almost any sustained approach to the family by professionals appears to pay off in improved parental quality of life—particularly when the child is of prekindergarten age. As we will note throughout this text, interventions are effective only if they have sufficient intensity and duration.

1-6e The Influence of Culture and Community

Culture refers to the attitudes, values, customs, and languages that family and friends transmit to children. These attitudes, values, customs, and languages have been passed down from generations of ancestors and have formed an identifiable pattern or heritage. The child is embedded in the family, its habits, and its traditions; this is as true for the child with special needs as for other children. Although the child may be only slightly aware of these cultural influences, it makes a world of difference to the child's experiences if his or her family is fourth-generation American or first-generation Irish, Mexican, Italian, Nigerian, or Taiwanese.

Families' religious beliefs, child-rearing practices, attitudes toward authority, and so forth can often be traced to their cultural identity. Therefore, school personnel need to understand and honor that cultural background in order to form positive relationships with the families. Children from diverse cultural backgrounds often may encounter conflicting expectations and values in the home and in the school. We can easily assume that the differences between school and family are due to family idiosyncrasies, when in fact they reflect the long history of that family in the cultural background of parents and grandparents. Teachers can help children by becoming aware of the wide range of norms represented in their classrooms and communities. When values fostered by the school, such as competitiveness and willingness to work at a desk with a minimum of talking conflict with a cultural preference for cooperation and for lively discussion, tensions may arise between families and school expectations. Such tensions may increase with the additional concerns for a child with disabilities.

In order to be more culturally aware, we often must become more self-aware (Turnbull & Turnbull, 2002). Teachers need to be aware of what factors shape their own cultural views and values. This builds an understanding that personal cultural beliefs and traditions that work well for them may not necessarily work for others. The child's cultural context and the family's beliefs and values must be honored, and this starts with identifying the strengths of the culture and family. Whatever the immediate problems the family and the exceptional child may have, they also have many strengths. A family's ability to make the child feel loved and accepted, a willingness to seek support from friends and counselors, a strong religious faith, and a caring extended family (Turnbull & Turnbull, 2002) are strengths that should be respected as a foundation for building a support system for the child.

The impact of environmental forces varies as the child grows: initially the family is predominant in caring for the child and acts as a link between the child and the larger environment (see Figure 1.6 on page 16: The Context/Ecology of the Exceptional Child). The support of the family continues to be important but is joined by other factors as the child enters school.

1-7 Transition to Community

As the child grows older, the peer group becomes a major force. Adolescence, with its focus on social development and career orientation, is a special challenge for the child with exceptionalities. Potential rejection or bullying by the peer group can have a powerful influence on the adaptation of the child with disabilities or the child with special talents (as it can on any vulnerable and self-conscious adolescent).

Finally, society, which includes the culture and community along with the work environment, influences the student who is trying to make the transition from school to a relatively independent lifestyle. Throughout their lives, many adults with exceptionalities will be in contact with a support system that includes advocates, educators, friends, and service providers. In addition, representatives of the larger society (such as government leaders) often make rules that determine whether the exceptional person receives needed resources or has the opportunity to succeed at some level of independence.

The most current legislation actually requires planning for the post-school period together with representatives from community agencies once the child with exceptionalities reaches age 16. This ensures that there is a clear plan for transition from school to work or to other training opportunities, so that students with exceptionalities continue positive actions for their future.

1-7a Community Resources

The type and number of resources available within your own community to assist families who have a child with a disability are often quite extensive but are usually hidden from the casual observer. Suppose you have been approached by a neighbor whose 3-year-old has just been diagnosed with autism. She now asks you—as the person who knows about special education and related subjects—where she can go to get some help.

To extend your own knowledge of relevant agencies you might track down and report on all of the currently available community agencies or individuals who might be able to provide some help for your neighbor and her family. Be sure and note the techniques that you used in your search.

Moral Dilemmas in Special Education

The presence of exceptional children in our families and our communities can raise any number of moral and ethical questions. We present for your consideration one of these in each chapter.

MORAL DILEMMA

The Cost of Educating Children with Disabilities

The education of children with disabilities inevitably costs more than the education of children without disabilities. This is true because of the need for smaller teacher–student ratios in many cases, more support personnel, and technology to meet the needs of these students. This extra expenditure is a point of contention with some parents and citizens. Their views may be summed up one or more of these ways:

1. Why should the school be spending more tax dollars for these students when my own child has many unmet needs?
2. Why spend this extra money on students who will have to struggle to maintain themselves in society and may never be able to contribute to society?
3. Why not spend the money on the brightest students? They will be the leaders who will discover new cures for diseases or improve our economy.

How would you respond to these questions from the perspective of (a) a school board member responsible for the education budget, (b) a tax-paying citizen, and (c) the parent of a child with disabilities?

Summary

- The major categories of exceptionality include children with intellectual differences, communication differences, learning disabilities, sensory differences, behavioral differences, multiple and severe disabilities, physical and health differences, ADHD, and autism.
- Exceptional children show both interindividual (among children) and intraindividual (within themselves) differences. Both kinds of differences require special adaptation by the educators at school.
- Early identification of exceptionalities is critical for providing appropriate interventions.
- The special needs of children can be described through an information processing model involving input, central processing, output, executive functioning, and emotional context.
- The number of culturally diverse children in special education requiring special program efforts is disproportionately large.
- The RtI model provides three layers of intervention depending on the degree of severity of the needs.
- The adjustment of siblings of children with disabilities can be improved through programs of intervention.
- Family empowerment gives parents more influence on the special programs established for their children and requires rethinking of the traditional roles played by professionals and parents.
- Cultural attitudes, values, customs, and language are often embedded in families and must be taken into account when educators and other

professionals work with exceptional children from a variety of cultural backgrounds.
- Families from diverse cultures may have differing values and child-rearing practices, which compounds the issues of adaptation for children with special needs.

Future Challenges

Every generation leaves, as its legacy to the next generation, certain problems for which solutions have not been found. There are many issues in the field of special education that today's professionals have been unable to resolve. The end-of-chapter sections titled "Future Challenges" briefly describe widely debated topics as a beginning agenda for the current generation of students, who will face these issues in their professional or private lives.

1. **Who is identified as exceptional?**
   The boundary line separating children with exceptionalities from nonexceptional children has become blurred where children with mild disabilities are concerned. Yet legislation and the courts call for eligibility standards to clearly separate children who should receive special education from those who should not. How do we distinguish, for example, between the child who is emotionally disturbed and the child who is experiencing a temporary behavior problem? The RtI model may help with students who are having difficulties but who do not require special educational placement or services, but how will we appropriately use these tiers of support?
2. **What is the impact of the family on children with special needs?**
   For many years, special educators focused on the child with exceptionalities. Increasingly, we have become aware that the child is only one component in a complex family and ecological system. We understand that many elements within that system can have a positive or negative impact on the child. How can special education incorporate this understanding into our personnel preparation and educational programs to help us build constructive relationships with the family?
3. **How should a student's cultural and linguistic background be honored in the educational approach to children with special needs?**
   We have only begun to consider how a child's cultural background will influence an appropriate education. With the increase of multicultural and multilingual students within our schools, this is becoming even more important. With few bilingual and bicultural teachers available who also have training in special education, we face a continuing challenge to build cultural awareness. How can we recruit a more diverse workforce for special education?

TeachSource Digital Download Access online

Key Terms

child with exceptionalities p. 4
culture p. 24
ecological model p. 16
family-centered model p. 19
high-incidence disabilities p. 13
individualized education program (IEP) p. 7
information processing model (IPM) p. 9
interindividual differences p. 6
intraindividual differences p. 7
low-incidence disabilities p. 14
medical model p. 16
response to intervention (RtI) p. 8

Resources

References of Special Interest

Donovan, M., & Cross, C. (2002). *Minority students in special and gifted education*. Washington, D.C.: National Research Council. A report from a special panel brought together by the National Academy of Sciences to address the disproportionate numbers of minority students in special education programs for children with disabilities and also for children who are gifted. The panel explores whether such disproportions in fact exist and, if they do, why they exist and what can be done about this issue. The panel concludes that such disproportions do exist and proposes better integrated general education and special education programs, increased teacher training in sensitivity to cultural differences, high-quality early childhood intervention programs, and increased research.

Kaufmann, J., & Hallahan, D. (Eds). (2011). *Handbook of special education*. New York, NY: Routledge. A comprehensive review of all aspects of special education with 57 separate chapters dealing with the education of exceptional children. Separate sections deal with history, legal aspects, specific categories of exceptionality, student assessment, policy and leadership, instructional issues for students with high incidence exceptionalities, instructional issues for students with low incidence exceptionalities, transition to adulthood, parent and family issues, early identification and intervention, and cultural and international issues. Each chapter is written by a recognized expert in his/her specialty and represents the best current view of these topics.

Odom, S., Horner, R., Snell, M., & Blacher, J. (Eds.) (2007). *Handbook of developmental disabilities*. New York, NY: Guilford Press. A collection of experts from multidisciplinary backgrounds have assembled a synthesis of current research on developmental disabilities as a prelude to more effective action. The topics range from infancy to adulthood and from education to genetics. This is a valuable sourcebook for those working in this field.

Salvia, J., Ysseldyke, J., & Bolt S. (2010). *Assessment in special and inclusive education* (11th ed.). Boston, MA: Houghton Mifflin. One of the problems in identifying children with special needs is the lack of knowledge about acceptable measuring instruments. This volume provides a wide variety of informal and formal methods of assessment and several chapters discussing the broad topic of general assessment itself. The authors include developmental appraisals of infants, toddlers, and preschoolers. Also included is a chapter on outcomes-based accountability assessment, which is a topic of growing interest in education.

Turnbull, A., & Turnbull, H. R. (2006). *Families, professionals and exceptionality: A special partnership* (4th ed.). Upper Saddle River, NJ: Pearson/Merrill-Prentice Hall. A comprehensive portrait of the relationship of families to professionals in the tasks of helping children with disabilities reach levels of self-determination. The authors argue that there should be a true partnership between parents and professionals in planning and executing special education plans for children with special developmental problems.

Journals

Exceptional Children, Council for Exceptional Children (CEC)
www.cec.sped.org
Exceptionality
www.tandfonline.com

Journal of Special Education
www.proedinc.com
Teaching Exceptional Children
www.cec.sped.org

Professional Organizations

Council for Exceptional Children (CEC) **www.cec.sped.org**

BATING
SM ACT
UND $$$ 4
SM NOW
EARCH
Time
This is a National
EMERGENCY
Autism Researc
NOW
ARTON
LENCED
OUR
GIVE US
BACK
OUR

CHAPTER 2

Children with Exceptionalities and Social Institutions: Government, Courts and Schools

Standards Addressed in This Chapter

All of the CEC Standards are addressed within this chapter. Please see the inside book covers for the complete list of the standards.

CEC

FOCUS QUESTIONS

2-1 How has society at large responded to children with exceptionalities over the years?

2-2 What government legislation supports and protects students with disabilities?

2-3 How have the courts influenced the development of educational services for children with disabilities?

2-4 What are some organizational and instructional ways in which schools can modify programs for children with special needs?

2-5 How will we adapt to children from different cultural backgrounds who also have special needs?

2-6 How do we assess the effectiveness of these special adaptations we have introduced?

2-7 What are the special requirements for ensuring effective transition for the child with exceptionalities from school to community?

In Chapter 1, we discussed the nature of children with exceptionalities and their surrounding ecology of family, peers, and culture. In this chapter, we look at the responses of three major social institutions—government, courts, and schools—to the needs of children with exceptionalities. How a society feels about its membership, particularly about citizens who are different, is expressed through such institutions. See Figure 2.1, which briefly explains the impact of each social institution on children with exceptionalities.

AP Images/Tony Gutierrez

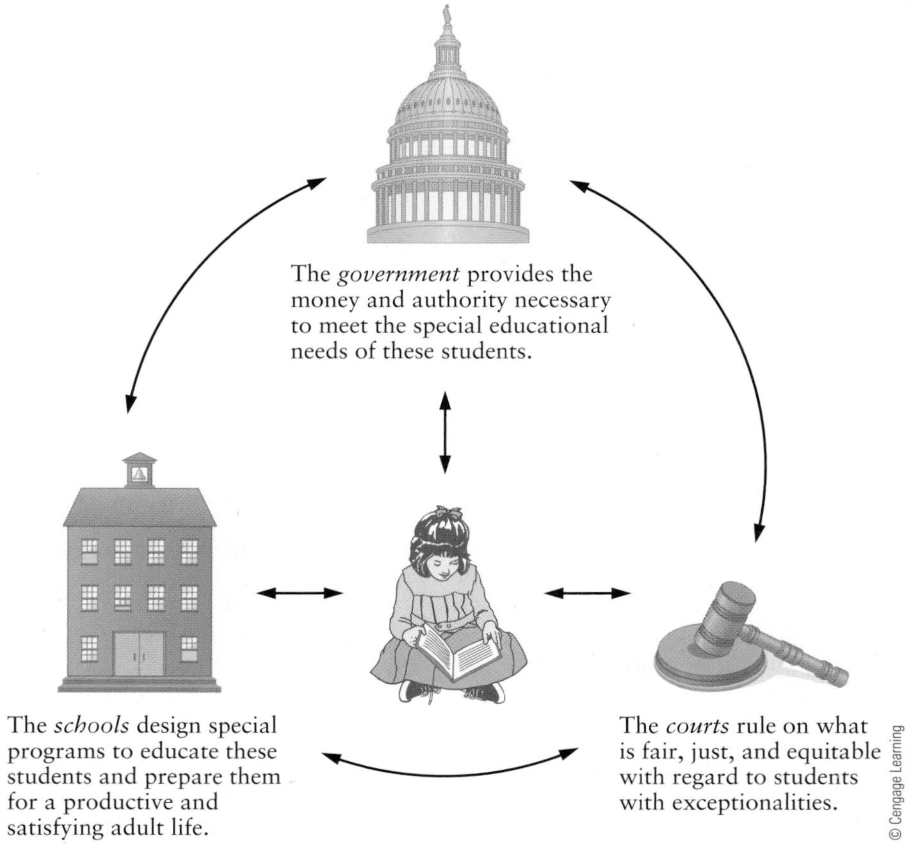

Figure 2.1 The Exceptional Child and Social Institutions

TeachSource Digital Download Access online

Each of the social institutions depicted in Figure 2.1 has its own rules and traditions that influence how decisions are made and how conclusions are reached. This chapter touches briefly on how each of them affects the child who is exceptional in our society. Take, for example, Sam.

Sam is a 5-year-old with Down syndrome, a genetic but not hereditary condition that will affect his entire life. He has developmental disabilities and other problems caused by his genetic patterns. Yet how Sam will fare in life will depend to a large degree on the environmental circumstances around him—family, school, community, and other societal forces such as government and legislation.

Will Sam do better in a loving family? In a neighborhood with some comfort and resources? In a school program that recognizes his needs and adapts the program to meet his needs? Of course!

No matter what the degree of exceptionality, how the child will eventually adapt to life is determined in large measure by how the environmental forces outside the child facilitate or inhibit his or her development. That is why we spend so much time studying these outside forces, which we refer to as the **ecology of the child**, or the context of the child.

We begin this chapter with an overview of society's attitudes toward the education of individuals with exceptionalities, so that we can better understand how schools work to address their needs.

2-1 Societal Responses to Children with Exceptionalities

During the past century, enormous changes have taken place in the way society treats children with exceptionalities, moving from rejection, to the charitable isolation of children with disabilities, to the acceptance of them as contributing members of society. The current level of acceptance has few precedents, representing a much more enlightened view than was evident even in the immediate past. The notion of educating *every* child to achieve his or her greatest potential is a relatively new idea.

Before World War II, individual states were involved in a limited way in subsidizing programs in public schools for children with sensory disabilities (blindness, deafness) and physical impairments. Some states helped organize and support classes for children who had intellectual and developmental disabilities or behavioral problems. After World War II, many states expanded their involvement, providing financial support for special classes and services to local schools for children with all types of disability. This expansion caused two problems that many believed could only be solved by federal legislation.

First, these new and larger programs created a personnel scarcity in the late 1940s and early 1950s. Professional special educators were in short supply, and the field of special education was not firmly established. Second, because not all states expanded their involvement in special education, organized parents' groups began asking why children with disabilities and their parents should be penalized because they lived in a particular state or a particular region of a state. Were not U.S. citizens (in this case, the parents of children with disabilities) entitled to equal treatment anywhere in the United States? Should parents, in addition to the challenges of having children with special needs, be forced to move their families to a community in which special education resources were available because no local resources existed? The blatant unfairness of the situation called for attention at the federal level.

2-2 The Role of Government

For more than 150 years, we have relied on our public school systems to educate about 89 percent of our school-age children (Planty et al., 2009). Public schools have been supported by the nation's taxpayers as a commitment to the future of our society.

Major social institutions that have had a long-lasting effect on the education of children with exceptionalities have been the state and federal governments. The executive branches and the legislatures have the responsibility to create policies, draft laws, and find the necessary money for the special services and extra expenses involved in educating children with exceptionalities. Legislation as a vehicle for change (Gallagher, 2006) has a way of shortening discussions and disputes. If you, as an educator, do not perform as the legislation states, you are no longer just showing your disagreement, you are breaking the law!

Federal legislation clearly was needed, both to provide resources to bring qualified people into special education and to equalize educational opportunities across the country. But that legislation was not easy to obtain, since it violated a strong American tradition of education as a state and local responsibility. In spite of this barrier, organized parents' groups, with the support of other interested citizens, convinced Congress that they needed help. This help was finally granted through a series of laws.

The advocacy of parents helped to secure the rights of individuals with disabilities

Michael Debets/Demotix/Corbis

2-2a A Summary of Special Education Legislation

Public Law 88-164

In 1963, Public Law (PL) 88-164 authorized funds for training professionals to work with children with special needs and for research and demonstration (the illustration of best practices) for students with intellectual and developmental disabilities (IDD) and deafness. The law represented a strong initiative by President John F. Kennedy, whose interest was heightened by his sister's IDD. These first efforts were followed by many others, and from that small beginning emerged thirty years of legislation to ensure that all children with disabilities have access to an appropriate education.

That flood of legislation served notice that the federal government accepted responsibility for providing support and resources for children with disabilities and for encouraging the states to carry out their basic responsibilities.

Public Law 94-142

In 1975, Congress passed **PL 94-142**, the Education for All Handicapped Children Act. The measure, which took effect in 1977, was designed "to assure that all handicapped children have available to them a free appropriate public education which emphasizes special education and related services designed to meet their unique needs" (Education for All Handicapped Children Act, 1975, p. 35). See Table 2.1, "Six Key Provisions of the Education for All Handicapped Children Act," for the key provisions of this legislation.

To carry out the provisions of this law, the federal government authorized the spending of up to $3 billion by 1982, promising much larger sums of money to aid the states than had previously been provided. However, by 1990, the government was only spending about $1 billion a year. In return for this aid, states were required to show evidence that they were doing their best to help children with disabilities receive needed services. Specific provisions in the law placed substantial pressure on public school systems, demanding more in the way of assessment, parental contact, and student evaluation than most school systems had been accustomed to providing.

Not surprisingly, many educators protested the burden that these new laws placed on them. But this law has become part of the educational landscape. In the

TABLE 2.1 Six Key Provisions of the Education for All Handicapped Children Act (1975)

- **Zero reject.** All children with disabilities must be provided a free and appropriate public education.
- **Nondiscriminatory evaluation.** Each student must receive a full individual examination before being placed in a special education program, with tests appropriate to the child's cultural and linguistic background.
- **Individualized education program.** An individualized education program (IEP) must be written for every student with a disability who is receiving special education. The IEP must describe the child's current performance and goals for the school year, the particular special education services to be delivered, and the procedures by which outcomes are evaluated.
- **Least restrictive environment.** As much as possible, children who have disabilities must be educated with children who are not handicapped.
- **Due process.** Due process is a set of legal procedures to ensure the fairness of educational decisions and the accountability of both professionals and parents in making those decisions.
- **Parental participation.** Parents are to be included in the development of the IEP, and they have the right to access their child's educational records.

TeachSource Digital Download Access online

past three decades, the federal government moved from little involvement in special education to becoming a major partner in local and state programs for students who have disabilities, expanding the reach of PL 94-142 through additional legislation.

Public Law 99-457

The Education for All Handicapped Children Act (PL 94-142) was, in fact, misnamed. It was not meant for all children of *all ages*. It became increasingly evident that early intervention was important, both for the children with exceptionalities and for their families, and pressure increased for the law to include younger children.

PL 99-457 (Education of the Handicapped Act Amendments of 1986) provided that opportunity by allocating federal funds for the states to develop plans and programs for children and their families *from birth on*. The title of the Education of the Handicapped Act was changed to the **Individuals with Disabilities Education Act**, or **IDEA**. The impact of IDEA is discussed throughout the text.

Federal legislation ensures that young children with special needs receive the intervention that they need.

Individuals with Disabilities Education Act 2004 (IDEA 2004)

IDEA 2004 is the reauthorization of the original legislation (Education for All Handicapped Children Act, PL 94-142) designed to strengthen and improve earlier versions. Some of the major changes in IDEA 2004 involve the following:

- *Quality of personnel.* Special education specialists must hold full state certification as special education teachers and have a license to teach. They must demonstrate subject-matter competence in the academic programs they teach.

- *IEP standards (section 1400).* IEPs (see more discussion later in the chapter) must reflect scientifically based instructional practices, cognitive behavioral interventions, and early intervention services, as appropriate. They must include plans for the use of assistive technology and short-term objectives for children with disabilities who take alternative assessments.
- *Transition planning.* A transition plan must be included in all IEPs for students at age 16 and for younger students if appropriate. **Transition planning** must include instruction, community experiences, development of employment, and other post-school adult-living objectives.

One of the key features of this legislation is that it funded many of the support elements that provide quality special education. Notably, it supported the training of special education teachers and higher education personnel who were training these teachers. It supported research and demonstration projects as well as outreach efforts to ensure that research findings made their way into the classroom. The act also funded technical assistance projects and parent education initiatives. In short, it provided the necessary educational infrastructure that was critical to the operation of a modern educational system.

In viewing the 35 years that this legislation has been in place in one form or another, Yell, Katsiyannis, and Bradley (2011) concluded, "the IDEA has clearly met its original goal to open the doors of public education to students with disabilities" (p. 75).

Other important pieces of legislation play a role in the life of students with disabilities.

Section 504 of the Rehabilitation Act of 1973 (PL 93-112)

RtI

This legislation has been brought into play when the rights of individuals with disabilities have been denied or interfered with. The key provision of the act says that it is illegal to deny participation in activities or programs solely because of a disability. Individuals with disabilities must have equal access to programs and services. One of its advantages is that children who might not meet the stringent criteria for IDEA 2004 may still be judged eligible for services under Section 504.

Problems such as failing grades, a pattern of suspensions, and chronic misbehavior may qualify a child for additional support under **Section 504**. This law acts as a bridge between general and special education and may be a first step to the response to intervention (RtI) model, mentioned in Chapter 1, so that the three-tier RtI model of support can be brought into play for children who don't quite meet the qualifications for special education.

Americans with Disabilities Act of 1992

The **Americans with Disabilities Act** of 1992 (PL 101-336) extends civil rights to persons with disabilities. These rights are guaranteed without regard to race, color, national origin, gender, or religion through the Civil Rights Act of 1964.

These three pieces of legislation—IDEA 2004, Section 504 of the Rehabilitation Act, and the Americans with Disabilities Act—make clear that American society is determined to see that children with disabilities have equal access to educational resources and cannot be discriminated against solely on the basis of their disabilities.

Public Law 107-110: No Child Left Behind Act of 2001

Sometimes a piece of legislation is so important that it affects children with disabilities even if they were not the target of the legislation. The **No Child Left Behind (NCLB)** Act of 2001 has had an impact on all schoolchildren and a special impact on children with disabilities. It was the major education legislation in the George W. Bush administration. Its purpose was to hold schools and educators responsible for bringing students to a minimum level of competency.

The NCLB Act requires schools to present test data to prove their effectiveness. This causes problems for some children with disabilities, who have a difficult time gaining a year academically for every year spent in school, and for their teachers, who must deal with such unrealistic expectations.

Imagine a rule that says that every child at a school should be able to run the 100-yard dash in 14 seconds or less. If the school is unable to meet the standards, and if more children every year do not meet the standards, the school will be disciplined and have its funds removed. We know that there are children who, for a variety of reasons, will never be able to run the 100-yard dash in 14 seconds, no matter what the physical education department does.

You may well imagine what happened with NCLB when the standard of 100 percent proficiency on the part of students and schools was proposed. While many exceptional children can respond well to the setting of higher academic performance goals, some students with disabilities could not meet these standards no matter how hard they tried. A number of attempts have been made to provide alternative assessments for children with disabilities (about 3 percent of children enrolled) so that students with disabilities can participate in the overall assessment in meaningful and appropriate ways.

NCLB created a different problem for students with special gifts and talents in that the tests create no challenge, and the standards can usually be reached with little or no effort (see Chapter 10). In addition, because the classroom teachers must focus more time on helping other students reach basic standards, they often do not have time to stimulate students with special gifts and talents through unique projects or assignments.

TeachSource Video Connection

Aligning Instruction with Federal Legislation

Watch this video case, in which a principal, teachers, and a student intern discuss modifying instruction to take federal legislation into account. Questions about the impacts of IDEA and NCLB are raised by the new intern, and other general education teachers and special education teachers chime in with their viewpoints. After listening to this discussion, reflect on how federal legislation impacts education practice. What are the pros and cons of federal educational legislation like IDEA?

Watch online

Sometimes the legislation that is passed may have contradictory purposes and goals, leaving educators puzzled as to which one should prevail in their system. This seems to be the case with IDEA 2004 and NCLB, passed by the Congress at different times and for different purposes.

IDEA 2004 continues a long tradition in special education of differentiating the programs for students identified as having a disability. NCLB sets standards for accountability for all students, including most students with disabilities.

The central issue here is how far into the educational programming of the student both of these ideas should be followed. NCLB seems to assume high standards for secondary and middle schools with the assumption that most students will seek a postsecondary learning site. IDEA 2004 assumes that major planning for transition to the community and vocational placement should be taking place as early as middle school. How can students with mild intellectual disabilities, learning disabilities, emotional disturbance, ADHD, and so on pursue both goals?

American Recovery and Reinvestment Act of 2009

One of the clear results of the 2008–9 recession was the passage of the **American Recovery and Reinvestment Act**, whose goal was to stimulate economic activity in a number of areas, including financial and social institutions, and education, to ensure the long-time economic health of our nation. This resulted in large funds provided to the states under IDEA on a one time basis to improve the delivery of quality of early intervention services. Infants and toddlers with disabilities from

President Barack Obama signed the American Recovery and Reinvestment Act, which provided millions of dollars in funding for early intervention services.

birth to age 2 received $500 million in federal funds, and children ages 3 to 5 were provided $400 million in federal funds.

Because these were one time funds, they were directed to activities such as Child Find—a data system to track children, improve delivery of services, and establish accountability standards for young children with disabilities. It is important to note that children with disabilities were included in the omnibus effort of the federal government to strengthen the health and economy of our nation.

Federal Actions for Students with Special Gifts and Talents

Except for a brief period in the 1970s, there has been little movement at the federal legislative level to provide resources for the education of children who are gifted. The Javits Act (PL 100-297)—named after U.S. senator from New York Jacob Javits, who showed early interest and support—provided a small sum of money to support research and demonstration programs that focused on the special needs of gifted students from economically disadvantaged circumstances, from culturally or linguistically diverse families, or with disabilities (twice-exceptional). The Javits programs have helped with the development of alternative identification methods designed to measure intellectual ability in special populations more adequately (see Chapter 10 for a discussion of this movement).

2-3 The Role of the Courts

Another of society's social institutions, the court system, has played a significant role in the lives of children with exceptionalities and their families. It is the duty of the courts to rule on the interpretation of the laws and regulations generated by the executive and legislative branches. If the law says that every child is entitled to a "free and appropriate public education," how does that translate at the community level? Does that mean that a school cannot expel a child with disabilities? Many important court decisions have formed the foundation for special education.

The basic issue here is that children with special needs deserve a **free and appropriate public education (FAPE)**, just as do all children in the United States. If that right is being abridged, or if other inequities are being created, citizens can appeal to the courts for justice and equity. During the past four decades, a series of legal cases has solidified the rights of children with exceptionalities and their guaranteed right to FAPE.

A landmark case (1972) that began a series of court decisions in favor of children with exceptionalities and their right to FAPE was the *Pennsylvania Association for Retarded Children (PARC) v. Commonwealth of Pennsylvania* lawsuit and decision. In this case, the court decided that children with IDD could not be excluded from school and did have a right to FAPE and that when the Pennsylavania state constitution said "*all* children are entitled to a free public education," the term *all* did, in fact, refer to *all* children, including children with disabilities.

This movement toward judicial action was, in part, a recognition of the success of the Civil Rights movement in using the courts to establish their educational rights.

TABLE 2.2 Court Cases Affirming the Rights of Children with Disabilities

- A child with disabilities cannot be excluded from school without careful due process, and it is the responsibility of the schools to provide appropriate programs for children who are different (*Pennsylvania Association for Retarded Children v. Commonwealth of Pennsylvania,* 1972; *Goss v. Lopez,* 1974; *Hairston v. Drosick,* 1974).
- The presumed absence of funds is not an excuse for failing to provide educational services to children with exceptionalities. If sufficient funds are not available, then all programs should be cut back (*Mills v. Board of Education,* 1972).
- Children should not be labeled "handicapped" or placed into special education without adequate diagnosis that takes into account different cultural and linguistic backgrounds (*Larry P. v. Riles,* 1979).
- Bilingual children with exceptionalities need identification, evaluation, and educational procedures that reflect and respect their dual-language backgrounds (*Jose P. v. Ambach,* 1979).
- A child with disabilities is entitled to an appropriate, not an optimum, education (*Board of Education v. Rowley,* 1982). The Rowley decision was the first court decision that suggested that there was a limit to the resources that children with exceptionalities could expect.
- A subsequent case to the Rowley decision made it clear that such services, though not optimal, must be more than *de minimus*—that is, must provide sufficient support so the child with disabilities can benefit educationally (*Polk v. Central Susquehanna Intermediate Unit 16,* 1988).
- The post Rowley period is crowded with cases trying to determine just how much benefit is enough to satisfy the FAPE requirements. Zirkel (2013) summarized these cases by questioning whether the benefits are being interpreted too liberally—for example, finding that two months' worth of growth in a ten-month period is sufficient to satisfy the educational benefits clause. There is also a tendency to ignore procedural violations if there are seen to be "educational benefits." Zirkel calls for professional elevation of the standard of FAPE to make sure the goals of court decisions have been met.

In 1954, with the classic school desegregation case *Brown v. Board of Education,* the courts began to reaffirm the rights of minority citizens in a wide variety of settings. If court decisions could protect the rights of one group of citizens, they could do the same for another group: those with disabilities. Soon, supporters of people with disabilities were working to translate abstract legal rights into tangible social action through the judicial system.

Class action suits have been influential in changing the status of children with disabilities in the United States. A class action suit provides that legal action taken as part of the suit applies not only to the individual who brings the particular case to court but also to all members of the class to which that individual belongs. That means the rights of all people with disabilities can be reaffirmed by a single case involving just one child. The rulings in several court cases have reaffirmed the rights of individuals with disabilities and have defined the limits of those rights (see Table 2.2).

2-3a Inclusion and Funding Issues

After establishing the basic rights of children with disabilities to a free and appropriate public education, the courts then turned to the issues of **inclusion** (bring children with exceptionalities into regular classrooms) and **least restrictive environment** and to what an appropriate program for children with exceptionalities should be. The results are a mixture of rulings, some supporting a strong version of inclusion and some supporting a continuum of services (McCarthy, 1994):

- A child with a hearing disability was allowed to attend a school several miles from home instead of a neighborhood school because the centralized program at the special school better met the child's needs (*Barnett v. Fairfax County Board of Education,* 1991).

- A child with Down syndrome was placed in a general education program rather than in a special education class because of the presumed priority of inclusion in IDEA (*Greer v. Rome City School District*, 1991).
- A court ruled that it is the responsibility of the school district to demonstrate that the child's disabilities are so severe that he or she will receive little benefit from inclusion or will be so disruptive as to keep other classmates from learning (*Oberti v. Board of Education of the Borough of Clementon School District*, 1993).

Clearly, these rulings reflect the specifics of each individual case and the interpretation of local or district courts. It may take a Supreme Court decision to provide more general guidance on the issue of what "appropriate" means for education of children with exceptionalities. Nevertheless, when the courts speak, people listen; because court decisions represent the law as we currently know it, they must be obeyed.

The late 1990s saw an increased number of court cases concerning the provision of services for children with autism, with parents battling the schools for additional services for their children (Lord, 2001). The results of these court cases depended on local circumstances, with either side (parent or school) prevailing depending on the facts of the case.

2-3b Appropriate Special Education Services

During the last few years the questions raised in court cases have focused on whether the services recommended by the student's IEP committees were adequate or appropriate, or implemented appropriately. There were a few cases of *predetermination* (the school system had already made up its mind as to what it was going to do before meeting with the parents—a violation of proper procedure). They include the following:

- In a court case in Maine, a child with Asperger's syndrome (a form of autism discussed in Chapter 5) was denied special education services because she was performing well academically. She had attempted suicide and was determined by a psychiatrist to be depressed. The court determined that she should have special education. (*L.I. v. Maine School Administrative District*, 2007).
- A child with autism was awarded reimbursement for private school costs because the judge found that the public school system knowingly and repeatedly failed to provide an appropriate educational program *(Henrico County School Board v. R.T.*, 2006).

2-3c Parental Involvement

One of the themes that the courts strongly endorse is the importance of parents playing a key role in the FAPE their children with disabilities receive. For example, the parents are to be involved in the development of the Individual Education Program (IEP) for the child. In one case (*Drobnicki v. Poway United School District*, 2009), the school district scheduled an IEP meeting on a date when the student's parents could not attend; the district held the meeting anyway and told the parents they could attend via speakerphone. The U.S. Court of Appeals declared that this was a denial of the student receiving a FAPE.

In another case (*Winkleman v. Parma City School District*, 2007), the Supreme Court unanimously ruled that parental participation in the special education process is crucial to ensuring that children with disabilities receive a FAPE. The importance of parental participation in educational planning for their child should be clear to everyone.

Just as laws have to be enforced and money has to be appropriated, so court decisions have to be executed. The court decisions noted in the previous list created the expectation that something would be done, but they did not guarantee it. Closing down state institutions, reorganizing public schools, and providing special services to all children with disabilities are substantial and costly changes. They raised a serious problem for program administrators: Where would the money come from for implementation? Ultimately, school and local leaders turned to Washington, pressuring Congress to appropriate funds to help pay for the changes that the courts were demanding. Even with federal assistance, implementation has come slowly.

2-4 Educational Responses for Students with Exceptionalities

Most of us consider ourselves experts on the schools. After all, haven't we spent twelve or more years of our lives in them? Unfortunately, as students, our contact with the schools, in most instances, was limited to specific teachers and classrooms. Sometimes there was a principal to administer "corrective action" if our behavior got out of hand. We were only dimly aware of policies or standards that were influencing the teachers and their behavior.

We typically have never thought of the school as a social institution, even though schools are one of the most significant of all our social institutions. They remain one of our country's assets in the 21st century, in the economic and political competition that we will face internationally.

Schools in large measure are a mirror reflecting our society as a whole. Most of the values taught or demonstrated there are the values of the dominant sectors of society. Many of the problems encountered in the schools, such as lack of motivation, drug use, and violence, are part of the larger societal fabric.

Our discussion of schools as institutions focuses on the policies that influence teachers and other staff coping with students with disabilities and students with special gifts and talents. Five major tasks face the schools:

1. Finding the child with special needs
2. Identifying and specifying these needs in individual cases
3. Organizing special programming to meet these needs
4. Proving that the special programming works
5. Facilitating a proper transition to the community

In most instances, the policies and standards that are followed to accomplish those goals are made collaboratively, with many persons involved, including the classroom teacher and the child's parents. Sometimes these rules are made in the state capitals or in the executive branch of the federal government.

The legislation has set the expectation that children with disabilities will have a free and appropriate public education. The courts have reaffirmed those rights and specified some of the conditions under which these rights must be met. It is now up to educators to provide the framework by which benefits can flow to these students.

McNulty and Gloeckler (2011) have outlined five key elements by which schools can reach these high expectations:

1. **Ownership:** Understanding among staff that students receiving special education services are the responsibility of all.
2. **High Expectations:** Understanding by administrators, faculty, and students that all students will be challenged and expected to perform to the best of their ability.
3. **Intervention Systems:** Policies, procedures, and protocols to ensure that struggling learners meet academic and/or behavioral expectations as measured by improved performance.

4. **Inclusion/Collaborative Teaching:** Teaching methodologies in which students receiving special education services are included in the general education classrooms and have access to both content and special education expertise.
5. **Organizational/Professional Development:** Successful programs for all struggling learners depend on alignment to and access to standards-based curriculum instruction and assessment and data-driven professional development to support teachers in achieving goals.

One of the educator's tasks is to demonstrate that these noble procedures and goals have been met.

The trend toward accountability, a term used to determine whether educators have done what they said they would do for their students, has forced special education to demonstrate not only that children with exceptionalities are receiving special services, but also whether the students have profited from a special program as expected.

The focus on accountability has raised the question regarding which of two seemingly contradictory purposes should be emphasized. IDEA 2004 proposed the need for specially designed instruction (meaning shaping or creating lessons to meet the special needs of the individual who has those needs), which is to be spelled out in the IEP. However, IDEA 2004 *also* wishes to ensure the children with exceptionalities have access to the general curriculum. This would mean that exceptional children will be included in regular class activities to the extent that they can master the basic facts and knowledge that all students are expected to master. The fact that the vast majority of children with exceptionalities are to be included in statewide testing programs (only a small percentage, 3 percent, are allowed to take alternative assessments) indicates that the schools are expected to attain *both* of these desirable goals—individual plans and access to general curriculum—and that it is the responsibility of the schools to achieve these results in individual circumstances.

2-4a Finding the Child with Special Needs

A child may be referred for special education services for any of a variety of reasons; most often referrals are made on the basis of observations by school staff that this child differs from his peers in a significant way that is affecting his or her learning in school.

Sometimes the school will administer screening tests in reading or arithmetic in the early grades in an effort to discover children who need special help before they have identified themselves to their teachers through either failure or extraordinary success in school. For example, Paul, age 8, has been referred for special education services because his third-grade teacher, Mrs. Parker, claims he is insolent, talks back to her, is not mastering his reading and math skills, and is continually disturbing the other children. Maybe Paul acts this way because he has a serious learning disability or behavioral disorder, or maybe he and the teacher have just started off on the wrong foot. He may be reacting in a predictable way to his inability to do the schoolwork (which may seem uninteresting to him anyway), and Mrs. Parker may not know how to cope with Paul's frustrations.

In such a situation, many school systems establish a **prereferral committee**, or a child study committee, to find ways of coping with a child's behavior short of a referral for special education services (Buck, Polloway, Smith-Thomas, & Cook, 2003). In this case, the assistant principal, a master teacher, and a psychologist meet with Mrs. Parker to see what she might be able to do to help Paul adjust. Not every child having trouble adjusting to school is a candidate for special education.

TABLE 2.3 Educational Adaptations

Adapting the learning environment	One can change the physical setting in which special services are delivered to make the instruction more likely to be effective.
Adapting the curriculum	It is often necessary to modify the curriculum content of the lessons to meet the needs of children with exceptionalities who are performing markedly below or above the rest of the class.
Adapting teaching strategies	Special strategies are needed for coping with behavior and attentional problems and for organizing and presenting content to meet the needs of students with exceptionalities.
Adapting assistive and instructional technology	Special assistive technology devices help students with exceptionalities to communicate and receive information; instructional technology devices aid them in mastering necessary knowledge and skills.

TeachSource Digital Download Access online

In Paul's case, several weeks have gone by with no appreciable improvement in his behavior despite the modifications his teacher has made, so a formal referral is made, calling for a comprehensive assessment of Paul and consideration for special education. Even if Paul is not eligible for special education services, he may still need educational help—perhaps in Tier II of the RtI model.

2-4b Planning for Children with Special Needs

It's important to realize that the reason special education exists is *not* that regular education has failed. Classroom teachers and general educational programs simply cannot respond fully to the special needs of children with exceptionalities without a substantial change in the structure, program, and staffing of the typical classroom.

Instruction can be adapted to the **interindividual** and **intraindividual differences** found in children with exceptionalities in several ways. Table 2.3 provides a brief view of the major adaptations included in special education.

2-4c Individual Education Programs (IEP)

Once the students with special needs have been identified, then a major effort is undertaken to assess those needs and plan for meeting those needs within the framework of the school. These can be done in two major ways: (1) organizationally to change the learning environment and the personnel needed and (2) instructionally through changing the curriculum and instructional strategies necessary to meet the students' instructional needs.

One of the ways of identifying individual needs is the **individualized education program (IEP)**. Once you remove the child from the regular classroom, there still remains the problem of the differentiation of the educational program. Should the program just be what the special education teacher is able to come up with from her or his own experience?

To counteract this vagueness, Gallagher (1972) proposed a special education contract for each student that stated specific goals for each student, the parental participation in the plan, and a means of determining whether the goals had been met. These procedures were codified in the Education for All Handicapped Children Act (1975), which required that each child must have an individual plan

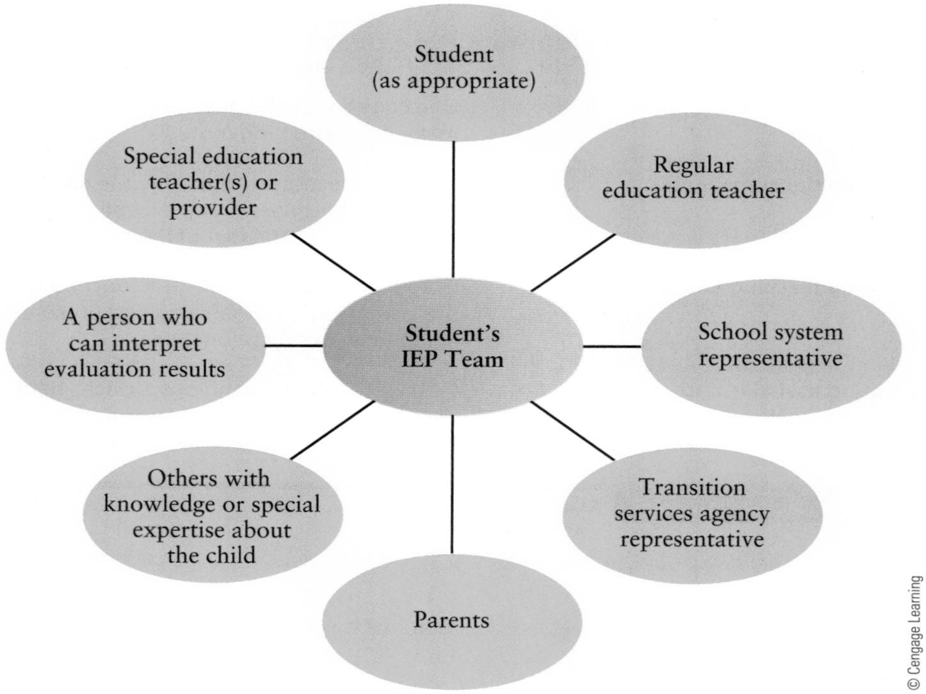

Figure 2.2 A Student's IEP Team

TeachSource Digital Download Access online

to meet his or her needs. Extensive regulations have been written to determine who makes the plans, who carries out the plans, and who determines the success of the plans.

One of the unique features of the IEP is not only the plan itself for each individual student with disabilities but also how the plan is constructed. The members of the team, as prescribed by law, include:

1. Parent or guardian of the child
2. One regular educator with responsibility for implementing the plan
3. A special educator with responsibility for implementing the plan
4. A principal or administrator who takes responsibility for seeing to it that the plan is implemented
5. Other personnel whose specialized knowledge can be helpful in constructing a plan (e.g., school psychologist, social worker, and so on; see Figure 2.2)

The required presence of the parent or guardian is a clear sign that the IEP is expected to take into account the wishes and feelings of the family of the student as well as the educators involved.

Table 2.4 outlines the major parts of the IEP as provided by the U.S. Department of Education (2004). As a specific example, an IEP sequence for a child who has a reading disability might be as follows:

1. ***Present level of performance (PLOP):*** Reads first-grade material at 20 to 30 words per minute with between 5 and 10 errors; guesses at all unknown words.
2. ***Service to be provided:*** One-to-one tutoring in highly structured reading program; five sessions weekly, 45 minutes each; provided in private, quiet setting.
3. ***Annual goal:*** Given a 500-word story at third-grade reading level, student will read 80 to 100 words per minute with 0 to 2 errors.

TeachSource Digital Download

Several full IEP examples can be accessed online.

TABLE 2.4 Individualized Education Program (IEP)

The IEP is a written document that is developed for each eligible child with a disability. It includes:

- A statement of the child's present levels of academic achievement and functional performance, including:
  - How the child's disability affects the child's involvement and progress in the general education curriculum (i.e., the same curriculum given to nondisabled children) or for preschool children
- A statement of measurable annual goals, including academic and functional goals designed to:
  - Meet the child's needs that result from the child's disability, to enable the child to be involved in and make progress in the general education curriculum
  - Meet each of the child's other educational needs that result from the child's disability
- A description of how the child's progress toward meeting the annual goals will be measured
- A statement of the *special education and related services* and *supplementary aids and services,* based on peer-reviewed research to the extent practicable, that are to be provided to the child, or on behalf of the child, and *a statement of the program modifications or supports* for school personnel that will be provided to enable the child:
  - To advance appropriately toward attaining the annual goals
  - To be involved in and make progress in the general education curriculum and to participate in extracurricular and other nonacademic activities
  - To be educated and participate with other children with disabilities and nondisabled children in extracurricular and other nonacademic activities
- An explanation of the extent, if any, to which the child will *not* participate with nondisabled children in the regular classroom and in extracurricular and other nonacademic activities
- If the IEP team determines that the child must take an alternate assessment instead of a particular regular state or districtwide assessment of student achievement, a statement of why:
  - The child cannot participate in the regular assessment, and
  - The particular alternate assessment selected is appropriate for the child
- The projected date for the beginning of the services and modifications and the anticipated frequency, location, and duration of *special education and related services* and *supplementary aids and services* and *modifications and supports*

SOURCE: Office of Special Education Programs, U.S. Department of Education, 2004.

TeachSource Digital Download Access online

IEPs and Transition

Surveys have shown a number of former special education students having problems adjusting to adulthood in the community (see U.S. Department of Education, 2004). Because of these difficulties, a section has been added to the IEP for students 16 years and older that addresses transition planning. This plan should be in effect when the child turns 16, or younger if determined appropriate by the IEP team, and updated annually thereafter. The IEP must include the following: appropriate measurable postsecondary goals based upon age-appropriate transition assessments related to training, education, employment, and, where appropriate, independent living skills. The transition services (including courses of study) needed to assist the child in reaching those goals must be specifically provided.

Another addition that can be made to the standard IEP is a **behavior intervention plan (BIP)** for those students who have been excluded from school for more than ten days for disciplinary reasons. Students with these intense behavioral needs should have a **functional behavioral assessment** that considers events preceding the precipitating cause. The BIP must include positive behavior intervention and strategies to help the student back into the academic community. It should also include a clear statement of the targeted behaviors to be increased (e.g., time on task), the intervention strategies to be used, and the quantitative outcomes to be achieved (Bateman & Linden, 2006). IEPs are particularly useful in cataloging the range of positive behavior strategies and the hopeful consequences of those strategies.

A number of attempts have been made to bring together "access to the general education curriculum" and the "meeting of individual needs" in inclusive settings for children with disabilities. For example, a junior high science program in an inner-city neighborhood was designed to include students with disabilities by establishing teams of special education and general education teachers and constructing a variety of hands-on materials and tasks to aid in comprehension. Crucial to the programs was a 100-hour training program for 15 three-person teams to prepare them for team activities in the classrooms and to aid in bonding personnel to a common purpose and common curriculum. Fifteen students with a diagnosis of severe emotional and behavior disturbances (E/BDs) or serious learning disabilities (LDs) were included in the 114 students involved.

The results indicated that the students with disabilities had the same passing rate (69 percent) as the general education students (from a neighborhood school in a poverty setting), and the social adjustment during the program was good, with discipline referrals and attendance figures within acceptable limits (Cawley, Hayden, Cade, & Baker-Kroczynski, 2002).

2-4d Adapting the Learning Environment

Often, a special learning environment is necessary to help some children with exceptionalities master particular content and skills. Making changes in the learning environment, however, has repercussions throughout the entire educational system. This may be one reason organizational modifications are the subject of greater controversy than are changes in either content or skills.

The Inclusion Movement

Inclusion has been the most significant movement in special education over the past three decades. As an educational philosophy, it essentially says that children with exceptionalities should be *a part of, not apart from,* general education. The question that still bothers both special educators and general educators is how the philosophy of inclusion can be made operational in so many different schools in so many different communities. Additional questions include:

- Does inclusion mean that the child with exceptionalities is always to be placed in the general education classroom?
- Does inclusion mean that the essential responsibility for the education of the children with exceptionalities is in the hands of the general classroom teacher?

The concept of least-restrictive environment means that teachers attempt to educate a child in the organizational setting that maximizes the chances that the child with exceptionalities will respond successfully to the educational goals and objectives set for him or her. It should *not* be imagined, however, that the emphasis on inclusion has brought all children with exceptionalities back into the general education classroom.

The legislation and court cases supporting inclusion have clearly had an effect. If the existing trends are maintained, even more students will likely receive supports and services in inclusive classrooms than today. Our challenge will be to provide the special services and support needed to educate children with exceptionalities in those inclusive classrooms.

Inclusion in Context

Part of the inclusion process depends on what resources will be available to help general education classroom teachers. Will special education teachers be available

Ellen Senisi/The Image Works

Group discussion in an inclusive classroom.

in the classroom with the general education teacher for a significant amount of time to help with special instruction? Will paraprofessionals be present to provide necessary assistance to the children with special needs, particularly students with physical disabilities? Will general educators receive personnel preparation for their new roles in working with children with special needs?

Those who support inclusion generally believe that supportive resources will be available for the general education teacher, whereas critics point to many situations in which the support forces are not there (Hunt & McDonnell, 2007). An alternative to full inclusion emphasizes providing a continuum of services based on each child's individual needs. The RtI approach, with its tiers of service, can help provide this continuum of services.

Social Relationships in the Inclusive Classroom

The formation of social relationships is an overarching goal for those supporting the inclusion movement, in addition to mastery of certain academic and technical skills. This is the position of The Association for Persons with Severe Handicaps (TASH), which advocates for inclusion. The policy of full inclusion follows this path of reasoning: If we are to have, as a major goal, the social integration of persons with disabilities into adult society, then the school environment should foster the development of social skills, personal friendships, and relationships among children with and without disabilities. These skills are available to nondisabled persons in the natural course of their educational experiences. Box 2.1 provides a portrait of a girl with autism that illustrates the importance of intervention for the development of students' social skills.

2-4e Organizing Special Planning to Meet Needs

The Information Processing Model in Identifying Needs

The information processing model (IPM) introduced in Chapter 1 can be used to identify special areas requiring educational attention, such as children with visual problems or children with learning disabilities. It also could be used to highlight the issues for individual children like Dianne.

Dianne is a second grader who has performed poorly in the first grade for no obvious reason. As a candidate for special education, Dianne was given a variety of

BOX 2.1 EXCEPTIONAL LIVES • EXCEPTIONAL STORIES

Inclusion for Caryn

Caryn is a 13-year-old girl who has been diagnosed with mild autism. She attends seventh grade in a midwestern suburban public school. Caryn's parents can be considered middle to upper middle class, and both have university degrees. Both she and her only sibling, a younger brother, have been identified as having autism. Both have received special education services throughout their public school education. Caryn is fully included in the classroom and receives speech and language services as well as the services of a special education teacher. Her brother has more intensive needs and requires greater accommodations and services.

Unlike many children with autism, Caryn does not demonstrate intellectual or developmental disabilities. Testing has revealed that Caryn's intellectual ability and academic achievement are in the average range. She can be described as a solitary child who enjoys horseback riding. Caryn has often told her parents, "I'm a loner. I like to be with animals more than people." While an interest in horses can be typical for a child of her age, her range of interests is restricted, and she will "get stuck" on the topic of horses and their care.

The social requirements of family get-togethers are also difficult for her. She will greet everyone only if promised she can go to her room afterward. Caryn does not seek social interactions and will often avoid situations in which she must interact with others. Until the second grade, Caryn never entered the classroom nor went to her seat directly. In an effort to avoid peer interactions, she would circle the room along the wall until she reached her seat. Up until age 10 or so, she observed others and played in parallel. It has only been within the last two years that she has started to initiate social interaction with her peers.

tests and observed in the classroom. Her first-grade teacher was also interviewed. The intent was to rule out possible causes for her poor academic performance.

As ◗ Figure 2.3 indicates, Dianne's vision and hearing test results were normal. She was not judged as having emotional difficulties—although her frustration was growing about her inability to do her work. Her general academic aptitude fell into the normal range, so the planning team was left wondering why Dianne couldn't read. The central problem (revealed by diagnostic tests and observation) is her inability to translate visual symbols from print to understanding, which would indicate a learning disability. Dianne's learning disability requires special attention and tutoring to help her translate these important visual symbols into meaning.

As Figure 2.3 illustrates, Diane's central problem of processing information can lead to secondary problems. If she is having trouble reading, this will obviously impact her writing and perhaps her peer relations (social interactions) and may even cause her to feel depressed and unhappy (emotional context). So one problem in the IPM can easily lead to others unless they are contained or remediated.

In Diane's case, but not necessarily with other children with the same exceptionality, she may lose her ability to make good decisions in school, her executive function. This is why school systems need support services to back up the general education teacher.

In the past decades, we have increasingly recognized that quality education requires more than just well-prepared teachers. A series of support services are needed to help these students with special needs (Gallagher, 2006; Mainzer, Deshler, Coleman, Kozleski, & Rodriguez-Walling, 2003).

2-4f The Need for Collaboration

The special needs of children with exceptionalities require the knowledge and skills of a large number of disciplines to devise a comprehensive plan. In medicine alone, pediatricians, geneticists, orthopedists, neurologists, and many other specialists may be helpful in individual cases. Then there are educators, psychologists, sociologists, social workers, special educators, speech/language therapists,

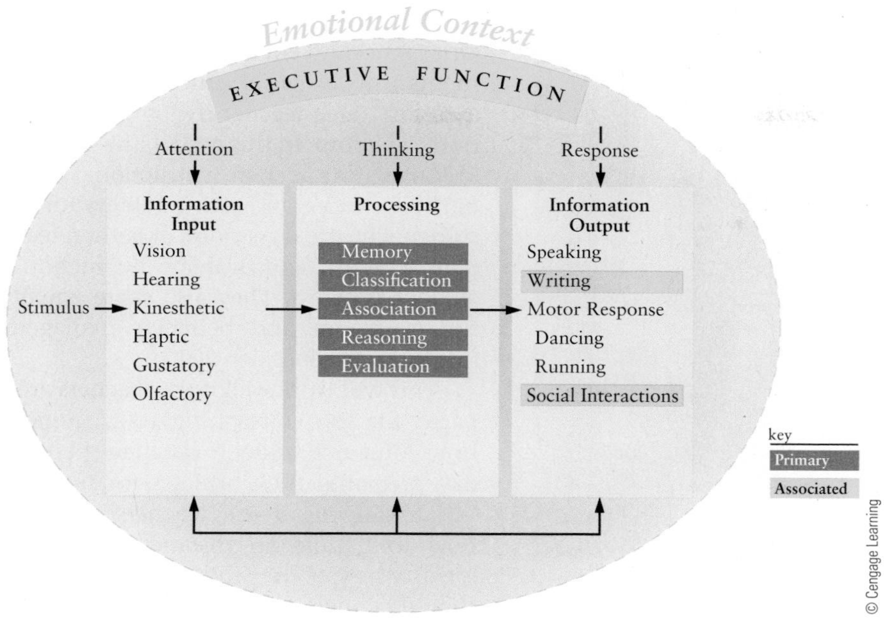

Figure 2.3 Dianne's Information Processing Model

TeachSource Digital Download Access online

occupational therapists, and others who may have needed knowledge and skills to add to a plan.

Think of Larry, who has a mild physical impairment with suspected brain injury, a hearing loss, and a communication problem, and who is not learning at his age level. How will we meet his needs except in some form of collaborative services?

It has always been difficult to bring all of these various specialists together to chart out a plan such as an IEP, because they work in different areas and institutions—hospitals, schools, universities, and so forth. This is one of the important jobs of the director of special education.

Introducing the Team Approach

Similar to the multidisciplinary approach described earlier, we endorse the view that education of children with exceptionalities is a *team game*. Professional collaboration becomes critical as the vehicle for bringing quality educational services to children with special needs. While we can have some feelings of nostalgia for a picture of thirty students and a fourth-grade teacher, no one should really expect one general education teacher to cope with the needs of thirty children, three of whom will likely need special education services, five or six more who will need adaptations to support them in the regular education curriculum, and some who may be advanced several years in some academic areas.

What we really need to ask is whether the education professionals and paraprofessionals (trained aides who assist teachers) have been prepared to play the roles necessary for good teamwork. Most of the general education teachers at work now have been prepared to act independently, with little team experience. Even with the development of an IEP, the emphasis is often on limited professional interaction.

We don't expect college professors to teach one course in English, another in nuclear physics, and another in African geography. In this light, our demands on elementary and middle school teachers to handle multiple content and process areas seem far from reasonable. If we hope to meet the needs of all children, then we must expect teachers to become used to working collaboratively with their colleagues, each of whom brings something special to the table for planning for children with exceptional needs.

MR Bob Daemmrich/The Image Works

Instruction can be adapted to the differences found in exceptional children in several ways—by varying the learning environment, the content of lessons and the skills being taught, and by introducing technology that can meet special needs.

Team Teaching

One of the most effective **co-teaching** arrangements pairs a special education teacher with a content area teacher in the general education classroom. In this model, the general and special educators share instructional responsibility, resources, and accountability for all the students in the classroom. Together, teachers plan, present, and evaluate instruction and student progress. They also share equally in the classroom and behavior management (McNulty & Gloeckler, 2011).

This will work well if the teachers are prepared for the co-teaching roles (remember how long our athletic coaches spend each day preparing their athletes for teamwork). What happens if the teachers disagree on how to handle an instance of misbehavior or whether the students with disabilities should be included in group projects or what their roles in those groups should be? All of this needs to be worked out in advance. Has time been allotted to help co-teachers reach accommodation beforehand? It should not be assumed that two strong persons can spontaneously come forward with easy decisions without some rules of the game set up before they start.

2-4g Support Services

For all of these special organizational and instructional changes to work, we will need to have an array of support services to aid the regular school staff. In many ways these support services resemble the well-organized system supporting the medical practitioner. Think about how limited your own physician would be without laboratories and x-ray technicians to help with diagnosis, active pharmaceutical enterprises producing new effective drugs, hospitals where special treatments can be applied, or medical schools that do important research on new techniques and produce new generations of qualified physicians. So when some say, "I have a really good doctor," they actually mean "I have a good health-care system."

If we do not provide that hard-working general education or special education teacher with a similar collection of support services, then we are placing our teacher in the same situation the physician would be in if deprived of his or her supports. One version of a quality support system consists of the components listed in Table 2.5.

The Office of Special Education Programs (OSEP) in the U.S. Department of Education has supported a number of organizations that provide additional help to parents and professionals seeking ways to help children with disabilities. One of these is the National Dissemination Center for Children with Disabilities, which provides a wide range of information upon request, including background of legislation, definitions, fact sheets on specific disabilities, and where one can go to obtain additional information.

National Dissemination Center for Children with Disabilities
http://nichcy.org

2-4h Curriculum and Instruction for Students with Special Needs

Even after we have made necessary organizational changes, we still face the challenge of how we will change the instruction to meet the specific needs of the exceptional child.

TABLE 2.5 Special Education Support Systems

Personnel preparation	The importance of programs designed to prepare specialists cannot be overestimated, and many institutions of higher education have cooperated in providing such programming.
Technical assistance	Continued support for the classroom teacher and administrators has been achieved through such organizations as Regional Resource Centers and the National Early Childhood Technical Assistance Center (NECTAC).
Research and program evaluation	There is a continual need to develop better techniques for diagnosing children with special needs and evaluate programs of effectiveness.
Communication	With the growing use of the Internet, websites can help disseminate information. URLs for selected websites have been placed in the margins throughout this book.
Demonstration	Sometimes it is important for teachers and administrators to actually see new ideas and practices in action. There is a series of demonstration centers for children with disabilities that offer programs illustrating techniques for teachers and administrators.
Data systems	An often-overlooked aid is a system of data collection that provides information about the availability of specialists, the number and types of students needing special assistance, and program effectiveness.
Comprehensive planning	The need for long-range government planning has been well accepted. The issue is how to coordinate the various support elements so that educational resources are available in the right place and at the right time.

Adapted from Gallagher, J., & Clifford, R. (2000). The missing support infrastructure in early childhood. *Early Childhood Research and Practices,* 2(1), 1–24.

Common Core State Standards

COMMON CORE STATE STANDARDS

One of the most important initiatives of the current educational scene has been the development of the **Common Core State Standards (CCSS)**. Stimulated in part by the relatively poor performance of U.S. students in international comparisons, the CCSS was designed to clearly state what skills and knowledge are expected from K–12 students in language arts and mathematics. The initiative was designed by the Council of State School Officers and the National Governors Association to produce a set of standards on language arts and mathematics for each grade level.

Teams of teachers, educators, and content specialists, drawing on already existing state standards, drafted the CCSS. These standards are going to challenge many students with disabilities severely; helping students toward these goals will require teamwork and support services.

In recognition of these problems, the creators of these standards included a message for special education. Namely, while the CCSS present what is to be learned, they do not say how these things will be taught. They assume "that how these standards are taught and assessed is the utmost importance in reaching this group of students." They urge the incorporation of the following types of supports:

- Supports and related services designed to meet the unique needs of these students and to enable them to access the general education curriculum (IDEA 34 CFR #300, 34, 2004).
- An Individual Education Program (IEP) which includes annual goals aligned with and chosen to facilitate attainment of grade-level academic standards.
- Teachers and specialized instructional support personnel who are prepared and qualified to deliver high-quality, evidence-based, individualized instruction and support services.

While the CCSS go into great detail regarding the knowledge and skills that the student is expected to learn at each level, they do not provide any advice as to how these are to be accomplished (see Table 2.6 for example).

COMMON CORE STATE STANDARDS

Think about how a teacher with a child who is autistic or has a math learning disability will help this student to meet the standards. Notice that the sixth-grade standards, in particular, assume a great deal of prior mastery of basic skills in

TABLE 2.6 Examples of Common Core State Standards

English Language Arts & Literacy in History/Social Studies, Science, and Technical Subjects	
Grade 3 Writing Standard 3	Write narratives to develop real or imagined experience or events using effective technique, descriptive details, and clear event sequences. **a.** Establish a situation and introduce a narrator and/or characters; organize an event sequence that unfolds naturally. **b.** Use dialogue and descriptions of actions, thoughts, and feelings to develop experiences and events or show the response of characters to situations. **c.** Use temporal words and phrases to signal event order. **d.** Provide a sense of closure.
Grade 6 Reading Standard 9	Compare and contrast texts in different forms or genres (e.g. stories and poems; historical novels and fantasy stories) in terms of their approaches to similar themes and topics.
Mathematics	
Grade 3 Measurement and Data Standard	Solve problems involving measurement and estimation of intervals of time, liquid volumes, and masses of objects. **1.** Tell and write time to the nearest minute and measure time intervals in minutes. Solve word problems involving addition and subtraction of time intervals in minutes, for example, by representing the problem on a number line diagram. **2.** Measure and estimate liquid volumes and masses of objects using standard units of grams (g), kilograms (kg), and liters (l). Add, subtract, multiply, or divide to solve one-step word problems involving masses or volumes that are given in the same units, for example, by using drawings (such as a beaker with a measurement scale) to represent the problem.
Grade 6 Geometry Standard	Solve real-world and mathematical problems involving area, surface area, and volume. **1.** Find the area of right triangles, other triangles, special quadrilaterals, and polygons by composing into rectangles or decomposing into triangles and other shapes; apply these techniques in the context of solving real-world and mathematical problems. **2.** Find the volume of a right rectangular prism with fractional edge lengths by packing it with unit cubes of the appropriate unit fraction edge lengths, and show that the volume is the same as would be found by multiplying the edge lengths of the prism. Apply the formulas $V = l \times w \times h$ and $V = b \times h$ to find volumes of right rectangular prisms with fractional edge lengths in the context of solving real-world and mathematical problems. **3.** Draw polygons in the coordinate plane given coordinates for the vertices; use coordinates to find the length of a side joining points with the same first coordinate or the same second coordinate. Apply these techniques in the context of solving real-world and mathematical problems. **4.** Represent three-dimensional figures using nets made up of rectangles and triangles, and use the nets to find the surface area of these figures. Apply these techniques in the context of solving real-world and mathematical problems.

order to reach student success. Students with emotional difficulties or who have hearing or vision problems pose special problems. It seems clear that a team of educators and assistants collaborating together will be necessary to reach success on these goals.

As we will discuss in more detail in further chapters, it is how the schools organize themselves to meet such problems, as well as the skills of individual teachers, that will determine the meeting of these goals, or any other standards that may be proposed.

Each of the following chapters will comment on how the CCSS may be met with the particular exceptionality. Tests are being developed to measure the attainment of CCSS and are expected to be ready in 2014–15. It will surely be a challenge for the schools to attain good results, especially with the fiscal restraints facing many states.

Building on Developmental Strengths

Children with learning problems used to be presented as having widely varying developmental weaknesses, and those weaknesses became the focal point of special education efforts to try to make the children's developmental patterns more even. The focus was largely on correcting the deficit or fixing what was "wrong with the child." So if a child who was deaf and missing oral language were approached, an enormous effort was made to help him or her to talk, and other developmental areas, such as cognition and social processes, were often ignored or downplayed.

We now realize that we can be more effective by analyzing a child's *strengths* and focusing a therapeutic program around these strengths. Therefore, now increased efforts are being made to find and support the child's and family's strengths so that these can help mitigate the areas of challenge.

Adapting Teacher Strategies

Much of the preparation of special educators deals with adapting instruction to the needs and levels of the students. This need for teacher flexibility is exemplified by the **Universal Design for Learning (UDL)** approach, a teaching strategy to build flexibility into the instruction so that the products and environments can be usable by the largest possible number of students. UDL promises three crucial steps to be taken to make inclusion work:

1. Provide multiple ways to access information, including text, audio clips, and video.
2. Provide multiple methods that allow students to interact with new information and develop new skills through text, audio, video, technology, and so forth.
3. Provide multiple methods for students to communicate their understanding of a given topic or acquisition of a particular skill through multiple ways (Russell, Hoffmann, & Higgins, 2009).

Considerable help will be required to translate these principles into workable classroom reality and transform the print-bound materials that have formed the basis for the usual education curriculum. The Office of Special Education Programs (OSEP) funded the Center for Applied Special Technology (CAST), whose task was to develop technology to provide diverse means of delivering information.

CAST, in turn, established the National Instructional Materials Accessibility Standard (NIMAS), whose purpose was to produce alternative presentations of materials that could be received by students with a wide variety of individual

Center for Applied Special Technology (CAST)
www.cast.org

needs. One of the major strategies was to digitize textbooks to make them accessible through text-to-speech technology, Braille, or other visual means for those who cannot learn through the standard print methods (Rose & Meyer, 2002).

The next task was to alert special education teachers and curriculum specialists about how they could utilize these new materials and methods. A major technical assistance program for states, disability experts, and publishers was undertaken in an effort to provide training and information to a growing number of educators about this new technology. NIMAS guides the production and electronic distribution of digital versions of textbooks and other instructional materials, as well as conducts workshops and technical assistance for special and general educators across the country. The activities of institutes such as CAST and NIMAS will make the future a more productive one for children with special needs.

In UDL, the assistive supports are built in rather than added as an afterthought. One of the key examples of UDL flexibility is closed captioning allowing persons with hearing problems to read the text at the bottom of the screen. The same message is being delivered through two separate channels—visual and auditory. UDL also allows flexibility in student expression. Instead of giving a paper-and-pencil answer, a student may use drawings or illustrations or respond through a computer.

A careful analysis of four secondary schools in four different states illustrates the UDL approach (Wallace, Anderson, Bartholomay, & Hupp, 2002). After extensive observations of general education students and special education students, the authors reached the following conclusions:

- Merely including students with disabilities in the general education classroom is not enough to ensure their success.
- The school administration in each of the schools must support team teaching with special and general education teachers.
- A significant amount of time must be spent guiding students in their preparation for learning and teaching them directly, using a variety of strategies, including technology.
- Teachers must know a variety of instructional strategies in order to address the diverse learning needs of students, and they need to know how to work with each other to effectively implement the strategies (p. 357).

In short, success in UDL is neither an accident nor attributable to good luck. It requires extensive planning, preparation, and teamwork. These plans may be made in Tier I of the RtI model for all classroom students and will also be incorporated in Tiers II and III for students with more intense needs. Chapters 3 to 13 each contain a Digital Download illustration of how the Common Core State Standards can be applied (using UDL) to the category of disability discussed within the chapter.

2-4i Technological Assistance for Instruction

Special education has often led the way in the acceptance and use of technology in education. That achievement may well be due to the unique challenges that special educators face. Because they are educating children with special needs, they have been willing to try new devices, such as computers adapted to special needs, hearing aids, print magnifiers, and machines that trace eye movements as the student reads.

There are two quite different uses of technology for children with disabilities: assistive and instructional technologies.

Assistive Technology

Assistive technology is designed primarily to allow the child with special needs to gain *access* to information. For the person who is blind, it provides Braille readers and typewriters; for the person who is deaf, hearing aids; for the person who cannot speak, communication boards for pointing to and composing messages. Assistive technology can be as sophisticated as a device that translates print into oral language or as simple as a headband and a pointer that allow students who have cerebral palsy to point to text or communication boards. Such devices have dramatically improved individual children's ability to receive and transmit information effectively, and are most often used with children with moderate to severe disabilities that create major barriers to communication. Many of the subsequent chapters include examples of the uses of assistive technology. We often think of assistive technology as being sophisticated, complicated, or computer-driven, but this is not always the case. Assistive technology devices, in fact, can be classified as low-, middle-, or high-tech.

- Low-tech devices may include nonelectronic devices like pencil grips, adaptive spoon handles, and picture boards (these may not involve technology at all!).
- Middle-tech devices include things like audiobooks, word-processing computers, sound recorders, and other uncomplicated mechanical devices.
- High-tech assistive devices are usually specifically designed to support an individual's needs and may include speech recognition software, electronic communication devices, and mobility technologies for guiding wheel chairs.

With the support of assistive technology, individuals with disabilities can often participate fully in many activities (Gersten & Edybum, 2007).

The National Assistive Technology Research Institute suggests that when considering what kind of assistive technology would be useful we:

- identify the environments where the student lives, works, and plays.
- determine the functional areas where support would be helpful.
- select the assistive technology device that can be used across all settings to maximize functioning (Bausch, Ault, & Hasselbring, 2006).

It is also important to remember that the best device is not always the most high-tech. Sometimes a lower-tech option like a communication picture board is more useful than a sophisticated communication device. The selection of the right device also depends on the demands of the environment in combination with the developmental level of the individual (Campbell, Milbourne, Dugan, & Wilcox, 2006). As the child grows and/or the demands change, the assistive technology support must be adapted and modified as well. When assistive technology is needed, the child's IEP should describe what and how this is to be provided and include a plan for periodically reviewing the appropriateness of the device.

Each chapter of this text includes a discussion of how assistive technology can be used to enhance the lives of individuals with special needs.

Purestock/Jupiter Images

The effective use of technology is one important goal for instruction.

Instructional Technology

Instructional technology is developed primarily as a means to deliver content and instruction in an appropriate manner to children with exceptionalities.

Major attempts are being made to go beyond the traditional transmission of knowledge and to use technology as a means to aid children with exceptionalities in thinking and problem solving. As an example, Hasselbring (2001) points out that a student may understand how the special characteristics of a camel may help the animal survive desert sandstorms, yet fail to understand that this survival illustrates the phenomenon of adaptation. When asked about the concept of adaptation, the student may not realize that her knowledge of camels is relevant or is a good illustration of the term.

Legislation (IDEA, 2004) mandates the mastery of technology on the part of special education teachers, and so teachers must now consider the appropriateness of assistive and instructional technology as tools for intervention. The technology can provide access to data and other programs. Even more important, computers allow children to learn at their own rate and provide immediate feedback and reinforcement. The child's learning becomes more active and self-directed.

AbleData: Assistive Technology
www.abledata.com

2-5 Cultural Differences and Exceptionalities

Research and experience has shown us that we need to pay special attention to students who have exceptionalities (such as autism or learning disabilities) and also come from diverse cultural backgrounds with different values and family expectations (Garcia, Ortiz, & Sorrells, 2012).

2-5a Cultural and Language Diversity and Assessment

Special attention should be paid to the possible test biases caused by the assumption that the student has had a set of standard experiences in the mainstream culture (Klingner, Blanchett, & Harry, 2007). As the number of children from Latino families rapidly increases, so does concern about the appropriate referral of these students to special education services. As pointed out by Klingner and Harry (2006), the RtI three-tier model may have the potential for more appropriate placement and planning.

2-5b Assessment and Culture

It is easy to understand that a child who does not have English as a first language can be poorly assessed with an achievement test written in English. What are we testing in such a situation—the child's vocabulary or his or her cultural experience (Salvia, Ysseldyke, & Bolt, 2012)?

A number of attempts have been made to promote a nonbiased assessment for children from different cultures, including the use of interpreters, "culture fair" tests, separate norms, and so on—all of which have their drawbacks. Trends have been toward supplementing standardized tests with alternative assessments, informal procedures, or the use of a mix of formal and informal measures to try to capture the child's range of abilities. The real problem may lie not in the tests themselves but in their interpretations (McLaughlin & Lewis, 2001; Salvia, Ysseldyke, & Bolt, 2007).

Consider Jorge, a 10-year-old Hispanic child with learning disabilities that prevent him from grasping the reading process. Jorge comes from a rich tradition of a close-knit family with common interests and loyalty. The family is wary about the Anglo school Jorge is attending. When teachers and psychologists of a culture different from the family's tell the family that something is wrong with Jorge's approach to school, are they reflecting a prejudice against Jorge because of his Hispanic background and his bilingual family? Are they going to help Jorge, or is this a way to prevent Jorge from getting a proper education? Will Jorge's father, misunderstanding the school's message, put even *more* pressure on Jorge to do well in school, assuming that his son is not giving proper effort to his school lessons?

BOX 2.2 Concerns about Assessment for Culturally and Linguistically Diverse Students

1. *Is there a higher incidence of children with special needs or giftedness among some racial and ethnic groups?* Yes. Disproportionate numbers of minority students are living in poverty. Major differences in measured aptitude between groups are documented at kindergarten entry.
2. *Does schooling contribute to these differences found in racial and ethnic groups?* Yes. Schools with higher concentrations of low-income minority students have fewer well-trained teachers and fewer resources.
3. *Does the current referral and assessment process reliably identify students with special needs and gifts, or is it biased by race and ethnicity?* The answer to this is not clear, although it does seem that minority status increases likelihood that the scores on assessment measures may be depressed.
4. *Is placement in special education a benefit or a risk? Is that outcome different by race or ethnic group?* There are insufficient data for answering the question, but there are substantial data that show that early identification and intervention are more effective than later identification and intervention.

Adapted from Donovan, M., & Cross, C. (2002). *Minority students in special and gifted education*. Washington, DC: National Academy Press.

The opportunities for misunderstanding from one culture to another are great and can substantially complicate the original learning problems faced by the exceptional child.

2-5c The RtI Model and Culturally/Linguistically Diverse Students

RtI

Many students for whom English is a second language have difficulty learning in American schools and may be referred to special education as a result. The RtI model Tier II, which allows for additional support for learning short of referral to special education, should be effective in this situation. The major problem, according to Klingner and Harry (2006), is the assumption that instruction is being adequately provided in Tiers I and II. Their qualitative study of 12 schools through observation in the classroom and in child study teams did not confirm that good instruction was provided in either tier; consequently, some of these children were referred to special education anyway.

There has been such concern about the assessment of culturally or linguistically diverse students that a panel was established by the National Academy of Sciences to answer key questions of assessment (Donovan & Cross, 2002). Box 2.2 highlights some of the panel's findings.

The National Academy of Sciences report clearly calls the current policy of "wait to fail" before referring the student for help unwise. Screening mechanisms exist for early identification of children at risk for reading and behavior problems and should be used to help place students in the proper tier or program.

We address this issue of ethnic and racial groups and their interaction with special education in many of the subsequent chapters concerning individual categories of children with special needs.

2-6 Proving That Special Programs Work: Accountability

The word accountability throws a mild chill into every educator. The general public tells us that we are to be held responsible for the students whom we release from the educational system. No longer will the general public take the educator's

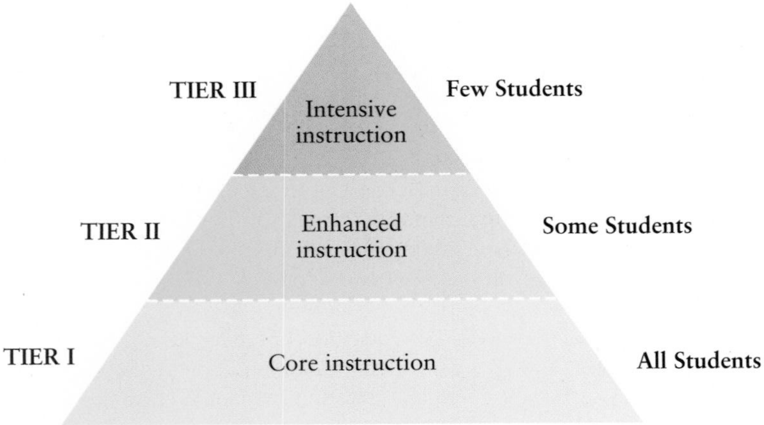

Figure 2.4 Response to Intervention (RtI) Model
Source: Salvia, J., Ysseldyke, J. & Bolt, S. (2007). *Assessment: In special and inclusive education.*

word about what progress is being made; it wants to be shown. The public wants proof that education and special education produce good results, and it does not react well when told how difficult it is to produce that proof, however valid the reasons (Gallagher, 2006).

In the field of educating children with exceptionalities, the goals of IEPs might be quite different from one child to another, so aggregating results into a total report on the special education program may be difficult. For example, if Mary is trying to achieve social acceptance goals and Sam is working on spelling, it would be hard to assess Sam's progress with a social acceptance scale or Mary's progress with a spelling test, and it is inappropriate to add up all the scores of the special students on these measures as a way of judging progress.

2-6a Assessment

One of the major tasks of special education is to assess both individual students and the effectiveness of the special programs. Student assessment is designed to capture the strengths and weaknesses of individual students and to determine whether the student is eligible for special education services or support through the RtI model approach (see Figure 2.4). This is another reason why we need a team of specialists to make proper assessments.

Assessment is a major part of the RtI model presented here. In Tier I there is universal screening of children in the early grades to find those students who may need special help. There is then a diagnostic assessment of those students who have been identified by the screening to enable the schools to plan an appropriate program for those students. In addition, there is periodic monitoring of students in Tier II and Tier III to measure progress and to determine if the students are receiving appropriate support. Finally, there is the use of assessment to determine if expected gains are achieved by groups of children as well as the individual children with special programs.

The increasing use of **high-stakes testing** has created special problems for children with exceptionalities because important decisions are based on the results of such tests—decisions as to whether the student receives a diploma or passes from one grade to the next. The Council for Exceptional Children, the major professional association for children with special needs, wants policies that hold programs for children with exceptionalities accountable, as long as the measures used are appropriate:

a. All students with exceptional learning needs shall be included in all assessment and accountability systems and shall have available the opportunity to participate in general assessments.
b. Only assessment processes and instruments that have been developed and validated on student samples that included students who have exceptionalities and that validly demonstrate their performance shall be used (Council for Exceptional Children, 2003, sec. 4, pt. 3, p. 137).

One of the few attempts to actually tease out the effects of high-stakes testing (so called because the results of the tests influence student placement) was done by Christenson et al. (2008) who surveyed 249 educational personnel in 99 schools across 19 states on the effects of statewide testing on children with and without disabilities.

One of the strong results was the belief among directly involved educators that high-stakes assessment has a positive effect on what students were taught. The authors speculated that this finding might be the result of increased attention being paid to curriculum.

A negative result was the increase of attention paid to testing (time for testing, for preparing for the test, and so forth) and the resulting limited instruction time of teachers. The effects seemed to apply to both children with and without disabilities.

A number of people and institutions have struggled over how to ensure that Jerry, with his cerebral palsy, or Paula, with her limited vision, can be adequately assessed. A series of accommodations such as reading test questions aloud or giving students with special needs more time has been suggested (Lazarus, Thurlow, Lail, & Christensen, 2009). While there is wide variation from one state to another, there is general agreement on extending time limits and seeking tests that meet the Universal Design for Learning model.

Some new approaches have appeared to supplement the standard achievement tests. They bear such names as *performance assessment, authentic assessment,* and *real-life assessment.* Because performance is knowledge put to use, **performance assessment** is a measure of the applications of knowledge. If a student is asked to write an essay on a particular topic, that essay can be the basis for a performance assessment. Similarly, if a student is asked to conduct a research project or produce an oral presentation on a topic, that assignment could be the basis for a performance assessment.

Authentic assessment involves the typical classroom performance of the student, rather than a contrived task. Quite typically, it might be an examination of a student portfolio providing evidence of student performance over time. In this way, we have an assessment in real time, using classroom work and assignments as the basis for evaluation.

These forms of evaluation still leave the task of determining just what level of performance is acceptable or outstanding. Often such judgments are rather crude 3-point or 4-point scales ranging from *excellent* to *unacceptable*. Added to that would be a substantive critique of writing style or scientific procedures revealed through the authentic assessment.

2-6b Student Expectations

One of the sources of tensions between No Child Left Behind and IDEA involves student expectations. If special education has done a good job, then what should we expect in student performance? NCLB seems to expect all or nearly all children with disabilities to be performing at grade level. It seems like a reasonable expectation, but is it?

We can take the case of Jim, who is typical of a large number of students with mild disabilities. Jim, at age 12, has been falling progressively farther behind each year of school until now—he is performing at a third-grade level while in the sixth grade. Is it reasonable to expect that next year, with the help of special education, a miracle drug, or any other intervention, Jim will be performing at the sixth or seventh-grade level?

To show this kind of growth, Jim would have to leap three grades in one year after years of inefficient learning and consequent low motivation. If he doesn't make such a gain, does that mean that the special education program has failed? We do have a responsibility to reverse the negative trends that Jim has shown and we must find ways to support his growth and performance. These positive gains would be a highly desired outcome and one we would be proud of.

Special education, as well as general education, should be held accountable for student performance. But the goals should be in line with what we have learned about developmental patterns and the various forces at work that influence educational performance.

BOX 2.3 Case Example: Transition Planning Goals for Paul's IEP

Paul, who has a continuing reading disability, has special concerns about getting a driver's license, which is necessary to his employment. Therefore, the following transition plans will be added to his IEP:

Present Level of Performance (PLOP): Paul has been driving on a learner's permit but worries about passing the written test needed for his license.

Special Education: Paul will seek from the Division of Motor Vehicles any accommodations made for students with disabilities and will take special instruction in map reading and route highlighting.

Goal: By March 1, Paul will be given a practice exam and will score 70 percent or better. Given a city map, Paul will highlight common routes he follows to work and routes to the mall, downtown, and so forth. By March 15th, Paul will take the licensing exam.

MORAL DILEMMA

The Inclusive Classroom

Two parents are discussing the merits of inclusion (keeping children with disabilities in the regular classroom with their age group). The first parent says, "It is the right thing to do. They should be with their same-age peers. If they are separated, they will get an inferior education. No one will really care what happens to them, and they will feel that they are being segregated and will have bad feelings about themselves as a result."

The second parent nods her head and then says, "Yes, but if they are in the regular class, they will demand the attention of the classroom teacher, who won't be able to give her attention to the other students, and they may well be a disruptive force in the classroom that will downgrade the education of all students. We know the schools will say they have special personnel to help, but we all know it won't be enough."

Both parents turn to you, a preservice teacher, and ask you what you think. Your response is ...

2-7 Transition from School to Work or Advanced Education

The number of graduates from special education programs who are unable to gain employment has sensitized professionals to the need for more direct services to bridge the gap between school and community adjustment. Specially trained personnel now have direct responsibility for helping students during this period.

As noted earlier, IEPs for older teenagers must include a plan for transition services. The following case example provides one illustration of the use of transition services to help Paul get a driver's license, critical for many jobs that he is capable of doing. His reading difficulties may cause setbacks on the state exam for the license, and thus he will need special tutoring and sample exams, with the necessary practice to give him the confidence to pass. In this case, accountability is fairly direct. If he passes the exam, the transition plan will be successful.

Other transition planning may involve direct collaboration with potential employers to prepare students for transition or with vocational schools to help with postsecondary training. Box 2.3 provides a look at Paul's IEP transition goals.

The three major social institutions—legislatures, courts, and schools—have played important roles in rescuing exceptional children from an unproductive childhood and limited adult life, and have opened the door to a more promising future. They have translated the phrase "all children should have a free and appropriate education" into workable procedures. We still have much to learn about exceptional children and how they best intersect with these social institutions, but the past progress has been encouraging.

Summary

- The social institutions of government, schools, and the courts all have important roles to play in the education of children with special needs.
- Legislation is the vehicle for providing additional resources for children with special needs and also creates the structure that educators must use.

- Court decisions have validated the rights of children with developmental disabilities to a free appropriate public education.
- Courts now require school systems to have strong documentation before moving a child with disabilities from the general education classroom.
- There is a clear trend for more children with disabilities to be placed in the general education classroom now than there was 10 years ago.
- *Inclusion* refers to educational situations in which children with disabilities are educated with same-age peers; one major goal is social integration.
- The response to intervention (RtI) approach, which provides three levels of service rather than two (special education and general education), seems to provide a more effective model for aiding children in need of help in the academic setting.
- An individualized education program (IEP) defines the nature of a child's academic situation, the program's long-term goals and short-term objectives, needed services, and criteria for evaluation.
- In addition to well-prepared teachers, a support system of educational services is needed to provide continued assistance for those teachers.
- Technology can serve two separate purposes for children with disabilities. Assistive technology enhances routine functioning and communication. Instructional technology aids in the delivery and support of instruction.
- Universal design for learning (UDL) provides alternative pathways for instruction and expression for children with special needs.
- The special needs of culturally and linguistically diverse children in special education require specific attention.
- Program assessment is an important part of special education programs.
- Effective transition from education to community is recognized as critical because it is the end product of our efforts.

Future Challenges

1. **What is the future role of the courts in protecting the rights of children with exceptionalities?**
   During the last part of the 20th century, the courts played a significant role in affirming the rights of children with exceptionalities to a free and appropriate public education. But who is to determine what is "appropriate"? Now that the courts have ruled in the *Rowley* case that it is sufficient for the schools to give reasonable help, clarification is needed as to how much is enough. It is unlikely that the courts have the professional knowledge to make such decisions.

2. **How can we build an educational infrastructure that will support education of children with exceptionalities?**
   As the administration of education in the United States has grown from local to state to federal levels, there has not been the opportunity to insert many systemic components into the educational enterprise, such as technical assistance or program evaluation or personnel preparation. These are all necessities for children with exceptionalities. We recognize the importance of an educational infrastructure just as we accept the need for infrastructure in medicine and transportation. But how will it be institutionalized in education: through legislation, court decisions, or administrative actions?

3. **How do we meet the requirements of No Child Left Behind and the vocational needs of children with disabilities?**
   There seems to be great value in planning a vocational job-oriented program for children with disabilities in the secondary schools, perhaps even beginning in middle school. This requires a different curriculum and activities.

But the requirements of NCLB to receive the common curriculum and be tested on it is in conflict with the needs of these students. How will the schools reconcile these differing objectives?

TeachSource Digital Download Access online

Key Terms

American Recovery and Reinvestment Act p. 37
Americans with Disabilities Act p. 36
assistive technology p. 55
authentic assessment p. 59
behavior intervention plan (BIP) p. 45
class action suits p. 39
Common Core State Standards (CCSS) p. 51
co-teaching p. 50
ecology of the child p. 32
free and appropriate public education (FAPE) p. 38
functional behavior assessment p. 45
high-stakes testing p. 58
inclusion p. 39
individualized education program (IEP) p. 43
Individuals with Disabilities Education Act (IDEA) p. 35
instructional technology p. 55
interindividual differences p. 43
intraindividual differences p. 43
least-restrictive environment p. 39
No Child Left Behind (NCLB) p. 36
performance assessment p. 59
PL 88-164 p. 34
PL 94-142 p. 34
PL 99-457 p. 35
prereferral committee p. 42
Section 504 p. 36
transition planning p. 36
Universal Design for Learning (UDL) p. 53

Resources

References of Special Interest

Eisenman, L., & Ferretti, R. (Eds.) (2010). Changing conceptions of special education [Special issue]. *Exceptional Children, 76*(3). An entire issue of the journal is devoted to changing views of special education that have emerged through federal legislation and educational experience. In particular, it focuses on the tension created by laws such as No Child Left Behind and the special needs of children with exceptionalities. The special role played by the response to intervention (RTI) model is also discussed, including its role in the blurring of the lines of special education. An important reference for reviewing current policies.

Gallagher, J. (2006). *Driving change in special education.* Baltimore, MD: Brookes. An attempt to supply a new approach to providing services through special education. The focus is on the necessary infrastructure of support services needed for quality programs. The author uses the engines of change, legislation, court decisions, administrative changes, and professional and parent initiatives as the vehicles for the discussion of needed change.

Martin, E. (2013). *Breakthrough: Federal special education legislation, 1965–1981.* Sarasota, FL: Bardorf & Co. A personal remembrance by the man who was a key player in the development and implementation of federal legislation for children with disabilities through four administrations. Portrays the difficulties of seeing legislation through the complex networks of the federal government and stresses the role that personal relationships play in that process. A revelation to those not familiar with this process.

National Research Council (2002). *Minority students in special and gifted education.* Washington, DC: National Academy Press. A comprehensive report examining issues that lead to the disproportionately high representation of culturally and linguistically diverse students in special education and to their disproportionately low representation in gifted education. Complex factors that create additional risk for children living in poverty are presented. These risk factors are discussed in terms of their impact on students' achievement and behavior in school settings. Recommendations for policy and practice are offered.

Salvia, J., Ysseldyke, J., & Bolt, S. (2012). *Assessment* (12th ed.). Boston, MA: Cengage Learning. A comprehensive book that covers all aspects of assessment, including both formal and informal measures, and that provides a basic discussion of measurement and its various problems. A special chapter is provided on how to adapt tests to accommodate children with disabilities. Special chapters are devoted to the assessment of perceptual-motor skills, socioemotional behavior, and adaptive behavior.

Turnbull, H., Stowe, M., Turnbull, A., & Schrandt., M. (2007). A 35-year retrospective and a 5-year prospective based on the core concepts of disability policy. In Odom, S., Horner, R., Snell, M., & Blacher, J. *Handbook of developmental disabilities.* New York, NY: The Guilford Press. A comprehensive review of the core concepts in public policy for children with developmental disabilities as revealed through legislative actions and judicial decisions. Eighteen core concepts are considered, including freedom, inclusion, integration, family-centered services, and accountability, and their development through public policy.

Journals

Teaching Exceptional Children
www.cec.sped.org/bk/abtec.htm/

Remedial and Special Education
www.proedinc.com/journals.htm/

Journal of Special Education
www.proedinc.com

Educational Leadership
www.ascd.org

Exceptional Children
www.cec.sped.org

Journal of Special Education Technology
http://jset.univ.edu

Professional Organizations

Council for Exceptional Children **www.cec.sped.org**

The National Assistive Technology Research Institute **http://natri.uky.edu**

Technology and Media Division of the Council for Exceptional Children
www.tamcec.org

PART 2 High-Incidence Exceptionalities

CHAPTER 3

Early Intervention Supports and Services

Standards Addressed in This Chapter

CEC

All of the CEC Standards are addressed in this chapter. Please see the inside book covers for the complete list of the standards.

FOCUS QUESTIONS

3-1 In what ways did research change historical beliefs about child development and set the stage for early intervention?

3-2 What is early intervention, and why is it so important for young children with disabilities?

3-3 Why is a "family-centered" approach to early intervention so critical?

3-4 How do we identify children who are in need of early intervention shortly after birth and during their toddler years?

3-5 What are the five developmental domains that states use to define developmental delays in young children?

3-6 What educational responses are needed for young children with disabilities?

3-7 What kinds of supports are needed to help families navigate the transitions in services for young children?

The eight chapters in Part Two are devoted to children who make up between 8 and 9 percent of the population of school-age children in the United States. Chapter 3 looks at the needs of young children and early intervention, while Chapters 4 through 10 focus on children identified with intellectual and developmental delays, autism spectrum disorders, learning disabilities, attention deficit/hyperactive disorders, emotional and behavior disorders, communication disorders, and gifts and talents. The high numbers of children with these exceptionalities reinforce the critical need for the supports and services that are described in these chapters.

The birth of a child is a wondrous event. It is a time filled with expectation, anticipation, and excitement. It can also be an overwhelming time for parents as they learn how to meet the needs of their newborn child. The challenges of feeding, changing, and calming a newborn can feel daunting, especially when parents are trying to manage all of this in a sleep-deprived state. Under the best of circumstances, the anxiety of caring for a newborn can be intense (Nugent, Keefer, Minear, Johnson, & Blanchard, 2007).

Newborns enter the world with a vast array of skills and abilities that will help them negotiate their early lives. The newborn prefers visual stimuli with clearly contrasting patterns; orients early to the mother's face and voice, recognizing these as distinct from a stranger's; and is biologically wired to seek social contact (Nugent, Keefer et al., 2007). These early skills and abilities help the newborn and the mother form a bond that is critical to both during the first few weeks of life (Brown & Conroy, 2011). The mother, father, and other primary caregivers learn together how to communicate with and respond to the needs of the infant. During this process, the mother gains confidence when her baby is happy, calm, and responsive, and the baby begins to thrive within this supportive environment (Quesenberry, Ostrosky, & Corso, 2007). All of this takes place in the greater context of the family and the environmental circumstances within which the family lives (Brown & Conroy, 2011).

The newborn and the mother, family, and environment form a set of complex relationships that are an interdependent system and that facilitate the optimal development of the child (Brown & Conroy, 2011; Center on the Social and Emotional Foundations for Early Learning [CSEFEL], 2010b); Dunst, 2007; Guralnick, 2005; Fox, Carta, Strain, Dunlap, & Hemmeter, 2010). When challenges exist within any of these components (the child, the mother and family, or the environment), these challenges can affect the health and well-being of the baby (CSEFEL, 2010b; Dunst, 2007; Fox et al., 2010; Guralnick, 2005; Reis, 2003). The purpose of **early intervention** is to provide necessary supports and services to optimize the child's development as early as possible. In this chapter, we explore the world of early intervention, looking at the supports and services that are available to help ensure that each family has what is needed for the optimal development of their child. We look at what it takes to support the development of physically and mentally healthy young children who can explore and learn with confidence (CSEFEL, 2010a). We review the history of early intervention, look at early childhood as a developmental period, explore the risk factors and stressors that can lead to difficulties, and examine the roles of families and professionals working together to meet the needs of young children.

3-1 History of Early Intervention

Although the benefits of early intervention are widely accepted today, this has not always been the case. Early intervention supports and services are a logical extension of early childhood programs, which have a long history in the United States, beginning in the late 1930s (Noonan & McCormick, 2006). Historically, programs known as nursery schools or preschools were an outgrowth of psychologists' concerns for children's mental health (Cairns, 1983), which psychologists believed was fostered by positive child-rearing practices during the first years of life (Anastasiow & Nucci, 1994). Children with disabilities, however, were excluded from most of these programs until the 1960s. The prevailing opinion was that little could be done for a child with disabilities because intelligence and abilities were fixed at birth and therefore could not be changed. As a result of this belief, parents were encouraged to place children with disabilities in institutions and orphanages, where they often received only custodial care. Special schools for children with sensory disabilities (hearing and vision) were beginning to emerge at this time as well; we will learn more about these in subsequent chapters.

In the 1930s, the belief that nothing could be done to improve outcomes for children with disabilities was dramatically challenged when Drs. Harold Skeels and Harold Dye performed a seminal research study (Noonan & McCormick, 2006). These researchers found that children who were placed in foster homes or who were adopted fared much better than did a comparable group of children who remained in an orphanage (Skeels & Dye, 1939). The fostered-adopted group achieved normal intelligence, whereas many of the institutionalized children were classified as "mentally retarded" (today we use the term "intellectually and developmentally delayed" for children with cognitive challenges). Amazingly, these gains seemed to hold for the fostered-adopted group into adulthood (Skeels, 1966). Samuel Kirk (1950), lead author of this text, further demonstrated that preschool experience could increase the rate of mental development and the social skills of children who were classified as "mentally retarded." The belief that children's potential was fixed at birth was beginning to give way to the exciting idea that, with the right supports and services provided early on, we could significantly improve outcomes for children who were "at risk" (Dunst, 2012).

The importance of early intervention was not well understood until l late in the 20th century.

A major longitudinal study looking at the impact of early intervention, the High/Scope Perry Preschool Study, expanded our understanding of the need for early intervention (Schweinhart et al., 2005). In this study, 123 African American children, born in poverty and identified as at risk for school failure, were assigned at ages 3 and 4 to either an intervention or control group (these assignments were primarily random, however some children attended their neighborhood child-care center). The intervention group received the High/Scope participatory learning approach in preschool, whereas the other half received normal preschool services. The long-term outcomes—looking at these individuals as adults at age 40—showed positive gains for the group that attended the High/Scope preschools (Schweinhart et al., 2005). The reported positive gains included 19 percent fewer arrests, 20 percent more high school graduations, and 20 percent higher earnings for the group who attended the High/Scope preschools (Schweinhart et al., 2005).

One of the longest running studies of the importance of early intervention is the Abecedarian Study that began in 1972 and continues through today (Campbell, Pungello, Burchinal et al., 2012; Campbell, Pungello, Keyserling et al., 2012; Campbell & Ramey, 1995; Campbell, Ramey, Pungello, Sparling, & Miller-Johnson, 2002). The Abecedarian study randomly assigned infants (4.4 months on average) into two groups in order to examine the impact of quality early child care on children from economically disadvantaged families (Campbell, Pungello, Keyserling et al., 2012). One of the groups of children received enriched, high-quality child care through the preschool years, and included some special curricular opportunities (Sparling, 2007). The second group of children received traditional child care. Both groups of children have been followed into adulthood. This seminal study showed that early intervention can have long-term positive benefits.

As young adults, the enriched group earned reading scores 1.8 grade levels higher and math scores 1.3 grade levels higher than the control group. They were more than twice as likely to enroll in a four-year college or university (36 percent to 14 percent) and were less likely to have their first child at age 18 or younger (26 percent versus 45 percent) (Campbell & Ramey, 1995; Campbell et al., 2002; Campbell, Pungello, Burchinal et al., 2012). A follow-up study of the groups as adults showed the experimental group was less likely to report depressive symptoms (McLauglin, Campbell, Pungello, & Skinner, 2007); had more years of education, higher job prestige, and were more likely to be employed (Campbell, Pungello, Burchinal et al., 2012; Campbell, Pungello, Keyserling et al., 2012). Researchers concluded that the high-quality early childhood programming can have a long-term positive impact on cognitive development, academic performance, and later adult educational attainment and vocational success (Campbell, Pungello, Burchinal et al., 2012; Campbell, Pungello, Keyserling et al., 2012).

One of the best sources of how caregiver practices can influence child development is the Kauai Longitudinal Study, conducted from 1952 to 2000 (Werner & Smith, 1992; 2001). The study followed individuals from their prenatal care through age 40 and demonstrated that many children who were at risk for developmental delays could achieve success (Werner, 2000). The study showed that child-rearing practices such as providing a home environment of psychological warmth, low physical punishment, responsiveness, verbalness, and intentional encouragement for development can help at-risk children achieve normal milestones (Werner, 2000). These child-rearing practices help mitigate the negative effects of a difficult or abnormal birth (Kolvin, Miller, Scott, Gatzanis, & Fleeting, 1990; Rutter, 2000; Werner, 2000). These seminal studies paved the way for the acceptance of early intervention as critical for improving outcomes for children with disabilities. Legislative support would follow, setting expectations for early intervention systems to support practice (Hebbeler, Spiker, & Kahn, 2012).

3-1a Legislation on Early Intervention

Legislative support for young children with disabilities began in 1968, when Congress passed the Handicapped Children's Early Education Assistance Act (HCEEAA; Gallagher, 2000). This act set up twenty model programs, including Head Start, across the United States to demonstrate how working with children with disabilities could improve their lives. During the 1970s and 1980s the legal rights of young children with disabilities were addressed in legislation. With the passage of PL 99-457, federal funding was extended to support children with disabilities and their families from birth on (Hebbeler et al., 2012; Noonan & McCormick, 2006). You may want to look back at Chapter 2 as you think about the legislation for young children in the context of other laws.

Today, the needs of young children are addressed in two sections of the 2004 Individuals with Disabilities Education Act (IDEA). Infants and toddlers (children from birth to age 2) with disabilities and/or developmental delays are addressed in IDEA, Part C, which encourages states to develop comprehensive, coordinated, multidisciplinary early intervention systems (Council for Exceptional Children, 2007; Guralnick, 2005; Hallam, Rous, Grove, & LoBianco, 2009). Children with disabilities age 3 through 5 are addressed in Part B of IDEA, which provides funds for states to ensure that all preschool-age children with disabilities receive special education and related services (Council for Exceptional Children, 2007). The 2004 reauthorization of IDEA further emphasized the need to provide services to all members of the family, recognizing the importance of the family in the child's development (Council for Exceptional Children, 2007; Hebbeler et al., 2012). IDEA 2004 requires transition planning across the early years, because services for children from birth through age 2 and for children ages 3 through 5 are currently addressed in different ways, and thus families often have to navigate complex networks of agencies as their children move across the age span of early childhood (Rous & Hallam, 2006). Navigating these complex networks is essential, however, because securing the services and supports needed for the family and child can be critical for a child's optimal development.

While as a nation we have made significant progress in establishing service delivery systems to meet the needs of young children, there is still much work to be done (Hebbeler et al., 2012). Questions remain regarding the quality of services (Kasprzak et al., 2012) and equitable access to services that are available (Guardino, Buddin, Pham, & Cho, 2010). The goals of IDEA, however, now go beyond just access to services requiring that states demonstrate positive outcomes for services provided (Kasprzak et al., 2012). One early childhood leader, Carl Dunst (2012) has called for re-examination of Part C to bring the focus back to the "essential characteristics of practices (experiences, opportunities, activities, etc.) and how and why they are expected to have specific outcomes based on empirical evidence" (p. 31). What remains clear is the importance of early intervention for young children and their families.

3-2 What Is Early Intervention and Why Is It So Important?

Throughout this text we stress that the earlier we begin to intervene on behalf of the child with exceptionalities the more likely we are to see successful outcomes (Coleman, 2011). Early intervention has also been recognized as important through the laws, as noted above. Let's look at what early intervention is and explore further *why* it is so important.

3-2a Defining Early Intervention

Early intervention consists of sustained support to the family, to the caregivers, and to the child with developmental delays and/or disabilities, during her/his early years, in order to promote optimal development for the child (Dunst, 2012; Noonan & McCormick, 2006). In some states the definition of early childhood extends to children through age 7, and first and second graders are included within this population. In this chapter, however, we focus on children's earliest years—from conception through age 5. Early intervention supports and services may address the needs of the child and the child's family during pregnancy, infancy, and the prekindergarten years (Rous & Hallam, 2006).

3-2b Why Is Early Intervention So Important?

The first years of life are a critical developmental time, laying the foundation for all that is to come (Bailey, Raspa, Humphreys, & Sam, 2011; Coleman, 2011). From birth to the age of 3, the brain develops rapidly (Sandman & Kemp, 2007; Shonkoff & Phillips, 2000). Information from the environment is stored in pathways in the brain that are ready to receive it. During this period, the basic "self" emerges through a dynamic relationship with caregivers and the environment, and this provides the foundation for autonomous emotional functioning (Guralnick, 2005). Language emerges during these early years, and during this time the child learns how to cope with the world. The infant is learning at a staggeringly fast rate, and the rapid development of the brain in these early years sets the stage for all further learning. If information is not provided through experience, the brain's neural pathways are unused; conversely, if enriched experiences are provided, they actually help build a more efficient brain (Freberg, 2006; Sandman & Kemp, 2007; Shonkoff & Phillips, 2000).

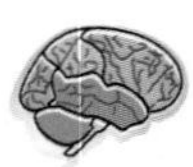

Neurology and Brain Development: Neonatal, in Infancy, and During Early Childhood

During fetal development, the brain grows at an amazingly rapid rate, estimated to be 50,000 to 100,000 neurons per second; creating an extensive network that forms a system for learning (Given, 2002). Around half of these nearly 200 billion neurons will die off during the fifth month of gestation, ensuring that only neurons that have made connections are preserved (Sousa, 2011). At birth, the infant immediately begins to use this learning system to make sense of the world (Smith, 2005). From the moment they are born, babies tend to show a preference for humans. They respond to faces, voices, and smells and have a special preference for their mother (Nugent, Keefer et al., 2007). Newborn babies get bored and look away when visual stimulus repeats too often. Very early on, infants learn to imitate the facial expressions and gestures of their caregivers (Smith, 2005).

The brain is preset for learning, and each experience the infant has reinforces this predisposition (Center on the Developing Child, 2013). The brain seems to be hardwired for the learning of language (Given, 2002). Language develops spontaneously and naturally for most children. With little formal instruction, a child learns to understand and imitate the sounds of the language she hears each day (Given, 2002). But language learning, like all areas of brain development, can be enhanced by favorable environments where caregivers talk with the child and offer lots of positive reinforcement to the baby (Smith, 2005). One of the reasons that early intervention to support children with disabilities is so important is that during the early years, birth though age 6, there are "windows of opportunity" or sensitive time periods where learning in a particular area is optimal. These sensitive time periods are not rigid, and the brain does have a significant amount of plasticity (that is, the ability to reorganize itself and shift learning functions from one area to another). Learning is easiest, however, if done within the optimal window (Sousa, 2011). When interventions are activated by age 3, for example, many children with speech difficulties are problem free by age 5 (Roth, Troia, Worthington, & Handy, 2006). The first step in early intervention is identifying children who need additional supports and services.

3-2c Profiles of Two Children Who Need Early Intervention Supports and Services

Children can need early intervention supports for a wide variety of reasons. We look at two children, Jennifer and Tyron, to see how needs for early intervention can differ from child to child.

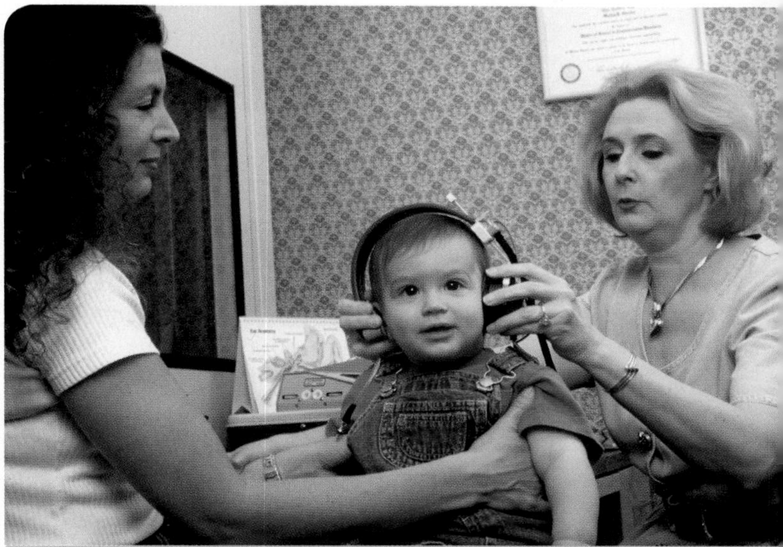
Robin Sachs/Photo Edit

Assessing the child's strengths and needs is essential to planning appropriate interventions.

Jennifer

Jennifer was born at 28 weeks' gestation and is a preterm infant. Her parents were told that she would need to spend her first few months in the hospital's neonatal care unit with oxygen support because her respiratory system was immature. Jennifer's early birth and prolonged hospital stay were very stressful for her mother, Sandra, and her father, Tony. Sandra and Tony knew that the pregnancy was considered to be high risk because of Sandra's age and health (Sandra is 38 and has type 2 diabetes), and so they had prepared early for their daughter's birth; but no prior knowledge could prepare them for the anxiety and worry they faced as they watched their tiny daughter fight for her life. Sandra and Tony felt helpless, knowing there was little they could do for Jennifer. They visited the hospital every day, and the neonatal care nurses encouraged them to hold and feed Jennifer on these visits. In the early weeks, Sandra often left the hospital in tears, feeling that she had let Jennifer and Tony down by not being able to carry the pregnancy to full term. When they finally were able to take Jennifer home, both parents were concerned that they would not be able to meet her needs. The family was referred to the local early intervention program, and home visits were set up through the visiting nurse's agency. These supports were critical to building Sandra and Tony's confidence in their parenting. We will meet Jennifer again later in the chapter to see how she is doing.

Tyron

Tyron's need for early intervention was not recognized until several months after his birth. He had been carried full term, and there were no complications. His early development seemed relatively normal and because Tyron was their first child, Michael and Laura were not really sure what to expect. Laura had gone back to work when Tyron was 3 months old, and things had settled down in the family routine. When Tyron was 10 months old, however, Laura started to feel uneasy. Tyron seemed different from some of the other babies in the child-care center. When Laura would go to pick him up he was fine, but he did not seem to know her in the same way the other babies recognized their mothers. She watched as other mothers called out their children's names when they entered the room and she saw how their children's faces brightened at the sight of their mothers. She also noticed that the other babies responded to their mothers' voices with smiles and "baby talk." Tyron was calm but seemed not to realize that she was there to pick him up. At first Laura kept her worries to herself, reassuring herself that Tyron seemed content and was just quieter than other children. Because Laura had had mixed feelings about going back to work, she also felt that maybe it was somehow her fault that Tyron did not seem to recognize her. When she finally shared these worries with Michael, he reassured her that Tyron seemed fine to him. But Laura continued to feel that something was not right. To reassure her, Michael agreed that they should talk with Tyron's pediatrician, Dr. Nolan, on their next visit, his one-year well-baby checkpoint.

In preparation for this visit, Laura made a list of her concerns about Tyron: "He does not recognize his name when I call to him; he does not seem to know me when I come to get him; unless he is upset, when his tantrums can be fierce, he's so quiet. And he does not seem to want to play with us; he seems not to hear us when we talk to him—could he be deaf?" As she reviewed her list, she felt that maybe she was being silly, and she hoped the pediatrician would tell her not to worry. Tyron's health checkup went well. He had gained some weight, and everything seemed normal. Dr. Nolan was surprised when Laura burst into tears when she asked if there were any concerns. Laura was also surprised by the intensity of her feelings as she described her fears about her son's behavior. Dr. Nolan listened carefully and jotted down notes into Tyron's file. When Laura had finished, Dr. Nolan shook her head and said, "Well, this is probably all normal, and Tyron is likely just fine, but, Laura, I think we would all feel better if we looked into your concerns a bit further." After an initial screening showed some problems, Dr. Nolan recommended that a full assessment for possible developmental delays be completed with Tyron.

One way to think about Tyron's needs is the information processing model (IPM), which describes how the brain works as the child takes in information (input), works with this information (processing), and shares information through a variety of means of communication (output). Information processing also involves the executive function, or the decision-making role of learning. In addition, all of this takes place within the context of emotions. (See Figure 3.1, Tyron's Information Processing Model.)

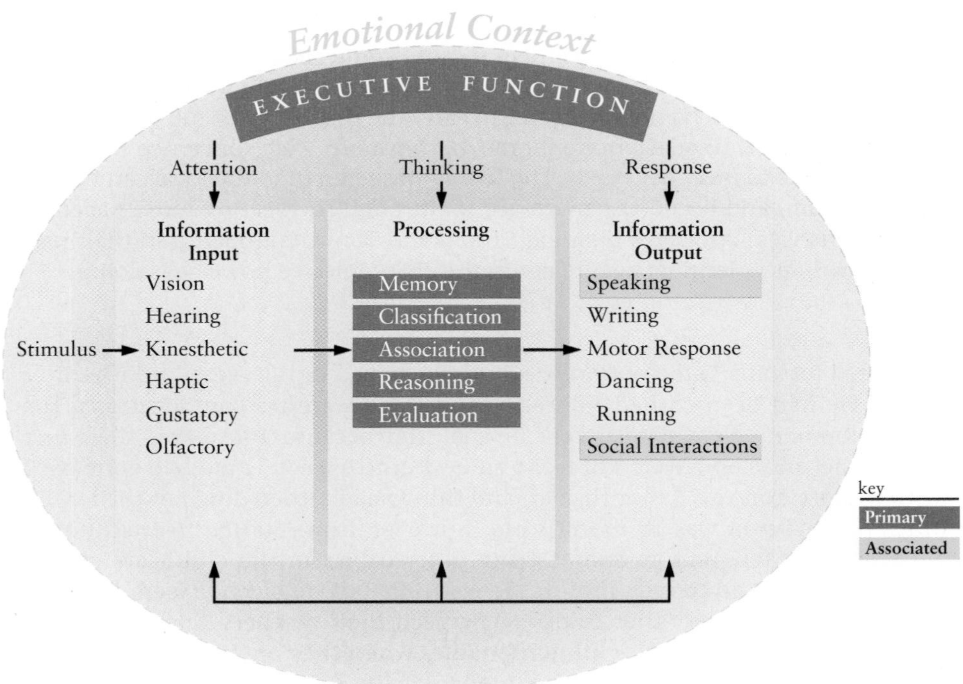

Figure 3.1 Information Processing Model for Tyron

TeachSource Digital Download Access online

After the meeting with Dr. Nolan, Laura left feeling both relieved that her concerns had been validated and something would be done and also more worried that something might be wrong with her son. Laura and Michael met with a multidisciplinary team to help with the assessment. The results from this assessment showed that Tyron did in fact have some developmental delays, confirming Laura's worst fears. The team also recommended that a follow-up assessment be completed when Tyron was 2 years old. The family immediately began working with the multidisciplinary team to develop an individualized family service plan (IFSP) to meet Tyron's needs. We will learn more about the multidisciplinary team and the plan they developed for Tyron later in the chapter.

As we can see from Jennifer and Tyron's stories, the needs for early intervention can vary widely from child to child. The shared theme, however, is that the child and family need additional supports to help them thrive and the sooner they receive early intervention support the better the outcomes are likely to be. Later in the chapter we will learn about these supports and how they can be delivered.

3-3 Family-Centered Support as Part of Early Intervention

A critical component of early intervention is strengthening the parents' capacity to meet their child's needs (Bailey, Raspa, & Fox, 2012; Bailey et al., 2011; Campbell, Sawyer, & Muhlenhaupt, 2009; Dunst, 2007; Turnbull & Turnbull, 1997). **Family-centered early intervention** means working with families as partners, respecting their strengths, values, and decisions, while supporting their ability to meet their child's needs (Bailey et al., 2012; Fleming, Sawyer, & Campbell, 2011). This is critical because the parents or caregivers are central to the well-being of the child (Friend, Summers, & Turnbull, 2009; Campbell et al., 2009; Dunst, 2007). While family-centered services are widely viewed as optimal, implementation, or putting these ideas into practice, has been challenging (Bailey et al., 2012; Bailey et al., 2011; Fleming et al., 2011).

Supporting parents as they learn to care for their newborn and toddler is a critical part of ensuring the child's mental health (Fox et al., 2010; Sopko, 2009). Early responsive relationships that form positive attachments with the primary caregiver are the foundation for the infant and toddler's social and emotional well-being and mental health (CSEFEL, 2010b). The nonprofit organization Zero to Three (2009) defines infant mental health as "the developing capacity of the child from birth to age three to: experience, regulate, and express emotions; form close and secure relationships; and explore the environment and learn, all in the contexts of family, community, and cultural expectations for young children.

Center on the Social and Emotional Foundations for Early Learning
http://www.vanderbilt.edu/csefel/

"Infant mental health is synonymous with healthy social and emotional development" (CSEFEL, n.d., p. 1).

The Family-Centered Approach and Cultural Diversity

Successful early intervention must address and honor the family's needs to be placed at the center of the work and family members' goals and opinions (Fleming et al., 2011; Parette & Petch-Hogan, 2000; Turnbull & Turnbull, 1997). Each family is unique and has a set of strengths, resources, and challenges that must be considered. Economically stressed families may not have access to health care, may experience food scarcity, and may lack basic resources for child care (Guardino et al., 2010). Many families also need support in recognizing the early warning signs for developmental delays (Fleming et al., 2011). Gaining the family's trust is essential as professionals work to encourage parents to accept proven practices for their child (Dunst, 2007; Banks, Milagros, & Roof, 2003).

Centering the intervention within the family is essential because the family is fundamental to the development of any child, with or without disabilities (Dunst, 2007). The key to success is the ability of the parents or caregivers to relate to the child and to provide a responsive, caring environment. Most parents will provide the kind of environment their children need, and if a child is disabled, the parents will seek out professionals and learn desired methods of facilitating growth. As professionals, it is our job to make sure that we get to know each family's unique and culturally specific beliefs about their child and what their child needs to thrive.

Cultural responsiveness is essential when working with families (Fowler, Ostrosky, & Yates, 2007). Exploring the following questions is an important part of assessing the appropriateness of services for children and families from a variety of cultural backgrounds:

1. What is the child's primary language, and how is it used in the home?
2. What are the parents' expectations as to the use of language to communicate? How is language use valued in the home?
3. What are the preferred strategies of learning: verbal, nonverbal, observation, imitation?
4. To what degree is the family acculturated? Do they agree or disagree about cultural values and mores?
5. What goals does the family have for the child?

Nuestros Niños Project
http://nnrp.fpg.unc.edu

Understanding the family context is critical to understanding the child (Castro, Garcia, & Markos (2013). Through effective collaboration, families and professionals can provide optimal support for young children with disabilities and help them thrive. The Nuestros Niños website shares helpful information on working with children who are bilingual.

Olmsted et al. (2010) found that families who completed the Family Outcomes Survey (rating their experiences with early intervention) in Spanish indicated lower outcome attainment and lower perceptions of helpfulness of the intervention than families who completed the survey in English. They also found that, for the Spanish language group, family-centered practices were significantly related to family outcomes. Looking at families' perceptions of outcomes and services is a critical first step to improve cultural responsiveness in family-centered work.

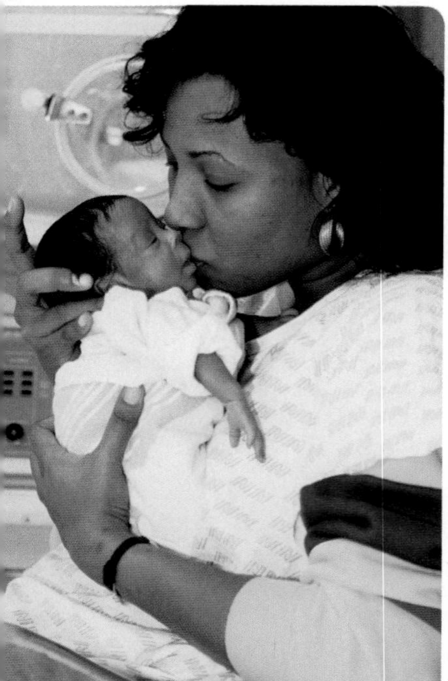

Annie Griffiths Belt/Corbis

Parents are key to the success of early interventions for the child

3-3a Early Intervention in "Natural Environments"

IDEA (2004) stipulates that early interventions should be provided, to the maximum extent possible, in **natural environments**, or settings that are typical for children who do not have disabilities (Noonan & McCormick, 2006).

Natural environments for young children can include the home, the family's place of worship, parks, playgrounds, grocery stores, child-care centers, and preschools (Campbell et al., 2009). These settings provide an authentic context for learning and practicing the child's targeted skills, such as self-feeding, pulling-up to walk, vocabulary building (Stremel & Campbell, 2007). Providing early intervention support within the child's natural environments is key to family-centered approaches and is also critical to building strong family partnerships. When interventions are provided in the home, for example, they can become part of the family's daily routines and activities (Trivette & Dunst, 2010; Campbell & Sawyer, 2007). Supporting the family as the family members provide for the child with special needs is essential to family-centered early intervention (Basu, Salisbury, & Thorkildsen, 2010). Seven key principles for practicing within natural environments (see Table 3.1) have been identified by the Workgroup on Principles and Practices in Natural Environments (2008), sponsored by the Office for Special Education Programs Technical Assistance.

TABLE 3.1 Seven Key Principles for Working in Natural Environments

1. Infants and toddlers learn best through everyday experiences and interactions with familiar people in familiar contexts.

Key Concepts

- Learning activities and opportunities must be functional, based on child and family interest and enjoyment
- Learning is relationship-based
- Learning should provide opportunities to practice and build upon previously mastered skills
- Learning occurs through participation in a variety of enjoyable activities

2. All families, with the necessary supports and resources, can enhance children's learning and development.

Key Concepts

- All means ALL (income levels, racial and cultural backgrounds, educational levels, skill levels, living with varied levels of stress and resources)
- The consistent adults in a child's life have the greatest influence on learning and development—not early intervention providers
- All families have strengths and capabilities that can be used to help their child
- All families are resourceful, but all families do not have equal access to resources
- Supports (informal and formal) need to build on strengths and reduce stressors so families are able to engage with their children in mutually enjoyable interactions and activities

3. The primary role of the service provider in early intervention is to work with and support the family members and caregivers in a child's life.

Key Concepts

- Early intervention providers engage with the adults to enhance confidence and competence in their inherent role as the people who teach and foster the child's development
- Families are equal partners in the relationship with service providers
- Mutual trust, respect, honesty, and open communication characterize the family-provider relationship

4. The early intervention process, from initial contacts through transition, must be dynamic and individualized to reflect the child's and family members' preferences, learning styles, and cultural beliefs.

Key Concepts

- Families are active participants in all aspects of services
- Families are the ultimate decision makers in the amount and type of assistance and support they receive
- Child and family needs, interests, and skills change; the individual family service plan (IFSP) must be fluid and revised accordingly
- The adults in a child's life each have their own preferred learning styles; interactions must be sensitive and responsive to individuals
- Each family's culture, spiritual beliefs and activities, values, and traditions will be different from the service provider's (even if from a seemingly similar culture); service providers should seek to understand, not judge
- Family "ways" are more important than provider comfort and beliefs (short of abuse/neglect)

5. IFSP outcomes must be functional and based on children's and families' needs and priorities.

Key Concepts

- Functional outcomes improve participation in meaningful activities
- Functional outcomes build on natural motivations to learn and do; fit what's important to families; strengthen naturally occurring routines; enhance natural learning opportunities
- The family understands that strategies are worth working on because they lead to practical improvements in child and family life
- Functional outcomes keep the team focused on what's meaningful to the family in its day-to-day activities

(Continued)

TABLE 3.1 Seven Key Principles for Working in Natural Environments (*Continued*)

6. The family's priorities, needs, and interests are addressed most appropriately by a primary provider who represents and receives team and community support.	
Key Concepts	• The team can include friends, relatives, and community support people, as well as specialized service providers • Good teaming practices are used • One consistent person needs to understand and keep abreast of the changing circumstances, needs, interests, strengths, and demands in a family's life • The primary provider brings in other services and supports as needed, assuring outcomes, activities, and advice are compatible with family life and won't overwhelm or confuse family members
7. Interventions with young children and family members must be based on explicit principles, validated practices, best available research and relevant laws and regulations.	
Key Concepts	• Practices must be based on and consistent with explicit principles • Providers should be able to provide a rationale for practice decisions • Research is ongoing and informs evolving practices • Practice decisions must be data-based and ongoing evaluation is essential • Practices must fit with relevant laws and regulations • As research and practice evolve, laws and regulations must be amended accordingly

SOURCE: Workgroup on Principles and Practices in Natural Environments. (2008, March). *Seven key principles: Looks like/doesn't look like.* OSEP TA Community of Practice-Part C Settings. Work group members: Susan Addision, Betsy Ayankoya, Mary Beth Bruder, Carl Dunst, Larry Edlerman, Andy Gomm, Barbara Hanft, Cori Hill, Joicey Hurth, Grace Kelley, Anne Lucase, Robin McWilliam, Stephanie Moss, Lynda Pletcher, Dathan Rush, M'Lisa Shelden, Mary Steenberg, Judy Swett, Nora Thompson, Julianne Woods, Naomie Younggern.

The intent of natural environments is to facilitate learning through experiences in daily activities and routines (mealtimes, out-of-home shopping, and so on). The early childhood special educator provides parents with strategies to maximize their child's learning in their daily activities and routines and helps identify learning opportunities in the home and community (Trivette & Dunst, 2010; Jung, 2003).

Therapists, teachers, and other interventionists often provide services in the home for a number of reasons (Campbell & Sawyer, 2007). A common belief among many educators is that education should take place in the setting in which the skills will be used; hence, the home is the functional setting for very young children. Infants spend most of their time sleeping, and it is not practical to take them to an early intervention program that offers educational and therapeutic practice. In addition, parents who are going through the process of accepting their child's disability may be most comfortable in their own home setting (Trivette & Dunst, 2007; Basu, Salisbury, & Thorkildsen, 2010). In some rural areas, early childhood special education centers may be a long way from the home, and parents would spend much valuable time traveling instead of interacting with and caring for their child. Furthermore, the caregivers' primary responsibility is to establish in-the-home routines that will facilitate the child's development.

The first person to visit the home may be a home health nurse who works with the caregivers to help them understand their child's disability, child development in general, and parenting practices. The home health nurse may also help the parents coordinate other therapies and may help to identify a curriculum for the child and family (Nugent & Blanchard, 2006). In the process, the home visitor provides emotional support for and contact with the family. Tammy, a home health nurse, visited Sandra and Tony, Jennifer's parents, during her first few months at home and provided critical supports to help Sandra and Tony meet Jennifer's needs. The home visitor can also act as a service coordinator and help the parents apply for additional services for the child or the family.

Some additional services may be provided by occupational or physical therapists, who visit the home once a week to teach the caregivers to position, carry, sit, bathe, feed, and generally care for the child. Promoting a child's competence through family routines and community activities also facilitates his or her movement into child-care programs (Bruder & Dunst, 2000; Dunst, 2007). The teacher can facilitate learning through the embedded material in the routine activities of the classroom, such as snack time, bathroom use, entering, and leaving (Carta & Kong, 2007; McWilliam & Casey, 2008).

The age span addressed by early intervention typically includes children from birth through age 5, and, as we saw with Jennifer and Tyron, the need for early intervention can be identified at any point during this time. Some disabilities are recognized very early on—at the birth of the child or even prenatally—whereas other needs do not become apparent until later.

3-4 Detecting Potential Problems

Can a physician or other professional tell whether an infant has a disability or is at risk for a disabling condition within the first few minutes of the child's birth? When a child is born, the physician administers the first screening test to determine whether the infant has any identifiable problems or abnormalities (Nugent, Blanchard et al., 2007). Screening tests are simple tests that are easy to administer and that separate infants without serious developmental problems from those who have a disability or are suspected of being at risk for a disabling condition (Anastasiow, Frankenburg, & Fandall, 1982). The first infant screening is done in the hospital at one minute and five minutes after birth. This screening is known as the **Apgar test**, after Virginia Apgar, who developed it in 1952.

In administering the Apgar test (see Figure 3.2), the physician examines the infant's heart rate, respiratory effort, muscle tone, and general physical state, including skin color. A blue cast to the skin, for example, may indicate breathing

	Score		
Characteristic	0	1	2
Heart rate	Absent	Slow (fewer than 100 beats per minute)	Over 100 beats per minute
Respiratory effort	Absent	Slow or irregular	Good; baby is crying
Muscle tone	Flaccid, limp	Weak, some flexion	Strong, active motion
Color	Blue or pale	Body pink, extremities blue	Completely pink
Reflect irritability	No response	Frown, grimace, or weak cry	Vigorous cries, coughs, sneezes

Note: Letters in Apgar are an acronym for the test's five criteria: A = Appearance, P = Pulse, G = Grimace, A = Activity level, R = Respiratory effort.

Figure 3.2 The Apgar Test
Source: From Shaffer/Kipp. *Developmental Psychology*, 8th ed. © 2010 Wadsworth, a part of Cengage Learning, Inc. Reproduced by permission. www.cengage.com/permissions.

or heart problems. Jaundice at birth is indicated by a yellow cast to the skin and eyes. A serious disorder, jaundice reflects the failure of the liver to filter the blood adequately because of its immaturity; as a result, bilirubin can accumulate. Many infants with jaundice recover in about a week. In more serious cases, the infant is placed under fluorescent lights for a day or two. This light treatment helps the infant process the bilirubin until the liver can function normally.

An infant with a below-average Apgar score at one minute or five minutes after birth is monitored by the physician to determine whether a disability or medical problem exists and whether medical intervention is needed. Lower than average Apgar scores are not necessarily predictive of disabilities, but they do serve to alert the physician that the infant may have special needs.

Because hearing impairments should be detected as soon as possible in order for the child to make desired developmental progress, universal hearing assessment is recommended at birth.

More recently the newborn behavioral observations (NBO) approach is being introduced to help parents and professionals understand the preferences and vulnerabilities of the newly born infant (Nugent, Keefer et al., 2007). The NBO approach can be used in a variety of settings and helps sensitize parents to the competencies and needs of their baby. This approach builds on naturalistic observations of the caregiver and infant to help create an optimal support system for both the family and the child (Nugent, Blanchard, & Stewart, 2007). Using the NBO, the clinician partners with the parent to understand the infant and models strategies to help the parent gain confidence and parenting skills (Nugent & Blanchard, 2006). Through a series of observations, an understanding is formed of the infant's unique traits and temperament, and this knowledge allows the parents to better respond to their baby's needs. The patterns revealed by the NBO approach can also help parents and clinicians decide whether further developmental assessments are needed (Levine, 2006). Some observations made for baby Jennifer (who we met earlier) are shown in Table 3.2.

TABLE 3.2 Summary of Jennifer's Newborn Behavior Observation (NBO) Findings

Observation	Recommendations
Jennifer's sleep pattern seems to be reverse, sleeping during busy day and wakeful during quiet night.	Transition her gradually by reducing daytime stimulation (e.g., light and sound) so that she becomes accustom to sleeping in dark/quiet.
Jennifer's muscle tone is somewhat problematic; she has difficulty with rooting, sucking, and grasping.	Use feeding cues (e.g., stroke cheek) to strengthen feeding response; use touch and contact to strengthen grasp
Jennifer responds to voice, but does not visually track or respond to other sounds.	Use activities to support visual and auditory response and to strengthen social interactions.
Jennifer is difficult to soothe when she is crying.	Work to provide comfort while encouraging self-soothing (e.g., touch and talk to her, allowing her to calm down).
Jennifer's activity level is low.	Support interactions and play activities.

Strengths: Jennifer recognizes mother's voice and responds to this. She is beginning to adjust to the new environment.

Challenges/Areas needing support: Continues to need support for appropriate sleep patterns, feeding and grasping, and social interactions

Additional Comments: Remember that Jennifer is still not full term, and she is doing really well for her age!

TeachSource Digital Download Access online

BOX 3.1 EXCEPTIONAL LIVES • EXCEPTIONAL STORIES
Welcome to Holland

I am often asked to describe the experience of raising a child with a disability—to try to help people who have not shared that unique experience to understand it, to imagine how it would feel. It's like this....

When you're going to have a baby, it's like planning a fabulous vacation trip to Italy. You buy a bunch of guidebooks and make your wonderful plans. The Coliseum. Michelangelo's David. The gondolas in Venice. You may even learn some handy phrases in Italian. It's all very exciting.

After months of eager anticipation, the day finally arrives. You pack your bags and off you go. Several hours later the plane lands. The flight attendant comes in and says, "Welcome to Holland."

"Holland?" you say. "What do you mean Holland? I signed up for Italy. I'm supposed to be in Italy. All my life I've dreamed of going to Italy."

But there's been a change in the flight plan. They've landed in Holland, and there you must stay.

The important thing is that they haven't taken you to a horrible, disgusting, filthy place, full of pestilence, famine and disease. It's just a different place.

So you must go out and buy new guidebooks. And you must learn a whole new language. And you will meet a whole new group of people you would never have met.

It's just a different place. It's slower-paced than Italy, less flashy than Italy. But after you've been there for a while and you catch your breath, you look around and you begin to notice that Holland has windmills, Holland has tulips. Holland even has Rembrandts.

But everyone you know is busy coming and going from Italy, and they're all bragging about what a wonderful time they had there. And for the rest of your life, you will say "Yes, that's where I was supposed to go. That's what I had planned."

And the pain of that will never, ever, ever go away, because the loss of that dream is a very significant loss.

But if you spend your life mourning the fact that you didn't get to Italy, you may never be free to enjoy the very special, the very lovely things about Holland.

In addition to the services for young children with identified disabilities, early intervention may be provided for children from birth through age 2 who have developmental delays. Box 3.1 looks at one parent's journey to accept her child's disability.

3-5 Children with Developmental Delays

In the United States, **developmental delays** are defined by each state, and can occur in any of the five critical domains: cognitive, communicative, social-emotional, motor, and adaptive development (see Figure 3.3). The purpose of early support for children who may have developmental delays is twofold: first, to optimize early development; and, second, to prevent secondary problems from emerging (Neitzel, 2011).

Figure 3.3 The Five Critical Domains of Development
Source: a. Jordygraph/Dreamstime.com b. Brebca/Dreamstime.com c. Pavla Zakova/Dreamstime .com d. Noam Armonn/Dreamstime.com e. Orangeline/Dreamstime.com

Infants develop at varying rates. Some sit at 6 months of age, others at 4 months, and still others at 8 months (Lundy, 2003). Some walk early, and some walk late. These variations are the major reason for being cautious when deciding whether an infant or toddler has developmental delays. Further, cultural beliefs about child rearing will influence when children hit certain developmental milestones. Families have differing thoughts about the child's independence versus dependence, and these beliefs will shape expectations for walking, self-feeding, safe boundaries for independent exploration of the environment, and time needed for self-regulation before intervening when the child is distressed (CSEFEL, 2010b). Understanding and honoring these beliefs is essential for successful culturally responsive family-centered interventions (Castro et al., 2013; Trivette & Dunst, 2010; Unger, Tressell, Jones, & Park, 2004).

Delays in development are identified by comparing a child's development in the five key domains with the development of other same-age children. The average ages of a task's accomplishment are put together in a **developmental profile**. If, for example, a child does not sit, stand, walk, or speak within the age range at which most children in his or her culture have acquired these skills, a disability or developmental delay is suspected (Neitzel, 2011). So what are some typical developmental milestones? Figure 3.4 shows some milestones for typical development that can serve as benchmarks for concerns regarding a child's development.

Although understanding typical developmental milestones is helpful when we are learning about children with special needs, a chart such as the one in Figure 3.4 can make things seem rather simplistic and static. We must remember that the early development of a child is anything but simplistic and is certainly not static (Neitzel, 2011).

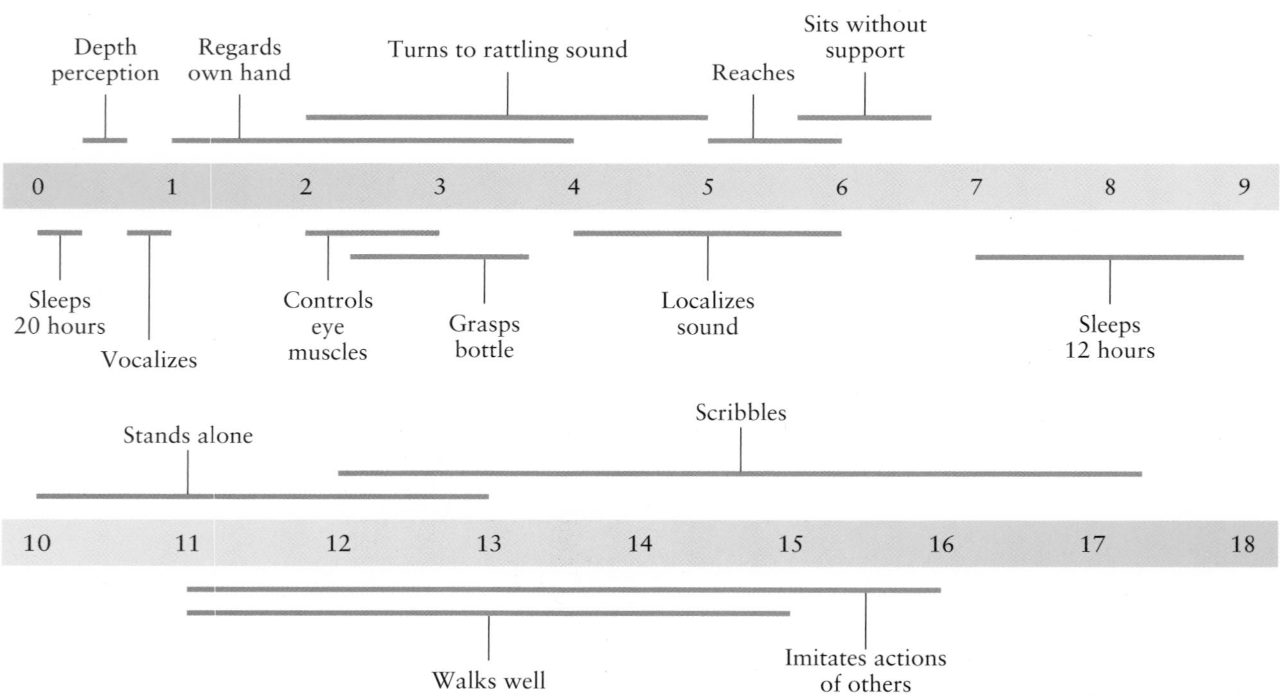

Figure 3.4 Typical Developmental Milestones (in Months)
Source: From www.brainconnection.com/topics/?main=fa/child-brain. © Posit Science Corporation. Reprinted by permission.

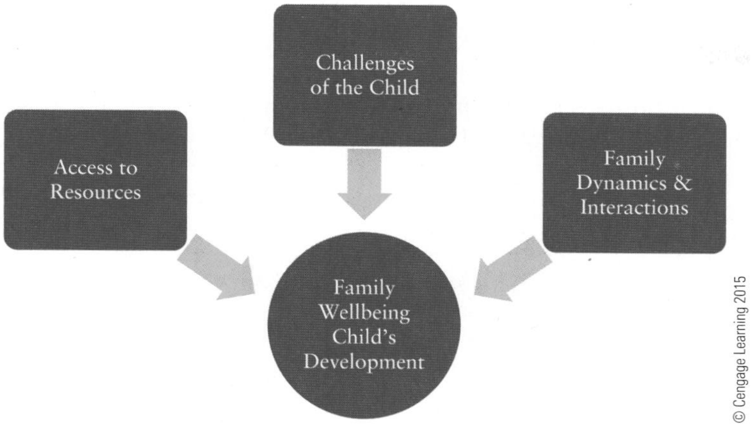

Figure 3.5 Stressors on the Family System that May Impact Child Development

Children develop through a series of interactions with their family and other caregivers and with their environment (Castro et al., 2013; Guralnick, 2005; Hebbeler et al., 2012). These constant interactions shape who the child is and influence who he or she is becoming. When the early care and environment are optimal, the child's development is enhanced. This is one reason why early intervention is family-centered and works to enhance the capacity of the family to meet the child's needs (Dunst, 2007). When stress enters the picture, the child's development may be compromised (CSEFEL, 2010b). Figure 3.5 shows how stressors can affect these relationships, jeopardizing the optimal development of the child (Guralnick, 2005).

In Figure 3.5, we can see that stressors may include inherent challenges for the child. Remember Jennifer and the challenges she faced as a preterm infant. Jennifer's challenges were not over when she was finally discharged to go home. At home she continued to have difficulty with feeding, and her sleep patterns seemed to be reversed. She was most alert and wakeful at night when things were quiet and seemed to be drowsy and fussy during the day. Jennifer also cried a great deal, and it was very difficult to calm her down. Her mother Sandra felt like nothing she did for Jennifer seemed to be right, and this growing feeling of incompetence made her wonder whether Jennifer may have come home too soon. The visiting nurse, Tammy, was well versed in the newborn behavioral observation system (Nugent, Keefer et al., 2007), and she was able to remind Sandra that Jennifer's physical development was still catching up to her full-term birth date and that Jennifer was likely to become overstimulated very easily. Tammy also helped Sandra understand that during Jennifer's earliest weeks of life she was in a busy, noisy, neonatal unit and that this activity actually helped Jennifer sleep. Sandra used this information to begin adapting the environment to gradually allow Jennifer to sleep with less external stimulation. Throughout this process, Sandra's confidence began to grow.

For Jennifer and her family, her preterm birth and early complications placed her at risk for developmental delays and added stress to the system, making the early parenting patterns more complicated. Stress can also be added to the system in other ways. Sandra and Tony are fortunate because they have good health-care benefits that cover 80% of most medical costs. Because of Jennifer's prolonged hospital stay, however, the family was left with a substantial bill in spite of their insurance and with the family's decision that Sandra would quit her job to take care of Jennifer, the family finances are very challenged. These additional stress factors create more worry for Sandra and Tony, but they have the emotional resources to cope with these difficulties and are committed to figuring things out. As the number of stress factors increases for a family, however, it can put the child at greater risk for developmental delays.

3-5a What Puts Children at Risk for Developmental Delays?

Infants are considered as being at risk for developmental delays because of low birth weight, prematurity, or the presence of serious medical complications. Researchers have identified three general categories of conditions that put children at risk: genetic disorders, events occurring during pregnancy and birth, and environmental stressors (Batshaw, 2002).

Genetic Disorders

Genetics is one of the most exciting areas in which new knowledge is increasing our understanding of human development. The Human Genome Project has led the way in helping us understand the role of genes in human variation, including how and why cognitive disabilities occur (Tartaglia, Hansen, & Hagerman, 2007).

The first opportunity to detect potential genetic disorders, in fact, occurs before conception, in **genetic counseling**. A counselor interviews the prospective parents about their families' histories of disabilities and analyzes samples of the clients' blood to determine whether they carry any problematic genes that might be passed on to their children. Individuals may choose to receive this counseling before a child is conceived. A genetic counselor can calculate the probability or odds of a couple's having a child with a disabling condition or a genetic disorder (March of Dimes, 2013), *but the counselor cannot guarantee whether the child will be born with or without disabilities*. If the parents have a high probability of having a child with disabilities, the expectant mother may choose to have additional testing to determine whether the child she is carrying may have a disability. Because genetic counseling is relatively new, we have yet to explore all the ethical issues that knowledge of genetic problems can create for individuals and for society.

Events during Pregnancy and Birth

The second broad category of conditions that may put infants at risk are events that occur during pregnancy or during the birth. The health and well-being of the mother are critical to the prenatal development of the infant. Under optimal conditions the fetus will develop normally during the gestation period. If the mother becomes ill, is malnourished, or consumes harmful substances, the health of the fetus can be jeopardized. Prenatal care is critical because it alerts mothers to the potential dangers of certain drugs and diseases (Schonberg, 2013). If the mother contracts German measles or chicken pox during pregnancy, for example, this can damage the fetus. Fortunately these diseases can be prevented by currently available vaccines. The most common maternal illness that causes difficulties with fetal development is diabetes. Controlling diabetes during pregnancy can prevent the occurrence of many disabilities (March of Dimes, 2013). Doctors may also limit the use of some over-the-counter and prescription medications during pregnancy to prevent complications for the fetus.

Substance abuse by the mother or father can be linked to behavior problems and disabilities in children. The use of alcohol during pregnancy may result in the infant having **fetal alcohol syndrome or spectrum disorder** (Brown,

Olson, & Croninger, 2010). Expectant mothers who use heroin may give birth to premature or low-birth-weight infants. These infants may exhibit severe drug withdrawal symptoms and will likely be at risk for disabilities. Heroin and cocaine appear not to cause disabilities in utero, but they often lead to premature births, and the problems associated with low birth weight and prematurity may lead to physical or behavioral irregularities as these children mature (Eichenwald & Stark, 2008). In addition, children whose mothers use drugs tend to be more emotionally and developmentally delayed than the children of nonusers. If the expectant mother smokes two packs or more of cigarettes a day, she risks giving birth prematurely or having a low-birth-weight infant. Major national campaigns have been mounted to discourage pregnant women from smoking and using substances that may harm their fetuses (March of Dimes, 2013).

Environmental Risks

Environmental risk factors, the third area for concerns, are conditions and occurrences in the life of the child and the child's family that interfere with the child's development. Environmental risk factors are the major cause of disabilities for young children. Two well-known environmental factors that interfere with development are poverty and child abuse (March of Dimes, 2013).

Poverty can increase the risk factors for a child in many ways. Women who live in poverty are likely to have insufficient medical care (including prenatal care), poor housing, and inadequate nutrition. In the absence of prenatal care, potential disorders that a physician could detect and treat are missed. Single mothers are at greater risk for living in poverty because they do not have the financial support of the father. If the expectant mother is a teenager living in poverty, she is at great risk of having a premature or low-birth-weight infant, who is in turn at great risk for a variety of disabilities. Young parents who are unaware of the child-rearing strategies that facilitate development face particular risks in rearing low-birth-weight or premature babies, because of the complications connected to their infant's needs. Other risks occur when family resources are too limited to provide adequate nutrition, medical care, and housing (Unger et al., 2004). These social conditions can, however, be addressed, and preliminary studies have shown that teenage mothers who live in economically advantaged homes, have good prenatal care, and receive emotional support from their spouses or families are more likely to give birth to healthy infants (Anastasiow, 1982; March of Dimes, 2013).

If you think back to Guralnick's system of interactive components that affect the child's development (Figure 3.5), you will remember that a lack of financial resources is one of the major stressors that can jeopardize the family's ability to meet the child's needs. When the family is stressed, the caregiving relationship with the child is more likely to be fragile, and the child is more likely to be neglected or abused (CSEFEL, 2010a; Dunlap et al., 2006; Friend, Summers, & Turnbull, 2009).

Many of us may find it hard to understand the existence of child abuse. How can an adult physically harm a baby or a young child, particularly one with disabilities? Yet most of us cannot imagine the stress that parents of children with disabilities face. Imagine a child who cries constantly and is inconsolable. For hours during the night, the parents try everything they can think of to calm him. They walk him, feed him, and bounce him, but nothing works. Throw into the equation additional stress factors such as a difficult marriage, pressures at work, and no prospect that tomorrow will be any better than today, and you have the potential for child abuse.

In 2011, an estimated 680,000 children were abused or neglected, and 11 percent of these children had diagnosable disorders (U.S. Department of Health and Human Services, 2012). Research suggests that children with disabilities are abused more often than other children (U.S. Department of Health and Human Services, 2006; 2012; Hibbard, Desch, & The Committee on Child Abuse and Neglect and

Council on Children with Disabilities, 2007). Physical punishment is strongly associated with child abuse, and Zigler, Finn-Stevenson, and Hall (2003) report that 60 percent of cases of child abuse evolved from situations in which parents were attempting to discipline their children physically.

When the circumstances of the family are very stressful, life is a challenge. These environmental risk factors are some of the most difficult stressors for a family to cope with, and they often feel overwhelming and insurmountable. Supporting vulnerable families to help them meet the needs of their child is central to the child's optimal development and mental health (Unger et al., 2004).

As we learn more about mental health, we understand how critical the early years are to the child's overall well-being and future success (CSEFEL, 2010b). Young children's mental health is critical for school readiness and positive long-term outcomes (Dunlap et al., 2006; Kauffman Early Education Exchange, 2002; Thompson & Raikes, 2007). Because of the critical role mental health plays in children's success, many early childhood programs are implementing programs that target the social and emotional development of young children. One model that is widely used to support social and emotional development of young children is the Pyramid Model (Hemmeter, Fox, Jack, & Broyles, 2007). We will learn more about this in the Educational Responses section later in this chapter. Optimal child development is dependent on how several factors come together to create a dynamic system (remember Figure 3.5 that either supports or inhibits children's well-being).

These factors include the child, the caregiver/family, and the environmental circumstances. Stressors can enter this system at any point and can make the child and family more vulnerable. Because optimal child development must be viewed in light of this system, the supports and services provided to enhance a child's development must address each component of the system. This is why one goal of family-centered early intervention in natural settings is to support the family with knowledge and skills that help them draw on their strengths as caregivers (Campbell et al., 2009; Dunst, 2007). One organization with a 37-year history of providing support to children and families is The Early Childhood Technical Assistance Center (ECTA, at the FPG Child Development Institute, University of North Carolina at Chapel Hill), whose mission is: to strengthen service systems to ensure that children with disabilities (birth through 5 years) and their families receive and benefit from high-quality, culturally appropriate, and family-centered supports and services. You may wish to visit the ECTA Center website to learn more about how these support systems are organized.

The Early Childhood Technical Assistance Center
www.ectacenter.org

3-5b Child Find for Children Who Need Early Intervention

Not all disabilities can be recognized prenatally or at birth, and so most states have developed extensive **Child Find** networks to help locate young children who may need additional supports in their early years.

Child Find is a critical component of the law. IDEA 2004 requires that states identify, locate, and evaluate all children from birth to age 21 who are in need of early intervention services or special education (ECTA, 2013). Some state Child Find programs involve a continuous process of building public awareness to increase the referral and identification of children and families in need of early intervention supports. Child Find programs include the elements given in Box 3.2.

Child Find services are coordinated at the state level with services for infants and toddlers covered under Part C of IDEA and with services for preschool children who require special education covered under Part B. This means that some states must coordinate two agencies that have responsibilities for services as the child progresses from birth through preschool. Ideally every child in

BOX 3.2 Elements of State Child Find Initiatives

- Definition of target population(s): How the state defines *development delays* will determine which children are eligible for services
- Public awareness campaigns: Outreach to parents, caregivers, and the community is essential to finding children who may need additional support
- Referral and intake processes: Each state has a system to manage this process
- Screening and identification procedures: These will vary from state to state
- Eligibility determination criteria: These policies guide decision making about which children will receive services
- Tracking and monitoring services: Evaluating the system of service providers is key to ensuring that it is successful
- Interagency coordination: Because Child Find services often involve multiple agencies (such as Head Start, public schools, child mental health), it is essential that these organizations work together to address child and family needs.

U.S. Department of Education Child Find Project, 2007

need of early intervention is "found." Unfortunately, the likelihood of being found for early intervention differs by gender, race, and economic status:

- Girls with special needs are less likely to be identified before kindergarten.
- African American children are less likely than any other race to be identified early (while being more likely to be disproportionately overrepresented in school-age children with disabilities), and
- English language learners are less likely to be found than non-English language learners (Guardino et al., 2010).

Bob Daemmrich/The Image Works

The parent and professional work together to observe the infant's strengths and learn how the infant communicates.

Children from low-socioeconomic-status households and those from homes where English is not the primary spoken language are also less likely to be represented in early intervention populations (Morgan, Farkas, Hillemeieir, & Maczuga, 2012). These data indicate that the very children who could most likely benefit from early intervention are the least likely to be found, so their families are the least likely to review the support they need to help their children be ready for school success.

In a study of five southern states, Morrier and Gallagher (2012) found that in one state (North Carolina) American Indian while in another state (Arkansas) African-American children were overrepresented in preschool special education programs, whereas white, Asian, and Hispanic children showed no disproportionality across the states. Taking a closer look at inclusionary placement within preschool special education, Morrier and Gallagher (2012) found wide variance across the five states in where children were being served. They found that the most likely placement for all children was "full-inclusion." However the second most likely was "no-known-inclusion," with "partial inclusion" being the third most likely placement option. They did not find any disproportionate representation by race for the full-inclusion or partial inclusion settings.

Appropriate identification for children from culturally/linguistically diverse families remains challenging as we work to balance the need for early supports and services to meet with success against the biases that may overidentify some children. Because the provision of early intervention for young children can be crucial to their future success, Child Find programs must do a better job identifying children for services. Once a child is found, the next step is to determine whether he is eligible for early intervention and determining what services should be provided. The following sections share educational responses for young children with developmental delays and disabilities.

3-6 Educational Responses for Children Needing Early Intervention

In this section, we look at how services and supports can be provided to children and their families. With most disabilities and developmental delays we can improve outcomes for children through carefully planned and implemented intervention programs. The goal of all early intervention supports and services is to help young children develop to their full potential. Ideally, early intervention takes place within an environment that is both inclusive and naturalistic. As noted earlier in this chapter, family-centered practices that engage parents and caregivers within the home setting provide support for the child's development using typical activities and routines (Campbell & Sawyer, 2007; Sandall, Hemmeter, Smith, & McLean, 2005; Trivette & Dunst, 2010).

3-6a Organizational Structures to Support Young Children

If prekindergarten (pre-K) were to become more accessible and an increasing number of children were able to enter school earlier, more children with developmental delays and disabilities would gain access to the supports and services they need to meet with success (Campbell, Pungello, Burchinal et al., 2012; Pianta, 2007). Unfortunately, many states have decreased their commitments to early childhood education in response to economic pressures. State funding for pre-K dropped by over half a billion dollars in 2011–2012 (Barnett, Carolan, Fitzgerald, & Squires, 2012). Currently, 40 states provide some type of publicly funded prekindergarten services; however 27 of these reported that funding had significantly decreased (Barnett et al., 2012). Even within states that provide support for pre-K, these services do not reach all children with developmental delays or disabilities. Even inclusive child-care settings may not provide the supports and services needed; thus, full and meaningful inclusion has not been accomplished for many children (Grisham-Brown, Hemmeter, & Pretti-Frontczak, 2005).

Children with disabilities need a program that focuses on all of their developmental needs. Most children with disabilities are, in other ways, like children without disabilities, and they have similar needs. This makes inclusion an even more important service option, particularly if the inclusive classroom is high in quality.

Quality of Early Childhood Services

The overall quality of the preschool classroom is clearly linked to successful outcomes for children (Gallagher & Lambert, 2006; Kasprzak et al. 2012; Pianta et al., 2005). Factors typically associated with a high-quality preschool classroom include low child-to-teacher ratios, high education levels for teachers, positive social interactions, and appropriate academic stimulation. In other words, a high-quality classroom provides a safe and nurturing emotional environment with rich and stimulating opportunities for learning. Research from child-care studies suggests that the curriculum in high-quality programs is associated with cognitive and language gains, as well as gains in social and emotional development (Love et al., 2003). Lower levels of aggression and fewer problem behaviors occur among children in high-quality programs. The curricula of these programs focus on children's self-determination, choice making, and initiative taking (Erwin & Brown, 2003), thereby encouraging them to interact with the environment (people and objects) in appropriate ways. Two useful scales have been used to assess quality care: the Infant/Toddler Environmental Rating Scale (for birth through age 5; Harms & Clifford, 1980) and the Early Childhood Environmental Rating Scale (ECERS; Harms, Cryer, & Clifford, 1990). These scales assess the appropriateness of classroom practices, the quality of teacher-child interactions, and the general classroom environment. What is clear is that most effective programs are child-centered, include developmentally appropriate practices, and are intensive in nature (Hallam, Rous, Grove, & LoBianco, 2009).

Seminal studies have shown that high-quality child care and early intervention classrooms result in positive cognitive and language development (Burchinal, Peisner-Feinberg, Pianta, & Howes, 2002; Burchinal et al., 2000; Love et al., 2003). Evidence indicates that children who enter a well-planned, intensively structured program during the first five years of life and stay in that program for a long period of time make the greatest gains and suffer the least loss (Guralnick, 1998).

After 25 years of building systems of support for early intervention and early childhood special education, we must now refocus on the quality of the services we provide (Hebbeler et al., 2012).

RtI Approaches for Young Children

RtI

IDEA is also influencing our thinking about how we meet the needs of young children with disabilities and developmental delays in early childhood through the use of response to intervention (RtI) approaches (The Division for Early Childhood of the Council for Exceptional Children [DEC], National Association for the Education of Young Children [NAEYC], & National Head Start Association [NHSA], 2013). The philosophy of early intervention is central to the RtI approaches being used with school-age children, and we are now seeing adaptations of RtI for preschool children (Coleman, Roth, & West, 2009; Barnett et al., 2006; Coleman, Buysse, & Neitzel, 2006a). RtI models for pre-K focus on universal screening and progress monitoring data to look at the child's needs, on the use of evidence-based practices to respond to these needs, and on working with the family to help the child become successful (Hojnoski, Caskie et al., 2009; Hojnoski, Gischlar, & Missall, 2009; Coleman, Buysse, & Neitzel, 2006b). **Evidence-based practices** are those that have been shown to work through research, practitioner wisdom/experience, and alignment with family values. Later in this chapter, we will see how Tyron's teachers collect and use data on his class participation and his use of words to ask for things in order to help them target support and monitor his progress.

Pre-K RtI approaches that are most compatible with early intervention for preschool children include a focus on providing a high-quality learning environment, an emphasis on providing supports to children as soon as a difficulty emerges rather than waiting for a formal label, tailoring instruction to meet the child's needs, and working with parents to provide support (Coleman et al., 2009; Coleman et al., 2006a; West, 2011; Odom, Buysse, & Soukukou, 2011). The use of intervening hierarchies, or tiered service delivery, is also compatible with current early childhood approaches (Brown, Odom, & Conroy, 2001; Coleman et al., 2009; DEC, NAEYC, & NHSA, 2013; Fox et al., 2010; Fox, Dunlap, Hemmeter, Joseph, & Strain, 2003; VanDerHeyden & Snyder, 2006).

RtI Action Network Pre-K site
http://www.Rtinetwork.org/Pre-K

TABLE 3.3 Levels of Support Provided in Tiers I, II, & III within an RtI Framework

	Definition	Focus	Goals	Roles of Parents and Professionals	Assessment Strategies
Universal **Tier I:** Effective core curriculum and intentional teaching	***Curriculum and instruction*** that is focused on all domains of learning and development, and is guided by observation and assessment	***All*** children need a suppoRtIve and enriched learning experience	Provide ***high-quality early-childhood instruction*** to meet the academic and behavioral needs of all children in the classroom	***Classroom teachers and staff*** plan and implement core curriculum and instruction; collaborating and communicating with families	Universal screening ***three times each year*** (e.g., fall, winter, spring)
Targeted **Tier II:** Group and embedded instruction	***Explicit instruction:*** content-specific curricula (e.g., math, literacy, phonic awareness) and instructional approaches (dialogic reading) ***Embedded instruction:*** environmental arrangement, curricular modifications, peer support	***Some*** children identified on the basis of universal and periodic screening need additional support to achieve success	Provide ***targeted instruction*** through additional supports and opportunities to practice skills within small groups, or as part of daily routines and for additional enrichment for learning	***Specialists*** assist ***teachers; parents*** receive progress reports and engage in a collaborative problem-solving process with early childhood staff	Progress monitoring to ensure adequate progress and learning ***every 8–10 weeks***
Intensive **Tier III:** Intensive and individualized instruction	***Individualized instructional strategies:*** prompting, modeling, physical assistance, giving a directive and waiting for a response, combined with ***explicit and embedded approaches***	A ***few*** children need additional intensive support or enrichment to achieve success	Provide ***intensive instruction*** through individualized instructional strategies to support or enrich learning	***Expanded team of professionals and parents*** develop more intensive plans for individual children and make decisions about referral for further evaluation; parents receive more frequent reports and engage in the collaborative problem-solving process with teachers and other professionals	Progress monitoring to ensure adequate process and learning ***every 4–6 weeks*** ***Referral*** for further evaluation if needed

TeachSource Digital Download Access online

RtI approaches for preschool children often use a three-tiered framework for meeting needs. Each tier is described in Table 3.3. As the needs of children increase and/or become more complex, the responses made to meet these needs must become more explicit and more intense.

Universal Tier I for Young Children

Within the Universal support level, Tier I, high-quality learning environments are in place; universal screening is done to look at all children's needs; and periodic progress monitoring is used to see how each child is doing. Children not thriving within this environment may need more support to help them learn. A Summary of *UDL Supports for Early Intervention* can be accessed online.

TeachSource Digital Download

Targeted Tier II for Young Children

At the Targeted support level, Tier II, we begin to see teachers using more embedded activities and more explicit instruction. In Tyron's case, the speech-language therapist has suggested a variety of activities that can be done within the day to promote communication and enhance Tyron's learning. One activity, called "turn taking," is being used during story time. The teacher gives four children two cards each. Each child's cards are a different color. The teacher reads a story and prompts the children to take turns with their comments. After a child has talked, she places one of her cards in the center. The child must then wait until at least two other children have taken their turns to talk and have placed their cards in the center before she can talk again. With Tyron, the teacher also prompts him with a specific question about the story.

Intensive Tier III for Young Children

Because Tyron has significant language delays, he also receives services at the Intensive level, Tier III. The speech-language therapist works with Tyron three times per week. Sometimes she works with a small group of children in Tyron's class, sometimes she models strategies to enhance communication during daily routines, and sometimes she provides intensive individualized activities. Tyron's parents have also been given strategies to enhance his communication in the home and other naturalistic environments.

The Pyramid Model at Vanderbilt University
http://www.vanderbilt.edu/csefel/

Tiered approaches to supports are also used when the primary need of the child falls within the area of behavior. A summary of *RtI Approaches for Early Intervention* can be accessed online.

TeachSource Digital Download

Behavioral Support Models for Inclusive Environments

The Pyramid Model, a multitier approach to supports that aligns with an RtI framework, helps teachers establish a positive nurturing environment for all children while providing additional support for any child whose behaviors continue to be challenging (Fox et al., 2003, 2010, 2011). A nurturing environment that fosters positive relationships combined with classroom practices that minimize or prevent the need for disruptive behaviors (that is, children feel safe and know that their needs will be attended to; adult–child relationships support and nurture prosocial interactions) is the foundation for all children (Brown & Conroy, 2011; Fox, Strain, Dunlap, & Hemmeter, 2010; Hemmeter et al., 2007). When children need additional support to overcome challenging behavior, teachers and parents work together to create a **behavioral support plan** (Squires & Bricker, 2007). The key to behavioral support planning is understanding the ABCs of a child's behavior: *A*, the **A**ntecedent (e.g., event or circumstance) that triggers the child's difficult behavior; *B*, the **B**ehavior that is causing problems; and *C*, the **C**onsequences of the behavior for the child, the adults, and others who are impacted by the behavior (Squires & Bricker, 2007).

Through an analysis of the child's behavior, the adults look at the antecedents or trigger(s) for the challenging behavior; what, when, and how the behavior is initiated (the context) and an examination of the behavior itself; the purpose for the behavior; what the child is trying to achieve or communicate; what the child needs; why the child is acting in this way. Finally, the adults look at the consequences of the child's behavior. They identify strategies to minimize the triggers (for example, planning for transitions and giving five-minute warnings to children so that they know what is coming next) and to teach replacement behaviors so that children have positive ways to express their needs (for example, asking with words when they want a toy instead of grabbing it). Through the use of this careful planning, teachers and parents can structure the environment to minimize challenging behaviors and promote positive interactions.

Because of Tyron's language delays, he does not use words to ask for toys and things that he wants and often just grabs these away from other children. As you can imagine, this gets him into difficulty when other children become upset! Tyron's teachers and parents worked together to examine this behavior so they could plan to support Tyron as he learns to use words to ask for what he needs and wants). This level of support falls within Tier III of RtI.

The Individualized Family Services Plan

Finding the right combination of supports and services for each child and his or her family is critical, and this process involves the development of an **individualized family service plan** (IFSP) (Xu, 2008). The IFSP is similar to the individual education plan (IEP) that is developed for older children (see Chapter 2). Because infants and toddlers with disabilities can be found in different settings (private child-care centers, Head Start programs, public prekindergarten classrooms, and so forth) it can be difficult to tell who is responsible for developing and carrying out the IFSP. A service coordinator is key to helping the family access and navigate the system of support that is available. The service coordinator oversees the development and implementation of the IFSP.

IDEA, Part C: Legal Requirements of the IFSP

Part C of IDEA requires that an IFSP be developed for each child from birth through 2 years of age who is diagnosed as disabled, developmentally delayed, or at risk for delays. When the child qualifies for early childhood special education services, such as Early Head Start, at 3 years of age, an IEP generally takes the place of the IFSP.

IDEA, Part C, requires that IFSPs be constructed to include the following:

- A statement of the infant's or toddler's present levels of physical development, cognitive development, communication development, social-emotional development, and adaptive development, based on objective criteria
- A statement of the family's resources, priorities, and concerns relating to enhancing the development of the family's infant or toddler with a disability
- A statement of the major outcomes expected to be achieved for the infant or toddler and the family, and the criteria, procedures, and timelines used to determine the degree to which progress toward achieving the outcomes is being made and whether modifications or revisions of the outcomes or services are necessary
- A statement of specific early intervention services necessary to meet the unique needs of the infant or toddler and the family, including the frequency, intensity, and method of delivering services
- A statement of the natural environments in which early intervention services shall appropriately be provided, including a justification of the extent, if any, to which the services will not be provided in a natural environment
- The projected dates for initiation of services and the anticipated duration of the services
- The identification of the service coordinator from the profession most immediately relevant to the infant's/toddler's or family's needs (or who is otherwise qualified to carry out all applicable responsibilities under Part C) who will be responsible for the implementation of the plan and coordination with other agencies and persons
- The steps to be taken to support the transition of the toddler with a disability to preschool or other appropriate services (Council for Exceptional Children, 2007)

The focus on the family is an important outgrowth of the findings of early childhood intervention programs: children with disabilities are children in families, and family members may need educational, financial, or emotional support to be able to provide the best setting, support, security, and stimulation to help children with disabilities or developmental delays achieve their potential (Trivette & Dunst, 2010; Xu,

2008; Dunst, 2007; Sandall et al., 2005). The family may need help locating, obtaining, and implementing the services specified in the IFSP; in fact, the family will need access to a multidisciplinary team of specialists who can help meet the needs of the child. Examples of family service plans can be found on Nebraska's Family Service Planning website. You may wish to visit this site to see how these plans are created.

Nebraska's Individual Family Service Plan
www.ifspweb.org

Collaboration and the Multidisciplinary Team

The law also recognizes that families who have children with disabilities need more than friendly neighbors or relatives to help them. They may need a variety of services from specialists and a service coordinator who can help them locate, obtain, and implement the services specified in the IFSP. Children who qualify for services under IDEA must have been identified, screened, and diagnosed by a multidisciplinary team as having a disability known to be associated with developmental delays or as being at risk for the occurrence of developmental delays. Under the guidance of a service coordinator the term *multidisciplinary* means that we must draw from the knowledge and skills of more than one professional in working with the family and child. The child may need physical therapy to improve motor function, speech-language therapy to assist control of the muscles involved in speech, and educational programming to support cognitive development. Thus, a **multidisciplinary team** working in an early intervention program might include a member of each of these professions. The team always includes a parent or guardian as a key member who helps inform the team of the child's and family's needs and helps shape the service plan so that it will meet these needs. Individuals who may serve on the multidisciplinary team working with infants and young children with disabilities are listed in Table 3.4.

TABLE 3.4 Possible Multidisciplinary Team Members

Parent(s)/guardian(s)	Share knowledge of the child and the family culture/values
Audiologist	Determines hearing abilities
Ophthalmologist	Determines vision abilities
Early childhood developmental specialist	Plans and administers educational services and coordinates special therapies and supports
Physician	Determines whether biological or health problems exist and plans treatment
Nurse	Provides a plan for adequate health care
Occupational therapist	Promotes individual development of self-help skills, play, and autonomy; provides needed therapies
Physical therapist	Enhances motor development and suggests prostheses and positioning strategies; provides needed therapies
Psychologist	Provides a comprehensive document of the child's strengths and weaknesses and helps the family deal with the stress of having a child with disabilities
Social worker	Assists the family in implementing appropriate child-rearing strategies and helps families locate services as needed
Speech and language pathologist	Provides necessary assessment plan for needed therapies and delivers services to facilitate communication skills

TeachSource Digital Download Access online

Parents Helping Parents Resource Center
www.php.com

Early childhood programs are essential for kids with special needs.

Each team will comprise the specific individuals needed to address the child's unique needs. In most cases the child will receive between two and four services (Hebbeler et al., 2007). Putting the multidisciplinary team together can be challenging given the variety of child-care settings for young children (family-based, center-based, Head Start, and public schools), and the role of the service coordinator is critical.

Ideally the team works together to gather and review information about the child's and family's needs so that a comprehensive and workable plan can be developed to address these needs. Let's look at how this process worked for Tyron and his family when he was first diagnosed with developmental delays. His teacher, after consultation with Tyron's parents, contacted the state coordinator for Child Find to initiate the formation of the team. (You may want to locate the Child Find services website for your state to see how you could secure support for a child like Tyron if you were his teacher.)

You may remember that Tyron's mother, Laura, was the first one to become concerned about his behavior. She was worried that he did not seem as responsive as his peers at the child-care center. Tyron's pediatrician, Dr. Nolan, listened to her and suggested that Tyron have a comprehensive assessment to determine what was going on. This assessment required the involvement of a multidisciplinary team. Tyron's hearing and vision were tested; his motor control, self-help skills, and sensory integration were assessed; and his overall communication and social skills were reviewed. Tyron's parents filled out a lengthy questionnaire, and his teachers completed some observational notes documenting Tyron's behavior under a variety of circumstances. An early childhood developmental specialist with extensive experience working with children with developmental delays and possible autism observed Tyron at his child-care center and at home. When all of this information had been gathered, the team met to review Tyron's needs. The team confirmed Laura's worries and determined that Tyron was indeed showing some delays; it diagnosed Tyron with developmental delays in communication and social-emotional domains. The team agreed that his progress should be followed closely and monitored for possible autism spectrum disorders (Boyd, Odom, Humphreys, & Sam, 2010). Identifying Tyron's needs, however, was just the first step for the team. The most important work was yet to come as the team worked to implement Tyron's plan.

3-6b Curriculum and Instruction for Young Children

Once Tyron's needs had been formally identified, the team's next step was to determine what interventions should be put into place to meet these needs. Because Tyron was only 1½ years old, he still qualified under part C of IDEA for an IFSP. You may remember from the information processing model (Figure 3.1), that Tyron's difficulties include processing (he seems to need more time to think things through) and that he also has challenges with output (speaking and social interactions). The team worked to create an IFSP that would meet the family's needs, agreeing that Tyron's plan would focus on communication and social skills (see ▶ Figure 3.6). Tyron's parents met with a speech-language therapist to learn ways that they could prompt and facilitate Tyron's communications.

Tyron would receive support for speech and language three times per week, and his child-care teacher would make sure to focus on language and communication with Tyron during the class activities and routines. Tyron's parents would set up more play times and would encourage his use of words to communicate. The team agreed to monitor Tyron's progress and to reevaluate his needs within six months. Using data to chart progress is critical for decision making (Hojnoski et al., 2009; Luze & Hughes, 2008).

Qualification for Services

Tyron has been identified with significant developmental delays with possible autism; the team will reassess Tyron within six months to determine progress and additional needs.

Family's Concerns and Desired Priorities

- Tyron's lack of recognition and greeting Mom when she picks him up from preschool
- Tyron's inability to play and engage with others (adults and other children)
- Inability to use words to communicate needs, to avoid frustrations and "melt downs"
- Mom wants more time with Tyron, feels she is working too much and that this is interfering with her ability to meet Tyron's needs
- Dad is concerned about Tyron's ability to get along with others and play

Child and Family's Strengths

- Tyron is a contented child who can entertain himself for long periods of time
- Both parents enjoy Tyron and are committed to meeting his needs. The family also includes grandparents, aunts, uncles, and cousins who love and support the parents and Tyron

Child's Present Levels of Development

- 12-months health check showed no difficulties with Tyron's vision, hearing, and overall health. Tyron's cognitive abilities also seem to be on target; however, these are more difficult to assess because of delays in communication and social engagement.
- Tyron shows significant delays in his expressive language (i.e., his use of words to express his thoughts, needs, and wants). Tyron's receptive language (his understanding of what others say to him) is difficult to gauge because he does not engage socially with others.
- Tyron's self-help skills seem to be on target; he feeds himself when finger food is prepared, he holds the sippie cup to drink, and he can help with dressing. However, parents say they are usually in a hurry and just dress him themselves.
- Tyron's fine and gross motor skills are not significantly delayed.

Goal/Outcome

1. Tyron will engage in more social-play with parents, family, and other children (increase from baseline of 1 to 4 exchanges per-day as documented by parents and teachers).
2. Tyron will show a 20% increase his use of words to express thoughts, needs, and wants.

Figure 3.6 Tyron's Individual Family Service Plan

TeachSource Digital Download Access online

Tyron's progress monitoring chart (Figure 3.7) shows how his teachers collected and used data on his use of words and his participation in class activities. Using the Individual Growth and Development Indicators (IGDIs), the team was able to see that Tyron used fewer words than the other children his age.

His teachers began supporting his use of language during daily routines reminding Tyron to "use his words" when he wanted something and asking simple questions like "which cracker do you like the best?" to get Tyron to talk more. You can see that while Tyron's use of language increased over time, he still needs more support for this and for his participation in daily activities. The progress-monitoring and word charts will help Tyron's teachers and parents see how things are going so that they can plan for next steps when they meet.

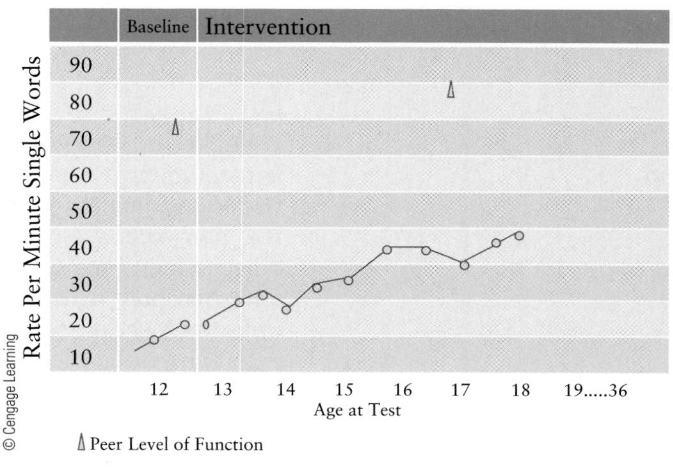

Figure 3.7 Tyron's Progress Monitoring Chart

Tyron's needs, like those of most children, will best be met through inclusion in his preschool and supports in his home.

Inclusion for Young Children with Disabilities

Early intervention laws are designed to promote inclusion in the broadest sense. Inclusion takes many forms and varies as to whether the child spends the total day or a portion of the day with typically developing youngsters, but what is critical is that the child is meaningfully engaged with nondisabled peers (Grisham-Brown et al., 2005; Casey & McWilliam, 2008). Inclusion is primarily designed to promote social relationships between children with disabilities and those without disabilities and to facilitate optimal access to learning opportunities through access to a standard academic curriculum.

COMMON CORE STATE STANDARDS

While a set of Common Core State Standards has not yet been developed for pre-school children, there are accepted practices for instruction to help children reach identified benchmarks for learning (Cabell, Justice, Konold, & McGinty, 2010; Fantuzzo, Gadsden, & McDermott, 2010; Kleeck & Schuele, 2010). **Blended practices** is one approach that draws from both general early childhood and early childhood special education and allows teachers in inclusive classrooms to meet the needs of all of their children (Grisham-Brown et al., 2005).

Figure 3.8 shows how teachers plan to meet the needs of their children by embedding specific goals within the classroom activities. Let's fast forward and picture Tyron as a preschool child at age 4. We can see that language is still an area of challenge for Tyron, but now his preschool teacher is focusing on a variety of communication strategies. She is helping Tyron use symbols to express his thoughts and is also prompting Tyron to use his words. The use of **embedded instruction** (i.e. the use of a child's daily activities to teach and reinforce key skills) helps us meet the needs of children with disabilities in the context of the inclusive classroom. Activity-based, embedded approaches are particularly useful in promoting and enhancing young children's social competence (Squires & Bricker, 2007).

One of the major dilemmas for inclusion is how to deliver services that are sufficiently intense within an inclusive classroom (Hallam et al., 2009). Ensuring that the child gets support that is both intense and sustained enough to make a difference is compounded by problems with the family's ability to access services. In 35 percent of states, for example, Medicaid will not cover physical therapy, occupational therapy, or speech-language therapy, thus many children are denied access to the very interventions that would help them meet with success in school (Hallam et al., 2009). Once again we can see the impact that poverty can have on a child's trajectory for success.

Importance of Learning Through Play

We have known for some time that the natural manner in which all children learn is through play (DiCarlo & Vagianos, 2009). Play is naturally-occurring, spontaneous engagement with objects, ideas, or people (Lifter, Mason, & Barton, 2011). It is particularly crucial for young children, who are innately curious, to look at objects, manipulate (for example, shake or rattle) them to see what they will do, and then play with them. Play is used in most early childhood programs. Play is important because it stimulates children's thinking, their motivation, and their social-emotional development (Frey & Kaiser, 2011). Many young children with disabilities, however, tend to spend their time observing rather than interacting during playtime (McWilliam & Casey, 2008). "Play" for young children with disabilities is often more solitary and functional, involving less imaginative activities.

Learning Goals for Tyron
Time Period: September-November

Curriculum Area	Tyron's Goal	Outcome Goal
Language (Expressive)	Uses words to ask for what he wants during play time	Communicates wants and needs
Language (Receptive)	Does what he is asked to do when following class routine	Understands simple multi-step directions (e.g. time to clean-up, put things away, and come to circle time)
Early Literacy	Repeats rhyming poems	Understands word sounds and rhymes
Early Math	Gives each child one snack item during snack time	Uses one-to-one correspondence (e.g. one child one snack item)
Self-Management	Cleans-up his materials after activities	Uses good work habits
Social and Emotional	Identifies basic feeling of the main character in the story during story time	Understands basic feelings of others (e.g. happy, sad, angry)
Perceptual Motor	Climbs on Jungle Gym during outside time	Develops gross motor skills

Figure 3.8 Embedding Learning Goals within Class Activities

Examples of functional play include rolling a toy car or sipping from a toy cup, where the object is used as it was designed. This type of play is less complex and is less likely to stimulate higher levels of thinking and problem solving. Engaging young children in symbolic or imaginative play (e.g., making a meal in the cooking center and feeding the family) helps build abstract thinking, language, and decision making. In encouraging higher-level learning, the importance of toys and play activities cannot be overemphasized (Frey & Kaiser, 2011; Lifter et al., 2011).

Early studies have concluded that children with disabilities tend to be less active (more passive) and less curious about the world around them; they have fewer coping skills with which to respond to environmental demands; therefore, an interventionist may have to teach a child with disabilities how to play so the child can use play to learn (Anastasiow, 1996; Field, 1989; Frey & Kaiser, 2011; Zeitlin & Williamson, 1994). Many positive social outcomes result from providing children with toys, allowing them to choose toys, and encouraging them to play with other children, with or without disabilities (Lifter et al., 2011). Engaging children through play enhances their interactions with each other and promotes communication (Frey & Kaiser, 2011; McWilliam & Casey, 2008).

Children learn through play and develop through interactions with their environment.

Higher level social play can be encouraged by providing dress-up clothes, a housekeeping corner, blocks, and puppets, as well as encouraging group block play. The National Parent Network on Disabilities catalog has toys that have been specifically adapted for children with disabilities. A high-quality learning environment will provide plenty of developmentally appropriate learning experiences for children through engaging them in the context of "play" (Lifter et al., 2011).

High-quality child care draws on what we consider to be developmentally appropriate practices.

Developmentally Appropriate Practices

Concern over the education of young children led the National Association for the Education of Young Children (NAEYC) to publish guidelines for **developmentally appropriate practice (DAP)** (Coleman, 2011; NAEYC, 2009). Developmentally appropriate practices meet the children where they are, responding to children's needs with appropriate supports and enhancements so that they can thrive (NAEYC, 2009). This means that teachers must get to know each child so that meaningful learning experiences can be planned that are both challenging and achievable. The use of multiple forms of data is critical to getting to know the child and planning to meet the child's needs (Hojnoski et al., 2009). All five of the developmental domains must be considered in planning for the child's needs.

Although special educators agree with the goals of DAP, their list of suggested practices includes more teacher-directed suggestions. For example, the activity-based intervention program (Carta & Kong, 2007), though consistent with the goals of DAP, looks for opportunities to embed the teaching of specific skills that the child has not mastered (Grisham-Brown et al., 2005). The major difference between the approaches resides in how one engages the child (McWilliam & Casey, 2008). Child engagement is defined as the amount of time the child spends interacting within the environment in a way that is developmentally and contextually appropriate (McWilliam & Casey, 2008). Special educators recognize that children with disabilities do not always readily engage and often have to be taught to do so (Casey & McWilliam, 2007).

TeachSource Video Connection

Watch the video "Assistive Technology in the Inclusive Classroom: Best Practices." Jamie uses a variety of assistive technology supports to help her learn and communicate. As you watch the video, think about the following questions: What kinds of low- and high-tech supports does Jamie use, and how does each help her learn and communicate? How does the use of assistive technologies impact the teacher, the other children, and the curriculum being taught?

What would be some examples of assistive technologies you might use to help Jamie learn about one-to-one correspondence in math (for example, five children get one cookie each; how many cookies will you need)?

Watch online

Assistive Technology for Young Children

Assistive technology (AT) includes any item or device that helps the child participate in more detail and function more independently within the environment (Mistrett et al., 2006). The use of assistive technology may improve the child's quality of life (More & Travers, 2013).

Often we think of computers when we hear "technology," and while computers may be one aspect of assistive technology, there are many other forms that AT can take—ranging from low-tech to high-tech (Bausch, Ault, & Hasselbring, 2006). The following are various forms of AT:

- Low-tech AT items can include nonelectronic devices like a specialized spoon grip and cup to help a child with self-feeding, or story boards with pictures and words to help a child learn key concepts for early literacy.
- Medium-tech AT options may include easy-to-operate mechanical devices like switch-operated toys and manual wheelchairs.

- High-tech supports can be very sophisticated electronic devices such as voice recognition programs and communication supports.

Finding the right level of AT support for each child is important—especially given the cost associated with many high-tech devices (Simpson & Oh, 2013). Families and teachers work together to analyze which tasks and skills the child needs help with, and select an appropriate support device to meet the child's level of functioning and needs (Castellani & Warger, 2009). As part of Tyron's support for communication, the speech pathologist uses pictures with words on them to help him express what he wants and needs in the classroom. His parents also use these to support his communication at home. These picture boards are an example of low-tech assistive technology that can support a child's communication.

To increase Tyron's participation in circle time, for example, his teachers created a "circle time book" (Simpson & Oh, 2013). The book had visual prompts for each circle time activity (e.g., what would little bear wear today? what is the weather? and what day is it today?). During circle time Tyron would point to the pictures to answer the questions and his teacher would prompt him to use his words. Having the circle time book kept Tyron more engaged and encouraged him to learn even more words. With young children no matter how well developed our assistive technology is, it can never take the place of human interactions (More & Travers, 2013).

nandana de silva/Alamy

Young children often adapt quickly to the use of technology for learning, communicating, and playing.

3-7 Navigating Transitions in Early Childhood

Navigating the change of service providers for early intervention may be a daunting task for families as they work to maintain supports for their child (Rous & Hallam, 2006). During the early years families may need to shift service providers three or four times as their child moves from hospital to early intervention to preschool and eventually to kindergarten (Rosenkoetter, Hains, & Fowler, 1994; Rous, Myers, & Stricklin, 2007; Rous, Hallam, McCormick, & Cox, 2010). Transitions are a time of change, and even at their best they can be stressful (Pianta, Cox, & Snow, 2007). For a family with a child who has disabilities, this stress is likely to be greatly intensified, as their fears about their child's well-being may make changes even more worrisome (Rous & Hallam, 2006). IDEA requires the development of a transition plan to support families during these changes and to ensure that children receive

TeachSource Video Connection

Copyright © 2015 Cengage Learning

Watch the video "Preschool IEP and Transition Meeting." Mark is getting ready to make the big move from preschool to kindergarten! His teachers and parents are meeting to look at his needs and plan for a smooth transition. As you watch the video, think about the following questions: How did Mark's teacher, Ann, set a positive tone for the meeting and why is this so important? What questions might Ann ask of Mark's parents to make sure that their concerns are addressed and that their ideas are incorporated into the planning?

This was a multidisciplinary team meeting; who was involved and what roles did they fulfill in helping to plan for Mark's needs?

Watch online

MORAL DILEMMA

Using Genetic Counseling

Shelia and Shea had been married for two years and were beginning to talk about starting a family. Although they wanted to have children, both of them were concerned that they might have some complications. Shea's family had a history of sickle cell anemia. They wondered whether they might pass this on to their own children. They decided to go for genetic counseling. During the session, the counselor asked for family histories and then reviewed the results from the blood work they had completed prior to the visit. The counselor explained that the information she could share with them could *not* tell them whether they would have a child with disabilities and that it could only give them an idea about the likelihood of problems. The counselor told Shelia and Shea that they both had "sickle cell trait," which meant that they were carriers of the sickle cell gene. Because they both carried the problematic gene, the counselor told them they had a 25 percent chance of having a child with sickle cell anemia. Shea asked about the likelihood of his sister carrying the sickle cell gene, because he knew that she and her husband were also thinking about having children. The counselor said that it was possible that Shea's sister also carried the gene. Shelia and Shea had been given a lot to think about, but the first thing Shea wanted to do when they got home was to call his sister and share their news with her. Shelia was not certain that he should let his sister know that she might also carry the sickle cell gene.

Should Shea inform his sister that she might be a carrier? What problems could having this information create for her (personal, social, health insurance, and so forth)? Is it better to know or not to know? If Shea decides to tell his sister, what should he say?

uninterrupted services as they move through their early years (Rous & Hallam, 2006).

Remember when Jennifer (the preterm infant presented earlier in the chapter) was finally ready to go home from the hospital? After weeks of worry, her parents, Sandra and Tony, had mixed feelings about finally taking Jennifer home. They worried that they would be unable to meet her needs and keep her safe. The first phase of intervention, the initial medical support, was ending, and the second phase started with home visits and home-based support. This support was provided through the state's Part C coordinator (remember that IDEA Part C is the section of the law that covers children from birth through age 2). This first transition was successful, and over the first three years of Jennifer's life, Sandra and Tony learned to trust their home-health nurse and the members of the multidisciplinary team they worked with as they struggled to meet Jennifer's needs. They were very comfortable with the family service plan that had guided the support they had received. So their concerns were natural when Jennifer was about to turn 3 and they had to change her services. Fortunately, a plan was developed to help create a smooth transition from Part C to Part B services (for preschool children).

Under Part B, Jennifer qualified for an IEP because she was still showing developmental delays in motor functioning and cognitive abilities. The multidisciplinary team recommended continued physical and occupational therapies and helped the family identify the inclusion prekindergarten programs close to their home. Although kindergarten is a long way off for Jennifer, her parents are already thinking about this fourth transition.

The transition to formal schooling in kindergarten is recognized as a landmark event by millions of families across the country (Pianta et al., 2007). This normal developmental milestone may be more difficult for children with disabilities and their families. A smooth transition depends on several factors coming together. Moving from early child care to kindergarten is a critical step for young children, and carefully formulated transition plans can facilitate their adjustment and success in school. Successful transition requires communication among the preschool teacher, the parents, and the kindergarten teacher, preferably before the child enters the class. It should be a collaborative process in which past experiences are linked to future goals (Rous et al., 2010).

The readiness of the child, as discussed earlier, is critical, but the readiness of the school to receive the child is just as important. School strategies that can facilitate this transition include sending letters home to parents, holding open-house visits, calling parents, and making home visits. One difficulty is that families who need support during this transition (those who live in poverty, those who reside in urban and rural communities, and those who have children with disabilities) may in fact receive fewer services. Transition planning for children with disabilities who are receiving early intervention is essential and a transition plan should be developed and implemented by a team (Rous & Hallam, 2006). Transition planning for a smooth entry into school is key to ensuring that gains made by early intervention are not lost.

Summary

- Early intervention is now widely accepted as essential to improving outcomes for children with disabilities and developmental delays.
- Early intervention consists of sustained and systemic efforts to provide support to the family, caregivers, and child to promote optimal development for the child.
- Early intervention may begin before pregnancy with the mother-to-be receiving appropriate medical care and support.
- At birth, physicians will check for the infant's overall functioning and health and will initiate any supports needed based on the results of the initial tests.
- Family-centered approaches are key to the success of early interventions because the parent or caregiver is critical to the child's well-being.
- Supports and services for children and families must address all components of the child's needs and must be culturally responsive to the families.
- Child Find is a critical component of the early intervention system as it helps locate children and families who need support.
- A multidisciplinary team helps identify the child's needs and develops a plan to respond to these needs: an IFSP for children from birth to 3 years; an IEP for children age 3 and older.
- Inclusion and naturalistic environments are key components of how and where early intervention services are provided.
- The RtI approach for young children focused on the use of data to plan developmental appropriate supports and enhancements to ensure that learning is both challenging and achievable.
- Supporting children and families during transitions is essential to ensuring a smooth delivery of supports and services.

Future Challenges

1. **What would be the impact if maternal health care were universal?**
   Primary prevention through prenatal care is not available to all expectant mothers, particularly those who live in poverty. However, in the fall of 2010, the Obama administration's Affordable Care Act directed all health plans, including Medicaid, to provide prenatal screening and counseling for expectant mothers. But even when it is available, some individuals do not take advantage of it. If prenatal care were provided universally, it could markedly reduce the number of premature and low-birthweight children who are at risk for disabilities. Is the new policy enough to ensure the most healthy pregnancies possible? What strategies would we need to employ to ensure access to these services for all mothers-to-be?

2. **How can we provide appropriate supports and services for families of children with disabilities?**
   Having a child with disabilities has a profound impact on the family system. The additional stress, need for resources, and time spent in caregiving can all take a toll on the family's ability to meet the needs of the child. How can we support the family to help them be successful? What are the health care/insurance, social support, and education needs of families? How can these be provided in ways that address families' cultural values?

3. How can we increase the quality of early child care in the United States?
Increasing numbers of children are receiving early child care, and a number of these children require early intervention supports and services. How can we ensure that all children have access to high-quality child care and early intervention if they need additional supports? How would universal prekindergarten affect the well-being of children?

TeachSource Digital Download Access online

Key Terms

Apgar test p. 77
behavioral support plan p. 89
blended practices p. 94
Child Find p. 84
developmental delays p. 79
developmental profile p. 80
developmentally appropriate practice (DAP) p. 96
early intervention p. 66
embedded instruction p. 94
evidence-based practice p. 87
family-centered early intervention p. 73
fetal alcohol spectrum disorder p. 82
genetic counseling p. 82
individualized family service plan (IFSP) p. 90
multidisciplinary team p. 91
natural environments p. 74

Resources

References of Special Interest

Bailey, D., Raspa, M., Humphreys, B., & Sam, A. (2011). Promoting family outcomes in early intervention. In J. Kauffman & D. Hallahan (Eds.), *Handbook of Special Education* (pp. 668–684). New York, NY: Routledge. The importance of promoting positive family outcomes within the complex system of early intervention is discussed. The authors examine key family outcomes including: understanding the child's strengths and needs; knowing legal rights; supporting the child's development/learning; maintaining support systems; and accessing community resources. Family-centered principles in practice are also discussed.

Campbell, F.A., Pugnello, E.P., Burchinal, M., Kainz, K., Pan, Y., Wasik, B. H., ... Ramey, C. (2012). Adult outcomes as a function of an early childhood educational program: An Abecedarian project follow-up. *Developmental Psychology, 48*(4), 1033–1043. The Abecedarian Project was designed to study the impact of intensive early childhood education for children in low-income families. This article examines educational, economic, and social-emotional outcomes for adults (age 30) who were first enrolled in the Abecedarian Project as infants. Policy implications are also discussed.

Castro, D., Garcia, E., & Markos, A. (2013). *Dual language learners: Research informing policy*. Chapel Hill: The University of North Carolina, Frank Porter Graham Child Development Institute, Center for Early Care and Education-Dual Language Learners. This paper discusses key research on appropriate supports and services for children who are dual language learners and offers recommendations for policy makers at the district, state, and national levels.

Keilty, B. (2010). *The early intervention guidebook for families and professionals: Partnering for success*. New York, NY: Teachers College Press. This practical guide is a useful resource for families and professionals who work with infants and toddlers in early intervention. It is based on research, policies, and practices for young children with developmental disabilities and those who are at risk.

Hebbeler, K. & Spiker, D. (2011). Cost effectiveness and efficacy programs. In C. Groark, & S. Eidelman (Eds.), *Early childhood intervention: Shaping the future for children with special needs and their families* (vol. 1, pp. 173–207). Santa Barbara, CA: Praeger. This chapter evaluates the cost effectiveness of early intervention programs. It includes a brief summary of terms and analyses that are used in making evaluations and discusses current and future trends.

Odom, S. L., Horner, R. H., Snell, M. E., & Blancher, J. (Eds.) (2007). *Handbook of developmental disabilities*. New York, NY: Guilford Press. This is a comprehensive reference on research related to children with disabilities. It reviews our current understanding of the field of study for developmental disabilities: the health, neuroscience and genetics, and practice related to meeting the needs of children and families.

Sandall, S., Hemmeter, M. L, Smith, B. J., & McLean, M. E. (2005). *DEC recommended practices: A comprehensive guide for practical application in early intervention/early childhood special education*. Missoula, MT: Council for Exceptional Children, Division for Early Childhood. The Division for Early Childhood of the Council for Exceptional Children gives clear guidelines for best practices for young children with disabilities. This book is an important handbook for all those who work with young children and their families.

Technical Assistance Center on Social and Emotional Intervention (2007). *Practical strategies for teaching social emotional skills* [DVD]. Available from http://www.challengingbehavior.org. This 28-minute DVD highlights many practical strategies and approaches that early childhood personnel and families can use to systematically target social emotional supports that build young children's skills in making friends, problem solving, asking for help, talking about feelings, and managing their emotions. The strategies rely on a three-stage approach to supporting young children's social-emotional development by (1) introducing and practicing a skill, (2) building fluency and competency with a skill, and (3) ensuring there is maintenance of a skill.

Turnbull, H. R., Shogren, K., & Turnbull, A. (2011). Evolution of the parent movement: Past, present and future. In J. Kauffman & D. Hallahan (Eds.) *Handbook of special education* (pp. 639–653), New York, NY: Routledge. This chapter provides an overview of how parents helped shape policies and practices for children with disabilities. The "parent movement" is described; its impact on securing educational rights for children with disabilities is tracked from pre–P.L. 94-142 through current times.

Young Exceptional Children Monograph Series. Missoula, MT: Council for Exceptional Children, Division for Early Childhood. These topical monographs cover all the essential areas related to services for young children with disabilities. These are essential references for practitioners and families.

Journals

Journal of Early Intervention
www.dec-sped.org/Journals

Young Exceptional Children
www.dec-sped.org/Journals

Early Developments
www.fpg.unc.edu/resources

Professional Organizations

FPG Child Development Institute
www.fpg.unc.edu

Center for Response to Intervention in Early Childhood
www.ctriec.org

The Beach Center on Disability
www.beachcenter.org

Division for Early Childhood of the Council for Exceptional Children
www.dec-sped.org

March of Dimes Resource Center Birth Defects Foundation
www.modimes.org

National Information Center for Children and Youth with Disabilities
www.nichcy.org

Parents Helping Parents Resource Center
www.php.com

Head Start
www.nhsa.org

CHAPTER 4

Children with Intellectual and Developmental Disabilities

Standards Addressed in This Chapter

CEC

All of the CEC Standards are addressed within this chapter. Please see the inside book covers for the complete list of the standards.

FOCUS QUESTIONS

4-1 Who were key pioneers in the early evolution of the field of intellectual and developmental disabilities (IDD)?

4-2 How do educators define IDD?

4-3 What are some of the biological and environmental factors that can cause IDD?

4-4 What are some characteristics of children with IDD?

4-5 How are children with IDD identified?

4-6 What are important educational interventions related to students with IDD?

4-7 What are some of the problems students with IDD may have in making the transition to the community?

The category of **intellectual and developmental disabilities (IDD)**, formerly termed **mental retardation**, has evolved though many changes over the last century. Since 1908 there have been ten changes in the definition, and even the current definition has received its share of criticism. There seem to be two reasons for this dynamic state: the proliferation of research, which is a strong change agent, and the changes in the way society views IDD and those who have it (Greenspan & Switzky, 2006).

Mary Evans Picture Library/The Image Works

Maria Montessori was a true pioneer in the education of young children.

4-1 A Brief History of Intellectual and Developmental Disabilities

Organized attempts to educate children who learn slowly began less than two hundred years ago. A French physician, Jean Itard, tried to educate a young boy who had been found living by himself in the woods—the so-called Wild Boy of Aveyron. Although Itard's attempts to tutor the boy met with only modest success, one of his students, Edouard Seguin, later extended Itard's approaches and became an acknowledged leader of the movement to help children and adults with IDD.

Another notable person in the field, Maria Montessori (1912), worked with young children with IDD using what is now called *sense training*. This approach uses the visual, auditory, tactile, gustatory, and olfactory senses to help preschool-age children learn about the world around them. Today, versions of Montessori's methods are still used at the preschool level for all children, although her original work was with children who had IDD. This is yet another example of how the education of children with disabilities may benefit all children eventually.

4-1a What Is in a Name?

Between 2006 and 2007, the key professional organization in this field, the American Association on Mental Retardation, changed its name to the American Association on Intellectual and Developmental Disabilities (AAIDD). It also changed the title of its key journals; now the names refer to the basic condition as intellectual and developmental disabilities rather than mental retardation. This name change was made, in part, to eliminate the negative connotations that had been attached to the previous term (Taylor, 2007). Current efforts are being made to change all references in legislation from mental retardation to intellectual and developmental disabilities.

Not only the professional community and the courts have objected to the term *mental retardation*; those who have been designated "mentally retarded" also take issue with the label:

> A lot of people on the outside world would run and make fun at "retarded people"....but when you get in the position of being the person they are making fun of it's different. That's why I won't poke fun at anybody. I have lived with that. I understand that if I had somebody poke at me, I wouldn't like it.
>
> I think I was sort of an outcast because when I was growing up everyone was calling me retarded. It was hard to deal with.
>
> I never thought of myself as a retarded individual but who would want to? I never had that ugly feeling down deep (Snell & Voorhees, 2006).

4-2 Defining Intellectual and Developmental Disabilities

Over the past decades, emphasis in the diagnosis of intellectual and developmental disabilities has shifted from strictly a measurement of cognitive abilities (primarily IQ tests) to a mix of *cognitive abilities* and *adaptive behaviors*. This change has been due in part to the realization of the role played by the environment (particularly elements of poverty) in the development of mild IDDs. Educators do not

TABLE 4.1 Defining Intellectual Disability

The current definition of intellectual disability by the AAIDD (2013) is as follows:
Intellectual disability is a disability characterized by significant limitations both in intellectual functioning and in adaptive behavior, which covers many every day social and adaptive skills. This disability originates before the age of 18.

merely try to help a child adjust to his or her disability; they also try to intervene early in a child's life to keep the condition from becoming more serious or from even appearing at all.

Table 4.1 highlights the current definition of mental retardation, now IDD. It refers to two separate domains in which limitations must be found before a person can be identified as having IDD. The first area is significantly *below average intellectual functioning*; the second domain reflects limitations in three general indicators of *adaptive skills*:

- Conceptual, mainly the use or misuse of language and self-direction;
- Social, problems in interpersonal relationships such as gullibility and naiveté, and
- Practical, including the ability to use money, travel in the community, and personal care.

Most special educators and psychologists see the wisdom of using the dual criteria (*intellectual below average/developmental delay* and *adaptive behavior deficits*) in identifying mild IDD.

The Diagnostic Manual (Schalock, 2010) also stresses the importance of having a "system of support" available to cope with the special needs of a child with IDD. The context of the child can determine his or her ability to adapt positively or negatively, and this can have a lifelong impact (as discussed in Chapter 1). The term *developmental disabilities* includes mental and physical limitations for which the child is likely to need lifelong support from a variety of health, social, and educational agencies.

4-2a Levels of IDD

One traditional way to further classify children with IDD has been to indicate the level of delay. IQ scores are used as ranking measures as follows:

- Mild (IQ 50–70)
- Moderate (IQ 35–50)
- Severe (IQ 20–35)
- Profound (IQ below 20)

A more functional approach has been to indicate the intensity of support needed by the individual. The four levels of intensity of support roughly match the four levels noted above (mild, moderate, severe, and profound).

4-2b Levels of Support

The formal definition given in the previous section reminds us that both intrinsic function and external support should be taken into consideration. The individual's level or intensity of support needed to operate effectively is shown in Table 4.2.

TABLE 4.2 Intensity of Support for Persons with IDD

The levels of support a person who has an intellectual or developmental disability may need are:

- *Intermittent* refers to support as needed, but that is not necessarily present at all times.
- *Limited* refers to support provided on a regular basis for a short period of time.
- *Extensive* support indicates ongoing and regular involvement.
- The *pervasive* level of support describes constant, high-intensity help provided across environments and involving more staff members than the other categories.

Adapted from Greenspan, S., & Switzky, H. (2006). *Forty-four years of AAMR Manuals.* Washington, D.C.: American Association on Mental Retardation.

The intensities of support are measured as *intermittent, limited, extensive,* and *pervasive* (Greenspan & Switzky, 2006).

Care must be taken that such identification must not limit the planning and opportunities developed for the child with IDD. The question remains how we determine levels of function and need. IQ testing serves the purpose of determining the level of mental functioning that the student shows, but it also can be used to determine the student's cognitive strengths and weaknesses. Students who are identified as having IDD reveal a wide range of performance that can then be used to direct the individualized education program (IEP) by focusing on the strengths revealed by the student (Bergeron & Floyd, 2006).

4-2c Adaptive Skills

The current emphasis on the environment and the context of the child has resulted in an extended attempt to distinguish among various categories of adaptive behavior. The key components of adaptive skills have been reduced to three major categories: conceptual skills, social skills, and practical skills (see Table 4.1 for a list of subsets of the skill sets).

It is possible to have a low IQ score and still possess usable adaptive skills, be self-sufficient in the community, be able to interact reasonably with other citizens, and maintain a part-time or full-time job. Under such circumstances, an individual would still be below average intellectually, but would not be considered "intellectually or developmentally disabled." The lowest score on an IQ test that a child with an intact, undamaged nervous system would achieve is not 0, but about 65 or 70. Any score lower than that is generally an indication of some type of damage to the nervous system.

Greenspan (2006) believes that there is a central element within the broad category of adaptive behavior that catches the essence of children and adults with IDD: "It is vulnerability to social exploitation owing to the inability to understand other people, especially when their motives are malevolent but disguised as benevolent" (p. 215). This failure to understand the feelings and thoughts of others is called a lack of **Theory of Mind**. The concept of being able to understand the feelings and thoughts of others is one we will meet again when we discuss autism spectrum disorders.

This vulnerability or gullibility, a desire for approval, can reveal itself in situations where the person with IDD, in a desire to be compliant, will agree in a police interrogation to things he or she hasn't done. This vulnerability may also lead a young person to fall victim to the false affection of others, which may lead to physical abuse or rape.

4-2d Prevalence

One of the striking changes over the past decades has been the reduction in the number of children classified as having IDD, from 3 percent (MacMillan, Siperstein, & Heffert, 2006) to 2 percent and now to about 1 percent (Polloway, Patton, & Nelson, 2011). Such a change does not mean that there are fewer children with disabilities, but rather that differential diagnosis has changed the label on these students from mental retardation or intellectual disability to autism or learning disabilities or emotionally or behaviorally disturbed. There remain substantial differences in the prevalence of IDD reported by individual states, representing perhaps the amount of service provided for these students rather than actual population differences.

4-2e Cultural Differences

In this category, there is a clear disproportion of minority students classified as IDD. We need to ask ourselves, why are we surprised at such a result? If poverty is a central factor in the causation of some disabling conditions, could it be an important factor with IDD?

If in fact poverty plays a role in creating the IDD conditions, then it becomes particularly important to press for early education experiences for children from economically disadvantaged families. If 4-year-old Mike has working parents who are out of the home most of the time, where will he get the language interchanges or other parent-child experiences that develop school readiness? If Mike's family is on the borderline of poverty, why should we have to wait for Mike to fail in the first or second grade before taking action? Head Start is one of those programs designed to counter the negative factors for children in environments like Mike's.

Mike may well be identified as mild IDD during this early childhood period. Part C of the Individuals with Disabilities Education Act (IDEA) of 2004 actually provides the basis for help with infants and toddlers with handicapping conditions, but organized developmental programs to support early development are still rarely found outside of major research efforts (Dunst, 2007).

Lauren Shear/Science Source

Children with IDD are children first—with some special characteristics that require educational attention.

4-2f Measuring Intelligence and Adaptive Behavior

How do we measure intelligence and adaptive behavior? Unless we have adequate measures of these concepts, we still are in a difficult position in diagnosing IDD. The development of intelligence measures actually can be traced back to Alfred Binet in France, who was given the task of finding children who were not capable of responding to the traditional educational program in France in the early 20th century.

Later individual tests of intelligence were developed by Lewis Terman (the Stanford-Binet Intelligence Scales) and David Wechsler (Wechsler Scales of Intelligence). The Stanford-Binet was originally designed to test the "g" factor, or general intelligence; it has lately branched out to test multiple abilities. The Wechsler scales generated subtests measuring verbal and performance IQs, which allowed psychologists to develop a profile of strengths and weaknesses for further planning (Salvia, Ysseldyke, & Bolt, 2007).

A third test, the Woodcock-Johnson Tests of Cognitive Ability, has recently received considerable attention. There are also nonverbal intelligence tests that have been developed primarily to help assess students who have verbal difficulties or have English as a their second language. The Peabody Picture Vocabulary Test is an example of such a nonverbal measure, where the student is shown four pictures and then asked which picture most closely resembles the verbal clue (such as a train).

A more current version of these adaptive rating scales is the Vineland Adaptive Behavior Scales (Sparrow, Cichetti, & Balla, 2006). Completed by a parent or guardian, it covers communication, daily living skills, socialization, motor skills, and maladaptive behavior. The Vineland results seem to match fairly well with other adaptive scales, although it does not include items on gullibility.

The closer one gets to all of these measures, the more cautious one becomes about using the data from them unsupported by other diagnostic information. A fine collection of test and scale reviews may be found in the text by Salvia, Ysseldyke, and Bolt (2007), *Assessment in Special and Inclusive Education.*

4-3 Biological and Environmental Causes of IDD

A large number of possible causes of IDD have been cited, including genetic malfunction, toxic intrusions, neurological damage and even environmental factors, such as poverty. We review some of the major ones here, but all of them negatively influence the development of cognitive and social abilities needed to adapt to the world without help. Whatever the original cause of the condition, the cognitive and social problems that are its end product call for educational adjustments. Therefore, similar educational strategies may be used with children whose disabilities result from widely differing causes.

4-3a Genetic Factors and IDD

The question of how a tiny gene can influence the complex behavior of children and adults has puzzled scientists for many years. The breakthroughs of James Watson and Francis Crick helped explain the functions of DNA and RNA. Because of them it is now possible to provide a general answer to that question. Watson and Crick discovered that genes influence the proteins that are critical to the functioning of organ systems that determine behavior (Tartaglia, Hansen, & Hagerman, 2007). Thus, genes can influence the development of anatomical systems and their functions—the nervous system, sensory systems, musculature, and so on.

Do certain patterns of genes predetermine certain types of behavior? Are we unwitting automatons driven by mysterious bursts of chemicals? Not really. No particular gene or protein forces a person to drink a glass of whiskey, for example, but some people have a genetic sensitivity to ethanol that may increase their tendency to become active drinkers. Similarly, genetics plays a special role in some types of IDD.

Down Syndrome

One of the most common and easily recognized genetic disorders is **Down syndrome.** The child in the photograph shows the physical manifestations of Down syndrome, resulting in a somewhat flattened facial profile. It occurs once in every 600 to 900 live births, and results from a genotype that features three copies of chromosome 21 (see Figure 4.1). The genotype is often responsible for mild or moderate IDD and often includes a series of other medical complications as well. Even here, environment seems to play a role, as there is a clear link to maternal age and Down syndrome, with older mothers more at risk for having a child with Down syndrome.

Burger/Phanie/Age footstock

Children with Down syndrome share similar physical features resulting from their genotype.

Phenylketonuria

Normal growth and development in the embryo and fetus depend on the production of enzymes at the right time and place. When enzymes are not produced, or fail to perform their normal functions, a number of unfavorable developmental conditions can result. These conditions are called *inborn errors of metabolism*. One of them is **phenylketonuria (PKU)**, a single-gene defect that can produce severe retardation. In PKU, the absence of a specific enzyme in the liver leads to a buildup of the amino acid *phenylalanine,* with serious consequences.

PKU is an unusual genetic disorder in that it can be modified by environmental treatment—a special diet. The diet is very strict, however, and many families have difficulty holding to its requirements. PKU can be detected at birth, and every state has established a screening program to identify children with PKU so that they can be started on an appropriate nutritional regimen early (Simonoff, Bolton, & Rutter, 1998). As children with PKU grow, they can eat only small quantities of

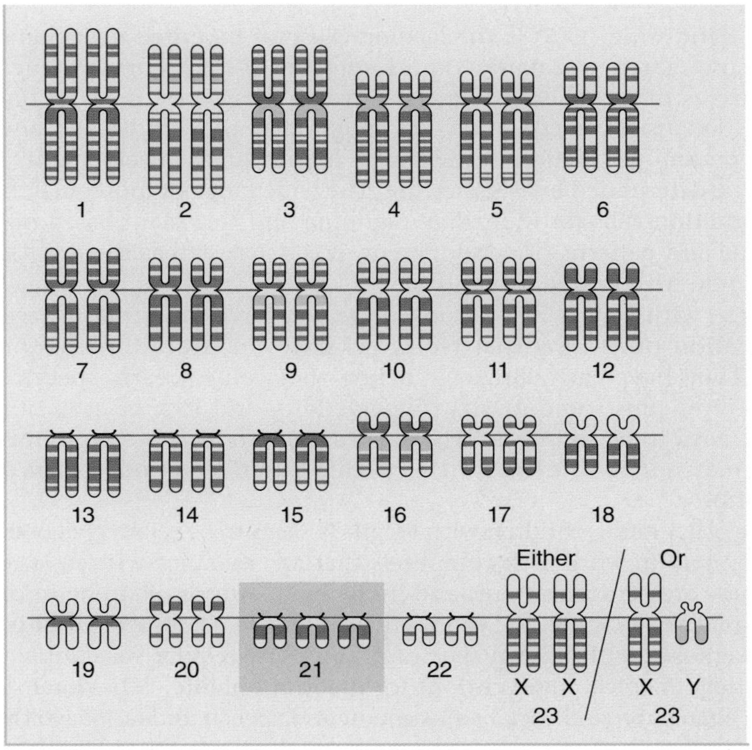

Figure 4.1 Down Syndrome
From FREBERG. *Discovering Biological Psychology,* 1E. © 2006 Cengage Learning. Reproduced by permission.

BOX 4.1 A Child with Fragile X Syndrome: Early Identification

Amy Tyler noticed a problem with her son Max within weeks of his birth. He was not easy to comfort and always seemed to keep his hands clasped. When he was 6 weeks old, Amy tried unsuccessfully to get Max to look at her when she clapped her hands. At 15 months, Amy's doctor expressed concern that Max's language development was behind. She took Max to an early intervention service provider, who recommended that he be tested at the local children's hospital. At 20 months, Max was diagnosed with Fragile X syndrome (FXS).

Compared with most families of children with FXS, the Tylers were fortunate. Max was diagnosed with FXS earlier than most children. According to a Frank Porter Graham Child Development Institute study, the average child with FXS is not diagnosed until nearly age 3, and many others not until much later. Had these children been identified earlier, they would have been immediately eligible for early intervention services under IDEA 2004.

SOURCE: Frank Porter Graham Child Development Institute, University of North Carolina at Chapel Hill. (2004). Screening newborns for Fragile X. *Early Developments, 8*(2), 11–13. Reprinted by permission of Frank Porter Graham Child Development Institute.

high-protein food (such as meat and cheese) but can have fruits and vegetables (low protein). Peer pressure, however, can often pull children off this restrictive diet. The importance for children of staying on this strict diet can be judged by the following facts: The earlier treatment is begun, the less will be lost in intelligence scores. Children with PKU who abandon the diet at school age suffer social and intellectual setbacks. Mothers with PKU can have a high proportion of children with birth defects unless they maintain this diet.

Fragile X Syndrome

Fragile X syndrome (FXS) is the leading cause of inherited developmental disability, resulting from a mutation on the long arm of the X chromosome. It affects about twice as many males as females—overall prevalence is about one in four thousand. Extensive investigation has found that the condition causes a deficiency in protein production necessary for normal brain development. The diagnosis can be determined by DNA testing. The wide range of individual differences in this condition calls for individual planning and treatment based on a child's own profile and patterns of development. Box 4.1 describes the early identification of a child with Fragile X syndrome.

Children with Fragile X syndrome appear to have strengths and weaknesses in information processing that require changes in educational planning and strategy. They have early language delays that call for early speech and language therapy, plus some ADHD (hyperactivity and lack of attention) symptoms that need to be addressed. They also appear to have memory disorders, so a teacher may not be able to count on a child's memorization of facts (Ornstein et al., 2008).

RtI

On the other hand, children with Fragile X seem to be relatively good at object recognition and in work with computers that can enhance written language. Of course, these are generalizations, and individual patterns of strengths and weaknesses should be documented. Children with Fragile X (30 percent of whom can also be diagnosed with autism spectrum disorders) require substantial multidisciplinary help: medical interventions for mood instability, behavioral support to help with aggression and social adjustment, and speech and language therapy for conversational skills. These supports would usually be a part of Tier III services in the response to intervention (RtI) model. With appropriate team efforts, meaningful developmental improvements can be shown with Fragile X in students (Tartaglia, Hansen, & Hagerman, 2007).

4-3b Toxic Agents and Causation

The remarkable system whereby a pregnant mother transmits nutrients through the umbilical cord to her fetus is also the highway by which many damaging substances can pass to the developing child. Drugs (including alcohol) and cigarette smoke are prime examples of **teratogens**, which include any agent that causes a structural abnormality following fetal exposure during pregnancy.

Fetal Alcohol Syndrome

For centuries we have been generally aware of the unfavorable effects that alcohol consumption by the mother may have on her unborn child. About 7 out of 10,000 births result in **fetal alcohol syndrome (FAS)**, which produces moderate retardation and behavioral problems such as hyperactivity and inattention.

Way too few women are aware of the potential consequences of drinking while pregnant. The National Organization on Fetal Alcohol Syndrome (2004) presents three key facts:

- When a pregnant woman drinks, so does her baby.
- The baby's growth can be altered and slowed.
- The baby may suffer lifelong damage.

This is not to say that these outcomes are inevitable, but drinking increases the chances that such outcomes will occur.

The Effects of Lead

Ingesting heavy metals, such as lead, cadmium, and mercury, can result in severe consequences, including IDD. Most attention is currently focused on lead, and much of the lead that enters the brain comes from the atmosphere. One of the most effective steps that has been taken on a societal level is the reduction of lead amounts permitted in gasoline. This reduction resulted in a lowering by one-third of the average lead levels in the blood of U.S. men, women, and children. The reduction in lead levels paralleled the declining use of leaded gasoline, showing how public policy can have a positive impact on children (Beirne-Smith, Ittenbach, & Patton, 2001).

Infections

The brain begins to develop about three weeks after fertilization. Over the next several weeks, the central nervous system is highly susceptible to disease. If the mother contracts **rubella** (German measles) during this time, her child may be born with IDD and other serious birth defects. A rubella vaccine that is now available has drastically reduced the number of children with defects caused by rubella. Children and adults are also at risk of brain damage from viruses that produce high fevers, which in turn destroy brain cells. **Encephalitis** is one virus of this type. Fortunately, it is rare, as are other viruses like it.

4-3c Neurology and Brain Development

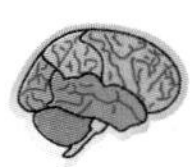

What does the brain have to do with developmental disabilities? Everything. Thanks to new methods of investigation, we have been successful in discovering more about this organ and IDD. For example, "It is well established that the brain forms new neurons in response to environmental stimulation. Remarkably, exposure to novel information can rewire the brain" (Dong & Greenough, 2004). The notion that the brain can be rewired through experiences can be good news for educators who are trying to create experiences that can have an impact on children with IDD.

The technique of magnetic resonance imagery (MRI) can show brain activity in action. The electric activity of the brain will change when a child is doing an arithmetic problem, for example, and we can see where in the brain this activity is taking place. Many research endeavors are underway that promise to answer the questions about how brain activity is different in children with IDD. Such discoveries can open doors to our understanding of cortical activity that previous generations had been unaware of. We are on the edge of a major leap in knowledge that promises changes in diagnoses and in education of individuals with IDD (Sandman & Kemp, 2007).

4-3d Environmental Factors That Influence IDD

There has long been an enormous gap between what we know about the brain and its function and the set of behavioral symptoms by which we define IDD. With current advances in understanding the central nervous system, we are able to make some reasonable assumptions about the links between the nervous system and behavior. Experience also influences the development and maintenance of certain structures and connections in the brain. The implications are exciting. If the development of the nervous system is not preset by genetic factors, then the nervous system can grow and change as the individual experiences new events (Dong & Greenough, 2004).

This means that environment and human interactions can play a role in neurological and intellectual development. The influence of experience on brain development has been largely confirmed (Jensen, 2008; Sameroff, 1990). We have already seen the results of various early intervention programs in Chapter 3. Some children who are on the borderline of IDD classification can be helped through environmental enrichments, though they may still need support in Tier II of the RtI model.

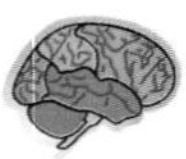

Psychologists such as Hunt (1961) and Bronfenbrenner (1989) have long championed the idea that the experiences young children have in their families and their surrounding social systems can have a significant impact on their development. It remains for educators and special educators to take such knowledge and transform it to the developmental benefit of children—the earlier the better (Dunst, 2007).

We also must not forget that there remains an interactive role for genetics in the mild category of IDD. As we learn more from research such as the Human Genome Project, we become more conscious of the continued interaction between environment and genetics. A study of 3,886 twins (Spinath, Harlaar, Ronald, & Plomin, 2004) focused on pairs who ranked in the lowest 5 percent in verbal and nonverbal abilities. The researchers found twin concordance (when one twin had the condition, the other did as well) for mild mental impairment in 74 percent of the monozygotic (single-egg) twins; this happened in only 45 percent of same-sex dizygotic (two separate eggs) twins. Such a finding suggests that genetics, as well as experience and environment, plays a role in mild IDD.

4-4 Characteristics of Children with Intellectual or Developmental Disabilities

4-4a Two Students with IDD

Let us meet two students who have IDD. Bob, a student with mild IDD, is a 10-year-old of average physical development; his mental functioning, however, more closely resembles a 7-year-old in understanding. The information processing

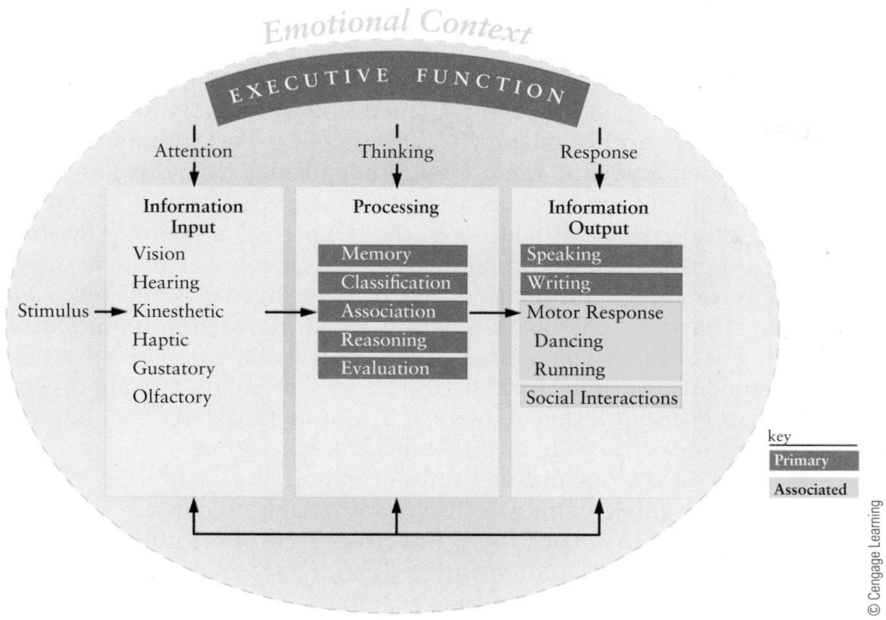

Figure 4.2 **Information Processing Model for a Child with Mild IDD**

TeachSource Digital Download Access online

model (Figure 4.2) shows where the major problems are in Bob's development. His ability to use his memory, associate concepts, and problem-solve are limited (his Wechsler IQ is 67). These primary problems have resulted in secondary problems, including an inability to participate in peer activities and a lack of motivation for academic performance.

His family lives at a borderline poverty level. His father is an unskilled laborer and his mother is a part-time sales clerk in local stores. They both love Bob, but they are having such problems with their own lives that they often can't give him the support that he or his siblings need. If we were to use the scale of "Intensity of Needed Support" (Table 4.1), Bob would probably require both intermittent and limited professional attention.

Jasmine is also a 10-year-old. She has been diagnosed with Down syndrome. She is at the IDD moderate level, and she has made limited academic gains in primary school. Jasmine clearly needs support provided on a regular basis, and this support will continue into adulthood. Her fifth-grade teacher is working to integrate her within the general classroom setting but finds that Jasmine requires substantial help from the special education teacher. Both teachers worry about her ability to fit into the middle school environment next year. Her family has more resources than Bob's, but her parents are still quite puzzled about how to help Jasmine, who has a pleasant and unassuming personality. Her challenges within the information processing model seem similar to Bob's, only more intense. Like many children with Down syndrome, she is delayed in language development but has relative strengths in social relationships. Everyone seems to like Jasmine.

Although there is an impressive range of behavior that can be shown by children in this exceptionality, there are some areas of the information processing model that seem to be particularly affected even in two children as different as Bob and Jasmine.

4-4b The Information Processing Model and Special Characteristics

Earlier we explained that a child's ability to learn about his or her world happens through the processing of information. As there is a great diversity within categories of children with special needs, there are variations in the impact of IDD from one child to another—including how well they are able to process information.

The most obvious characteristic of children with mild or moderate IDD is their limited cognitive ability, or the central processing of memory, association, classification, reasoning, and evaluation (see Figure 4.2). This limitation inevitably reveals itself in their academic work. These students may lag by two to five grades in language-related subjects (such as reading or social studies).

Unless the student has an additional disability (e.g., a learning disability or autism), the input or receptive abilities would not likely be seriously impaired. It is the ability to absorb information, not to sense it, that is affected. Children with IDD often have difficulty with memory, which can stem from limitations in understanding. It is hard to remember what you never understood. Most typically developing students use "rehearsal" as a memory aid, saying a string of words or a poem to themselves until they remember it. Children with IDD are less likely to use this method unless they are directly taught how to do so.

Classification, or the organization of information, is also affected for children with IDD. Children in elementary school learn quickly to cluster or group items into useful classifications: chairs, sofas, and tables become furniture; apples, pears, and oranges become fruit. Children with IDD tend to need direct instruction and much practice to learn classification. For example, a teacher may need to explain how a car and train are similar before a child with IDD can classify them both as means of transportation. Reasoning and evaluation are contributors of information that may also need extra attention for children with IDD.

The executive function is particularly affected in children with IDD. Their ability to make good decisions and make good judgments with the information available is limited. Because of central processing differences, children with IDD may have difficulty expressing themselves (*output processing*). Differences in speaking and writing in turn can influence social interactions. All of these information processing functions are listed separately in the model (Figure 4.2) but are actually closely intertwined in practice.

The emotional context is also linked closely to IDD (see Figure 4.2). But whether that link is due to negative academic experiences or part of the neurological and genetic conditions that lead to IDD is not clear. What is apparent is that the **learned helplessness** (the feeling that one is powerless to cope with a challenge) that some children with IDD display causes continual academic difficulties and can be addressed with educational programming.

4-4c Cognitive Processes

One of the questions posed by researchers in this area is: Do children with IDD follow the same developmental patterns of cognitive growth, only slower, or do they have a unique pattern of development? Weisz (1999) synthesized the results of many experiments and came to the conclusion that the evidence strongly supports a similar developmental sequence for children with IDD—only developing slower than a typical student. If the child with IDD consistently fails on tasks, does he or she have a tendency to quit trying because of a feeling built up by consistent failure in academic tasks and situations? Think of your own abilities in some sports. If you are not able to kick the ball well in soccer and cannot run fast, isn't there a strong tendency to abandon that game in favor of something that provides some measure of success? Several studies that matched children with IDD with nonidentified children of the same mental level indicated that following failure experiences, the children with IDD showed a significant decline in the use of effective problem-solving strategies (Weisz, 1999). This issue of learned helplessness becomes a significant challenge in inclusion because children with IDD are often faced with the fact that their performance does not match those of typically developing children in the classroom.

4-4d Ability to Acquire and Use Language

The ability to develop language is one of the great achievements of humans, and there has always been curiosity as to how, if at all, language development is changed or modified in children and adults with IDD. The close link between language and cognition has long been noted along with their reciprocal interactions. Not only is language limited by cognition, but cognition (especially thinking, planning, and reasoning) is also limited by language (Fowler, 1998). In addition, limited input and an impoverished language environment during the language-learning years can add up to an impoverished linguistic system.

Kali Nine LLC/Getty Images

Learning to work together is a key part of the educational process.

4-4e Ability to Acquire Emotional and Social Skills

We know that emotional and social difficulties can undermine vocational and community adjustment. We are also aware that emotional and behavior problems probably lower the level of social acceptance for children with IDD in comparison with their peers in the classroom.

As has been the case with language development, studies on social development have focused on the specific problems of children with special causal factors of IDD such as Down syndrome (Kasari & Bauminger, 1998). A range of studies has revealed many problems in peer relationships for children with IDD. With the current emphasis on inclusion, it is particularly important to find ways to improve the social relationships of children with IDD, as the formation of relationships is one of the key purposes of inclusion. Certain skills appear to be important for social acceptance. They include sharing, turn taking, smiling, attending, and following directions. A person with social competence uses such skills appropriately in social situations.

TeachSource Video Connection

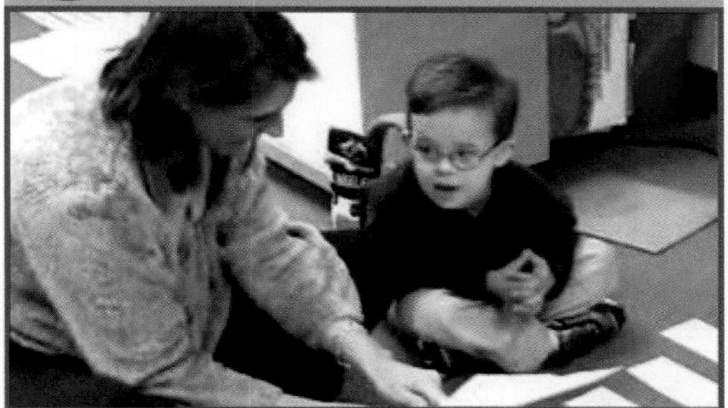

Watch the video "Serving a Student with Down Syndrome in an Inclusive Classroom." This video is a good depiction of how a collaborative team of general educators, special educators, and parents can work to modify general education goals to meet the special needs of Bobby, a first grader with Down syndrome. After watching the Video Case, reflect on the benefits and drawbacks for Bobby in the inclusive classroom. What difficulties does he face? What is he gaining from his environment?

Watch online

4-4f Social Adaptation

Because social adaptation, or adjusting to living in accordance with cultural demands, has become critical for the child with IDD both in the classroom and later in vocational settings, it is important to determine what barriers stand in the way of social adaptation. A study on the interpretation of social cues was most revealing in this regard (Leffert, Siperstein, & Millikan, 2000). One hundred seventeen students in elementary grades, with and without IDD, were shown videotapes depicting various social conflicts (including a child knocking a book off another child's desk accidentally and another child being rejected when wanting to join a group on the playground). The students watching the videotapes were then asked for their reactions.

The children with IDD were much more likely to interpret the child who knocked over the book in the first scene as being mean. They were focusing on the negative outcome of the event and ignoring social cues that would indicate that the event was an accident. They also more often referred to an adult authority to solve the social crisis rather than suggesting social strategies for resolving the incident.

These results suggest one reason that children with IDD are sometimes not well received in peer groups and also point the way to some necessary curricular additions for them. Children with IDD clearly need practice in identifying social cues so that they can better interpret social situations; practice through role-playing or discussions about useful strategies for social interaction is essential. One of the helping roles that the special educator, working as a collaborator with the general education classroom teacher, can play is to provide such experiences in small-group situations and help children with IDD work out their own strategies for appropriate social response.

4-5 Identification of Children with IDD

The first step in adapting the standard educational program to meet the needs of children with IDD is to identify the children who need special help. How do we find a child in need of special education services? Although referrals can come from many different sources, most students with IDD come to the attention of special education services because they have failed in school. The inability of the children to adapt academically or socially to the expected standards of their age group sets off alarm bells in the teacher and calls for action.

Until recently, the response to these alarm bells was a diagnostic examination by the school psychologist to determine whether the child was eligible for some form of special education. Now many school systems use a prereferral team, which may include the classroom teacher, the principal, someone from special education, and relevant other special personnel. The team tries to help the classroom teacher devise some adaptation of the general classroom program to cope with the student's problems without more intensive (and more expensive) intervention (Salvia, Ysseldyke, & Bolt, 2007). If the school is using the RtI model, the team may suggest Tier II supports for the child. If the student makes no apparent gain as a result of the recommendations of the prereferral team, the child may then be referred for more detailed diagnostic examination by the psychologist and, if found eligible, placed in more intensive special education services with an IEP decided on by the multidisciplinary IEP team working with the child's parents.

What is the purpose of a **multidisciplinary team**? Each team member brings important information to an IEP meeting. Members share their information and work together to write the child's IEP. The team membership always includes the general education teacher, a parent, and the special education representative. Also included, depending on the nature of the child's needs, can be a speech and language pathologist, school psychologist, school principal, occupational therapist, the student, and others as appropriate. Each person's information adds to the team's understanding of the child and what services the child needs.

4-5a One or Two Populations?

There are special educators who insist that children with IDD at the mild level of intensity, like Bob, need to be considered as a separate population from other children with IDD like Jasmine (MacMillan et al., 2006). Earlier, in definitions by Tredgold and Doll, even mild IDD was considered incurable because genetic causes were assumed to be at the heart of these difficulties (Spitz, 2006). The more environment has assumed a role in the development of disability, the more professionals believe that cure or improvement should be considered possible.

Haywood (2006) also discusses the question of subdividing this large category of IDD for the purpose of education and treatment:

> Mental retardation (IDD) is not a single entity and can only be further misunderstood if we insist upon regarding persons who are profoundly retarded and multiply handicapped under the same broad concepts that govern our conception of persons who are barely discriminable from those who actually escape the "retardation" label altogether (p. 306).

The rest of this chapter focuses on what steps can be taken to help children like Bob and Jasmine reach an independent or semi-independent adulthood with a high degree of self-sufficiency.

4-6 Educational Responses for Students with Intellectual and Developmental Disorders

Children with IDD present a clear and continuing challenge to educators. The serious cognitive and adaptive deficiencies faced by these youngsters mean that the general education program has to be supplemented by both organizational and instructional adaptations if they will reach our goal for them of independent or semi-independent living as adults.

Figure 4.3 provides the data from the Data Accountability Center (2013) on the educational settings for students with IDD. About half of the students are in the regular classroom most of the day. About half of the students spend less than half of their day in a regular classroom; the number of students spending time outside the regular classroom increases as students enter secondary school.

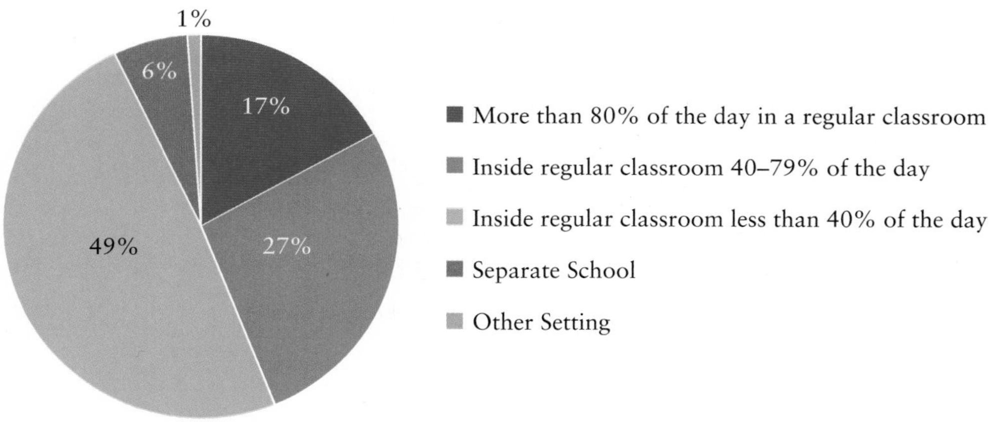

Figure 4.3 Educational Settings for Children with Intellectual and Developmental Disabilities
Source: Data Accountability Center. (2011). *Part B Educational Environments 2011* [data file]. Retrieved from http://www.ideadata.org/PartBEnvironments.asp

The suggested modifications presented here are aimed at children with mild and moderate IDD. The needs of the most severely impaired will be addressed in the chapter on children with multiple handicaps (Chapter 13).

4-6a Organizational Structures to Support Students with Intellectual and Developmental Disorders

Children with IDD Have Potential

As we seek strategies and proper learning environments for children with IDD to succeed in school, we should remind ourselves that their limitations in information processing are only relative. Although the child's ability to remember or associate ideas may be limited, it is not absent. With proper instruction and teacher support, Bob and Jasmine can learn and become productive adults. Most of us learn much about the world through incidental learning (observations or imitations). We don't have to receive direct instruction to know to run to first base instead of third, to stay away from Mike on the playground when he is angry, or not to talk when the teacher is explaining something. Children with IDD can learn these things as well, but it often takes direct instruction, practice, and special learning environments for them to master the skills necessary to navigate their environments.

RtI

The special needs of children with IDD call for some special modifications in their learning environments.

RtI Approaches for Students with IDD

The RtI model is brought into play at all three levels, or tiers, for children with IDD.

Universal Tier I for Students with IDD

At Tier I, the inclusive classroom, attention still needs to be given to ensure that the key lesson elements have been mastered, and additional practice is needed for children with IDD so that they don't fall behind and become confused and discouraged. A special education teacher can be valuable here in proposing adaptations that fulfil the goal of **Universal Design for Learning (UDL)**, learning the same concepts through different methods or approaches.

Table 4.3 provides a description of some aids and services that can be used by UDL. These include diverse means of presenting material, multiple means for student expression beyond the usual spoken or written response, and multiple means for engaging the student in learning.

TABLE 4.3 Universal Design for Learning (Supplementing Aids and Services)

Multiple Means of Representation	Multiple Means of Expression	Multiple Means of Engagement
digital talking books	art work	computer use
text to speech	drama, acting out	design for individual student's interests
graphic depictions	music	mnemonic strategies
flow charts	video	student directed
		self-monitoring
		cooperative learning

Adapted from Wehmeyer, M. (2006). Universal Design for Learning: Access to the general education curriculum and students with mild mental retardation. *Exceptionality, 14*(4), 215–235.

Proponents of inclusion (the practice of including children with disabilities in the regular classroom) want the child with disabilities to be welcomed into a community of equals in the classroom. Implementation of inclusion requires teamwork from support personnel to assist the classroom teacher, who otherwise would have to bear sole responsibility for inculcating such values.

How does inclusion work in actual practice? We obviously don't expect the special educator to have mastered all of the content fields in the middle school curriculum (English, social studies, math, and science). Where will he find appropriate content material for special exercises or tasks for children with disabilities? How will he manage the content area instruction?

This is where the team approach becomes necessary. Working with the general education teachers who provide the content for lessons, special education teams can make modifications to meet the needs of the student or suggest ways for the general education teacher to present lessons to include these students. Increased responsiveness of students like Bob and Jasmine can be important rewards for the staff's collaborative efforts.

The U.S. Congress left little doubt as to its preference for education in the general education classroom for all children with special needs with the following language (from the IDEA amendments of 1997 and repeated in IDEA 2004):

> To the maximum extent appropriate, handicapped children, including children in public or private institutions or other care facilities, are educated with children who are not handicapped, and that separate schooling, or other removal of handicapped children from a regular educational environment occurs only when the nature or severity of the handicap is such that education in regular education classes ***with the use of supplementary aids and services*** cannot be achieved satisfactorily [20 U.S.C. §1412(5)(B)].

Teachers in inclusive classrooms should be able to call on reading specialists, special education personnel, school psychologists, school counselors, physical and speech therapists, other classroom teachers, math and science teachers, and a variety of other people to participate in the classroom to help the classroom become more flexible and relevant to the needs of all students. The RtI model, with its tiers of support, can be most useful in meeting these needs and utilizing these specialists. A Summary of *UDL Supports for Students with IDD* can be accessed online.

TeachSource Digital Download

Targeted Tier II for Students with IDD

Tier II may include special lessons for small-group instruction for students with IDD in social skills or in making good choices, conducted by knowledgeable staff. These choices will necessitate removing children for a time for this special instruction, but Bob, and especially Jasmine, need this special small group experience for reading and math lessons and social skills.

One of the goals of this small group instruction is to get children with moderate handicapping conditions to begin to read and realize that print can represent real things. Lemons and Fuchs (2010) engaged 24 children with Down syndrome in one-on-one tutoring for two 30-minute periods, five days a week for six weeks.

The peer tutors without developmental disabilities received extensive training and were audiotaped to ensure that the intervention was proceeding appropriately. For example, the student with IDD would read a passage at her or his level of difficulty.

Bob Rowan/Progressive Image/Corbis

Individual lessons to fit their needs are important for children with IDD.

Errors would be met with the correct word stated by the tutor and then repeated by the student with IDD. The students were provided with many rewards in terms of points, which they used to purchase balloons, pencils, stickers, etc. About half of the children seemed to reach a level where word recognition and phonemic identification was possible. This program also demonstrated how much effort and commitment is necessary to reach this level of beginning reading for children with moderate disabilities. Research findings suggest that changes in the **learning environment** alone do not make a striking difference. Many studies have tested the effectiveness of inclusive education for children with IDD, but the information derived from such studies is not necessarily educationally significant, as few of the studies discuss the nature of the program the students received. This is surely just as important as, if not more important than, "where" the student has been placed (Guralnick et al., 2006).

Intensive Tier III for Students with IDD

The greater the degree of disability, the more likely a child like Jasmine will need a special learning environment in order to learn distinctively different material. In this special setting, a special education teacher can provide a distinctive curriculum for a small group of children, typically no more than fifteen. The curriculum may include exercises in personal grooming, safety, pre-primary reading skills, or any other subjects not needed for the typically developing child in the regular classroom. These life skills are highly appropriate for a child like Jasmine, whose cognitive development is limited and will need these life skills to reach a level of independence.

One of the first efforts to develop long-range plans for child and family came forth from the IEPs, to increase the collaboration between professionals and parents and to ensure thoughtful consideration about how children would be served within the general and special education program.

One of the major changes in the educational planning for children with disabilities is a shift from focusing on their deficits and disabilities to documenting their developmental and personal strengths, to plan the most effective educational intervention. Students with limited verbal proficiency may be able to express themselves through dance or through other arts, or they may be relatively proficient in working with their hands, as in carpentry (Bateman & Linden, 2006).

Table 4.4 shows briefly some of the IEP goals and objectives for Micah, a 10-year-old with mild IDD with resistant behavior but with clear strengths as

TABLE 4.4 Micah's IEP Goals and Objectives (Chronological Age = 9;8, IQ = 67)

Area	Annual Goals	Short-Term Objectives
Academic	Micah will increase his reading and math scores by one year each on standard tests.	• Reciprocal teaching will be used to improve his reading performance and peer-adult interaction by 25 percent. • Will create his own addition and subtraction problems.
Social	Micah will reduce his resistant and oppositional behavior episodes by one-half by end of school year.	• Positive behavior supports will be used to decrease the basis for oppositional behavior. Resistant episodes charted should be down by 25 percent.
Physical	Micah will be involved in team sports to encourage sharing and cooperative behavior.	• Micah will be invited by physical education teacher to play after-school soccer. Number of confrontations and resistant behaviors will be counted and reductions noted.

TeachSource Digital Download Access Micah's full IEP online.

well. Micah's strong communication skills will be brought forth in the **reciprocal teaching** model to improve his academic performance. Here, Micah is the teacher and the teacher is the student. By teaching the lesson himself, Micah should gain more insight into the content by playing a different role.

His good physical skills are also taken advantage of by encouraging him to play soccer and, through that experience, to improve his respect for rules and his peer interactions while under adult supervision.

Even with Tier III support, some students with moderate IDD may not be able to master the standard curriculum and may have to be given individualized instruction in a special education setting for at least a part of the day or even in a separate setting (Bambara & Knoster, 2005). For instance, Jasmine could be given social skills practice with her special education tutor.

A totally separate environment may be necessary for children with moderate or mild IDD at the secondary level, where the focus is on vocational skills and preparation for the transition from school to work or post-secondary training. A Summary of *RtI Approaches for Students with IDD* can be accessed online.

TeachSource Digital Download

4-6b Curriculum and Instruction for Students with Intellectual and Developmental Disabilities

COMMON CORE STATE STANDARDS

There has been much discussion about the most desirable curriculum for children with IDD. Should the content be modified from that given to the average child? If so, where in the educational sequence should the branching take place? In secondary school? In middle school? Or should the curriculum be different from the beginning? The important questions to be answered in the development of curricula for students with IDD are: What are our goals? What are our immediate objectives to reach that goal?

For students like Jasmine, who have moderate IDD, reasonable goals are to:

- Learn to read at least the "survival words" *(stop, poison, restroom, school bus,* and so on). (You may create a list of survival words for your community.)
- Master basic arithmetic and understand the various denominations of money.
- Learn social skills, such as the ability to work cooperatively with others.
- Develop some leisure-time activities and skills.
- Communicate effectively with persons such as storekeepers and community helpers.
- Learn work skills to be partially or fully self-supporting in adulthood.

The more difficult curriculum decisions must be made for children like Bob, with mild IDD, who can be expected with appropriate support to reach a middle school level of skills and knowledge. The curriculum in the early grades will be the Common Core State Standards (CCSS)—supplemented by adaptations (such as more time to master the material) needed for his success.

Table 4.5 shows some sample math and literature examples for third-grade students. It is clear that even at this young age some level of adaptation will be necessary for children with disabilities if this is going to work. Thompson et al. (2010) comment, "Planning individualized supports requires thoughtful and regular analyses of student characteristics and environmental contexts. Although educators from a variety of disciplines can make contributions, it would be logical for the special education teacher to take the lead in serving as the primary facilitator of this process" (p. 177).

But when Bob gets into middle school and secondary school, the problems change. Table 4.6 gives an example of two Common Core State Standards from middle school to indicate how far out of Bob's abilities these standards now become. Not only would trying to implement these goals be a great frustration for Bob and his teachers, there is a real question of how relevant they are for Bob's career goals and abilities.

TABLE 4.5 CCSS and Students with IDD (Third-grade Math and Reading)

Standards (Math)	Sample Tasks
Tell and write time to the nearest minute, and measure time in minutes.	It is now 11:00 am and the teacher says we will break for lunch in 50 minutes. What time will we have lunch?
Develop understanding of fractions as numbers.	Have a number line from 0 to 8. At what point would you put ½, ¼, ¾?
Standards (Reading)	
Distinguish your own point of view as opposed to the view of authors.	Lucy, in the classic Peanuts comic, has a clear opinion of Linus and Charlie Brown. Explain where you agree and disagree with her and why.
Standards (Writing)	
Write narrative on imaginative experiences, with descriptive details and clear event sequences.	Bob is asked to write a story on what he would like to happen that hasn't happened, and describe it in detail.

TABLE 4.6 CCSS and Students with IDD

CCSS.Math.Content.8.F.A.3 Interpret the equation $y = mx + b$ as defining a linear function, whose graph is a straight line; give examples of functions that are not linear. *For example, the function $A = s^2$ giving the area of a square as a function of its side length is not linear because its graph contains the points (1,1), (2,4) and (3,9), which are not on a straight line.*

CCSS.ELA-Literacy.W.9-10.8 Gather relevant information from multiple authoritative print and digital sources, using advanced searches effectively; assess the usefulness of each source in answering the research question; integrate information into the text selectively to maintain the flow of ideas, avoiding plagiarism and following a standard format for citation.

SOURCE: National Governors Association Center for Best Practices, Council of Chief State School Officers. (2010). Common core state standards for English language arts & literacy in history/social studies, science, and technical subjects. Washington, D.C.: National Governors Association Center for Best Practices, Council of Chief State School Officers.

At what point does the student with mild IDD, like Bob, branch off into a separate secondary school program that is designed to provide work skills rather than academics that are more designed to help the student reach the next level of education? Inclusion advocates do not expect students with mild or moderate IDD to take advanced high school physics or calculus. It is in the secondary program that attention is traditionally paid to community adjustment and work skills.

If all children are required to meet the same challenging standards, this is surely not good news for students with IDD who do not do well on high-level conceptual material. For some students with IDD, a secondary program focused on learning community living is most appropriate. Yet the No Child Left Behind legislation insists on including most children with disabilities in these CCSS assessments, following these principles:

- All students should have access to challenging CCSS standards.
- Policymakers and educators should be held publicly accountable for every student's performance.

Although the federal government, through No Child Left Behind, requires assessment of all students, it is clear that alternative or modified assessments must be made for some students with disabilities. The number of students allowed an alternative assessment option was originally 1 percent of all students. Later a new rule was established that "states could have an alternative assessment for an additional 2 percent of students who evidence persistent academic differences and thus are working toward 'modified achievement standards'" (Salvia, Ysseldyke, & Bolt, 2007, p. 660).

This percentage still amounts to only 3 out of 10 students discussed in this text, so the clear expectation is that the majority of students with exceptionalities will be expected to take the state tests for content competence. For example, Bob would be expected to take the state tests, while Jasmine might receive alternative or modified assessments because her academic program is significantly different from the standard course of study.

© istockphoto.com/Chris Schmidt

Play can be an important element of a child's learning.

What do alternative assessments look like? Typical examples are:

- ***Portfolio assessment:*** An assessment of a compilation of selected work of the student over the year that links to the standards.
- ***Performance assessment:*** An assessment of tasks performed by the students, linked to the standards.
- ***Teacher observations:*** Descriptions or formal ratings of the student as connected to the standards.

States have the responsibility of showing how the results of modified assessments fit into the required annual yearly progress (AYP) for the school.

Teacher Strategies

In addition to curriculum modification, the teacher and team may find it necessary to modify the assignments and teacher-student interactions. This may mean that the teacher adjusts the level of difficulty of tasks to fit the level of development of the child with IDD. For example, in math, if the rest of the class is doing complex multiplication or division problems, the child with IDD may be given addition and subtraction problems at his or her level of comprehension. Or in a cooperative learning situation, teams of four or five students might be working on a particular problem related to the early American colonists in our country. The child with mild IDD could be given a task such as finding pictures of colonial life to be used in a report, and other students would be challenged with a more complex question, such as why these settlers abandoned their homeland to come to the New World. Sometimes differential lessons are referred to as **tiered assignments**—that is, assignments of varied difficulty that allow the child with IDD to participate meaningfully in the group activity.

When the general education teacher is using differentiation, it becomes important to have the special education teacher help design tiered assignments. Failure to differentiate lessons for the child with IDD runs the risk of discouraging the child, who faces failure once again in the academic setting (see the earlier discussion on learned helplessness).

Case Study: Audrey

Audrey and her parents have been told that she will be part of a program at school called inclusion that will bring Audrey into the regular fifth grade, even with her diagnosis of mild IDD. Previously she was in a school program where she spent an hour or more each day with a special education teacher who worked with her in areas of language and basic arithmetic. She was achieving at the third-grade level.

Her parents felt gratified that Audrey would now be with all the other fifth graders, but worried, too. Would she get along with the other children? How could she keep up with the other students, when she was reading at only a third-grade level? The school principal told Audrey's parents that Audrey would be seeing her special education teacher for some lessons—but within the general education classroom. The fifth-grade classroom teacher worried about the very same issues as the parents, knowing that having Audrey in a seat in her class didn't mean that Audrey would find friends there or that she would be happy. How will she differentiate the CCSS to meet Audrey's needs? Will she need to use UDL to help her grasp some of the concepts? One major task for this teacher is to make Audrey feel at home, feel like part of the class. A second is to ensure that she receives individualized instruction to meet her needs. Making inclusion work for Audrey will require much professional teamwork.

Two key areas where students with IDD will need additional support are language/communication and social skills.

Language and Communication

There is a substantial effort underway in elementary schools to help children with mild and moderate IDD use language as a tool for communication and reading as an essential skill. Teaching students the most common sounds represented by letters and a strategy for sounding out words, such as explicit phonics, has proven effective for children with IDD (Browder et al., 2007). In math instruction, the use of money management can be role-played in "banks" and "grocery stores" to teach the use of addition and subtraction.

Language exercises for children with moderate intellectual impairment like Jasmine aim to foster the development of speech and the understanding and use of verbal concepts. Communication skills focus on the ability to listen to stories, discuss pictures, and tell others about recent experiences. Two important areas of study are the home and the community. Children learn about holidays, transportation, the months of the year and days of the week, and how to contribute to home life. Teachers may make use of dramatization, acting out a story or a song, playing make-believe, and using gestures with songs, stories, and rhymes.

Social Skills

Social skills are a critical component of the preschool and primary school curriculum for children who have IDD, but instruction at this level should be informal. Skills such as taking turns, sharing, and working cooperatively can be embedded into their daily activities.

In preschool settings, the lunch table is an excellent location for teaching social skills. Here, youngsters learn table manners, as well as how to pass and share food, help others (e.g., pouring juice), and wait their turn. The lunch table is also a good place to review the morning's activities and talk about what is planned for the afternoon or the next day. Although the teaching is informal, it is both effective and important to the child's social development.

Because, as previous studies have indicated, children with IDD have difficulty establishing social acceptance in the classroom and in their other social environments, we need to prepare them by practicing social skills. A major effort to do this was a study conducted with 45 children with IDD (IQ ranging from 50 to 80, ages 4 to 6) that introduced, over two years, individualized programming in play groups, increased parent-child interaction, and coaching on social skills (Guralnick, Hammond, Conner, & Neville, 2006). This comprehensive effort to improve the social skills of developmentally delayed students, in the authors' words, "produced only modest results with children with lower cognitive abilities benefitting the most" (p. 352). There was some reduction in the children's negativity and reduction in unusual play patterns in the children with the lowest measured abilities.

This study shows again that interventions to change the behavior of children and students must be intense and administered over a considerable amount of time for there to be manifest improvement. There is no simple pill to take to improve social skills and relationships.

Children with IDD sometimes have difficulty transferring or applying ideas from one setting to another. Thus, we teach some needed social skills directly (such as greeting of other students). It is likely that we have to think for a while to recall the coping strategies we use without conscious effort (e.g., in meeting strangers, breaking unpleasant news, communicating with someone we haven't seen for a long time, or telling someone that he is intruding on our space and time). These skills are the lubrication that allows each of us to move smoothly through our daily contacts and tasks. Someone who is markedly lacking or awkward in social skills stands out in a crowd. Many children with IDD need direct instruction in social skills if they are to establish an effective personal and community adjustment.

Bob, for example, usually got too close to the person he was speaking to. Thus, he made the other person uncomfortable but was not aware of this reaction. Through role-playing a number of social situations with Bob and others, the teacher was able to establish that each person has a personal space that is not to be invaded without permission (e.g., to kiss an aunt good-bye). Such social rules may seem trivial, but their importance is magnified substantially when they are violated.

It is important that the sense of privacy is established and understood when the child begins to cope with sexual relationships. Parents and other adults worry about the susceptibility of young people with IDD to sexual abuse or unwanted sexual contact merely because they lack the social skills to fend off others in sexual encounters (the gullibility factor). Therefore, some type of counseling and role-playing of relationships or situations with the opposite sex should be a part of the curriculum for students with IDD.

To meet the socialization goal of inclusion, special educators have developed a series of activities that enhance social contact and learning. In peer-buddy systems, a classmate may help a classmate with disabilities negotiate the school day; peer support networks help students become part of a caring community; and in circles of friends, an adult facilitator helps potential peer buddies sensitize peers to the friendship needs of students with disabilities.

Positive Behavior Interventions and Supports

One of the most effective moves made for children with IDD has been the introduction of **positive behavior interventions and supports (PBIS)** in educational programming. Behavior problems and disruption have, unfortunately, been a major part of the lives of too many children with IDD. It may be that these children have been reacting to their inability to live up to adult expectations at home and at school. Unfortunately, the teacher response to disruptive behavior is often punitive, which compounds the problem.

The strategy of PBIS advocates that, when faced with some form of behavior disruption, the teacher should focus on human motivation, not just on human behavior. For example, Micah, a student with mild IDD who we met through his IEP discussion on page 122, has shouted "No!" to the teacher's request to pick up his reading book. Why would Micah do such a thing, considering that it will surely bring unpleasant reprimands? What hidden rewards must Micah receive from this situation that would cause him to burst out like that? There must be rewards of some sort, or he wouldn't have done it.

BOX 4.2 Micah's Functional Assessment

1. What were the environmental circumstances surrounding Micah's outburst? (Micah had an altercation with Sylvia at lunchtime, which upset him a lot. He has not been doing well in his reading exercises in past days. He feels the teacher has been too demanding of him, and his father gave him a hard time at breakfast this morning.) Any or all of these might be the cause.
2. Develop some hypotheses about the motivation for Micah's behavior. Is he trying to avoid reading recitation time, at which he has been doing poorly? Is this a general reflection of his fight at lunchtime? Has his relationship with the classroom teacher soured, and he wants to strike back? Is school or the classroom an unpleasant place to be and he wants to get out?
3. Let us test one of the hypotheses by changing the environmental circumstances. Instead of Micah reciting in a group, the teacher's aide, Mrs. Rosseli, who Micah likes very much, will take him aside and work with him one-to-one with his reading lesson so that he will not show his deficiencies to the entire classroom. If we are right, Micah's events of resistance should be reduced, and his reading may even improve.

TeachSource Digital Download Access online

The goals of PBIS are to achieve (1) improved academic performance, (2) enhanced social competence, and (3) safe learning and teaching environments (Eber, Sugai, Smith, & Scott, 2002). The seeking of the "why" of human behavior has traditionally been the role of the psychologist and the psychiatrist—not the teacher, who has immediate circumstances to deal with. Once Micah has been settled down, after either a quiet talk with the teacher or a short visit to a quiet place, it can pay to reflect on the *why* of the situation. The teacher or a child study team can take some time to analyze the event, particularly if it is only one of many resistant actions taken by Micah. Micah's **functional behavioral assessment**, presented in Box 4.2, shows how we can come to understand his behaviors.

We will take regular measurements of Micah's behavior and chart these changes coincident with the change in environment that we have made. If there is no reduction in Micah's resistant behavior, we might move on to another hypothesis and test it (e.g., by not including Sylvia in small-group work). Once we have found an environmental change that works (that is, reduces the undesirable behavior), we can see whether it generalizes to other situations and employ it there.

Scaffolding

In **scaffolding**, the teacher or aide models the expected behavior and then guides the student through the early stages of understanding. As the student's understanding increases, the teacher gradually withdraws aid (hence the name scaffolding). The goal is to have the student internalize the knowledge and operate independently.

Reciprocal Teaching

Reciprocal teaching is an educational strategy where small groups of students and teachers take turns leading a discussion on a particular topic. This exercise features four activities: questioning, clarifying, summarizing, and predicting. In this strategy (as in scaffolding), the teacher models how to carry out the activities successfully. The students then imitate the teaching style while the teacher plays the role of the student. In this way, students become active players in a role they find enjoyable.

Cooperative Learning

Interestingly, emphasis has switched from a focus on one-on-one instruction for the individual student with special needs, as represented in the policies for an IEP, to the importance of student participation in **cooperative learning** or team-assisted individualization (Browder et al., 2007).

RtI

Group instruction may actually be more advantageous than one-on-one instruction because of the economy of teacher effort, students learning how to interact with peers, and students learning from peers. Small-group instruction (RtI Tier II) is the mode for the regular classroom if the students with special needs are to be included (King-Sears & Carpenter, 2005).

Motivation

One of the most important questions facing the teachers of children with IDD is how to motivate them to learn. There are many reasons that they may not be motivated in school. Bob, for example, comes from a home in which there is little interest in school learning. He is 10 years old and has had a few years' experience in school. But those years have not been full of positive experiences. Bob has known a lot of failure, and failure is a distinct turnoff for most children and adults. Building on Bob's strengths becomes important to avoid feelings of learned helplessness.

Self-Determination

One of the long-term goals for students with IDD is **self-determination**, or the ability to set personal goals and to take appropriate actions to achieve them. The capability of making choices and solving problems within the range of their abilities is an often-stated IEP goal (Wehmeyer, 2006).

Practice at decision making can strengthen the executive function in the information processing model. If the teacher makes all the decisions for the student about what to do next or what to read, this undermines this key ability for adult adjustment.

Teaching strategies for self-determination is a priority for children with IDD. A total of 891 elementary and middle school teachers in six districts were asked whether they valued and provided instruction in seven self-determination domains: (a) choice attainment, (b) decision making, (c) goal setting and attainment, (d) problem solving, (e) self-advocacy and leadership, (f) self-awareness and self-knowledge, and (g) self-management and self-regulation skills (Stang, Carter, Lane, & Pierson, 2009). Both general educators (elementary and middle school) and special educators clearly stated self-determination as a curricular priority, although special educators rate it somewhat more important than general educators. A call has been made to blend these goals into the elementary program and to stress these strategies more in personnel preparation.

While Bob's program will focus on general education, Jasmine faces a different situation. Many special educators believe that for students with moderate to severe IDD, the fundamental goal should be not the mastery of knowledge or academic skills but the mastery of adaptive behaviors such as social skills, communication skills, and work skills. After all, they ask, who cares very much whether Jasmine reaches third-grade or fourth-grade mastery of academic skills? If it is most important for Jasmine to develop adaptive skills that will serve her well in adulthood and in the world of work, she should participate in cooperative learning exercises—not necessarily to learn what the other students learn but to experience positive social interaction and learn how to work constructively with others.

A problem-solving strategy can be taught that helps the student achieve more independent behavior. It requires some practice.

1. Find the problem (problem).
2. Discover as many options as possible (option building).

3. Choose the option you think is best (best option).
4. Act on the choice (action).
5. Judge the effectiveness of the choice (success or no success).

Another skill related to **self-management** is choice making. Josh may be asked, "Would you like to complete your work at your desk or at the table? Would you like to do your math now or after lunch?" Such choice making gives the student a sense of being in control. Of course, once the decision is made, it should be honored (Bambara & Koger, 2005). The outcome of these problem-solving and choice-making activities is students with more self-confidence who are more in control of their environment.

© iStockphoto.com/1MoreCreative

Intensity and duration are key elements in carrying out IEPs.

Effectiveness of Intervention

As with other programs in special education, we are interested in knowing how much and in what ways intervention is paying off for children with IDD. Guralnick (1997) has summarized the literature on early intervention and concluded that the basic question, "Can intervention make a difference?" has been answered and that the answer is yes. Our task now is to determine the relative effectiveness of various models of intervention.

Bryant and Maxwell (1999) reviewed a series of studies that attempted to chart gains from special programming for these children. They found support for an *intensity and duration-of-treatment* effect. In other words, the heavier the dose of educational treatment, the greater the children's gains. The same can be said for the length of time that the treatment is applied: the longer, the better. As a matter of fact, when special treatment stops, there is a tendency for the children to lose some of the gains they have made.

We might make an analogy with diabetes in that the patient must *keep receiving treatment* (insulin or other medication and adherence to diet) in order to get the desired results. What we have learned is that special education needs to be intensive and ongoing for the children's initial gains to hold.

Fidelity of Special Programs

With the establishment of such strategies as the Individual Education Program (IEP) there has been concern as to whether such strategies are really being carried out as intended. This is particularly true of the IEP, which represents the key to much of what is intended for children with IDD. Christle and Yell (2010) reviewed the literature to see if IEPs were really developing plans that conferred "meaningful education benefit."

They found reports that IEPs in many instances failed to develop meaningful annual goals, failed to develop ways to monitor student progress, to offer adequate and appropriate educational services or show modifications to the general education program. Most serious of all was the discovery that individual IEPs were using "stock computer generated IEPs" without changing them to meet a student's unique needs. Many of these errors would tend to take away the proposed value of the IEP strategy itself.

Powers et al. (2005) gathered 399 IEPs from a number of communities to look at how adequately the **transition plans**, which are key to community adjustment, were being formulated. They found that in 24 percent of the cases the transition plans were missing and in many of the others the participation of transition specialists and vocational rehabilitation personnel was low. They suggested that the schools needed to improve collaboration with adult service agencies, among other suggestions.

Christie and Yell (2010) summed up the situation by urging more attention be paid to the formation of the IEP and that "the only way school district personnel can prove that an IEP is in substantive compliance with the law is to have data to show that a student has made educational growth in his or her special education program" (p. 122).

Assistive Technology for Students with IDD

The rapid development of technology linked to education provides a variety of opportunities for children with disabilities. As we have discussed earlier in the text, these technological aids can be divided into two areas: assistive and instructional. Assistive technology exists to help the child with disabilities gain access to the information needed for learning. Instructional technology is used to help the student learn that information.

Many students with IDD have difficulty reading. **Hypertext software** programs can provide assistance to learners with words they do not recognize or understand. In such programs the student can select the unknown word. The student can make the computer read and define the word and read the definition. Some programs may also have pictures to support the meaning of the word. For example, a hypertext program could be created for vocabulary found in a general science class. A student could independently study the pronunciation and definitions found in the science curriculum through the use of a program that provides words and definitions in an auditory format.

Although assistive technology can provide the avenue through which knowledge can be accessed, instructional technology provides the means for presenting content in alternative approaches (such as in UDL); as such, the computer is a critical tool for the special educator.

For the child with IDD, the computer is actually a window on the world, given capable instruction in its use and the availability of appropriate software. As Foshay and Ludlow (2005) point out, "computers can be the means of curriculum modification, to facilitate the access to content areas such as science and social studies in the academic curriculum and to develop peer relations through interactive games and collaborative learning" (p. 101).

Sometimes children with IDD need additional multimedia stimulation to master concepts. For example, the Doppler effect, often illustrated by a whistle of an approaching and then departing train, may be more richly portrayed through audio and video formats that can be repeated to ensure that the student has mastered the concept.

Technology allows a child to avoid learned helplessness by allowing him access to knowledge and allowing him to complete required tasks. Students with mild IDD can use text-to-speech software, so that the student can listen to the information as it is read by the computer. In computational math, a student can use WebMATH, which gives instructional support for solving math problems.

WebMATH
www.webmath.com

Do not be deceived, however. Much teacher or teacher aide time must be invested in preparing the student for the proper use of the computer for learning. Still, through the Assistive Technology Act (P.L. 105-394), Congress provided funds for obtaining hardware and also requires, through IDEA 2004, that IEP committees take technology needs into account when developing IEPs for the student in question. It is highly likely that special education programs for teachers in training will be spending larger and larger amounts of time on the uses of technology in the classroom.

BOX 4.3 EXCEPTIONAL LIVES • EXCEPTIONAL STORIES
Eunice and Me

I sometimes wonder what was going through Eunice Kennedy Shriver's head when she came up with the idea of Special Olympics and turned her backyard into a day camp for disabled kids. They say it was for Rosemary, her older, learning-disabled sister. That Eunice saw how difficult things were for Rosemary and was inspired by her struggle, and that she also saw that including Rosie with the right support worked out well. It is certainly true that having a disabled person in your life can really alter your perspective. You become very familiar with the dark underside of the world, the realm of "can't do" and "will never be."

My autistic son is 18, and I have been jamming my foot into closing doors all his life: from the renowned doctor who shrugged and pronounced him "retarded" to the synagogue that would not let him have a Saturday bar mitzvah to the local principal who was afraid to have him attend her school.

One day, however, a door swung open wide where we least expected it: sports. Nat tried a gymnastics class run by Special Olympics. The coach was inexperienced with autism but full of energy and patience. She worked him hard and got him to the State Games that summer. We experienced the odd sensation of feeling both proud of our son and being able to trust others with him. Then, at 14, Nat learned how to swim on the local Special Olympics swim team, and it was the first time he ever seemed to look forward to something. "Swim races, swim races," he would say over and over, with a huge grin. Now, at 18, Special Olympics taught him how to be a part of a basketball team.

Our life with Nat is often very hard, but at Nat's sporting events it is not. There, he's just another team member playing his hardest. Nat is just one of the guys, and we are like everyone else. There is no "can't" in Special Olympics. Whether she knew it or not back then, I think that this is what Eunice Shriver had in mind when she set up the day camp. Even though the Special Olympics athlete's pledge is "let me be brave," the secret is, at Special Olympics, we parents don't have to be.

SOURCE: This essay aired on November 16, 2007, on WBUR-FM. Susan Senator is the author of *Making Peace with Autism: One Family's Story of Struggle, Discovery, and Unexpected Gifts*. Boston: Shambhala, 2005. Reprinted by permission of 90.9 WBUR, Boston's NPR News Station.

4-7 Transition from School to Work and Community

4-7a Special Olympics

A goal of almost everyone, regardless of their educational philosophy, is to increase community contacts and interaction for students with IDD. There is a manifest advantage in these students interacting in the community in which they will live as adults.

One of the most successful of these ventures is a program called Special Olympics, which uses the format of the Olympic Games but in which all the persons participating have developmental disabilities. The program was begun in 1968 by Eunice Kennedy Shriver, a sister of President John F. Kennedy. It has grown to an international event, with several thousand participants and many thousands of spectators. The purpose of the games is to allow children and adults with disabilities to participate in races, swim meets, field events, and team games and to feel what other athletes feel in competition, in winning and losing—an experience they rarely are able to achieve elsewhere. It has received substantial community support and is touted as one of the largest athletic events now operating, second only to the traditional Olympics. Box 4.3 gives an example of how the Special Olympics affected one student.

4-7b Transition to Adulthood

The ultimate goal of transition is for students with IDD to achieve independence in the community. To reach such a goal, we need to organize our resources along four separate lines (Odom, Horner, Snell, & Blacher, 2007):

- Systematic planning over several years
- Careful attention to the development of essential skills

BOX 4.4 Ryan's Readjustment

Ryan, a 22-year-old with mild IDD, was referred to an occupational therapist after unsuccessful community-based job placements. Several professionals recommended that he return to a sheltered day program for "work skills training."

While working with a new occupational therapist, Ryan said he'd like more jobs similar to the ones he had previously lost due to excessive absence or poor performance. Ryan was capable of doing the necessary tasks for those jobs but had seemed to lose interest in them very quickly.

He took a look at some new job ideas on video and was excited about the possibility of working as a housekeeper at a motel. It wasn't easy to find an employer who was willing to give him a try. But one motel owner agreed to give Ryan a job on a 30-day trial basis. It took only a short time for Ryan to become one of the most efficient and reliable housekeepers on the motel's staff. His employer was so impressed that she requested other people with disabilities seeking employment.

Ryan had many successes at this job. He was named Employee of the Month and given a cash bonus, and later he was promoted to "second floor supervisor" and given a raise. Ryan eventually moved up to supervising a group of motel employees without disabilities

Adapted from Blair, B. (2000). Ryan's story: From job placement challenge to employee of the month. *Teaching Exceptional Children, 32*(4), 47. Copyright by the Council for Exceptional Children. Reprinted with permission.

- Assistance in the transition process, and
- Ongoing support in adulthood.

An acceptable quality of life depends on income, a sense of self-worth, and social connections provided through work, so there are many people responsible for supporting a student with IDD in the adult community. Ryan's experience, described in Box 4.4, is one example of what can be done.

4-7c Studies on Transition

There are a growing number of studies on how students with IDD are doing in adult life. The news is mixed. A seminal study looking at 8,000 youths with disabilities, the National Longitudinal Transitional Study of Special Education Students (Blackorby & Wagner, 1996), has established a baseline for future results. Researchers used a careful sampling design to ensure that their sample was nationally representative and generalizable to the population as a whole, as well as to students in 11 disability categories. Large samples of youngsters with disabilities from 300 public school districts and from 25 state-operated schools for children who are deaf or blind were surveyed and interviewed. In addition, a subsample of more than 800 parents of youths who had been out of secondary school between two and four years was interviewed.

What happened to youths identified as having IDD?

Half of the students with IDD graduated from high school; the rest either dropped out or aged out of school. The reasons for dropping out of school appeared to be related to behavior rather than to academic performance. Twenty-eight percent of the students who dropped out had serious discipline problems.

What about responsibilities at home?

Youths with IDD had roughly the same amount of household responsibilities as youths in other disability categories. Although the number of students with IDD who were performing in an unsatisfactory fashion at home was not encouraging, their adaptation seemed to be at the same level as that of students with other disabilities.

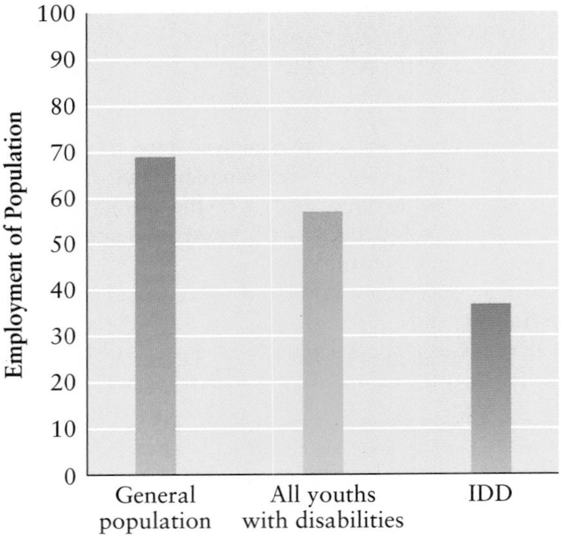

Figure 4.4 Youths Competitively Employed 3–5 Years Out of School
Source: Wagner, M. M., & Blackorby, J. (1996). Transition from high school to work or college: How special education students fare. *The Future of Children, 6*(1), 103–120.

What about living independently?

In the first or second year after secondary school, fewer students with IDD were living independently than were students with other disabilities. For example, 24 percent of adults with IDD were living independently three to five years after high school (Blackorby & Wagner, 1996).

Figure 4.4 indicates the percentage of youths with IDD who were competitively employed within three to five years after they left school. On the graph, the general population of students shows a 70 percent rate of employment, and when all the figures for youths with disabilities are included, slightly more than half are competitively employed. In contrast, the number of youths with IDD is between only 30 and 40 percent. Yamaki and Fujiura (2002) took a national profile of U.S. adults with IDD living in community households and found an employment rate of 28 percent, with typical jobs found in service occupations (i.e., cashier) or unskilled labor. These low-income jobs mean that people with IDD will continue to rely on family or public support (Stancliffe & Lakin, 2007). Affordable housing, stable employment, and transportation are keys to independence.

Table 4.7 provides a series of events for secondary students who have IDD. Basically, by getting a part-time job at age 16, enrolling in vocational classes at age 17, and setting vocational goals at age 18 the student is preparing for a transition to work and the community. It does not make much sense to continue to enroll students with IDD in traditional secondary courses, many of them designed for college-preparatory programs, when transition to work is a more appropriate goal.

In another study, Newman et al. (2009) reported that only 14 percent of young adults with IDD lived independently and only 28 percent were involved in community activities. Nevertheless, 33 percent reported being stopped by police and 14 percent reported spending at least one night in jail. There is, however, substantial literature reporting that young adults with IDD can be successful in the workplace given appropriate training and opportunities (Snell et al., 2009).

Such results have convinced special educators that assistance for many students with IDD has to be continued beyond the school years if the goals of becoming self-sustaining and independent are to be achieved. Accordingly, there has been more attention paid to the transition years between school and vocational work (and adulthood). Although inclusion appears to be a viable goal for children with IDD through middle school, a strong transition plan must be established early in the child's program.

The lesson here is that we cannot release young people with IDD from school and expect them to adjust to a working environment without support and planning. With organized training programs and support services, many of these individuals can adjust well. The support resources fall into four categories:

- *Individuals:* skills, competencies, the ability to make choices, money information
- *Other people:* family, friends, coworkers, cohabitants, mentors
- *Technology:* assistive devices, job or living accommodations, behavioral technology
- *Services:* habilitation services that can be used when natural resources are not available

TABLE 4.7 Planning for Secondary Students with IDD

AT AGE 16
Find and hold a part-time job in school or in the community.
Write transition knowledge into the IEP meetings.
Invite adult service providers to IEP meetings.
Discuss how long student will attend high school—for four years or until age 21.
Attend information night meetings about future planning.
AT AGE 17
Enroll in vocational education classes.
Establish a graduation date.
Write transition goals into IEP.
Invite adult service providers to IEP meetings.
Investigate guardianship procedures and determine what is in the best interest of
AT AGE 18
Apply for SSI and Medicaid card.
Apply to adult service provider. Take time to visit all providers to find the best match.
Schedule a vocational evaluation to better assist in determining the child's interest and setting a vocational goal.
Write transition goal in IEP. Discuss services needed for best transition from high school to adult services.
Attend a job fair

Adapted from Goldberg, A.M. (2004). Transition timeline. Retrieved from www.ndss.org. Reprinted with permission.

4-7d Family Support

One of the common feelings of parents whose children have IDD is loneliness. They feel different from their neighbors and often do not know how best to help their child. An important resource designed to help them cope can be an organized parents' group such as The Arc of the United States (established in 1951 as the National Association for Retarded Citizens), a national organization with many chapters throughout the country. It is able to provide access to resources for parents and to advocate for them and for their children. Often another parent who has been through the same experience can be a valuable friend and confidante, and parents' organizations such as The Arc have well-developed support help. Visit The Arc's website for leads to a wide variety of useful information.

The Arc of the United States
www.thearc.org

One of the strategies that professionals use to help families cope with the extra stress that often accompanies living with children with disabilities is respite care. **Respite care** is the provision of child-care services so the parents are freed for a few days of their constant care responsibilities. Parents who may not have had a "day off" from child-care responsibilities for years greatly appreciate such assistance. Respite care is an effective way of reducing parental depression and stress and enabling parents to be more effective in their role (Botuck & Winsberg, 1991).

Too often in the past, when professionals said they were involved with the family, they really meant only the mother. We now realize the importance of relating to the father as part of the family unit. This is especially true in light of evidence that the typical father tends to play less of a family role when there is

MUMS: National Parent-to-Parent
www.netnet.net/mums

a child with disabilities (Blacher & Hatton, 2007). Some direct counseling and support for the father in his role may be important in achieving the sustainable daily routine that seems so necessary to keeping the family on an even keel. It is helpful to have a male counselor participate here.

A popular program called MUMS: National Parent-to-Parent Network matches a trained "veteran parent" (someone who has experience as a parent of a child with disabilities) and a "referred parent" (one who is dealing with the issues for the first time). Today, there are 650 Parent-to-Parent programs serving nearly every state. An example of what such a program can mean comes from a referred parent:

> Parent-to-Parent has been my lifeline. When I first heard the diagnosis, I was devastated. Well-meaning doctors and nurses, as well as friends and family, simply did not understand. It was only when I finally connected with another parent through the Parent-to-Parent program that I could begin to hope for a future for us all. My veteran parent was generally there for me whenever I needed her (Turnbull & Turnbull, 1997, p. 181).

We have tried to portray the diversity of students that fall under the category of intellectual and developmental disabilities (IDD). The causes for the condition are multiple, but as educators we face the student who results from these genetic and environmental forces. Such diversity requires differential adaptations, and such diverse adaptations require a team approach in planning and implementing a program. The general rule that success depends on the intensity and duration of programming certainly applies here.

MORAL DILEMMA

Inclusion and Student Harassment

A teacher in training, Mr. Bascomb, has been concerned about Carlos, a 9-year-old who has just moved into town with his family. Carlos joined the fourth-grade class under the school policy of inclusion, although he clearly was not performing at the same level as the other students. The other students have noticed this as well and have begun to comment about it. Today, while on the playground, a group of boys more or less surrounded Carlos and made some comments that he was a "dummy" and a "retard," asking why he didn't go to a school where he belongs. Carlos clearly didn't know how to handle the situation and tried to slip away from his tormentors.

What is Mr. Bascomb's responsibility in this situation? What should he say to the boys who were harassing Carlos? When they have dispersed, what should he say to Carlos? How should the incident be reported to the classroom teacher, who has been having troubles of her own getting Carlos oriented? Develop a dialogue between Mr. Bascomb and the boys; Mr. Bascomb and Carlos; and Mr. Bascomb and the classroom teacher. How should Carlos's parents be involved?

Summary

- Pioneers such as Itard and Montessori laid the groundwork for current educational practices.
- The current definition of children with intellectual and developmental disabilities (IDD) focuses on two major components: intelligence and adaptive behavior. An educational diagnosis of IDD depends on the characteristics of the child and on the demands of the social environment.
- Many factors contribute to the development of IDD. They include genetic abnormalities, toxic agents, infections, neurological damage, and negative environmental factors.
- There are different developmental levels found in children with IDD, and those levels determine the educational placement and strategies that meet the child's needs.
- Children with IDD have difficulty processing information. For many, the problem lies in limited memory, perception, reasoning, classification, and the way they organize information and make decisions. Children with IDD often have a general language deficit and specific problems using interpretive language.
- Early intervention programs are one means of preventing IDD caused by environmental factors, but they are not a cure-all for the effects of poverty and social disorganization in the home. They are an important first step; the earlier, the better.
- The IEPs of children with IDD are encouraged to stress strengths that can lead to positive accomplishments.

- The elementary and secondary curricula for students with IDD emphasize academic skills, communication and language development, socialization, and prevocational and vocational skills. The emphasis, particularly for students with moderate IDD, is on functional language.
- By reducing failure, increasing success, and modeling appropriate behaviors, teachers can improve the attitudes and behaviors of children with IDD.
- Families with a child with IDD may need support and assistance in their attempts to cope with the challenges they are presented. This could be both from professionals and from other parents in similar situations.
- Planning and vocational training are needed to ease the transition of those with IDD from school to work. Many of these students make good adjustments as adults, often with community help.

Future Challenges

1. What aspects of the culture of poverty influence developmental delay?

We know that a disproportionate number of children growing up in a culture of poverty show early developmental delays. We don't yet know what factors, or interaction of those factors, in that culture are responsible. Our current emphasis on preschool development and intervention promises better answers to this puzzle in the near future.

2. How can positive employment prospects be increased?

The future of students with IDD depends as much on the environment or context in which they live as on their education and training. The increasing complexity of modern society casts a shadow over the goal of independence for these students, although many may be able to get jobs in the service sector.

3. How can more effective instruction be offered to students with IDD who come from a variety of cultures?

The changing demographics of the American population make it certain that more and more students from different cultures and ethnic backgrounds will be referred for special education services. Some will be mislabeled because of the difficulties of communication; others will find it difficult to adapt to classrooms in which the demands are high and not in line with their own experience or even their family values. Special educators need to develop greater understanding and sensitivity to the cultural diversity of families bringing children to the schools in order to serve the students well.

4. How can inclusion and the best community options be achieved?

By including individuals with mild IDD in the general education classroom at the secondary level, we limit them to a standard curriculum. Yet these students need special instruction in prevocational and survival skills. How do we balance the benefits of inclusion with these special vocational needs?

TeachSource Digital Download Access online

Key Terms

central processing p. 116
cooperative learning p. 129
Down syndrome p. 111
encephalitis p. 113
executive function p. 116
fetal alcohol syndrome (FAS) p. 113

fragile X syndrome (FXS) p. 112
functional behavioral assessment p. 128
hypertext software p. 131
inclusion p. 121
instructional technology p. 131
intellectual and developmental disabilities (IDD) p. 105
learning environment p. 122
learned helplessness p. 116
mental retardation p. 105
multidisciplinary team p. 118
phenylketonuria (PKU) p. 111
positive behavior interventions and supports (PBIS) p. 127
reciprocal teaching p. 123
respite care p. 135
rubella p. 113
scaffolding p. 128
self-determination p. 129
self-management p. 130
teratogen p. 113
Theory of Mind p. 108
tiered assignment p. 125
Universal Design for Learning (UDL) p. 120

Resources

References of Special Interest

Schalock, R., Bothwick-Duffy, S., Brodley, V., Berntinx, W., Coulter, D., Craig, E., . . . Teager, M. (2010). *Intellectual disability: Definitions, clarifications, and systems of support* (11th ed.). Washington, D.C.: American Association for Intellectual and Developmental Disabilities. This impressive volume represents the results of 10 years of work to recast the definition of children with intellectual and developmental disabilities. There is a special emphasis on the need for systems of support to provide the special services needed for those children.

Agran, M., & Wehmeyer, M. (2005). *Mental retardation and intellectual disabilities: Teaching students using innovative and research based strategies.* Boston: Merrill/Prentice Hall. A review of the many kinds of special intervention techniques to be used with children with IDD. Special attention is paid to positive behavior supports and the teaching of problem-solving techniques to build the capacities of these students.

Lakin, K., & Turnbull, A. (Eds.). (2005). *National goals and research for people with intellectual and developmental disabilities.* Washington, D.C.: American Association on Mental Retardation. This volume puts into writing the conference findings from 200 national experts who wished to summarize the progress that has been made over the past few decades in providing multidisciplinary assistance for children with IDD and their families. The National Goals that were agreed upon provide a basis for special programming and policies for such students.

Odom, S., Horner, R., Snell, M., & Blacher, J. (2007). *Handbook of Developmental Disabilities.* New York, NY: The Guilford Press. This volume contains 30 chapters dealing with all aspects of children with developmental disabilities written by ranking experts in their own specialty. There are special sections on early intervention, issues in genetics and neurology, behavior supports, family issues, post school and adult issues, and others.

Polloway, E., Patton, J., & Nelson, M. (2011). Intellectual and Developmental Disabilities. In J. Kauffman & D. Hallahan (Eds.), *Handbook of Special Education* (pp. 175–186). New York, NY: Routledge. A good summary of our current knowledge of the IDD condition, focusing on causation and assessment. Educational practices, trends, and issues are given comprehensive treatment. Good source for those looking for an authoritative view on where the field is now.

Switzky, H., & Greenspan, S. (Eds.). (2006). *What is mental retardation?* Washington, D.C.: American Association on Mental Retardation. A comprehensive view by many different experts on the problems of defining and implementing the concept of intellectual and developmental disabilities (IDD). The role of the environment and adaptive behavior are explored, with widely varying views on the appropriate answers.

Journals

American Journal on Intellectual and Developmental Disabilities
aaidd.allenpress.com/

Education and Training in Intellectual and Developmental Disabilities
www.cec.sped.org

Intellectual and Developmental Disabilities
www.aaidd.allenpress.com

Research in Developmental Disabilities
www.elsevier.com

Professional Organizations

American Association on Intellectual and Developmental Disabilities
www.aaidd.org

Association for Retarded Citizens (The Arc) **www.thearc.org**

National Down Syndrome Society **www.ndss.org**

United Cerebral Palsy Association **www.ucp.org**

causes of autism, major legislative initiatives aimed at addressing the challenge of autism (the Combating Autism Act of 2006), and active advocacy groups of

BOX 5.1 Exceptional Lives Exceptional Stories

Mike Dolan was a poster boy of a child. With his blond, curly hair and clear blue eyes, he was, as neighbors and relatives said, a beautiful 2-year-old. But Mike's parents were worried about him. Something was clearly wrong with their child. He wasn't talking as 2-year-olds do. He made a series of repetitive physical motions with his hands. And, above all, he didn't interact socially with his parents or others the way he should. For example, he didn't look directly at people when they talked to him, and he appeared not to pay attention to many of the things his parents said to him. He seemed preoccupied with his toy trucks and would play with them incessantly. When he wanted something, such as a glass of milk, he would go to the refrigerator, grab a carton, and hand it to his mother rather than ask.

Finally, Mrs. Dolan decided to take him to the family pediatrician. Dr. Phinney examined Mike and found nothing physically wrong with his development, with the exception of some motor coordination difficulties. However, having seen a child with similar behavior two months before, the doctor suggested that the Dolans take Mike to a university clinic with a multidisciplinary staff who could review Mike's needs.

Mike was evaluated by physicians, psychologists, and speech pathologists at the university clinic. Then they met with the Dolans and explained that in their judgment, Mike had a condition known as *autism*. The lack of communication, his inability to interact socially, his obsession with particular toys, and his strange motor movements all pointed in that direction. It was fortunate that the Dolans had come to them so soon. Early intervention was essential, and it would be important to begin a treatment regimen right away.

The Dolans had many questions. What was this condition? What had caused the autism? Could future children that they might have contract the condition as well? Could it be cured, and if so, what would the treatment be? Mrs. Dolan wanted to know whether the schools could handle a child with this condition or whether Mike would need to go to a special school.

These are all good questions—ones that any parent might ask in a similar situation. Awareness of autism, with its patterns of symptoms, has grown. Now a child like Mike can be diagnosed by age 2 or even earlier.

Autism Society of America
www.autism-society.org

parents and professionals (Autism Speaks and Autism Society of America) who have been calling attention to these children and their educational and health needs. Mike Dolan exemplifies many of the special characteristics of children with autism.

5-1 History of Autism

Autism was first brought to our attention by Leo Kanner (1943), a psychiatrist at Johns Hopkins University. He described a group of children who did not relate to others, had delays in speech development, engaged in repetitive behavior, were upset by changes in routines, and so forth:

> In October 1938, a 5-year-old boy was brought to my clinic from Forest, Mississippi. I was struck by the uniqueness of the peculiarities which Donald exhibited. He could, since the age of 2½ years, tell the names of all the presidents and vice presidents; recite the letters of the alphabet forwards and backwards; and flawlessly, with good enunciation, rattle off the Twenty-Third Psalm. Yet he was unable to carry on an ordinary conversation. He was out of contact with people, while he could handle objects skillfully. His memory was phenomenal. The few times when he addressed someone—largely to satisfy his wants—he referred to himself as "You" and to the person addressed as "I." He did not respond to any intelligence tests but manipulated intricate foamboards adroitly. (Kanner, 1943, p. 93)

Later on, in England, Michael Rutter (1996) reported a study that compared children diagnosed as autistic with children who displayed other emotional disorders. He found three characteristics that almost always were present in the children with autism but only occasionally in children with emotional disorders:

1. Failure to develop social relationships
2. Language retardation with impaired comprehension
3. Ritualistic or compulsive behaviors

5-2 Defining Autism Spectrum Disorders

Autism spectrum disorders are a variety (or *spectrum*) of related disorders that affect a child's social development and ability to communicate and that include unusual behavioral manifestations such as repetitive motor movements. Included in the category of autism spectrum disorders are Rett syndrome, pervasive developmental disorders–not otherwise specified (PDD–NOS), Asperger's syndrome (observable in high-functioning children with autism-like symptoms), and childhood disintegrative disorders, which cause children to regress in their development (such as in a child who once had speech but is no longer communicating).

Rett syndrome is a condition included within autism spectrum disorders because its symptoms resemble autism. It is a progressive neurological disorder in which individuals reveal a loss of muscle functions, hand flapping, and autistic behavior. Symptoms appear in children 6 to 18 months old, and educational treatment is similar to treatment for autism.

Pervasive developmental disorder–not otherwise specified (PDD–NOS) refers to a group of disorders characterized by delays in the development of socialization and communication skills. Individuals with PDD–NOS usually have some but not all of the full symptoms of autism and, as a result, may not be diagnosed until later on in childhood.

Asperger's syndrome (AS) has gained much public interest over the past few years due to increased interest in the general condition of autism and to its increased prevalence. Named in 1944 for Viennese physician Hans Asperger, this autism spectrum disorder is characterized by an observable developmental imbalance. On one hand, children with Asperger's can be of average or superior intelligence; on the other, they are unfailingly years behind in their social development.

In addition, students with AS may have a preoccupation with certain subjects almost to the exclusion of other subjects (for instance, the solar system or computers) and can become experts in a narrow field that includes things but not people. They may also show stereotypical behavior, such as "hand flapping," and various nonfunctional rituals, such as insisting that the objects on a shelf always be in the same place and order (Attwood, 1998). In addition, awkwardness in motor skills is often a part of Asperger's syndrome.

▶ Figure 5.1 shows the various conditions that, together, make up the autism spectrum disorders as now seen by the latest Diagnostic and Statistical Manual (DSM-5) of the American Psychiatric Association. The major difference from earlier versions is that Rett syndrome and Asperger's syndrome are no longer considered separate, if associated, conditions. All now fall under the Autism Spectrum Disorders category.

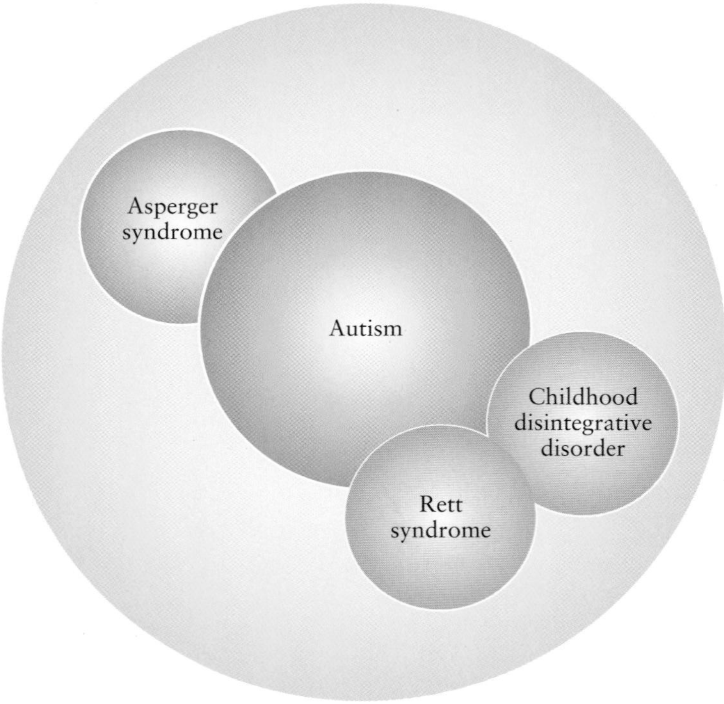

Figure 5.1 Autism Spectrum Disorders
Based on Lord and Risi, "Diagnosis of Autism Spectrum Disorders in Young Children," in A. Wetherby & B. Pizant (Eds.), *Autism Spectrum Disorders*, 2000, p. 12.

TeachSource Digital Download Access online

5-3 Causes of Autism

During the 1970s and 1980s, it became popular in the social sciences to emphasize the effects of environment on children and adults. Now, with the growing capabilities of genetic research, it seems clear that many conditions that produce special needs in children are linked to an intertwining of genetics and environment. Conditions such as Fragile X syndrome, intellectual and developmental disabilities, attention-deficit hyperactivity disorder (ADHD), and dyslexia (and all learning disabilities), as well as autism, all seem to have genetic components (McGuffin, Riley, & Plomin, 2001).

5-3a Genetics and Autism

The genetic search for the causes of autism has shown remarkable progress in recent years. We no longer search for the magic gene that might be the cause. Instead, a complex collection of genes and environmental interactions appear to be implicated.

One line of evidence for a genetic cause for autism lies in the observation that autism appears to run in families (Newschaffer et al., 2007). A more dramatic finding (see Figure 5.2) of the role of genetics is the discovery that monozygotic twins (with an identical genetic makeup) are much more likely to both have autism than dizygotic twins (where the genetic makeup of the twins is different).

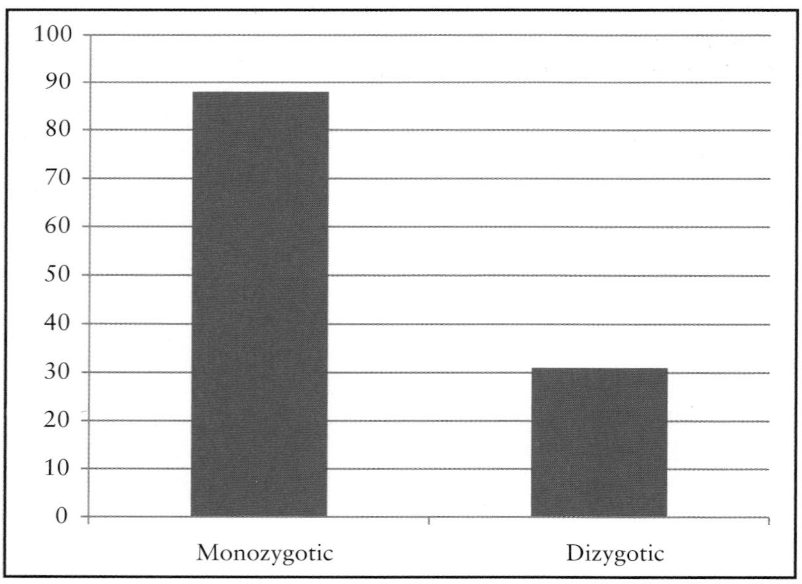

Figure 5.2 Genetic Concordance of Twins with Autism
Source: Rosenberg, R., Law, J., Yenskyan, G., McGrady, J., Kaufman, W. & Law, P. (2009). Characteristics and concordance of autism spectrum disorders among 277 twin pairs. *Archives of Pediatric and Adolescent Medicine, 163*(10), 907–914.

One problem in finding the genetic causes of autism has been gathering a large enough sample of children with autism to give confidence in the findings. Greatly aiding this search is a consortium of 13 universities that have cooperated in identifying 2,000 families (the Simons Simplex Collection) in which the child with autism has no siblings or parents with the condition. Investigators are collecting histories from these families and seeking the genetic factors that separate the SSC children with autism from their relatives (Fischbach & Lord, 2010). This collection of families promises to be a rich supply of continuing data for the immediate future.

5-3b Mistaken Causes of Autism

With the advance of more sophisticated diagnostic tools, several previously held ideas about the causes of ASD have been abandoned. One of these was that the mother's coldness or lack of emotional feelings for the child had resulted in the child's social distancing. An unfortunate term, "refrigerator mother," had been used to describe this situation (Bettelheim, 1978). Not only was this insulting to mothers who were already stressed, but it was also totally incorrect. The term apparently came from observations of the frustrations of the mother being unable to establish social contact with her child.

Another discredited theory is that thimerosal, one of the ingredients in vaccinations, might have some side effect causing the ASD. This idea has been widely circulated in the public press and has resulted in some parents fearing to get vaccinations for their child. Thimerosal as a possible cause of ASD has been studied extensively by scientific panels and found to be without merit (Taylor et al., 2002). Nevertheless, such ideas die hard, and Mike's parents agonized over whether to vaccinate him until they were convinced by their pediatrician that the danger of thimerosal in vaccinations is far less than going without protection from childhood diseases. The pain and confusion caused by these discredited ideas underline the importance of scientific studies to test various propositions to keep the public informed.

5-3c Neurology and Brain Development: Recent Findings Related to ASD

The presence of unusual symptoms in children with autism spectrum disorders has suggested that some neurological dysfunction or genetic factors or a combination of both are at play. The rapid development of magnetic resonance imagery (MRI) has allowed us to literally peer into the brain for the first time and observe its functioning.

The Center for Cognitive Brain Imaging at Carnegie-Mellon University is one center for examining the brain function of children and adults who have been diagnosed with autism. Marcel Just, director of the center, has observed that important cognitive, language, and social skills require many parts of the brain to work together. Just and Varma (2007) believe it is the white matter of the brain that contains the cables that connect parts of the brain that hold the key to the functioning of the individual with autism.

Another line of investigation involves the discovery of mirror neurons. These are neurons that fire not only when a person acts (bouncing a ball, for instance) but also when the person sees someone else act. **Mirror neurons** have been assumed to be the basis for human imitation. Mirror neurons are important because imitation of others seems so difficult for children with autism to perform. The lack of ability to imitate motor or speech production is, in fact, one of the diagnostic signs for the presence of autism (Winerman, 2005).

5-4 Identifying Children with Autism

5-4a Diagnosing Autism: DSM-5

A substantial development in who may be called a child with autism may result from the latest *Diagnostic and Statistical Manual for Mental Disorders* (DSM-5) released in 2013. This manual, created by the American Psychiatric Association as a guide to professionals, has become a road map for clinics and schools to establish official diagnoses. More importantly to parents, it may determine whether their child is eligible for special services.

The current version represents some substantial shifts from the DSM-IV. Table 5.1 reveals the four key elements of the new diagnosis criteria. There will now be one category of Autism Spectrum Disorders. No longer will there be separate diagnoses for Asperger's Syndrome or PPD-NOS.

TABLE 5.1 DSM-5 Criteria for Autism Spectrum Disorders

An individual must meet criteria A, B, C and D:
A. Persistent deficits in social communication and social interaction across contexts, not accounted for by general developmental delays.
B. Restricted, repetitive patterns of behavior, interests, or activities.
C. Symptoms must be present in early childhood (but may not become fully manifest until social demands exceed limited capacities).
D. Symptoms together limit and impair everyday functioning.

SOURCE: American Psychiatric Association. (2013). Diagnostic and statistical manual of mental disorders (5th ed.). Arlington, VA: Author. Retrieved from http://dsm.psychiatryonline.org

Included under criterion A are deficits in nonverbal communications for social interaction and deficits in developing and maintaining relationships. Criterion B includes repetitive speech and motor movements, excessive adherence to routines, and overreaction to sensory stimuli like noises.

These new criteria are causing concern in the existing autism community. For example, there is no question that Mike Dolan with his serious communication disorders clearly meets the criteria for deficits in communication and social interaction. His stereotyped speech plus his need to have the blinds in the windows of his bedroom always at precisely the same level when he goes to sleep to prevent a tantrum, fulfills the second criterion. He showed these unusual characteristics before the age of 3 (criterion C) and they are clearly impairing his everyday functioning (criterion D) so he meets all of the criteria for an autism diagnosis.

But what about Tim Page, a well-regarded writer for the *New Yorker* magazine, who had previously been diagnosed with Asperger's syndrome? Or Temple Grandin, a well-known lecturer on her autism, who has made a successful career out of designing equipment for the care of farm animals? Would their Asperger's symptoms or high-functioning autism meet criterion D, "limiting and impairing everyday functioning," for diagnosis?

These are far from casual questions because it may mean that children like Tim or Temple may have trouble getting funding for services under the new criteria, particularly criterion D. A different category, "social communication disorders," has made its appearance to identify children who have autism-like qualities but fall short of meeting the new criteria. Will this tend to reduce the number of diagnoses of autism spectrum disorders or reduce special education services?

5-4b Prevalence of Autism

The prevalence of autism spectrum disorders has been steadily rising as the spotlight of attention focuses on them. Fombonne (2003) reviewed the data in ten countries and estimated a prevalence of 4.8 per 10,000, or about 1 in every 2,000 children. Other estimates suggest it may be as high as 1 in every 1,000; Blumberg et al. (2013) estimate 1 in 50 children is diagnosed with ASD. The number of children with autism may now exceed the number of children with Down syndrome and children with Fragile X syndrome. Autism has moved from a low-incidence condition to a high-incidence condition (see Chapter 1)—similar to children with intellectual and developmental disabilities (IDD) or emotional disturbance.

Experts explain that they do not necessarily see a major epidemic of autism striking the country. Instead, the rise seems due to an increased sensitivity to the condition so that children who had previously been labeled "mentally retarded," emotionally disturbed, ADHD, and so forth are now correctly diagnosed as children with autism. Also, children with high-functioning autism and/or Asperger's syndrome have been added to the total. In short, it probably has been professionals' ability to differentially diagnose the ASD condition that has resulted in the increase in the prevalence, a trend that may be reversed by DSM-5.

One of the puzzling aspects of ASD is the disparity in the ethnic and gender distribution of diagnoses. It is reasonably well established that there are four or five boys diagnosed for every one girl diagnosed. Such a distribution speaks powerfully for the involvement of a genetic factor in the condition (Fischbach & Lord, 2010).

But there is another difference in prevalence that seems to be more related to environmental factors. Mandell et al. (2007) found that African Americans are 2.6 times less likely to receive an autism diagnosis than were White children. How can that be? It seems that African-American children were more likely to be diagnosed as having a conduct disorder or an attention disorder and only after several visits were they correctly identified as autistic. Also, it appears that African-American children are identified much later in the developmental sequence and often do not get the early intervention treatments that are so effective. There seem to be some prior predispositions of the diagnosticians that pull them away from a diagnosis of autism for African-American children (Mandell et al., 2002).

5-4c The Importance of Early Identification

Early identification of children with autism is one of the key elements of treatment. The development of language and social skills is critical from ages 18 months to 3 years. These skills, in addition to imitation of motor behaviors and using eye gaze to communicate, must be fostered during this time. If we wait for the child's autism to be discovered in kindergarten, we have lost valuable time that will be difficult to recover.

Fortunately, a number of studies have shown that diagnosticians have the ability to correctly identify children with autism at age 2 or earlier (Baron-Cohen et al., 1996; Lord, 1995; Stone et al., 1999). This ability affords an early opportunity to begin therapy in language functioning and improvements in peer relationships. It is important for parents and pediatricians to be aware of the existence of such diagnostic services in their communities so that this early identification and treatment can be carried out.

Pediatricians use basic screening tests to identify children who may require further evaluation. Children with autism have difficulty with *pretend play* (such as pretending to drink from a teacup), *imitating adult behavior* (such as rapping on the table), and *pointing at objects on request* (such as pointing at the dog). In addition, pediatricians may note repetitive motor movements that have no context. A child's failure to respond well in these instances is often the cue to enter into a more comprehensive examination of child and family.

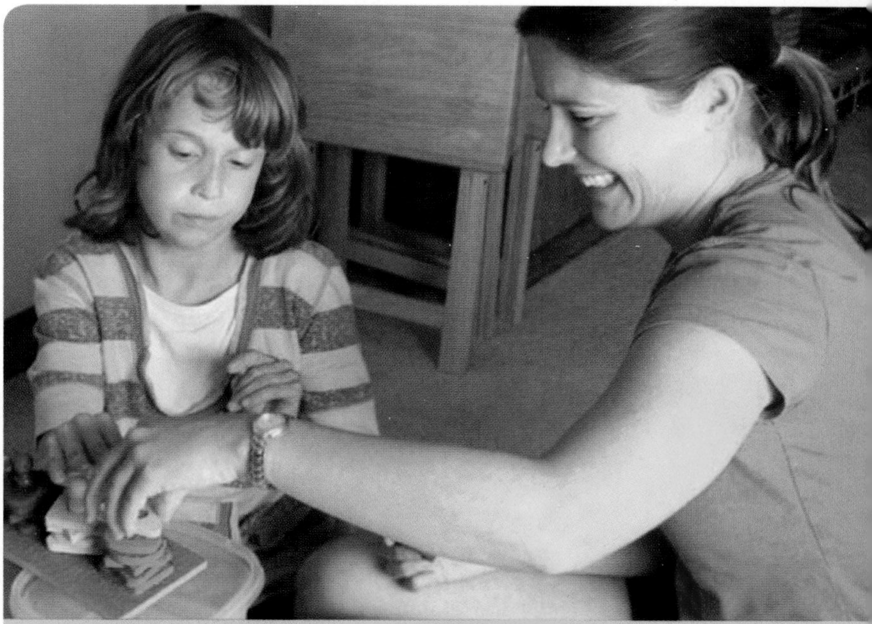

Early identification and intervention allows younger children with ASD to make significant gains. The therapist above is helping this young girl with autism to learn the skill of turn taking.

5-5 Characteristics of Children with Autism

Many have wondered what might be the fundamental mechanisms at the heart of the problems observable in children with autism like Mike Dolan. What is behind the inability to socialize or to communicate effectively with others?

5-5a Theory of Mind

One of the indicators of a fundamental developmental disability in children with autism has been lack of **Theory of Mind**, the ability of human beings to understand the thinking and feelings of other people that's necessary for understanding, predicting, and shaping the behavior of others. Typically developing 4-year-old children have a developing Theory of Mind, unlike children with autism (Twachtman-Cullen, 2000).

One example of a test of Theory of Mind is known as the Sally and Anne Test (see Figure 5.3). In this test, the child watches while a doll named Sally puts a marble in a round box and leaves the scene. While she is away, the other doll, named Anne, moves the marble to the square box sitting beside the round box. On Sally's return, participants are asked to predict where she will look for her ball. To answer correctly, one must be able to understand what Sally's mental state would be—namely, that since she put the ball in the round box, she would expect to find it there.

Most children as young as 4 can correctly guess where Sally will look. But children with autism have a great deal of difficulty with this test. This suggests that they are not able to get inside Sally's thinking processes. Children with autism often do poorly on such tasks that depend on understanding the feelings or thinking processes of others. An analysis of a series of studies on this topic (Yirmiya, Erel, Shaked, & Solomonica-Levi, 1998) revealed that children with autism have a major fundamental deficit in the development of Theory of Mind compared with typically developing children. They seem even less able to do these tasks than children with intellectual and developmental disabilities who also have deficits in Theory of Mind ability.

Figure 5.3 Theory of Mind: An Illustration
Source: Based on *Understanding autism*. Geoffrey Cowley, NewsWeek July 25, 2000.

5-5b Behavior

One of the consequences of a limited ability to communicate, common among children with autism, is frustration, often expressed through acting out or aggressive behavior. Such behaviors complicate the instructional program for children with autism and even result in burnout or emotional exhaustion for teachers.

Kanne and Mazurek (2011), using the large sample of children with autism obtained through the Simplex consortium of university programs and clinics, were able to gain data on 1,380 children with autism. They found a high rate of aggressive behavior (35 percent) that was not related to age or measured ability but seemed linked to self-injurious behavior, repetitive behaviors, and increased levels of social and communication deficits. This aggression seems to be spontaneous and not planned. Reports of children with ASD being involved in criminal behavior or assaults often turn out to be cases of **comorbidity** (more than one disorder—in this case a mix of autism and emotional disturbance); the aggression comes from the emotional disturbance rather than the autism side of the comorbidity.

However, given such a high prevalence, teachers and IEP planners need to be alert to aggressive behavior in these children. Aggressive behavior almost always complicates treatment and educational programs and needs to be part of the IEP recommendations.

5-5c The Information Processing Model

Figure 5.4 provides a portrait of the various elements of information processing that are likely to be affected in children with ASD. The sensory or receptive abilities seem to be affected by the inability to moderate incoming experiences.

Hypersensitivity to Sensory Stimuli (Input)

One of the characteristics shared by many persons with autism is a **hypersensitivity to noises in the environment.** It almost seems as if they have lost the ability to modulate sounds, as these sounds come through with terrifying impact. The following quote from Temple Grandin, an adult with autism, illustrates this:

> Loud, sudden noises still startle me. My reaction to them is more intense than other people's. I still hate balloons, because I never know when one will pop and make me jump. Sustained high-pitched motor noises, such as hair dryers and bathroom vent fans, still bother me, lower frequency motor noises do not. (Cowley, 2000, p. 53)

In addition to sound sensitivity, sensitivity to stimuli can extend to the tactile—some children with autism are sensitive to touch and will shy away from relatives hugging them or from being touched by others—and to other sensory

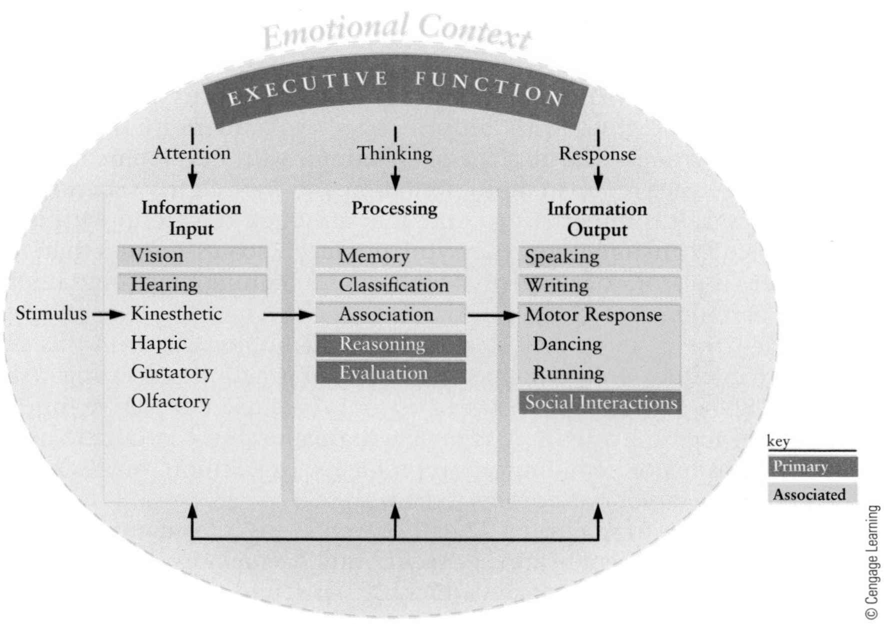

Figure 5.4 Information Processing Model for Children with Autism Spectrum Disorder

TeachSource Digital Download Access online

© Monkey Business Images/Shutterstock.com

Sustained support for children with ASD is essential to help them develop skills needs for success.

systems, such as the visual (seeking out or avoiding visual stimulation), oral (limited food repertoire, excessive chewing or mouthing of objects), and so forth. Such behavior can easily be misinterpreted and compound the social difficulties such children face.

Central Processing

As seen within the information processing model, most individuals with ASD have trouble with important thinking skills like decision making, problem solving, executive function, and the more complex mental processes of reasoning and evaluation. However, the memory and classification areas seem less involved, and a child with high-functioning autism can collect an amazing body of information about specific content areas (such as marine life or various forms of transportation). When asked to use that information in social contexts like the classroom, however, the child shows clear limitations.

Response Mode (Output)

Children on the autism spectrum also have difficulty with a range of motor skills such as gross motor skills (running and jumping, for instance), fine motor skills, and motor planning (moving one's body in space). Although children with ASD may meet motor milestones on time, their movements can appear stiff or clumsy.

An example of a motor task that is particularly difficult for children with ASD is motor imitation. Stone, Ousley, and Littleford (1997) compared the ability of children between 2 and 3 years of age to imitate actions of adults, from pushing a toy car across a table, to clapping hands, to opening and closing fists, to banging spoons on a table. Three groups matched for mental age were tested: a group of 18 children with autism spectrum disorders, 18 children with developmental delays, and 18 children with average development. The results clearly indicated that the abilities of the group with autism were sharply inferior in motor imitation to other two groups. The abilities of the group with developmental delays approached the average group in motor imitation and were clearly superior to the group with autism. It is important to note that although the group with autism had great difficulty in imitating, they still produced scores greater than zero. Therefore, there is reason to believe that with careful training they could improve their current performance.

As we review the puzzling behavior of Mike Dolan noted earlier in this chapter, we need to consider what is happening in his information processing system. As shown in Figure 5.4, he seems to have major problems in executive function. He has difficulty focusing attention, is unable to organize his thinking to address problems, and has major communication problems. In addition, his background of socioemotional adaptations appears to be weak.

It is also important to note what functions well in his information processing system. Mike has no problem hearing or seeing, and his memory for the things he likes or wants ("Where are the cookies and milk?") is sound. Except for some hand flapping, his motor skills seem acceptable, if somewhat uncoordinated. We can activate the relative strengths in his information processing as a base for instructional planning.

Although there are great individual differences in youngsters with ASD diagnosis, the problems described here are found at the heart of many of their learning problems. Therefore, a major focus of special education procedures must be on improving attention and communication skills in children with ASD.

5-6 Educational Responses for Students with Autism Spectrum Disorders

The two major educational responses are organizational and instructional in nature and follow here.

5-6a Organizational Structures to Support Students with ASD

One of the themes of this text is that special education is a team game. In other words, no individual teacher should be expected to meet the needs of students alone. This is especially true in cases involving children with ASD, where it is necessary for a team of multidisciplinary personnel to diagnose and plan treatment. Also necessary are modifications in the **educational infrastructure**—organizational changes involving personnel preparation, technical assistance, research, and evaluation—to ensure continuing support. As you can see from Figure 5.5, children with ASD are found in a variety of educational settings.

RtI Approaches for Students with ASD

The range and the intensity of autism spectrum disorders in individual children make it likely that all three tiers of the response to intervention (RtI) model will be brought to bear on these issues.

RtI

Universal Tier I for Students with ASD

As we have noted before, Tier I is not merely the general education class without any additions. At the least, the general education teacher needs to be sensitized to the special needs of children with autism and have some instructional strategies to cope with problems that might arise in that setting. It is likely that some degree of consultation with a specialist in autism is necessary if the child with

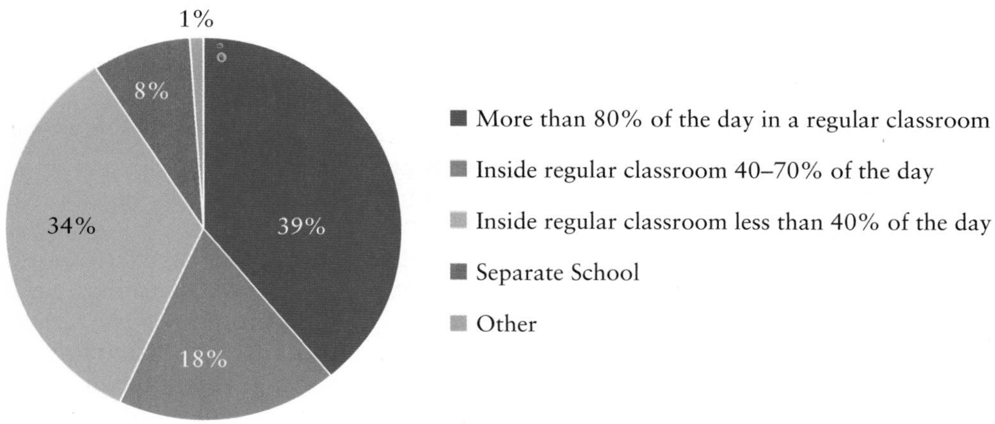

Figure 5.5 Educational Settings for Children with ASD
Source: Data Accountability Center. (2011). *Part B Educational Environments 2011 [data file]*. Retrieved from http://www.ideadata.org/PartBEnvironments.asp

autism is to remain in Tier I. George, a 9-year-old fourth grader, has a mild form of ASD and is placed in the regular classroom with some outside professional help. Mrs. Holcomb, his teacher, is bothered by George's verbal outbursts in the class and her inability to form a social contract with George regarding his lessons and behavior.

She needs a specialist in autism to help her with suggestions on behavior control and in adapting lessons. The Universal Design for Learning (UDL) is a good idea (similar curriculum but different delivery methods) but means little without the practical knowledge of how to modify the standard curriculum to take into account George's behavior and academic lagging. Given some qualified help, Mrs. Holcomb can create a good learning environment for George.

Another example of Tier I is the implementation of schoolwide positive behavior supports, a system of universal expectations for all students stressing core values of respect, responsibility, and safety. Such a system, with positive reinforcements for behavioral demonstrations of such values together with predictable consequences for behavior infractions, has shown to be helpful in creating a positive atmosphere for learning for all students (Horner et al., 2009). A Summary of *UDL Supports for Students with ASD* can be accessed online.

TeachSource Digital Download

Targeted Tier II for Students with ASD

Tier II might be devoted to small-group or individual lessons built around **applied behavior analysis (ABA)**, discussed later in this section, to help the child develop language and learn some social skills. Obviously, having a person specially trained in the use of ABA will be necessary. Special educators who have experience interacting with children with autism should be close by, if not directly involved.

Sally, an 8-year-old, has a moderate form of ASD that calls for some Tier II support, even though she may not be qualified for a full-scale diagnosis of ASD. Sally's inability to learn to share with others and difficulty working on cooperative tasks may be addressed by matching her with a small group of children to practice these skills. Someone with special knowledge of the development of social skills may be called upon to conduct these small-group activities focused on social learning. This specialist can also consult with Sally's third-grade teacher about Sally's behavior in the classroom and the rules to establish to help her interact positively with her peers. George can be provided with similar Tier II experiences.

Intensive Tier III for Students with ASD

In Tier III, full-scale intensive work with special educators will be called for. The more intense the symptoms are, the longer the time period needed to help the student by providing some alternative behaviors for these students. Most specialists in this field believe that 20 hours a week or more of special programming over a number of months or years will be needed to make a difference—a measure of how difficult these sessions can be before some tangible results can be expected (Lord, 2001).

Bob is in the fourth grade, and his unusual behavior and academic issues have been long recognized. He has a definite diagnosis of ASD and may need more intense programs than either George or Sally. He should receive Tier III services for 20 hours or more, with primary responsibility for his education given to a special educator with a background in autism. This intensive program may have to go back to the fundamentals of language development and give attention to help Bob establish the basis of learning that he has not yet acquired. A Summary of *RtI Approaches for Students with ASD* can be accessed online.

TeachSource Digital Download

Major Centers for Children with Autism

The special nature of this condition has led to the development of centers for research and treatment in which multidisciplinary staff members can collaborate. Listed here are some of the most well-known.

UCLA Young Autism Project

This program has used the principles of applied behavior analysis or operant conditioning to directly provide positive rewards for appropriate behavior. In this way, the child learns to pay attention to adults, to imitate, and to use language for social purposes. This one-on-one interaction, with trained students or parents, is often an intensive and painstaking process. Lovaas, director of the UCLA Center on Autism, insists that 40 hours a week be spent on working directly with children with ASD to ensure that they can be ready for first grade with typically developing children. The approach requires teaching many discrete skills, which are then chained into functional routines (Olley, 1999).

The applied behavior analysis (ABA) approach that has been a central part of the Lovaas method has been utilized by many others in the field who have adopted it and established treatment programs of their own. Subsequent results (Butter, Mulick, Metz, 2006; Sallows & Graupner, 2005) confirm the usefulness of the ABA approach for many young children with autism. Other investigators have suggested that initiated communication, allowing the child to begin the interaction based on his or her needs, is more effective. The Applied Behavior Analysis approach is based upon the behavioral model of B.F. Skinner (from 1938), which presents the antecedent-behavior-consequences sequence. Once the behavior to be changed is identified (Bob putting his materials away, for instance), the teacher can try to modify the antecedents through prompting (handing the books to Bob), and introducing differential reinforcement (such as praising Bob for doing a good job or withholding praise if he performs poorly).

UCLA Young Autism Project **http://www.semel.ucla.edu/autism**

TEACCH—University of North Carolina at Chapel Hill

TEACCH is a statewide program in North Carolina with seven regional centers. Intensive work is done with parents to help them become teachers of their own child with autism. Pictures and other visual symbols are used extensively to help communicate with the child. The communication curriculum is based on behavioral principles but applied in more naturalistic settings (home and child care centers) (Schopler, Mesibov, & Hearsey, 1995).

TEACCH has also developed an extensive curriculum (Eckenrode, Fennell, & Hearsey, 2007) that includes domestic skills, such as cleaning, cooking, and putting things away, and independent living skills, such as using calendars, hygiene, handling money, and so on. TEACCH makes parental counseling available to help parents cope with stress that is caused not only by daily stressors but also by their growing concerns about what their child is going to do in adulthood and how as parents they can help them on this path. Individual counseling for children and youth with high-functioning ASD is also available.

TEACCH University of NC at Chapel Hill **www.teacch.com**

LEAP—University of Colorado at Denver

This program, at its base, attempts to improve the social behavior of children with autism. The curriculum emphasizes independent play and social interaction in naturally occurring routines. Social skills are taught as discrete skills such as "play initiation." Applying the program in an integrative setting with typically developing children allows practice in social skills. LEAP has used peer-mediation skills intervention, training typically developing peers to enhance social interaction with children with autism. Numerous studies have demonstrated the effective acquisition of social skills by preschool children with autism via this method (Strain, Kohler, & Goldstein, 1996).

LEAP, University of Colorado at Denver **http://depts.washington.edu/pdacent/sites/ucd.html**

Pivotal Response Model—University of California at Santa Barbara

This program often starts with discrete trial behavior analysis, similar to the UCLA model, but then moves on to a goal of social and educational proficiency in natural settings. The goal is to achieve change in pivotal areas that have broad generalizations. The emphasis is placed on self-management, motivation, self-initiation, and other abilities that can be transferred from one situation to another. Koegel and Koegel (2007) have developed specific curricula with an emphasis on parental involvement to obtain their reported positive results.

These four comprehensive approaches are only some of the widening professional efforts to cope with ASD. These initiatives are encouraging because of the reports of successful gains in each (Odom, Rogers, McDougle, Hume, & McGee, 2007). These comprehensive programs stress the differences between their programs and others providing similar services, but we should also consider their similarities. In a typical preschool program, all children face the daily greeting of teacher and peers, a morning snack, reinforcement of the classroom rules, a lunch break (a fine time for natural lessons of conversation and social skills), nap time, and leaving for the day. These events are roughly similar from one program to another, even with the differences in therapeutic approaches noted by their program leaders. This may be one reason they all report favorable outcomes with little to distinguish them from one another.

5-6b Curriculum and Instruction for Students with Autism Spectrum Disorders

Autism and the Common Core Standards

COMMON CORE STATE STANDARDS

As noted earlier, the Common Core State Standards (CCSS) provide guidance as to what knowledge and skills are required for students to master in English and mathematics at each grade level. How do they intersect with the needs of students with ASD? The CCSS require teachers to address two of the key elements in the ASD characteristics: perspective taking and social communication. For example, from the writing standards for fifth grade:

> Write opinion pieces on topics or texts supporting a point of view with reasons and relevant evidence.

Here the student is forced to take the perspective of others and address the idea that other people have different ideas, thoughts, and beliefs. Teachers must help the student with ASD understand how to take the perspective of others (develop Theory of Mind) to do this task. The speaking and listening standards for K-2 are an example of a way the CCSS address social communication:

> Participate in collaborative conversations with diverse partners about grade level topics and texts with peers and adults in small or larger groups. Follow agreed upon rules for discussions (e.g. listening to others and taking turns speaking about the topics and texts under discussion).

Meeting such standards will be difficult for students with ASD and will require time and many examples. There is good reason to believe that many of these children can meet these challenges through the team approach and special instructional strategies. Table 5.2 provides some additional reactions to the CCSS materials and requirements.

Early Childhood Strategies

The emphasis on early diagnosis means that educational programming for the child with autism should begin early—sometimes as early as 2 years of age. During the preschool years, the goals are to help the child master basic skills

TABLE 5.2 CCSS Classroom Behaviors and Evidence-Based Strategies

Sampling of CCSS	Classroom Behaviors	Evidence-Based Strategies
Ask and answer questions to seek help, obtain information, or clarify something that is not understood. K.3 Speaking and Listening	Student may not be able to initiate asking for help or clarification. May sit and do nothing. May try to escape or avoid the task.	Naturalistic intervention Peer-mediated instruction and intervention
Describe how characters in a story respond to major events and challenges. 2.3 Reading Literature	Student may struggle to answer correctly in response to questions about character perspective and responses.	Social narratives of social stories Comic strip conversations
Write narratives to develop real or imagined experiences or events using effective technique, descriptive details, and clear event sequences. 5.3 Writing	Student may have difficulty separating fact from fantasy.	Prompting Visual supports
Analyze how particular lines of dialogues or incidents in a story or drama propel the actions, reveal aspects of a character, or provoke a decision. 8.3 Reading: Literature	Students have difficulty determining how dialogue or incidents in a story propel a character's actions.	Social narratives of social stories Comic strip conversations
Write narratives to develop real or imagined experiences or events using effective technique, well-chosen details, and well-structured event sequences. 11-12.3 Writing	Student may have great difficulty organizing writing with well-structured event sequences and instead may focus on unimportant details.	Visual supports

Constable, S., Grossi, B., Moniz, A., & Ryan, L. (2013). Meeting the Common Core State Standards for students with autism: The challenge for educators. *Teaching Exceptional Children, 45*(3), 6–13.

that provide the foundation for future learning. The child must be able to communicate with others, so a major building block is to help him or her attain a ***functional communication system.*** Second, the child must be able to interact socially with adults and peers, so ***basic social skills*** (paying attention when others speak, not pushing people out of the way, and so forth) should be learned and practiced.

The inability of children with autism to imitate or learn through observation means that they do not learn as well as other children do through **incidental learning** (i.e., learning that occurs but is not explicitly taught). Typically developing children, through observation and imitation, learn not to run to third base when they hit the ball or not to go to the front of the line in the cafeteria. Such basic life lessons have to become part of the special curriculum for children with autism—some of whom can learn them only through direct teaching.

Greenspan and Wieder (2006) make an important observation about teaching to the strengths of the child. The key point is that the treatment has to be based on the top of the range. If the child can walk sometimes, then he can walk. If the child can relate with others sometimes, then she can relate, and we can help her relate more often (p. 25). So, when we say that children with autism

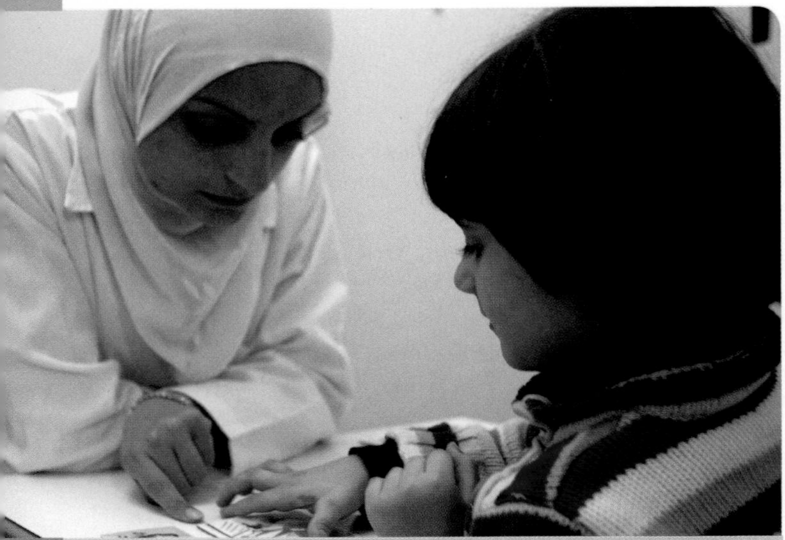
ALI JAREKJI/Reuters/Landov

Supporting the child with ASD communication skills is critical to the development of social skills.

have difficulties in creating social relationships, it does not mean that the ability to do so is totally absent. It may mean that we have to put more energy and effort into nurturing such skills. The same is true of motor skills or language. A deficit is not an absence of a skill; it represents a delay or shortage.

In some cases in which the child is unable to respond even at this basic level, an approach known as augmentative and alternative communication (AAC) and assistive technology may be used. This approach includes supporting existing speech. Extensive use may be made of pictures displayed on communication boards so that the child, by pointing to the pictures, can communicate his or her wishes. AAC provides ways to communicate needs and can prevent the development of nonadaptive child behavior, such as head banging, biting, throwing objects, and so on, when children are frustrated with their inability to communicate in standard ways.

Inclusion in Context: School-Age Children with Autism

Children with autism at school age will undoubtedly have an IEP planned for them by a multidisciplinary team. There must surely be someone on the team who knows something about autism and its special issues. We would not think of planning for a child who is deaf without engaging a specialist in the education of children with hearing disabilities, yet too often we engage in a program for children with autism with only minimal expertise present.

It is important for the teacher to know that when things get difficult someone will be available to help. Few things can be more depressing to teachers than believing themselves totally alone in attempting to help the children with autism and feeling that the instructional responsibility is not shared.

The academic lessons that the child with autism receives can be planned in advance by a team of teachers and aides so that they fit the child's own developmental level. The assignments can be short and not complex, so that the child can see progress and success in these appropriate tasks.

One would expect that each IEP would have some special plans for improving the social skills of the child and would also pay some attention to his or her language development, together with specific plans to cope with disturbing behavior patterns, if they are present.

Sam, now in fifth grade, attended a rural school where teachers tried their best but were unfamiliar with ASD or the remedial techniques that might help him. His behavioral problems became worse. His parents moved to a more suburban setting that had more support personnel who formed a team approach to address Sam's difficulties.

Table 5.3 shows some elements of an IEP that might be planned for Sam. Such planning necessitates the presence of specialized assistance, consultation, aides, and others for the general education teacher if it is to work, because few such teachers have the skills or background knowledge or time to carry out the program unaided. Because Sam is behind in fundamental reading and mathematical skills, some specific attention is paid to special ***tiered assignments*** (assignments adjusted to the developmental level of the child).

Sam's social skills are in substantial need of improvement. Placing him in a small group stressing cooperative learning is one approach to giving him experience working with others toward a common goal. The question as to what Sam's

TABLE 5.3 IEP Elements for Sam

Area	Goals	Short-Term Objectives
Academic	1. Sam will improve reading skills to third-grade level. 2. Sam will master fundamentals of addition and subtraction.	1. Sam will complete a book relevant to class topics but directed to his limited reading skills. 2. Sam will be given tiered assignments to match his developmental level in arithmetic. He will reach 90 percent correct level in addition and subtraction problems with two numerals.
Social	1. Sam will improve his social skills. 2. Sam will reduce by one-half his episodes of challenging behavior (fighting).	1. Sam will be placed in cooperative learning groups that have been primed to include him in activity. 2. Functional behavior assessment will be carried out by a specialist to determine appropriate replacement behaviors for Sam.
Behavioral	1. Sam will reduce by 50 percent the repetitive movements with his hands (hand flapping).	1. Tasks will be chosen that will require Sam to use his hands in a constructive manner. 2. The teacher will reduce sensory overload and provide calming periods for Sam.

TeachSource Digital Download Access online

fighting is achieving for him (perhaps security, revenge, attention, or status) can be addressed through a functional behavioral analysis. We may be able to discover Sam's motivation and prepare some substitute or alternative behaviors to replace the fighting while still obtaining the same psychological result for him. One detriment to Sam's social adjustment has been his "hand flapping," which seems to emerge when he is under stress. His classmates view this repetitive motor movement with his hands as "weird," and that doesn't improve his social standing. It seems appropriate to work on all of these problems simultaneously, and that also requires more personnel than just one classroom teacher in this situation.

Creating Structure

There are a variety of changes recommended for the direct instruction of children with ASD. There has been a consistent call for teachers to use Evidenced-Based Practices in their instruction of children with autism. It is one thing to call for such practices and quite another to provide the means for the teachers to follow through on such requests. Odom et al. (2010) have identified 24 specific evidence-based practices (such as prompting or reinforcement) and have developed instructional modules that illustrate and elaborate on each of the practices. This is the type of follow-through that will tend to ensure that teachers will execute evidence-based practices.

One example of an evidenced-based practice that addresses the difficulty a child with autism often has confronting unorganized environments is an approach called "structured teaching" (Mesibov, 2009). The desire for structure among children with ASD can be met by visual representations for the day ahead. Figure 5.6 shows two types of schedules that can bring structure and security to the student. In Paul's case, the sequence is presented in language so that he can check off each event as it occurs and can read the next upcoming event.

For other students like Jordan, a visual representation of the day provides the structure needed. Jordan has a card with a large checkmark on it, and as each event occurs, he moves the checkmark next to the action and can see what is coming next. Such scheduling can bring necessary routines to the child's attention and allow him or her to live in a predictable world. Of course, it is up to the teacher to see to it that these sequences are honored in practice, or the student with ASD will be plunged into a chaotic world again.

Creating a consistent physical environment around the child (everything is in the same place from one day to another) can be another source of security. A daily schedule and a consistent environment are critical for a child with autism to feel secure. Many children with autism need structure and order so that they can proceed academically. Although children with high-functioning autism or with Asperger's syndrome can have generally good proficiency in language, they tend toward literal interpretation, which causes a lack of understanding of jokes that depend on plays on words, metaphors, or common idioms such as these (Attwood, 1998, p. 77):

Has the cat got your tongue?

Keep your eye on the ball.

You're pulling my leg.

Pull yourself together.

The literal-mindedness of the child with autism lends an appearance of naiveté that can interfere with socialization.

Improving Social Skills

Because one of the prime areas concerning the education of children with autism is the lack of social sensitivity and social skills that most typical children display, there have been many attempts to counteract that lack. Of course, children with autism are not totally devoid of social skills. McGee and her colleagues (McGee, Feldman, & Morrier, 1997) found that young children with autism engage to some degree in play, social participation, and social interaction, but they do so much less often than typical children of the same age. Neihart (2000) suggests frequent use of diagrams, visualization, and pictograms in the lessons provided to children with Asperger's syndrome or to high-functioning children with autism, as they think best in concrete and literal pictures.

For instance, a picture such as that shown in photo below, may portray one student helping another student to clean up a mess or put toys or books away. The teacher can use the picture to show students how friends behave. Similar pictures portraying physical confrontations can be used to illustrate unacceptable

Social skills is an important component of the program for children with ASD.

Heidi Velten/Mauritius/SuperStock

behaviors. Thus, pictures can become the basis of role playing, where children act out situations and then discuss with the teacher the merits of the various approaches taken. In some cases the teacher may play one of the roles or ask peers to play out the social interaction. If the child sees himself or herself in these pictures, then some necessary insight has been achieved.

The teacher can use social stories, which involve the child writing a very short story that describes a specific social situation with which the child struggles. These social stories are designed to teach the cues and behaviors for specific social situations.

One attempt to intervene on behalf of children with autism was a study in which photographs of various play areas were identified and the children with autism were asked to pick the areas where they intended to play (Morrison, Sainato, Benchaaban, & Endo, 2002). Their choices of photographs of play areas were placed on a bulletin board, and the children were encouraged to follow their choices.

Children with autism can follow a schedule with encouragement, and the result was that children with autism engaged more effectively in interactive play with other children. However, because it is challenging, teachers have to be proactive in designing activities that increase the play and social behavior of the child with autism.

McConnell (2000) concluded that promoting social interaction development should be a routine component of any comprehensive treatment program for children with autism.

Functional Behavior Assessment

One of the favorite educational strategies designed to cope with some of the behavior manifestations of autism is **functional behavior assessment**. Instead of concentrating on the specific behavior of the child, the teacher, therapist, or parent tries to assess the meaning of the behavior to the child. This has been referred to as the ABC approach:

- Antecedents—What preceded the behavior
- Behavior—The nature of the event
- Consequences—What happens as a result of the behavior

If Mike hits or bites other people, then in addition to dealing directly with the behavior, the educational team tries to understand how his behavior seems to benefit him. Is he using this as a means for gaining attention, for communicating some need that he is unable to express verbally? If we can understand why Mike hits or bites, we can then try to help him use alternative means for attaining his goals.

This does not mean, of course, that Mike is allowed to continue to hit people while his behavior is analyzed, but if these attacks have become a constant problem, it means trying to deduce the motivation behind them and substituting some more acceptable ways, or **replacement behavior**, for him to achieve his goals. For example, if Mike's behavior is aimed at obtaining parental or teacher attention, perhaps a small bell to ring when he wants his parents' attention or a physical sign such as raising his arm in class could be substituted for the hitting and biting. This search for the child's intentions has proven to be more effective in modifying the child's actions than using direct punishment for unacceptable behavior (see Chapter 8 for more information).

Assistive Technology for Students with ASD

The importance of communication to the child with autism is universally agreed upon. When the child does not develop speech and receptive language in the usual fashion, a wide variety of devices (called augmentative and alternative communication; AAC) are tried to augment or increase the child's communication skills (Fossett & Mirenda, 2007). This may include the Picture Exchange Communication System (PECS) or, on occasion, teaching the child some elements of American Sign Language.

Picture Exchange Communication System (PECS) **http://www.pecsusa.com/pecs.php**

Sometimes a communication board is used so that basic communication is established between child and adult. The child can communicate basic needs

TeachSource Video Connection

Watch the video "Tyler: Augmentative Communication Techniques for a Kindergarten Student with Autism and Language Issues." This video describes how teachers modify their instructional strategies and classroom environment to meet the needs of Tyler, a kindergarten student with autism. After watching the Video Case, reflect the ways these strategies make it easier for Tyler to communicate. Are their potential drawbacks to the use of such strategies? How can these strategies change Tyler's educational outcomes?

Watch online

and feelings, and the adult can respond in kind. The use of photographs to aid in this type of communication is increasing. Children with autism may learn eye-hand coordination using a computer mouse, while a touch screen helps a child understand sending commands to the computer by using a tactile approach.

Voice output communication aids (VOCA) store recorded messages that the child can trigger. These can range from a series of twenty messages, each twenty seconds long, to complex messages that can be changed according to the situation so that the student can participate.

The improvement of communication devices often has a favorable effect on controlling or reducing challenging behavior because some challenging behavior seems to be caused by the inability to communicate needs and wishes. Augmentative communication aids that set up pictorial or written schedules help the individual to follow predictable sequences (Wood, Lasker, Siegel-Causey, Beukelman, & Ball, 1998), which in turn helps reduce stress and challenging behaviors.

In addition to using assistive technology to support communications skills for children with autism, programs are being developed to teach social skills (Moore, Cheng, McGrath, & Powell, 2005; Lacava, Golan, Baron-Cohen, & Myles, 2007). In one study, robotic dolls were used to help children learn appropriate social interaction (Dautenhahn & Billard, 2002). Children engaged in structured interactions with a humanoid robot, Robota, to learn about turn taking, imitation of behaviors, and appropriate social exchanges. This work holds promise for helping children with autism generalize interactions from inanimate objects to humans.

Another software package, *Mind Reading: The Interactive Guide to Emotions*™, has been used to help children with Asperger's syndrome recognize emotions and plan appropriate responses to emotions (Lacava, Golan, Baron-Cohen, & Myles, 2007). With *Mind Reading,* students are shown pictures of individuals displaying complex emotions (insincerity, ambition, intimacy, and so forth) and are guided through an understanding of what these states mean. The voice accompanying the picture also helps students learn how to "read" various communications when the words do not match the messages (such as "you look *wonderful*" said with sarcasm). Initial studies show that this kind of software holds promise for helping children with autism expand their understanding of Theory of Mind (Lacava, Golan, Baron-Cohen, & Myles, 2007).

Autism Intervention Effectiveness

Of the two types of interventions, focused intervention practice and comprehensive teaching models, there are growing bodies of evidence as to effectiveness. In the **focused intervention practice**, which is short term with specific goals (such as to reduce random motor behavior or to increase verbal language output) the results are positive regarding the use of ABA (Odom, Boyd, Hall, & Hume, 2010).

In the case of the **comprehensive treatment models** like TEACCH, there are similar positive results reported but with little to distinguish between the effectiveness of models. Seida et al. (2009) summarizes these results:

> There is evidence of positive outcomes for many of the interventions examined in systematic reviews of ASDs, suggesting that some form of treatment is favourable to no treatment.... There is little evidence of the relative

effectiveness of these interventions; therefore, uncertainty remains about "best practices" for the treatment of autism. (p. 103)

There is good reason to tailor the treatment to the individual needs of the child and good reason to believe that systematic intervention will pay off in meaningful developmental outcomes, particularly when the treatment is begun early in the preschool years (Odom et al., 2012).

One of the other favorite intervention techniques has been early intensive behavioral intervention (EIBI) for children with autism spectrum disorders. The controversial Lovaas study (1993) stirred much interest and critique and resulted in a large number of replications of his work. There were so many studies that a number of meta-analyses (which are documents synthesizing the results of groups of studies on the same topic) have been completed. Five of these were reviewed by Reichow (2012) who concluded:

> The results of the synthesis show there is much supporting evidence for the treatment of social deficits in autism. However, the methods and results of this synthesis do not permit conclusions about the superiority of one treatment over another. (p. 161)

The extensive reviews of literature devoted to evaluating comprehensive programs has allowed for some clear conclusions regarding these programs and the strategies they used. These conclusions are summarized in by the National Standards Project (2009) (see Table 5.4). This report was compiled by professionals working together through the National Autism Center and was reviewed by over fifty specialists in autism.

TABLE 5.4 National Standards Project Approved Treatments for Students with Autism

Antecedent Package (99 Studies)	The modification of situational events that typically precede a target behavior. Treatments falling into this category reflect research in applied behavior analysis (ABA), behavioral psychology, and positive behavior supports.
Behavioral Package (231 Studies)	Reduce problem behavior and teach functional alternative behaviors or skills through the application of basic principles of behavior change.
Naturalistic Teaching Strategies (32 Studies)	Use primarily child-directed interactions to teach functional skills in the natural environment.
Peer Training Package (33 Studies)	Teach children without disabilities strategies for facilitating play and social interactions with children on the autism spectrum.
Pivotal Response Treatment (14 Studies)	PRT, Pivotal Response Teaching, and Pivotal Response Training focuses on targeting "pivotal" behavioral areas—such as motivation to engage in social communication, self-initiation, self-management, and responsiveness to multiple cues.
Schedules (12 Studies)	Present a task list that communicates a series of activities or steps required to complete a specific activity.
Self-Management (21 Studies)	Promote independence by teaching individuals with ASD to regulate their behavior by recording the occurrence/non-occurrence of the target behavior and securing reinforcement for doing so.
Story-Based Intervention Package (21 Studies)	Describe the situations under which specific behaviors are expected to occur. Social Stories™ are the most well-known story-based interventions, and they seek to answer the "who," "what," "where," and "why" in order to improve perspective taking.

SOURCE: National Standards Project. (2009). Randolph, MA: National Autism Center.

The development of social skills in children with autism is one of the most popular intervention techniques. Reichow and Volkmar (2010) reviewed 66 studies done after 2000 involving a total of 513 subjects; 56 of the studies were of single subject design. The use of social skills groups and video modeling were prominent techniques. The authors concluded that the development of social skills groups and video modeling have now reached the point where they can be called evidence-based practices. The vast majority of studies showed clear gains in social skills by the students involved.

5-7 The Role of Families and Communities

5-7a Family Involvement

Most programs put major emphasis on **family involvement**, although the nature of the involvement may vary from one program to another (Gresham, Beebe-Frankenberger, & MacMillan, 1999; Mesibov, 2006).

To provide an appropriate education for their children, parents of children with autism need specialized skills. Prime among these are the mastery of specific teaching strategies, such as ABA, that enable them to help their child acquire new behaviors. Parents also need an understanding of the nature of autism and how it influences their child's learning patterns and behavior. They need to know special education laws and regulations and how to negotiate these on behalf of their child.

In addition, some parents need help coping with the emotional stress that can follow from having a child with a significant developmental disorder. Many parents of children with ASD have become autism experts in their own right and create their own books, websites, and blogs in order to share information and support with other parents. Visit the website of author Susan Senator for an example of a high-quality website and blog authored by a parent of a child with ASD.

www.susansenator.com

The siblings of children with autism can have their lives seriously disrupted, and they should be considered part of a comprehensive treatment program (Konidaris, 1997). Because siblings are often enrolled in the same school, a sensitive teacher can sometimes help a child respond to questions about his or her sibling's autism (Lord, 2001), but professional help for siblings should still be sought out by parents when the need is present.

One of the promising attempts to modify the behavior of young children with autism focuses on the relationship between the parents and the child. Mahoney and Perales (2003) report a yearlong intervention with 20 young children with autism spectrum disorders (80 percent under the age of 3, the rest under 6). The approach is a **relationship-focused intervention (RF)** that encourages parents to use responsive interaction strategies (such as taking turns) during routine interaction with their children. Parents of children with autism were seen in one-hour sessions for an average of 30 sessions. The parents were taught a variety of techniques for responsive interaction with their child, and they reported using these strategies with that child at home for about two hours a day.

The authors reported significant improvements in social-emotional functioning that included decreases in detachment and underactivity and increases in social competence, including empathy and cooperation. The authors concluded that enhanced maternal responsiveness encourages children to use the behaviors necessary to attain higher levels of social-emotional and developmental functioning.

Systematic efforts to train parents to use cognitive behavior therapy (CBT; challenging irrational cognitions, Socratic questioning, logical rationales, and so forth) have been reported to be effective in increasing self-help skills and reducing student anxiety. A sample of 17 families received three months' treatment and were compared with similar groups of students (N=223) who were put on a waiting list for three months (Drahota et al., 2011). The treatment families showed clear advances in daily living skills and an accompanying reduction in anxiety compared to the wait-listed families, though not approaching normal child expectations. Once again, systematic treatment of any style and approach appears to result in positive gains but not cures.

It is extremely important that the parents be encouraged, or they may give up attempts to communicate with the child following initial frustrations and failure. A fine example of practical help for parents is shown in Box 5.4, "Holiday Tips for Families Living with Autism."

We can sum up the family issues for the child with autism as follows:

1. Parents can learn how to teach adaptive skills and manage the behavior of their child with autism.
2. For some families, having a child with autism creates measurable stress, and support services should be available for the parents.
3. Parents' use of effective teaching methods for their child with autism can have a measurable impact on the reduction of family stress.

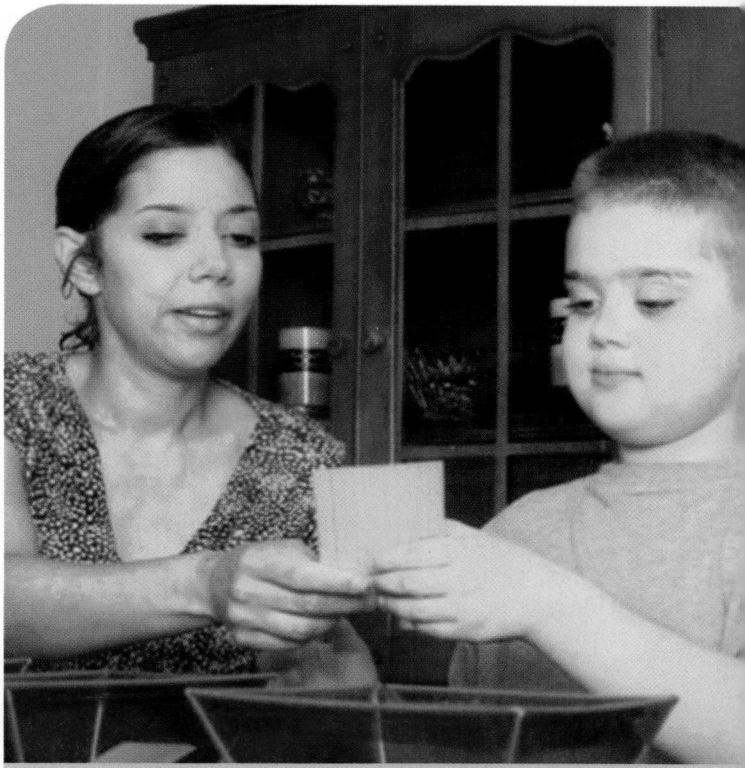

It is important for parents and family members of individuals with ASD to spend enjoyable leisure time with them. This child with ASD is playing a card game with a favorite aunt.

Many parents of children with autism have found to their dismay that although legislation has established their children's right to a free and appropriate public education (FAPE), this does not mean that these laws and regulations will be implemented at the local level. The huge expense (often $20,000 to $60,000 per child) of the intensive treatment programs have led local schools to plan for something less than the intensive treatment that many Lovaas followers and others insist on. Indeed, the National Academy of Sciences' report, *Educating Children with Autism,* recommends no fewer than 25 hours of treatment a week for young children with ASD—far fewer than the 40 insisted on in the Lovaas program (Lord, 2001).

Friend, Summers, and Turnbull (2009) reviewed the existing literature and concluded that "intervention research suggests that parent training programs improved parenting skills and parent satisfaction and reduced parental stress" (p. 468). Naturally, success in "two-generation" programs (child and parent) depends on the intensity and relevance of the program involved.

5-7b Transition to the Teen Years and Young Adulthood

What happens to children with ASD when they become young adults? The National Academy of Sciences report (Lord, 2001) calls for more longitudinal research, but the truth is that the field has paid much more attention to young children with autism than to what happens to them when they leave school for the adult world.

It is easy to see why there has been so much attention to early childhood. There have been positive results from early intervention studies. However, the

BOX 5.4 Holiday Tips for Families Living with Autism

The holiday period can be a stressful time for those on the autism spectrum, because it is a breach in their daily routine. However, if we anticipate the holidays and what they entail before they arrive, the person with autism can be made more comfortable and at ease—ensuring joy for all throughout the holidays.

"Everyone in the Car!": Starting Off on Successful Outings

- To help day trips run more smoothly, travel in two cars so that one person can return home with your loved one on the autism spectrum if he or she gets distressed.
- Eat before leaving home or bring food with you.
- Bring a quiet toy or books to a restaurant, religious service, or other social activity.

"We Are Going to Grandma's!": Tips for Social Gatherings

- When going to large social gatherings, arrive early to let the person on the autism spectrum get accustomed to the growing number of people.
- If the child becomes distressed during a social gathering, pick a quiet place to go or take him or her out for a walk.
- When visiting someone's home, ask for breakables to be removed from reach; think carefully about visiting those who refuse to accommodate your request.
- Bring a preferred item, favorite toys, or stuffed animals to a family gathering or other social event.
- Before going to a family event, look at individual pictures of family members and teach your child their names.
- Before going to a social event, use "social stories" and practice simple courtesy phrases and responses to questions, either verbally, with pictures, or with gestures. ("How are you?" "I am fine." "How is school?" "Good.")
- Let trusted others spend time with your child if they volunteer.
- Ask for help if you need it. Families and friends are often eager to participate.

"Do We Have to Go to the Mall?": Shopping Without Stress

- To help your loved one with autism get used to malls, go early before the stores open. Walk around, get familiar with the building, buy a snack when the stores open, and leave. Extend the amount of time at the mall each time you go.
- When shopping, be positive and give small rewards, such as a piece of candy, for staying with you.
- To teach your child not to touch things when shopping, visit a clothing store or another store with unbreakable objects; this gives him or her an opportunity to model behavior and minimize risk.
- When shopping, bring a helper to have an extra set of eyes and hands until you are confident of a safe experience.
- Provide headphones or earplugs to the person with autism spectrum disorder to moderate the noise and activity around him or her.

National Standards Project. (2009). Randolph, MA: National Autism Center

result of this emphasis on early life and schooling, and the relative newness of this field, means that we have all-too-little information on the long-term adaptation of such children and are forced to fall back on anecdotal reports from adults with autism. An elevated rate of depression in adults with autism is possible, and this depression sometimes necessitates medical and psychiatric attention.

The general recommendation for vocational placements stresses the strengths of the child with autism and downplays the social problems. The requirement in the Individuals with Disabilities Education Act (IDEA) of 2004 for beginning planning for adult adjustment in the IEPs of teenagers with disabilities seems very appropriate here. We would expect these students with autism to be working with computers or going into engineering or a similar occupation that downplays social interaction and emphasizes focused work. Others with high-functioning autism have successfully made adaptations to the social needs of their jobs.

Currently, information is still being gathered about what happens to the greater number of children with autism when their time in school is finished and they must find a way into the larger world. We do have some individual memoirs by persons with autism (Grandin, 2011), which remind us that even though the basic condition remains, these adults have made effective adaptation and are gainfully employed. One of the next steps, surely, is to determine how we can help youths with autism to make the shift from school to work.

5-7c Public Policy: The Courts and Legislation

The importance of the courts in the development of programs for children with special needs has been noted in previous chapters. In no other category have the courts played such a significant role than with children with autism. A total of 19 cases were brought into federal court between 1998 and 2002 as a result of disputes between parents and school districts on the appropriate way of educating autistic children (Nelson & Huefner, 2003).

In many instances, the parents insisted that the school district employ a particular method, such as ABA, whereas the school system wished to provide an alternative training program. The parents' intensity of feeling is not hard to understand because the Lovaas program, which uses ABA, has claimed that children under this program have reached "normality" in many instances. The school districts, however, aware of the high expense and the stringent requirements of the Lovaas approach, have often sought alternatives to this method (or have tried to do it with less expense). This has resulted in parental distress and legal disputes.

In general, the courts have been unwilling to substitute their judgment for that of the school system as to what was appropriate for an individual child, assuming that the districts worked closely with the parents and followed the provisions of IDEA 2004. One case established the legal standard for sound education policy in these disputes (*J. P. v. West Clark Community Schools,* 2002):

1. Can the school district articulate its rationale or explain the "specific benefits" of using that approach for the given child?
2. Do the teachers and special educators involved have the necessary experience and expertise to do so successfully?
3. Are there "qualified experts in the educational community who consider the school district's approach to be at least adequate under the circumstances"?

If the answer to these questions is "Yes," the school system will prevail in such disputes.

Until there exists a much larger cadre of specially trained teachers or other support personnel capable of meeting the needs of children with autism, it is likely that these disputes will continue.

MORAL DILEMMA

Jerry's Situation

Jerry Boyd, age 8, has been diagnosed as having high-functioning autism and has the various solitary interests that mark this condition. He loves playing computer and video games but pays little attention to his peers. He has no interest in team games or in attending birthday parties or other social functions of his class and age group.

This is upsetting to Mrs. Boyd, his mother, who thinks that this lack of interest in social matters will hurt his adjustment later on in school and community. She has embarked on campaigns to have friends sleep over. She also enrolled Jerry in dance classes and encourages him to participate in Little League baseball.

So far, Jerry couldn't care less about his mother's campaigns and wants her to stop. Mr. Boyd, his father, is uncertain whether to support Jerry in his wishes or to support his wife, who has Jerry's long-range adjustment in mind.

What should the Boyds do? What is your strategy? If Jerry was your student, how would you advise his parents?

5-7d How Legislation Affects the Education of Children with ASD

Over the past few years, a growing number of parents and advocates became concerned that their children with ASD were not receiving proper education and treatment within the public schools. They also wondered whether the Centers for Disease Control and Prevention and other authoritative voices were giving appropriate weight to the concerns of those who believed that diet or vaccines were possible causative factors of ASD.

In 2006, this alliance of parents and professionals was able to persuade Congress to pass the Combating Autism Act of 2006 (P.L.109-416), and President George W. Bush signed it into law.

This act:

- authorizes establishment of regional centers of excellence for autism spectrum disorders research
- authorizes activities to increase public awareness of autism, to improve the ability of health care providers to use evidence-based interventions, and to increase early screening for autism
- calls on the Interagency Autism Coordinating Committee (a state multidisciplinary group) to enhance information sharing

This bill was reauthorized in 2011, showing the continuing interest in the Congress on this issue.

Summary

- Autism is a pervasive developmental disorder affecting communication and social development and causing, at times, a variety of unusual behaviors and unusual reactions to sensory stimulation.
- There are clear indications of neurological and genetic factors in causes of autism. No environmental factors, such as vaccinations or family patterns, have been implicated.
- The change in diagnostic standards (DSM-5) may remove services for children with high-functioning autism or Asperger's syndrome.
- This condition of autism can be recognized in a child as young as 2 years of age. Beginning intensive treatment for language development and social skills immediately is strongly recommended.
- The prevalence of children with autism spectrum disorders appears to be steadily rising. It now is estimated at 1 in 88, or even more. The reason for the increase is not clear. It may be that we are now identifying as autistic many children who previously would have been labeled differently (e.g., developmentally disabled). Or there may be a genuine increase in autism, for reasons not yet known. The gender ratio remains constant: Four or five times as many boys with autism are found as girls.
- The ability to read the feelings and needs of others (Theory of Mind) is diminished in children with ASD.
- Applied Behavior Analysis is a treatment of choice for forming the basis for social and cognitive learning.
- Focus on social skills development includes changes in environment, the teaching of collateral skills, direct social skills training, or peer-mediated intervention.
- Improvements in communication are often carried out in natural environments, both home and school, using the child's natural interests in play to develop and expand communication.
- For children without the use of language, augmentative and alternative methods of communication are employed, such as pictures that are organized especially for communication.
- Many programs of treatment for ASD exist, and all report clinical successes in terms of improving social and academic skills, but we still need careful research to document these treatments and their long-term effects.
- Despite the variety of approaches, all major treatment programs include common elements, such as similar curriculum content, structured teaching environments, predictable routines, functional approaches to problem behavior, and the teaching of transition skills to prepare children for kindergarten.
- The major problems with implementation in the schools are the high costs of such treatment and the lack of trained personnel to administer it.
- We need more information on the transition to adulthood and adult adjustment of children who were given early help through the schools.

- Both the courts and legislation have acted to protect the rights of families with children with ASD and provide resources for their education and treatment.

Future Challenges

1. **Will there be enough trained personnel?**
   The education of children with autism requires very special preparation. Few teachers, whether in general or special education, have mastered the methods of applied behavior analysis or the other instructional strategies designed to enhance the social development and communication skills of children with autism. How will these needs for trained personnel be met?

2. **Will new medical treatments become available?**
   To date, medical or pharmaceutical treatments have had uncertain effects on children with autism. With our increasing sophistication and understanding of brain function and the genetic code, can there be some future help for families affected by autism?

3. **Who will pay for expensive educational treatments?**
   One of the issues that has not yet been solved, or even confronted, is where the funding for these projects will come from. If one takes the clinical advice that children with autism should have 25 to 40 hours of special instruction weekly, and 1 in 100 children have this condition, how do we pay for all the trained personnel needed (Schwartz & Sandall, 2010)? There are simply not that many specially prepared personnel to meet the demand, and schools and special educators need to adapt their programs to take this into account.

   Similarly, budgets at local and state levels for general and special education are already seriously stretched. Such a demand for extensive clinical services would be met with skepticism, if not opposition. In addition, the report by the National Standards Project (2009) includes some emerging treatments that look promising but do not yet have the evaluation evidence to justify their inclusion in the established treatments. In a relatively short time, we have demonstrated that the treatments listed in Table 5.4 pay off as evidence-based approaches.

4. **Where is the special programming for adolescents with ASD?**
   While we are developing impressive adaptations for early childhood and elementary age children with ASD, the literature is almost silent about adaptations in all three of the RtI tiers for adolescents with ASD. This is a major problem, as the environments in secondary education are so different, with the emphasis on content specialists and even movement between classes (including the social milieu that secondary school creates). One big thrust in special education has to be in programming for these adolescents and in planning for their transition into further schooling or the world of work.

TeachSource Digital Download Access online

Key Terms

applied behavior analysis (ABA) p. 152
Asperger's syndrome p. 143
comorbidity p. 149
comprehensive treatment models p. 160
focused intervention practice p. 160
functional behavioral assessment (FBA) p. 159
hypersensitivity p. 149
incidental learning p. 155
mirror neurons p. 145
pervasive developmental disorders–not otherwise specified (PDD–NOS) p. 143
relationship-focused intervention (RF) p. 162
replacement behaviors p. 159
Rett syndrome p. 143
Theory of Mind p. 148

Resources

References of Special Interest

Grandin, T. (2011). *The way I see it* (2nd ed.). Arlington, TX: Future Horizons. A unique perspective on autism by a successful businesswoman who has autism and now wishes to share with others her experiences growing up, including the difficulties she had fitting into the cultural environment that was unaware of or unsympathetic to her condition.

Koegel, R., & Koegel, L. (Eds.). (2007). *Pivotal response treatments for autism.* Baltimore: Brookes. Stresses the importance of teaching and intervention under naturalistic environmental conditions in the home, community, and school. Using multidisciplinary programming with an emphasis on parents, this book stresses the redirection of disruptive behaviors using functional assessment with self-management strategies and the fostering of social interactions with typically developing peers.

Mesibov, G. B., Shea, V., & Schopler, E. (with Adams, L., Burgess, S., Chapman, S. M., Merkler, E., Mosconi, M., Tanner, C., & Van Bourgondien, M. E.). (2005). *The TEACCH approach to autism spectrum disorders.* New York: Kluwer Academic/Plenum. This text provides a detailed description of TEACCH, one of the well-known organized programs for young children with autism and their parents. A wide variety of curriculum suggestions are presented for teachers and parents on domestic and independent living skills. This program includes strong efforts to help parents join in the treatment program looking forward to adulthood.

Padiyar, K. (2009). *Targeted, taunted, tormented: The bullying of children with autism spectrum disorders.* Boston, MA: Massachusetts Advocates for Children. A report focusing on a special problem faced by children with ASD. These children are especially vulnerable to bullying, as they have few psychological and physical defenses. These interviews with parents leave little doubt that their children have suffered serious bullying, and the parents expose the issues with the educators' responses to these events.

Volkmar, F., & Wiesner, L. (2009). *A practical guide to autism: What every parent, family member & teacher needs to know about autism.* Hoboken, NJ: John Wiley. A much-needed description of the causes and treatments of autism aimed at persons with little technical knowledge of the disorder. The book stresses the importance of educational and behavior treatments that have been shown to produce positive results. Also includes references to other books on the subject.

Journals

Journal of Applied Behavior Analysis
http://onlinelibrary.wiley.com/journal/10.1002/(ISSN)1938-3703
Journal of Autism and Developmental Disorders
http://link.springer.com/journal/10803
Journal of Child Psychology and Psychiatry
http://onlinelibrary.wiley.com/journal/10.1111/(ISSN)1469-7610
Topics in Early Childhood Special Education
http://tec.sagepub.com/

Professional Organizations

Autism Network International **http://www.autreat.com/**

Autism Research Institute (ARI) **www.autism.com**

Autism Society of America **http://www.autism-society.org/**

Online Asperger's Syndrome Information and Support (OASIS) **http://www.aspergersyndrome.org/**

National Dissemination Center for Children with Disabilities (NICHCY) **www.nichcy.org**

CHAPTER 6

Children with Learning Disabilities

Standards Addressed in This Chapter

All of the CEC Standards are addressed within this chapter. Please see the inside book covers for the complete list of the standards.

CEC

FOCUS QUESTIONS

6-1 What is the history of the learning disabilities field?

6-2 What are some characteristics of children with learning disabilities?

6-3 How are learning disabilities defined and identified, and what are some of their causes?

6-4 What challenges do we face in working to identify students whose primary language is not English?

6-5 How does the information processing model help us understand learning disabilities?

6-6 What educational responses are needed to help students with learning disabilities meet with success in school?

6-7 How does a child with learning disabilities impact the family?

6-8 What kind of supports will students with learning disabilities need to be successful in college, in the workplace, and in adult life?

Children with learning disabilities are both puzzling and paradoxical. In spite of near-average or higher-than-average intelligence, students with learning disabilities often find school to be very difficult. Just as the term learning disabilities implies, these children struggle to learn and often need additional supports to help them succeed in school. Andrew, for example, is a bright and talkative third grader who loves to socialize with his friends. When books are read to him he understands and remembers all the details and often asks intriguing questions. His teacher noticed this and felt that Andrew should be a very capable student, yet his independent reading level was barely at the first grade. At first his teacher assumed that he was just being lazy, but when she saw how frustrated he was becoming with reading, she decided there might be more to it, and indeed there was: Andrew has a learning disability.

The reasons that children with learning disabilities do not do well in school have fascinated and baffled researchers and practitioners in the fields of reading, cognition, speech and hearing, neurology, learning, vision, audition, and education. Not all children with learning disabilities have the same set of challenges. Most have difficulty learning to read, spell, and write. Others have trouble with math or with attending to information and completing tasks. Some have difficulty with all academic areas. In this chapter, we look at the history of learning disabilities, how learning disabilities are defined, and how the school and family can work together to create a climate of success for individuals with learning disabilities.

6-1 A Brief Historical Overview of Learning Disabilities

The phrase *learning disability* was coined in 1962 by Samuel Kirk, the first author of this text. It came to life during discussions at a 1963 conference with concerned parents and professionals that focused on students who in spite of average or above-average intelligence seemed to be encountering substantial difficulties in school. Prior to 1962, these students had been labeled with terms such as *minimal brain dysfunction, Strauss syndrome*, and *brain injured* (Lerner & Johns, 2012). From Kirk's perspective, students with learning disabilities were a heterogeneous group who shared one commonality: All had a neurologically based problem that affected learning in various ways (Cortiella, 2009; Hallahan & Mock, 2003; Pullen, Lane, Ashworth, & Lovelace, 2012).

The assumption that a learning disability has a neurological basis is sound, but it is hard for teachers to use "neurological anomalies" as evidence when they are trying to decide whether or not a student has a learning disability. There may come a time in the not-too-distant future when brain studies will be part of the identification process, but currently we must rely on a student's behavior and performance to help us determine the presence of a learning disability (Chandrasekaran, Hornichel, Skoe, Nicol, & Kraus, 2009; Sternberg, 2008). Because of this limitation, the students we currently identify as having learning disabilities are a very diverse group: They include those with assumed neurologically based learning problems (the group that Samuel Kirk was focused on) *and* students who are not performing well for other reasons (including poor motivation, problems at home, challenges faced due to external factors such as poverty, teacher-student personality conflicts, and so forth). This situation has made the category of learning disabilities a "catch-all" for students who need additional support in school. Many of the students currently identified with learning disabilities do *not* have an underlying neurological base for their difficulties. This group of students has been identified as learning disabled because of **unexplained underachievement**. We explore this further when we discuss how we define learning disabilities (Fuchs, Fuchs, Mathes et al., 2002).

for these students they don't need a special educator

6-2 Characteristics of Children with Learning Disabilities

While all children have unique patterns of strengths and challenges, children with learning disabilities face more dramatic combinations. They are like snowflakes; each has his or her own unique structure, combining strengths and needs to form an individual pattern. Children with specific learning disabilities vary in their academic, personal, and social characteristics. Students Tonya and Ray (discussed in the following paragraphs) show the variation that children with learning disabilities often exhibit.

Tonya: Tonya is a fifth grader with a measured IQ score of 135. Although this score places her in the gifted range intellectually, she still struggles with many academic tasks. Tonya is a **twice-exceptional** (2e) learner. She is a solid reader but a very poor speller. Tonya also has difficulty with handwriting, and so, although she can talk in great detail about subjects of interest, she has a very hard time writing about them. Tonya also struggles with organizing her thoughts and her written products are messy and very hard to follow. Even when she seems to be committed to a writing project, like her report on the NASA space program (Tonya would like to be an astronaut), she refuses to revise her work to strengthen it. Because of these challenges, she often tries to distract the class with off-topic discussions and refusal to complete work that she claims is "boring" when she becomes frustrated. This disruptive behavior has led to some social isolation, as Tonya's classmates, especially in the gifted education program, do not want to get into trouble because of her behavior. Tonya's teacher is frustrated with her; she sees how bright she is when she is participating in discussions and wonders why she can't apply herself more diligently when she is writing. She is also puzzled by Tonya's refusal to complete work that should be relatively easy for her and feels that she might need more discipline—both at school and at home. Later in the chapter we explore how specific writing strategies, computers, and assistive technology can be used to help Tonya become more successful.

Ray: Ray's case looks very different from Tonya. Ray has average intelligence but encounters extreme problems with reading, spelling, and writing (sometimes called **dyslexia**). He has a hard time organizing his ideas and is frequently distracted. His reading problems are so severe that he is almost a nonreader. Because of his poor academic performance, his classmates believe he is "stupid." In spite of these academic problems, Ray excels in one area: art. Ray is very creative and loves hands-on building projects. In fact, he happily volunteers for all art projects. His teacher feels that he needs a great deal of support for learning and is grateful for the resource teacher's help with Ray. The resource teacher has expertise in working with students with special needs. She works with Ray and a small group of students with similar needs for an hour each day, and she also helps Ray's general classroom teacher adapt her lessons to provide more support for Ray. Together, both of Ray's teachers are looking for ways to use his strength in art to bolster his self-esteem and build more social support for him with his peers.

Richard Hutchings/PhotoEdit

Social situations can be challenging for children with learning disabilities as they struggle to find ways to fit in with their peers.

Both Tonya and Ray have learning disabilities, and yet each has a unique combination of strengths and challenges. Students with learning disabilities have difficulties with processing information, and this can lead to problems across several areas including language development, academic learning, motor coordination, social and emotional self-regulation, and focusing attention (Horowitz & Stecker, 2010). Because learning disabilities can impact any area of processing, it is difficult to portray a "typical" child with learning disabilities. Figure 6.1 shows us that Ray has difficulties involving **executive processing**, understanding auditory input (hearing letter sounds, following directions given orally, and so forth), memory (especially for things he hears), and both speaking and writing as ways to share his ideas. The secondary areas that cause difficulties for

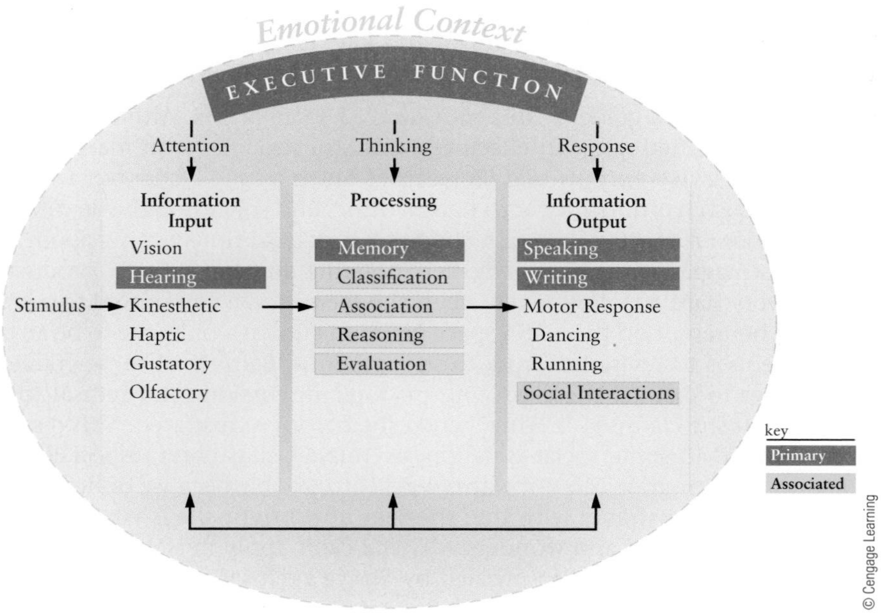

Figure 6.1 Ray's Information Processing Model

TeachSource Digital Download Access online

Ray are more generalized. Because of his challenges with both memory and focus or attending, he struggles with all of the deeper processing areas (classification, association, reasoning, and evaluation). He also has had difficulties with social interactions that require processing a lot of auditory information (such as tone of voice, inferential intent of words, and emotional content of the message). As you can see in Figure 6.1, Ray's challenges are pretty pervasive. The good news is that he has strong visual and kinesthetic skills, and these are what help him with his art.

Table 6.1 shows some of the major characteristics that students with learning disabilities often share. In looking at these characteristics, it is important to remember that individuals with learning disabilities will have their own unique combination of strengths and challenges.

Because of these differences, each student with a learning disability will need specialized supports to be successful in school. These supports are often described

TABLE 6.1 Sample Characteristics of Students with Learning Disabilities

Language Development

- Delays in learning to speak
- Difficulties with naming objects and word retrieval
- Voice modulation (loud/soft; tone) may be problematic
- Limited vocabulary and word usage

Reading

- Delays and difficulties with skills (phonemic awareness, word recognition, comprehension)
- May have stronger listening comprehension
- Slow reading rate
- Substitutes words or leaves out words when reading

TABLE 6.1 Sample Characteristics of Students with Learning Disabilities (*Continued*)

Written Language

- Avoids or dislikes writing and copying tasks
- Reverses letters and words
- Uneven and poorly spaced/shaped penmanship
- Poor spelling

Math

- Difficulty with arithmetic facts and skills
- Challenges with telling and estimating time
- Problems with memorizing information
- Difficulty with interpreting graphs and charts

Social and Emotional

- Difficulty interpreting and understanding others' moods/feelings
- Problems with self-control and impulsivity
- Difficulty with realistic goal setting
- Challenges understanding peer and group expectations

Gross and Fine Motor Skills

- May be awkward or clumsy
- Difficulty with buttons, hooks, snaps, zippers, shoelaces
- Awkward pencil grasp
- Dislikes and avoids games with balls, bats, moving parts

SOURCE: Horowitz, S., & Stecker, D. Checklist for Learning Disabilities. © 2011 National Center for Learning Disabilities, Inc. All rights reserved. Adapted with permission. For more information, visit LD.org.

in either an individualized educational program (IEP) or a 504 plan, as discussed in Chapter 2. Later in this chapter, we will explore how teachers and parents can work together with the child to promote success, but first we take a look at how learning disabilities are defined by law, how students are identified, and what some of the causes of learning disabilities are.

6-3 Defining and Identifying Learning Disabilities and Looking at Causes

More than fifty years have passed since Samuel Kirk used the term *learning disabilities* to describe children who, despite average or above average intelligence, seemed to be encountering problems with school (Coleman, Buysse, & Neitzel, 2006a). At that time Kirk believed that these children would likely be a very small subset of children with disabilities. Little did we know that children with learning disabilities would become the largest group of students served by our special education programs. Current estimations indicate that 3.4 percent of the school-age children who receive special education are categorized as learning disabled (U.S. Department of Education, 2011). This represents a substantial reduction in the numbers of students identified as learning disabled. The specific reason for the decrease is not known. It may be due in part to the use of RtI approaches, which allow schools to provide Tier I and II supports for students without formal identification. It may also, however, be motivated by attempts to save money, as additional funds are needed to provide services for students who are identified with special needs. This downward trend in identification warrants further study to better understand its impact on students with learning disabilities (Reynolds & Shaywitz, 2009). While the numbers of children identified as learning disabled is going down, this is still the largest category within special education (Cortiella, 2009).

One possible explanation for the high numbers is the way we have defined learning disabilities. The U.S. Department of Education (2004) gives us the following definition:

> SEC. 602. DEFINITIONS.
> (29) SPECIFIC LEARNING DISABILITY.
>
> (A) IN GENERAL. The term "specific learning disability" means a disorder in one or more of the basic psychological processes involved in understanding or in using language, spoken or written, which disorder may manifest itself in the imperfect ability to listen, think, speak, write, spell, or do mathematical calculations.
>
> (B) DISORDERS INCLUDE. Such term includes such conditions as perceptual disabilities, brain injury, minimal brain dysfunction, dyslexia, and developmental aphasia. . . .
>
> (C) DISORDERS NOT INCLUDED. Such term does not include a learning problem that is primarily the result of visual, hearing, or motor disabilities, of mental retardation, of emotional disturbance, or of environmental, cultural, or economic disadvantage.

This is a theoretical definition and must be "operationalized" to help us actually identify students with learning disabilities. To operationalize this definition, most states have developed formulas that hinged on the discrepancies between intellectual abilities (IQ) and achievement and/or performance. The magnitude of these discrepancies was thought to indicate the degree of underlying disability affecting a child's psychological processing. Each state set up its own formulas for determining the degree of the discrepancy. Tonya, for example, is a bright girl who is doing poorly in school. Her poor performance may be due to a learning disability, or it may be due to any number of other things (e.g., a lack of interest in school, teachers who are inexperienced, challenges due to poverty, or even problems with home and family). Some educators believe that the use of discrepancy models to identify students with learning disabilities has broadened the category to include any child who experiences problems with learning. Many students have been labeled as learning disabled because they are underachieving in school and there is no apparent reason for their lack of success (Fuchs, Mock, Morgan, & Young, 2003; Gerber et al., 2004; Kavale, Holdnack, & Mostert, 2005). Partly because of this, the category has remained large, as the learning disability label has often been given to any student about whom teachers feel would benefit from some level of systematic support.

The following concerns highlight several problems with the discrepancy model as it is used to identify children with learning disabilities:

1. Discrepancies between IQ and achievement/performance are often difficult to measure with children in pre-K through third grade.
2. Discrepancies between IQ and achievement/performance may exist for any number of reasons; thus, this approach is really just helping us find children with "unexplained underachievement" that may or may *not* be due to a learning disability.
3. To find discrepancies we must wait until the gap between IQ and achievement/performance is wide enough to measure, and this means that we must wait until the child has experienced substantial failure with learning.
4. The "wait-to-fail" model creates a situation in which the primary problems a child is experiencing get worse and are frequently compounded by

secondary problems with behavior, self-concept, and academic readiness (Coleman, Buysse, & Neitzel, 2006b).

Because of these problems with the discrepancy model, many educators maintain that the ways we identify and serve students with learning disabilities within both general and special education are not working. Some states have moved away from this approach entirely (Kavale, Spaulding, & Beam, 2009; Fuchs & Fuchs, 2006; Vellutino et al., 1996).

Some educators believe that it will take a major paradigm shift to get back on track so that the needs of students with learning disabilities can be met (National Association of State Directors of Special Education [NASDSE], 2005; Fletcher, Denton, & Francis, 2005). The response to intervention (RtI) approach, described in Chapters 1 and 2, was initially conceived as a way to help us identify and serve children with learning disabilities (NASDSE, 2005).

Purestock/Getty Images

Learning disabilities will impact the individual across their life time and students will need sustained support to meet with success.

6-3a Learning Disabilities: The Paradigm Shift to RtI

RtI

The reauthorization of the Individuals with Disabilities Education Act (IDEA; reauthorized as the Individuals with Disabilities Education Improvement Act, 2004) reflects this change in thinking about how we define and serve students with learning disabilities. IDEA 2004 includes an RtI approach as one option that schools can use to identify students with learning disabilities. The new language is part of Section 614, the section that addresses evaluations, eligibility determinations, individualized education programs, and educational placements:

> (b) EVALUATION PROCEDURES.
>
> (6) SPECIFIC LEARNING DISABILITIES.
>
> (A) IN GENERAL. Notwithstanding section 607 (b0, . . . when determining whether a child has a specific learning disability as defined in section 602 (29), a local educational agency shall not be required to take into consideration whether a child has a severe discrepancy between achievement and intellectual ability in oral expression, listening comprehension, written expression, basic reading skill, reading comprehension, mathematical calculation, or mathematical reasoning . . . .
>
> (B) ADDITIONAL AUTHORITY. In determining whether a child has a specific learning disability, a local educational agency may use a process that determines if the child responds to evidence-based intervention as a part of the evaluation procedures described in paragraphs (2) and (3) (IDEA, 2004).

It is important to note that the language of the law does *not* preclude a review of the student's strengths and challenges as part of a comprehensive educational evaluation of the student's needs (Fuchs & Fuchs, 2007). This section allows the use of information that shows how a child has responded to **evidence-based interventions** *as one part of a comprehensive evaluation of students' needs* (Kame'enui, 2007). This approach is called *Response to Intervention (RtI)*. The need for comprehensive evaluations assessing students' needs is even more important within an RtI approach because understanding *why* children are unable to learn is key to reshaping our educational supports to help them succeed. In addition to being comprehensive, a Supreme Court decision emphasizes that the evaluation of the student's

general educators are not equipped to do so. Don't have the training needs must be done in a timely manner to ensure that supports and services can be put in place as early as possible (*Forest Grove School District vs. T.A.*, 08-305, 2009).

The RtI model, as noted in previous chapters, focuses on prereferral prevention and intervention and on recognizing the needs of students so that we can deliver appropriate supports and services through a collaborative approach (President's Commission on Excellence in Special Education, 2002). While RtI began as an alternative route for identifying students with learning disabilities, it has grown into a school improvement movement focused on building collaborative approaches to meeting students' needs (Whitten, Esteves, & Woodrow, 2009).

The RtI approach allows early and intensive interventions based on students' needs without waiting for children to "fail" in the third grade (Whitten, Esteves, & Woodrow, 2009; Gersten et al., 2008; Fuchs & Fuchs, 2007; Fuchs, Fuchs, Mathes et al., 2002; Fuchs, Mock et al., 2003; Jenkins & O'Connor, 2002; Vaughn & Fuchs, 2003). The third grade often seems to be the critical year for students with learning disabilities, since during this year students are expected to make the shift from "learning to read" to "reading to learn." This means that classroom activities usually become more complex and students are expected to function with more autonomy; putting additional pressure on students with learning disabilities.

If we think about Ray's experience in school, we can see how the RtI approach would have been useful. Ray, as you may recall, is a fifth grader who is struggling in school; he has severe problems with reading, spelling, and writing. In the early grades Ray's teachers hoped that he would catch up to grade level if he worked a little harder. They did not refer Ray for an educational assessment to initiate special education services because, although he was falling behind, his teachers did not yet see an acute discrepancy between his abilities (which were average) and his performance (somewhat below average). It was not until Ray was in the third grade that he qualified for learning disabilities services, at which point he was finally failing. With the RtI approach, Ray's teachers would have been able to activate supports and services as soon as they noticed that he was encountering difficulties; they would not have had to wait for a formal label of learning disabilities (Gersten et al., 2008). Ray would have had more intensive instruction provided in small groups, as Tier II interventions, early on, and his teachers would have initiated formal assessments and **progress monitoring** as soon as they realized that he was continuing to fall behind. Ray's learning disability would have been identified, but he would not have had to fail in third grade in order to get the help he needed. To help us get a fuller picture of Ray's learning disabilities, let's look at the related area called dyslexia.

A multidisciplinary team works to develop the Individual Education Plan for each student.

6-3b Dyslexia

Currently, dyslexia is accepted as a disorder within the learning disability population, defined by the International Dyslexia Association as follows:

> Dyslexia is a language-based learning disability. Dyslexia refers to a cluster of symptoms, which result in people having difficulties with specific language skills such as spelling, writing, and pronouncing words. Dyslexia affects individual's throughout their lives; however, its impact can change at different stages in a person's life. It is referred to as a learning disability because dyslexia can make it very difficult for a student to succeed academically in the typical instructional environment, and in its more severe forms, will qualify a student for special education, special accommodations, or extra support services. (International Dyslexia Association, 2013).

The major conclusion is that children with dyslexia have brains that operate differently from the brains of children without dyslexia (Maisog et al., 2008; Shaywitz & Shaywitz, 2008; Willingham, 2008; Willis, 2008). Although persons with dyslexia have difficulties in language-based tasks (reading, spelling, writing, and phonological awareness), many have well-developed abilities in visual, spatial, motor, and nonverbal problem solving. Ray's problems with learning could be called *dyslexia* because his specific learning disabilities are in the language area with great difficulty learning to read. It is important to remember that not all children with learning disabilities have dyslexia and that dyslexia is often considered a medical term, whereas *specific learning disability* is used in educational settings. Ray also has a great deal of difficulty with paying attention in school, and his mind often seems to wander, which causes difficulties for him in school and is a source of frustration to his teachers. Ray's difficulties are extreme enough that his teachers feel he may also have an attention-deficit disorder, discussed in Chapter 7. Many individuals with learning difficulties will also have attention-deficit disorders (Silver, 2010).

Children with learning disabilities often excel with hand-on interactive learning experiences.

6-3c Importance of Early Recognition of Children with Learning Disabilities

Recognizing young children who may show early indications of learning disabilities is important so that support can be provided for their development (Neitzel, 2011; Coleman, Roth, & West, 2009). The National Joint Council on Learning Disabilities (2006) states that "the purpose of early identification is to determine which children have developmental problems that may be obstacles to learning or that place children at risk." They further recommend systematic observations of a child's behavior and abilities over time as an important way to document possible early learning disabilities.

One clinical observation tool that is being developed to help with this is the *Early Learning Observation & Rating Scale* (*ELORS*) (Coleman, Gillis, West, 2011; Coleman, West, & Gillis, 2010). The *ELORS* is a concerns-based observation tool that helps teachers and parents gather and share information about young children who may have learning disabilities (Gillis, West, & Coleman, 2010a) Using the *ELORS*, teachers and parents can systematically rate their concerns from 1 (little or no concern) to 4 (great concern) across seven developmental domains. The seven areas of development are perceptual and motor, self-management, social and emotional, early math, early literacy, receptive language, and expressive language (Gillis, West, & Coleman, 2010b). Ten examples of typical developmental tasks are provided for each domain, and teachers and parents use these to rate their levels of concern. Table 6.2 shows a sample of the items for each domain.

International Dyslexia Association
www.interdys.org

This *ELORS* focuses on seven areas of development that are associated with children who have learning disabilities (Gillis, 2011). Significant difficulties for a young child within any of these seven areas should be a cause for parental and teacher concern. Social validity studies with the *ELORS* teacher and parent versions showed that it is perceived as very helpful and that it may be used during the

TABLE 6.2 Sample: Early Learning Observation and Rating Scale (ELORS)

Teacher-Individual Child Form	4 (great concern) 1 (little or no concern)			
Domain of Learning: Perceptual and Motor				
Eye-hand coordination	1	2	3	4
Large muscle coordination	1	2	3	4
Drawing simple shapes (such as circle, square)	1	2	3	4
Dressing skills (zippers, buttons, shoes, socks)	1	2	3	4
Domain of Learning: Self-Management				
Adjusting to changes in routine	1	2	3	4
Transitioning from one activity to another	1	2	3	4
Understanding the consequences of behaviors	1	2	3	4
Using words to solve problems with peers	1	2	3	4
Domain of Learning: Social and Emotional				
Playing cooperatively with other children	1	2	3	4
Expressing frustration appropriately	1	2	3	4
Maintaining friendships	1	2	3	4
Showing a range of emotions (e.g., happy, worried, sad)	1	2	3	4
Domain of Learning: Early Math				
Naming numbers	1	2	3	4
Showing understanding of one-to-one correspondence	1	2	3	4
Determining which of two groups of objects has more	1	2	3	4
Showing understanding of basic time sequences	1	2	3	4
Domain of Learning: Early Literacy				
Interest in reading activities	1	2	3	4
Identifying words (such as "STOP" on a stop sign)	1	2	3	4
Remembering names of letters	1	2	3	4
Learning letter sounds	1	2	3	4
Domain of Learning: Receptive Language				
Paying attention to speech in the presence of background noise	1	2	3	4
Responding to verbal requests	1	2	3	4
Following simple three-step directions	1	2	3	4
Requiring modeling or demonstration	1	2	3	4
Domain of Learning: Expressive Language				
Expressing wants, needs, and thoughts verbally	1	2	3	4
Size of vocabulary	1	2	3	4
Length of typical sentences	1	2	3	4
Retelling details of a story	1	2	3	4

SOURCE: Coleman, M. R., West, T., & Gillis, M. *Early learning observation and rating scale (ELORS): Teacher-individual child form.* Adapted with permission. For more information, visit LD.org.

collaborative problem-solving discussions within the RtI approach (West, 2011; Gillis, West, Coleman, 2010b). The *ELORS* may prove to be a useful tool; however, more research is needed demonstrate its validity.

6-3d Causes of Learning Disabilities

No one has discovered a single cause of learning disabilities. Studies that focus on subgroups within the larger population of children with learning disabilities have identified some neurological differences associated with their learning problems (Hynd, 1992; Lyon, 1995; Pullen et al., 2012; Rourke, 1994).

Although no one is quite sure what causes learning disabilities, some evidence indicates that learning disabilities may be genetic, as they seem to "run in families."

Genetics of Learning Disabilities

Genetic patterns for children with learning disabilities have been noted in family relationships, and chances are good that their parents, grandparents, aunts and uncles, or other relatives will also have learning difficulties (Paracchini, Scerri, & Monaco, 2007). Researchers are currently working to isolate the genetic markers for learning disabilities, and these may help us better understand the link between biology and learning (Cope et al., 2005). All learning disabilities, however, cannot be attributed to genetic causes. Some learning disabilities may stem from environmental factors and/or from inadequate prenatal health care, which may influence brain development.

The Brain and Learning Disabilities

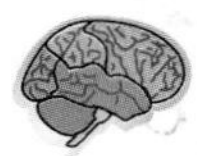

The brain is hardwired for learning, so what happens when an individual has a learning disability? Neurologists believe that the organization of the brain is different when a learning disability is present (Hoeft et al., 2006; Maisog et al., 2008; Shaywitz & Shaywitz, 2008). Remember that while the brain functions as a whole, each area of the brain takes on specialized tasks (Freberg, 2006). Studies using imaging technology have found differences in the brain structure of students who have reading problems, attention deficits, and auditory processing difficulties compared with their nondisabled peers (Castellanos et al., 2002; Willingham, 2008; Willis, 2008). We still do not understand how these structural anomalies affect information processing. In these studies, the brain scans show different patterns of activity for children with dyslexia compared to children with no reading difficulties during reading tasks (Hoeft et al., 2006). One encouraging finding is the emerging evidence that when children are given explicit and intense instruction on reading skills (phonological awareness, decoding, and so forth), their brain scans show similarities to the scans of their nondisabled peers in how their brains process information (McCandliss & Noble, 2003). Although there is a significant evidence of brain abnormalities for children with dyslexia, we still do not know the specific impact and causal link of these differences with learning problems (Hoeft et al., 2006).

6-3e Prevalence of Learning Disabilities

Although learning disabilities have an impact at all ages, we focus our discussion of prevalence on school-age individuals from 6 to 21 years old. The U.S. Department of Education (2011) reports that 3.4 percent of individuals ages 6 to 21 are receiving special education and/or related services because of specific learning disabilities. While learning disabilities remain the largest category of disability among children, the numbers of identified children has declined, and during the last decade the number has dropped 1 percent (National Center for Education Statistics, 2012).

This decline may be due to several factors including early interventions to support children as they learn to read, changes in definitions and identification practices, and the use of research-based instructional methods (Cortiella, 2009). However, as noted earlier, we need more information about the impact this downward trend is having on students with learning disabilities (Reynolds & Shaywitz, 2009).

In spite of these declines, learning disabilities remain the largest category of disability among all racial and ethnic groups. However, there are differences in identification patterns across groups. The *28th Annual Report* indicates that American Indians/Alaska Natives, black non-Hispanic, and Hispanic students are somewhat more likely to be identified as having learning disabilities, whereas identification is somewhat lower for white non-Hispanic and Asian/Pacific Islanders. These patterns continue to remind us that the identification process we use must be fair and equitable so that we do not inadvertently overidentify children from some racial and ethnic groups (Sullivan, 2011).

6-4 Appropriate Identification of Bilingual Children

RtI should be given by a special educator who speaks child's language

With the demographic shift in the United States, Hispanics are currently the largest minority group (15.4 percent of the population) and approximately 20 percent of school-age children come from homes where a language other than English is spoken (Cartledge, 2011). Appropriate identification of children with learning disabilities whose first language is not English presents a special challenge (Sullivan, 2011; Spear-Swerling, 2006). The National Longitudinal Transition Studies found an increase in learning disabilities identification, from 1.3 percent in 1987 to 15.4 percent in 2001, for students ages 15 to 17 whose primary language was not English (Cortiella, 2009). This increase may reflect the demands faced by students who must communicate in two or more languages, and it likely contributes to the disproportionate representation of Hispanic students with learning disabilities (Ortiz, 2001; Spear-Swerling, 2006). Because mastering more than one language is difficult in and of itself, bilingual assessments of the child's abilities and skills are critical to understanding if learning disabilities are present (Banks, 2012). The dual language demands faced by children who are bilingual will be examined in-depth in Chapter 9, but the following example of Juan illustrates some of the challenges we have been discussing.

Juan is a high school student whose primary language is Spanish. While he is a hard worker and seems to like school, he is struggling with the demands of reading in the academic subjects. His teachers are concerned about this and feel that he may have a learning disability. They are reluctant to refer him for special education because they also feel that his reading problems may stem from his dual language usage. More and more students like Juan are being supported by being taught specific strategies for reading in the content areas within Tier II of the RtI model to help them meet with success (Deshler et al., 2001).

Juan's teachers decide to intensify support for him using embedded vocabulary development opportunities (Ortiz, 2001), specific guidance on paraphrasing key readings to build understanding (Deshler et al., 2001), and instruction on writing using self-reflection (such as reading aloud what you have written to check the meaning) to guide and model the writing process (Graham & Harris, 2009). The decision to provide this extra support for Juan was made by a team of teachers including the English language learners specialist, the special education teacher, and his general education teachers. In the meeting, Juan requested additional support with his homework, and the team agreed that he should participate in the student support program offered either before school, during lunch hours, or after school, through the RtI services. Because Juan relies on the school bus and has after-school responsibilities

BOX 6.1 EXCEPTIONAL LIVES • EXCEPTIONAL STORIES
A Painful Situation

A bad year
Without bad people really
No one exactly to blame
Just a sequence of events
A class that didn't belong to me
And I not belonging to it
The round peg in the square whole [*sic*]
So slowly I faded out
At first just the field trips and their ilk
Then for part of the day
And finally completely
As words sprang and papers vanished
I became more and more lost and confused
And most of all sad
So the round peg
Found a round whole
And so the story ends
At least it was without villains

(unpublished poem by Shane Wilder, 2004)

Shane was born in 1992 and has lived in Albuquerque his whole life. He began writing in the second grade, when he won the New Mexico PTA Reflections Fair. Years later one of his stories, "To Top It All Off," about his experience of having a learning disability, was placed in the Library of Congress. In 2005 and 2006, Shane was recognized as an All-American Scholar. But in spite of these academic successes, Shane's early life was filled with struggles in school. His parents captured Shane's dilemma this way: "In the early elementary school grades, Shane experienced profound failure and, in our view, a lack of understanding that a student could have a substantial learning disability and also be intellectually gifted. This was especially confusing for some teachers because his primary area of disability identified was in reading and written language, and yet these are also the primary areas of his giftedness." Like other students who are *twice-exceptional*, Shane is gifted in several areas, but these strengths are combined with areas of great challenge. In Shane's case, he has a specific learning disability that affects reading. In fact, through fourth grade, Shane was essentially a nonreader, and he describes his difficulties this way: "It all began in the second grade. That was when I realized that I couldn't read, write, or keep track of things like other kids could. Thus I sort of fell out of regular education, first into a special education class at my school and eventually into Mr. Higgins's twice-exceptional class."

Shane kept his love of language and learning alive by getting his books on tape. According to his parents, "Shane continued to be a motivated learner, but he became very discouraged about his daily failure at school. At home he discovered books on tape, which greatly helped his mental state as he was able to read the books he loved independently and continue to learn new words and ideas that were so important to him." One of Shane's teachers in middle school said, "Shane's passion for language would be remarkable in any teenager but is astounding when coupled with the severe learning disability that made reading 'with his eyes' a struggle at best and, for most of his elementary years, an impossibility. How could a boy who faced years of failure—and at times stinging humiliation—maintain his love of books? Thank heavens for books on tape!" The books on tape allowed Shane to use his strong listening comprehension, his outstanding ability to think, and his natural curiosity about life to continue learning.

Marci Laurel

Shane was also fortunate because the Albuquerque Public Schools has one of the finest programs for students who are twice-exceptional. As Shane's struggles in school increased, his parents sought out ways to help him:

> We were so very fortunate at that time to meet Dr. Dennis Higgins. Shane was eventually transferred to the school where Dr. Higgins was teaching a model elementary school classroom for students who were identified as both gifted and having an area of disability. Shane felt "at home" from the moment he stepped into this classroom and, with the love and guidance, became willing to try again to be a "successful" student.

Shane talks about his journey back to school success this way:

> It began with learning to accept school again once I got to Mr. Higgins's class. This occurred by beginning my time in Mr. Higgins's class with very little work and a lot of support for those few things. In Mr. Higgins's class I slowly learned, one, to catch up in skills that I have missed and, two, to persist in things that were hard. As well, I had a series of reading teachers who had varying levels of success, until the final one who taught the Wilson Program, which was exceedingly dull and boring, but it had its desired effect. By working two hours a week one-on-one with the teacher, I finally learned to read in the fifth grade.
>
> I am currently doing well in the ninth grade, where I take honors English, analytical biology, and a "gifted" health class but also study skills (a.k.a. resource room special education support). The most important support for being successful in challenging academic classes at this point are my IEP modifications, especially those that allow a teacher to accept my work based on content that might otherwise be disqualified because of spelling and/or conventions of writing. Books on tape are and always will be the most important adaptation for me because, even though I can now read at an expected level, it is still slow and less effective; therefore, I rely on audiobooks for most of my reading. The final modification of great relevance is the ability to either use voice activation software (which is new to me) or dictation for long written work.

He added that although he does not have any "sage" advice, he would suggest that others who struggle with twice exceptionalities should "find Dr. Higgins or his clone!"

to his family, Juan decided to attend the lunch hour support session. He also planned to talk a few of his friends into going with him so he would have a small group to eat with during the lessons.

Identification practices for children whose first language is not English go beyond simply making sure that the specific assessments are valid and reliable. We also must make sure that these assessments are fair (Banks, 2012). Fairness comes into play in ensuring that the primary language is used for the assessment and that the individuals conducting the assessments are culturally competent (Banks, 2012). Our goal is to make sure that the assessments reflect the student's actual abilities and that we capture strengths as well as areas of concern (Banks, 2012).

Box 6.1 shares the experience of one student with learning disabilities, Shane.

6-5 Using the Information Processing Model to Understand Learning Disabilities

The IPM is not the only way to describe learning, but it is a useful way to think about learning in the presence of a learning disability (Sternberg & Grigorenko, 2002; Willingham, 2008). The IPM shows the components of learning and how they are impacted by a learning disability. The IPM also gives us direct insight into strategies we can use to support student learning. The four major components (input, processing, output, and executive function) operate in the context of an emotional environment that influences the processing of information (Immordino-Yang & Damasio, 2007). Each component performs an important function related to learning, and optimum learning takes place when the components function smoothly as one system. A learning disability can be explained as a glitch in this system. Let's look at each component and explore what the glitches mean for students.

6-5a Problems with Input

When the learning difficulty occurs because of input glitches, a sensory perceptual problem exists. Unlike sensory acuity problems, perceptual problems cannot be corrected with glasses or hearing aids. Those with **visual perception** problems can experience figure-ground (seeing an object against the background), closure (completion of a figure), and spatial relationship problems. Any one of these problems can make learning very difficult. If they are combined with auditory perceptual difficulties—figure-ground auditory problems (hearing speech against background noise) or difficulties in sound discriminations and/or sound recognition—then learning becomes even more difficult (Lerner & Johns, 2012). Andrew, the first child we met in this chapter, has visual perceptual problems that make reading very difficult. His **auditory perception**, however, is strong, so he can understand information that is read to him. Ray, as noted earlier, has the opposite pattern: strong visual perception with weak auditory perception.

Jim West / PhotoEdit

Technology can be used to support children's learning when they have visual or auditory perception difficulties.

In addition to perceptual problems, some individuals with learning disabilities experience sensory integration difficulties. Sensory integration involves the ability to use two or more senses simultaneously and smoothly (Lerner & Johns, 2012). A student's inability to listen and take notes during class is an example of a sensory integration dysfunction because this task requires blending auditory perception and tactile or **proprioceptive** (an awareness of where your body is in relation to the space around it) actions.

A final area of concern with this component is oversensitivity to sensory input; this may mirror the difficulties faced by some children with autism (see Chapter 5). Lights, sounds, smells, and tastes may become overwhelming. When this **heightened sensitivity** affects the sense of touch, it is called **tactile defensiveness**, in which touch can trigger acute discomfort. For individuals who are tactually defensive, a light or soft touch seems to be more uncomfortable than firm contact. In a typical busy classroom, it is easy to see how a student with these sensory sensitivities would experience difficulties.

6-5b Problems with Processing or Thinking

When problems with learning primarily affect processing or thinking, we see difficulties with memory and with organizing ideas or thoughts in meaningful ways. Problems in these areas can be especially frustrating for students and their teachers. Although Ray's problems occur in several areas, the most difficult of them involves his inability to organize his thoughts and ideas. This inability creates great challenges across most school tasks, and it is only when he can be creative in the arts that he feels truly at home. Tonya, on the other hand, excels in her thinking; she seems to thrive in the world of ideas, and she has a great memory. Her struggle comes when she must write her ideas down. Let's look at glitches that affect memory and information retrieval and then at the problems with organizing thoughts.

The division of memory into sensory, short-term, and long-term memory helps us understand how students process different tasks (Swanson & Sáez, 2003). See Figure 6.2 for an information processing model of how memory works. Our **sensory memory** can hold large amounts of information for a very short period of time (2 to 3 seconds). We use **short-term memory** to remember the directions and steps for solving a math problem while simultaneously doing the calculations. **Long-term memory** stores information that we have made our own to draw on for future use. Problems with any of these forms of memory lead to major learning difficulties (Swanson, Zheng, & Jerman, 2009). However, the greatest impact occurs when students struggle with long-term memory storage and retrieval.

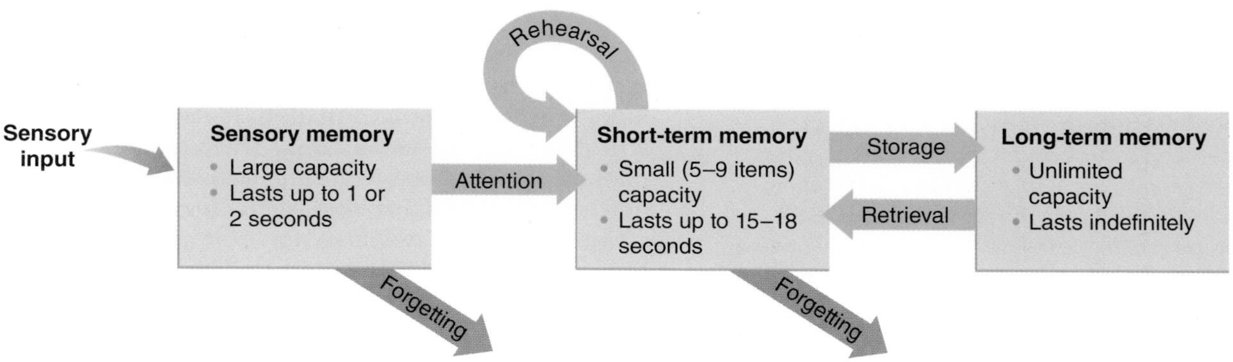

Figure 6.2 The Atkinson-Shiffrin Model of Memory
Source: From FREBERG. *Discovering Biological Psychology*, 1E. © 2006 Wadsworth, a part of Cengage Learning, Inc. Reproduced by permission.

Another way to view memory is to consider how the information is stored. We typically store information in three kinds of memory: semantic, episodic, and physical/motor (Lerner & Johns, 2012).

- **Semantic memory** stores concepts, words, symbols, and generalizations. This is the most frequently used form of memory in school.
- **Episodic memory** is our ability to recall whole scenes or episodes from our past. When we experience episodic memory, we feel we are "right back there" with all senses engaged. Often episodic memories are triggered by smells. When you smell lavender perfume like your grandmother wore, you are immediately transported back to the times she read to you while you sat on her lap. Episodic memories are often associated with strong emotions that can be either positive or negative.
- **Motor memory** is our ability to program our body movements. Our bodies learn patterns and retain them for future use. We learn to ride a bicycle, play the piano, or write our names. Some motor memories seem to last after we no longer use them—thus the expression "It's like riding a bike."

When an individual has a learning disability that affects memory in any form, school can be a challenging place.

In addition to memory, the processing component includes thinking. Students work with the information to interpret and combine it with prior knowledge as they create meaning for themselves by constructing their own understandings. Original ideas are born in this stage that allow the learner to move beyond the known into new areas of thought. It is in this component of the IPM that real learning takes place.

When problems occur in thinking, they are likely to stem from an inability to organize thoughts in meaningful ways (classifying, forming associations, using reasoning abilities, and so forth). In other words, ideas remain fragmented and disconnected so that patterns and relationships across ideas never jell into useful concepts. Interestingly, when information is stored in memory as isolated bits and pieces, it is more difficult to retrieve and is less useful for thinking (Coleman, 2005). Structuring teaching around concepts and big ideas is useful in helping our students reduce retrieval problems (Ellis, Farmer, & Newman, 2005). This is discussed further later in the chapter.

Learning, according to the IPM, is a function of how well an individual processes the information. Deep processing is necessary to understanding information so that it can be used in meaningful ways. Deep processing occurs when we transform the information to make it ours (Willis, 2008). Such processing might include forming categories where new information is linked with existing information. It also includes analytical and evaluative thinking. The ultimate transformation occurs when we use the information to create new ways of thinking and share these new understandings with others. Ray, for example, has a hard time getting new information to "stick." In preparation for an upcoming social studies test, his mother spent several nights helping him study by quizzing him on vocabulary and dates. During the study sessions, he seemed to be getting the information, and everyone

TeachSource Video Connection

Watch the video "Managing an Inclusive Classroom: High School Math Instruction." This video shows a general classroom teacher and special educator working together to assist students in an inclusive high school classroom. They use a variety of strategies to help support all their students. What are some of the strategies that they use or recommend to other teachers who work with students with learning disabilities? How might some of these strategies help target potential problems with information processing?

Watch online

was discouraged when he all but failed the actual test. Ray had not processed the information deeply during his study time, and so he was not able to apply his learning when it came to the test. On the other hand, after he completed his social studies project—a topographical map of his state showing its different regions, populations, and products—he was able to remember and discuss everything he had learned in great detail. For Ray, this hands-on art-related project helped him process the information more deeply so that he could remember and use what he had learned. Sharing information, or using what you have learned, is represented in the output component of the IPM.

6-5c Problems with Output

For some individuals with learning disabilities, the problem is primarily output, or the expression of ideas and thoughts, which can take several forms.

When output problems affect speech, they may be called *developmental aphasia* because the symptoms mirror those of a stroke patient with speech difficulties. These problems include word retrieval and speech fluency, which can make communication difficult.

A second form of output glitch involves the motor mechanics of handwriting (Berninger & Amtmann, 2003). The easiest way to understand this is to imagine that the connection between the brain and the hand is not efficient. There is "static on the line," which makes it difficult for the hand to know what to do and for the brain to understand what the hand has done. If you think back to Tonya's profile, you will remember that this was one of her challenges. Difficulties with handwriting are sometimes called **dysgraphia**, which literally means *bad writing*. To produce legible products, these students have to "draw" their letters and form them into words. This process is very taxing and cannot be sustained for general work. When dysgraphia is combined with visual and auditory perceptual problems or sensory integration difficulties, note taking during lectures and copying from the board are virtually impossible.

Another form that output learning disabilities can take is an inability to both understand and produce gestures and facial expressions that correspond with feelings and emotions. In this case, individuals have difficulty interpreting emotional nuances that are communicated through facial expressions and body language. Because a tremendous amount of information is communicated nonverbally through looks and body positions, an individual who does not "read" these clues is at a distinct disadvantage when communication is required.

Individuals with these problems may also have a *flat affect* (an absence of expression on the face) that can limit their ability to express needs and wants, thus making communication more problematic. Social situations can be quite painful for these individuals, creating an early pattern of social avoidance.

6-5d Problems with Executive Functions

As we discussed earlier, the executive function, or **metacognition**, is the decision-making component of this model. Decisions are made about

- What input to notice or screen out
- What strategies to use to store information or whether the information needs to be stored
- How useful the information is
- How ideas and understandings will be expressed

Metacognition also includes **self-regulatory skills** (Wery & Nietfeld, 2010; Hidi & Ainley, 2008). We monitor ourselves so that we can continuously adapt our thoughts, speech, and actions to accomplish our goals. Self-regulatory skills help us adapt to the environment and are essential (Wong, 2004; Zimmerman & Schunk, 2008). Self-regulation implies that an individual is in control of and responsible for his or her own actions. In addition to its importance for learning, self-control is also a key ingredient in social success. Impulsivity can lead to disastrous results: essentially leaping before looking. In learning, self-regulation allows us to monitor our understanding. Good readers, for example, continuously monitor their comprehension and work to make sense of their reading (Pierangelo & Giuliani, 2006). When something is not clear, good readers loop back and reread the passage. Poor readers, on the other hand, often fail to recognize that something does not make sense. Even when they do recognize the problem, they often fail to initiate a strategy such as rereading to help them make sense of the text (Wery & Nietfeld, 2010). In addition to problems with self-regulation, difficulties with the **executive function** can show up as **attention deficit/hyperactivity disorder** (ADHD), as will be discussed in Chapter 7, and it is not unusual for students with learning disabilities to also have ADHD.

6-5e Emotional Context of Information Processing

Emotional context is critical to our understanding of how students learn (Immordino-Yang & Damasio, 2007; Campos, Frankel & Camras, 2004). The IPM usually describes learning as a purely cognitive activity, but this is not how learning really takes place (Jensen, 2008). Both one's emotional environment and internal emotional state have a dramatic impact on one's ability to learn (Shattell, Bartlett, & Rowe, 2008; Willis, 2008). When the emotional environment is harsh or we perceive it as dangerous, our internal emotional states become acutely stressed and defensive. Neither this environment nor the internal state it produces is optimal for learning. Think for a moment of a time when you were trying to learn something new or to perform a task under a great deal of pressure and stress. Perhaps you were taking an exam, or maybe you were learning to drive. Take yourself back to that time and try to remember how you felt. Can you see how strong emotions can affect our ability to learn and to perform with success? In fact, strong negative emotions have an impact on all aspects of our ability to process information, coloring our perceptions, scrambling our thinking, interrupting our ability to communicate, and, perhaps most importantly, clouding our judgment or executive functioning (Lewis & Stieben, 2004). As our understanding of neurology develops, we see that emotions and cognition are interwoven and cannot be viewed separately (Zimmerman & Schunk, 2008).

Individuals with learning disabilities may be even more vulnerable to toxic emotional environments than other students because their internal emotional states are often less secure (Shattell et al., 2008). Repeated experiences of failure and frustration can lead to **anticipatory anxiety** in the face of new situations, even when the situation is not particularly stressful (Levine, 2003). This anticipatory anxiety can sabotage success by undermining self-confidence at the start of a new experience. Anticipatory anxiety can also lead to heightened sensitivity and defensiveness, which further erode an individual's ability to respond to new situations and opportunities.

Thus far we have discussed the impact of the emotional context on cognition, but the emotional context also affects social situations. When an individual has a learning disability that affects his or her ability to read and understand social cues, social situations can feel threatening because people are often very unpredictable. The individual may have difficulty reading and understanding social cues due to this unpredictability.

In a classroom, students' success is directly related to their skills in understanding and interpreting the teacher's expectations. Most students know when they are about to "cross the line" with a teacher and pull back enough to prevent negative consequences. Students who have learning disabilities that affect their understanding of social cues and who have difficulty with self-regulation may often find themselves in trouble. This tendency further exacerbates the anxiety response in the face of similar situations. When you are fairly certain that you will get in trouble and you don't know how to prevent it, you can become anxious when anticipating the future.

Put yourself in the shoes of Tonya, Juan, or Ray for a moment and think about how their frustrations, fears, and anxieties compound their difficulties and make learning even harder for them. The importance of a positive emotional climate for learning is discussed later in the chapter.

Giving students with learning disabilities lots of choices can help them find books that they want to read.

6-5f The Information Processing Model as a System

Although each part of the IPM has been discussed separately, the components work together as a system. Each component influences and is influenced by others in a continuous feedback loop. An anomaly or problem in one area will have an impact on other components.

For example, a student with a visual processing problem that affects *closure* will have a difficult time recognizing the differences between the letter pairs *a/u, n/h, a/d, h/b, a/g, c/o, a/q, c/d, t/f, i/l, i/j, o/p, r/n,* and *v/y*. If he or she has a problem with *visual rotations* and *mirror images,* then the following letter pairs will become difficult: *b/d, q/p, q/g, u/n, h/y, m/w,* and *g/p*. With these moderate perceptual difficulties, reading becomes a struggle. The individual spends the majority of his or her time and energy sorting the letters and decoding the words. This leaves little room for understanding meaning, which is essential for moving information into short-term memory (see Figure 6.2). Moderate problems with input will also hamper processing and thinking, making it difficult to learn. This will inhibit output (the ability to share what has been learned), because the information has not been deeply processed and stored in long-term memory. In contrast, for good readers, the decoding becomes automatic. This automaticity means that while they are reading, they can also process the information; they can think about what they are learning. When all the components work together, this facilitates understanding and keeps the IPM operating smoothly. In addition to the influences of each IPM component on the others, disabilities are further complicated because of the multiplicity of problems. Remember that when we use the term *learning disability* we are referring to a wide range of learning problems that coexist with a variety of learning strengths. Therefore, each student with a learning disability will have a unique profile and will need an educational environment that can address these differences. It is not unusual, for example, for a student to have problems with visual perception, short-term memory, sequencing information, organizing thoughts, and handwriting. This same individual might be strong in auditory perception, creative insights, and talking. In fact, this combination reflects Andrew's learning profile; we will see how we can address Andrew's needs in the next section, which shares educational responses for students with learning disabilities.

6-6 Educational Responses for Students with Learning Disabilities

Throughout this chapter we have looked at the multiple ways that a learning disability can affect a student's ability to learn. We have noted that the category of learning disabilities includes individuals with widely different strengths and needs. Because of these unique needs, an IEP or 504 plan that links educational interventions and supports to the specific needs of each student is often needed. The following section on educational responses shares organizational structures or supports and instructional strategies for meeting the needs of students with learning disabilities.

6-6a Organizational Structures and Support for Students with Learning Disabilities

Where Are Students with Learning Disabilities Served?

Figure 6.3 shows how the services for students with learning disabilities are provided across both general and special educational settings. The majority of students with learning disabilities (57.2 percent) spend most of their time in general education classes. Twenty-two percent of students with learning disabilities receive services in the regular classroom for 20–60 percent of the day. A much smaller percentage of students with learning disabilities (15.4 percent) spend over half of their school day in settings other than the general classroom,

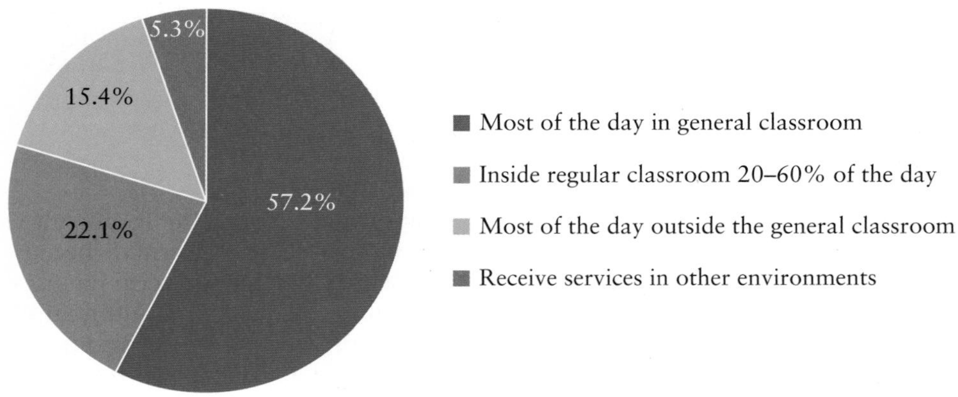

Figure 6.3 Educational Settings for Children with Learning Disabilities
Source: Data Accountability Center. (2011). *Part B Educational Environments 2011 [data file]. Retrieved from http://www.ideadata.org/PartBEnvironments.asp.*

and 5.3 percent receive services in a different environment (U.S. Department of Education, 2009).

As you can see from Figure 6.3, the vast majority of students with learning disabilities receive all or most of their education within the general education setting. There is a continuing trend toward full inclusion for students with learning disabilities, with an increasing number of students spending most of their time in general education classrooms. Students with learning disabilities typically participate in the same learning activities, focus on the same core standards, and take the same assessments alongside their nondisabled peers; however, skilled teachers use a variety of strategies to support students successfully (Cortiella & Burnette, 2009).

One of the questions increasingly being asked is: What evidence do we have that special education for children with learning disabilities shows positive results? This is particularly important because these programs increase the cost of education for students who are identified. A primary question is: Do we know how to provide remedial programs that get positive results for children in academic difficulty? The answer to that question is yes (Torgeson, 2009; Vellutino et al., 1996). Students with an intense program devoted to their individual needs make significant academic gains, often catching up with their academic peers.

The second question then is: Can children with learning disabilities make such gains in the general inclusive classroom? After all, inclusion is not a remedial program; it is a place. So can an intensive remedial program be instituted in this setting? There is serious doubt expressed about that. Zigmond, Kloo, and Volonino (2009) report on four separate settings in Pennsylvania schools where they tracked children with learning disabilities. In each instance, there were only minor changes made by the classroom teacher, not the intense and individual changes needed.

What about placing the children with learning disabilities in a resource room? After all, this too is just a place, not remediation. Vaughan and Fuchs (2003) suggest positive outcomes are not seen unless a well-organized remedial program is put into place. McLesky and Waldron (2011), reviewing the whole question, concluded that the inclusive classroom is not the only setting needed for children with learning disabilities. They state that "most elementary students with learning disabilities require intensive high quality instruction in a part-time special education setting that is delivered by a teacher with specialized skills to make adequate academic progress in basic skill areas" (p. 53).

So while the general inclusive classroom can provide positive support and social skills experience for students with learning disabilities, a specially trained teacher needs to implement a targeted remedial program if our additional costs are to yield important benefits. While full inclusion for students with learning disabilities is the trend, we have yet to demonstrate the success of this approach, which relies on skilled teachers using a variety of strategies to support students (Cortiella & Burnette, 2009).

RtI Approaches for Students with Learning Disabilities

RtI

The RtI approach to meeting students' needs builds on collaboration between general and special education across the **intervention hierarchy**, or tiers of support. Students with learning disabilities will often receive supports and services at each tier of RtI as teachers work to match instruction to the learning needs of the student through systematic progress monitoring (Bush & Reschly, 2007). Students receive support at the different tiers based on the intensity of their needs, and movement across the tiers is determined by the students' responses to the supports offered. Figure 6.4 shows the RtI triangle with it's three tiered format.

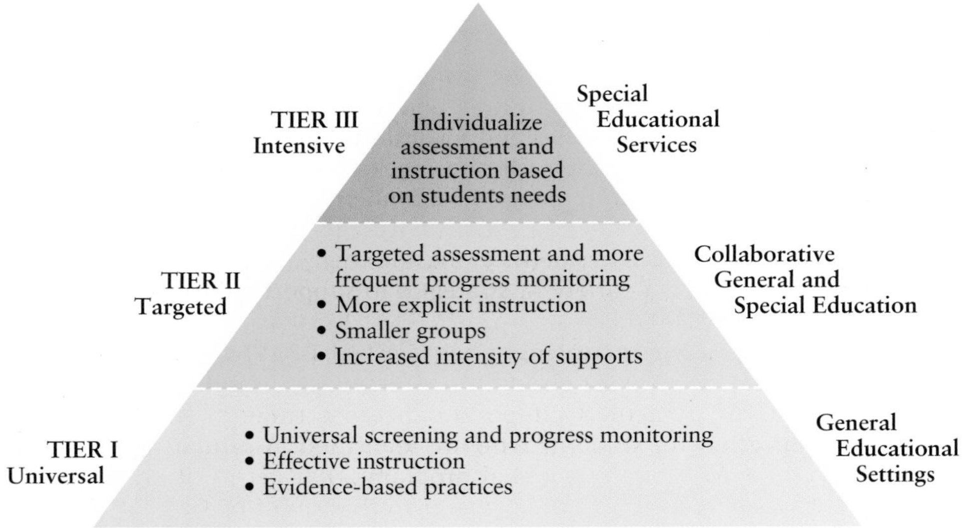

Figure 6.4 Intervening Hierarchy for RTI
Adapted from www.nasdse.org/projects.cfm?page projectid=23. Reprinted by permission of National Association of State Directors of Special Education.

Universal Tier I for Students with Learning Disabilities

The general education classroom is the primary prevention and intervention site for all students. Effective teaching using evidence-based curriculum and pedagogy creates a high-quality learning environment in which most students should be successful. Teachers intentionally plan for their students, responding to their needs. General classroom teachers use universal screening and periodic progress monitoring to check on the needs of their students (Compton, Fuchs et al., 2006). Progress monitoring at Tier I helps teachers determine whether their students are making appropriate gains in their learning. Teachers may use performance outcome measures that align the overall learning goals (often called curriculum-based measures) to monitor progress, or they may use work sampling, in which tasks are drawn directly from the learning activities and are used as evidence of a student's mastery or needs.

Andrew is struggling in third grade because his reading skills are weak and he is now failing to make his grade. His teachers are exploring whether to have him tested for learning disabilities so that they can provide additional support and help him get back on track. If his teachers had been able to recognize his needs and respond to them earlier using an RtI approach, Andrew might have had a better chance of success and might not have had to fail the third grade. Let's look at what would have happened for Andrew if he had attended a school where an RtI approach was used.

We will start with what Andrew's kindergarten classroom would have looked like. Ms. Brown, Andrew's kindergarten teacher, uses a guided reading approach to help all her students get ready to learn to read. This approach focuses on early reading skills, including print awareness, phonemic awareness, vocabulary building, word recognition, reading fluency, and reading comprehension. At the beginning of the year, as part of the schoolwide screening, Ms. Brown assessed all of her students on letter naming, letter sound recognition (phonemic awareness), word recognition, story retelling (retelling the story from memory after it had been read aloud), and story sequencing (placing pictures in order to show the story as it was told). Andrew had a very difficult time with most of these skills, but he was very good at story retelling and picture sequencing. Ms. Brown noted Andrew's initial skill levels in each area and began her instruction with Andrew. She also sent a note home to Andrew's parents asking them to read with and to

Andrew as often as possible. She included two books that she thought might interest Andrew, with a list of questions to be used in discussion of the books. Andrew was placed with a group of his classmates who all needed to strengthen their early reading skills. For six weeks Ms. Brown collected weekly progress monitoring data on letter naming, letter-sound matches, and word recognition. At the end of this period she used this information to review what her students had mastered. At this point, she realized that Andrew was not making appropriate gains in his phonemic awareness and that he was falling further behind his classmates in word recognition. Ms. Brown decided that Andrew's needs required even more intensive instruction, so she brought Andrew's file to the kindergarten team meeting. In addition to the kindergarten teachers, the team meeting included the school's reading specialist and special education teacher. At the team meeting, it was decided that Andrew would benefit from short-term intensive instruction on letter recognition and phonics and that Andrew would receive reading support with Tier II "targeted" services. A Summary of *UDL Supports for Students with LD* can be accessed online.

TeachSource Digital Download

Targeted Tier II for Students with Learning Disabilities

As the intensity of the students' needs increases, the level of support to meet their needs must also increase. In Tier II, general and special education come together to provide the support needed. Interventions at Tier II are characterized by instruction that is more explicit or directive, along with expanded learning opportunities that are embedded in the students' daily learning experience. Learning supports at Tier II are often provided in smaller groups to increase the intensity of the instruction, and the frequency of progress monitoring is also increased. Tier II learning activities act as supplements to Tier I and are designed to correct problems early and to prevent further problems from developing. The general classroom teacher works with specialists to design and implement Tier II interventions. Through this collaborative process the team selects **standard protocol** interventions and works together in a problem-solving mode to determine what else should be done for the child. Progress monitoring in Tier II is used to see whether the intervention has been successful and to help in determining whether the child needs more intense supports (Fuchs & Fuchs, 2006).

In Andrew's case, he joined two other students who worked three times a week with the reading specialist on mastering letter-sound matches (phonemic awareness) and word recognition. An evidence-based curriculum was selected to teach these skills, and this support was provided in addition to all the early reading instruction that Andrew received in his general classroom. Andrew's progress on both skills was monitored three times per week, and records were kept to show his **slope of improvement** (see ▶ Figure 6.5).

A meeting was held with Andrew's parents to share Andrew's progress and discuss his needs. Andrew's parents suggested that they could help more with word recognition and wondered whether there might be any computer software that they could use for this. They also asked his teachers to remember his outstanding memory for stories that were read to him, and together they decided to use this strength to help him develop a word bank of his favorite words from the stories he heard. Andrew created a notebook with pages for each letter and began adding words the next afternoon after story time. In addition, his teacher helped him write a sentence using each word, and Andrew drew a picture in his word bank showing the part of the story in which this word occurred (see ▶ Figure 6.6).

Andrew's teaching team met again with his parents to review his progress at the end of nine weeks. It was decided that, although Andrew had made substantial progress in both his phonemic awareness and his word recognition, he still needed the intense support to be successful. The team also agreed that more information about Andrew's learning needs should be gathered through a comprehensive evaluation. The planned evaluation included individual assessments of

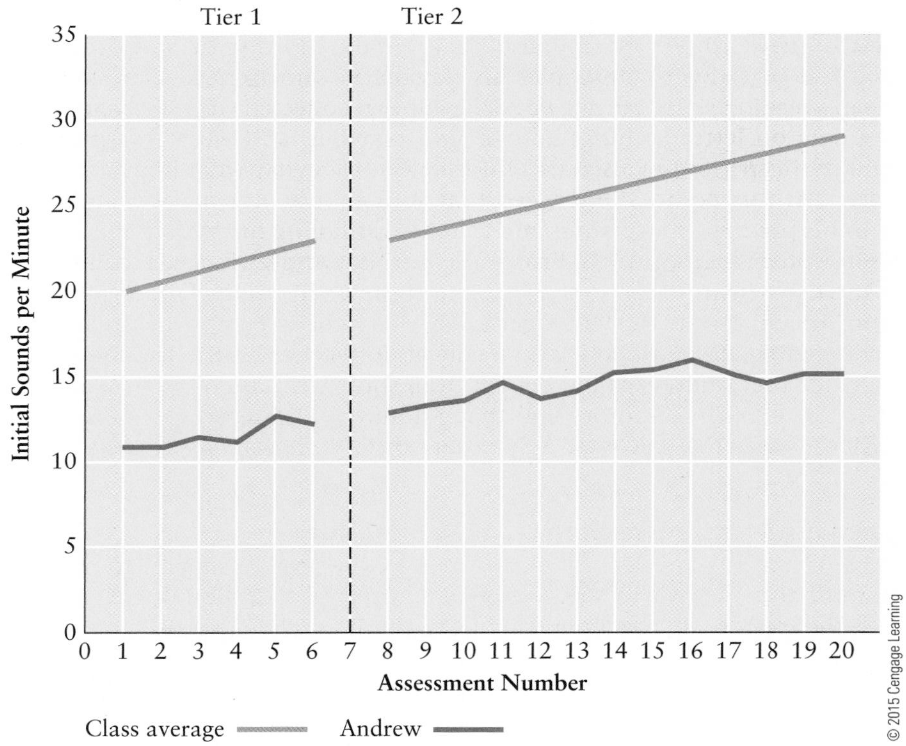

Figure 6.5 Andrew's Progress Monitoring Chart

Figure 6.6 Sample Page from Andrew's Word Bank

Andrew's listening, thinking, speaking, reading, writing, spelling, and math—the seven domains identified in the legal definition of specific learning disabilities. An occupational therapist was brought onto Andrew's team to assess his handwriting, sensory integration, and motor skills. These assessments, in combination with the progress monitoring data, gave a comprehensive picture of Andrew's strengths and challenges to help the team determine how to meet his needs. The assessment would also be used to decide whether Andrew would need the more intensive services provided through the school's special education program.

Intensive Tier III for Students with Learning Disabilities

When the results of Andrew's assessments had been compiled, the team met again. This time the team members reviewed all of the assessment information and discussed Andrew's eligibility for special educational services. Andrew's assessment verified the observations that his teachers and parents had made and helped them understand the complexity of his needs. Andrew's strengths and challenges placed him in the above average range and also showed that he was eligible for learning disabilities services. The psychological report indicated that "Andrew's reading and writing deficits will impact all academic areas. But in spite of these problems, he understands concepts easily, has an advanced spoken vocabulary, and demonstrates superior verbal abilities. Andrew's listening comprehension is advanced, and his critical thinking is strong." The areas of difficulty included significant delays in visual-motor integration, early reading skills, and writing, and moderate difficulties with early math achievement. This information, along with the progress monitoring data, indicated that Andrew should be identified for special education services for learning disabilities. The team agreed that an IEP would be needed for Andrew to help him with the transition to first grade. A Summary of *RtI Approaches for Students with LD* can be accessed online.

TeachSource Digital Download

6-6b Curriculum and Instruction for Students with Learning Disabilities

Students with learning disabilities can be successful in school. Often the curricular adaptations and instructional modifications that help students with learning disabilities meet with success are also helpful to other students. As you read through the next section, think about Andrew, Tonya, Ray, and Juan, students you have met in this chapter, but also think about other students you have worked with. How might the strategies suggested here be useful in helping any student meet with greater success in school?

Strategies That Work to Support Students with Learning Disabilities

Earlier in this chapter we looked at the **Information Processing Model (IPM)** as a way to think about the impact that a learning disability can have. Table 6.3 shows strategies that can help address difficulties with each component of the IPM system. These strategies have been organized to show how the Universal Design for Learning (UDL) can be integrated with the IPM. UDL, as you recall, includes multiple ways to represent information, multiple ways to engage the learner, and multiple ways to assess learning. UDL corresponds directly with the Information Processing Model's input (representation of information), processing (engagement of the learner), and output (assessment of learning). Each of the strategies chosen for inclusion in Table 6.3 has an evidence basis Taken together, these strategies form a set of options that can be matched to the student's needs.

TABLE 6.3 Meeting the Needs of Students with Learning Disabilities: Information Processing and Universal Design for Learning

Input	UDL Representation
	Books on tape
	Manipulatives
	Video/Pictures
	Graphics/Charts
	Story boards
	Timelines
	Matrixes
	Highlighting
	Color coding
	Large font/bold
	Audio files
	Tactile graphics
	Use of all senses

(Continued)

TABLE 6.3 Meeting the Needs of Students with Learning Disabilities: Information Processing and Universal Design for Learning (*Continued*)

Processing		**UDL Engagement** Kinaesthetic Activities Discussions Debates Plays/Drama/Dance Music/Song Building models Writing activities (Journals, Poetry, Stories, Reports, Plays, Essays) Role Playing Simulation Games Critical Thinking Creative Thinking Research Skills Data Collection Data Analysis	
Output			**UDL Assessment** Discussions Debates Plays/Drama/Dance Drawing/Sculpting Music/Song Building models Experimentation Writing activities (Journals, Poetry, Stories, Reports, Plays, Essays) Charts/Graphs Pictures/Photos
Executive Function	Graphic organizers Thinking maps Concept maps Learning frames Outlines Chapter headings Advance organizers Syllabi Study guides Highlighting Prompts (verbal, visual)	Thematic lessons Big ideas Concept-based learning Metacognitive strategies Learning strategies Study skills	Rubrics (with open areas of student choice) Self-assessments Self-selected products
Emotional Context	Safe environment Structured rules Encouragement Rewards vs. punishment	Choice of activities Interest-based assignments Support available Study buddy Breaks for movement	Use of non-punitive assessments that reward student growth Risk-taking environment Recognition of effort Separate grades for content and form

Table 6.3 shows strategies to help with input difficulties. Remember that students with learning disabilities have problems with perception, or how the brain interprets the information, not with acuity or the ability of the sensory organ to take in stimuli. Ray, for example, has severe auditory processing difficulties. This means that it is very hard for him to take in information when he is reading or listening; but remember that Ray is very good with hands-on projects. The strategies that will support Ray need to focus on using multiple pathways for processing the information.

Some students with learning disabilities have problems with processing information, or thinking. Processing problems make it difficult for students to organize their thoughts and ideas and to retrieve information that they have learned. Ray has a very hard time with memory, and he often finds organizing his ideas to be a daunting task. What strategies given in Table 6.3 do you think would help Ray with his memory and organization of ideas?

Problems with output often create difficulties such as those faced by Tonya, who struggles with handwriting. Her behavior is becoming increasingly more disruptive as her frustration escalates. Reviewing Table 6.3, what kinds of things might be put in place to reduce Tonya's frustration with output difficulties, while supporting her strengths in thinking or processing? Some of the most challenging difficulties faced by students with learning disabilities are those that affect the executive function abilities. Ray has difficulty with maintaining attention and is impulsive. What strategies in Table 6.3 might help Ray develop better self-regulatory skills?

The emotional context within which individuals learn is also key to understanding the IPM. Thinking about Juan, how can his teachers create the emotionally supportive environment he will need to thrive in school? Often, when we begin to look at how we can support students with special learning needs, we find that the same strategies would benefit many of our other students. How would all of our students' learning be enhanced if some of the strategies you have identified for Andrew, Ray, Tonya, or Juan were more broadly implemented in general education classrooms?

TeachSource Video Connection

Watch the video "Including Students with High-Incidence Learning Disabilities: Strategies for Success." In this clip, an elementary teacher demonstrates and discusses how she works with students with learning disabilities. How does the use of graphic organizers help support these students, particularly those with executive function difficulties? What are some of the other educational adaptations she uses in her classroom? What other strategies might you recommend?

Watch online

Access to the Common Core Standards: Universal Design for Learning

COMMON CORE STATE STANDARDS

The National Research Center on Learning Disabilities at the University of Kansas has an outstanding website that gives evidence-based strategies for working with students with learning disabilities. Table 6.4 shares universal design strategies that can be used to give students with learning disabilities access to the Common Core State Standards.

Educational adaptations should be designed to minimize the impact of the disability while maximizing the student's ability to be successful. Accommodations that help the student become more autonomous and independent are optimal. The responsibility for learning and for self-regulation ultimately rests with the individual, but it is the job of educators to provide the support needed so that the individual can thrive (Berkeley, Scruggs, & Mastropieri, 2010).

National Center on Student Progress Monitoring
www.studentprogress.org

National Research Center on Learning Disabilities
www.nrcld.org

Assistive Technology for Students with Learning Disabilities

Assistive technologies play a key role in supporting students with learning disabilities (Dell, Newton, & Petroff, 2008). Assistive technology helps support students by minimizing the impact of their disability (Castellani & Warger, 2009). Students with learning disabilities can benefit from an array of assistive

TABLE 6.4 Using Universal Design Principles to Give Students with Learning Disabilities Access to the Common Core State Standards

Common Core Standard	Multiple Representations	Multiple Engagements	Multiple Assessments
Reading Standard Informational Text #9, Integration of Knowledge and Ideas, Grade 4 Integrate information from two texts on the same topic in order to write or speak about the subject knowledgeably.	Advance Organizers Text/Narrative Graphic Organizers Charts, Pictures, Tables Web-based Text Audiobooks Bold/Large Font Color-Coded Text for Main Ideas	Direct Instruction on Content & Strategies Reading using SQ3R (Survey, Question, Read, Recite, Review) Note Taking (outline headings) Discussions Small Group Applications Seminars Debates Develop Graphic Organizers: compare/contrast, concept webs, pros & cons, timelines, visual representations of information Writing Activities Prepare Presentations (PowerPoint, etc.)	Written Products (including note cards, outlines, concept webs, & drafts) Oral Presentations Charts, Graphs, Pictures Compare/Contrast Graphic Organizers Blogs Threaded Discussions online Documentary Film Letter to the Editor Mock Briefing for Decision Makers
Math standard #2, Operations and Algebraic Thinking, Grade 4 Multiply or divide to solve word problems involving multiplicative comparison, e.g. by using drawings and equations with symbol for the unknown number to represent the problem, distinguishing multiplicative comparison from additive comparison.	Hands-on Materials Charts, Graphs, Pictures Drawings Real-World Application Highlighted Problems (key words in color) Flash cards: Words to Math Symbol or Operations	Direct Instruction on Concepts with Modeling of Problem-Solving Strategies (I do, you all do, you do!) Use Hands-on Manipulatives Create side-by-side comparing Multiplication & Addition Create flash cards Draw Pictures Representing Process Use Calculators for Checking Create word problems based on real-world data collection Math talks on when to multiply rather than add Develop rhyme or rap on multiplying vs. adding	Traditional Written Assessment of Problem solving Student developed word problems on concepts Drawings, Pictures, Charts, Graphs Math Talks Students find real-world examples of when multiplication would be more efficient than addition

TeachSource Digital Download Access online

technologies including text-to-voice readers, audiobooks, calculators, voice-activated software, voice recorders, and electronic spellers. The role of assistive technology is to help learners become more autonomous in learning so that they can function more independently. Tonya, for example can use the computer with spell-check for her writing. This will allow her to revise more easily and should prevent most spelling errors. Each child's IEP or 504 plan should specify the assistive technology needed.

Technology and Media Division of Council for Exceptional Children
www.tamcec.org

Summary of Evidence-Based Practices for Students with Learning Disabilities

While each student is unique, there are some instructional approaches that we know help students with learning disabilities to master new content. Research supports teaching that is explicit, strategic, scaffolded, and metacognitive (Berkeley, Scruggs, & Mastropieri, 2010; Coleman, 2005; Deshler et al., 2001; Ellis et al., 2005; Faggella-Luby & Deshler, 2008; Graham & Harris, 2009; Maccini, Mulcahy, & Wilson, 2007; Wolgemuth, Cobb, & Alwell, 2008).

- **Explicit teaching** involves using language that is both precise and concise, giving clear examples of what is to be learned (avoiding vague, disorganized, and cluttered presentations of information), and providing schemas that show the organization of ideas to be learned (Berkeley, Scruggs, & Mastropieri, 2010; Fuchs et al., 2004; Gersten, Chard, Jayanthi, Baker, Morphy, & Flojo, 2009; Maccini et al., 2007; Scheuermann, Deshler, & Schumaker, 2009).
- **Strategic teaching** includes mnemonics, organizational strategies (such as graphic organizers, advance organizers, and outlines), and specific approaches that facilitate memory, making connections across information being learned, and the ability to apply information within new contexts (Berkeley, Scruggs, & Mastropieri, 2010; Deshler, Robinson, & Mellard, 2009; Gersten et al., 2009; Gildroy & Deshler, 2008; Wolgemuth et al., 2008).
- **Scaffolding** of instruction includes moving from concrete to abstract; from simple to complex, and from supported to independent (Coleman, 2005; Deshler, Robinson, & Mellard, 2009; Ellis et al., 2005).
- **Metacognitive approach** to teaching means helping students understand how to "think about their thinking" as they work to solve problems, activate or select strategies to use, and anchor learning in their memory. It also helps students with self-regulatory skills that facilitate learning (Coleman, 2005; Ellis et al., 2005; Deshler et al., 2001; Faggella-Luby & Deshler, 2008; Graham & Harris, 2009; Maccini et al., 2007; Wery & Nietfeld, 2010; Wolgemuth et al., 2008).

How does teaching that is explicit, strategic, scaffolded, and metacognitive fit with what you know about learning as information processing? The responsibility for learning and for self-regulation ultimately rests with the individual, but it is the job of educators to provide the support needed so that the individual can thrive. Fortunately, the child's family can play a critical role in the support system.

6-7 Family and Support Issues

Families are a critical part of the support system for individuals with learning disabilities. Because a learning disability is often not identified until the child reaches school age, the adjustment of the family to the child's needs comes later than it will in some other areas of disability. Families of children with learning disabilities are at risk themselves if they lack social support and are undergoing stress in coping with their child's disability. Because learning disabilities seem to run in families, parents may feel guilty that they have genetically passed this on to their child. Parents may also be struggling with some of the same problems that their child is experiencing, and so they may feel ill-equipped to help.

Families provide support to help their child find success.

© Ronnie Kaufman/Blend Images/Corbis

However, families are unique, and often they display amazing strengths as well as needs. Many recognize that their child with learning disabilities needs to be taught strategies (executive functions) for learning, as well as information and facts. Families are also key in convincing their children with learning disabilities that they are not "stupid" or "lazy," and families can play a major role in challenging their children to persist in the face of academic challenges (Shattell et al., 2008). Families know their child the best, so they are uniquely positioned to help teachers know what their child may need.

Teachers working closely with families can develop an IEP or 504 plan for the child. Strong partnerships with parents help both the teacher and the parents understand the child's needs. The parents play two key roles for their child with learning disabilities (Baum & Owen, 2004). The first is as an advocate for the child, working to ensure that the school addresses their child's needs. As teachers, it can sometimes be difficult when parents ask us to change our practices to better meet the needs of their child. But it is critical that we listen. If we have formed a strong partnership with the parents, we can work together, and the parents' knowledge of their child can help us meet the child's needs.

The second key role of parents is to create a support system at home to provide a safe and loving environment with the necessary structures for the child's success. Table 6.5 shows a few things parents can do to support their child with learning disabilities. Although the suggestions in Table 6.5 may seem like solid ideas for any family, the consistency, organization, and positive tones are even more critical for the healthy development of children with learning disabilities. The major task of every family with children is to prepare them for a meaningful life. This is no different for families who have a child who has learning disabilities.

Parenting is a full-time job, and it continues as the child moves through adolescence and young adulthood. For students with learning disabilities, family support during these transitions is critical.

TABLE 6.5 Ideas for Parental Support for Students with Learning Disabilities

- As much as possible, create a consistent household schedule for daily routines (bedtimes, wake-up times, dressing, leaving for school, meals, room cleaning, TV time, chores, and so forth).
- Develop clear guidelines for expected behavior framed from the positive (what you want, rather than what you don't want), and place these in a chart or contract if needed for a reminder.
- Consistently reinforce expectations from a positive point of view and, if necessary, develop consequences for inappropriate behavior. Consequences should be naturally linked to behavior. For example, if a child breaks a toy out of anger, the consequences may be to clean up the mess and to give one toy away to a child who does not have many toys. For a teenager who stays out too late and does not call, the consequence may be grounding for a week with no phone privileges.
- Use prompts and checklists for normal chores if needed (prepare a get-ready-for-school checklist to use the night before).
- Organize, organize, organize!
- Set up things you need for the next day the night before (put clothes out, make lunch, gather everything by the door, etc.).
- Provide a quiet study place and time.
- Check to see that homework has been done and verify that the agreed-on amount of time has been spent working on assignments.
- If needed, seek out the help of a tutor or study coach.
- Help your child regulate blood sugar with healthy snacks and foods.
- Help your child get appropriate exercise to regulate mood and stress.
- If medications are needed, monitor these and their impact.
- Monitor TV time, programs watched, computer time, and Internet access.
- Communicate your love and appreciation of your child often and in very concrete ways.
- If there are other siblings in the family, make sure that their needs are also addressed, and do not set siblings in competition for your approval.

TeachSource Digital Download Access online

6-8 Transitions to Postsecondary Life for Individuals with Learning Disabilities

The transition from adolescence to young adulthood can be a difficult time for anyone (Levine, 2005). The normal struggles with independence, identity formation, and lifestyle choices are compounded when a disability is added. The challenges of transition to adult life can be even more daunting for Latino or other immigrant youth with learning disabilities who face barriers due to language, citizenship status, and lack of community resources (Povenmire-Kirk, Lindstrom, & Bullis, 2010). Studies of risk-taking behaviors indicate that compared with their peers without learning disabilities, adolescents with learning disabilities engage more frequently in risk-taking behaviors such as smoking, using marijuana, acts of delinquency, aggression, and gambling (McNamara & Willoughby, 2010). Students with learning disabilities may also use passive coping strategies (ignoring the problem and hoping it will just go away) (Firth, Greaves, & Frydenberg, 2010). Given the increased likelihood of risk-taking behaviors in combination with limited coping strategies, counseling support may be important for adolescents with learning disabilities when they face difficult life choices.

MORAL DILEMMA

Classroom Modifications

Students with learning disabilities often need modifications in their assignments in order to minimize the impact of their disabilities and to facilitate their success. Kevin's IEP, for example, includes extended time on exams, no penalty for spelling errors on essays written in class, and the ability to use the computer for extensive written work. You are Kevin's high school English teacher, and one of your students has protested that giving these accommodations to Kevin is not fair. The protest is growing, and now several students have voiced their resentment of "Kevin's special treatment."

How will you handle this? What are your personal beliefs about this issue, and how will your beliefs affect your professional decisions? What does "fair" mean in the educational context for individuals with special learning needs?

High school dropout rates are significantly higher for individuals with learning disabilities than for their nondisabled peers (Zablocki & Krezminen, 2013). Dropping out of high school can have significant negative impact on life outcomes, limiting job opportunities and reducing income, while increasing unemployment and the risk of incarceration or arrest (Zablocki & Krezmien, 2013). Two factors associated with high dropout rates were disciplinary exclusions (being expelled from school or placed in suspension) and lower than average grades (Zablocki & Krezminen, 2013). When we reflect on the challenges of students like Ray and Juan we can understand how staying in school can sometimes feel overwhelming. Our responsibility as educators is to find ways to support the student's success through appropriate accommodations (Jung & Guskey, 2010). The development of solid transition plans during middle school helps increase the likelihood that the student will graduate (Landmark & Zhang, 2013).

Transition plans must take into account the student's current levels of performance, interests and aptitudes, postsecondary goals, and transition activities. These plans must also address who is responsible for implementing the plan and how the plan will be reviewed (Landmark & Zhang, 2013; Lerner & Johns, 2012). The plan may focus on transition to work or on postsecondary educational opportunities. Plans must also consider the student's cultural context and needs (Povenmire-Kirk et al., 2010). Unfortunately, the quality of the transition plan seems to differ for groups of students. Landmark and Zhang (2013) found that the student's ethnicity influenced the level of compliance with best practices evidenced in the student's transition plan. They found that plans for African-American students were less likely to be compliant on family involvement and employment preparation, and the plans for Hispanic students lacked compliance with annual goals. Thus, we see that students who will likely need the highest level of quality support for success both in high school and in their transition to adult life often receive less appropriate support (Balcazar et al., 2012; Lo, Mustian, Brophy, & White, 2011; Shumate, Campbell-Whatley, & Lo, 2012).

For many students with learning disabilities, school has been a place where they have struggled. Therefore, decisions about postsecondary options are filled with mixed emotions. Yet in spite of these challenges, students with learning disabilities are attending college in growing numbers (Coleman, 1994; DaDeppo, 2009; Kosine, 2007; Kravets, 2006). Colleges and universities that receive any federal funds may not discriminate against students with disabilities in their admissions policies; they are also legally required to provide support for students with disabilities if they are accepted. In spite of this requirement, supports and services vary widely from campus to campus and graduation rates for students with learning disabilities continue to lag behind those of their nondisabled peers (DaDeppo, 2009; Kirby, Silvestri, Allingham, Parrila, & LaFave, 2008). A solid support system at the college level is important for students with learning disabilities, because college is different from high school. Think of the many things that you, as a college student, are expected to do that were never part of your high school experiences (Kirby et al., 2008). Now imagine the impact these differences would have on you if you were also coping with a learning disability. Not all students with learning disabilities will go to college; many will choose other options. The most important thing is that during their early educational years we have prepared them for the many opportunities that will come their way in life, so that they can make sound personal decisions and meaningful contributions to those around them.

Summary

- The field of learning disabilities has evolved over many years as we come to understand more about child and brain development.
- Individuals with learning disabilities are a heterogeneous group, and they each have their own unique set of strengths and challenges.
- A comprehensive evaluation that includes overall cognitive abilities and academic achievements in combination with progress monitoring data is essential to accurately diagnose and plan services for students with learning disabilities.
- Although the origins of learning disabilities are largely unknown, the most commonly accepted cause is a problem related to how individuals process information at the neurological level.
- While the incidence of students identified with learning disabilities has gone down, this remains the largest group within special education.
- Determining if an English language learning student has a learning disability can be difficult, because of the challenges children face when mastering two or more languages. Because of this, a bilingual assessment is important.
- The information processing model (IPM) can be used to help understand learning disabilities and to help us plan interventions and supports to help students overcome their challenges.
- Recognizing the early indications of a learning disability allows for support to begin before a child has met with failure.
- The response to intervention (RtI) approach promotes the collaboration between general and special educators needed to fully support students with learning disabilities.
- Most students with learning disabilities are served in general education classrooms with appropriate modifications outlined in their IEPs or 504 plans to help them be successful.
- Evidence-based teaching approaches include the use of explicit, strategic, scaffolded, and metacognitive strategies to support learning.
- Instructional and assistive technologies can greatly minimize the impact of a learning disability.
- Families of students with learning disabilities are critical both in their advocacy role and in the home support they provide for their child.
- Because adolescents with learning disabilities often show poor judgment and engage in risk-taking behavior to a greater extent than their nondisabled peers, counseling support may be needed.
- More and more students with learning disabilities are attending college and finding ways to use their strengths in meaningful and productive lives.

Future Challenges

1. **How will the use of RtI affect the identification of students with learning disabilities and decisions about services for them?**
   As RtI becomes more widely used, patterns of identification and services are likely to change. We do not yet know what the full impact of this will be for students with learning disabilities. The following questions will need to

be addressed: How will RtI change which students are identified? Will RtI reduce the current overrepresentation of students from culturally diverse families? How will collaborative services be delivered in ways that ensure that the needs of students with learning disabilities are met? What will be done for those whose needs are in math or in other nonreading areas? How will parents' rights continue to be addressed as RtI becomes more prevalent?

2. **Increasing numbers of students with learning disabilities are attending colleges. What should be done to ensure smooth transitions and comprehensive services in the postsecondary setting?** The wonderful news is that more and more students with disabilities are attending colleges. The difficulty is that institutions of higher education may not be fully prepared to meet the needs of these students. Questions that will need to be answered include: How can we make sure that colleges and universities are equipped to meet the needs of students with disabilities? What changes are needed in institutional policies (e.g., admissions, drop-add periods, support services, housing, full-time student criteria, and so forth) in light of this changing student population?

3. **How can the needs of twice-exceptional students be addressed?** As more students are recognized as being twice-exceptional—that is, gifted and with disabilities—supports and services need to be developed to address their complex needs. We need to ensure that we nurture and address the strengths of twice-exceptional students through challenging learning experiences while providing appropriate supports for the areas of disability at the same time. How can collaborative teams work to include specialists in the education of students with special gifts or talents, to address the needs of twice-exceptional students?

TeachSource Digital Download Access online

Key Terms

anticipatory anxiety p. 188
attention deficit/hyperactivity disorders p. 188
auditory perception p. 184
collaborative problem-solving p. 181
dysgraphia p. 187
dyslexia p. 173
episodic memory p. 186
evidence-based interventions p. 177
executive processing p. 173
executive function p. 188
explicit teaching p. 199
heightened sensitivity p. 185
information processing model (IPM) p. 195
intervening hierarchy p. 191
long-term memory p. 185
metacognition p. 187
metacognitive approach p. 199
motor memory p. 186
progress monitoring p. 178
proprioceptive p. 185
scaffolding p. 199
self-regulatory skills p. 187
semantic memory p. 186
sensory integration p. 185
sensory memory p. 185
short-term memory p. 185
slope of improvement p. 193
standard protocol p. 193
strategic teaching p. 199
tactile defensiveness p. 185
twice-exceptional p. 173
unexplained underachievement p. 172
visual perception p. 184

Resources

References of Special Interest

Division for Learning Disabilities. (2007). *Thinking about response to intervention and learning disabilities: A teacher's guide.* Arlington, VA. This publication of the Council for Exceptional Children's Division for Learning Disabilities is a brief, user-friendly guide to how the RTI approach can be used with students who have learning disabilities. It provides an excellent overview for teachers who will be working to implement RTI in their schools and classrooms.

Trail, Beverly (2010). *Twice-exceptional gifted children: Understandings, teaching, and counseling gifted children. Waco, TX: Prufrock.* Comprehensive guidance is provided for teachers, parents, and students on how to cope with the complexities of gifts in combination with areas of extreme challenge. The use of student case stories brings the book to life and makes the strategies presented readily applicable for use with students who may face similar difficulties.

Lerner, L., & Johns, B. (2012). *Learning disabilities and related mild disabilities: Teaching strategies and new directions (12th ed.).* Belmont, CA: Wadsworth Cengage Learning. This is the definitive text on learning disabilities, written by leading authors in the field. It shares the current strategies and ideas for identifying and serving students with learning disabilities and those with mild disabilities. It is a critical body of work that forms an essential foundation for teachers who work with these students.

Schumaker, J. B., & Deshler, D. D. (2010). Using a tiered intervention model in secondary schools to improve academic outcomes in subject-area courses. In M. R. Shinn & H.M. Walker (Eds.), *Intervention for achievement and behavior problems in a three-tier model including RTI.* Bethesda, MD: National Association of School Psychologists.

Journals

Learning Disabilities Research and Practice. A publication of the Division for Learning Disabilities, Council for Exceptional Children
www.TeachingLD.org

Learning Disability Quarterly. The journal of the Council for Learning Disabilities **www.cldinternational.org.**

Journal of Learning Disabilities. A publication of the Hammill Institute on Disabilities, 512-451-3521.

Twice Exceptional Newsletter.
www.2enewsletter.com
An excellent resource for teachers and parents.

Professional Organizations

National Research Center on Learning Disabilities **www.nrcld.org**

Division for Learning Disabilities, Council for Exceptional Children **cec.sped.org**

National Center for Learning Disabilities **www.ncld.org**

Learning Disabilities Association (LDA) **www.ldanatl.org**

Council for Learning Disabilities **www.cldinternational.org**

CHAPTER

7

Children with Attention Deficit/Hyperactive Disorders (ADHD)

Standards Addressed in This Chapter

CEC

All CEC standards are addressed within this chapter. Please see the inside book covers for the complete list of the standards.

FOCUS QUESTIONS

7-1 How has the field of education for students with attention deficit/hyperactive disorder (ADHD) evolved?

7-2 What characteristics of students with ADHD can impact their learning and life success?

7-3 What is the definition of ADHD, how are students identified, and what are some causes of ADHD?

7-4 How is ADHD related to other areas of disabilities (e.g. learning disabilities, emotional and behavior disorders, communication difficulties)?

7-5 What are some of the pros and cons of using medication to address the challenges of ADHD?

7-6 What educational responses are needed to address the needs of students with ADHD?

7-7 How can families help support children with ADHD?

7-8 What challenges do youth with ADHD face in their transition from school to work and adult life?

Mermet/Photononstop/Glow images

"He is in constant motion, his energy is non-stop and his exuberance is sometimes overwhelming!" "She seems to be in a world of her own… it is hard to get her to focus and even though she is bright, tasks often remain half done."

Have you met these children? Have you taught these children? Do you know these children? Children with **attention deficit/hyperactive disorder (ADHD)** can find life, and especially school, a bit daunting. For some it is hard because their energy is difficult to harness, others have a hard time maintaining focus, and some struggle with both of these challenges. The major symptoms of ADHD—inattention, impulsivity, and hyperactivity—can lead to an inner chaos that manifests in fidgety, loud, disorganized, disruptive, off-task, or daydreaming behaviors, and missing or incomplete work. Children with ADHD form one of the largest groups of exceptional learners, and teaching them can test our stamina and our patience! In this chapter we will explore the field of ADHD, learn about the nature and causes of the disorder, and identify the needs of children with ADHD and explore how these needs can be met to support their success in school and life.

7-1 History of the Field of ADHD

The field of ADHD largely evolved through the medical community, as early as 1798, with physicians taking the lead in describing patients who seemed unusually fidgety, inattentive, and/or unruly (Rooney, 2011). After a 1917–1918 epidemic of encephalitis (acute inflammation of the brain), physicians saw an increase in patients with these symptoms; the term "minimum brain damage" came into use to describe this cluster of symptoms (Patterson & Spence, 1921). Dr. Kurt Goldstein (1936, 1939) noted that soldiers who had experienced traumatic brain injuries during World War II suffered from disorganization, perseveration, hyperactivity, and problems with figure-ground focus (discerning the foreground object from the background of a picture).

Educators began to describe children with similar behaviors in the 1930s and 1940s. Alfred Strauss studied children who were thought to have brain damage, and the term "Strauss Syndrome" was used to describe the cluster of characteristics shown in Figure 7.1 (Strauss & Lehtinen, 1947). William Cruickshank worked

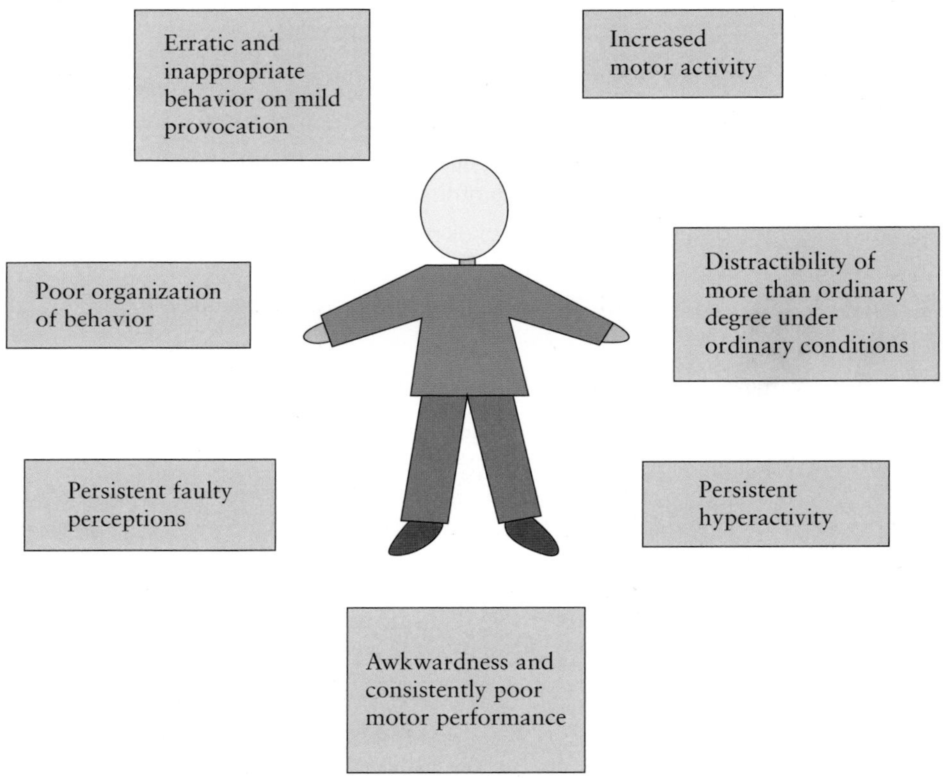

Figure 7.1 Strauss Syndrome, Early Description of Children with ADHD
Source: Baum, S., Olenchak, R., & Owen, S. (1998). Gifted student with attention deficits: Fact and/or fiction? Or, can we see the forest for the trees? *Gifted Child Quarterly*, 12(2). 96–104.

to identify educational strategies for children who were hyperactive and distractible, and his work helped lay the foundation for interventions we see in use today (Cruickshank, Bentzen, Ratzenburg, & Tannhauser, 1961).

The term minimal brain damage or dysfunction was replaced in the 1960s as the focus shifted to the child's hyperactivity. Today we recognize two forms of difficulties within the cluster we call attention deficit/hyperactivity disorders (ADHD): inattention (the inability to attend and focus) and hyperactivity (problems with impulsivity and self-regulation). Some individuals have a combination of challenges that include both inattention and hyperactivity/impulsivity.

Educators are involved in the identification of children with ADHD and with providing supports and services needed for their success. Physicians, however, are still taking the lead in looking at causes for ADHD, studying the brain and genetic links, helping parents and teachers identify children, and exploring the use of medications to help treat the symptoms. As with all children with exceptionalities, it takes a team!

7-2 Characteristics of Children with ADHD

ADHD presents in a variety of ways depending on the specific combinations of challenges and strengths for each child. Some children struggle most with attention and focus but do not seem to be hyperactive or to have excess energy. Other children are little dynamos whose energy seems to be impossible to contain. Some children like Angelina, below, struggle with both inattention and hyperactivity, making routine activities very challenging. Although many children encounter periodic problems with attention and follow-through, individuals with ADHD face lifelong challenges and need a variety of supports to help them be successful. The characteristics of children with ADHD are given in the *Diagnostic and Statistical Manual of Mental Disorders 5 (DSM-5)* (see Box 7.1). According to the American Psychiatric Association (APA; 2013b, p. 1), "ADHD is characterized by a pattern of behavior, present in multiple settings (e.g. school and home), that can result in performance issues in social, educational, or work settings." ADHD symptoms, which must present prior to age 12, fall into two categories: inattention and hyperactive/impulsive (see Box 7.1 on page 210). Children must have at least six symptoms, while older adolescents and adults must have five or more symptoms (APA, 2013a).

In reviewing these symptoms, it is easy to see why school would be difficult for a student with ADHD.

7-2a Let's Meet Angelina

Angelina, who is 6 years old, has ADHD. She is easily distracted and often distracts other students. Angelina makes careless mistakes in her work and seems to daydream much of the time. She is often out of her chair, sharpening a pencil, going to the supply table, or just wandering around the room. It is hard for her to concentrate in school, and her teacher refers to her as a "wiggle worm" and a "day dreamer." Angelina's parents feel that she is careless, and they find it frustrating that she cannot follow through with simple household chores, like feeding Binx, her cat, unless she is prompted several times. Her parents feel that they have become "nags" and that Angelina is changing from their fun-loving little girl into an angry and unhappy child. If you review the indicators of ADHD in Box 7.1, you will see that Angelina has several of the symptoms. Angelina's symptoms include failing to give close attention to the details and making careless mistakes, having difficulty sustaining attention, not following through on instructions, avoiding

BOX 7.1 Symptoms of Attention-Deficit/Hyperactivity Disorder

Note: Symptoms of inattention, hyperactivity, and impulsivity must have persisted for at least six months and occur in multiple setting (such as home, school, work) to a degree that is maladaptive and inconsistent with the developmental level of the individual.

Inattention

- Fails to give close attention to the details or makes careless mistakes in schoolwork, work, or other activities
- Has difficulty sustaining attention in tasks or play activities
- Does not seem to listen when spoken to directly
- Does not follow through on instructions and fails to finish schoolwork, chores, or duties in the workplace (not due to oppositional behavior or failure to understand instructions)
- Has difficulty organizing tasks and activities
- Avoids, dislikes, or is reluctant to engage in tasks that require sustained mental effort (such as schoolwork or homework)
- Loses things necessary for tasks or activities (e.g., toys, school assignments, pencils, books, or tools)
- Is easily distracted by extraneous stimuli
- Is forgetful in daily activities

Hyperactivity

- Fidgets with hands or feet or squirms in seat
- Leaves seat in classroom or in other situations in which remaining seated is expected
- Runs about or climbs excessively in situations in which it is inappropriate
- Has difficulty playing or engaging in leisure activities quietly
- Is often "on the go" or acts as if "driven by a motor"
- Talks excessively

Impulsivity

- Blurts out answers before questions have been completed
- Has difficulty awaiting turn
- Interrupts or intrudes on others (e.g., butts into conversations or games)

SOURCE: From *Diagnostic and Statistical Manual of Mental Disorders* 5th ed., TR.

tasks that require sustained mental effort, leaving her seat, being easily distracted, having difficulty playing quietly, and waiting her turn. Her ADHD symptoms include both inattention and hyperactive/impulsive challenges, and Angelina's difficulties impact her functioning at home and at school. To better understand the way ADHD impacts learning, we can look at the Information Processing Model (shown in ▸ Figure 7.2) for Angelina.

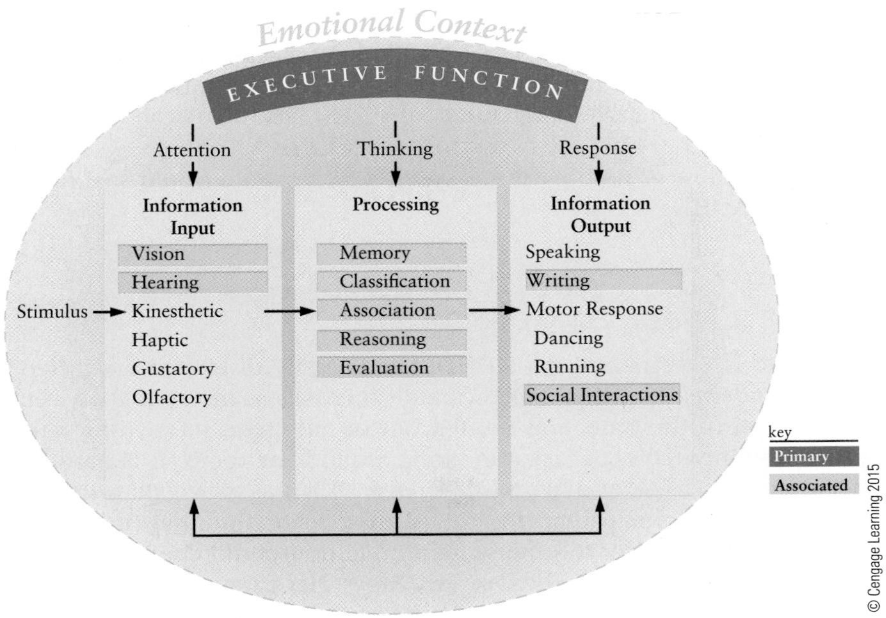

▸ **Figure 7.2 Information Processing Model for Angelina, a Child with ADHD**

TeachSource Digital Download Access online

7-2b Information Processing Model and ADHD

While the primary difficulties for children with ADHD are related to the executive function, individual children with ADHD show a range of executive function deficits (Lambek, Tannock, Dalsgaard, Trillingsgaard, Damm, & Thomsen, 2011). Some of the tasks that are managed by our executive function include: making plans, keeping track of time, keeping track of more than one thing at a time, integrating past knowledge for current decision-making, evaluating ourselves and our work, knowing when we need to ask for help, and regulating our behaviors. Since the executive function oversees attention, decision making, and self-regulation, all other areas of information processing are also impacted by ADHD. It is as though the child's ADHD throws a blanket over her or his ability to process information; sometimes medications can lift this blanket. Figure 7.2 shares the information processing model for Angelina, a child with ADHD. Angelina has the combined form of ADHD with inattentiveness and hyperactivity, and we can see that several areas of information processing are impacted, including all of the central processing areas and also social interactions.

For children with ADHD, distractibility occurs because they are unable to screen out stimuli that are irrelevant to the present task. Therefore, all input seems to be given equal weight, and the information-processing system can be overwhelmed. Imagine being in a store with 45 televisions tuned to 45 different channels. Trying to watch only one program would be difficult because all the TVs are producing sound and visual images that are competing for your attention. This is similar to the experience that individuals with ADHD have when environmental stimulation is abundant. For an individual with ADHD, like Angelina, a typical busy classroom may be challenging with its numerous distractions. This is the world as she knows it, and it is no wonder that she finds it overwhelming at times.

7-3 ADHD Definition, Identification, and Causes

The definition of ADHD has undergone several changes as our understanding of how children learn and our knowledge of neuroscience have increased (Nigg, Tannock, & Rohde, 2010). The federal regulations for special education, the Individuals with Disabilities Education Act of 2004 (IDEA 2004), include attention deficit disorder or attention deficit/ hyperactivity disorder within the category of "Other Health Impairment," shown in Box 7.2.

Each area included within other health impairments is medically related, with diagnosis and treatment under the care of a physician. Each also has educational repercussions that will likely impede the child's ability to be successful in school if educational support is not provided. This is why they are included in the educational regulations for children with disabilities. Doctors and mental health workers rely on the *Diagnostic and Statistical Manual of Mental Disorders (DSM-5)* to guide their identification of ADHD (see Box 7.1, presented earlier).

The *DSM-5* (APA, 2013a), places ADHD within the cluster of Neurodevelopmental Disorders, which also includes Learning Disabilities, separating ADHD conceptually from oppositional defiant and conduct disorders. This organization emphasizes the relationship between the difficulties children experience with attention and impulsivity, which are behavioral concerns, and problems with learning or academic outcomes (Tannock, 2013). Ability to attend (to pay attention) overlaps with ability to learn; children with ADHD may find learning more difficult, while children with learning disabilities may also have problems attending and/or controlling their impulses. Throughout this chapter we will explore the comorbidity of ADHD with other areas of exceptionality, examining the relationships and overlap

BOX 7.2 Federal Regulations for Other Health Impairments

(9) Other Health Impairment means having limited strength, vitality, or alertness, including a heightened alertness to environmental stimuli, that results in limited alertness with respect to the educational environment, that:

(i) Is due to chronic or acute health problems such as asthma, attention deficit disorder or attention-deficit/ hyperactivity disorder, diabetes, epilepsy, a heart condition, hemophilia, lead poisoning, leukemia, nephritis, rheumatic fever, sickle cell anemia, and Tourette syndrome; and

(ii) Adversely affects a child's educational performance

SOURCE: Individuals with Disabilities Education Improvement Act of 2004, PL 108-446, U. S. Department of Education, Washington, DC.

TeachSource Digital Download Access online

Fuse /Getty Images

Parents often seek help from their pediatrician when they firs suspect that their child may have ADHD.

across areas of concern. **Comorbidity** is the coexistence of other areas of disability or other mental health concerns along with the primary disorder, making diagnosis and treatment more complicated. Comorbidity is particularly important, as ADHD may exist with several other disabilities and disorders, including learning disabilities, emotional and behavior disorders, communication disorders, and other mental health challenges (National Institute of Mental Health [NIMH], 2008).

7-3a Identification of Students with ADHD

Students with ADHD can legally qualify for services through the Other Health Impaired category (see Box 7.1) of IDEA 2004 or they can be found eligible for services through Section 504 of the Rehabilitation Act (1973). Under IDEA, students receive an individualized education plan (IEP) while under the Rehabilitation Act students get a 504 plan for support; these will be discussed later in the chapter. The process for identification is similar regardless of the path to eligibility for services. Students who do not qualify under the requirements for IDEA may still be eligible for support through 504.

Identifying a student as having ADHD should be a team effort, with input from key individuals who know the child well and can document behavioral, social, emotional, and academic impacts of the disability across a variety of settings. Parents and teachers often provide information through an observational checklist showing how the student performs and indicating areas of concern (Rooney, 2011). Parent reports have been shown to be very reliable (Ramtekkar, Reiersen, Todorv, & Todd, 2010). Student input can also be key to helping with identification because students themselves can share information directly related to their experiences. Table 7.1 shares some sample items from the Conners-3 Scale (Conners, 2008), a rating scale for identifying ADHD. A descriptive list of several other rating scales can be accessed online.

Many of the checklists have parent and teacher versions, and a few also have a student version to gather input. All of the scales help establish patterns of behavior. In looking specifically at the intensity and duration of this behavior, we can determine if the child has ADHD. Identifying students through checklists and rating scales can be challenging, however, because perceptions can sometimes be biased. One area where potential bias may influence referrals for ADHD is gender. In school- or

TABLE 7.1 Sample Items from the Conners Scale (Conners-3)

Conners-3 ADHD Rating Scale: The following are sample items from the Conners-3 Teacher Rating Scale, used for students ages 6–18. The full scale contains 113 items. Respondents consider the student's behavior for the last month and select 0 for *not true at all*, 1 for *just a little true*, 2 for *pretty much true*, and 3 for *very much true*. A separate scale is used for parents' responses; students ages 8–18 may also complete a self-report form. In addition to ADHD, the Conners-3 also addresses comorbid disorders such as Oppositional Defiant Disorder and Conduct Disorder.

Category	Sample Item
Inattention	3. Has a short attention span.
	37. Doesn't pay attention to details; makes careless mistakes.
	44. Is sidetracked easily.
	60. Avoids or dislikes things that take a lot of effort and are not fun.
	86. Gets bored easily.
Hyperactivity/Impulsivity	1. Leaves seat when he/she should stay seated.
	4. Fidgets or squirms in seat.
	9. Blurts out answers before the question has been completed.
	26. Talks out of turn.
	83. Talks nonstop.

SOURCE: Conners, C. K. (2008). *Conners-3 teacher assessment report*. North Tonawanda, NY: Multi-Health Systems, Inc.

community-based settings, boys are identified two to three times more often than girls, and the girls who are identified often have higher levels of impairment (Coles, Slavec, Bernstein, & Baroni, 2012). Coles et al. (2012) found that teachers' interpretations of student needs were different for boys and girls. Fifty teachers were given eight matching vignettes, four girls and four boys, depicting students with ADHD. They were asked to rank how likely they would be to refer each child for treatment and to indicate their treatment preferences. Box 7.3 gives a sample vignette for Michael and one for Michelle, showing two students who met the criteria for ADHD given by the *DSM-IV* (APA, 2000; the guidelines in use at the time of the study).

Teachers in the study rated girls like Michelle as having more severe impairments than boys like Michael, when hyperactivity and opposition defiant disorders were included in both vignettes. This is an indication that the teachers saw these behaviors as more "abnormal" for girls than for boys. The authors concluded that hyperactive and impulsive behaviors were more likely to lead to teacher referrals in general and that when these were displayed by girls, the impairments were perceived as more serious (Coles et al., 2012). They also indicate that girls with ADHD more often show symptoms of inattention-without-hyperactivity and that perhaps this is why girls may be overlooked by teachers.

7-3b Families from Culturally/Linguistically Diverse Backgrounds

Another area of potential bias is with the identification of children from culturally/linguistically diverse and/or economically disadvantaged families (Gerdes, Lawton, Haack, & Dieguez Hurtado, 2013). Using some rating scales, African-American

BOX 7.3 Vignettes of Michael and Michelle, Two Students with ADHD

A. Michael is a 9-year-old boy. His teacher describes him as having difficulty keeping his attention focused in work and play activities. Michael often makes careless mistakes in his work and fails to pay close attention to details. Although he is obedient and seems to understand instructions, Michael frequently fails to complete his assigned duties, work, and chores. In addition, Michael seems to avoid work that requires sustained mental effort, such as schoolwork and homework. When spoken to directly, Michael often appears to not listen, as if he is off in a daze. It is likely that Michael's inability to sustain attention contributes to his difficulty in organizing everyday tasks. Michael experiences the same problems both at home and at school, and has been this way since before kindergarten.

B. Michelle is a 9-year-old girl. Her teacher describes her as forgetful in her daily activities as she frequently loses or misplaces items necessary for tasks and activities, such as notebooks, books, pencils, keys, or gym shoes. It is likely that Michelle's forgetfulness contributes to her difficulty in organizing her daily duties, work, and activities. As well, Michelle displays difficulty in keeping her attention focused during tasks and leisure activities, as she is easily distracted by people, events, and trivial details in her environment. Furthermore, she displays a tendency to procrastinate and is often reluctant to begin or engage in challenging academic and mental tasks, such as written work. Michelle experiences the same problems both at home and at school, and has been this way since before kindergarten.

SOURCE: Coles, E. K., Slavec, J., Bernstein, M., & Baroni, E. (2012). Exploring the gender gap in referrals for children with ADHD and other disruptive behavior disorders. *Journal of Attention Disorders, 16*(2), 101–108.

students are twice as likely to be identified with ADHD (Flowers & McDougle, 2010). The concerns for identification patterns of ethnic minority and poor children are complex:

- Are we over identifying some students because the rating scales are primarily designed for and normed with white, middle-class students?
- Do additional risk factors for children whose families live in poverty increase the number of children with ADHD?
- How do the family's cultural expectations of child behaviors impact their view of what is "appropriate"?

Researchers are exploring these questions to help us understand how ADHD identification interacts with the family's culture and economic status.

Basch (2011) looked at the impact of ADHD identification on urban poor students, noting the increased likelihood of identification for ADHD as well as higher absenteeism and dropout rates for these students. The students also experienced more social rejection and greater difficulties with peer relationships than students without ADHD. The difficulties of urban poor students with ADHD are compounded, because while there is higher likelihood that they will be identified as ADHD, they are less likely than white, middle-class students with ADHD to receive consistent pharmacological therapy to help them manage their symptoms (Basch, 2011; Pastor & Reuben, 2005). Flowers and McDougle (2010) reviewed rating scales to look at their use with African-American children. Data supported the use of the Terry and the Vanderbilt Attention-Deficit/Hyperactivity Disorder scales for diagnosing African-American students with ADHD. The authors call for greater cultural sensitivity, more representative normative samples, and an increased awareness of the need for culturally appropriate assessment tools for use in the identification process of students with ADHD.

Gerdes et al. (2013) looked at culturally appropriate assessments for Latino children and found that there were potential problems with the use of rating scales primarily designed for white families. They looked at the Disruptive Behavior Disorders Rating Scale Spanish version (DBD-S) and found that while both subscales (Inattentive and Hyperactive/Impulsive) were psychometrically sound, the Hyperactive/Impulsive scale may not be culturally appropriate for some Latino families. While the family's degree of acculturation must be considered, Latino families, relative to Caucasian families, may hold different beliefs regarding mental health problems. Latino families may hold more collectivist values, may emphasis spiritual origins for mental health difficulties, and may believe in an external locus of control (that is, the problems are not intrinsic to the child) (Skinner, Correa, Skinner, & Baily, 2001). This combination of beliefs and values may predispose Latino families to be more accepting of the child's behaviors. Gerdes et al. alert us to the fact that just because an instrument is technically sound does not mean that it is a culturally appropriate assessment. They call for a combination of diagnostic approaches, including a focus on the child's functional behaviors (e.g. how they relate to their peers, academic achievements) in addition to the current focus on the ADHD symptoms (such as failing to give close attention to the details).

Going Beyond Checklists

In addition to observational checklists and rating scales, intelligence and achievement tests are often used to show patterns of performance that are associated with ADHD. Box 7.4 shares Dr. Emily King's thoughts on what psychologists can look for during their assessments of children for ADHD.

There are many facets to a comprehensive assessment used to determine if a child has ADHD. Parents, teachers, and other adults provide observational documentation of the child's behavior across different settings and input may also be included from the child. Assessments will often include measures of cognitive abilities and achievement, like those described by Dr. King. Taken together this information is used to establish the intensity and duration of the behaviors to determine if a child has ADHD.

Complications Impacting Identification of Children with ADHD

Identification is complicated because there is no single test that indicates ADHD. Diagnostic decisions need to be made by a licensed health professional, following the guidelines given in the *DSM-5* (2013, see Box 7.1) and using information from multiple sources (NIMH, 2008). Health professionals need to rule out other possible causes for the child's difficulties. Other causes of inattention, impulsivity, and hyperactivity that need to be ruled out can include:

- Undetected seizures that may be associated with other medical conditions
- Middle ear infections that cause hearing problems
- Undetected hearing or vision difficulties
- Any medical problem that could affect thinking or behavior
- Learning disabilities
- Anxiety or depression
- Significant or sudden changes in the child's family, school, or environment (NIMH, 2008).

Symptoms of ADHD can vary depending on the age and gender of the child and cultural expectations of behavior can also influence identification; individuals within a given category may vary greatly (Frick & Nigg, 2012). Questions that a specialist asks to determine if the child's symptoms warrant formal identification as ADHD include:

- Are the behaviors excessive and long term, and do they affect all aspects of the child's life?
- Do they happen more often in this child compared with the child's peers?
- Are the behaviors a continuous problem or a response to a temporary situation?
- Do the behaviors occur in several settings or only in one place, such as the playground, classroom, or home? (NIMH, 2008, p.6).

Symptoms also fall along a continuum ranging from mild to severe, and often individuals who do not meet the diagnostic criteria for ADHD are still in need

BOX 7.4 What Do Psychologists Look For When Assessing a Child for ADHD?

Emily King

Dr. Emily King is a licensed psychologist and the owner of an independent private practice in Raleigh, North Carolina, where she provides psychological evaluation, therapy, and consultation services for children, adolescents, and families. She has extensive experience working with children with learning disabilities, ADHD, oppositional behavior, anxiety, depression, Autism Spectrum Disorders, and developmental disabilities. Dr. King is experienced in conducting psycho-educational evaluations, developing academic-based interventions, and consulting with teachers and parents to improve children's functioning by supporting their emotional, behavioral, and academic success. She also conducts cognitive and memory assessments as part of a multidisciplinary team at the Diagnostic Teaching Clinic at North Carolina State University. Dr. King received her Ph.D. in School Psychology from the University of North Carolina at Chapel Hill after completing an internship in a large urban-suburban school district in Houston, Texas. She continued her post-doctoral training in the public schools in Houston before returning to Raleigh to practice psychology. You can contact Dr. King through her website at www.dremilyking.com.

What assessments do you typically use for intelligence and achievement when diagnosing a child's ADHD?

The most common evaluation instruments for intelligence, or cognitive ability, are the Wechsler scales and the Woodcock-Johnson Tests of Cognitive Abilities, 3rd ed. (WJ-III Cog). Other cognitive batteries include the Differential Ability Scale, 2nd ed. (DAS-II) and the Stanford-Binet Intelligence Scales, 5th ed. (SB5). Let's look at the Wechsler scales to see how they can be used in the assessments of children with ADHD.

The Wechsler scales include the following:

1. Wechsler Preschool and Primary Scale of Intelligence, 4th ed. (WPPSI–IV)
   — for ages 2 years, 6 months to 7 years, 7 months
2. Wechsler Intelligence Scale for Children, 4th ed. (WISC-IV)
   — for ages 6 years, 0 months to 16 years, 11 months
3. Wechsler Adult Intelligence Scale, 4th ed. (WAIS-IV)
   — for ages 16 years, 0 months to 90 years, 11 months

I most commonly use the WISC-IV for school-age children. The WISC-IV provides four index scores, which together determine a full scale intelligence score. Here is a summary paragraph I include in all of my reports describing the WISC-IV:

> The WISC-IV measures an individual's ability using ten core and five optional subtests which are grouped into the following four global areas: Verbal Comprehension Index, which evaluates a child's ability to respond orally to questions, Perceptual Reasoning Index, which assesses a child's ability to manipulate concrete materials or process visual stimuli to problem-solve non-verbally, Working Memory Index, which measures a child's short-term memory, and Processing Speed Index, which assesses the efficiency of a child's cognitive processing. These four areas then yield a Full Scale score indicating a child's overall ability.

The most commonly used achievement instruments are the Wechsler Individual Achievement Test, 3rd ed. (WIAT-III) and the Woodcock-Johnson Tests of Achievement (WJ-III). Another commonly used achievement instrument in the public schools is the Kaufman Test of Educational Achievement, 2nd ed. (KTEA-II). Each of these tests yields standard scores related to reading, mathematics, written expression, and oral language.

What patterns are you looking for within these assessments that indicate the child might have difficulties with attending or impulse control?

A test examiner most often uses clinical observations of behavior during the administration of these tests to determine impulse control or attention concerns. In regards to impulse control, for instance, children may impulsively grab test materials or be extremely eager to begin testing before having received the directions or test prompt. Some individuals may have an impulsive response style where they quickly give a response, then change their response after looking at all the options on the page of a visual task, for instance. At times, an individual's struggles with impulsivity or inattention may be exacerbated when presented with a challenging academic task, such as writing, and they may need verbal prompts repeated in order to ensure they have heard the directions. In regards to inattention, examiners also use clinical observations during testing sessions to determine if the individual is overly distracted by extraneous noises in the environment, needs directions repeated, or needs support to remain on task. For instance, some children become easily distracted by testing materials on the table or other items in the testing room and begin talking about those items rather than the task at hand.

Using the WISC-IV as an example, examiners often look for weaknesses on the Working Memory Index, which contains two auditory short-term memory tasks, when concerned about attention issues. If a child has difficulty focusing or maintaining a steady work pace due to distractibility while completing the Processing Speed tasks (both timed pencil and paper tasks), his or her score may be impacted by this behavior, which would be noted through the examiner's clinical observation.

Additionally, a memory test can be used to help determine attention/concentration. Commonly used memory scales include the Wide Range Assessment of Memory and Learning, 2nd ed. (WRAML2) and the Children's Memory Scale (CMS). Both tests ask an individual to complete visual and verbal memory tasks, some

BOX 7.4 What Do Psychologists Look For When Assessing a Child for ADHD? (*Continued*)

presented within a context, such as a story or picture, or without a context, such as a word list or visual design. The WRAML2 also has two specific tasks, one presented visually and one verbally, measuring attention and concentration. .Each task requires attention and allows the examiner to observe an individual's behavior and approach to these tasks.

An additional test often given to identify attention concerns is the Conners' Continuous Performance Test II Version 5 (CPT-II V.5; Conners, 2013). The CPT-II involves an individual responding to a series of target letters presented on a computer screen. Results indicate the likelihood of an individual having attention difficulties and can be used in conjunction with parent and teacher rating scales when investigating characteristics of an attention disorder. The CPT-II can also be used to learn more about individuals with impulsivity or activity control concerns.

Children with Attention Deficit/Hyperactivity Disorder (ADHD) often perform lower than expected on working memory tasks, given their performance in other areas. While a low score on working memory tasks does not directly indicate a diagnosis of ADHD (observations and teacher/parent report across settings must be gathered), children with ADHD often benefit from having memory testing in order to determine any strengths or weaknesses in their learning profile so that teachers can best plan how to teach them new information.

SOURCE: Interview with Dr. Emily King, Licensed Psychologist, Wake County, NC conducted by Dr. Mary Ruth Coleman. Reprinted by permission.

of supports to be successful. For students who do not meet the criteria, the RtI approach discussed later in the chapter may be of great help, with targeted Tier II supports that do not usually require formal identification.

Prevalence of ADHD

It is difficult to establish with any precision the actual prevalence rates for students with ADHD (Ramtekkar et al., 2010). Some of the factors that make it difficult include:

- Students who are diagnosed in private or clinical settings may receive medication/support and may not be included in school special education counts.
- ADHD is part of the Other Health Impaired category and counts for this category include several other areas of concern, making it hard to parse out the specific count for ADHD.
- Many students with ADHD receive supports through 504 plans, or targeted support at Tier II within an RtI approach, and so they do not appear in the school counts for special education (Rooney, 2011).
- Comorbidity of ADHD, when it is the secondary area of disability, further complicates the count.

Because of these challenges, we see wide variance in reported numbers of students with ADHD.

Prevalence rates for ADHD vary; estimates suggest 3–7 percent of school-age children, or approximately 5 million children ages 5–17, have some degree of ADHD (Pastor & Reuben, 2008). However, because symptoms of ADHD manifest on a continuum from mild to severe, only around 1 percent of these children are likely to be counted as qualifying for special educational services. Boys (12 percent) are more than twice as likely to be identified as girls (5 percent) (Pastor & Reuben, 2008). Students from families with higher educational levels (Merikangas, He, Brody, Fisher, Bourdon, & Koretz, 2010) and those receiving Medicaid health insurance (Centers for Disease Control and Prevention, 2010) are more likely to be identified. White (non-Hispanic) children comprise the largest group of children with ADHD, 4.1 million (representing 8.7 % of all white students); however, given the larger proportion of black children at 904,000 (9.8% of all black students) we see that these children are more likely to be identified as ADHD than white children. Only 5 percent (659,000) of Hispanic or Latino children are identified with ADHD and no information was given for children of Asian or Pacific Islander backgrounds (Pastor & Reuben, 2008). These data show that there are differences across groups of children with regards to identification of ADHD.

7-3c Neurological, Genetic, and Environmental Causes of ADHD

ADHD is a complex disability with possible neurological, genetic and/or environmental causes. These causes often overlap influencing the degree and specific manifestation of the dysfunction. While it is impossible to completely untangle the causes of ADHD, we can look at each area separately to get a sense of why some individuals have ADHD and how the specific manifestation of the problems can differ from one person to another. We can also begin to see how genetics and environment may influence identification patterns, leading to higher rates for boys and for children living in poverty.

Neurological Causes of ADHD

Several studies examining differences in brain size, structure, development, and function have established a clear neurological basis for ADHD. In their meta-analysis of 55 studies, Cortese et al. (2012) found that when compared with typically developing children, the brains of individuals with ADHD seem to develop more slowly, reaching key maturation points somewhat later, and that the size of some brain areas is smaller. These findings were replicated in additional studies by Shaw et al. (2011), and Qui et al. (2011). Studies with MRI (magnetic resonance imaging) show differences in brain structure and function that seem to be linked to problems with executive functioning including off-task behaviors, attention, planning, sequencing for problem solving, time management, and the ability to keep future consequences of present actions in mind (Qui et al., 2011; Mostofsky, Reiss, Lockhart, & Denckla, 2010). ADHD-related dysfunctions are impacted by multiple neurological systems. These systems include higher-level cognitive functioning, sensorimotor processing, and use of the "default network" involved in mental focus (Cortese et al., 2012; Konrad & Eickhoff, 2010). As the brain develops, the areas of dysfunction change, showing differing patterns of impact for children and adults (Frodl and Skokauskas, 2012). Gender differences must also be kept in mind; because most of the neurological studies have been done with males, we need to remember that we may see somewhat different patterns for females with ADHD (Frodl and Skokauskas, 2012). Researchers are currently working to establish the genetic factors underlying the neurological differences of students with ADHD (Durston, 2010).

Because of genetic factors, it is not unusual for both fathers and sons to have ADHD.

Genetic Causes for ADHD

ADHD runs in families; approximately one-third of the fathers who were diagnosed in childhood have a child who is also diagnosed (Rooney, 2011). Twin and family studies have shown that ADHD is highly heritable and work is underway to establish the genetic factors involved (NIMH, 2008). According to Durston (2010) genetic factors can account for up to 80 percent of phenotypic variance. **Phenotype**, the set of observable characteristics of an organism, includes physical form, development, and biochemical make-up. Because clear phenotypical differences have been established for the brains of individuals with ADHD, mapping these differences to genetic factors should be possible. While multiple genes may contribute to the phenotype of ADHD, no genome-wide significant associations have been firmly established (Neale et al., 2010; U.S. Department of Education, 2008a). Work continues on several gene candidates that offer promise for establishing the genetic basis for ADHD (Neale et al., 2010). Our genes, however, only provide a blueprint for our development, and genes alone do not determine our specific outcomes. The environment also contributes to how our personal strengths and weaknesses will evolve.

Environmental Causes for ADHD

Environmental factors that are potentially linked with ADHD include cigarette and alcohol use by the mother during pregnancy, premature birth, high levels of exposure to lead, and brain damage or injury (NIMH, 2008; U.S. Department of Education, 2008a). Commonly held beliefs about the role of sugar and food additives as causes of ADHD have also been studied. These studies seem to discount the role of sugar in increasing symptoms of ADHD, but they do provide some support for the role of food additives in increasing symptoms of hyperactivity (NIMH, 2008). Food additives like artificial colors and preservatives may be linked to increased activity levels. Further research is underway to explore these findings (NIMH, 2008).

7-4 Comorbidity: ADHD and Other Areas of Disability or Concern

As we have discussed earlier in this chapter, the condition of ADHD often coexists with other categories of disability and other mental health disorders. Current estimates indicate that between 40 and 60 percent of children with ADHD will have an additional area of concern (Anastopoulos et al., 2011). Almost one-third of all children with ADHD have learning disabilities, and many experience difficulties with reading, math, and written communications (U.S. Department of Education, 2008a). Other commonly occurring areas of disability include emotional and behavioral disorders and communication disorders (U.S. Department of Education, 2008a). Mental health concerns are also frequently associated with ADHD; these include: conduct disorders, oppositional defiant disorders, mood disorders, anxiety, depression, bipolar disorder, sleep disorders, bed-wetting, substance abuse, tics, and Tourette Syndrome (Rooney, 2011; U.S. Department of Education, 2008a). There also seems to be a linkage between aggressive behavior and ADHD, putting children at increased risk for social difficulties and school failure (Rooney, 2011). The challenge of the mental health worker or clinician is to determine what symptoms belong to the ADHD, which ones reflect any associated disorders, and which ones may be associated with both ADHD and the secondary condition.

Children and Adults with Attention-Deficit Hyperactivity Disorder
http://www.chadd.org

Children with comorbid disorders seem to have poorer overall function than children with ADHD alone (Booster, DuPaul, Eiraldi, & Power, 2012). Different patterns for social and academic performance are associated with internalizing disorders (mood or anxiety disorders) and externalizing disorders (such as oppositional defiant and conduct disorders). Children with comorbid externalizing disorders have more difficulties with social interactions, and children with both externalizing and internalizing disorders have greater problems with homework and academics (Booster, DuPaul, Eiraldi, & Power, 2012). Self-regulation problems and emotional liability are also associated with ADHD, and these may lead to the secondary problems we see with internalizing disorders (Anastopoulos et al., 2011). Not surprisingly, children with any other condition comorbid with their ADHD show increased academic difficulties (Barnard-Brak, Sulak, & Fearon, 2011). As the number of comorbidities increases, the need for cross-sector coordinated care also increases. This care must be tailored to the specific pattern of strengths and challenges faced by the individual child and family (Larson, Russ, Kahn, & Halfon, 2011).

7-5 Using Medication for ADHD Symptoms

Rasheed, an 8-year-old, has been diagnosed with ADHD and with some aspects of EBD (emotional behavioral disorders) as well. The most frequent description of Rasheed is that he is "out of control." His constant activity seems almost "driven," according to his mother. Rasheed's doctor, impressed by the intensity of his behavior, has prescribed Ritalin as a way to calm Rasheed and help him control his behavior so that he has an opportunity to learn. The Ritalin seems to help Rasheed control his impulsive behaviors, but his mother worries about possible side effects from taking medicine. Many individuals with ADHD may benefit from medications to help them focus and sustain their attention; however, there may also be some drawbacks to this, and Rasheed's mother is correct to be concerned. Rasheed's teachers are aware that he is taking Ritalin, and they are helping his parents keep track of any changes in his behaviors to monitor the impact of the medications.

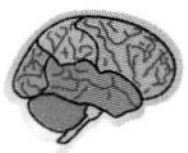

Pharmacological interventions for ADHD are one of the most common treatments. While medication will not make them learn, for some children it may give them an opportunity to learn. An estimated 66 percent of the children with ADHD between the ages of 4 and 17 received medication as at least part of their treatment. Children between ages 11 and 17 showed the highest prevalence for medication and boys were almost 3 times more likely to take medication than girls (Centers for Disease Control and Prevention, 2011). The most typical medications prescribed for children with ADHD are stimulants, which may seem counterintuitive; why would you give stimulant medication to a child who is already hyperactive, impulsive, or who has difficulty controlling his or her behavior? Stimulant medications, used with children with ADHD, are believed to affect the portion of the brain that produces **neurotransmitters**, the chemical agents at the nerve endings that help move electrical impulses among nerve cells (U.S. Department of Education, 2008a). The boost that stimulants give in neurotransmitter production increases the child's capacity for attending, controlling their impulses, and reducing their hyperactivity (U.S. Department of Education, 2008a). A list of ADHD medications that are approved by the U.S. Food and Drug Administration is given in Table 7.2.

Nonstimulant medications that are sometimes used with children with ADHD include anti-depressant, antipsychotic, anti-anxiety, and mood-stabilizing drugs. While medications seem to have a beneficial effect for many children with ADHD, they are not without problems. All drugs will have some side effects. The most common side effects for stimulant medications include: decreased appetite/weight loss, insomnia and sleep problems, nervousness, mild headaches, and stomachaches (NIMH, 2008). Less common, but more serious, side effects can include: slowed physical growth, tic disorders, problems with thinking or social interactions, and increased suicidal thoughts (NIMH, 2008). When we read the list of possible side effects, we can understand why some parents, like Rasheed's mother, and some children are concerned about taking medications.

Side effects can often be avoided or minimized. Adjustments can be made in the type of medication, the dosage levels, and the time and manner the drug is taken. The determination of medication protocols is the responsibility of medical personnel and is *not* done by educators. Educators, however, do have a clear role in helping to monitor the effects of medication. The feedback teachers give helps doctors

TABLE 7.2 FDA-Approved Medications for ADHD

Trade Name	Generic Name	Approved Age
Adderall	amphetamine	3 and older
Adderall XR	amphetamine (extended release)	6 and older
Concerta	methylphenidate (long acting)	6 and older
Daytrana	methylphenidate patch	6 and older
Desoxyn	methamphetamine hydrochloride	6 and older
Dexedrine	dextroamphetamine	3 and older
Dextrostat	dextroamphetamine	3 and older
Focalin	dexmethylphenidate	6 and older
Focalin XR	dexmethylphenidate (extended release)	6 and older
Metadate ER	methylphenidate (extended release)	6 and older
Metadate CD	methylphenidate (extended release)	6 and older
Methylin	methylphenidate (oral solution and chewable tablets)	6 and older
Ritalin	methylphenidate	6 and older
Ritalin SR	methylphenidate (extended release)	6 and older
Ritalin LA	methylphenidate (long acting)	6 and older
Strattera	atomoxetine	6 and older
Vyvanse	lisdexamphetamine dimesylate	6 and older

SOURCE: National Institute of Mental Health. (2008). Attention Deficit Hyperactivity Disorder (ADHD). Bethesda, MD: Author.

ensure that the child is taking the proper dosage, at the most effective times, and in the most efficient ways. Still, parents and children have to weigh the pros and cons of medication as they make their decisions. The story in Box 7.5 shows one child's path to identification as ADHD; in Michael's case pharmacological support is a key part of the intervention plan that will help him meet with success.

While medication is considered a key part of multimodal treatment for ADHD, it is prescribed less often for Latino and African-American children (Pastor & Reuben, 2005). As noted earlier, children from African-American, Latino, and poor families remain underserved even when identified (Pastor & Reuben, 2005; Basch, 2011; Gerdes et al., 2013). Gerdes and colleagues (2013) identified several barriers to services for Latino families:

- lack of health insurance
- lack of reliable transportation
- inability to pay for child care
- immigrant status
- difficulties with proficient use of English
- lack of trust for mental health providers, and
- lack of bilingual/bicultural mental health providers.

BOX 7.5 EXCEPTIONAL LIVES • EXCEPTIONAL STORIES

Meet Michael

Michael is in the third grade at Southside Elementary School. His teachers and parents are concerned about his high activity level, distractibility, and impulsivity. While his parents had noticed these concerns dating back to his early development, they always viewed him as just being "all boy" and while it was often exhausting, they appreciated his active engagement with the world. These symptoms, however, were now impacting his learning, especially in writing.

Wechsler Intelligence Scale for Children, 4th ed. (WISC-IV)

Scales/Subtests	Index/Scaled Score*	Percentile Rank	Descriptive Category
Verbal Comprehension	114	82	High Average
Perceptual Reasoning	121	92	Superior
Working Memory	99	46	Average
Processing Speed	85	16	Low Average
Full Scale	**109**	**73**	**Average**

*Index and IQ scores between 85 and 115 are considered average.

How was Michael identified?

Michael is the middle child with an older brother and younger sister. His family history is significant for ADHD and learning concerns. Michael's parents reported that he has always been an active boy, jumping and climbing off things when he was a toddler and sometimes being a safety concern when running from his parents in public as a young child. Michael's sunny personality kept everyone engaged but his parents worried that his fearlessness of strangers could lead to trouble and they tried to keep a close eye on their little boy.

Michael was able to follow routines in preschool and Kindergarten, but had some difficulty sharing due to his impulsivity with grabbing toys from others. He also had difficulty remaining still during circle time. While Michael appeared to be a smart child, in the first and second grades he had difficulty remaining focused to complete tasks and often needed to get up and move around for frequent breaks. By third grade, however, the demands of school seemed to be overwhelming him. He was becoming easily frustrated, unhappy, and had alarmed his parents by saying on several occasions that he "hated school!" His parents and teachers were concerned and wanted to know more about his needs; they referred him for additional assessments. The school psychologist prepared a learning profile of Michael, showing the following results.

Based on cognitive testing, Michael showed some strengths and needs within his profile. He has strong verbal and visual reasoning abilities, yet his working memory is relatively weaker and there is some concern with his processing speed score, which indicates that Michael works slower than others his age on timed pencil and paper tasks. These results are commensurate with concerns regarding Michael's writing, which seems to be a struggle for him. While standardized achievement testing ruled out a writing disability, concerns remain regarding Michael's writing as he is below grade level in this area.

Parent and teacher rating scale results indicated significantly elevated scores in the areas of inattention and hyperactivity/impulsivity on the Conners-3, indicating that Michael is exhibiting more frequent behaviors in these areas than others his age. Based on his reported history, rating scale results, and examiner observations, Michael was diagnosed with Attention-Deficit/Hyperactivity Disorder, Combined Type (ADHD).

The school-based IEP team met to discuss these results and Michael's needs. The IEP team included Michael's parents, his classroom teacher, a special education teacher, the school psychologist, and a school administrator. The school psychologist reviewed Michael's cognitive testing, rating scale results, and the resulting ADHD diagnosis, and the team began thinking about Michael's needs. While Michael's test results did not indicate a specific writing disability, he continues to struggle in this area. His IEP team discussed that Michael is often disorganized and distracted during writing tasks and also appears to have difficulty with handwriting, all concerns that frustrate Michael during writing tasks. Based on his below-level performance and poor

Some of these barriers are likely to impact African-American children and children from urban poor families as well. Thus, we find that the very children who are most at risk for identification as ADHD are also most likely to receive the lowest levels of supportive interventions once they have been identified (Pastor & Reuben, 2005; Basch, 2011, Gerdes et al., 2012).

BOX 7.5 EXCEPTIONAL LIVES • EXCEPTIONAL STORIES
Meet Michael (*continued*)

grades in writing, the IEP team concluded that Michael's diagnosis of ADHD appeared to be significantly impacting his academic performance in writing, and therefore he qualified to receive special education services as a student with an Other Health Impairment.

What are Michael's strengths and challenges?

Strengths:

- Visual processing skills
- Reading and math skills
- Energetic social personality
- A leader in athletics

Michael's challenges include:

- Difficulty remaining seated during class
- Easily distracted by others around him and extraneous noises in the hallway
- Difficulty getting organized and started on tasks, especially writing
- Difficulty completing work due to talking to others and playing with items in his desk
- Often impulsively calls out in class or bumps into others in line when having trouble standing still
- Difficulty remembering to bring completed homework back to school

What supports might be helpful for Michael?

Several modifications were put in place by the IEP team to support Michael's academic and behavioral success, including the following:

- Preferential seating away from distractions and close to the teacher
- Frequent reminders to remain on task either provided by the teacher or by a timer on his desk
- A basket of fidget toys he can play with while sitting on the floor listening to the teacher
- One-on-one assistance from a special education teacher as needed to support his writing needs
- Permission to dictate writing assignments into a recorder, then copy them to his paper
- The opportunity to use the computer for writing assignments to keep him engaged and on task
- Shortened assignments, such as one writing prompt at a time, to encourage his compliance with getting started on tasks
- Permission to take frequent breaks to get a drink of water or complete a job, like running an errand for the teacher
- Consultation with the school's occupational therapist to determine handwriting needs
- Home-school chart to provide positive reinforcement for writing down homework assignments and returning completed work to school

The IEP team recommended that Michael receive direct instruction from the special education teacher to support his organization and writing skills. The special education teacher worked with his classroom teacher to set a time for Michael to join a small group of students for focused work on how to be organized for success. She also provided one-on-one support for Michael's writing; teaching him to use Inspiration software to organize his ideas in prewriting and word processing to draft his papers for easier revision. Michael learned the revision process and began to take pride in his written work. Michael's parents continue to work with him during homework tasks and other multistep activities, such as chores at home. He benefits from using visual supports such as lists to remember his routines in the morning and evening, and he also benefits from the use of timers at home.

Michael also benefited from pharmacological management of his ADHD symptoms under the care of his pediatrician. His medicines helped him remain focused, lowered his energy level, and decreased instances of impulsivity during the school day. Michael said that he felt like "his brain was his own" when he took his medicine and that he "could decide what it was going to do!" His teachers and parents also saw the difference. With his medicine Michael was better able to sustain his focus and self-regulate his behavior. This in turn seemed to reduce his anxiety and frustration. Michael was going back to the happy-go-lucky boy his parents had known him to be! With careful planning and support Michael is learning to manage his ADHD and it looks like he will have a successful year.

SOURCE: Provided by Dr. Emily King, Licensed Psychologist, Wake County, NC. Reprinted by permission.

It is important to remember that medication does not cure ADHD and it is only effective while it is being used. In addition to medication it is critical for children with ADHD to receive appropriate educational, behavioral, and emotional support to help them thrive.

Students with ADHD often find attending in class difficult and teachers often feel these students just "day dream" instead of listening.

7-6 Educational Responses for Children with ADHD

Two federal laws guarantee a "free and appropriate public education" (FAPE) for students with ADHD (see also Chapter 2): the Individuals with Disabilities Education Act (IDEA) and Section 504 of the Rehabilitation Act of 1973. Students with ADHD may qualify for supports and services under one of these. There are some different requirements, however, depending on whether service eligibility is through IDEA or Section 504. Table 7.3 offers a comparison of the requirements.

Section 504 eligibility is often a good choice for students who can be successful in school with minor changes and accommodations while eligibility through IDEA 2004 may be better for individuals with more intense or wider-ranging needs for support. In addition to considering the level of support needed for

TABLE 7.3 Comparison of IDEA 2004 and Section 504 for Students with ADHD

	IDEA 2004	Section 504
Source	Special education and related services guarantees free and appropriate public education for students with disabilities.	Federal Civil Rights statute: Non-discrimination against children with disability; guarantees free and appropriate public education (FAPE)
Required Document	Eligible students receive an individualized education plan (IEP) including (1) goals for the child based on his or her current level of performance, (2) educational placement, (3) descriptions of services provided, (4) how progress will be measured	Eligible students receive a 504 plan that outlines (1) appropriate accommodations, (2) evidence-based interventions, (3) related services giving students with disabilities an equal opportunity to succeed.
Eligibility	Other Health Impaired category; students may also qualify under Specific Learning Disabilities or Severe Emotional Disturbance.	A physical or mental condition that substantially limits a "major life activity" such as school, established before, not after, intervention.
Evaluation	A complete evaluation is required with authorized parental consent. Students must be evaluated at least every three years unless school or parents agree this is not needed. Parents do not have to pay for evaluations. If parents do not agree with the results of the school evaluation, they may be entitled to an independent evaluation at no cost.	Information from a variety of sources (parents, teachers, doctors, students, etc.); a medical diagnosis is NOT required; parents' participation is not an entitled right and depends on school district procedures/policies.
Discipline	Even if suspended or expelled a student is guaranteed FAPE; may be expelled up to 10 school days, meeting (manifestation determination) to establish relationship of behavior to disability; any student who brings a weapon, engages in buying, selling, or carrying illegal drugs may be suspended for up to 10 days.	May be suspended or expelled for up to 10 days; after 10 days (consecutive or not) a "manifestation determination" meeting must be held to determine if child's disciplinary behavior is related to his or her disability; if yes, alternative placement must be found. Exceptions: (1) illegal drugs or alcohol relinquishes all 504 rights; (2) firearms removal immediately to alternative setting with meeting after 10 days.

Data from Children and Adults with Attention-Deficit/Hyperactivity Disorder (CHADD). (2012). What we know #4: Educational rights for children with ADHD in public schools. Landover, MD: Author.

TeachSource Digital Download Access online

the student's success, parents and teachers should also understand that specific requirements for implementing 504 plans can vary from school to school and that parental rights are not guaranteed under Section 504. Both IDEA 2004 and Section 504, however, do require that schools provide students with appropriate supports and services. The vast majority of students with ADHD will be served within general education classrooms with consultation support from special education teachers and/or related service providers.

7-6a Organizational Structures to Support Students with ADHD

Placing students with ADHD on a trajectory for success requires intense, engaging, and sustained multimodal support (Bussing et al., 2012). **Multimodal support** is a three-pronged approach using pharmacological/medical support (discussed earlier), behavior therapies, and academic interventions (Fabiano et al., 2010). It takes a team to provide supports needed; for students with ADHD this team may include medical and mental health specialists in addition to educators and parents. Systemic district, school, and classroom structures must be in place to deliver and sustain this kind of support (Bussing et al., 2012).

RtI Approaches for Students with ADHD

RtI

The difficulties faced by students with ADHD impact both academic success and behavioral/social outcomes. Students with ADHD experience significantly lower academic achievement, levels of class placement (more remedial classes), and rates of homework completion, while simultaneously showing higher absence and tardy rates, class failure, and dropout rates (Kent et al., 2011). Peer and social relationships are also challenging for individuals with ADHD (CHADD, 2003). Academic and behavioral successes seem to be directly related. When a student is meaningfully engaged in learning and is meeting with academic success, he/she is less likely to act out. By the same token, when a student is able to self-regulate his/her behavior, make friends, and feel socially accepted, he/she is better able to meet with academic success. Because of this many schools are working to support academic and behavioral outcomes for students with ADHD, combining RtI and **Positive Behavioral Interventions and Supports (PBIS)** approaches in **Multitiered Systems of Support**. The use of multitiered approaches (RtI and PBIS) has been shown to reduce suspension, expulsion, and dropout rates for students with ADHD (U.S. Department of Education, 2008b). Further, these approaches can facilitate the home/school partnerships so important to the success of students with ADHD (U.S. Department of Education, 2008b).

We can see the importance of this for a student like Rasheed, now in middle school, who is facing some serious academic and social challenges. Rasheed will need both academic and behavioral support at all three levels (Universal, Targeted, and Intensive) to be successful. Let's see what that might look like.

Universal Tier I for Students with ADHD

Tier I supports are typically provided within the general education classroom. These often begin with **Universal Design for Learning (UDL)** strategies that support learning for all students. Rasheed's middle school team, whose motto is "We are the winning team!" has worked together to establish "The Team Rules" (see ▶ Figure 7.3) that share expectations. These are consistently used across classrooms and all students know the consequences for inappropriate behaviors.

Having a consistent set of expectations that are clearly and explicitly shared is a starting place for all students. Rasheed's teachers have also structured their

The Team Rules

Show Respect for Others By:

- Not Interrupting, raising your hand to speak in class, and being courteous

Be Prepared By:

- Completing work on time, having your materials ready, and keeping track of your assignments

Be a Good Citizen By:

- Helping others when you can, asking for help when you need it, and working to get along with others

Figure 7.3 The Team Rules

classrooms into "zones" for various activities. The team knows that the red zone is for small group activities and the expectations are posted for group work. The blue zone is for quiet individual work, and the green zone is for whole class time. Teachers also alert the students when specific behaviors are expected; for example, during a seminar discussion students are not expected to raise their hand before they speak, but they are expected to use courtesy with their peers. For Rasheed, this new way of interacting was actually disconcerting, and his behavior began to deteriorate without having the clear rule of "raise your hand." Because of this, his teachers decided to offer some targeted support, Tier II, for some students, including Rasheed.

TeachSource Digital Download

Targeted Tier II for Students with ADHD

Targeted supports, delivered either within the general classroom or in another setting, are designed to help students with specific needs to learn skills such as how to participate in a seminar discussion versus a whole-class general discussion. In a seminar discussion the expectations include: no raised hands, free flow of ideas, and courtesy when others are talking. For a whole-class general discussion the expectations are: raise your hand before you talk, wait for the teacher to call on you, and listen to others. For some students who have learned the "rules" it can be difficult to understand situations where the rules do not apply. Rasheed's teachers modeled the appropriate behavior for the seminar, gave students practice time with immediate feedback, and developed a set of discussion guidelines for the students so that they would be able to participate in the classroom seminars more comfortably. After practicing these skills in a small group with direct support, Rasheed was able to participate in the seminar with his classmates.

Intensive Tier III for Students with ADHD

Rasheed also receives more intensive support for his behavioral needs at Tier III. The school counselor has been working with a group of students on appropriate social skills, particularly those needed for friendships within mixed gender groups. The group meets during lunch on Tuesdays and Thursdays. The counseling group offers a safe place for the students to talk about concerns and to practice their social skills. They use role play to experience different points of view, a technique that has been really helpful. The group has even taken field-trips to local restaurants and movie theaters, which has been really fun for Rasheed and his peers. Rasheed is learning how to interact with others in appropriate ways, which has given him more confidence. A wonderful by-product of this group work is that a friendship has evolved between Rasheed and another student, Collin! A Summary of RtI Approaches for Students with ADHD can be accessed online.

TeachSource Digital Download

Special Programs: After School, Saturdays, and Summer

Support provided during the school day to help students with ADHD may need to be augmented with more intense interventions after school, on Saturdays, or through summer camps. Special programs offer a structured context to address learning strategies and/or behavioral needs like peer relationships. Interventions delivered within special programs can be strictly controlled to maintain consistency and a high degree of **fidelity of implementation** (using interventions specifically as they are designed). Because these programs do not take place during the school day, they can focus on increasing the intensity of instruction, providing time for scaffolded practice of new skills, and monitoring the effectiveness of the intervention (U.S. Department of Education, 2008b). Group size can be adjusted using small groups for instruction to improve on task behaviors (Hart, Massette, Fabiano, Pariseau, & Pelham, 2011). Parent support classes can be integrated with these special programs to promote consistent support for the child. Special programs can also be used to support teachers' professional development, giving classroom teachers a chance to observe and participate in structured interventions to help them learn how to implement similar strategies with their students. More information about special programs for students with ADHD can be found on the websites listed in this section.

Center for Children and Families, University at Buffalo
http://ccf.buffalo.edu/default.php

The Incredible Years
www.incredibleyears.com

7-6b Curriculum and Instruction for Children with ADHD

Planning to address the instructional needs of students with ADHD begins with an assessment of their strengths and challenges (McLaughlin, 2012). For students with ADHD, "instructional needs" will usually include academic interventions *and* behavioral therapies; assessment information will be needed from both areas. This information lays the foundation for accommodations to help the student meet with success. While some information from the identification process may be useful, often additional information is needed to help us understand the student's needs in the classroom. This means that we may have to collect our own data for planning instruction. Let's look at one student, Sarah (see Box 7.6), to see the typical kind of information we might get from her identification information so we can begin thinking about how to plan for her instructional needs.

What we can see with Sarah's story is that she definitely has strengths as well as difficulties, and that while she can be successful, she will need some support. Table 7.4 shares the steps we can follow to get a planning process started if we have a student like Sarah in our class.

If Sarah were a student in your class, and you followed these planning steps you would learn a lot about her strengths and needs and you would likely be

BOX 7.6 Sarah's Story

Sarah is in the 10th grade at Sample High School. She currently receives accommodations through Section 504 of the Rehabilitation Act of 1973 due to a diagnosis of Attention-Deficit/Hyperactivity Disorder, Predominantly Inattentive Type (ADHD). She was diagnosed with ADHD in the third grade.

How was Sarah identified?

Sarah is the younger of two girls who live in a supportive home. She has a family history of ADHD but no family history of learning concerns. Sarah's parents reported that she met all developmental milestones within expected timelines. However, her parents also reported that when Sarah was 5 years old, she had difficulty following multistep directions during everyday routines, her Kindergarten teacher reported that she would "zone out" during circle time, and her parents recalled that she needed repeated reminders to stay seated to eat meals or complete tasks such as craft projects. Despite these concerns, Sarah appeared to be a bright child who learned well during her early years. Her parents became more seriously concerned in the third grade, when the academic curriculum became more challenging. Sarah appeared to have difficulty maintaining focus during subjects that were challenging and began to withdraw or "space out" in class. Sarah also began to forget to turn in homework assignments even though they were completed. However, she continued to compensate with her intelligence and energetic nature and was able to maintain acceptable grades. But was she working up to her potential? Cognitive testing yielding the following results.

Wechsler Intelligence Scale for Children, 4th ed. (WISC-IV)

Scales/Subtests	Index/Scaled Score*	Percentile Rank	Descriptive Category
Verbal Comprehension	128	97	Superior
Perceptual Reasoning	123	94	Superior
Working Memory	88	21	Low Average
Processing Speed	118	88	High Average
Full Scale	**120**	**91**	**Superior**

*Index and IQ scores between 85 and 115 are considered average.

Based on cognitive testing, Sarah is clearly a bright girl with strong verbal and visual reasoning skills. She is able to process pencil and paper tasks just as well as others her age according to her performance on processing speed tasks. However, she exhibited a weakness in working memory that, based on the examiner's observations, was related to her difficulty attending to these verbal memory tasks. Further, Sarah's teacher and parents noted a significantly elevated level of concern in the areas of Inattention and Executive Functioning (i.e., planning) on the Conners-3, indicating that she was exhibiting more inattention, distractibility, and difficulty planning ahead than other girls her age. Based on these results, as well as a parent-reported history of inattention and distractibility across settings prior to the age of 7 years old, Sarah was diagnosed with ADHD, Predominantly Inattentive Type.

SOURCE: Interview with Dr. Emily King, Licensed Psychologist, Wake County, NC conducted by Dr. Mary Ruth Coleman. Reprinted by permission.

able to help her thrive in your class. Box 7.7 shares what the Sarah's school team recommended.

The key to helping students with ADHD learn is threefold: identifying the strengths and needs of the child, selecting appropriate instructional approaches, and implementing these consistently to support the child's learning (U.S. Department of Education, 2008b). Instruction for students with ADHD must be **explicit**, clearly organized and clearly presented; **contextual**, embedded within a meaningful sequence of learning that activates prior experience and knowledge; and strategic, supporting learning with specific approaches that are directly taught (mnemonics for memory, for instance) and other metacognitive approaches.

Edwin Ellis and his colleagues suggest that we use a scaffolded approach to instructing students with ADHD that builds increasing levels of autonomy for the

TABLE 7.4 Steps for Instructional Planning for Students with ADHD

What to do...	Why do this?	How to use this...	Advice
Get to know the student, review the student's file (IEP or 504 plan) looking for patterns of strengths and challenges, talk with the student, observe in class.	This helps us see the big picture so we can understand what the student is facing and how we can best support his or her learning.	Think about how the student's strengths can be used to help him or her learn and what difficulties his or her challenges might create in your class.	Try to put yourself in the student's place and picture what would help him or her to be successful in your class.
Identify the ideas offered in the IEP or 504 plan that could help the student meet with success in your class; ask the student what has worked before.	Ideas that have been successful in the past may be the best starting place.	Think about which ideas or strategies will be most effective with your content areas and style of teaching and start with these.	Remember that IEPs and 504 plans are legal documents designed to help us meet the student's needs and we must implement these.
Identify the BIG Ideas you want to your students to understand; these themes or concepts are the most important overarching ones that guide your instruction.	Knowing the BIG ideas that you are teaching will help you and your students organize the facts and skills into meaningful wholes and will reduce fragmentation and isolated ideas.	Structure your lessons around these BIG ideas and share this structure with your students to show them how ideas are related (use graphic organizers to explicitly show this structure).	When we use BIG ideas to organize our teaching it helps make learning more meaningful and it facilitates memory because information is organized around a central theme.
Consider what additional information about the student you will need to plan your instruction of specific content knowledge and skills. At this point focus on skills and check on the student's baseline readiness.	While the IEP and 504 plans are a good starting place, they often will not have the specific data you need on skills levels to plan your instruction.	Look at your specific teaching/learning goals and design curriculum-based assessments of the skills needed for success. Use these as checkpoints for progress monitoring. You are looking for error patterns that will show you where to start.	Don't make this harder than need be—remember you are checking readiness skills for the lesson. If you are teaching reading, use vocabulary words and/or a read-a-loud; for math use a few problems; for writing use prompts to check skills. (These may already be part of your curriculum.)
Plan for supported instruction using UDL ideas (see Table 7.5). Plan for the student's specific supports and enhancements.	If you plan ahead to address the student's needs, your class time is less hectic, more productive, and students are more engaged in learning.	Think about how you can use multiple ways to (a) represent the content, (b) engage the learner, (c) assess learning. Also think about the FUN Factor: will learning be active and enjoyable?	When students are actively engaged they learn more and their behavior improves.

TeachSource Digital Download Access online

learning (Ellis, Farmer, & Newman, 2005). He characterizes this way of teaching as three levels: "I do it," the students watch and the teacher explains both the process and her thinking; "Y'all do it," pairs or small groups of students engage in helping each other practice the new skill or information; and finally, "You do it," the student reaches a confidence level to work independently. This approach is highly engaging and allows the student to work toward mastery with a feeling of confidence. While these instructional guidelines are excellent for all children, they are essential for students with ADHD who can easily get lost if our instruction is vague, disorganized, or boring.

BOX 7.7 Sarah's Story, Continued

So what happens for Sarah?
The school-based team met to discuss these results and Sarah's needs. The team included Sarah's parents, her classroom teacher, a special education teacher, the school psychologist, and a school administrator. The school psychologist reviewed Sarah's cognitive testing and rating scale results and discussed her classroom observations of Sarah. While Sarah met diagnostic criteria as a child with ADHD, Predominantly Inattentive Type, she was able to maintain her grades by compensating with her intelligence. The school-based team concluded that Sarah would benefit most from remaining in the regular education setting, yet she would likely need several accommodations to support her symptoms of ADHD. Therefore, the school team did not feel an IEP was appropriate, but agreed that Sarah would benefit from a 504 plan in order to support her learning.

What are Sarah's strengths and challenges?
Sarah's strengths were as follows:

- Verbal and visual processing skills
- Social skills
- Energetic personality
- Enjoys performing on stage

Sarah's challenges included:

- Difficulty maintaining attention to verbal discussions
- Easily distracted by social interactions with peers and extraneous noises in the hallway
- Weakness in recalling information learned outside the context of a story, such as memorizing spelling words, math facts, or vocabulary words
- Difficulty turning in her homework and staying organized

What supports might be helpful for Sarah?
Several accommodations were put in place by the school-based team to support Sarah's academic and behavioral success, including the following:

- Preferential seating away from distractions and close to the teacher
- Frequent reminders to remain on task either provided by the teacher or by a timer on her desk
- Chunking assignments into smaller parts so they do not feel so overwhelming
- Discussions with her teacher about concepts learned to help her connect newly learned information with personal experiences and/or previously learned information

Sarah was quite successful throughout elementary school with these accommodations. The school-based team met each year to review the supports in order to determine if they were still appropriate. In middle school, Sarah learned to self-monitor by setting her own timer and no longer needed reminders from her teachers. Her parents also consulted with a psychiatrist, who recommended medication management for Sarah's inattention symptoms, which proved to be very helpful for her. She also benefited from after-school tutoring to maintain her focus and get homework done before leaving school for the day. Added accommodations in middle school included having a home-school chart where Sarah's teachers signed off on homework assignments being recorded and her parents signed off on completed homework being placed in her backpack. Sarah was able to earn points for her success and redeem them for special outings on the weekends.

Sarah is now in the 10th grade. While she continues to struggle with symptoms of ADHD, such as inattention to verbal lectures, distractibility from peers, and disorganization, she has developed many coping strategies from the support she received through her 504 plan. She continues to need accommodations such as using timers when completing her work to keep her on task, preferential seating to keep her seated away from distractions, and a written copy of the teacher's notes so that she can follow along during the lecture. These supports have allowed Sarah to be academically successful despite her ADHD symptoms.

SOURCE: Interview with Dr. Emily King, Licensed Psychologist, Wake County, NC conducted by Dr. Mary Ruth Coleman. Reprinted by permission.

Strategies: Four Variables for Success

Learning strategies that promote success can be organized under four variables: time, structure, support, and complexity (Coleman, 2005). These variables can be modified to match the student's strengths and needs. Some students, for example, just need a little more time to meet with success; others need more structure or support. All students deserve content that is complex, meaningful, and appropriately challenging. The goal is to keep the complexity level of the concepts as high as possible while providing the time, structure, and support the student needs to be successful (Coleman, 2005). Figure 7.4 shows how these variables are related and gives examples of how each can be modified to help students with ADHD be successful in our classrooms.

Time is our most flexible resource and it is the easiest one to change, yet in schools we often use time very rigidly. With a little planning, however, we can adjust the time we use for direct instruction, guided practice, and independent practice to better match the needs of our students (McLaughlin, 2012). We can offer additional time for students who need it while shortening the time for others who have already mastered the content. To do this we must, of course, know our students' strengths and needs, and this is why our first step in planning is assessment (the data collection outlined in Table 7.4). We also need a classroom that is set up for **differentiated instruction** so that students can be working on modified assignments when needed.

Structure encompasses the content, the process, and the learning environment. Structuring the content helps to make it more explicit for our students (U.S. Department of Education, 2008b). We can add more structure to the content by organizing it around big ideas, using focus questions, and graphic organizers (see other strategies in Figure 7.4). These strategies help our students see concretely what the information is and how it is connected with other information they have learned or are learning. We can add more structure to the process of learning by helping our students use **task analysis**, breaking large complex tasks into the smaller steps needed to complete them (U.S. Department of Education, 2008b). Imagine the panic that Sarah feels if she is assigned a ten-page research paper. Without support, Sarah will likely feel so overwhelmed that she will give up. We can use task analysis to help her identify the steps she will need to follow to write the paper:

- Selecting an approved topic
- Compiling appropriate sources
- Reading, annotating, and making notes from these sources
- Developing a thesis statement or main theme
- Identifying evidence that supports and or refutes this theme
- Outlining or using a web to organize the paper
- Drafting the paper
- Getting feedback on the first draft
- Revising the paper (perhaps going back through the feedback/revision process)
- Completing the final draft

We may also need to structure the process by teaching Sarah study skills and developing a timeline with checkpoints with her to help her stay on target. The great news is that while explicitly developing and teaching these strategies to Sarah, many other students in our class are likely to be more successful!

Finally, we can structure the learning environment to help students with ADHD focus. We can reduce distractions (such as tennis balls on chair feet to minimize noise, use of headphones with soft music, reduced clutter and visual stimuli in the classroom). We can also set up the physical environment to facilitate whole-group, small-group, and individual activities. By structuring the classroom environment we help all of our students work more productively.

TeachSource Video Connection

Watch the video "Edward: Instructional Modifications for a Gifted Student with Attention Deficit Hyperactivity Disorder." This video is a good depiction of how we can use task analysis (breaking large tasks into manageable chunks) and how graphic organizers support learning for students with ADHD. After watching the Video Case, reflect on how these strategies might also help other students in Edward's class. What other strategies would you suggest Edward's teachers use to help him be successful? How might his teachers also nurture Edward's giftedness?

Watch online

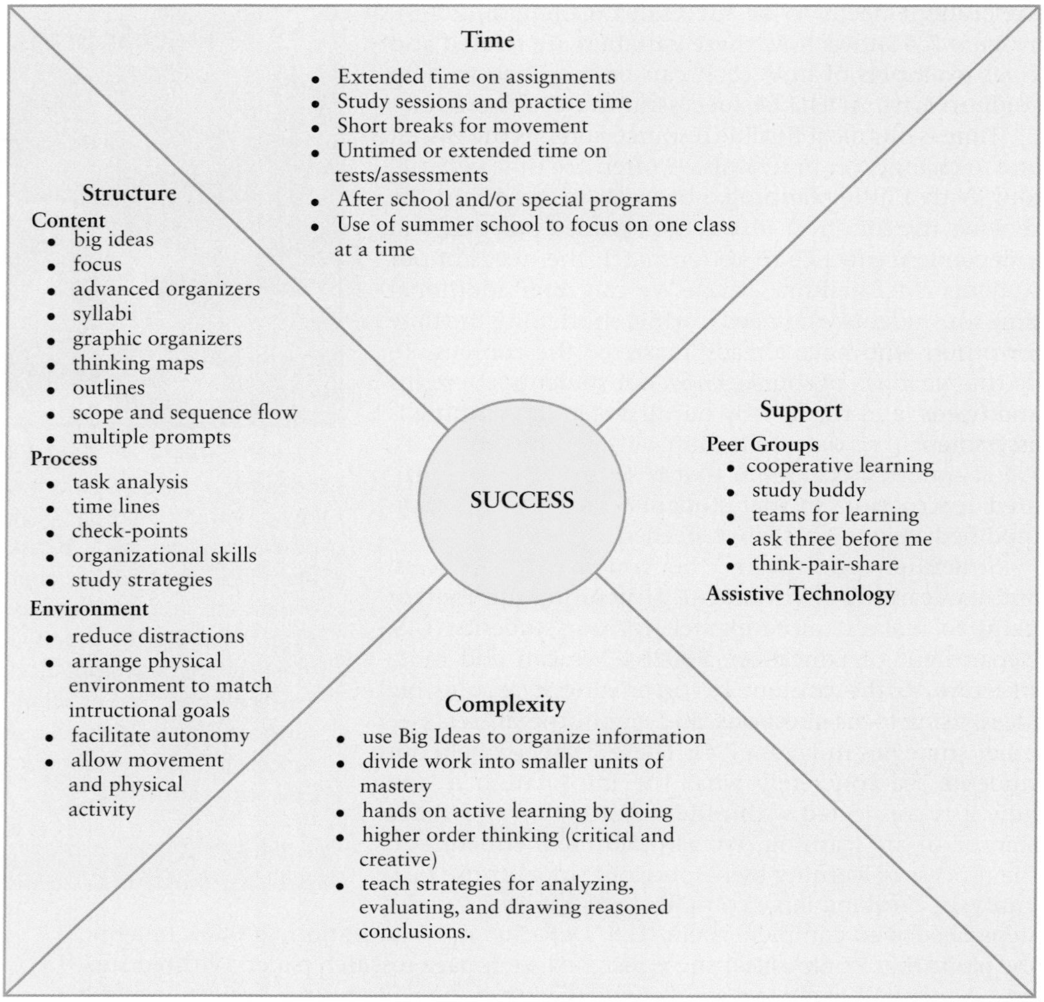

Figure 7.4 Four Variables for Success
Coleman, M. R., Four Variables for Success. *Gifted Child Today*, 26(1), 22–24.

TeachSource Digital Download Access online

The third variable for success is support. Support can be provided in several ways. We can provide more direct instruction, targeted interventions (Tier II), and intensive interventions (Tier III). Peer support can also be helpful through activities like cooperative learning groups or study buddies. There are, however, some pitfalls to peer support that we need to keep in mind: some students really prefer to work alone and will do much better on their own, while some students are easily distracted and may need to work in pairs. Also, peer support should allow all students to be meaningful engaged in learning, and peer support does not take the place of our teaching. Additional support can also be provided through assistive technology, discussed later in this section.

The fourth variable for success is complexity. More complex content requires that our students think about what they are learning rather than just memorizing isolated facts. With complex thinking, students are asked to identify meaningful patterns and relationships across ideas. Students analyze and evaluate information and learn to draw reasonable conclusions based on evidence. Complexity also involves the use of creative thinking as students combine ideas in new ways. The Common Core State Standards (CCSS) discussednext are complex standards that set high expectations for learning. When a student is struggling to meet high standards, we often tend to reduce the level of content complexity in an effort to make things easier (McLaughlin, 2012). Instead of making the content easier, we can provide more time, structure, and support to help the student be successful while maintain higher expectations (Coleman, 2005).

Figure 7.4 is a graphic organizer showing how the four variables are related. As you look at it you will notice that time is at the top: it is the first and easiest variable to modify. Structure and support are directly across from each other and are directly related. If we have not provided the structure a student needs, then we will have to provide additional support (or help) for the student to be successful. On the other hand, if we have provided appropriate structure in the content, process, and environment, then the student is more likely to be able to complete the work autonomously. Complexity is at the bottom of the figure; it is the foundation that we are strengthening through the other variables. By providing the time, structure, and support needed we can keep the complexity level higher. Our job is to adjust each variable to allow for the right level of student autonomy.

Access to the Common Core Standards: Universal Design for Learning

COMMON CORE STATE STANDARDS

The CCSS present complex outcomes that students are expected to master. For students with ADHD this can be challenging but not impossible. Skills needed for complex learning tasks, like understanding causal relationships within a narrative, differ from tasks like word decoding or memorizing vocabulary. Bailey, Lorch, Milich, and Churnigo (2009) describe the following deep processing steps needed for the complex learning task "understanding causal relationships in a narrative":

1. Strategically allocate attention.
2. Select, encode, and interpret important information.
3. Use story structure to build understanding.
4. Retrieve relevant background information.
5. Generate inferences for interpreting information.
6. Monitor comprehension.

These processing skills for understanding causal relationships can be generalized to other complex tasks like understanding and interpreting social cues (Bailey et al., 2009). The difficulty that students with ADHD have is that while they *can* do deeper processing, they must be sufficiently engaged with the task to maintain adequate attention. Bailey et al. (2009) conducted a 21-month longitudinal study of attending behaviors for 132 students with ADHD under two conditions: toys present to distract attention and no toys present. They found that children with ADHD showed no improvement in factual recall when toys were present; recall of factual information did improve over time when no toys were present. More worrisome, however, was their finding that *no improvement in understanding causal relationships occurred in either condition* (toys present or no toys present). They conclude that because understanding complex ideas requires deeper, more effortful processing, students with ADHD are not likely to engage in this without specific support and prompting. They recommend direct and explicit instruction on how to make the meaningful connections necessary for building coherent understanding.

Once again we come back to the importance of keeping students with ADHD engaged with the task. Verret, Gauy, Berthiaume, Gardiner, and Beliveau (2012) found that when children with ADHD participated in a moderate-to-high-intensity physical activity program they seemed to be more engaged in classwork and teachers reported better ability to attend to their lessons. Movement and kinesthetic activity has also been shown to help children with ADHD remain engaged in learning (U.S. Department of Education, 2008b). Table 7.5 shows how we can use Universal Design for Learning (UDL) with the CCSS, helping students with ADHD engage and sustain the attention needed for deeper processing of information.

TABLE 7.5 Using Universal Design Principles to Give Students with ADHD Access to the Common Core State Standards

Common Core Standard	Multiple Representations	Multiple Engagements	Multiple Assessments
Writing Standard #7, Research to Build and Present Knowledge, Grades 9-10 Conduct short as well as more substantive research projects to answer a question (including a self-generated question) or solve a problem: narrow or broaden the inquiry when appropriate; synthesize multiple sources on the subject, demonstrating understanding of the subject under investigation.	• Provide several examples of well-written papers as models • Develop timelines, checkpoints, and research strategies • Use graphic organizers to show relationships among ideas (e.g. hierarchies, compare/contrast, main idea and supporting details) • Develop graphics to show ideas and data • Create pictorial outlines showing the flow of ideas • Discuss relationships among ideas and examples of support/evidence for conclusions	• Use software programs to help organize work (e.g. Inspiration) • Web-based research to locate reliable sources • Interview experts • Use color-coding for organizing notes and sources • Dictate ideas to capture thoughts • Use drama to portray ideas • Partner with another student to review work and get feedback • Draft, get feedback, revise	Written product Oral presentation of main ideas and supporting evidence Debate for students who have drawn different conclusions Photo essay or documentary film on topic
Math Standard, High School Geometry: Congruence, Experiment with transformations in the plane Know precise definitions... Represent transformations... Describe rotations... Develop definitions of rotations, reflections, and translations... Draw transformations...	• Written definitions • Pictures showing definitions • Use solid shapes and graph paper • Use mirrors to show reflections • Find examples of transformations in real life	• Use flash cards with concepts, definitions, pictures • Use manipulatives to explore transformations (e.g. shapes on graph paper, overhead projector) • Use movement to show the principles of congruence with a partner (e.g. playing shape charades) • Use computer software to experiment with and depict transformations • Draw transformations (use graph paper, tracing paper, software) • Work with a partner challenging each other to identify and replicate the sequence of transformations made to carry a given figure onto another	Use knowledge of congruence to build something (e.g. picture frame) Assess for knowledge of definitions (e.g. short answer, or matching test) Create a piece of art showing congruence or a lack of congruence, incorporating rotations, reflections, and translations if possible Create a photo essay of examples of congruence in real life (e.g. rotations, reflections, or translations) Assess for applications of knowledge of congruence (problem solving)

TeachSource Digital Download | Access online

Keeping students with ADHD engaged and on task is the first order of business, and the UDL principles help us with this. Sometimes, however, students with ADHD will be off task; in fact, Mary Fowler (2010) reminds us that we can *expect* off-task behavior if the tasks are too long, too hard, too boring, too repetitive, too vague, or if they require more skill than the student has. She encourages us to closely examine the tasks we assign our students to make sure that they are worthy of students being "on."

Assistive Technology for Students with ADHD

Students with ADHD can benefit from a variety of assistive technologies to help them stay focused and organized. Computer tutorials can be useful for practicing specific skills, because they give the student immediate feedback, use branching programs to redirect based on outcomes, and often use engaging game-like features to keep the students' attention. Another benefit to computer tutorials is that the student's "failures" are private and can be self-corrected. If the computer tracks progress, the teacher can use this record to monitor the student's learning. Technology that helps with organization is especially useful for students with ADHD. Calendars, daily schedules, to do lists, reminder prompts, pictures of work or exam schedules, and information files can be stored on smartphones or tablet computers. Tools like spreadsheets, PowerPoint presentations, and word processing are also helpful for organizing, analyzing, and communicating ideas.

In this ever-changing digital age, however, technology should be much more than just study tutorials or organizational tools. Technology at its best, according to Siegle and Mitchell (2011) should be integrated into the curriculum to support learning, enhance critical and creative thinking, and allow for authentic product development. Today's students use the Internet to access information on any topic at any time. Apps exist that allow them to compare prices of shoes, track sports teams, and follow key news events. Social networking media allow them to connect with others across the room and around the world. This high-tech environment offers fast ready access to, well, just about everything. How we can use these technologies to help students with ADHD is yet to be fully determined. Will the technologies keep students more engaged, or will they create greater distractions? Perhaps the students themselves will teach us how to help them thrive in this rich, interactive digital world.

Behavioral Interventions for Students with ADHD

Behavior therapy is a key part of the educational support needed for students with ADHD (Rooney, 2011). The goal of behavior therapy is to help students increase their positive behaviors while reducing behaviors that interfere with learning (NIMH, 2008). School-wide programs like Positive Behavioral Interventions and Supports (PBIS), described earlier, are ideal because they provide consistent expectations for students (Rooney, 2011). There are, however strategies that classroom teachers can use to support student's positive behaviors. Table 7.6 shares a list of evidence-based strategies for behavioral interventions that teachers can use with their students.

When the student's behavior is more problematic, specific behavioral intervention plans must be developed. Rasheed, the young man discussed earlier in the chapter, not only struggles with ADHD, he also deals with emotional challenges and aggressive behaviors. In elementary school, Rasheed needed a comprehensive and consistently implemented **behavior intervention plan** which began with a **functional behavioral assessment** to determine what was motivating his inappropriate behaviors (see Chapter 8 for a full description of this). Rasheed often used inappropriate behaviors to get attention from his teacher and to avoid tasks that he disliked. He was a master at getting the teacher to focus on him until she became so exasperated that she placed him in "time-out"; therefore, he achieved both his goals with his disruptions. His teacher's challenge was to find ways to shift this pattern by giving him attention for appropriate behavior and replacing "time-out" with "work-out" where Rasheed was placed in semi-isolation while he completed the expected work. Rasheed's elementary teachers helped him learn how to get attention through appropriate behaviors and taught him specific strategies to ask for help with his work. They also incorporated strategies like the ones in Table 7.6 in his intervention plan. One of the most important things they did, however, was nurturing positive relationships with Rasheed to make sure that he felt strongly connected to his teacher and classmates (Basch, 2011). Involving Rasheed and his parents in

- Using appropriate commands
- Using "when…then" contingencies (such as when your room is clean, then you can play baseball)
- Planning ahead for public outings and practicing appropriate behaviors
- Using "time-out" as a consequence for inappropriate behavior
- Using charts, points, and token systems to reward appropriate behaviors
- Using a school-home note system to communicate and track academic and behavioral accomplishments (CHADD, 2004).

National Resource Center on ADHD **www.help4adhd.org**

TABLE 7.6 Evidence-Based Behavior Intervention Strategies

Behavior Modification Strategies

- Premack Principle: "Eat your spinach before you get your cake"—rewards come after completion of required work.

BOX 7.8 Tips to Help Kids Stay Organized and Follow Directions

Schedule. Keep the same routine every day, from wake-up time to bedtime. Include time for homework, outdoor play, and indoor activities. Keep the schedule on the refrigerator or on a bulletin board in the kitchen. Write changes on the schedule as far in advance as possible.

Organize everyday items. Have a place for everything, and keep everything in its place. This includes clothing, backpacks, and toys.

Use homework and notebook organizers. Use organizers for school material and supplies. Stress to your child the importance of writing down assignments and bringing home the necessary books.

Be clear and consistent. Children with ADHD need consistent rules they can understand and follow.

Give praise or rewards when rules are followed. Children with ADHD often receive and expect criticism. Look for good behavior, and praise it.

SOURCE: National Institute of Mental Health. (2008). Attention Deficit Hyperactivity Disorder (ADHD). Bethesda, MD: Author.

Daily Report Card packets
http://wings.buffalo.ed/adhd

One system for establishing home-school communication is the Daily Report Card (DRC) (CHADD, 2004). Benefits of the DRC have been described as (a) increasing timely communications between school and home, (b) helping teachers and parents maintain the focus on IEP goals, (c) enhancing the use of data to monitor the child's progress, (d) increasing the likelihood of consistent rewards and consequences for behaviors, and (e) providing timely feedback to students on their progress (Fabiano et al., 2010).

A comparison study of students with ADHD randomly assigned to the "daily report card" intervention or to "business as usual" groups showed that the intervention did not result in significant achievement gains for the students (Fabiano et al., 2010). The authors conclude that the daily report cards' main value seems to be enhancing the home-school relationship and monitoring the child's progress; they recommend intensive academic interventions in addition to the DRC for students with ADHD (Fabiano et al., 2010).

Helping children learn to stay organized, follow a schedule, and control their impulses can be difficult. Parents are often juggling multiple family needs with work and other demands. Setting home routines and consistent expectations is a foundation for the child. NIMH (2008) offers the advice in Box 7.8 for families.

One of the primary responsibilities parents face is the decision about medications for their child. Meeting with physicians is critical, and weighing the pros and cons of medicines can be difficult. Parents will also be the ones who must monitor the impact of medications, with input from teachers. Keeping a behavior log is a useful way to track the impact of medications; parents and teachers make note of the child's eating, sleeping, and mood patterns as well as specific behaviors. This information is especially helpful when new medication is prescribed or there has been a change in medications (Subcommittee on Attention/Hyperactivity Disorder, Steering Committee on Quality Improvement and Management, 2011). As with all children, being a parent of a child with ADHD is a full-time job that continues throughout the child's life.

7-8 Transition to Post-secondary and Adult Life for Individuals with ADHD

The difficulties experienced by children with ADHD may change as they grow up; however, the challenges do not seem to diminish (Frodl & Skokauskas, 2012). Academic problems persist and may even increase (Bailey et al., 2009), social difficulties with peers may worsen (Wehmeier, Schacht, & Barkley, 2010), abuse of alcohol, drugs, and nicotine may emerge (Charach, Yeung, Climans, & Lillie, 2011), and individuals may be a greater risk for involvement with the juvenile justice system (Bussing, Mason, Bell, Porter, & Garvan, 2010). Biederman, Petty, Evans, Small, and Faraone (2010) studied the persistence of ADHD symptoms in a sample of 110 boys as they moved from childhood to young adulthood. They found that participants had more comorbid mental health and mood disorders, as well as higher levels of educational, workplace, and family adjustment problems than the control groups.

A disappointing trajectory for students with ADHD, however, is not written in stone. Protective factors for youth include: early intervention and support (Bussing et al., 2012), strong parenting (CHADD, 2008), and intensive educational support including strategies for coping and learning (Kent et al., 2011). An estimated 2–8 percent of college students have ADHD and many of them report that they struggle more than their peers without ADHD (Rooney, 2011). Students that seem to be successful in college report strong time management, organization, and study skills; the good news is that all of these skills can be taught (Rooney, 2011). Gifted students with ADHD seem to have educational outcomes that are more similar to their gifted peers than to their ADHD peers (Bussing et al., 2012). While teens and adults are often more likely to stop taking medicines (Kent et al., 2011), studies have shown that continued use of medication as part of a multimodal approach to regulate ADHD symptoms may be helpful (Wehmeier et al., 2010). To place a child with ADHD on the pathway toward a successful life it takes a concerted team effort. Early intervention, consistent and continued support for the child and family, and multimodal approaches that combine medicine, behavioral therapies, and educational interventions are needed to help children with ADHD grow into happy productive adults.

MORAL DILEMMA

Austin's behavior

Austin, a child in your fifth-grade class, is struggling. He has been identified with ADHD and his constant motion, impulsive outbursts, and disorganization are causing him difficulties and disrupting the learning of others. Austin's parents do not believe in medication and expect you to modify your classroom for Austin. While you have made several accommodations, Austin's behavior continues to create problems. You feel that he will not be successful in middle school given his current functioning. You have a conference coming up with his parents and are wondering how to share your concerns. What will you say?

Summary

- ADHD involves a combination of challenges which impact the individual's ability to sustain, attention, restrain impulsivity, and control activity levels.
- Although ADHD is a relatively recent term, educators and medical professionals have long recognized its symptoms.
- ADHD presents in a variety of ways, although it typically results in executive function deficits of some sort. Some students will suffer from inattention, others hyperactivity, and others from both. The *DSM-5*, released in 2013, is used by clinicians to make an ADHD diagnosis.
- Clinicians often use rating scales such as the Conners-3 to make an ADHD diagnosis in addition to clinical observation and other diagnostics, including intelligence tests. Input from parents and teachers is vital to correctly identifying students with ADHD, because the diagnosis cannot be made without confirmation that the ADHD behaviors are present in multiple settings (home and school).
- Students from culturally/linguistically diverse backgrounds are more likely to be misidentified as having ADHD or to be overlooked as having ADHD. Girls are also more likely to be overlooked as having ADHD.
- It is difficult to accurately count the number of students with ADHD due to the wide range of symptoms and the fact that ADHD is often comorbid with other disorders.
- ADHD is thought to have both neurological and genetic causes. Environmental factors also play an important role in the manifestation and management of ADHD symptoms.

- A multimodal treatment including medication, behavior therapies, and educational interventions is the most effective way to address the needs of students with ADHD.
- Students with ADHD may qualify for supports and services under IDEA 2004 or Section 504; some students may not qualify for services, but educators can still adapt instruction to meet their needs.
- Multitiered Systems of Support such as RtI and PBIS can provide the academic and behavioral support students with ADHD need to be successful.
- Instructional planning for students with ADHD should take into account the supports and services offered under IDEA 2004 or Section 504. Teachers should also work with other professionals such as the school psychologist or special education teachers to develop appropriate instructional strategies.
- Universal Design for Learning offers one way to make curriculum such as the CCSS accessible for students with ADHD. Time, structure, support, and complexity should all be considered as elements of effective instructional planning.
- Assistive technology can be used to help students with ADHD stay organized and on top of tasks.
- Modifications to the learning environment and evidenced-based behavioral modification techniques are also vital components of a successful strategy that meets the needs of students with ADHD.
- Families play a vital role in the success of students with ADHD. Schools can work with parents to support students' learning. The importance of support for parents of children with ADHD should not be overlooked.
- Students with ADHD can have productive, happy lives with support and a strong educational foundation.

Future Challenges

1. **Families are critical to the success of children with ADHD. How can we better support families in the development of strong parenting skills?**
   A substantial body of research shows that enhancing parenting skills is an evidence-based practice to help children with ADHD be more successful. Parent training programs exist; however, few parents participate in these. How can we make parent support and training programs more accessible so that more parents can participate in them?

2. **Although Latino, African-American, and poor children are at a higher risk for being identified with ADHD, they are also less likely to receive appropriate supports and services, especially medication as part of a multimodal approach.**
   How can we ensure that we are not inadvertently overidentifying children from culturally and linguistically diverse families because of biases in the identification process or assessment tools? And how can we simultaneously ensure that all children who do have ADHD have equal access to the interventions that will help them be successful?

3. **As we learn more about the interaction of genetic predispositions and environmental risk versus protective factors, how can we improve outcomes for students with ADHD?**
   Although there is a strong indication of genetic predispositions for ADHD, we also know that factors in the environment can act as either protective agents or risk enhancers. How can we identify these factors so that we can increase children's protective factors to minimize the impact of their ADHD?

TeachSource Digital Download Access online

Key Terms

attention deficit/hyperactive disorder (ADHD) 207
behavior intervention plan 235
comorbidity 212
contextual 228
differentiated instruction 231
explicit 228
fidelity of implementation 227
functional behavioral assessment 235
multimodal support 225
Multitiered Systems of Support 225
neurotransmitters 220
Positive Behavioral Interventions and Supports (PBIS) 225
phenotype 218
task analysis 231
Universal Design for Learning (UDL) 225

Resources

References of Special Interest

Hallowell, E. M. & Ratey, J. J. (1994). *Driven to Distraction*. New York, NY: Touchstone.This classic book is one of the first to describe what having an attention deficit disorder is like. The authors, who both have ADHD, share their experiences, challenges, and pathways to success. The case studies present excellent snapshots of individuals with ADHD and help the reader build an understanding of what ADHD is and how it can be addressed. For teachers and parents, this book remains a must-read.

Quinn, P. O. (2011). *100 Questions & Answers about Attention Deficit Hyperactivity Disorder (ADHD) in Women and Girls*. Sudbury, MA: Jones & Bartlett Learning.

Perhaps because there are more males identified with ADHD, girls and women often get left out of the discussion. This book serves as a resource for those interested in how ADHD affects girls and women, discussing the differences in symptoms, other accompanying conditions, and treatments that have been successful. Other books by Quinn include: *AD/HD and the College Student: The Everything Guide to Your Most Urgent Questions* (2012); and *ADHD According to Zoe: The Real Deal on Relationships, Finding your Focus and Finding your Keys* (2013) by Zoe Kessler and Patricia Quinn.

National Institute of Mental Health (2012). *Attention Deficit Hyperactivity Disorder*, NIH Publication No. 12-3572. Washington, D.C.: Author. This comprehensive report shares symptoms, causes, and treatments for students with ADHD. It reviews medications and includes a discussion of research that is currently underway to improve treatments for individuals with ADHD.

Journals

Journal of Attention Disorders
http://jad.sagepub.com/

Journal of the American Academy of Child & Adolescent Psychiatry
http://www.jaacap.com/

Organizations

American Academy of Child & Adolescent Psychiatry ADHD Resource Center) **www.aacap.org/cs/ADHD.ResourceCenter**

Children and Adults with Attention Deficit Hyperactivity Disorder (CHADD) **www.chadd.org/**

Centers for Disease Control and Prevention ADHD Resource Center **www.cdc.gov/Features/adhdresources/**

Council for Exceptional Children **www.cec.sped.org/**

National Institute of Mental Health **www.nimh.nih.gov/health/publications/attention-deficit-hyperactivity-disorder/index.shtml**

National Resource Center on ADHD **www.help4adhd.org/**

CHAPTER 8

Children with Emotional and Behavior Disorders

Standards Addressed in This Chapter

All of the CEC Standards are addressed within this chapter. Please see the inside book covers for the complete list of the standards.

CEC

FOCUS QUESTIONS

8-1 How did the field of education for children with emotional and behavior disorders (EBD) evolve?

8-2 How do we define children with EBD?

8-3 What are some proposed causes of EBD?

8-4 What are the characteristics of children with EBD?

8-5 What educational responses help meet the needs of students with EBD?

8-6 What role can the family and community play in supporting children with EBD?

Few experiences are as disturbing to teachers as trying to teach children who are chronically unhappy or driven to aggressive, antisocial behavior. Teachers feel distressed knowing there's a problem but often feel unsure what to do. Managing behavior problems in the classroom is rated as one of the most serious problems facing teachers.

Children with behavior problems carry a burden that children with other disabilities do not. We do not blame children who have intellectual and developmental disabilities or who have cerebral palsy for their different behaviors. But many people assume that children with behavior disorders *can* control their actions and *could* stop their disturbing behavior if they wanted to. The sense that they are somehow responsible for their disability colors how others respond to children with EBD: their peers, their families, and their teachers (Gresham, 2007).

8-1 History of Emotional and Behavior Disorders

We have always been painfully aware of children with behavior or emotional problems. Yet for generations there has been amazing variation in what were believed to be the causes of such behavior and, correspondingly, there have been a wide array of treatments. Two centuries ago, children with behavior problems were believed to be possessed by the devil, insane, or mentally retarded. When attention was paid to them at all, they were shut away in large institutions with very little effort directed to their education. The professionals who dealt with them were largely physicians or clergy (if they were "possessed," it was up to the "holy men" to cure them) (Kauffman, Brigham, & Mock, 2004).

In the late 1800s, children who were manifestly different from their age-mates were being put into special ungraded classes, with little attention paid to their individual or special needs. Jean Itard and Edward Seguin, both physicians, became important figures in treating children with behavior problems as well as children with intellectual and developmental disabilities, as there had been few other attempts to differentiate the two conditions.

After World War II, the responsibility for children with exceptionalities gradually shifted from the medical or mental health professionals to educators. The schools assumed greater responsibility for their treatment, and the treatment became increasingly behavioral and educational. As we became aware of the power of ecological and social factors to influence children's development (Chapter 2), treatment also included changing and improving their social and educational environment. This chapter discusses the current view of causes, as well as the methods and current curricula based on humanistic, ecological, and behavioral principles.

8-2 Emotional and Behavior Disorders: A Slippery Definition

It is not easy to define emotional and behavior disorders in children. There is no clear dividing line, such as an IQ score or the syndromes of autism spectrum disorders. Readers are tempted to skip lightly over technical matters such as definitions in order to get to the more meaty sections that describe students with exceptionalities and how to plan programs for them. We urge that you not do that in this case because the definition of children with EBD is inherent in many of the problems faced by this special field. Table 8.1 provides the legal definition of EBD as found in the Individuals with Disabilities Education Act (IDEA) of 2004. It is often easy to recognize oneself in this definition. After all, who among us has not been concerned with interpersonal relationships or depression or engaged in inappropriate behavior?

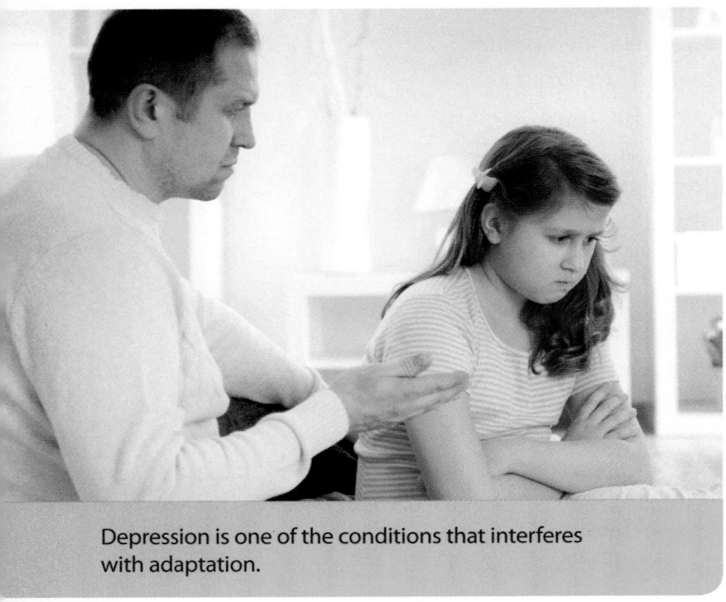

Depression is one of the conditions that interferes with adaptation.

What separates children with EBD from their more average peers is not the *kind* of behavior shown but the *intensity* and *duration* of that behavior. Everyone can be unhappy from time to time, but not every day or in many different circumstances. One problem with this definition is then how to separate those students who have a normal amount of unhappiness from those with such intense unhappiness that it threatens to swallow them up and destroy any attempt to perform academically. Where is

TABLE 8.1 Federal Definition of Emotional and Behavior Disorders

(i) *Emotional disturbance* means a condition exhibiting one or more of the following characteristics over a long period of time and to a marked degree that adversely affects a child's educational performance:

(A) An inability to learn that cannot be explained by intellectual, sensory, or health factors.

(B) An inability to build or maintain satisfactory interpersonal relationships with peers and teachers.

(C) Inappropriate types of behavior or feelings under normal circumstances.

(D) A general pervasive mood of unhappiness or depression.

(E) A tendency to develop physical symptoms or fears associated with personal or school problems.

(ii) Emotional disturbance includes schizophrenia. The term does not apply to children who are socially maladjusted, unless it is determined that they have an emotional disturbance under paragraph (c)(4)(i) of this section.

SOURCE: Individuals with Disabilities Education Improvement Act of 2004, Pub. L. 108-446, U. S. Department of Education, Washington, D.C.)

TeachSource Digital Download Access online

the dividing point? Another problem with this definition is in the final statement in Table 8.1, which states that the term "does not apply to children who are socially maladjusted unless it is determined that they have an emotional disturbance." Few professionals are in agreement with this statement; they believe that we should be trying to cope with both emotionally disturbed and socially maladjusted disturbed children (Cullinan, 2004). Gresham (2007) has suggested that lawmakers assumed that students who were acting out were doing so on their own accord and could stop if they wished to do so. Another line of thought has been that lawmakers, having passed legislation dealing with delinquency, thought that having two different kinds of legislation would create a confusing overlap. The schools have, by and large, handled this problem by assuming that any child showing serious behavior problems can automatically be assumed to be emotionally disturbed and thus eligible for treatment. Whether this is really true or not remains an open question.

The definition of emotional disturbance has another serious shortcoming. A number of observers have pointed out that the federal definition places *all* responsibility for the problem on the child and none on the environment in which the child exists, thus making it the responsibility of the special education program to change the *child* but not the *learning environment,* which may itself be considerably flawed (Nelson, Crabtree, Marchand-Martella, & Martella, 1998).

This chapter is divided into two main groups of students with EBD—those who externalize their difficulties (**behavior disorders**) and those who internalize them (**emotional disorders**).The term behavior disorder implies that the child is causing trouble for someone else. A serious emotional disturbance can be merely a manifestation of personal unhappiness. But almost all children reveal age-inappropriate behavior at one time or another. Moreover, a child's behavior is not the only variable that determines classification in this category. The person who perceives the child's behavior as "inappropriate" plays a key role in the decision. Clearly, some kinds of behavior, such as physical attacks, constant weeping, or unhappiness, and extreme hyperactivity, are unacceptable in any setting. But the acceptability of a wide range of other behaviors depends on the attitude of the perceiver.

Council for Exceptional Children's Division of Children with Behavior Disorders. **www.ccbd.net**

8-2a Cultural Perspectives on Defining EBD

In our pluralistic society, behavior that is acceptable in some groups or cultures is unacceptable in others. Can we say that a child's behavior is deviant if that behavior is the norm in the child's cultural group, even though *we* may find the particular behavior socially unacceptable? A definition of acceptable behavior must allow for cultural differences.

We noted earlier that the federal definition focuses on the child but not on the child's environment; however, the learning environment may be exactly what is at issue for a child who comes to school from a different cultural background with different lifestyles and family values. Let us introduce you to a few students.

Pete is a good example of a child with both academic and behavior problems that interfere with school performance. He has been a constant trial to his middle school teachers. He belongs to a gang known as the Griffins who, on occasion, terrorize other students in the school. They are suspected of stealing from local stores and perhaps dealing drugs in the school. Pete does not appear to be depressed or anxious, but his acting-out behavior causes great stress for his teachers and his parents.

Juan, a child newly arrived from Mexico, has trouble with the different ways he is supposed to react to authority. He is expected to look teachers in the eye when they are talking to him. But if he did that at home, he would be severely reprimanded because such eye contact would be considered defiance of parental authority. Juan's reaction to this very different environment may cause him to exhibit behavior within the range of the current definition of behavior disorder. That behavior would not be due to some underlying pathology but to the clash of cultural values between school and home (Harry & Klingner, 2006).

What treatment is prescribed for such a child? Should Juan be made to change his behavior patterns to fit the new environment, or should we try to reach an accommodation between the two? The issue of an individual child with maladaptive behavior may turn out to be an issue of clashing societies with a very different prescription for social remediation that extends far beyond the reach of special education.

The student caught between two cultures can still manifest behaviors that are certain to cause him or her trouble now, and in the future, in the school environment and in the community. In short, the problem may start out as a cultural clash, but it is transformed into a personal adjustment problem. Should the child receive some type of intervention? In this situation, it is appropriate to think of the entire family as the focus of attention. Increasingly, the family unit is involved in the attempts at behavior change in the child.

8-2b Misidentifying Students with EBD

There is one fact that everyone agrees upon: The rate of referral of minority students to programs for emotionally disturbed students is about 1.6 times that of white children. The question is why? While Sameroff (1990) reported risk factors for child development derived from the family and the social surroundings, Hart (2009) added another risk factor—the school setting itself. They reported on four case studies of minority children in programs for emotional development. In one, Kanita, a student in a school serving primarily low-income African-American students, was referred for disruptive and noncompliant behavior such as the following from an observation of her classroom:

> There is little student involvement. Some are looking at what their classmates are doing at the computer. At least one student is cutting paper while others look aimlessly around the room.... The boy sitting next to me keeps talking to Kanita, who is at the computer. Someone tells the teacher that Kanita is doing Math Corner on the computer and the teacher tells her not to. Kanita replies she is going to do it anyway. (p. 155)

The question is whether Kanita's "troubling" behavior represents "troubled" behavior as in emotional disturbance. Do behavioral problems mean emotional problems or only cultural influences? School personnel believed that Kanita's problems stemmed from her mother's months-long incarceration. In fact, observations in the home itself revealed Kanita was in a warm and supportive environment with other relatives. When Kanita was referred to a program for emotionally disturbed children, the ED teacher remarked that her behavior was quite acceptable. Kanita was mainstreamed and then later was placed in a program for gifted students. How many minority students like Kanita are wrongly referred to programs for emotionally disturbed children?

8-2c Prevalence of Children with EBD

There is a disturbing gap between the number of children with EBD receiving special services in the schools (between 0.6 and 1 percent) and the number of children who are judged to have either **serious emotional disturbance** or behavior disorders (variously estimated between 5 and 15 percent). Many of the judgments are subjective and left to local personnel; this is the reason it is hard to arrive at a definitive prevalence figure.

This is not to say, however, that there is not a core of children who can readily be identified as having emotional or behavior disorders. A child who attacks another child with a weapon such as scissors, a knife, or a hammer leaves little doubt; neither does a child who weeps five or six times a day without apparent cause. As always, confusion about whether a child is eligible for special services exists at the margin of the category.

When a first-grade teacher sees a child who harms others and damages property, who breaks the rules, fights, lies, and yells, the teacher first wonders what to do about this child, then worries about what is to become of him or her. Will he or she continue to show these aggressive tendencies? Will they fade away as the child gets older? Will the child, in fact, be in trouble with society as an adult?

8-2d Is the Prevalence of Aggression Long-Lasting?

One of the hopes of educators is that behavior problems and academic problems may ease or become less severe over time as the child physically and socially matures. But longitudinal studies tend to lessen that hope. One such study (Montague, Enders, & Castro, 2005) followed kindergarten students identified as at moderate or high risk for behavior and academic problems into later elementary and middle school. These students were primarily from culturally diverse and poor families.

The authors found that those at risk in kindergarten continue to be at risk for poor school outcomes that included truancy, delinquency, and school failure, through middle school. The critical importance of early intervention to support such children with EBD is obvious.

Another seminal longitudinal study, in which a sample of 297 male children was first assessed at age 6, then evaluated at each grade level through seventh grade, and finally evaluated through interviews at ages 19 and 20, provides some answers to these questions (Schaeffer, Petras, Ialongo, Poduska, & Kellam, 2003). The authors were able to sort children into four groups: *chronic high aggressive* (the child was aggressive when starting school), *moderate aggressive, increasing aggressive* (including those who seemed to become aggressive while in school and increased their aggressiveness over the years), and *nonaggressive*. ▶ Figure 8.1 shows the comparison of aggressive behavior in school with later adult consequences. The figure shows that almost three-quarters of the children in the chronically high aggression and

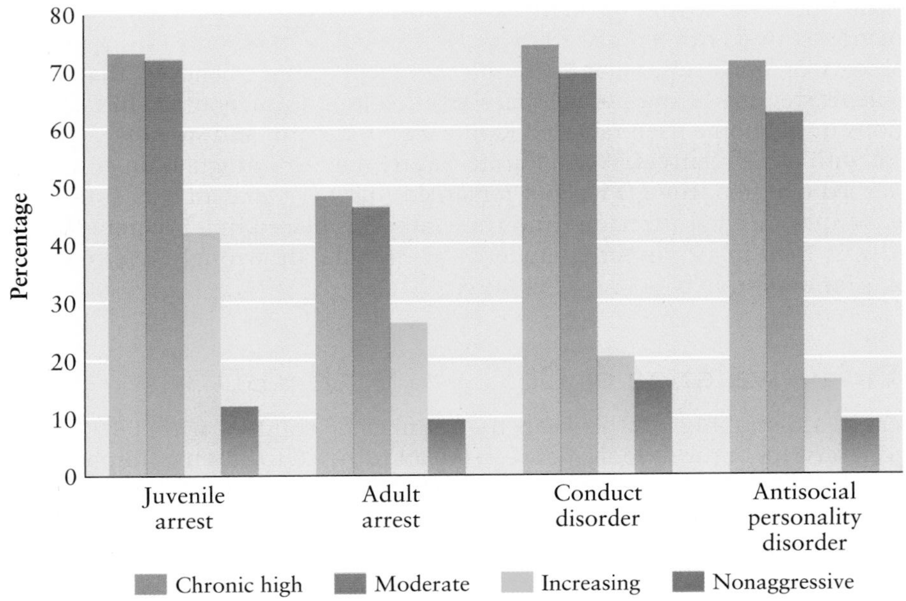

Figure 8.1 Predictor of Adult Aggressive Behavior Based Upon Behavior of Young Children

Source: Schaeff er, C., Petras, H., Ialongo, N., Pofuskea, J., & Kellam, S. (2003) Modeling growth in boys aggressive behavior across elementary school; Links to later criminal involvement, conduct disorder and antisocial personality disorder. *Developmental Psychology* 19, 1020–1035.

the moderate groups were arrested as juveniles and that half of them were arrested as adults. Also, almost three-quarters of the children in the chronically high aggressive and the increasing aggressive groups were identified as having conduct disorder or antisocial personality disorder that continued through young adulthood.

8-3 Causation of Emotional and Behavior Disorders

What causes EBD? Some ideas are harder to accept than others. One hypothesis is that future behavior is determined at birth. Many books and media have adopted the theme of the "evil child" (see the film *The Bad Seed*). The essential unfairness of such a concept repels us and makes genetic research findings harder to accept. Fortunately, we can now say that the final determination of adult behavior is a mix or blend of genetics and environment. Criminal behavior, for instance, is *not* fixed at birth.

What the genetic evidence does tell us, though, is that some children have a predisposition toward behaviors such as hyperactivity, attention problems, or impulsiveness. Those behaviors may call for some special educational or social environments to ensure that such predispositions do not flower into real behavioral problems.

8-3a Interaction Between Genetics and Environment

As we have learned more about the brain, we have come to realize that how we are wired at birth by genetics and prenatal conditions have much to do with our behavior and such characteristics as impulsiveness. On the other hand, we also know that children such as Matt—an active, aggressive, gifted boy who often lands in the principal's office—are not inevitably doomed to a life of aggression and hyperactivity. We also realize that more educational energy and resources will be needed to prevent such an outcome—more than are needed with typical children. An extensive review of the research of such topics (Beauchaine, Neuhaus, Brenner, & Gatzke-Kopp, 2008) concludes:

> [A]lmost all forms of psychopathology emerge over the course of development as a result of complex interactions between biological vulnerabilities and environmental risks, neither of which can be ignored in efforts to prevent the debilitation of psychiatric conditions (p. 762).

Although there clearly is some genetic influence in conduct disorders, particularly those associated with hyperactivity, inattention, and poor peer relationships, there is no reason to believe that environmental experiences cannot counteract those influences. What does seem clear is that there are two-way interactions between the various forces at work. That is, just as aggression can change psychosocial factors, so can psychosocial factors change levels of aggression.

8-3b Neurology and Brain Development

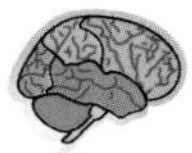

When children have extreme emotional and/or behavioral difficulties, the neural chemistry of the child's brain may need to be adjusted and medication may be considered as part of the treatment and support (National Institute of Mental Health [NIMH], 2010). When medication is considered for a child, the multidisciplinary team will need to include a physician (psychiatrist, neurologist, or pediatrician), and may often include a psychologist, a psychiatric nurse, and/or a behavioral therapist as well. As our understanding of brain development increases, we are better able to recognize and treat early stages of mental illness and emotional disturbances in children.

The use of **psychotropic** (affecting the neurosystem) medication is a part of the intervention support for young children, however, must take into consideration the related risks (NIMH, 2010). Some risks associated with medications include side effects like nausea, decreased appetite, excessive sweating, confusion, and dizziness (Bank, 2010). For children who are trying to manage extreme anxiety disorders, depression, obsessive-compulsive disorders, post-traumatic stress disorders, attention deficits, eating disorders, and schizophrenia, the benefits of medication may outweigh the risks. While the specific medication needed for an individual child will, of course, be identified by the child's physician, medications may include antidepressants, mood stabilizers, antipsychotics, and stimulants to support attention (Bank, 2010).

This medication creates a feeling of well-being and a sense of control (Bank, 2010). Young children respond to medications differently than older children and adults because their brains are developing so rapidly. As a result, they may metabolize medications at a different rate (NIMH, 2010). Since psychotropic medications affect the brain chemicals related to mood and behavior, children taking these medications must be closely monitored. Teachers also need to be aware of the child's medication and its potential side effects.

8-3c Risk Factors for Externalizing Disorders

There is a tendency to react to aggressive acts as isolated events at face value, especially under the pressure of many other things going on in the classroom. However, there is impressive data that suggest that our behavior is the result of integrated contributions of factors, both internal and external, and that these factors work together as a dynamic system.

Table 8.2 provides some **correlated constraints** that affect aggression, both positively and negatively (Farmer, Farmer, Estell, & Hutchins, 2007). On the positive side,

TABLE 8.2 Aggression and Correlated Constraints

Positive	Negative
Academic success	Academic difficulties
Positive peer relations	Attention problems
Athletic competence	Peer rejection
Supportive adults	Coercive family systems
Sufficient resources	Poor parental monitoring

SOURCE: Farmer, T., Farmer, E., Estell, D., & Hatchens, B. (2007). The developmental dynamics of aggression and the prevention of school violence. *Journal of Emotional and Behavioral Disorders, 15*(4), 197–208, copyright © 2007 by Sage Publications. Reprinted by permission of SAGE Publications.

good academic performance, good relationships with peers, the presence of supportive adults, and athletic competence all tend to interrelate with one another and operate as a brake on aggression. On the other hand, there is a series of negative constraints, also interrelated, that can predict aggression. A combination of academic problems, attention difficulties, coercive family relations, and poor parental monitoring all can operate as a dynamic system supporting aggressive behavior (Farmer et al., 2007).

When we realize that we are dealing with a correlated dynamic system of factors, we see the limited use of a single intervention—such as improving social skills, for example—in the face of this system of correlated constraints. These constraints have likely been in place for a large part of the developmental history of the student.

An extended literature review reveals a series of correlated constraints (factors related to one another that add to or reduce the challenges occurring) that predict internalizing behaviors such as anxiety, depression, self-hatred, and so forth. Some of these are the presence of a chronically ill sibling, other learning disabilities, poor social status, and parental divorce. These correlated factors also form a dynamic system that defies easy modification (Crews et al., 2007).

Sameroff and his colleagues (1993) conducted a family longitudinal study for ten years to examine the impact of environmental factors on the intelligence of children. Using an index of ten risk factors (including mother's anxiety, social supports, low income, minority) they concluded that the number of risk factors present were a better predictor of poor intellectual development than any of the individual risk factors. The cumulative effect of the risk factors made it difficult for the child to maintain normal or even development.

Family Risk Factors

One interesting indicator of a family risk factor is family violence, which includes child abuse. Children who experience such violence are more likely to inflict such violence on those weaker than they are in turn. The intergenerational aspect of this disorder is distressing. A child with serious behavior disturbance rarely comes from a stable home with warm and loving parents. And the child who is abused is likely to be an abusive parent and to reproduce the entire negative pattern unless the school or community intervenes (Mattison, 2004).

A generation ago, feelings were strong that parents were in large part responsible for their child's behavior problems. Today, many believe that the child's atypical behavior may cause parents to react in ways that are inappropriate and make the condition worse in a downward spiral of unfortunate sequential events.

Child Abuse

One of the environmental factors clearly related to EBD is child abuse. This physical and psychological mistreatment of children, mainly by parents, is so strongly predictive of EBD that unless preventive action is taken, we will see this misfortune repeated generation after generation. The enormous scope of the situation is not well known. As Barth and Haskins (2009) note:

> More than 3 million American children are investigated for child mistreatment each year, and 800,000 children, about 1 in every hundred, are identified by state agencies as having been abused or neglected. More than 1,500 children die as a result of this mistreatment (p. 1).

What is also not well known is that it doesn't have to be that way. We know techniques and treatments that can reduce this problem significantly through parent training and support (Forgatch, Patterson, Degarmo, & Beldavs, 2009). We spend a great deal more time teaching each other how to drive a car than how to parent—how to cope with stress and frustration without taking it out on vulnerable children.

Fighting is a problem if it is intense and over long duration.

Think about how your own parents learned how to cope with you and your worries and behaviors. If they were fortunate enough to have loving and caring parents themselves, this was a good start. In addition, there are methods, such as positive behavior supports, not well known to even the most caring parents, that can make a clear difference in the family, in the classroom, and in the community. We will discuss some of these methods later in the chapter.

The Family and Society

Bronfenbrenner (1989) focused on the family as a child-rearing system, on society's support or lack of support for that system, and on the effects of that support or lack of support on children (Chapter 2). He maintained that the alienation of children reflects a breakdown in the interconnected segments of a child's life—family, peer group, school, neighborhood, and work world. The question is not "What is wrong with children with emotional or behavior disorders?" but may be "What is wrong with the child's social system?"

The conflict between the values of those in authority in society (and in the school) and the values of their culture can create tension. For example, what does a child do who sees a friend cheating? Honesty—a valued societal ethic—demands that the child report the incident. But loyalty—also a valued cultural ethic—demands silence. Even more serious in its impact is the situation in which the peer group devalues education or pressures the individual to use drugs or violence.

School Risk Factors

The risk factor most frequently associated with social and emotional disturbance is below-grade achievement in school. Do these children act out *because* they are academically slow and not able to keep up with their classmates? Is their acting out a reaction to their failure in school? The idea is an interesting one, but the evidence does not seem to support it. For one thing, the aggressive behavior that gets these youngsters into trouble in school is clearly observable *before* they enter school.

Jim, for example, was in trouble in school as early as kindergarten. His school records are peppered with teachers' statements: "He seems bright but doesn't want to apply himself." "He's unmotivated and an angry little boy." "This boy will not take the time necessary to learn the basics." Jim had myriad correlated constraints: a **coercive family system** (the use of physical or psychological force for imposing will), peer rejection, academic difficulties, and attention problems.

Violence in the Schools

We said earlier that the schools are a mirror of our society. Whatever bright spots we see in society, such as a sense of optimism about the future, or whatever problems we see, such as the rise of drug use or extensive violence, are likely to show up in the classroom and schoolyard. We need to remind ourselves that over 55 million students are in school right now, or about one in every five citizens of this country. Since we see a great deal of violence in our communities, we should not be surprised to see it reverberating in our schools. Here are recent statistics on the kind and rate of violence in our schools:

- During the 2008–2009 school year there were 1,579 homicides among youth ages 5–18; 17 of those occurred at school. In 2008, there were 1,344 suicides among youth ages 5–18; seven of those occurred at school.
- In the first six months of 2009, 4 percent of students ages 12–18 reported being victimized at school, 3 percent reported theft, and 1 percent reported violent victimization.
- In 2009, about 10 percent of male students and 5 percent of female students in grades 9–12 reported being threatened or injured with a weapon on school property.
- During the 2007–2008 school year 10 percent of city schoolteachers and 6 percent of suburban or rural schoolteachers reported being threatened with an injury. Five percent of city schoolteachers and 3 percent of suburban or rural schoolteachers reported being physically attacked.
- During the 2009–2010 school year, 23 percent of public schools reported daily or weekly bullying among students; 9 percent reported widespread disorder on a daily or weekly basis.
- In 2009, 23 percent of students in grades 9–12 reported that drugs were offered, sold, or given to them.
- During the 2009–2010 school year there were 433,800 serious disciplinary actions taken in public schools; 74 percent were for suspensions of five days or more, 20 percent were transfers to specialized schools, and 6 percent were expulsions.

Source: U.S. Department of Education. (2011). *Indicators of School Crime and Safety*. Washington, D.C.: National Center for Educational Statistics.

TeachSource Digital Download Access online

All of these statistics can be misread, of course, to make schools appear to be a vast arena of misbehavior and conflict. In almost every case, the statistics on violence reported were much higher in the community at large than in schools, but they do remind us that violence is a part of students', teachers', and administrators' lives in the school setting.

Can we identify children prone to violence in schools? The answer is yes, and they can be identified quite early. Loeber and Farrington (1998) suggested that a small subset of juveniles commits virtually all of the serious offenses and that these students began their violent activities when quite young. Sprague and Walker (2000) suggest that 6 to 9 percent of children account for more than 50 percent of total discipline referrals and virtually all of the serious offenses. Furthermore, early discipline problems predict later adjustment problems quite accurately, so it is important to intervene as early as possible.

School Bullying

One of the most recent concerns with children with EBD has been **bullying** and what to do about it. There is little doubt that bullying has been a part of schools since the beginning of education. Only recently has it been a source of study and part of the special education programming.

Farmer et al. (2007) have identified three actors in bullying:

1. Bullies: Youth identified as bullies repeatedly perpetrate physical and social harm against their peers but are not bullied by their peers.
2. Victims: Youth who are identified as victims are routinely bullied by peers but do not bully peers.
3. Bully-Victims: Youth who are identified as bully-victims perpetrate bullying against peers and are also bullied by peers.

> Each of these behaviors has different motivations and reasons for appearing in the classroom or school environment, and each is often involved in the social status and interactions of individual students. Our task is to find the motivation behind behavior such as bullying and then change the rewards or sanctions behind such actions. Children with high-incidence disabilities are more likely to be a part of the last two types of bullying. Sometimes children with disabilities bully other marginalized peers as a way of deflecting social assaults against themselves.
>
> It is difficult for teachers busy with their lessons to tease out the social structures present in their classrooms. This, again, is a reason for a team approach. This team can present a brief screening instrument that targets a range of behaviors including aggression, disruption, noncompliance, and nonengagement in academic affairs. This data could be a base for planning so that we understand the process of peer inclusion and exclusion in the social system that lies at the base of much aggression and bullying.

It is hard to calculate the damage done when children go to school not to learn but to to worry about how to avoid the bully or bullies who physically threaten, extort money, or write hurtful or threatening e-mails. The size of this problem can be seen in ▶ Figure 8.2, which shows that in the sixth grade more than four out of ten students report incidences of bullying; even in the twelfth grade, one out of five report such behavior.

There is a gender difference, with boys experiencing physical bullying and girls receiving more psychological intimidation. We rarely know the extent of psychological harassment, but it surely can be deadly, as the story details. This involves not only individual teachers but the entire school faculty, which has the responsibility to curb such behavior. Teachers should point out to students that bullying

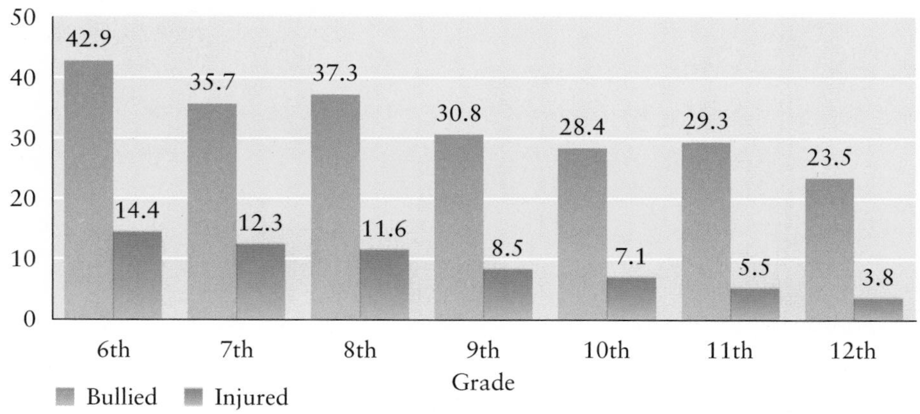

▶ **Figure 8.2 Percentage of Students Bullied and Injured from Bullying**
Source: Data from Table 11.2 in Indicators of School Crime and Safety: 2009; National Center for Education Statistics, U.S. Department of Education. Retrieved from http://nces.ed.gov

is not only wrong but also breaks the law when it becomes stealing, assault and battery, extortion, sexual harassment, and other criminal acts (National School Safety Center, 2002).

One approach to addressing bullying identifies school staff who are "safe contacts" from whom students can receive counseling and support and with whom they can feel free to share experiences. It is clear that school staff have the responsibility to act when such behavior is revealed.

The harm is done not only to the bullied but also to the bully himself or herself, who carries such behavior and sense of power into adulthood and will possibly commit more serious offenses. It is not just the bullied who need counseling but the bullies themselves. It is likely that the bully is working out his or her own psychological needs thought their use of power over others and so counseling would be of benefit to them.

Cultural and Ethnic Risk Factors

Many observers have noted the increased prevalence of culturally and linguistically diverse children who are identified as having social or emotional disturbances (Osher et al., 2004). However, there might be a clear *correlation* between ethnic background and behavior, this does not mean there is *causation*—that is, that their condition was caused by their ethnic or racial membership.

There is reason to believe that schools react differently to offenses committed by students from various ethnic backgrounds. Vincent, Swain-Bradway, Tobin, and May (2011) reported on the exclusion (suspensions and expulsions) policy of 77 different schools that were implementing school-wide positive behavior support procedures. Long-term exclusions (over 10 days) showed African-American students heavily overrepresented, while White and Hispanic students were underrepresented. These disproportions continued even after the school-wide procedures were implemented over two years.

Substance Abuse Risk Factors

One of the serious side problems of many children with behavior disorders is *substance abuse*. The public's attention is often directed to the use of exotic drugs, but the use and abuse of alcohol and tobacco are much more common. Substance abuse is a growing problem in U.S. schools; there is evidence (Davis, Kruczek, &

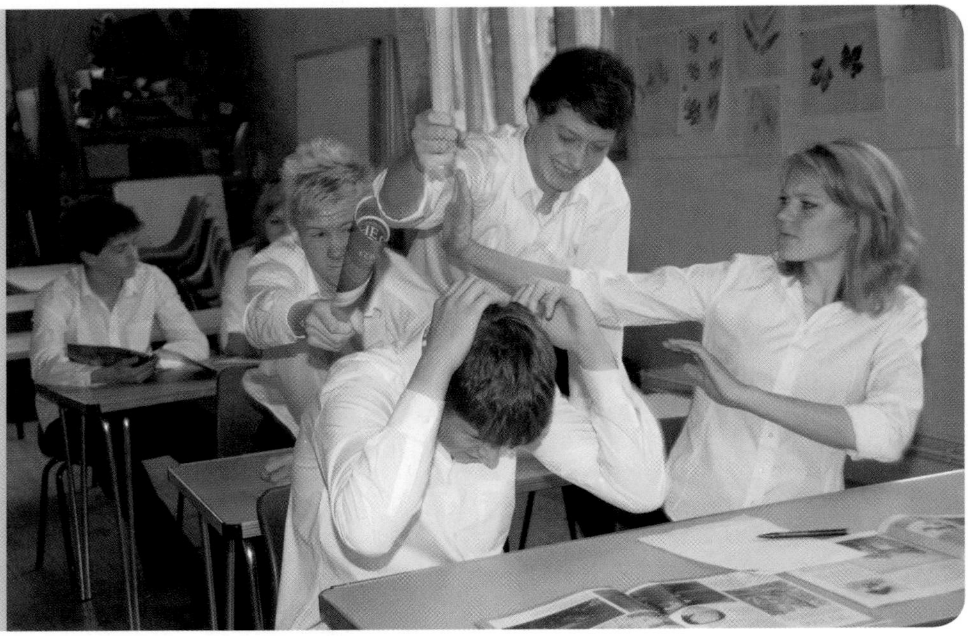

When a person is bullied everyone is negatively impacted... the bully, the victim, and the observers.

ACE STOCK LIMITED/Alamy

McIntosh, 2006) that children with behavior problems have rates of substance abuse higher than the rates of their peers in special education or in general education. In addition to the general teen culture that can encourage substance abuse in some communities, children or teenagers with behavioral and emotional problems often are influenced by a series of additional factors that may predispose them to substance abuse. These factors would include prescribed medication, chronic medical problems, social isolation, depression, and a higher risk of being in a dysfunctional family (McCombs & Moore, 2002).

One notable study is the longitudinal Pittsburgh Youth Study of inner-city boys. Substance use was classified into five categories: beer and wine, tobacco, hard liquor, marijuana, and other drugs. Tobacco was being used by 23 percent of the 13-year-olds, whereas beer and wine had already been experienced by 32 percent of those boys. By the time the boys in this study reached 13 years of age, 9 percent of them had used marijuana.

These investigators (Loeber & Farrington, 1998) found that the different levels of substance use correlated with the severity of delinquent acts. The factors that seemed to be most linked to substance abuse were low achievement, depressed mood, the presence of attention deficit disorders, and a lack of guilt on the part of the child about such substance use.

Substance abuse cannot be said to cause emotional problems or problem behavior, but it is clearly part of the syndrome of behaviors linked to early problems and later delinquency. Think about the characteristics of drug users: low self-esteem, depression, inability to handle social experiences, and stress. These same characteristics mark children with behavior disorders. Although the research is not yet clear, there may be a connection between the primary disability of a behavior disorder and the secondary disability of substance abuse. Despite this information, there appears to be little systematic effort to include prevention programs in the school curriculum for these students. Special educators, then, must know the signs of chemical dependency, what to do when they suspect drug abuse in their students, and how to work with drug treatment programs.

Violent Video Games

One of the recent developments in the culture of young people has been the proliferation of violent video games. Along with these games comes the inevitable question: Does the playing of these games have some kind of effect on young people who seem addicted to them? A synthesis of the various studies that have attempted to answer this question has emerged with a tentative positive answer (Anderson et al., 2010).

Recently, even the small effect presented by the anti–video games group has been questioned (Ferguson, 2013) on the grounds that the evidence is not sufficient to cause us to make definitive statements about the negative effect of these games. The Supreme Court recently agreed with that point of view (*Brown v. Entertainment Merchants Association*, 2011) saying the evidence is not clear as to the effect of these games and that we should not make legal decisions based on it. Whether the effect is small or nonexistent, it is clear that many other factors play a more important role in aggressive behavior than video games.

What Have We Learned About Externalizing Behaviors?

Rutter (2003), in summarizing what has been learned, also presented what we have yet to learn. These statements represent a challenge for the next generation of researchers and educators:

1. Most of the research falls well short of identifying the crucial mediators of the causal process or the effective elements of prevention or treatment.
2. We have only a very limited understanding of what is required to bring about beneficial change. It is evident that parental abuse and neglect provide

significant risks for children, but it is not obvious what would prevent abuse and neglect.
3. Even when we know which interventions are effective, we lack good means of ensuring that those who might benefit from the interventions participate.
4. Most research has focused on individual differences rather than on (a) differences in level, (b) why the crime rate now is much higher than in 1950, (c) why most forms of antisocial behavior are more common in males than in females, or (d) why the homicide rate in the United States is some dozen times the rate in Europe. (p. 376)

What can be done? First of all, we should consider what does *not* appear to work with the violent child. The "zero tolerance" approach adopted by many schools, which includes suspensions, expulsions, metal detectors, guards in the hallways, and so forth, seems to reduce violence only temporarily. This "zero tolerance" amounts to counter-hostility on the part of the school rather than an attempt to deal with the individuals. Of course, expulsions may solve a problem for the school administration but not that of the community, because violent youths can roam the neighborhoods, free of monitoring or supervision.

8-3d Risk Factors for Internalizing Disorders

Children who are anxious or withdrawn are likely to be more of a threat to themselves than to others around them. Since they usually are not disruptive, they generally do not cause classroom management problems. In contrast to children with conduct disorders, children who are anxious and withdrawn have problems with excessive internal control; in most settings they maintain firm control over their impulses, wishes, and desires. Children who are anxious and withdrawn may be rigid and unable to be spontaneous (Gresham & Kern, 2004).

Where do fearful children come from? We know that many of them have parents with similar problems. In addition, most professionals agree that chronic anxiety in children comes from being in a stressful situation, not being able to get out of the situation, and not being able to do anything to improve it. This inability to change the situation adds to feelings of helplessness and reinforces low self-image.

For students, a crucial examination looming on the horizon can create chronic anxiety. For younger children, anxiety can stem from homes in which they feel unwanted or are abused. Children are often too young to understand that their parents may be working out their own problems or that their parents' actions have little to do with them. All they understand is that no matter what they do, they are not getting praise or love from their parents.

Learned Helplessness

Learned helplessness in children is the belief that nothing they do can stop bad things from happening. Learned helplessness results in severe deterioration in performance after failure, as though the children have said to themselves, "It's all happening again." These children often have such low self-concepts that failure in a school task or a social setting only confirms for them their worthlessness and helplessness in the face of an unfriendly environment (Seligman, 1991).

The child's poor performance in the classroom may be much worse than he is capable of, simply because he is so pessimistic about himself and his abilities. Low self-esteem seems to be at the heart of much of the underachievement of children who are anxious and withdrawn.

Adolescents need to find their way out of learned helplessness through learning alternative coping mechanisms and being offered experiences designed to improve their feelings of self-esteem and self-worth. In these situations, as well as many others we have discussed, multidisciplinary teams of professionals are necessary.

Suicide

A strong feeling of hopelessness can be the predominant reason for teenagers to think about suicide or even attempt it. For some time, suicide has been one of the major causes of adolescent death. Today, it is the third leading cause of teenage deaths in the United States, with 272 deaths recorded and about eight times more suicides attempted. The ratio of males to females in such attempts is about 4:1 (NIMH, 2001). A number of suicides are also linked to substance abuse.

The following are some currently cited signs of a potential suicide:

- Extreme changes in behavior
- Previous suicide attempts
- Suicide threats and statements
- Signs of deep depression

Special education or general education teachers who note such signs should make referrals to appropriate crisis teams or mental health facilities. Most communities now have such services available. In addition, there is a National Suicide Prevention Lifeline (1-800-273-TALK; 1-800-273-8255) that is available 24 hours a day and seven days a week for emergency counseling (English and Spanish). The teacher remains the first line of defense in these crisis situations and needs to be alert for any signs that students may provide.

One effort to thwart suicide attempts has been the formation of crisis teams at both the school and the district levels. Team members learn procedures to cope with suicidal individuals, and the team has access to resources that it can bring to bear quickly. A teacher who sees the danger signs has the immediate task of providing relief from the feelings of helplessness or hopelessness that the student may be expressing and of instilling in the student some feeling of being in control. Some positive change, no matter how small, must be made to prove to the student that the situation is not hopeless.

The individualized education program (IEP) can be an effective guide for teachers who are trying to cope with children who show emotional or behavior problems. The IEP is shaped not only by the student's specific problem but also by available resources. The presence of professional consultants in the mental health area or of an active remedial program in the school gives both the assessment team and the parents more options to consider.

Dennis MacDonald/PhotoEdit

It takes a team to provide the interventions needed to help students with emotional and behavioral needs be successful.

Long-range treatment may demand services from community and mental health agencies, and teachers should be aware of good referral sources. For schools, the best method of prevention is an educational program that enhances feelings of self-worth and self-control. Explicit instruction in positive coping skills can be one way of providing feelings of self-control.

8-4 Characteristics of Students with EBD

8-4a Information Processing Model

As indicated in Figure 8.3, emotional and behavioral disorders have an impact on all aspects of information processing. Although visual, olfactory, and auditory abilities may test as normal, how the child perceives the stimulus may be altered. Pete, very aware of his power status in his group, may misinterpret actions and words of others as a threat to him and his status.

Anxiety and stress can influence all of the central processing mechanisms from memory to evaluation. The child's attempt to communicate through speaking and writing is clouded by either externalizing or internalizing concerns, as well as social relationships. Students' decision making (executive function) is at the mercy of the emotional forces working on them at any given time. In short, a child with emotional and behavioral disorders has serious problems in every major aspect of information processing.

Two students, Jim and Molly, both 8 years old, have information processing models that appear similar, but Jim is externalizing aggression while Molly is internalizing aggression. Jim has not been able to control his temper and seems to be in an angry rage most of the time. As a result, he is not able to fully use his good central processing skills—memory, reasoning, evaluation, and so forth—to apply to schoolwork. He comes from a father-absent family, and his mother appears disorganized and depressed. His social relations are poor, and he has been in a number of fights. His decision-making ability (executive

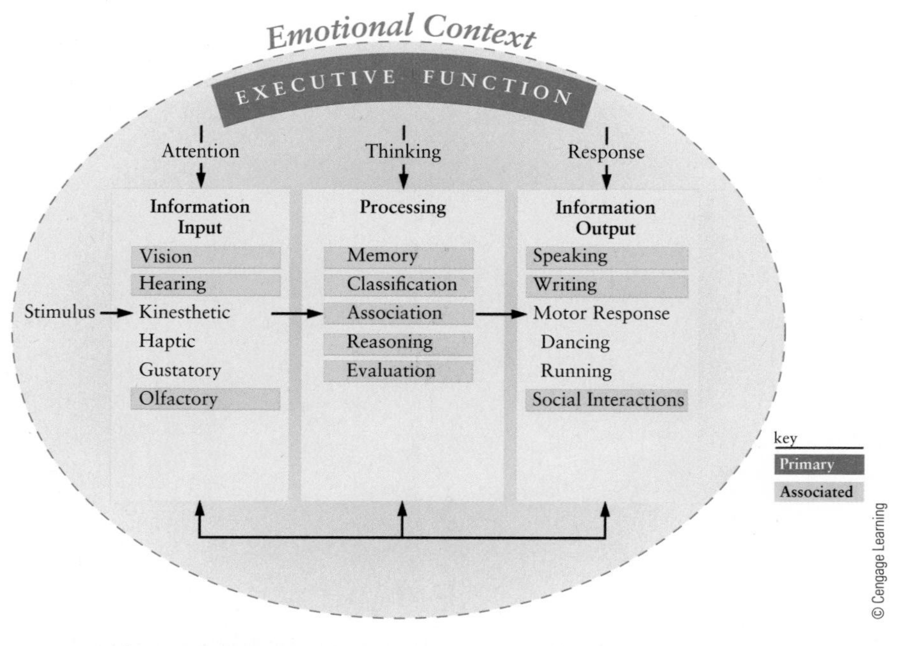

Figure 8.3 Information Processing Model for Students with Emotional and Behavior Disorders

TeachSource Digital Download Access online

function) appears to be overwhelmed by the waves of negative emotions sweeping over him.

A multidisciplinary team, including community mental health services, has been planning to place Jim in special learning sessions where he can get some self-confidence in his abilities, but there is a tough road ahead because Jim did not have the preschool care that might have helped considerably.

Molly also has central processing problems. She is depressed and in tears much of the time, so, like Jim, she is unable to use the abilities she has. She has seen a psychiatrist with minimal success, and her parents wish Molly had the social skills of her older sister, who seems to succeed effortlessly in academic and social settings. Molly is not the personal threat to her teachers that Jim is, because she does not challenge their ability to control the classroom. Nevertheless, her teachers are distressed by their inability to help her sadness and low self-concept. Again, a team of professionals from physician to psychologist to educator is needed to help turn around Molly's distress and her increasing levels of academic difficulties.

8-5 Educational Responses for Students with Emotional and Behavior Disorders

There has been a growing understanding that our school programs for children with emotional and behavior disorders (EBD) have not been crowned with success. For example, half of the students labeled EBD drop out of school, the highest rate of all disabilities. Twenty percent of students with EBD are arrested at least once before they leave school, and over half are arrested within a few years of leaving school (Lewis et al., 2010). Either we have started too late, do not have the right organizational approach or the right instructional strategies, or we do not apply them with sufficient intensity. We have good reason to believe that we have the right interaction strategies, so we need to see how we can organizationally and instructionally create the proper environment.

As seen in Figure 8.4, most children with EBD spend half or more of their day in the regular classroom. This might represent more the economics of education than a response to their needs, as treatment is expensive. Most of these students need an intense program; whether they can get it in the regular classroom is questionable.

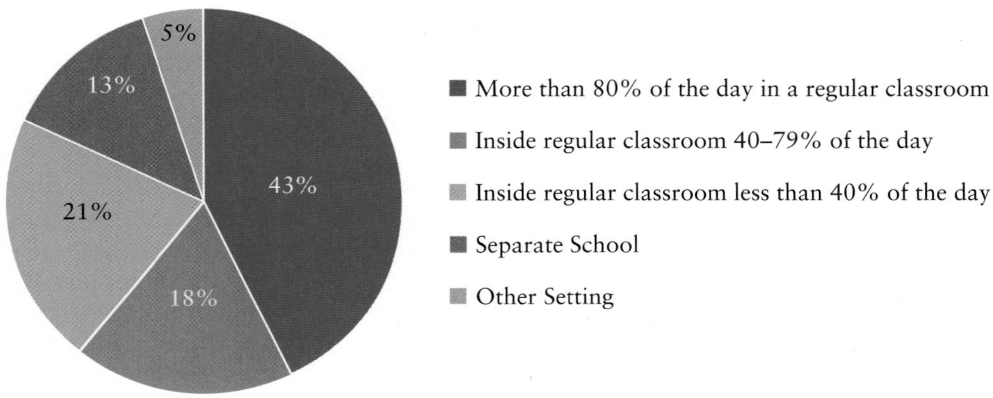

Figure 8.4 Educational Settings for Students with Emotional and Behavior Disorders
Source: Data Accountability Center. (2011). *Part B Educational Environments 2011* [data file]. Retrieved from http://www.ideadata.org/PartBEnvironments.asp

Furthermore, we have come to the realization that most of the parent and teacher behavior in the face of child misbehavior represents the wrong reaction and may even increase future misbehavior. Punitive responses or negative comments in the face of student actions do not help the social climate of the classroom or get positive reactions from students. For example, Mrs. Moore, after a morning of chastising Lucia for shouting in class, will relax when Lucia is quiet for once. But this is the very time she should be interacting in a positive way. "It is so nice, Lucia, to see you attending to your work." Since the "natural" response (punishment) turns out to be the ineffective one, a good deal of teacher preparation and parent training seems called for to help encourage a positive classroom and home environment (positive behavior supports) and to avoid making the problem worse with the "natural" response.

The **transactional theory** describes child development as an ongoing series of reciprocal relations, with a child's environment exerting influence on behavior, and the child's behavior in turn influencing the environment. If this theory holds, then the more we create a positive environment in the school, the better we can expect the child's behavior to be.

The educational responses here are divided by organizational strategies and instructional strategies to separate what the system can do and what the teacher can do.

8-5a Organizational Structures to Support Students with EBD

It is particularly important to identify children at the preschool age with symptoms of EBD because we have good evidence that preschool problems do not go away but persist and become more serious in later grades unless action is taken early (Egger & Angold, 2006).

The most common problems found at this age are ADHD, oppositional defiant and conduct disorders, anxiety disorders, and depressive disorders. We are not well equipped to apply diagnostic services and subsequent treatment at the preschool age, because preschool services, like child care centers, do not have the resources of the public schools. So it is important that teachers in early childhood be aware of the community mental health resources available.

There is a concern that "normal" aggression may be tagged as a sign of an emotional or behavior problem, so it must be clear that oppositional behaviors be *persistent, pervasive, and severe* to warrant mental health referral. (Still, only about one in four children who would be identified as emotionally and behaviorally disturbed are referred for treatment, representing a major gap in services (Egger & Angold, 2006). Some attention has been given to the issue of preschool depression, with the predominant symptoms being sad and irritable mood, low energy, eating and sleeping problems, and low self-esteem (Luby et al., 2003). These conditions are often **comorbid**; that is, they exist alongside other disorders such as anxiety and fearful feelings.

In one study, the special education outcomes of 3,608 children who had a preschool history of developmental disability were followed into the fourth grade. Over three-quarters of preschool children who had a designated disability continued to have a disability in fourth grade, but not necessarily with the same label. The most consistent of the labels was that of autism, with 87 percent of the children continuing with the same label. However, for preschool children identified as having an emotional disability, only 69 percent were still considered to have the same label; 18 percent at fourth grade were referred to as "specific learning disabled" and another 6 percent as having autism. The most flexible of the labels were those children described as having an "educable mental handicap" or a "mild intellectual or developmental disability." Five years later, only 20 percent

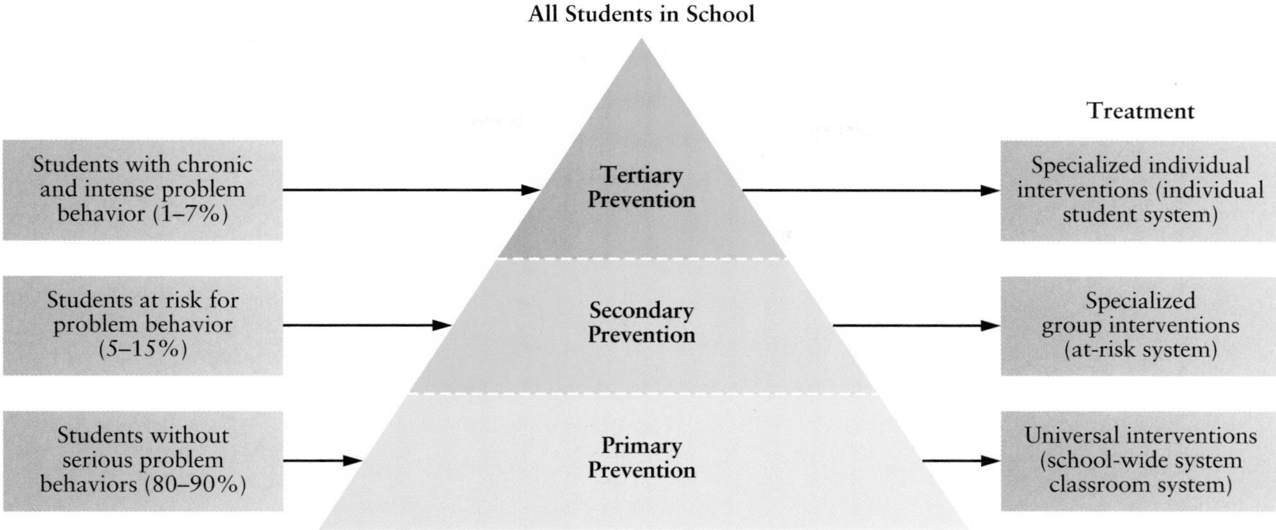

Figure 8.5 Response to Intervention, EBD
Source: Based on Sugai, G., & Horner, R. (2006). A promising approach for expanding and sustaining the implementation of school-wide positive behavior support. *School Psychology Review, 35, 245–259.*

retained the same label, while 36 percent were now described as being learning disabled, 11 percent emotionally disturbed, 7 percent autistic, and 13 percent speech impaired (Delgado, 2009).

For our purposes as educators, however, it is important to note that these children were still in academic trouble, whatever the labels. These findings indicate that the best plan may be to move ahead with IEPs that specify the student's difficulty and outline specific supports and services to meet the child's needs.

RtI Approaches for Students with Emotional and Behavior Disorders

RtI

How does the response to intervention (RtI) model fit into these various attempts to create a plan for behavior adjustment? Figure 8.5 reveals the RtI model for children with emotional and behavior disorders. The bottom of the RtI triangle (Tier I) is concerned with the universal interventions—the **school-wide behavior supports.** It should not be assumed that this band is represented by the usual classroom program. Instead, there may need to be a determined effort to ensure that the regular classroom *is* a place for healthy social interaction and the presentation of good mental health programming, as well as adequate content knowledge.

Three levels of behavioral support seem to be necessary for good school operation (Sugai & Horner, 2006). The first of these is **universal group behavior support** for most students. This involves establishing school-wide management strategies, setting rules and standards for expected student behavior in such venues as the cafeteria, the hallways, and the bus. Such an approach has been documented as sharply reducing office referrals for misbehavior (Lewis et al., 2010).

The Tier II activities (for about 5 to 15 percent of students) would apply the positive behavior supports through small-group work or individual tutoring. Such intervention should start as early as possible to prevent even more difficult behavior problems.

The Tier III activities involve a small number of students (1 to 7 percent), those with the most serious emotional and behavioral problems. They are dealt with on an individual basis with carefully designed IEPs and professional support to lessen the negative impact that the environment and bad personal interactions have had on these disturbed children.

Universal Tier I for Students with EBD

When we realize that poor academic performance is one of the key elements for children with EBD, our attention needs to be focused on all of the tiers of the RtI model. Included in Tier I must be a strong core reading program that is adaptable for students currently doing poorly (Simonsen et al., 2008). A consensus on school rules and classroom performance expectations is also part of the Tier I model. Such rules should be enforced schoolwide and applied in every classroom to give students a sense of stability and few surprises.

There has been a sharp increase in the number of research studies testing positive behavior approaches. For example, in a carefully controlled study, a three-year application of school-wide behavior supports in elementary schools in Hawaii and Illinois resulted in the improvement of the perceived safety of the school and the proportion of third graders meeting or exceeding the state reading assessment standards. A reduction in office discipline referrals was also noted (Horner et al., 2009). A Summary of *UDL Supports for Students with Emotional and Behavior Disorders* can be accessed online.

TeachSource Digital Download

Targeted Tier II for Students with EBD

If we are to urge teachers to abandon punishment and punitive responses to behavior problems (primarily because they don't work in the long run), then what will we replace them with? This is particularly relevant because the influential No Child Left Behind Act stresses the importance of evidence-based practices and research-supported procedures.

A review of such innovative practices includes positive behavior supports, functional behavior assessments, social skills instruction, and self-management practices (Lewis, Hudson, Richter, & Johnson, 2004). These reviewers point out that teachers must not only understand these techniques but also get ample opportunity to practice them! It is one thing to read a piece of music and quite another to play that piece with grace and style. Such performance requires quality monitoring of the necessary practice.

The history of **positive behavior interventions and supports (PBIS)** is recent, but its influence is growing rapidly across the country. The basic concept is that misbehavior should not necessarily be followed by punishment of one sort or another but with attempts to understand the causes or antecedents of the misbehavior (Dunlap & Carr, 2007). Then the teacher should introduce measures to create a positive environment that would make the misbehavior unnecessary. If we can create an educational climate in which personal needs and interests are being met, we will generate less of the anger and cruelty that so often accompanies social transgressions. None of these procedures is easy to learn or implement. The teacher in Box 8.1 hints at what a middle school teacher without such training may face.

Functional behavior assessment (FBA) is a key part of positive behavior supports. It can be described as a collection of methods for gathering information about a child's behavior that tries to answer the question "Why did he or she do that?" rather than, "What did he or she do now?" To answer this key question, a child study team may wish to seek the **antecedent behaviors** to the event and also to comprehend the child's understanding of the consequences of his or her actions.

Gresham (2007) describes five major ways in which unwanted behavior can accomplish certain goals for the individual child or adult:

1. Gain social attention (positive social reinforcement)
2. Gain access to tangibles or preferred activities (material or activity reinforcement)
3. Escape, delay, reduce, or avoid aversive tasks or activities (negative reinforcement)

BOX 8.1 Case Example: Mrs. Cabot

Mrs. Cabot, a sixth-grade teacher, does not necessarily believe in punishment as a way of restoring order in the classroom, but she sometimes is driven to it as a last alternative to chaos. What she may not realize is that Juan and Pete, her most troublesome students, would really prefer a calm and reasonable learning environment, too, if their needs were appropriately met. The question is how to keep Mrs. Cabot from reaching that level of desperation and how to have available to her alternative strategies for classroom control. She needs, and should have, professional supports to aid her.

4. Escape or avoid other individuals (negative social reinforcement)
5. Gain internal satisfaction (automatic or sensory reinforcement)

When Bobby suddenly hits another boy for being in his way or Sally tears up a drawing done by someone else, their motivation likely fits into one of these five categories, but which one? Careful observation may be required to discover which one and to plan alternative activities that will reduce the need for the unacceptable behavior (Fox & Gable, 2004). Bobby may be avoiding working with numbers, which he hates, whereas Sally may be trying to avoid Midge, whom she has just been told to work with. If we feel confident in our conclusions, then we can plan environmental changes or social activities that make such behavior unnecessary. You might recall some unusual behavior that you have seen over the past week. See if you can categorize it into one or more of the motives in the preceding list. Remember that all behavior is communicating something and it is our job to try and determine what need is being communicated. There is growing evidence that the use of Functional Behavior Analysis yields positive results, though it does not rid the child entirely of symptoms of behavior disorders. Goh and Bambara (2010) reviewed 83 case studies to determine the efficacy of Individual Functional Behavior Analysis (IFBA). These interventions were done in both self-contained special education settings and in general education classrooms. There were significant results obtained in both settings, but the effect was larger in the special education placement. They concluded: Functional based assessment (FBA) was found to be effective in reducing problem behaviors and increasing appropriate skills across diverse student populations and educational settings (p. 281)."

The use of team decision making was effective when part of the planning and implementation process. A similar meta-analysis was conducted by Gage, Lewis, and Stichter (2012) where over 69 studies of functional behavior assessment indicated a 70 percent reduction in problem behaviors and was effective across all student characteristics.

Intensive Tier III for Students with EBD

One of the most frequently used methods of modifying student behavior is **applied behavior analysis** (ABA), procedures that follow the work of B. F. Skinner on operant conditioning. In addition to the attention paid to the problem behavior, the procedure focuses on the *antecedents* to the behavior and the *consequences* following it; this is sometimes referred to as the A-B-C approach (antecedents–behavior–consequences). By modifying the antecedent behavior and the consequences that follow, we can often modify the behavior itself (Lewis, Lewis-Palmer, Newcomer, & Stichter, 2004).

For example, Matt has developed the disturbing habit of physically escaping from frustrating situations, and this means that teachers and administrators must be alert lest Matt leave school and take off into the surrounding neighborhood, leading his mentors on a long and exasperating chase. The answer that applied behavior analysis gives is to focus on antecedent behavior. What was happening immediately before Matt headed for the outdoors? If we discover it was direct conflict with one of the other boys in the class, we can take steps to reduce the likelihood of such conflicts or stop them before a crisis develops.

Also, if the consequence of Matt's sojourns is that the other students pepper him with attention when he returns to the room, the teacher can instruct the other students to ignore Matt when he runs away or to praise him for being a member of the group. Matt can even earn points in a token system for resisting the temptation to flee. Such points can later be turned in for rewards like time to listen to music or read special books.

It is not easy to always determine the antecedents and consequences of problem behavior. Once we are looking for them, however, we are often able to make a reasonable conclusion as to why the behavior is happening. There will be many students with diverse needs and capabilities in the same physical space; this fact makes even more necessary the establishment of a solid basis for school-wide behavior supports at the Tier I level in the RtI model. A Summary of *RtI Approaches for Students with Emotional and Behavior Disorders* can be accessed online.

TeachSource Digital Download

The Wraparound Approach

The **wraparound approach** makes extensive use of agencies outside the school program, though they are expected to include school personnel in the planning. The family is also a critical part of this planning if it is to work, and strong efforts are made to involve them (Eber, Sugai, Smith, & Scott, 2002). Because behavior problems seem to include many different dimensions of self, family, culture, and community, it makes good sense to try a multidisciplinary approach using professionals from education, psychology, psychiatry, social work, and perhaps other related fields, combined into a treatment team that produces a system of care (Eber & Keenan, 2004).

With regard to Jim, such wraparound planning might include counseling for his mother, who has become depressed about her inability to handle his behavior; some psychological counseling for Jim to help him understand the reasons for his hostile outbursts; and plans for the teacher to find some examples of success for Jim in his schoolwork so that he will get some satisfaction from being in school.

The plan focuses on the strengths of the student, as well as on attempts to mute any deficits in performance that the student may have. Although it is often used as a vehicle for maintaining the student in the general education classroom by bringing additional resources into that classroom, services might be delivered in a resource room or a self-contained special class if that represents the least restrictive environment for that student (Kerr & Nelson, 2002).

Teachers can use various strategies with students who have behavior disorders, but each strategy imposes costs or demands on the teachers, whether they are trying to communicate with students, support desirable behavior, or control problem behavior. For example, reminding a student about the rules of the classroom (RtI, Tier I) costs the teacher less in energy or effort than does conducting a group meeting on a problem behavior (Tier II). High-cost teacher behavior, however, may be needed to bring some benefits to the situation. Teachers often find themselves having to decide whether to use these high-cost strategies, and all sorts of factors—professional and personal—can affect the final decision.

Technical Assistance

One of the marks of the success of the positive behavioral intervention movement has been the establishment of the OSEP Technical Assistance Center on

Positive Behavioral Interventions and Supports, a collaboration between the U.S. Department of Education and 11 technical assistance units across the United States. The Center is based on the demonstrated success of PBIS in improving social behavior and academic performance as a practical classroom implementation. Its goal is to encourage the widespread implementation of PBIS through demonstration, dissemination, and evaluation.

8-5b Curriculum and Instruction for Students with EBD

While organizational strategies are important, their influence is diminished unless they are accompanied by effective instructional strategies. Once the teacher and the student are face to face, how does the teacher adapt the lessons to fit the special needs that the exceptional child brings to the classroom?

Access to Common Core State Standards: Universal Design for Learning

COMMON CORE STATE STANDARDS

Children with EBD, like Bob and Molly, are expected to meet the high levels of the Common Core State Standards (CCSS). But we also recognize that their disabilities may pose problems in meeting those standards, without special planning and assistance. In this instance, will the students' emotional problems keep them from adequately applying the logical analyses required by the CCSS? The CCSS presents the goal to be reached, but not direction on how to get there.

One instructional approach to help Bob and Molly access the CCSS is **Universal Design for Learning** (UDL). Providing instruction in different ways and allowing Bob and Molly to respond in alternative pathways, such as acting out the emotions of characters instead of writing a traditional report, could increase their acceptance of and success with the assignments. Ms. Rosselli, their teacher, is already prepared for a frustrated Bob to loudly protest about the unfairness of the assignments. Molly can be counted on to fold into her unhappiness as she prematurely gives up. The EBD specialist can be most helpful in assuring Bob through positive behavior supports and promising to look over his drafts so that he is not totally on his own. Ms. Rosselli assures Molly of her abilities as well.

The CCSS, like all standards, are dependent upon the particular approach from the educators in the classroom setting to make it a useful part of the curriculum. A group planning strategy, taking into account the individual needs of the students, would seem to be the way to approach these requirements for students with EBD.

As one example of how a teacher might use the principles of UDL to adapt the CCSS for a student with EBD, consider the first standard for fifth-grade writing:

> Write opinion pieces on topics or texts supporting a point of view with reason and information.
>
> a. Introduce a topic or text clearly, state an opinion, and create an organizational structure in which ideas are logically grouped to support the writer's purpose.
> b. Provide logically ordered reasons that are supported by facts and details.
> c. Link opinion and reasons using words, phrases, and clauses (e.g., consequently, specifically).
> d. Provide a concluding statement or section related to the opinion presented.

Such a standard could yield an assignment where the student with EBD expresses himself on the rules of the school or society that he finds irritating or o bnoxious

TABLE 8.3 Using Universal Design Principals to Give Students with EBD Access to the Common Core State Standards

Common Core Standard	Multiple Representations	Multiple Engagements	Multiple Assessments
Reading Standard for Literature, #6, Craft and Structure, Grade 7 Analyze how an author develops and contrasts the points of view of different characters or narrators in a text.	Text-based materials Movies, TV shows Cartoons Pictures Graphic organizers (characters' points of view) Highlighted text (colors for points of view) Story boards showing development of points of view	Direct instruction on points of view analysis Readings Identify words/phrases that show characters' points of view Compare/Contrast Charts Role plays/Drama Write poem or song sharing points of view Debates Discussions/Seminars Draw pictures depicting evolving points of view Application to real life, where people have different points of view	Written product on points of view Compare/Contrast Chart Dramatic presentation Write editorials giving contrasting characters' points of view Poem or song presenting evolving points of view
Math Standard Statistics and Probability, #6 Investigating Chance process and develop, use, and evaluate probability models, Grade 7 Approximate the probability of a chance event by collecting data...	Charts, Graphs, Pictures Hand-on Models Real-world examples Software for probability	Direct instruction on probability Dice roll predictions and charts Develop a model for predicting the likelihood of being dealt an ace in a five-card deal for five people using a standard deck of cards Develop real-world scenarios where knowing the probability of an event should help with decision making	Traditional assessments of problem solving Computer generated models of Probability Given a specific real-world scenario using probability, students can offer advice on the best choice or decision Discuss the ethics of games of chance

TeachSource Digital Download Access online

(rulings on bullying for instance). A teacher applying UDL might allow students to choose a written or performative response. Such responses can give the teacher or team insight on how students' feelings are driving their behavior and thinking and help adjust future interactions with them. Table 8.3 shows two further examples of how UDL can be used to provide access to the CCSS for students with EBD.

Sequencing Treatments

One question when faced with students with both reading and behavioral problems is which to address first or whether both should be tackled simultaneously. Cook et al. (2012) working with sixth- and seventh-grade students with both reading and behavioral problems, were able to try one treatment by itself and then both treatments simultaneously. Their findings indicate the superiority of the combined interventions:

> The results revealed that the whole, or combination of reading and behavioral interventions is greater than either of its parts. The implication of this finding is that school staff should attempt to intervene on both fronts when confronted with students with co-occurring reading and behavior problems. (p. 53)

One question often asked is what and how do you teach children with severe emotional disturbances. Cuenca-Sanchez et al. (2012) presented a model for reaching self-advocacy through persuasive writing. Using the POW+TREE model, they were able to obtain impressive gains for a small (N=10) experimental group of eighth graders, all of whom had been officially diagnosed as emotionally disturbed.

P-Pick my idea
O-Organize my notes
W-Write and say more
+
T-Topic Sentence
R-Reasons
E-Explanations
E-Ending

Using this model over a two-month period of time with small groups, the authors were able to demonstrate major gains in persuasive writing and increased satisfaction on the part of the students involved. The use of an organized model (POW+TREE) would seem to be one key to aid students who had limited academic success in previous settings.

Social Skills Training

One of the clear goals in remediation of emotional and behavior disorders is to improve the social skills of the student to produce socially acceptable learned behaviors such as cooperation, assertion, responsibility, empathy, and self-control. There has even been some suggestion that improvement in academic skills instruction, as much as social skills instruction, might improve the behavior of many students. One of the biggest problems has been the failure of **generalization**; that is, the student might learn a skill in one setting (e.g., proper greeting in a classroom) but be unable to generalize it to other settings, such as the playground. Gresham (1998) has proposed a contextual approach to teaching social skills that would take advantage of events that occur naturally in the school environment. Most social skills instruction in home, school, and community settings can be characterized as informal. Thousands of behavioral incidents occur in these settings, creating numerous opportunities for successful learning experiences every day.

A comprehensive review of social skills training and its effect on children with behavior and emotional disorders (Kavale, Mathur, & Mostert, 2004) found limited positive results and concluded that social skills training is still an "experimental intervention and needs to be rebuilt as part of a comprehensive treatment for students with EBD" (p. 459). This serves to remind us that it took years for many of these students to develop their dysfunctional behavior patterns, which cannot now be eliminated without substantial effort and professional attention.

Although the various attempts at meta-analyses (syntheses of past studies) of the effectiveness of social

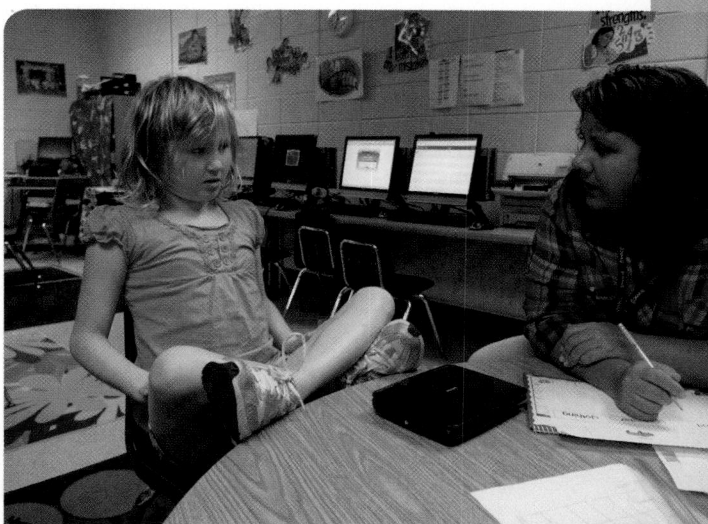

Robin Nelson/PhotoEdit

Social skills have to be taught explicitly for some children with EBD.

skills training have reported modest and sometimes discouraging results (see Kavale & Forness, 1999), a more recent study (Gresham, Van, & Cook, 2006) provides more encouragement. These authors suggest that the reasons for the small effects shown in previous studies were (1) lack of intensity of treatment and (2) failure to target the specific behaviors in need of modification.

The finding that "treatment intensity" is important has many applications in other special education attempts to modify behavior. Because of the chronic lack of resources for treatment, we are tempted to try to use as few resources as possible to get the changes we want. We lose faith in some methods because they were not provided in specific intensity or for a specific length of time with follow-up. The hard lesson is that it takes time and considerable effort to modify ingrained behavior patterns.

Cognitive Strategies Approach

Self-Monitoring, Self-Instruction

There is a family of strategies currently known as the **cognitive strategy approach**. Whether called self-monitoring, self-instruction, or self-control, these methods rely on the cooperation of the child and encourage the development of effective conscious coping skills. One attraction of these **self-management** techniques is that students who successfully apply them assume greater responsibility for their behavior instead of being externally controlled or "forced" to change by various kinds of conditioning (Polsgrove & Smith, 2004).

Suppose Pete has trouble staying in his seat. The first step is to teach him to recognize the behavior and then to record its frequency. Next, Pete negotiates a reward that is satisfying to him (perhaps some time to work on the computer) for staying in his seat for a specified period. Once he has shown the ability to control the behavior, he can be given the opportunity to control his own schedule and make decisions about the content or skills he would like to work on in the time slot.

There are several self-management techniques:

- **Self-monitoring** means keeping track of how often a target behavior occurs by checking a form at a predetermined time (Sheffield & Waller, 2010). For example, if Pete feels an aggressive attack coming on, he can note it in a journal. This helps him become increasingly aware of the clues that identify a potential outburst.
- **Self-instruction training** (SIT) is a strategy for teaching any sequential thinking skills such as problem solving, handling frustration, managing anger, or resisting peer pressure (Polsgrove & Smith, 2004).
- **Self-evaluation** asks the student to compare her behavior with some criteria and make a judgment about the quality of the behavior being exhibited; for example, "On a scale of 1 to 5, how much attention am I paying to the teacher?"
- **Self-reinforcement** means that the student rewards herself with a token or a tally after meeting some performance standard, such as avoiding aggressive outbursts for a set period of time. For example, a timer set for ten minutes that goes off without an aggressive outburst earns for the student a token that she can cash in later for game-playing time or a specially designed activity.

These techniques are designed to increase students' awareness, competence, and commitment to eliminating negative behaviors and to encourage the acquisition of constructive ones. For Pete, this means that the teacher works with him to improve self-awareness skills that will enable him to increase his own control over his hyperactivity or distractibility. One practical way of increasing students' personal responsibility is to let the students participate in developing their own IEPs (see Figure 8.6 with sample IEP goals for Pete).

The greatest advantage of this approach is that children gain self-confidence by exerting control of their previously out-of-control behavior. There is an important additional advantage. Many children with behavior disorders spend

Example IEP goals for Pete may include:

- Pete will work at his desk for 10 minutes 80% of the time.
- Given a class situation when Pete is evidencing inappropriate behavior, he will indicate, with modeling and/or prompts, his feelings (frustration, discomfort, fear), and a more appropriate behavior and language (i.e. "help me" or tap a student to get his attention and sign "please move" or "it's my turn" or indicate to teacher that he needs to regroup and organize himself), 80% of the time.

Figure 8.6 Sample IEP Goals for Pete

TeachSource Digital Download Access Pat's full IEP online

much of their time in the general education classroom. Many general education classroom teachers do not wish to, or feel they cannot, engage in the complex monitoring and recording of individual student behaviors that some of the other behavior-shaping techniques require. Once the students learn what they are to do in a self-management program, they can proceed with only modest teacher supervision.

How do all the approaches work with individual children such as Pete, who is having special problems with a fellow student, Jason? Part of Pete's volatility around Jason is a reaction to feeling left out. Pete is angry at being abandoned by Jason, who had been his friend when they were younger, and his behavior with Jason is a misplaced attempt at getting something: Jason's attention and friendship. At this point we can work with Pete to help him see how his aggressive behavior drives more people away from him. Part of the positive behavioral supports for Pete will include working with the school counselor on (1) recognizing the consequences of negative behavior and (2) developing specific **replacement behaviors** that will help him make and keep friends.

When we look at Pete's functional behavior assessment, we see that there are a few things we can do to modify the classroom environment and provide positive supports for his better behavior. We might, for example, establish a work carrel for Pete in which distractions are minimized and he has all supplies (such as pencils, Franklin speller, paper, etc.) in one place. This might help with his initial "out of the seat" behavior, but we need to go further if we want to address his task avoidance. We already know that Pete avoids tasks with reading and writing because they are very difficult for him, so we look for ways to support his academic progress with tasks that are at his level of development and thereby foster competence and success.

In addition to working on his IEP goals, we might establish a **behavior contract** with him that focuses on his interactions with classmates, especially with Jason. The contract might look like the "Behavior Contract for Pete" in Box 8.2.

What is most important about behavior contracts is that they are directed by the student: The student identifies specific objectionable behavior, articulates the impact of this behavior, identifies its consequences, and describes rewards for not indulging in it. This ownership, for students, is critical to helping them take responsibility for their behavior and for the impact it has on those around them. It is also essential to remember that the more specific a contract is regarding the targeted behavior, the more likely it is that the student will be able to succeed in changing it. So in Pete's case, the wording "leaving Jason alone" is much better than a vague phrase like "trying to get along with Jason." The reward, too, is critical: It should appear desirable to the student, but it should also foster positive growth. For Pete, the ability to invite other students to play a computer math game fosters growth in both academic and social skills. Finally, the consequence

BOX 8.2 Behavior Contract for Pete

Behavior and impact: I, Pete Walker, understand that when I start fights with Jason, I disrupt the class, I don't do my own work, I make my teacher mad at me, and Jason and I sometimes get hurt.

Target for change: This week I will work on leaving Jason alone.

Reward for change: If I do not get into a fight with Jason this week, I can pick three classmates to play my favorite computer math game with me on Friday during independent work time.

Consequence for no change: If I do fight with Jason this week, I will use my independent work time to do a classroom chore. That way, I can give something back to my classmates.

Date: 9/15/2010

Student Signature: ________________

Teacher Signature: ________________

TeachSource Digital Download Access online

for *not* fulfilling the contract must be logical and must be seen by the student as undesirable. In this instance, Pete's behavior disrupts the class and takes away class time, so it is logical that his consequence should give something back to the class.

Teacher Preparation

Policymakers differ as to whether the field of emotional and behavior disorders merits a specialist training program or whether it can be folded into the usual special education program.

What is needed in the situation described in Box 8.3 is not a "super teacher" but a *team* of professionals working together to meet the students' needs. Personnel preparation studies of teachers in the EBD field yield good news in terms of the increasing confidence that such prospective teachers have in controlling classroom behavior (Henderson et al., 2005). Teachers who work specifically with students with EBD respond positively to statements such as "I am skillful in managing behavior" and "I am skillful in collaborating with non-special education teachers, including prereferral interventions."

The bad news is that not enough teachers with special training in EBD are available. The teacher shortages in the EBD field are severe, as is attrition, causing many school systems to hire persons under emergency certificates to handle these responsibilities. SPeNSE (Study of Personnel Needs in Special Education, supported by the U.S. Department of Education) has conducted surveys that reveal the continued need for qualified personnel (Carlson, Klein, Schroll, & Wittig, 2002). Among other things, these results probably mean that some in-service training of general and other special education teachers in local districts should be provided by certified EBD teachers in such problematic areas as classroom management and behavior challenges.

The Support Teacher (EBD Specialist)

One innovative suggestion for supporting classroom teachers is to use a **support teacher**, a person with special education training in many of the approaches noted earlier. Such a teacher comes into the general classroom to support the teacher in working with children with special needs and sometimes takes responsibility for small groups of students. Obviously, a classroom teacher with 25 or 30 children cannot cope with all aspects of the classroom environment without help. Who can provide that help? The strategy rests on five assumptions and principles:

- Even a child who has serious behavior problems is not disturbed all the time. There are only certain periods during which the pupil cannot function in the larger group setting.

BOX 8.3 The Teacher and the Pressures of Inclusion

Anne, a devoted elementary schoolteacher in a local rural school district for 15 years, tells me that her job has become emotionally and physically overwhelming. After her school district moved to "full inclusion" several years ago, her fifth-grade classroom of 25 now includes two children diagnosed with autism, three with EBD, eight with learning disabilities (LD), and about five others with mild cognitive disabilities. Anne is not certified in special education, but she gets some support from a special education teacher who works with the children with autism and a child with LD about thirty minutes each day. Although the reading levels of the children range from preprimer to grade level, she is required by the state to use standard textbooks for the fifth-grade level. She is finding it an increasingly difficult struggle to meet the needs of such a widely diverse class of students and is seriously considering resigning her position at the end of the year.

SOURCE: From Polsgrove, L. (2003). Reflections on the past and future, *Behavioral Disorders 28,* 221–226. Reprinted with permission.

- Teachers need direct assistance. Consultation is one thing, but real help is something else. Psychologists and similar professionals might offer advice, but they do not know what it is like to try to administer a classroom that includes children who have behavior disorders.
- Direct-service support teachers should work full time in the school to which they are assigned, should not be itinerant, and should be trained as a special education teacher. The support teacher should not only be able to respond to the child who is in crisis but also be able to help all children with academic and emotional problems.
- Sometimes the support teacher can assist best by taking over the classroom while the regular teacher works through a phase of a problem with a child.
- Help should be based on the reality of how the child is able to cope with the classroom and not on categories, labels, or diagnostic criteria.

The support teacher generally uses techniques that are an extension of regular education procedures, emphasizing positive behavior supports. In addition, the support teacher is able to provide important liaison services that are not within the capabilities of the heavily burdened classroom teacher. Children with behavior problems often need the help of a multidisciplinary team of pediatricians, psychologists, and paraprofessionals, and the support teacher can be the case manager and coordinate these sources of assistance.

TeachSource Video Connection

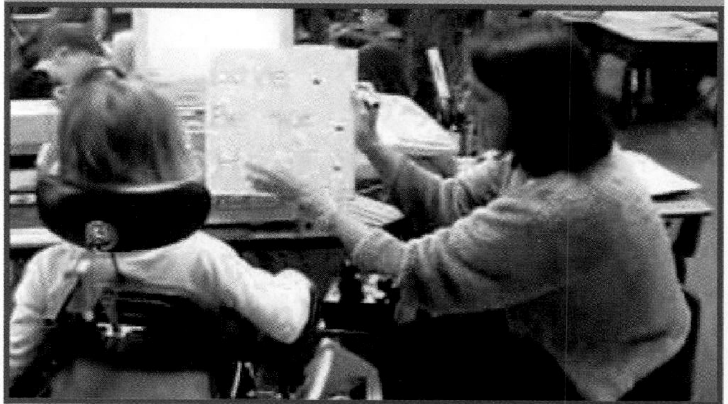

Watch the video "Brittany and Trisha: Teaching Strategies for Students with Emotional and Behavioral Disorders." This video describes the experiences of two students, Brittany and Trisha, and the teaching strategies their teachers have used to help them meet with success. After watching the Video Case, reflect on the strategies described in the video. How might you incorporate these strategies into your own teaching? What questions or concerns might you have about working with students with EBD in the classroom?

Watch online

Peer Tutoring

One of the instructional strategies in use with students with mild disabilities such as EBD is **peer tutoring**. Obviously, if peers can be helpful in improving the performance of children with disabilities, it could be a substantial boon for the teacher.

One of the most active and well-researched programs is the peer-assisted learning strategies (PALS) used primarily in elementary schools (see Fuchs et al., 1997). This approach consists of pairing students, one of whom is the player (student with a disability) and the other the coach (a student who has been prepared to help).

In 25-minute segments, the pairs meet to take turns in reading to one another, identifying words, and so forth.

Over a 15- to 25-week period, meeting four times a week, this approach has shown growth in reading that is sustainable over time for many, but not all, students. Much appears to depend on the nature of the students and the kind of preparation given to the tutors before beginning. One of the great potential advantages of such an approach is that expert outside help is not needed for its operation. Once classroom teachers have set up the pairs and the learning periods, they have only to monitor the progress periodically. This approach would be especially valuable in rural schools, where little outside help can be expected for the classroom teacher.

Peer Assisted Strategies
www.peerassistedlearning strategies.net

Senhoff and Lignugaris-Kraft (2007) reviewed 20 articles on peer tutoring at the secondary level and reported good results. These favorable results occur when the teacher spends some time in providing the tutors with a clear understanding on how to conduct lessons, how to provide feedback for correct responses, procedures for correcting errors, and so forth. Role-playing the tutor-tutee procedures seems particularly useful.

As with inclusion, it is not enough to ask one student to help another with his or her lessons. This peer tutoring approach requires considerable planning and preparation to be successful. One of the interesting side benefits is that the tutors themselves showed academic gains, reduced school absences, and increased positive social interactions. It seems that giving students increased responsibility in the academic setting pays off for both tutor and tutee!

Assistive Technology for Students with EBD

A number of technological aids can provide some supportive help for those working with children with behavior or emotional difficulties. Some take the form of board games that enhance social skills development with topics such as social greetings, handling anger at school and work, appropriate and inappropriate touching, good sportsmanship, and so on. In another classroom behavior game, students move around the board and are exposed to ten strategies that are positive solutions for managing anger. They include taking responsibility for one's own actions, encouraging self-control, and dealing with the acting-out behavior of others.

PCI Education
www.pcicatalog.com

Peer tutoring can have a beneficial impact if both students are engaged in learning.

A computer can be an especially useful learning tool for a student with a behavior disorder, because it provides an objective, neutral response to the child's sometimes provoking or challenging behavior. Children with long histories of social interaction problems may respond poorly to teacher feedback, particularly when criticism or correction is involved. Children who are adept at manipulating others can quickly change the focus of a discussion from their inadequate academic performance to the teacher's behavior. "Why are you always picking on me?" is a common theme. With a computer, however, the student must find a different approach.

Obviously, a computer is not able to interact emotionally with the child. If students have difficulty solving a problem, they must find out why and determine the right answer in order to proceed with the computer program. Students cannot resort to emotional manipulation or accuse the computer of being unfair.

Computer-assisted learning can support the child's academic performance by helping with spelling, word definitions, text-to-speech options for reading, and organizational support for writing down thoughts and ideas. Assistive technology support can help by increasing success and reducing stress for children with emotional difficulties (Edyburn, 2006).

8-6 The Role of Family and Community

The importance of the family, in both positive and negative ways, has long been recognized for children with EBD. This is one of the reasons parents play a significant role in the IDEA 2004 legislation. Table 8.4 summarizes the various interactions the family will have with the school.

As you can see in Table 8.4, parents must be fully informed about activities related to their child. Sopko and Reder (2007) provide detailed statements from the law itself that leave little doubt as to the intentions of the lawmakers.

A relatively new way of viewing the professional and parent relationship is by seeing it as a *partnership of experts*. The parents are experts on their own children and on those children's feelings and behaviors. They are case managers, policymakers, and legislative advocates. The professionals are experts in such general

TABLE 8.4 Parental Involvement in IDEA 2004

- Understand what consent is and provide informed consent for services under IDEA 2004.
- Be notified in advance about any proposed changes to a child's evaluation, IEP/IFSP, or educational placement, to ensure the opportunity to participate in meetings regarding the education of their child.
- Be informed about the process used to assess the child's response to scientific, research-based intervention, appropriate strategies for improved achievement, and the right to request an evaluation.
- Learn about disciplinary processes and disciplinary actions regarding their child.
- Receive a copy of the procedural safeguards, the evaluation report, the documentation of determination of eligibility, and a copy of the child's IEP at no cost.
- Be informed about the state procedures for filing a complaint and the right to records of hearings, findings of fact, and decisions.
- Permission to inspect and review all education records related to their child, and request that information be amended.

SOURCE: Sopko, K. and Reder, N. (2007). *Public and parent reporting requirements: NCLB and IDEA regulations*. Alexandria, VA: National Association of State Directors of Special Education.

MORAL DILEMMA

Emotional and Behavior Disorders

Mrs. Stern, a special education teacher working with children with behavioral disorders, has been on increasingly good terms with Ralph because she has listened quietly to Ralph's complaints and protests about the unfairness of life from his standpoint. Ralph has had numerous escapades in and out of school.

One day Ralph, a 12-year-old, asked Mrs. Stern to sit down and talk with him about a problem he was having. He asked Mrs. Stern to swear to keep secret what he was about to tell her, and she said she would. He then told her about his belonging to a gang that was systematically stealing from local Wal-Marts and drugstores. This activity was fairly limited in scope, and Ralph did not seem too concerned. Recently, however, drugs had entered the situation, with members of the gang urging Ralph to deliver drugs from their supplier to various other sites. Part of the reward for his being a delivery boy would be that he would get a small amount of drugs for his own use. Despite the pressure put on him by other members of the gang, he had resisted so far, but now he was being threatened with expulsion from the gang or worse. He wanted advice and perhaps moral support for his action.

What should Mrs. Stern do? She has already promised him confidentiality. What should she say to Ralph? What is her responsibility to the larger school and neighborhood community concerning the presence of drugs in and out of school? Write some dialogue that might follow in this situation.

fields as special education and mental health. Under these assumptions we can establish a relationship between the two parties with the best interests of the child in mind (Turnbull, Turbiville, & Turnbull, 2000).

A possible problem in establishing such collaboration or partnership emerges when there are cultural differences between families and professionals. Sometimes the parents of children from culturally and linguistically diverse families are seen by the professionals as "needing training" rather than as being full-fledged partners in the support efforts. A sense of learned helplessness felt by many parents has to be combated by the professionals, so that the parents can maintain self-respect and their desire to partner with professionals.

It has often been noted that parents are not issued a manual for parenting upon the birth of their child. Whenever children have special problems that prevent them from learning or socializing, the need for such parent training becomes obvious. One attempt to provide such guidance has been Triple P (Positive Parenting Program) designed by Professor Matt Sanders at the University of Queensland in Australia. Triple P focuses on self-regulation using DVDs to supplement written material.

There are four levels of increasing intensity as the problems increase. The fourth level involves active skills training and support, with application in home and community settings. A meta-analysis of the effectiveness of the work at the fourth level of Triple P (de Graaf et al., 2008) found the program effective with diverse families, types of problems and ages of children.

8-6a Transition and Life

One of the unsolved challenges involving the education of students with emotional and behavior disorders is their poor record of school completion, together with limited success in the vocational arena following school. The Office of Special Education Programs (2003) reported that only about 40 percent of students with EBD completed their secondary schooling. These findings suggest (1) the difficulty of entering a labor market with low and uncertain wages, (2) the possibility of trouble with the law, and (3) the unlikelihood of their seeking additional training on their own.

Triple P Program
http://www.triplep.net

The findings are consistent with those of earlier studies (Rylance, 1997; Valdez, Williamson, & Wagner, 1990). Kortering, Braziel, and Tomkins (2002) individually interviewed 33 students who were receiving services for behavior disorders to find out their perceptions of the problems with completing school. Students' responses, listed in Table 8.5, indicate that additional support is needed during the difficult transition period.

One of the goals for children with EBD is to help them complete their secondary programs and adapt meaningfully to their community or gain further education towards adult competence. It is clear that we must pay increased attention and commit resources to strengthen the bridges from school to community for children with EBD.

TABLE 8.5 Responses from Students with EBD on Staying in School

Are There Any Advantages or Disadvantages to Staying in School?	
Advantages	Better education and jobs. Getting a better job and better pay. Diploma means a better job. Good education and a job. So I can get in the army and get a job. You will get a better job. Good job.
Disadvantages	Getting into trouble with peers. A lot of homework and not much free time. Can't get a job. Can't work. Working in class is too hard. Don't get a lot of time with friends.
What Changes Would Help an Individual Student Finish School, and How?	
More Support	Help me pass. Help me with my homework. Help me get good grades. Give me more help. Help me control my anger.
What Changes Would Help More Students Stay in School?	
Curriculum	More detail in classes. Up-to-date books. Newer texts. Social studies books should be easier for kids in special education classes. Some of the books are too difficult. More fun things in class. Put tutors in [classes].

SOURCE: From L. J. Kortering, P. M. Braziel, & J. R. Tomkins. (2002). The challenge of school completion among youths with behavioral disorders: Another side of the story, *Behavioral Disorders, 27*, 142–154. Reprinted with permission.

8-6b In Conclusion

In many ways, teaching children with emotional and behavior disorders represents the most challenging of all exceptional children. These children can provide the most serious threat to the teacher's control and command of the classroom. They can have a dampening effect on the entire class. While working with children with learning disabilities can be frustrating, they do not represent a personal and direct threat to the self-image of the teacher as a person in command of his or her own feelings.

The positive behavior support strategies and positive reinforcement that teachers are expected to use seem contrary to the natural reaction you might have to threat or disobedience. Teachers have to prepare themselves to use the techniques that have been proven successful, even if they seem unnatural.

In those times of crisis, it is comforting to have collaboration with other team members whose expertise and support can help guide you through the rough patches you will surely experience. You have to remind yourself that this child in front of you is carrying the heavy burden of many past unpleasant experiences and his or her misbehavior is often a disguised cry for help.

Summary

- The definition of *emotional and behavior disorder* takes into account the intensity and duration of age-inappropriate behavior, the situation in which the behavior is exhibited, and the individual who considers the behavior a problem.
- Unlike children with other disabilities, children with EBD are often blamed for their condition. This affects their interactions with the people around them.
- Although less than 1 percent of schoolchildren are receiving special education services for EBD, the number of children who actually need those services is at least 5 percent and may range as high as 15 percent.
- In many instances, the causes of EBD appear to be a blend of neurology, genetics, and environmental factors.
- Children who externalize problems require different planning and intervention from those who internalize problems.
- Bullying in the schools has been a continuing problem. Serious physical violence is caused by a small percentage of students, many of whom can be identified at an early age.
- There is an increased prevalence of children from culturally and linguistically diverse families referred for special services for social and emotional disturbance. Favorable changes in the school environment for these children have positive results.
- Intervention for the child who is anxious and withdrawn should have as its primary objective instilling a sense of self-worth and self-control.
- Positive experiences play an important role in preventing suicide—a serious problem among students who are deeply depressed and withdrawn.
- The RtI model's three-tier approach provides the opportunity for students to move between intense treatment and less intense professional involvement as the situation requires.
- Social skills training has been a modest success and should focus on the need for generalization from specific training to general classroom behavior.
- Functional behavior assessment and positive behavior supports clearly seem to have favorable results.
- Self-management and self-control training has shown promising results. The wraparound approach, which features a multidisciplinary system of care, has also potential for positive results.
- Much remains to be done to assume good community adjustment following school for children with emotional and behavior disorders.

Future Challenges

1. What are the conditions for emotional health for culturally diverse students?

Despite findings of increased prevalence of social and emotional problems in culturally and linguistically diverse groups, the vast majority of such children are not so affected. A study of emotionally healthy children from these backgrounds and their families could help us understand and assist in the emergence of emotional health in these groups.

2. **Can increasing uses of multidisciplinary teams provide the necessary increase in services?**
   One serious condition limiting the delivery of quality educational services to children with behavior problems is the need for highly trained personnel. Unless a way can be found to use paraprofessional personnel, as has been done in applied behavior analysis programs, it will not be possible to provide the help needed by many students identified as having behavior problems.

3. **How early should we begin?**
   Research increasingly indicates the advantages to beginning education and therapy early in the child's life—and that includes family counseling. For children with emotional and behavior disorders, this would mean starting well before the school years. Ideally, some therapeutic treatment for children with EBD and their families should begin by ages 2 or 3. This often means arranging for relationships with pediatricians and other professionals, who frequently are the first contact that the family has about these problems.

4. **How can violence be prevented?**
   Longitudinal studies of children who are socially maladjusted and act out their aggressive feelings suggest strongly that they do not outgrow these tendencies. Unless something significant is done with these children or with the environment surrounding them (positive behavior supports), we can predict that aggressive children who hurt peers will become aggressive adults who hurt people. The need for large-scale intervention within the school, family, and neighborhood is clear.

TeachSource Digital Download Access online

Key Terms

antecedent behaviors p. 264
applied behavior analysis p. 265
behavior contract p. 271
behavior disorders p. 247
bullying p. 254
coercive family system p. 254
cognitive strategy approach. p. 270
comorbid; p. 262
correlated constraints p. 251
emotional disorders p. 247
functional behavior assessment (FBA) p. 264
generalization p. 269
learned helplessness p. 258
peer tutoring p. 273
positive behavior interventions and supports p. 264
psychotropic p. 251
replacement behaviors p. 271
school-wide behavior supports p. 263
self-evaluation p. 270
self-instruction training p. 270
self-management p. 270
self-monitoring p. 270
self-reinforcement p. 270
serious emotional disturbance p. 249
support teacher p. 272
transactional theory p. 262
Universal Design for Learning p. 267
universal group behavior support p. 263
wraparound approach p. 266

Resources

References of Special Interest

Dunlap, G. & Carr, E. (2007). Positive behavior supports and developmental disability: A summary and analysis of research. In S. Odom, R. Horner, M. Snell, and J. Blacher (Eds.), *Handbook of Developmental Disabilities*. New York: The Guilford Press. A review of one of the most popular and well-researched topics in the field of EBD. Positive behavior supports are a distinct departure for the traditional way of dealing with misbehavior and have the advantages of solid research findings.

Farmer, T., Farmer, E., Estell, D., & Hutchins, B. (2007). The developmental dynamics of aggression and the prevention of school violence. *Journal of Emotional and Behavior Disorders 15*(4), 197–208. A thoughtful portrait of the background of aggression by students who externalize their difficulties and the various strategies for coping with them in the school environment, perhaps the largest management problem faced by teachers.

Kauffman, J. & Landrum, T. (2009). *Characteristics of emotional and behavioral disorders of children and youth* (9th ed.). Upper Saddle River, NJ: Merrill. A fine review of what is currently known about students with EBD and the challenges faced by educators working with these students. These are two of the most respected professionals in the field. This text is an excellent stepping stone for students with a particular interest in this area.

Landrum, T. (2011). Emotional and behavioral disorders. In J. Kauffman and D. Hallahan (Eds.), *Handbook of special education*. New York: Routledge. A comprehensive review of both causes and educational programming for children with EBD. It provides a good summary of the various factors identified as linked to possible causes of the condition.

Reading and Writing Interventions for Students with, and at Risk for, Emotional and Behavioral Disorders [Special Issue]. (2010). *Behavioral Disorders, 35*(2), 81–184. There is a growing interest in the link between academic performance and emotional disturbance. This special journal issue explores a variety of studies and research syntheses dealing with academic performance of children labeled emotionally and behaviorally impaired. The results indicate a strong link between the two that require educational adaptations.

Journals

Behavioral Disorders
www.ccbd.net

Beyond Behavior
www.ccbd.net

Exceptional Children
sped.org/Publications/CEC-Journals/Exceptional-Children

Journal of Applied Behavior Analysis
seab.envmed.rochester.edu/jaba/

Teaching Exceptional Children
sped.org/Publications/CEC-Journals/TEACHING-Exceptional-Children

Journal of Emotional and Behavior Disorders
ebx.sagepub.com/

Professional Organizations

American Psychological Association
www.apa.org

Council for Children with Behavioral Disorders
www.ccbd.net

National Alliance for the Mentally Ill
www.nami.org
National Mental Health Association
www.nmha.org
Society for Research in Child Development
www.srcd.org

SRA/McGraw Hill
is on the
3
The Hen's Hat

CHAPTER 9

Children with Communication, Language, and Speech Disorders

Standards Addressed in This Chapter

All of the CEC Standards are addressed within this chapter. Please see the inside book covers for the complete list of the standards.

FOCUS QUESTIONS

9-1 How did the field of speech and language disorders evolve?

9-2 What are some characteristics of children with difficulties in these areas and how are communication, language, and speech defined?

9-3 How does typical language develop and what kinds of problems and/or disorders can affect communication, language, and speech?

9-4 Why must a child's culture and linguistic background be factored in when assessments and services are determined?

9-5 How do other disability areas impact communication, language, and speech disorders?

9-6 What educational responses are needed to support children with speech, language, and communication disorders?

9-7 What family and lifespan issues are important for individuals with speech, language, and/or communication disorders?

The desire to communicate seems as basic a human need as food. Communication begins early as infants work to make their needs known to parents. Initially, the infant uses cries, grunts, gestures, and facial expressions to get the message across. At 3 or 4 months of age, the baby begins cooing and babbling—using sounds that approximate speech and imitate the language the baby has been listening to from birth. Finally, at around 1 year, the first "words" appear. These first words are usually repetitions of sounds, such as *ma-ma, da-da,* or *pa-pa*. So is it any wonder that in many languages these words mean "mother" and/or "father"? Nothing is more exciting to parents than their infant's amazing ability to acquire speech and language in the first year of life.

Elizabeth Crews/The Image Works

When children show delays in language development or have difficulty producing speech sounds, early intervention is essential to improve their ability to communicate. In this chapter, we look at communication, language, and speech, examining the ways that children develop and the difficulties they encounter when they have problems in these areas. We look briefly at the history of the speech-language field; reflect on how we define communication, language, and speech; examine typical human development of language; review the disorders and disabilities that can affect these areas; and present strategies that can be used to support children and youths who have disorders in communication, language, and/or speech. Throughout this chapter, we discuss the impact that specific disabilities may have on a child's ability to communicate, use language, and speak.

9-1 History of Communication, Language, and Speech Disorders

The formation of the American Speech and Hearing Association (ASHA) in 1925 marked a significant point in the emerging field of speech-language pathology, but attempts to correct speech patterns and to enhance communication date back at least as far as the early Greeks in the fifth century bc (Coufal, 2007). In the United States during the 1800s, the focus was on elocution, or the ability to speak with elegance and propriety (Moore, 1802, as cited in Duchan, 2008). With the emergence of public schools, curricula for teaching elocution were developed, and some attention was given to helping students who had speech impediments. Alexander Graham Bell founded the School of Vocal Physiology in 1872 to help improve the speech of children who were deaf or who suffered from stuttering and/or articulation problems (Duchan, 2008).

American Speech and Hearing Association
www.asha.org

By the 20th century, the science of speech and communication began to influence practice. Early studies showing areas of the brain that were associated with speech and language began to emerge with the work of Paul Broca and Carl Wernicke. As Figure 9.1 shows, parts of the brain were named after Broca and

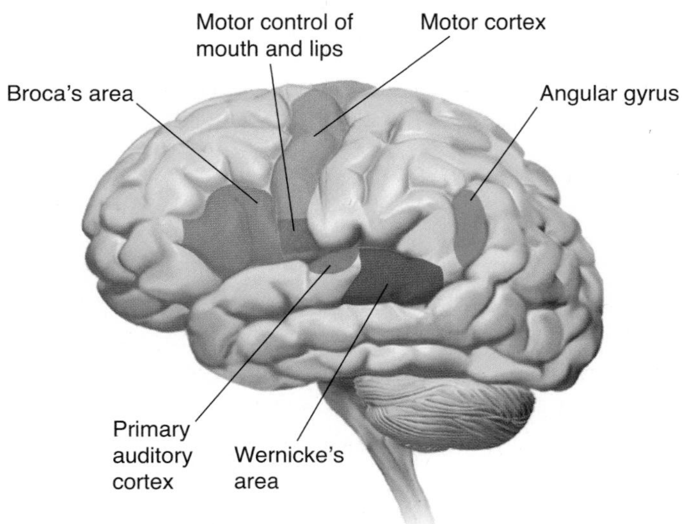

Figure 9.1 The Major Brain Structures Participating in Language
Source: Freberg, L. (2006). *Discovering Biological Psychology*, p. 392. Used by permission of Houghton Mifflin Harcourt Publishing Company.

Wernicke as a result of their pioneering work in this area. By the middle of the 20th century the conception of speech-language disorders began to move beyond the production of sounds to include the "inner language," or thoughts that underlie communication. Key contributors to the importance of symbol formation were Karl Goldstein, Helmur Myklebust, and Charles Osgood. Goldstein worked with aphasics, individuals who had lost or failed to develop language, whereas Myklebust concentrated on individuals with auditory processing difficulties. Osgood added the idea of a mental component to communication. Their combined work began to show that communication was complex, involving interactions among speech production, language development, and thought (Duchan, 2008).

9-1a Studying Brain Injury to Understand Language

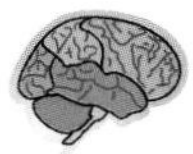

Neurologists often try to determine the specific function for areas of the brain by examining the impact of brain injury or damage. The generalized notion that language is largely associated with the brain's left hemisphere (see Broca and Wernicke's areas in Figure 9.1) is supported by the language disruption that occurs when there is a lesion or injury to the left hemisphere (Lansing et al., 2004). This pattern of hemispheric specialization, however, seems to be better defined for adults than for children (Bates et al., 2001). For young children, when the brain is still developing, there seems to be far more *plasticity*, which is the ability of the brain to compensate for and reorganize functions to draw on the nondamaged areas, than there is for adults (Bates et al., 2001). In their comparison of the effects of left hemispheric brain lesions on language for children and adults, Bates and her colleagues (2001) found that while adults showed the classic signs of aphasia (language loss) after their injuries, children did not seem to be impacted in the same way. In their study, they saw no differences in the language development of children, ages 5 to 8, who had either left- or right-hemisphere lesions. The language of children and adults with bilateral brain injury was severely impaired. These findings support the hypothesis that language outcomes, as a result of brain injury, differ for children and adults and depend on the extent of damage to both hemispheres.

9-1b Study of Linguistics

During the 1960s and 1970s, the field emphasized linguistics. Noam Chomsky led the way by examining the rules and sequences governing the acquisition of language (Chomsky, 1965). Over the last 30 years, the area of **language pragmatics**—ways that language is used to communicate in a variety of contexts—has emerged as a critical area of study (Duchan, 2008; Hyter, 2007). The social aspects of communication in everyday life also play a central role in our current thinking about speech and language disorders (Duchan, 2008; Olswang, Coggins, & Svensson, 2007; Salvia, Ysseldyke, & Bolt, 2007). Current research also focuses on the role of cognition in language development and the importance of learning as part of language acquisition (Hoff, 2004, 2009). Language acquisition, from the cognitive perspective, depends to a large extent on the child's exposure to language (Slobin, 2006). The more language a child hears, and the greater the complexity of this language, the more likely the child will learn the structural properties of language. From this perspective, providing language-rich environments is critical for young children. The impact of learning two languages for children growing up in bilingual or multilingual families or communities is also an emerging area of study. We will explore this issue in greater detail later in this chapter (Maguire et al., 2010). Since communication is so vital to being a member of society, life can be difficult for children who have speech and/or language disorders.

9-2 Characteristics of Students and Definitions of Communication, Language, and Speech

Communication is central to our ability to fit into society successfully, and when difficulties with language and/or speech interfere with communication, children often experience problems (Brinton & Fujiki, 2006). These problems can affect the formation of a child's friendships, school success, and self-esteem (Girolametto & Weitzman, 2007).

9-2a Characteristics of Children with Communication, Language, and Speech Disorders

While there are many different patterns of impact for challenges with communication, language, and speech, we can begin to understand some of the difficulties if we get to know two students: Johnny and Michelle.

Meet Johnny and Michelle, Two Students with Speech Disorders

Johnny: Johnny is a 10-year-old boy who has a moderate articulation and phonology disorder (he mispronounces specific sounds). A speech disorder may signal an underlying language problem, and a comprehensive assessment indicated that Johnny also has a language-related learning disability. Academically, he is performing below grade level on skills that require language mediation. Johnny also demonstrates a range of intraindividual differences. At this point, his sound substitutions and omissions are not so severe, and he can usually be understood, but his oral productions still call attention to his speech and sometimes set him apart from his peers.

Johnny's speech is characterized by consistent sound substitutions (w/r, as in *wabbit for rabbit;* t/k, as in *tome* for *come;* and l/y, as in *lellow* for *yellow*). He also sometimes omits sounds at the ends of words, including the sounds that represent verb tense and noun number (e.g., the final /s/ in *looks* and *cats*). When he was younger, his expressive language was delayed, and he spoke very few words until he was 2 years old. When he did begin to talk, his speech was almost unintelligible, and nonfamily members had difficulty understanding him. Johnny's receptive language, however, was excellent, and his understanding of language spoken to him allowed him to be an active member of a busy family with three older siblings. Careful listening to his conversational language reveals that he still omits articles and that his sentence structure is not as elaborate as that of most 10-year-olds.

Johnny is in a general classroom, RtI Tier I, but he seems reluctant to participate in class. It has not been determined whether this reluctance stems from his sensitivity to others' reactions, an inability to formulate speech and complex language to express his ideas, or both. When we look at Johnny's strengths, we note that he is bright and has strong athletic abilities and that he gets along well with other children. A sensitive teacher can do much to help Johnny feel comfortable in spite of his speech disorder and can help him develop a positive self-concept.

Michelle: Michelle also has difficulty with speech. Her problems, however, are not with articulation—that is, the pronunciation of words. Michelle has difficulty with speech fluency, and she often stutters when she is talking. Michelle's speech is characterized by sound repetitions (e.g., "W-W-W-What do you need?"), sound prolongations (e.g., "ShShShShould I go too?"), and a series of interjections that insert pause words into the sentence (e.g., "I can-um-um-you know-do this"). Sometimes when Michelle opens her mouth to speak nothing comes out. Michelle is a shy child by nature, and her difficulties with speaking have made her very hesitant to interact

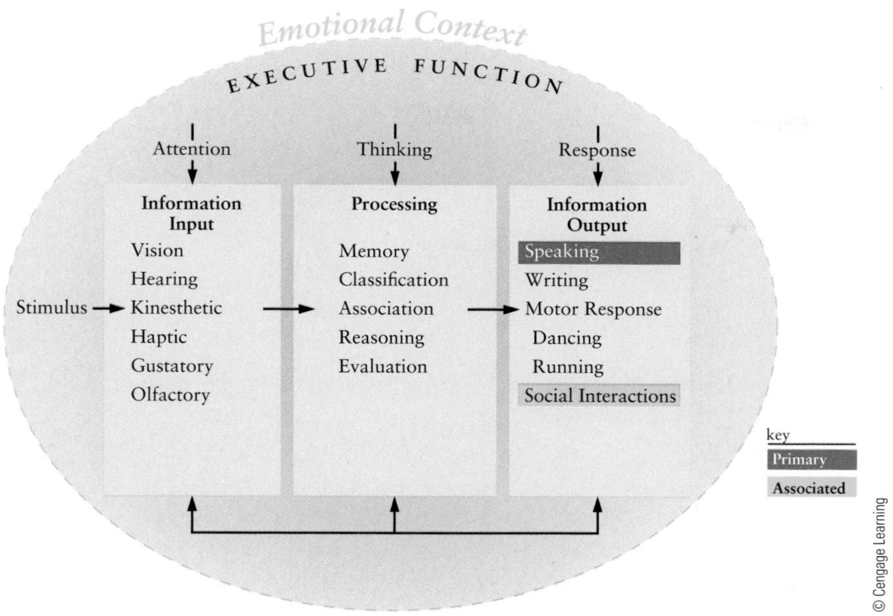

Figure 9.2 Michelle's Information Processing Model

TeachSource Digital Download Access online

with others. When Michelle was in the second grade, she had a teacher who made the situation even worse. Michelle remembers Mrs. Cooke forcing her to stand before the class and give her book report. Mrs. Cooke said loudly in front of the class, "Now, Michelle, just take a deep breath and talk slowly and you will be fine." When Michelle did begin to stutter, Mrs. Cooke interrupted her and said, "Just start from the beginning and you can get it right." Michelle was mortified by her continued difficulties in front of the whole class, and the more nervous she became, the worse her stuttering became. Finally, she was allowed to slink back to her seat and try to make herself invisible; she has tried hard to maintain her invisibility ever since.

One of Michelle's strengths is written language, and she has won several awards for her poetry. Michelle is comfortable talking at home, and her stuttering does not seem to be a problem when she is with her family. In school and other settings Michelle finds it very difficult to participate in conversations in which there are more than a few people.

The information processing model for Michelle indicates the areas that cause her the most difficulties, but it also shows her strengths (see Figure 9.2). While Michelle has difficulties with speech (output), and this can cause secondary problems with social interactions, her ability to receive information (input) and to process information (thinking) is just fine.

Both Johnny and Michelle have speech disorders, and both receive support from a speech-language pathologist. Later in the chapter we discuss the supports and services these children need to be successful, and we return to Johnny and Michelle to check their progress.

9-2b Definitions of Communication, Language, and Speech

Although we sometimes use the terms *communication, language,* and *speech* interchangeably, each means something different. The following definitions clarify how these terms are being used in this chapter and give us a shared platform for looking at the kinds of problems that can emerge with each of these areas.

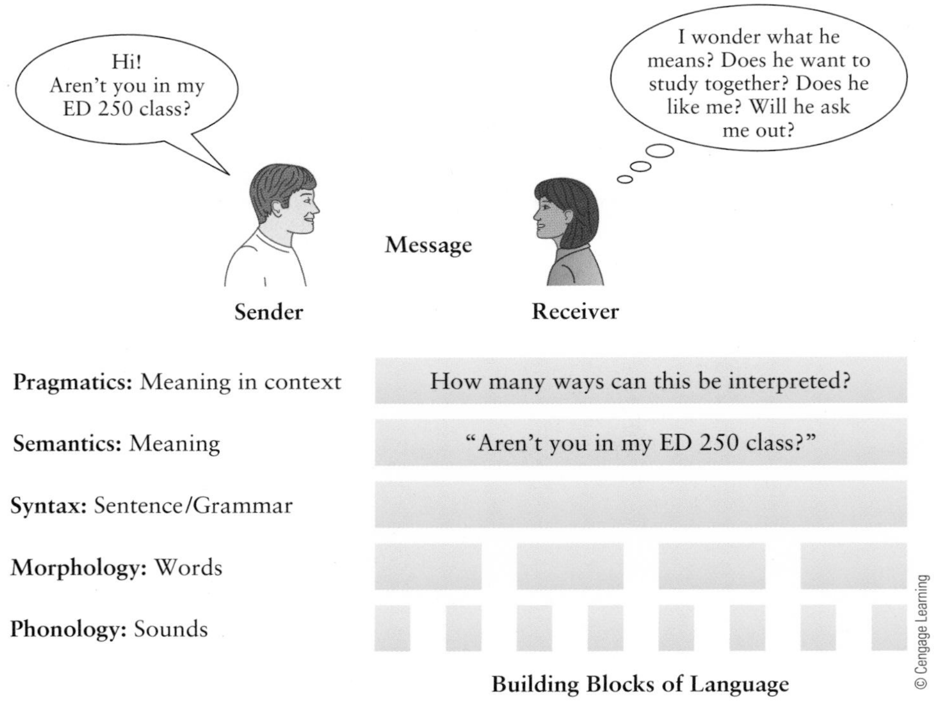

Figure 9.3 Has Communication Taken Place?

9-2c Communication

The ability to communicate is essential to our participation in society. It is what links us to others and helps us form a shared sense of belonging. **Communication** is the exchange of thoughts, information, feelings, and ideas, and it requires three things: a *sender*, a *message*, and a *receiver* (see Figure 9.3). This statement may seem like common sense, but it is important to note that communication has not taken place unless all three elements are in place *and* are working (Loncke, 2011). The sender initiates the communication and determines the message, and the receiver gets the message and must interpret it to understand what it means, thus completing the communication loop. If you think about the information processing model (IPM) you can see how communication involves input (hearing or seeing), central processing (thinking about and understanding), and output (speaking, signing, writing, etc.). Communication also involves the use of the executive function (decision making), and all of this takes place within an emotional context that must be factored in to correctly understand the message (Loncke, 2011). Communication problems can emerge when there are difficulties with any one of these elements.

There are many ways to communicate. Messages can be transmitted through writing, telegraphy, and pictures. As humans we also communicate through drama, dance, music, and all of the fine arts. Communication can be nonverbal, through gestures and facial expressions. Think of all the things you can express with just a look. Sign language uses an ordered form of gestures to convey meaning. The primary vehicle that humans use for communication, however, is spoken language.

9-2d Language

Lahey's classic definition of **language** as "a code whereby ideas about the world are represented through a conventional system of arbitrary signals for communication" is still viable today (Lahey & Bloom, 1988, p. 3). Through this definition we see that language, as a *code*, represents *ideas*, or mental constructs, and that these are *separate from the actual objects and events*. These mental constructs are inherent to the person and not to the word, object, or event. Further, Lahey's definition reminds us that language is symbolic; that it relies on signals, sounds, and signs to represent objects and events; and thus that it is an abstraction of these. And finally, through this definition we see that the primary function of language is to communicate.

Two kinds of language are involved in communication: receptive language and expressive language. **Receptive language** involves the ability to take in the message and understand it (that is, listening with understanding to oral language and reading written language with comprehension; input and central processing). **Expressive language** is the ability to produce a message to send; this typically involves speaking and writing (output). So, as part of communication, language is an organized system of symbols that humans use to express and receive meaning (Jusczyk, 1997; Salvia et al., 2007). Language systems evolved over time and largely replaced the innate communication system of gestures and facial expressions, which convey a more limited range of meaning. The key elements that help define a language can be thought of as belonging to three categories: form, content, and function.

Language Form

The form that a language takes can be seen in the sounds, the words, and the grammar that underlie the language (Salvia et al., 2007). Each language has its own individual form, or structure, but languages that share a common origin may be similar to each other in form (Gleason, 2005). **Language form** includes the following components.

1. **Phonology** is the sound system and patterns for the combinations of these sounds into speech.
2. **Morphology** is the rules that address how words are formed and the structure of words.
3. **Syntax** is the rules that guide how words are combined to form sentences and the relationships of components within the sentence.

A language's grammar is the combination of its morphology and syntax. The structure of a language helps convey the content. For example, in English we often use the sentence form article/noun/verb: "The cat pounced." When we see a sentence like this but with a word we do not know (in this case a made-up word): "The cat zupped" we understand that "zupped" is an action.

Language Content

The content of a language is the information being communicated. This is an essential element of language because the meaning of the symbols used is the heart of the message. **Language content**, or *semantics,* is the meaning of words and sentences. You may have heard someone say, when arguing a point, that something is "just semantics," dismissing a point of difference by implying that the ideas are the same regardless of the words used. This argument is incorrect, however. *Meaning is semantics*, and this may be the most essential aspect of language. Meaning, however, must be interpreted within the context of the communication.

Language Function

Language function, or use, addresses language as appropriate communication within a given society and a specific context. The two concepts that are critical to how language is used are language pragmatics and supralinguistics (Salvia et al., 2007). Language pragmatics address the social context in which the communication occurs. The social context is important because it helps clarify the meaning of the communication. Thus, the sentence "Can you feed the dog?" may mean one of the following:

Please feed the dog.

Are you physically able to feed the dog?

Do you have the resources needed to feed the dog?

depending on the circumstances and person to whom the question is addressed.

Pragmatics also addresses the different expectations for communication in different settings. Children are asked to use very different rules when they communicate in the classroom versus on the playground, and sometimes expectations for communication are different for the home and the school. To be successful we must learn to adapt our communications to the specific expectations in a variety of settings.

Supralinguistics is the sophisticated analysis of meaning when the literal meaning of the word or phrase is *not* the intended meaning (Salvia et al., 2007). Being good at supralinguistics means that one can understand sarcasm, indirect requests, subtle inferences, and figures of speech. This skill is also important for understanding puns, wordplay, and verbal humor. Because people often communicate with indirect language, individuals who have difficulty with this may be at a loss to interpret meaning and understand needs. For example, a teacher may say, while rolling her eyes, "Well, of course I *expect you* to talk out in class," when she means the opposite. A youngster who has difficulty understanding social cues and interpreting nonliteral language (such as sarcasm) will be very confused by this statement. This is one of the challenges faced by children with Asperger's syndrome (Hughes-Lynch, 2010).

Next, we discuss speech. When a given community selects a series of sounds to convey meaning, it creates speech. Spoken language can be used to convey abstract meanings and to address the past and future, as well as the present.

Speech

Speech is the systematic oral production of the words of a given language. Sounds become speech only when they produce words that have meaning. Speech has a rhythmic flow, with stress and intonation, and it uses words with stressed and unstressed syllables. We think of normal speech as combining articulation, fluency, and voice. **Articulation** is the clear pronunciation of words, **fluency** refers to the appropriate flow of the words, and **voice** is the intonation and quality of the production (pitch, loudness, and resonance). ▶ Figure 9.4 presents a simplified overview of the production of speech. A thought occurs in the brain; it is translated into symbols and sent to the larynx area for phonation and resonation, which takes place in the vocal tract; then air is sent to be modified by movements of the tongue and passage over the teeth and lips, which combine to form the sounds, words, and sentences of a particular language (articulation).
The thought transformed into words is received by a listener through hearing, in a process called **audition**.

The following four processes are involved in the production of speech:

- **Respiration** (breathing) generates the energy that produces sound.
- **Phonation** is the production of sound by the vibration of the vocal cords.
- **Resonation** gives the voice a unique characteristic that identifies the speaker (it is the product of sound traveling through the speaker's head and neck).
- Articulation is the movement of the mouth and tongue that shapes sound into phonemes (the smallest unit of sound), which combine to make speech.

Figure 9.4 displays where each of these processes occur in the human body. Both Johnny and Michelle have speech disorders, but it is important to remember that

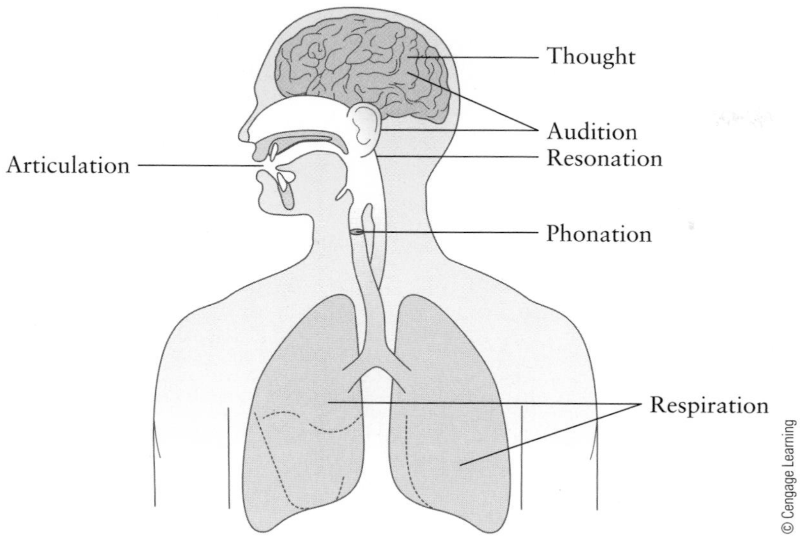

Figure 9.4 Processes Involved in the Production of Speech

a failure to appropriately interpret the context or setting can also lead to problems with communication and the pragmatics of language use (Loncke, 2011). Communication disorders often involve both language and speech disorders.

9-3 Typical and Atypical Language Development

An infant is innately programmed to communicate through smiles, eye contact, sounds, and gestures (the prelinguistic system). Most infants are very social beings and are motivated to relate to persons in their environment. The language system uses these talents. Parents and caregivers teach the child that people and objects have names and particular sounds to identify them. Early challenges with these prelingual behaviors can signal risks for later problems with language development (Loncke, 2011). Although the specific language that each child learns will depend on the language spoken in the home, the pattern of language development seems to be similar across languages. The aforementioned two aspects of language, receptive language and expressive language, are critical to a child's development. Understanding typical language development is essential to understanding when and how problems with language can manifest themselves.

Typically expressive language emerges in sequence from pleasurable sounds (such as cooing) and cries to babbling (e.g., da-da-da) and by around 1 year of age most children have one or two words (e.g. mama; bye-bye). From ages 1-5 language begins to take-off with simple sentences (such as "where kitty?" or "more cookie"), until at age 5 the child can communicate easily using the same grammar used by other family members ("I like ice cream. It be good!!").

Receptive language, the child's ability to understand spoken words, also follows a sequence from simple to complex. Infants enjoy eye contact and games like "peek-a-boo"; toddlers begin to recognize that spoken words stand for objects (shoe, cup, ball) and they can often follow simple commands (such as "Get your shoes so we can go the park"). Preschool children can usually follow two-step directions (Sit on the rug and get ready for story time), and they can listen to stories and respond to basic who, what, and where questions. By the time children start kindergarten (age 5) they should be ready to understand most of what is said in home and school settings.

Children may need additional support for language development.

RayArt Graphics/Alamy

There are many reasons, however, that a child's individual language progression may differ somewhat from this typical sequence. A bilingual child, for example, who is learning two languages at the same time may have fewer words in each language and so may appear to be delayed in vocabulary or language acquisition when only one language is assessed (Hoff, 2004; Hart, 2009; Brice & Brice, 2009). When words in both of the child's languages are considered, however, we get a more accurate understanding of the child's true vocabulary (Holt, 2005, Brice & Brice, 2009). Children who are bilingual may also be somewhat delayed in their phonemic awareness (the relationship between letters and sounds) and they may need additional time and support in early reading (Brice & Brice, 2009; Brice, Carson, & O'Brien, 2009).

The ability to communicate in more than one language is a strength that will ultimately be an asset to the individual (Barac & Bialystok, 2012). Because, however, bilingualism may impact the early development of language, children can be misidentified as having language delays when they are actually on target given the demands of learning two languages. During assessments, we must make sure that the child's language and cultural context are understood as we look at the child's needs (Hart, 2009; Hoff & Elledge, 2005). With the growing numbers of children from culturally and linguistically diverse families in today's schools, we must be extremely careful that we take the child's language background into consideration as we look at possible areas of concern (Guiberson et al., 2006; Salvia et al., 2007; Brice et al., 2009).

9-3a Disorders in Communication, Language, and Speech

It is important to distinguish among disorders in communication, language, and speech, because they have different origins and require different interventions. Table 9.1 gives the American Speech-Language-Hearing Association's (ASHA) definitions of these disorders. Communication disorders are often related to other areas of disability. Those related to hearing are discussed in Chapter 11. Communication difficulties also impact children with autism (Chapter 5), learning disabilities (Chapter 6), visual impairments (Chapter 12), and physical disabilities (Chapter 13). We will explore these relationships in greater detail later in this chapter.

TABLE 9.1 American Speech-Language-Hearing Association's Definitions of Communication Disorders Including Language and Speech

I. Communication Disorders	A **communication disorder** involves difficulties with receiving, sending, processing, and comprehending verbal, nonverbal, and graphic symbolic information. Communications disorders may be mild or sever and may co-exist with other areas of disabilities. **A.** A **speech disorder** involves the articulation of speech sounds, fluency, and/or voice. **1.** An **articulation disorder** speech sounds are distorted and may be unintelligible due to substitutions, omissions, or additions of phonemes. **2.** A **fluency disorder** the flow of speech is characterized by differences in rate or rhythm and the reputation of speech sounds, syllables, words or phrases. **3.** A **voice disorder** the quality of voice is atypical given the speakers gender and age; pitch may be too high or low, volume may be inappropriate, and differences my include resonance and duration of sound. **B.** A **language disorder** involves difficulties with any combination of spoken, written, and or symbol systems used to share ideas and messages. Langue disorders may impact understanding and use of (a) language form (phonology, morphology, syntax) (b) language content (semantics), or (c) language function (pragmatics).

Communication Disorders

Communication is often used as a general term to include pragmatics, speech, and language. Communication disorders disrupt the individual's ability to send, receive, and process information. If you think about the information processing model, you can see how problems with input could undermine an individual's ability to take in messages. Difficulties with processing can make understanding or interpreting the message hard, and output problems can make it hard to send a message. In some cases, the processing difficulties affect a child's ability to understand nonliteral meanings of words, and so the child misses the nuances of the communication. The brain's executive function system also oversees and monitors communication; so if there are problems with attending, communication will be difficult. The emotional context of communication can also contribute to an individual's inability to send, receive, and/or understand the message. Strong emotions, such as anger and high levels of anxiety, can make communication difficult. Remember Michelle, the girl we met at the beginning of the chapter, and how painful speaking in front of the class was for her because of her speech disorder? Speaking in front of the class became even more difficult as her anxiety increased when her teacher put pressure on her. Michelle's early experience with public speaking was connected with strong negative emotions that stayed with her and inhibited her desire to communicate for years to come.

Language Disorders

As explained earlier, culturally determined rules govern the form, content, and function of language. Table 9.1 shows that each element of language—phonology, morphology, syntax, semantics, and pragmatics—is a potential source of language disorders. For example, some children are able to express age-appropriate ideas in correct sentence structures but are not able to use accepted rules of morphology; they might have difficulty with pluralization (*foot-feet*), with verb tenses (*run-ran, walk-walked*), or with the use of prefixes (*pre-, anti-*).

Language involves both *reception* (taking in information) and *expression* (giving out verbal information and producing written language). In some manner, language is processed internally during both reception and expression, but language production and language comprehension do not always proceed at the same pace. Some children will speak but do not seem to understand the meaning of the sentence (Slobin, 2006). And remember from our discussion of the information processing model that processing errors interfere with all types of learning, including language learning.

The stages and sequences of normal language acquisition give clues to language disorders. But it is often difficult to determine a specific cause for a child's language disorder. Speech problems, developmental disorders, or other disabilities may all influence the child's ability to use language. Speech disorders are a specific form of language disorders that affect a child's ability to produce oral language.

Speech Disorders

Speech disorders may include problems with articulation and phonological processing, voice, and/or fluency, and may originate because of a physical anomaly such as a cleft palate.

Cleft Palate

One cause of speech disorders is a **cleft palate**, which is a congenital abnormality that occurs when the roof of the mouth has not joined completely during prenatal development (Lee, Law, & Gibbon, 2009). The incidence of cleft palate ranges from 1:500 to 1:2000 depending on racial and gender differences (Lee et al., 2009). The cleft may be only on one side (unilateral) or on both sides (bilateral) and is usually closed by surgery during the first 18 months of the child's life (Henningson et al., 2008; Priester & Goorhuis-Brouwer, 2008). While early surgery can repair the cleft, an estimated 50 to 75 percent of children born with a cleft palate will require speech intervention at some point in their life (Lee et al., 2009).

Smile Train
www.smiletrain.org

Maya Barnes Johansen/The Image Works

Repair of the child's cleft palate is essential to the child's language development.

Studies looking at the development of speech for children born with a cleft palate indicate differences in pronunciation, word usage, and vocabulary for children at age 2.5 to 3 years (Scherer, Williams, & Proctor-Williams, 2008; Scherer, D'Antonio, McGahey, 2008). Scherer, Williams et al. (2008) compared the early language development of children born with and without cleft palates and found persistent difficulties in vocalization and vocabulary for children even after their cleft palate had been repaired surgically. While the two groups of children (those born with and without a cleft palate) were similar in their frequency of early babbling, the complexity of the child's early babbling was significantly lower for children with cleft palates. The authors conclude, in part, that the children with cleft palates use fewer and less complex sounds and receive more limited motoric feedback from their babbling practice and that this limits their spoken word acquisition at 3 years of age.

Early intervention with a multidisciplinary team (including surgery, dentistry, audiology, and speech language pathology professionals, as well as parents) can help support speech acquisition (Henningson et al., 2008). Parents can also be taught to provide early intervention support to help their child's speech development (Scherer, D'Antonio et al., 2008; Priester & Goorhuis-Brouwer, 2008). The areas of speech therapy that are often needed for children born with cleft palates include disorders of articulation, phonological processing, and voice.

Articulation and Phonological Processing Disorders

Articulation disorders may range from a mild frontal lisp or a fleeting hesitation in words to mispronunciations of speech sounds that are so severe that speakers are unintelligible to listeners in their own community. Imprecise phoneme (sound) production or articulation errors include substitutions, distortions, omissions, and, infrequently, the addition of extra sounds.

When the intended phoneme is replaced by another phoneme, the error is one of *substitution*. Common examples are *w* for *r* (*wight* for *right*),

Kim Gunkel/E+/Getty Images

Lots of practice on speech sounds maybe needed to help children with articulation disorders.

t for *k* (*toat* for *coat*), and *w* for *l* (*wove* for *love*). The influence of multiple substitutions on intelligibility becomes apparent when *like* becomes *wite.* In other instances, a misproduction makes a phoneme sound different but not different enough to change the production into a phoneme with a different meaning. These productions are known as *distortions* (e.g., *bwu* for *blue*). When a disorder involves *omissions,* certain sounds are omitted entirely (*pay* for *play, ka* for *cat* or *cap*). Johnny, the boy discussed earlier in the chapter, had difficulties primarily with articulation. Even with intense early speech therapy, his speech was almost unintelligible until he was 8 years old.

Disorders of Voice

Voice is the production of sound in the larynx and the selective transmission and modification of that sound through resonance and loudness (you may want to look back at Figure 9.4 to remind yourself how speech is produced). When we talk about voice, we usually think of three characteristics: quality, pitch, and loudness (ASHA, 2008). We evaluate these characteristics in terms of the speaker's age, sex, and culture (Moores, 1996). A voice disorder is an inappropriate variation in one of these. Disorders of voice quality, generally called **dysphonia**, can be related to phonation, resonation, or both. Breathiness, hoarseness, and harshness are disorders of phonation. Problems with resonation include hypernasality (excessively nasal-sounding speech) and hyponasality (speech that sounds as if the speaker has a bad cold). For children born with a cleft palate, voice disorders often include hypernasality, hyponasality, audible nasal air emissions, and/or turbulence and difficulties with controlling voice quality (Henningson et al., 2008). Often phonation and resonation disorders are present in the same person, but they can be separate disorders. Pitch indicates whether the speaker is male or female, young or old. Pitch breaks, a common problem, occur in adolescents and affect boys particularly when their voices are maturing.

Disorders of Speech Fluency: Stuttering

Fluency is the flow of speech. The most common fluency disorder is stuttering, which is characterized by repetitions and prolongations of sound, syllables, or words; tension; and extraneous movement (ASHA, 2010). **Stuttering** is a complex speech disorder with a variety of assumed causes. Speech patterns often include:

- repetitions of words or word parts ("W-W-W- Where are we eating?")
- prolongations of speech sounds ("SSSSave me a chair.")
- interjections of sounds ("We can meet at um, um, you know, like, six o'clock.")
- stopped or blocked speech where the sounds will not come out (ASHA, 2010).

Stuttering is diagnosed when these disfluencies stand out and disrupt the person's ability to communicate. A skilled speech-language pathologist is needed to assess the speech patterns and develop and implement a support program to help individuals cope with their speech challenges. Treatment programs for people who stutter often focus on teaching behaviors to help them monitor and control speech rate, control breathing, and reduce tension during speaking (ASHA, 2010). Some researchers believe that there may be a genetic component to stuttering because more boys than girls have disfluencies in their speech (Dworzynski, Remington, Rijsdijk, Howell, & Plomin, 2007). Many children who stutter show spontaneous recovery by school age (Ward, 2008). But others, like Michelle, continue to have difficulties. As with most disabilities, early intervention (begun by the age of 3) can be very effective in reducing stuttering (Ward, 2008).

9-3b Prevalence of Communication, Language, and Speech Disorders

Because of the complexity of communication problems, it is difficult to get an accurate picture of how many communication disorders are speech disorders and how many are language disorders. Speech and language disorders affected over 1 million children in 2004, approximately 1.6 percent of children (U.S. Department of Education, 2011).

Determining prevalence figures can be difficult, however, because younger children, in kindergarten through second grade, may be overidentified due to mild speech delays. Prevalence figures also tend to be distorted because intellectual and developmental delays, cerebral palsy, hearing loss, and many other disabilities affect communication. Although a communication disorder may be secondary to another disability, it still requires treatment and therapy as part of a total special education program.

9-4 Importance of the Child's Cultural and Linguistic Context

Children learn to speak the language that is spoken in their homes and neighborhoods. They tend to use language to express their needs and thoughts in the same way that their parents or caregivers do.

9-4a Bilingual Learners

For children who are bilingual, the increased language demands may cause delays in vocabulary acquisition in each of the languages used. As noted earlier in the chapter, these delays are a normal by-product of learning more than one language. To accurately assess vocabulary development for bilingual children, we must include word counts for both languages used by the child (Brice & Brice,

2009). The word *ball* and *bola*, for example, must be counted as two words for the bilingual child, and thus, the actual vocabulary for bilingual children is often greater than that for the monolingual child.

There is also evidence that learning and using two languages may enhance the child's executive function (Bialystok & Viswanathan, 2009). Barac and Bialystok (2012) examined executive functioning for three sets of bilingual children, Spanish-English (n = 20), French-English (28), and Chinese-English (30), compared with monolingual English speakers (26). The nonverbal executive control task involved selecting the matching color or shape for a computer=presented stimulus, monitoring both the speed and accuracy with which the child could complete the task. This task measures the child's ability to maintain focus and task-switch from color to shape depending on the stimulus presented. The bilingual students outperformed the monolingual students on this nonverbal executive control task (Barac & Bialystok, 2012).

Brice et al. (2009) studied articulation and phonology for preschool bilingual (Spanish-and-English-speaking) children and noted differences in pronunciations for some phonemes. In these cases the use of two languages may cause interference patterns to emerge, when one language structure is imposed onto the other language. These differences may lead to the misdiagnoses of some children as having speech disorders. The articulation differences were further complicated by the various Spanish dialects used by the child (see discussion of dialect in a later section). The study highlights the need for speech-language pathologists with bilingual and bicultural experience to appropriately assess children who are dual language learners.

9-4b Language Differences

In some homes, parents use language in ways that are different from the language some teachers expect students to use. For example, teachers may demand explicitness in language (Justice, Mashburn, Hamre, & Pianta, 2008). Although the two sentences "He took it" and "Arthur took my truck" convey the same meaning, the listener has to be in the immediate environment to understand the former, less explicit communication. Children who have not been exposed to explicit communication in the home may have difficulty when they encounter a teacher who expects it. Teachers must be aware that differences in language usage such as this are not considered to be disorders. These differences can be addressed by teaching rather than by therapy. Comparing the child's communication skills with the skills of peers from the same cultural background helps us to avoid labeling the child as language impaired rather than language different (McCabe & Champion, 2010; Hart, 2009).

9-4c Dialects

The picture can be further complicated by differences in a child's language due to family, community, or regional accents and dialects. Variations in word usage, pronunciation (phonology), word order (syntax), and meaning (semantics) influence the child's use of language (pragmatics). A **dialect** is a variation of language that differs in pronunciation, vocabulary, or syntax from the literary form of the language.

The child's primary language must be considered when evaluation his or her pronunciation of English for speech articulation.

It is used and understood by a group within a larger community. Dialects reflect regional, social, occupational, and other differences: "He done sold his car"; "We be there"; "She be sick to her stomach." The use of a dialect is *not* a sign of a speech disorder but is part of the linguistic diversity of society (Hwa-Froelich, Kasambira, & Moleski, 2007). Saying "warsh" for "wash" is not a sign of a speech defect but a regional dialect. The following ASHA definition for communication differences and dialects reminds us that these are *not* considered to be speech or language disorders:

> *Communication difference/dialect* is a variation of a symbol system used by a group of individuals that reflects and is determined by shared regional, social, or cultural/ethnic factors. A regional, social, or cultural/ethnic variation of a symbol system should not be considered a disorder of speech or language. (ASHA, 2013a).

A dialect is very much a part of a child's self-concept, and teachers must react to it carefully. Teachers should model standard literary usage when speaking and encourage children to use it when reading aloud and writing, but they should allow children to use dialect in their informal speech if the intent of their communication is clear.

A major problem for teachers is that the existence of a dialect may mask a delay or disorder that will become increasingly difficult to diagnose the longer it remains undetected (Guiberson, Barrett, Jancosek, & Itano, 2006). Language assessment tools, however, are based on an average child's use of language, which is not necessarily the way language is used, taught, and encouraged in all families and communities; this can be problematic (McCabe & Champion, 2010). Speech-language pathologists and teachers need to learn what a specific community considers accurate pronunciation and usage, and then they can teach children the expectations for communication in different settings (Brice & Brice, 2009).

9-5 Disability Areas and Problems with Communication, Language, and Speech

Throughout this text we look at the ways that a disability can affect a person's life. The impact that a disability can have on an individual's ability to communicate with others is perhaps one of the most poignant of these effects. Table 9.2 shows the possible problems with communication, language, and speech that can coexist with other areas of disability.

Since problems with communication, language, and/or speech are often present along with other disabilities, the law requires that speech-language therapy be available as a related service for children with disabilities if they need it (CEC, 2010). **Related services** are defined as support services that are required to assist the child in benefiting from special education (CEC, 2010). In most cases, a speech-language pathologist will be part of the multidisciplinary team that helps in assessing the child's needs, in planning to address these needs, and in carrying out the services required to support the child. The early detection of problems related to communication, language, and speech is essential, because early intervention can make a significant difference in the outcomes for children with problems in these areas and for preventing secondary problems from emerging (Loncke, 2011).

TABLE 9.2 Possible Problems with Communication, Language, and Speech That May Accompany Disability Areas

Disability Area	Possible Communication, Language, and Speech Problems
Intellectual and Developmental Delays	Delayed language is a universal characteristic; disorders may be present in all aspects of speech production and with both expressive and receptive language.
Cerebral Palsy	Poor muscle control and difficulty breathing may result in communication difficulties ranging from speech disorders of articulation and voice to the inability to speak; may need augmented communication support. For many individuals language delays will also be present.
Learning Disabilities	Language difficulties can cause major problems in learning to read, write, spell, and do arithmetic. Problems with communication include understanding social cues, contextual needs, and interpreting nonliteral language.
Severe and Profound Multiple Disabilities	Difficulties with speech production. May experience delays in language development; may need augmented communication support.
Autism	Communication difficulties can stem from an inability to read and interpret social cues, facial expressions, and gestures; a lack of interest in communication; difficulties with interpreting nonliteral language and language delays may be present.
Deaf/Hearing Loss	Generalized language delays, alternative communication needs (such as sign language, cued speech, lip reading); may have articulation difficulties, voice problems, and limited use of speech.
Visual Impairments	Difficulties with language reception in reading; can require use of Braille or audio augmentation. Communication difficulties may be present if individual is unable to see social cues, facial expressions, and gestures. Abstract ideas (e.g., colors) may be hard to communicate if child has no vision.
Emotional and Behavioral Problems	Communication difficulties can arise from the inability to appropriately read social cues and from impulsivity related to difficulties with self-regulation. Language delays lead to further frustration and can exacerbate existing problems.

TeachSource Digital Download Access online

Augmentative communication systems must be individualized for each student.

BOX 9.1

EXCEPTIONAL LIVES • EXCEPTIONAL STORIES

Have you ever wondered what it would be like not to be able to communicate? It's very frustrating. It's very lonely. It hurts.

Think about it. You feel, you think, you know and understand the words, yet you cannot speak them. You hear everyone around you in an interesting conversation, but you cannot join in.

You cannot express any of the feelings or emotions that are just as deep inside of you as anyone else. You are furiously angry and you have to hold it in; or you are extremely happy and you can't show it. Your heart is so full of love you could just burst, but you can't share it. I know what it is like because for years I could not communicate or express myself. I am a 19-year-old girl. I have cerebral palsy and cannot talk. I do not have coordination in my hands to write or use sign language. Even a typewriter was out of the question when I was younger. I know what it is like to be fed potatoes all my life. After all, potatoes are a good basic food for every day, easy to fix in many different ways. I hate potatoes! But then, who knew that but me?

I know what it is like to be dressed in reds and blues when my favorite colors are mint greens, lemon yellows, and pinks. I mean, really, can you imagine?

Finally, help came! I was introduced to Blissymbols.

My life changed! Blissymbols were originally developed for a universal language, but they have been a miracle for me and others like me. Blissymbols are a combination of the written word and a symbolized picture that anyone can learn, which are displayed in a way that can be easily used. There was a tray strapped to my wheelchair. It was covered with a sheet of paper, which was divided into little blocks of words to form sentences. At last, I could communicate!

Naturally, one board could not hold all the words needed. I had to learn to make up my own, combining two or more words to mean another. As in "story sleep" for dream or "bad night horse" for nightmare.

My teachers started me on ten words a day to see if I could learn them. I learned as fast as they could give me new words. I was ready to communicate! I could even stutter! That's what my uncle calls it when it takes three or four tries to point to one word.

Once I mastered Blissymbols, I left the symbols behind and changed to words and sentences. I got my first computer. It was an Autocom™. I programmed my Bliss board into it and much more. It also had a printer. Finally, I could write!

Communicating for me has opened a lot of doors. It even let me act in a play. I have been a guest speaker at a Kiwanis Club meeting. It has done a lot more, too. There's help out there, just don't give up.

SOURCE: "Sara's Story" from *Keyhole Communique, 3*(3), May 1989.

Box 9.1 shares the story of a young girl's experience prior to being able to communicate her needs.

9-5a Assessment and Identification of Problems with Communication, Language, and Speech

A comprehensive evaluation of a child's ability to communicate will include an assessment of both receptive and expressive language strengths and needs. Because the demands of communication are complex, it is essential to assess each element of language to establish areas in which difficulties are encountered. Table 9.3 shows the language element that should be assessed and what it will look like for both receptive and expressive language.

A comprehensive evaluation will likely include both formal and informal assessments, combining standardized tests with systematic observations and recordings of spontaneous uses of language (Hyter, 2007; Olswang et al., 2007; Salvia et al., 2007). Formal assessments rely on diagnostic test and clinical evaluations done by a speech-language pathologist. As part of the informal assessment, teachers can make a key contribution to understanding the child's needs through their systematic observations of the child. The observations that a teacher makes of the child's language behavior during the course of typical classroom activities help the team gain a comprehensive portrait of the child's typical verbal and nonverbal communication patterns (Olswang et al., 2007). Teachers can further use their observations to shape the kinds of supports that will help strengthen the child's communication skills.

TABLE 9.3 Language Elements for a Comprehensive Assessment of Communication Difficulties

Language Elements	Receptive Language	Expressive Language
Phonology	Child has difficulties hearing different speech sounds.	Child's articulation of speech sounds is impaired.
Morphology and Syntax	Child has difficulty understanding grammar or language structure (not based on cultural dialect or linguistic differences).	Child uses inappropriate grammar or language structure (not based on cultural dialect or linguistic differences).
Semantics	Child has difficulty understanding needs, ideas, wants, feelings, and thoughts of others.	Child has difficulty expressing needs, ideas, wants, feelings and thoughts through language.
Pragmatics and Supralinguistics	Child has difficulty interpreting the speaker's motivations.	Child has difficulty adjusting communication to the social context and demands.

The speech-language pathologist is primarily responsible for the identification, diagnosis, and design of the treatment plan or curriculum, and the implementation of this plan for children with language and speech disorders. In doing this, the speech-language pathologist works as part of a multidisciplinary team. Coming together as a team is really important; the special educator and speech-language pathologist bring different expertise and experiences to the table. But because they have been trained in separate programs, it may take extra effort to combine their understandings of how to support the student's success. The team must consider several things as they evaluate the communication strengths and needs of the child. The child's age, general cognitive abilities, sensory acumen, experiences, and the family's primary language will all have an impact on the child's communication. When English is not the primary language of the child and/or the child's family, the assessment for possible problems with language is more complex.

Assessment of Children from Culturally or Linguistically Diverse Backgrounds

Children from homes in which English is not the primary language are likely to encounter difficulty in using English in school, but language pragmatics can be explicitly taught to minimize problems for the child due to differences in expectations between home and school (Brice, Miller, & Brice, 2006). When a language or speech disorder is suspected, children from cultures and communities that speak a language other than English need to be assessed by speech-language pathologists who are skilled in the child's primary language (Brice et al., 2009; Guiberson et al., 2006).

Ines is a 3-year-old child whose bilingual family lives in New Mexico. English is her primary language, but her range of English vocabulary and language proficiency is lower than would be expected for her age norms. In part, these lower scores reflect the impact of her dialect, called Spanglish, which varies from classic Spanish and includes some English. The school personnel will need to be knowledgeable about this dialect when they assess Ines's functioning (Brice et al., 2006). Ines is fortunate in some respects, as many children her age in New Mexico have not learned English and will not do so until they attend school. Ines's school success will depend on the skills of her teacher and the speech-language pathologist and on the cooperation and support provided by her family (Saenz & Felix, 2006).

Assessments of children who are bilingual should involve a specialist who is bilingual *and* bicultural. A speech-language pathologist who speaks the language of the child's home and who understands the child's cultural background can

TeachSource Video Connection

Watch the video "Bilingual Education: An Elementary Two-Way Immersion Program." As you watch this Video Case, reflect on how the teachers worked together to promote vocabulary development for their students. In addition, think about the ways they used the bilingual approach to reinforce concept development and enhance understanding. Which of the six guiding principles did you see demonstrated in the video? What might be some pros and cons of using a bilingual approach with children with communication disorders?

Watch online

more appropriately interpret the child's assessment results; this should help prevent misdiagnosis of communication, language, and speech disorders (Brice & Brice, 2009).

Great care must be taken that children from different cultures who speak a different language receive an accurate assessment by a person well versed in the children's language and cultural mores. For example, Spanish-speaking children who speak a Puerto Rican dialect make a number of phonological "errors" that are consistent with their dialect. If the dialect of these children is not taken into account, lower scores will be obtained (Goldstein & Iglesias, 2001; Brice & Brice, 2009).

When a native speaker of the child's language is not available to conduct the assessment, a mediator who speaks the child's language can be hired as a neutral person to assist the evaluator and help communicate with the family. During the evaluation, the mediator can relieve the family's stress by keeping the family informed about what is taking place (Saenz & Felix, 2006).

Six research-based guiding principles for working with preschool bilingual children have been identified by the Southern California Comprehensive Assistance Center. These six principles include:

- Using the child's home language as a foundation for cognitive development, learning about the world, and emerging literacy
- Creating a learning environment that facilitates social and emotional growth and affirms the child's cultural identity
- Supporting opportunities to allow one language to enhance the other language
- Building strong and effective home-school partnerships
- Providing high-quality professional development for adults on meeting the needs of English-language learners
- Using culturally, developmentally, and linguistically appropriate assessment (2005).

9-6 Educational Responses for Children with Communication, Speech, and Language Disorders

Students with communication, speech, and language disorders form a heterogeneous group with a wide variety of strengths and needs. They may be identified primarily for their challenges with speech or they may have another primary area of disability and therefore receive speech/language support as a related service. In either case, a multidisciplinary team will likely be involved in planning and delivering supports and services.

9-6a Organizational Structures to Support Students with Communication, Speech, and Language Disorders

Not all children with speech-language disorders are in special education classes. In fact, as shown in ◗ Figure 9.5, 87 percent of children with speech and language disorders spend the majority of their day in general education classes (80 percent

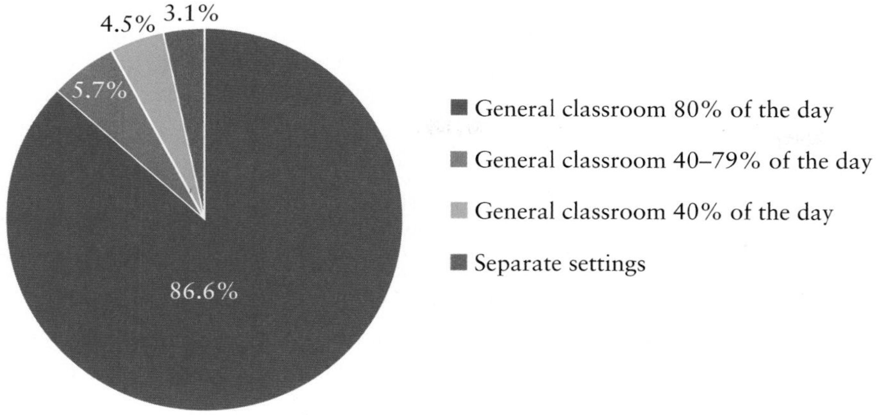

Figure 9.5 Educational Setting for Children with Communication Disorders
Source: Data Accountability Center (2011). *Part B Educational Environments 2011 [data file]. Retrieved from http://www.ideadata.org/PartBEnvironments.asp*

of their time or more); 6 percent are served in the general classroom for 40 to 79 percent of the day; only 4.5 percent spend about half their day outside of the general classroom and 3 percent are served in separate settings (U.S. Department of Education, 2009). Children with speech and language disorders are more likely than children with other disabilities to be served in the general classroom.

With the majority of children with communication, speech, and language disorders served within the general education program, multitiered approaches like RtI become very important to address the child's needs.

RtI Approaches for Students with Communication, Speech, and Language Disorders

RtI

The three levels of intervention that typically constitute the response to intervention (RtI) approach, when they are working well, provide a collaborative framework for meeting the needs of students with communication, language, and speech disorders (Sanger, Mohling, & Stremlau, 2012). The speech-language pathologist is central to the multidisciplinary team planning and implementing the interventions within an RtI system. The speech-language pathologist can help with screening, progress-monitoring, assessments, and interventions to prevent continued failure (Sanger et al., 2012). Collaboration among the multidisciplinary team across all three tiers is essential to helping the child meet with success.

Universal Tier I for Students with Communication, Speech, and Language Disorders

As previously mentioned, most children whose primary area of identification is speech and language are served in the general classroom. Inclusion is the typical option for the child with communication disorders, because most children with primary speech disorders respond well to the general education program if they receive additional help for their special communication needs. The general education classroom and inclusion with typically developing peers provides a rich language environment that can enhance the communication of all children.

You may recall that both Johnny and Michelle, the children presented early in this chapter, were students in a general classroom. You may also remember that Michelle's second-grade teacher's insensitivity led to a painful situation in which Michelle's stuttering caused her significant embarrassment. Michelle's current teacher in fifth grade, Ms. Boone, is much more aware of the difficulty that Michelle faces and has worked hard to make the classroom comfortable, engaging, and nonthreatening. Ms. Boone has modeled active listening for her students, and she praises them when they listen respectfully and patiently to each other without interrupting. This is particularly helpful to Michelle, because it has allowed her to feel more at ease talking. In addition, the children in the class have learned about the difficulties that Michelle faces, and they have been asked to show courtesy to Michelle when she is speaking by following these guidelines:

- Disregard short pauses or slow speech.
- Show acceptance of what has been expressed rather than how it was said.
- Treat Michelle like any other member of the class.
- Acknowledge Michelle's speech difficulties without labeling her.
- Help Michelle feel in control of her speech.

Not surprisingly, because of the open, honest, and compassionate way that Michelle's needs have been addressed, the class is very supportive, and Michelle is making leaps and bounds with her class participation.

Ms. Boone also uses a variety of cooperative learning strategies to promote student-to-student communication (Timler, Vogler-Elias, & McGill, 2007). The classroom environment is set up with engaging materials and small-group arrangements that promote conversations about what is being learned. Ms. Boone believes that learning is facilitated by social interaction, and so she has structured her classroom environment and routine to facilitate communication (Timler et al., 2007). Even with this language-rich environment in which the children's communication is intentionally enhanced, Ms. Boone knows that some of her students will need more support. She works closely with the school's speech-language pathologist, Mrs. Henley, to help her students with more intense needs. A Summary of *UDL Supports for Students with Communication Disorders* can be accessed online.

TeachSource Digital Download

Targeted Tier II for Students with Communication, Speech, and Language Disorders

In addition to Michelle, Ms. Boone's fifth-grade class has three students with language-related learning disabilities: two students who are English-language learners, Pedro and Gyanna, and one student with Asperger's syndrome, Drew. These children often seem reluctant to participate in the literature seminars that the class holds every other week. To help with this, Mrs. Henley works with a small group of children, giving them explicit instruction on the "language routines" used by Ms. Boone during literacy seminars (Ritzman, Sanger, & Coufal, 2006). She explicitly teaches them the rules of participation, and the students practice their new participation skills until they can use them comfortably (Timler et al., 2007). During the seminars Mrs. Henley prompts the students to remember their "participation rules" when they want to contribute. Eventually students are able to participate without explicit prompting. Pedro and Gyanna also work with the English-language learners' (ELL) teacher prior to each seminar to review key vocabulary that will be used and to explore answers to the questions that will be discussed. These preliminary activities help both children feel more confident in participating during the seminars.

To help Michelle become more comfortable participating in the classroom, Mrs. Henley and Ms. Boone use a similar approach called "planned participation," which gives Michelle time to prepare and practice what she wants to say. They also focus on Michelle's strength in poetry writing by creating a "Friday Poets Corner," in which students can share their poems. Classroom teachers can be particularly helpful to the child who stutter by working with the speech-language pathologist to create planned opportunities for the child to participate in speaking activities that are appropriate for practicing newly acquired fluency skills at increasing levels of complexity.

For some children, however, more individualized support is needed, and for these children Tier III services must be provided to help them be successful.

Intensive Tier III for Students with Communication, Speech, and Language Disorders

At Tier III, the services are specifically designed to meet the individual needs of the student. In most cases, the child's individualized education program (IEP) will specify the services needed and will determine the related services that are essential to his or her success. Because the needs of each child are unique, a speech-language pathologist must be prepared to deal with a broad range of disorders. The speech-language pathologist provides support for students who may have primary articulation, fluency, voice, and/or language disorders. The pathologist must also be able to address the problems found among children with cleft palate, intellectual and developmental delays, cerebral palsy, learning disabilities, and emotional disturbances; and students who are deaf (Hanks & Velaski, 2003). To address the wide variety of needs, the speech-language pathologist must be able to manage multiple roles (Ritzman et al., 2006). A Summary of *RtI Approaches for Students with Communication Disorders* can be accessed online.

TeachSource Digital Download

9-6b Curriculum and Instruction for Students with Communication, Speech, and Language Disorders

Speech-language pathologists increasingly are working directly with children in the general education classroom, supporting the academic program (Sanger et al., 2012). They may alert students to pay attention to verbal or written instructions, encourage them to ask pertinent questions and to participate in discussions, and assist them in responding in a culture- and classroom-appropriate fashion. The speech-language pathologist helps teachers facilitate communication with the child in natural settings, including the classroom.

Speech-language pathologists also use many techniques to promote the carryover of newly acquired communication skills into the classroom and everyday conversation. These techniques include children's notebooks prepared by therapists that are kept in the classroom for the teacher's regular review, weekly conferences with teachers regarding specific objectives, the use of devices and props as reminders, and carefully planned in-class "talking" activities. A major task of the communication specialist is to help the classroom teacher use these tools effectively, because the teacher's help is vital to success. The speech-language pathologist helps by suggesting strategies that encourage talk, expand talk, and model correct forms and usage. She may help the teacher set up effective peer-mediated social supports (Goldstein, Schneider, & Thiemann, 2007) and may help teach students self-advocacy skills so that they can communicate their needs (Ritzman et al., 2006).

The teacher's creativity in adapting classroom opportunities to foster ways of talking will help the student to generalize these new skills. The classroom is often the most appropriate setting for incidental and interactive functional teaching of communication skills (Fey, Windsor, & Warren, 1995).

Common Core Standards for Students with Communication, Speech, and Language Disorders

COMMON CORE STATE STANDARDS

Students whose primary area of concern is with speech or language disorders are most often served within the general education classroom and are expected to access the common core curriculum alongside their peers. Just as with all areas of disability, early and intense intervention is essential to seeing successful outcomes for the child (Wilcox, Gray, Guimond, & Lafferty, 2011).

Access to the common core curriculum can be challenging for children with language disorders that impact listening, talking, reading, and writing. Table 9.4 shares universal design for learning approaches that can support children with communication, speech, and language disorders in mastery of the curriculum.

TABLE 9.4 Using Universal Design Principals to Give Student with Communication, Speech, and Language Disorders Access to the Common Core State Standards

Common Core Standard	Multiples Representations	Multiple Engagements	Multiple Assessments
Reading Standard Literacy, #7, Integration of knowledge and ideas, Grade 6 Compare and contrast the experience of reading a story, drama, or poem to listening to or viewing an audio, video, or live version of the text. Including contrasting what they "see" and "hear" when reading the text to what they perceive when they listen or watch.	Advance organizers Text/narrative Graphic organizers for compare and contrast Pictures Video Dramatization Web-based text Audiobooks Vocabulary builders Use picture or iconic prompts for material (e.g,. an eye for narrative descriptions that promote visual images, and ear for words that evoke sounds)	Direct instruction on content, vocabulary, and strategies Reading text material with guided prompts for noting what you "see" and "hear" Listening to reading (with guided prompts) Watching dramatization or video (with guided prompts) Discussions Small group applications Debates Develop graphic organizers: compare/contrast Create visual representations of information or images Writing activities Prepare presentations (PowerPoint, etc.)	Written products (concept webs, drafts) Oral presentations Pictures of images seen Compare/contrast Graphic organizers Documentary film showing differences in perceptions Essay on the pros and cons of "reading" vs. "watching the video"
Math Standard, #1, Geometry, Solve real-world and mathematical problems involving area, surface area, and volume, Grade 6 Find the area of right triangles, other triangles, special quadrilaterals, and polygons by composing into rectangles or decomposing into triangles and other shapes; apply these techniques in the context of solving real-world and mathematical problems.	Hands-on materials Charts, Graphs, Pictures Drawings Real-world application Highlighted problems (key words in color) Flash cards: words to math symbol or operations	Direct instruction on concepts with meta-cognitive or "think-aloud" explanations of process Use hands-on manipulatives Create flash cards for formulas of area, surface area, and volume Draw pictures representing Use tangram forms to practice using triangles, squares, and rectangles to compose and decompose larger shapes Use calculators for checking Create word problems based on real-world data collection	Traditional written assessment of problem solving Student developed word problems on concept Drawings, Pictures, Charts, Graphs Math talks Students find real-world examples of when an area, surface area, or volume can be found by composing or decomposing the space into other shapes

TeachSource Digital Download Access online

Children who receive speech-language support as a related service, because they have another primary area of disability, will often have communication goals on their IEPs. In these cases the services provided by the speech-language pathologist will follow the IEP goals supporting the child and her or his teacher.

Specific Strategies to Support English-Language Learners

Understanding the linguistic competencies of children whose primary language is not English can be tricky. Earlier in the chapter we looked at a variety of things that make it more challenging to recognize language delays and disorders in children who are English-language learners, and so it should come as no surprise that meeting the needs of bilingual children can also be challenging. The strategies given here are meant to be a starting place for teachers and can provide a foundation for interventions at Tiers I and II.

These strategies address the two areas of language competency that ELL students need: (1) basic interpersonal communication skills and (2) cognitive/academic language proficiency (Bunce, 2003). In other words, children must be able to communicate with others socially, *and* they need the more specialized language skills required for success in school. Brice et al. (2006) offer the following ideas for teachers to help English-language learners strengthen their communication:

1. Build lessons around the child's background knowledge and bridge this to the new learnings.
2. Provide written copies of directions and key instructions and use pictures to show what is expected.
3. Ask prediction questions that are open-ended, to allow children to contribute a variety of knowledge (e.g., "What do you think . . . ?").
4. Teach study skills (such as note-taking, organization, and test-taking strategies).
5. Encourage students to ask questions and participate in discussions.
6. Model correct language forms and employ appropriate wait times (be patient and give 3 to 5 seconds or more to let students think) to allow students to respond.
7. Teach language routines to help the childrem in typical situations (e.g., asking questions, getting what they need, and providing information).
8. Use grammar drills and direct instruction to support skill development.
9. Practice formalized or structured speaking and allow students to "rehearse."
10. Allow for code switching and code mixing (the use of the primary language interspersed with English is natural as the second language emerges).
11. When students have reached a higher level of proficiency with English, use more complex sentences.
12. Explicitly teach vocabulary that is needed in the learning context.

Perhaps most importantly, in working to meet the needs of ELL children who have communication disorders we must establish a collaborative team that includes the classroom teacher, the bilingual education specialist, the special education teacher, the speech-language pathologist, and the child's parents.

Assistive Technology for Augmentative and Alternative Communication

When speech disorders are severe enough to make oral communication difficult, students will need additional assistive technology supports to help them communicate. Assistive technology includes approaches and devices that support communication and help people express their thoughts, needs, wants, and ideas (Leech & Cress, 2011). The primary forms of assistive technology for children with communication, language, and speech disorders are **augmentative and alternative communication** devices or approaches (ASHA, 2010). Augmentative communication strategies are often used to prompt or promote the development of speech by helping the child use words to communicate. Individuals with severe speech difficulties, however, can use augmentative or alternative communication to supplement or replace talking.

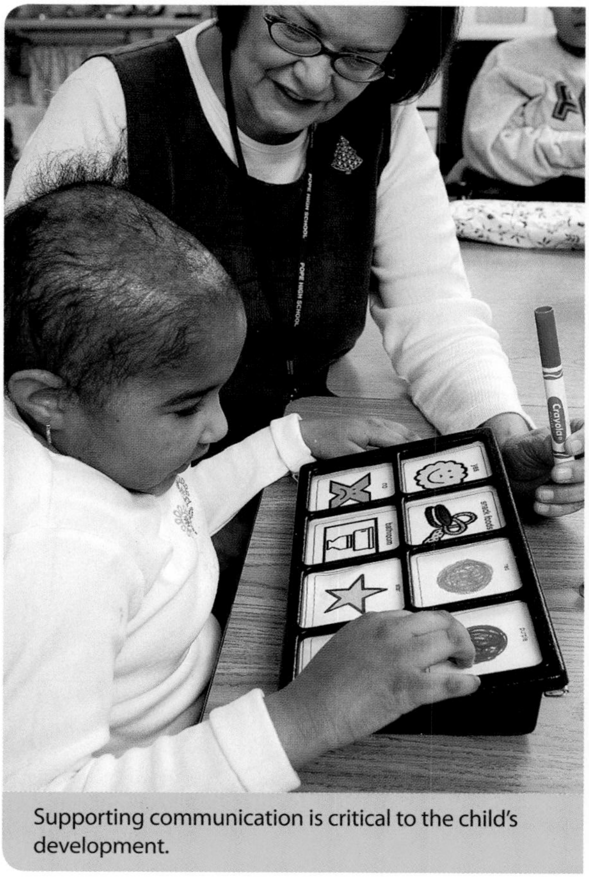

Robin Nelson/PhotoEdit

Supporting communication is critical to the child's development.

TeachSource Video Connection

Watch the video "Tyler: Augmentative Communication Techniques for Kindergarten Students with Autism and Language Issues." In this video, you will meet Tyler, his teacher Whitney Mead, and his speech-language pathologist, Becky Paden. Tyler uses the Picture Exchange Communication System (PECS), an augmentative communication approach, to help him express his thoughts, needs, and wants. As you watch this video, reflect on the strategies his teachers use to support Tyler's communication abilities. What strategies did Ms. Paden suggest that might be used with all children to enhance communication? How did Ms. Meade help her students develop their pragmatic language skills?

Watch online

Some communication systems do *not* provide voice output, so the person who is receiving the message must be physically present to understand what is being communicated. In other words, the communication must be seen—such as gestures, body language, sign language, and communication boards. Because of this, these communication approaches are not useful with telephones or for communication from room to room. **American Sign Language (ASL)**, an alternative communication system of gestures that contain meaning, is an example of a nonspeech communication system that is discussed in more detail in Chapter 11.

Other augmentative communication devices simulate or enhance speech. Assistive technology for communication varies in its level of sophistication. One device for supporting communication is the communication board. Communication boards vary in complexity from a set of simple pictures (e.g., pictures of a glass of milk and a glass of juice) to sophisticated groups of letters, words, pictures, and special symbols (Hart & Banda, 2010). More sophisticated communication boards produce speech when they are used.

Blissymbolics is a computerized communication system that uses graphic symbols or "blisswords" to help the child communicate. Figure 9.6 shows some sample blisswords that might be used for communication. Using Blissymbolics, children point to or touch the words they want and form sentences to express thoughts. This allows a child with severely limited speech to "talk." This is the system that Sara, who you met in the Exceptional Lives, Exceptional Stories section of this chapter, used to communicate. You may

Technology and Media Division of the Council for Exceptional Children
www.tamcec.org

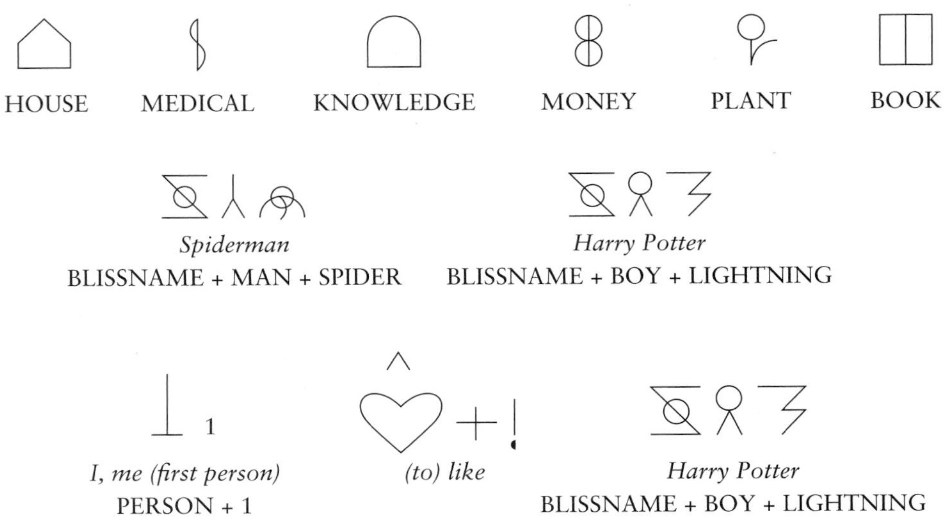

Figure 9.6 Sample Blisswords
Blissymbolics is a computerized communication system that uses graphic symbols or "blisswords" to help the child communicate. Almost any word in the English language can be described using a combination of blisswords.

want to revisit her story to think about how assistive technology can change someone's life. The picture exchange communication system is another way to augment communication, helping students increase their vocabulary and expand their communication. Tyler, a kindergartener with autism, uses this approach in the TeachSource video that you can watch as part of this chapter.

Blissymbolics
www.blissymbolics.org

Communication for a person using augmentative devices takes more time, energy, and skill; it also requires the listener to be an active, patient, and receptive communicator (Solomon-Rice & Soto, 2011). Adolescent students who used augmentative communication systems described "good" communicators as those who:

- treat me as a person who has things to say
- treat me like a teenager, not a baby
- give me time
- listen properly
- give me the option of saying "it is none of those"
- tell me if they do not understand me
- check with me to make sure they got my message
- do not finish my sentences for me
- are not afraid of me or my voice
- are able to use signs, my communication book, or other ways to communicate with me (Wickenden, 2011)

The students in this study also said that they could tell very quickly if the person they were talking with was going to be a good communicator or not (Wickenden, 2011). The principles these teenagers articulated are a solid foundation for good communication in general and offer excellent advice to anyone who wants to be a good communicator!

The most important thing to remember about the use of augmentative and alternative communication supports is that the more children communicates, the stronger their ability to communicate becomes. This means that we should support communication through a variety of means to enhance children's development.

9-7 Family and Lifespan Issues

Parents are the child's first teachers, and in no area is this more true than in the language a child develops. The child makes amazing progress in language during the first few years of life (Loncke, 2011). The parent or primary caregiver can do a lot to support early language development. In the first few years of life, talking with the child is essential. Talking about colors, counting, identifying the names of objects, playing word repetition games, and sharing nursery rhymes are all part of the early language stimulation of young children. The parent can also help the child become more aware of sounds by reinforcing the familiar sounds of the environment (e.g., "The clock goes tick-tick-tick"; "The car goes vroom!"; "What does the cat say?"). Reading with young children further extends their understanding of language and can be the perfect time for discussions of pictures, ideas, and actions in the story. As the child grows, it is important that early attempts to communicate are taken seriously. Children thrive when adults listen to them and seem interested in what they have to say (Loncke, 2011). Often grandparents play a special role in the child's life because they take the time to listen to the child and are genuinely interested in what the child has to say.

9-7a How Parents Can Support Their Child's Communication

If the child says "Wa doo," the parent may say, "I don't understand; tell me again." The child repeats "Wa doo," looking at the refrigerator. The parent then says, "Oh,

Technology can enhance communication in many ways.

Ableimages/Digital Vision/Getty Images

you want some juice," and gives it to the child. The parent can also be taught to use *recasting,* or modeling the correct pronunciation without correcting the child's speech. For example, in response to the question "What do we call that big cat?" the child says "a wion," and the parent says, "yes, that big cat is a lion." At no time does the parent interrupt the child and tell him or her, "Say *lion.*" Responses by the adult that build on what the child is communicating are also referred to as *following directives,* and they have been shown to facilitate the child's language development (McCathren, Yoder, & Warren, 1995). When adults follow the child's lead, talking about what the child is interested in, the child is likely to be more engaged in the conversation and will use and learn more words (Southern California Comprehensive Assistance Center, 2005; Justice et al., 2008).

When we focus on the social use of language (pragmatics) and stress functional communication, we can support language development in natural environments. Using an interactive approach, the interventionist—a parent, special education teacher, or speech-language pathologist—capitalizes on the natural inclination of children to talk about what they are doing, plan to do, or want to do. To encourage correct word and language use, the adult provides support while the child is eating, playing, or visiting community settings such as a grocery store (Hyter, 2007). Working in settings in which talking and listening occur naturally helps to increase the child's amount of talk. And the more the child talks, the more he or she will gradually gain accuracy and increase his or her vocabulary.

9-7b Transitions for Students with Communication Disorders

What lies ahead for the child who has a communication disorder? The answer to this question depends on the nature and severity of the disorder (Loncke, 2011). Children who have primary articulation disorders (that is, a speech or language disorder not associated with other disabilities) seem to have few related problems as adults. In contrast, follow-up studies of children with severe disorders show that some children with language deficits continue to have problems in academics, interpersonal relationships, and work (Durkin, Fraser, & Conti-Ramsden, 2012). Students with specific language impairments, for example, were more likely to aspire to manual tasks than their typically developing peers who aspired to professional roles (Durkin et al., 2012). What is clear, however, is that early support can help to minimize secondary problems and in some cases it can help a child overcome the speech disorders.

Important changes have come about in helping students with communication disorders make transitions from high school to college and the workplace. Many colleges and universities have support services and special programs for students with disabilities. Special clinics and help sessions are staffed by speech-language pathologists, learning disabilities specialists, and psychologists. Supports offered may include individualized techniques for note taking, class participation, and writing. Job coaches can help individuals with the pragmatics of work-related communication to allow individuals to be successful in employment settings (Montgomery, 2006). Augmentative and alternative communication systems can be developed to meet work-related needs, and assistive technologies can be used to support communication. Because communication is so critical to an individual's successes, every effort must be made to support effective and appropriate communication. Appropriate supports and interventions that are provided early and continued for as long as necessary can help individuals develop their communication skills.

MORAL DILEMMA

Children with Communication Disorders

Collaboration among classroom teachers, special education teachers, and speech-language pathologists is essential to providing the full support that a child with communication disorders needs across all three tiers of intervention. A good example of collaboration was presented in the Educational Responses section of this chapter (see pages 302–309). But collaboration is not always easy to accomplish. What can you do if one of the professionals who is key to the child's success will not work as part of a team? What are some of the personal and professional obstacles to collaboration, and how can you help a colleague overcome these? What should you do if you feel a child is being harmed by a colleague's resistance to collaboration?

Summary

- The formation of the American Speech and Hearing Association in 1925 was critical to the development of the field of speech and language disorders.
- Children with communication, language, and speech disorders have a wide range of strengths and needs that impact their learning.
- Communication is an essential part of being human, and it requires a sender, a message, and a receiver.
- Language is a code in which signs, sounds, and symbols represent feelings, ideas, and information.
- Language is both receptive and expressive and can be described as having form, content, and function.
- Language form includes phonology, morphology, and syntax; semantics refers to content; and function includes pragmatics and supralinguistics.
- Speech is the systematic oral production of the words of a given language.
- Processes needed to produce speech are respiration, phonation, resonation, articulation, audition, and symbolization/organization.
- Typically language development follows a pattern of emerging complexity moving from sounds to words and sentences that convey meaning.
- A language disorder is impaired comprehension or use of spoken, written, and/or other symbol systems.
- Speech disorders include problems with articulation, fluency, and voice.
- Understanding normal patterns of language acquisition is an important part of identifying children with language disorders.
- A comprehensive assessment is essential to identifying communication, language, and speech disorders.
- Since communication, language, and speech disorders often co-exist with other areas of disability, it is difficult to determine their prevalence in children.

- Understanding a child's cultural and linguistic background is necessary to correctly identify and support children with language disorders.
- Recognizing communication disorders in children whose primary language is not English can be challenging and may require a specialist who is both bilingual and bicultural.
- Individuals with disabilities may also have communication disorders.
- The role of the speech-language pathologist has expanded in the schools to include coteaching children within the general education classroom.
- Assistive technologies including augmentative or alternative communication devices, and approaches may be needed for individuals with limited speech.
- Parents and families can provide essential support for a child's development of language.

Future Challenges

1. **How can schools provide the time and resources needed to allow teachers to collaborate as they work to meet the needs of their students?**
   Collaboration between general education teachers and specialists is essential to supporting children with communication, language, and speech disorders, yet often teachers find this difficult to accomplish. Barriers to collaboration include a lack of time, limited shared resources, and difficulties with caseloads or class size. If we truly believe that collaboration is necessary, how can we find ways to support teachers and related service providers so that they can work together meaningfully?

2. **How can early intervention materials be made more available to parents and physicians?**
   Most speech disorders are not identifiable until a child reaches 2 years of age, when verbal language ability usually appears. Unfortunately, parents frequently do not recognize early signs of potential speech disorders in the prelinguistic stage. How can we make information on prelingual indicators of potential difficulty more available to both pediatricians and parents?

3. **How can we provide appropriate services for children with communication, language, and speech problems who are also English-language learners?**
   Our schools are serving increasing numbers of children whose primary language is not English. When communication, language, and speech problems exist in children who are bilingual, it can be more difficult for school personnel to recognize, identify, and meet the child's needs. How can we address the communication, language, and speech needs of bilingual children and their families?

TeachSource Digital Download Access online

Key Terms

American Sign Language (ASL) p. 306
articulation p. 290
articulation disorders p. 294
audition p. 290
augmentative and alternative communication p. 307
cleft palate p. 294
communication p. 288
communication disorders p. 293
dialect p. 297
dysphonia p. 295
expressive language p. 289

fluency p. 290
fluency disorders p.293
language p. 288
language content p. 289
language disorders p. 293
language form p. 289
language function p. 289
language pragmatics p. 285
morphology p. 289
phonation p. 290
phonology p. 289
receptive language p. 289
related services p. 299
resonation p. 290
respiration p. 290
speech p. 290
speech disorders p. 294
stuttering p. 296
supralinguistics p. 290
syntax p. 289
voice p. 290
voice disorders p. 295

Resources

References of Special Interest

Justice, L. (2013). *Communication sciences and disorders: A Clinical Evidence-Based Approach* (3rd ed.). Don Mills, ON, Canada: Pearson. This is a literacy-focused look at the development of speaking, listening, reading, and writing and the ecological impact of communication disorders at home, school, work, and within the community.

Clark, E. V. (2009). *First language acquisition* (2nd ed.). Cambridge, UK: Cambridge University Press. This textbook provides a comprehensive account of first language acquisition in children, beginning from birth. This edition includes recent research findings and a new chapter on the acquisition of two languages.

Wallach, G. P. (2008). *Language intervention for school-age students*: Setting goals for academic success. St. Louis, MO: Mosby. In this book, Wallach provides useful strategies that can help promote learning in students with learning disabilities. Theoretical and conceptual discussions are also included.

Paul, R. & Norbury, C. F. (2012). *Language disorders from infancy through adolescence: Listening, speaking, reading, writing, and communicating* (4th ed.). St. Louis, MO: Elsevier. A comprehensive presentation of assessment strategies for a wide array of speech-language disorders, as well as suggestions for intervention.

Journals

American Journal of Speech-Language Pathology
http://ajslp.asha.org/

Communication Disorders Quarterly
www.proedinc.com

Journal of Special Education Technology **http://www.tamcec.org/jset/**

Canadian Journal of Speech-Language, Pathology, and Audiology
www.caslpa.ca/english/resources/jslpa.asp

Journal of Speech, Language, and Hearing Research
http://jslhr.asha.org/

Topics in Language Disorders
http://www.topicsinlanguagedisorders.com

Language, Speech, and Hearing Services in Schools
http://lshss.asha.org/

Professional Organizations

American Speech-Language-Hearing Association (ASHA)
www.asha.org/

Division for Communicative Disabilities and Deafness
http://www.dcdd.us/

Council for Exceptional Children
www.cec.sped.org

Technology and Media Division of the Council for Exceptional Children
www.tamcec.org

CHAPTER 10

Children Who Have Special Gifts and Talents

Standards Addressed in This Chapter

All of the CEC Standards are addressed within this chapter. Please see the inside book covers for the complete list of the standards.

CEC

FOCUS QUESTIONS

10-1 Why should we care about educating students with special gifts and talents (SGT)?

10-2 What are the current components of definitions for children with SGT?

10-3 What are special characteristics of students with SGT?

10-4 How do we identify students with SGT?

10-5 What educational responses are needed to educate students with SGT?

10-6 What adjustments for postgraduate experiences are needed for students with SGT?

We can all picture the two or three most intelligent persons that we have ever met. We have been impressed by the breadth of their knowledge and skills and sometimes are envious of how effortlessly they learn or play an instrument. We may have even wondered where such talent came from. Was it merely a lucky roll of the genetic dice, or did their parents and teachers have something to do with the flowering of this talent? Were they always so superior in development? Are there others in our society who have great talent who, for a variety of reasons, have not been discovered or enhanced?

One thing is certain: As educators we need to do more than stand in awe of such abilities. We need to find ways to help students with special gifts and talents (SGT) develop and extend these creative abilities, because new art, new scientific inventions, and business innovations will likely come from their gifts and talents.

No matter how intelligent they are, these students won't discover algebra on their own, nor learn how to write a sonnet, nor play a saxophone or violin. Their special abilities are raw materials that need to be nurtured. This chapter describes these gifted and talented individuals and shares what we have learned about the best ways to educate them.

10-1 Why Should We Care about Students with Special Gifts and Talents?

Aside from the commitment to help all students do the best they can, why should we spend special time and resources on children with special gifts and talents (SGT)? We have learned that students with SGT can have an important impact on the future of our society.

The National Academy of Sciences assembled a distinguished panel composed of Nobel prizewinners, university presidents, and CEOs of major corporations to produce a report on the status of students with SGT in American society, with particular reference to math and science. This panel concluded with some serious concerns in a report, *Rising Above the Gathering Storm* (2007).

Following are some of the indicators the panel members noticed:

- U.S. 12th graders performed below average for 21 countries on a test of general knowledge in mathematics and science.
- In 2004, China graduated about 500,000 engineers and India graduated 200,000, as compared with 70,000 in America.
- In 2001, U.S. industry spent more on tort litigation than on research and development.

The following are a few of the many recommendations made by the panel:

- Create 10,000 four-year scholarships in math and science to capture the best minds in our society.
- Increase teacher training to stress innovation and creativity.
- Increase funds for research for a number of federal agencies, such as the National Science Foundation and NASA.

The National Academy of Sciences report was one of many efforts to alert the American public to the importance of educating students with SGT. Other efforts include:

- The Marland Report (Marland, 1972)
- *A Nation at Risk* (D. Gardner, 1983)
- National Excellence (Ross, 1993)
- Rising above the Gathering Storm (Committee on Prospering, 2007)
- Preparing the Next Generation of STEM Innovators (Bruer, 2010)

10-2 Definitions of Special Gifts and Talents (SGT)

The term *gifted* traditionally has been used to refer to people with intellectual gifts, and we use it here in the same way. Each culture defines *giftedness* in its own image, in terms of the abilities that culture values. Ancient Greeks honored the philosopher and the orator, and Romans valued the engineer and the soldier.

TABLE 10.1 Federal Definition of Students Who Are Gifted

Children and youth with outstanding talent perform, or show the potential for performing, at remarkably high levels of accomplishment when compared with others of their age, experience, or environment.

These children and youth exhibit high-performance capability in intellectual, creative, and/or artistic areas; possess an unusual leadership capacity; or excel in specific academic fields. They require services or activities not ordinarily provided by the schools.

Outstanding talents are present in children and youth from all cultural groups, across all economic strata, and in all areas of human endeavor.

SOURCE: Ross, P. (Ed.). (1993). *National excellence*. Washington, D.C.: U.S. Department of Education.

TeachSource Digital Download Access online

From a society's definition of giftedness, we learn something about the values and lifestyles of that culture. We also learn that the exceptional person often is defined by both individual ability and societal needs.

Although there have been a number of more recent attempts to craft a definition of giftedness, the definition in Table 10.1 still seems most acceptable.

In this definition, the phrase "show the potential for performing" means that we accept the idea that children can have special gifts without showing excellent performance. "Compared with others of their age, experience, or environment" means that we accept the important role of environment and context in developing students with gifts. The phrase "require services . . . not ordinarily provided" means that we expect that school systems will and should modify their services and programs to take into account the different levels of development of these students. "Outstanding talents are present in children . . . from all cultural groups, across all economic strata" means that we expect to find gifted abilities in all racial and ethnic groups and across all socioeconomic levels.

In the United States, early definitions of giftedness were tied to performance on the Stanford-Binet Intelligence Test, which Lewis Terman developed during and after World War I. Children who scored an intelligent quotient (IQ) score above an agreed-on point—such as 130 or 140—were called gifted. They represented from 1 to 3 percent of their age-group population (Terman & Oden, 1947).

Essentially, a high score on the Stanford-Binet or the Wechsler Intelligence Scale for Children (WISC) or on other intelligence tests meant that children were developing intellectually more rapidly than their age-mates. What was unique was not so much *what* they were doing as *when*, developmentally, they were doing it. A child playing chess is not a phenomenon, but a child playing chess seriously at age 5 is. Many

Bob Daemmrich/The Image Works

Chess is one game that can reveal special gifts and talents in young children.

children write poetry, but not at age 6, when most are just learning to read. Early rapid development is one of the clear indicators of high intellectual ability, and that is what intelligence tests measure.

Where we find that entire populations of countries are performing better on tests of ability than they had a generation before (Flynn, 1999), we must confront the notion that IQ scores are *not* fixed for an individual or a society but can be improved with education and experience. We are *not* limited in the number of highly intelligent students we can produce but have as a prospect a gradually increasing number of highly intelligent people—if we are wise enough to create the conditions for their development.

Some of the disputes about the definition of giftedness seem to be related to *when* in the developmental sequence we are talking about. When we are referring to preadolescent years, we are defining giftedness as *potential*; when we are referring to secondary years, we may add a requirement for *production* or *performance*.

Potential refers to a high level of cognitive ability. This remains an essential part of production, but added to that are other factors determining the outcome, such as motivation or personality. As discussed by Subotnik, Olszewski-Kubilius, and Worrell (2011) referring to the "talent development" viewpoint:

> General ability is necessary but not sufficient to explain optimal performance or creative productivity. It remains a component of talent development along with domain-specific abilities, psychosocial skills, motivation, and opportunity. (p. 14)

This combination of forces is referred to as **talent development**, with the end goal of adult eminence.

10-2a Eminence

Subotnik et al. (2011) suggest that eminence, meaning high rank or importance, should be the goal of gifted education. But does eminence refer only to those well known in society, such as movie stars or politicians?

Consider the following people:

- the first chair in the Cleveland Symphony
- a vice president of Bank of America
- a distinguished professor of literature at Duke University
- a senior engineer at NASA
- the U.S. ambassador to France

Most of us could not name even one from this group of people, but are they eminent? Would we be happy if our programs for students with SGT helped nurture these people, as they are all making important contributions to society?

10-2b One Gift or Many?

Should giftedness be regarded as one overriding general mental ability or as a series of special abilities? Howard Gardner is one of the latest of a group of psychologists to view giftedness as a series of special abilities (Ramos & Gardner, 2003). He has proposed a list of eight distinct and separate abilities called **multiple intelligences** that need specific educational attention: *linguistic, logical-mathematical, musical, spatial, bodily-kinesthetic, interpersonal, intrapersonal,* and *naturalist.*

Everyone knows persons who are particularly good at one or two of the abilities listed by Gardner but who are not superior in them all. Think of a student who is a math whiz but is not an expert in linguistic or interpersonal intelligence. Consequently, the educational issue becomes not only how to plan one *overall* program for students with SGT in many of these areas but also what should be done with students who have specialized talents in a single area such as mathematics, music, visual perception, or interpersonal relationships.

High ability is not the sole predictor of student productivity but only the base on which the student must build. *Extended practice, dedication,* and *high motivation to succeed* are the characteristics necessary to complete the portrait of a productive person. These are easily recognized components of the successful athlete or musician, and so this should be of no surprise to educators. The school and educators can play a significant role by exciting the student about learning, and providing resources and access to advanced knowledge that keep a student's high motivation alive.

© iStockphoto.com/skynesher
Small group work helps develop planning and explorative skills.

10-2c Children of Extraordinary Ability

It is generally accepted today that superior intellectual ability often predicts high academic performance and favorable personal adjustment. But doubts linger about the youngster of extraordinary ability—the 1 in 100,000 at the level of an Einstein. What happens to the rare students who are seven or eight years ahead of their age group in intellectual development?

One of the standard assumptions has been that once the threshold of an IQ of 120 or 130 is reached, intellectual or artistic production depends on other factors such as motivation and persistence. These characteristics are certainly important, but the notion that there is a ceiling on the importance of IQ level is incorrect.

Lubinski (2009) reported on over 2,000 students who represented the top 1 percent of ability drawn from the Study of Mathematically Precocious Youth project (SMPY). When these students were divided into quartiles, the top quartile was enormously more productive than the bottom, even within the top 1 percent. The top quartile received many more doctoral degrees, wrote more scientific articles, were named on more patents, had higher income, and had more literary publications than did the lowest quartile. As Lubinski commented, "Overall, there does *not* seem to be an ability threshold within the top 1%" (p. 353). So higher IQs can make a difference in performance. The great developmental distance between youngsters with SGT and their peers necessitates individual programs for them, not unlike the individualized education programs (IEPs) proposed for children with disabilities.

Extraordinarily precocious students represent one of our greatest and rarest natural resources. We must learn more about them to understand the origin of their giftedness and develop ways to help them adapt to an often difficult social environment.

BOX 10.1 EXCEPTIONAL LIVES • EXCEPTIONAL STORIES

Terry and Lenny

Thanks to Dr. Julian Stanley, who began the Study of Mathematically Precocious Youth (SMPY) in 1971, we have gathered a picture of children of outstanding ability over time. Two of the most outstanding are Terry and Lenny, whose mathematical abilities flourished early. The schools they attended and their parents were flexible enough to adapt to the special abilities of these boys.

Terry: Terry, who grew up in Australia, taught himself to read by watching *Sesame Street* at age 2. By age 3 he had learned to read, type, and solve mathematical puzzles designed for 8-year-olds. At age 5 he was placed in a split first- and second-grade class but took math with fifth graders. In three years he had mastered the elementary curriculum and was placed in eleventh-grade mathematics. He finished undergraduate work at age 15 and received a PhD in mathematics from Princeton University at age 21.

His parents and mentors took care that he had social interaction with his peers and was not distracted by the notoriety that accompanied his obviously unusual development. Terry's father commented on his friendly personality. When he was little he was liked by his classmates and teachers, and now he is equally liked by his colleagues, peers, and students. He is now a parent himself and a professor of mathematics at UCLA. When asked what advice he would give to other talented students, he said:

> Well, don't be afraid to explore and be prepared to learn new things continually. . . . I remember in high school thinking I understand what mathematics and physics were all about only to discover so many wonderful things about these subjects in college that I had no idea existed in high school. (p. 313)

Lenny: Lenny grew up in a university town in North Carolina. Lenny came to the attention of many people when, as a 10-year-old, he earned a perfect score on the SAT mathematics test. During his participation in SMPY, he was referred to as "the smartest kid in the United States," yet he was a friendly and gregarious boy interested in music and sports, interests he has carried into adulthood.

He excelled on various tests, obtaining a perfect score on the College Board Test of Standard English at age 11 and also on all three parts of the Graduate Record Examination. He led the United States team in the International Mathematical Olympiad and helped the team win two gold medals and one silver medal, the first time the United States was able to do so. He also won distinction in the National Spelling Bee and the Westinghouse Science Competition.

Unlike Terry, Lenny was not moved through the school program so rapidly, skipping only the third grade. His parents discouraged rapid acceleration in favor of good social and emotional development, although he took many university classes while in high school and eventually went to Harvard University at age 16. He now has his PhD from the Massachusetts Institute of Technology and is a professor at Duke University. Despite growing up on different continents, Terry and Lenny both had intelligent and well-educated parents who wished for their boys good achievement but also happy social and emotional development. They will likely make major contributions to mathematics and to our country's scientific advancement.

Not all stories of outstanding talent have such happy endings. One counterexample is provided by the early life of Norbert Wiener, another famous mathematics **prodigy**, or child who shows extraordinary development in his or her early years, who coined the word *cybernetics*. His unhappy childhood is detailed in his autobiography, *Ex-Prodigy: My Childhood and Youth* (Wiener, 1953).

What is clear is that such unusual talent has to be guided in an intelligent way with the education system remaining flexible and adaptive to these students' needs. If this occurs, there is no reason not to expect other happy stories such as those of Terry and Lenny.

SOURCE: Muratori, M. et al. (2006). Insights from SMPY's greatest child prodigies: Drs. Terrence (Terry) Tao and Lenhard (Lenny) Ng reflect on their talent development. *Gifted Child Quarterly 50*(4), 307–324.

10-3 Characteristics of Students with Special Gifts and Talents

10-3a The Information Processing Model

The information processing model for students with SGT differs considerably from that of the typical student. In this instance, the differences are assets rather than difficulties. In Chapter 8, on emotional and behavior disorders, we discussed *correlated constraints*—features that combined to cause a negative outcome. In the case of students with SGT, **correlated assets** exist, linking high IQ scores to favorable

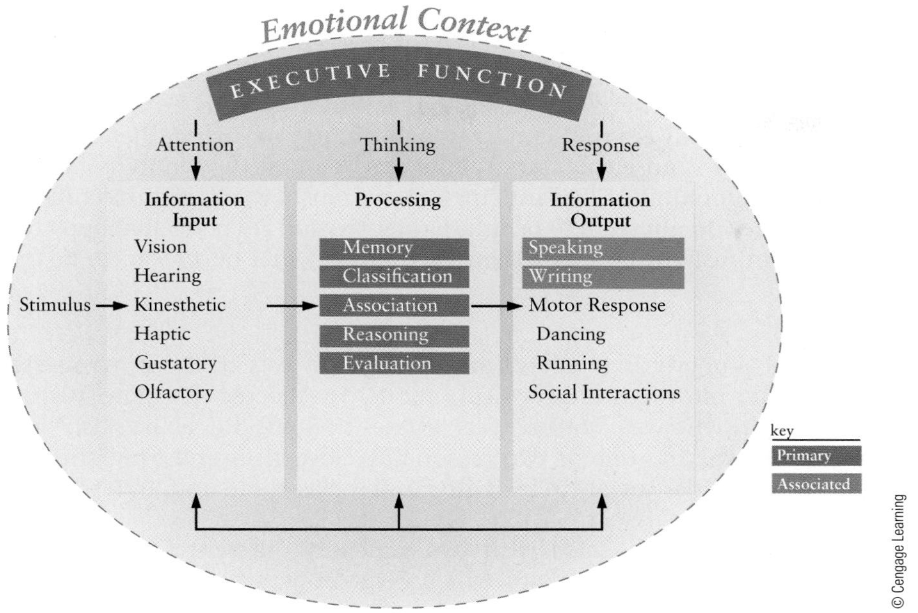

Figure 10.1 **Information Processing Model for Gifted Students**

TeachSource Digital Download **Access online**

physical, personality, and social factors. These students are generally more popular, have fewer physical problems, and have intact families.

As shown in Figure 10.1, the major assets of students with SGT are the central processing areas of *memory, association, classification, reasoning,* and *evaluation*. Because of these mental strengths, the output area of the model reveals an ability to speak well and write effectively. The ability to think more clearly should allow students with SGT to make better decisions in the *executive function* and to succeed in *emotional and social contexts,* although there are many exceptions to this generalization.

These correlated assets may pose a challenge to the teacher, as students with SGT may be bored with being taught facts and simple processes, making them markedly inefficient and overconfident from being told how smart they are. They bring home good grades, pleasing their parents, who are unaware of how their children are being shortchanged by the lack of challenge to their abilities.

10-3b Characteristics of Three Students with SGT

We would like you to meet three children: Cranshaw, Zelda, and Pablo. They are 10 years old and in the fifth grade. Cranshaw probably meets the criteria for intellectual, creative, and leadership giftedness; Zelda has intellectual gifts; and Pablo's gifts are hidden.

Cranshaw

Cranshaw is a big, athletic, happy-go-lucky youngster who impresses the casual observer as the "all-American boy." He seems to be a natural leader and to be enthusiastic over a wide range of interests. These interests have not yet solidified. One week he can be fascinated with astronomy, the next week with football formations, and the following week with the study of Africa.

His history in school has suggested that teachers have two very distinct reactions to Cranshaw. One is that he is a joy to have in the classroom. He is a cooperative and responsible boy who not only performs his own tasks well but is also a good influence in helping the other youngsters to perform effectively. On the other hand, Cranshaw's mere presence in the class also stimulates in teachers some hints of personal inferiority and frustration, as he always seems to be exceeding the bounds of the teachers' knowledge and abilities.

Cranshaw's family is a well-knit, reasonably happy one. His father is a businessman, his mother is an elementary school teacher, and the family is moderately active in the community. They anticipate that Cranshaw will go on to higher education, but they do not seem to be future-oriented and are perfectly happy to have him as the enthusiastic and well-adjusted youngster that he appears to be today.

Zelda

Zelda shares similarly high scores on intelligence tests to those manifested by Cranshaw. Her information processing model is reflected in Figure 10.1. Zelda is a chubby girl who wears rather thick glasses that give her a "bookish" appearance. Socially, she has one or two reasonably close girlfriends, but she is not a member of the wider social circle of girls in her classroom and, indeed, seems to reject it.

Teachers respond to Zelda with two generally different feelings. They are pleased with the enthusiasm with which Zelda attacks her schoolwork and the good grades that she gets. At the same time, they are vaguely annoyed or irritated with Zelda's undisguised feeling of superiority toward youngsters who are not as bright as she is.

Zelda's family has values that Zelda has accepted wholeheartedly but that are getting her into difficulty with her classmates. Her parents are college professors—her father in history and her mother in English literature. They seem to value achievement and intellectual performance almost to the exclusion of all other things.

Their social evenings are made up of intellectual discussions of politics, religion, or the current burning issue on the campus. These discussions are definitely adult-oriented, and Zelda is intelligent enough to be able to enter occasionally into such conversations. This type of behavior is rewarded much more by her parents than is the behavior that would seem more appropriate to her age level (Gallagher & Gallagher, 1994).

Cranshaw's social adjustment is as good as his academic achievement, but Zelda has social difficulties. She is not accepted by her age-mates and doesn't understand why. The pattern of development is different for each of these students because of differing environmental contexts.

Pablo

Pablo, a short, compact boy with enormous energy, is very different from Cranshaw and Zelda. As a matter of fact, in years past, he would not have been considered for SGT services at all. His gifts and talents would have likely gone unnoticed.

Pablo came to this country with his parents five years ago from Central America and speaks two languages, English and Spanish. His father works long hours on construction projects, and his mother stays at home with the four children. They were somewhat surprised when the school system told them Pablo was eligible for the program for students with special gifts and talents, but now they are very proud and want to help Pablo succeed in his new role.

Pablo is very athletic and physically active. He does best in school with tasks that require him to think, but his performance in English and related subjects, spelling and reading, lags somewhat behind his other abilities. The psychologist says that his IQ score of 120 represents a minimal estimate.

Pablo qualifies as having "hidden" gifts. His information processing model will show the same pattern as Cranshaw and Zelda (see Figure 10.1) but much less visible assets. The standard achievement measures would not show his abilities, but classroom observation and new teaching techniques, such as *problem-based learning*, allowed him to show his bright and inquiring mind and encouraged his teacher to refer him for further evaluation. If energy and effort mean anything, and they do, Pablo will be a success. He puts as much effort into his lessons as he does on the soccer field.

Pablo's teacher, however, will still have to be careful with his assignments, supporting his verbal skills while stressing his artistic contributions, which are considerable. It is not enough just to place Pablo in a group of students with SGT; the teacher must also be sensitive to his cultural background and linguistic differences and provide appropriate support if he is to thrive.

When we look at Cranshaw, Zelda, and Pablo, we are reminded that individuals within any category of exceptional children are first and foremost *individuals*. Each has his or her own pattern of strengths and areas of need. Indeed, within any category of exceptional children, the intraindividual differences of a single child can seem more important than the interindividual differences across the group. Nevertheless, we need to remember that what students with SGT all have in common is an advanced cognitive ability that will require teachers to provide a more challenging curriculum in these students' areas of strengths.

10-3c Neurology and Brain Development: What We Know about SGT

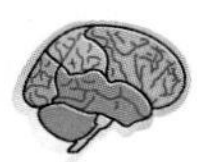

Most of the research on brain function has been devoted to what happens when the brain doesn't function well (Newman, 2008). But another significant question is: What happens when the brain is operating efficiently, as it does with children with SGT?

One of the original ideas from neurology was that the frontal lobes were linked to intellectual ability and executive function. Such functions as control processing, strategy formulation, and monitoring the contents of working memory fit into this category.

But more recent evidence from a variety of MRI studies now suggests that the neural basis of giftedness is distributed throughout the brain, and it is the "interconnectiveness" of the brain (those fibers that link one part to another) that determine high efficiency (Just & Varma, 2007). While there are areas within the brain that have specialized functions, it is the ability of these areas to work together in synergy that contributes to giftedness.

10-3d Genetic Factors and SGT

Are children born with SGT? Do outstanding abilities emerge no matter what opportunities or education a person has? What role does heredity play in giftedness? How important is the environmental context for the child with special gifts?

More than one hundred years ago, Francis Galton, in a study of outstanding Englishmen, concluded that extraordinary ability ran in families and was genetic in origin. (Galton overlooked the environmental advantage of being born into an upper-class family.) Ever since, there has been a strong belief in the powerful role that heredity plays in producing mental ability. Certainly, studies of twins and the close relationship of the abilities of adoptive children to the abilities of their biological parents demand that we recognize a hereditary element (Plomin, Defries, Craig & McGuffin, 2003).

One of the strongest arguments for hereditary influences on giftedness lies in the small—but still impressive—number of prodigies. These children perform as adults at a young age in music, dance, writing, and so on; their extraordinary talents cannot be explained by environmental conditions.

© Poznyakov/Shutterstock.com

Doing experiments is one way to exercise advanced thinking skills.

10-3e Family

Extraordinary talent may be shaped by heredity, but it is nurtured and developed by the environment. We have discussed the role that society plays in defining SGT and rewarding individuals with SGT. A more powerful influence, because it is closer, is the family. We stress that intellectual production takes more than talent; it also takes persistence, hard work, and desire. It is clear that the family plays a major role in the development of these traits (Webb, Gore, Amend, & DeVries, 2007).

10-3f Gender

The observation of gender differences in various aptitudes in students with gifts has been often noted, although such differences have sometimes been linked to differential encouragement and opportunity. Strand, Drury, and Smith (2006) analyzed a representative sample of 320,000 11- and 12-year-olds in the United Kingdom and found striking gender differences in favor of boys at the upper reaches of ability in quantitative reasoning. In general, males seemed more diverse, having both more high scores and more low scores than the girls.

The impact of gender on how students decide to manage their giftedness has been an area of interest to many scholars (Coleman & Cross, 2001; Kerr & Cohn, 2001; Reis, 2003; Roeper, 2003). Sociocultural standards regarding appropriate roles for boys and girls are very clear and may conflict with the emergence of giftedness in some instances. Let's look at how this might work for girls who have SGT.

For girls with SGT, the message to be "feminine," meaning to be passive, modest, dependent, nurturing, and unselfish, can conflict with their expectations of such factors as independence, risk taking, full development of their potential, assertiveness, and a certain degree of competitiveness. These conflicting messages can mean that some girls with SGT elect to camouflage their abilities in order to fit in better with society's expectations (Reis, 2003). Although societal messages have changed somewhat since the women's movement of the 1960s (Roeper, 2003), these dilemmas remain critical for many girls with SGT.

10-3g Social and Emotional Development

Despite their demonstrated ability to make friends and generally to adapt well, people who have SGT may shoulder some challenges that stem from their exceptionality.

A volume produced by members of the National Association for Gifted Children presented a summary of what was known about the social and emotional status of students with gifts (Neihart, Reis, Robinson, & Moon, 2002). There have been substantial differences of opinion with regard to the linkage of giftedness to such issues as depression, delinquency, perfectionism, suicide, and response to stress. Giftedness does not provide an inoculation against emotional problems. The question is whether it provides a buffer against them because of these students' cognitive abilities to solve problems and to examine their own feelings.

10-3h Perfectionism

Another characteristic that seems to be a part of the emotional and social lives of some students with SGT is **perfectionism**. Perfectionism is the combination of thoughts and behaviors associated with high standards or high expectations for one's own performance. From their earliest years, children with SGT tend to be successful in almost everything they try—because they are being underchallenged. If perfectionism becomes a neurosis, students can become "failure avoidant." Perfectionist students can have a depressive reaction if they receive a 95 on a paper instead of the usual 100. In such instances it is important for teachers and others to point out to the student that great accomplishments usually are accompanied by failure in some part of the process—and that 95 percent is not a failing grade!

Jack, who was used to doing well in everything, once struck out three times in a Little League game. He wept uncontrollably. "I'm a failure, a failure," he cried. He could not match his behavior to his expectations. Parents can sometimes help by recounting similar events in their own lives, letting the child know that everyone eventually faces these experiences.

10-3i Suicide

Cross (2013) pointed out that an increasing incidence of suicide among adolescents in general would seem to mean that the incidence would likely be increasing in the gifted population as well. There is some indication that youngsters who are extremely creative artistically are more vulnerable to mental illness than are their classmates with other academic gifts. Periodically the question arises about the relationship between emotional disorder and giftedness and between suicide and giftedness. It is clear that many well-known personalities, scientists, and artists, such as Vincent Van Gogh, have committed suicide, and periodically news stories appear about highly gifted students who have committed suicide. The question lingers.

Cross, Cassady, and Miller (2006) explored suicide ideation in 153 teenagers applying to a residential school for advanced mathematics and science and found no higher rates of suicide in this group than in the normal population. Since this was a select group of students of high achievement applying to such a school, however, it still leaves unanswered the question about underachievers with gifts and their emotional status. We will further discuss underachievers with SGT in a later section.

10-3j Do Special Gifts and Talents Persist into Adulthood?

One of the most often-asked questions about students with SGT is: What actually happens to them as adults? Do they continue to do well, or do they slump and become average or even underachievers? One way to answer that question is to use longitudinal studies that follow children with SGT into adulthood, which we now have.

Lewis Terman, a professor of psychology at Stanford University, turned his attention to children with SGT. In 1920, he began a study of 1,528 such children, which was to continue for more than sixty years!

Terman used teacher nominations and group intelligence tests to screen California students. He based the final selection of children on their performance on the Stanford-Binet Intelligence Scale. The characteristics of this group of high-IQ students were, on average, favorable in practically every developmental and socioemotional dimension. The group, with a few exceptions, did well not only in school and career but also in areas such as mental health, marriage, and character.

The final volume in the Terman series captures this population in their 60s and 70s (Holahan & Sears, 1995). The group continued to be superior in health, psychological well-being, and survival rates; when compared to the general population, the overall portrait was one of a privileged group of children who contributed substantially to their society as adults.

However, we have come to realize that Terman did not balance his sample of individuals with SGT. Through his identification process of young children using IQ tests as the tool for selecting students for his sample, he eliminated many potentially bright youngsters of low economic or immigrant status from the sample. For example, he failed to find two future Nobel Prize winners who were in school at the time of his study. We still do not have a record of what happens in adulthood to low-income or culturally diverse children who are gifted.

One of the recurring questions regarding longitudinal studies such as the one that Terman and his associates did is, Are the results due to the students or to the culture and times (the context) in which the study took place? A more recent study provides some information on this issue (Subotnik, Kassan, Summers, & Wasser, 1993). In the 1940s, a special elementary school was established at Hunter College in New York City. The school was highly selective in the students it enrolled. In educational attainment, the results were similar to those reported by the Terman group. Over 80 percent held master's degrees, and 68 percent of the men and 40 percent of the women held doctorates in medicine, law, or some other area. They were in good health, mentally and physically, and were earning incomes as impressive as their educational attainments would suggest.

One major difference between the Terman and the Hunter Elementary samples was in the careers of the women. The vast majority of the women in the Hunter Elementary sample were employed and were satisfied with their careers. Fewer than 10 percent were homemakers exclusively. The interviews made it clear that the women's movement (context again!) had a decided effect on their becoming more oriented to work outside the home.

Subotnik and the other authors of the study (1993) were somewhat disappointed by the lack of drive for success or for extraordinary achievement that they found in the Hunter Elementary group. Most members of the group seemed content to do their professional jobs and enjoy their social lives and the opportunities their vocational success provided. The well-rounded students had become well-rounded, complacent adults. One of them remarked,

> This is a terrible thing to say, but I think I'm where I want to be—terrible because I've always thought that there should have been more challenges. I'm very admired and respected where I work. . . . I don't want to be a senior vice president. . . . I want to have time to spend with my family, to garden, to play tennis, and see my friends. I'm very happy with my life. (p. 78)

The vast majority of these students became productive and useful citizens, and we might well ask whether we should expect more of them than that.

Another major study followed over 2,000 participants in the Study of Mathematically Precocious Youth over 20 years to see what happened to these students who fell in the top 1 percent of measured ability on the SAT at age 13 (Lubinski, Benbow, Webb, & Bleske-Rocheck, 2006). The results were comparable to the earlier study in terms of large numbers of these students attaining advanced degrees, even in their early thirties attaining more than five times the number of patents achieved in the general population and being prolific in writing scientific papers and literature.

10-3k Creativity

Creativity is a process that has fascinated educators and philosophers for centuries. How does one create something novel that was not there before? How did da Vinci, Picasso, the Brontë sisters, Einstein, DuBois, Curie, Fanon, Mozart, Suzuki, Shankar, and many thousands of others accomplish their outstanding works? Can we as educators discover and enhance these talents that seem to be at the apex of human endeavor?

One researcher defined creativity as the ability to generate ideas, products, or solutions that are considered novel and useful for a given problem, situation, or context (Beghetto, 2008). (Note the emphasis on usefulness; many people produce "novel" thoughts, but with little utility.)

The recognition is growing that creativity is not so much a personal characteristic as it is a process that blends both thinking and personality. Treffinger, Young, Selby, and Shepardson (2002) present four different dimensions of the creative process: generating ideas, digging deeper into ideas, courage to explore ideas, and listening to one's inner voice.

Generating ideas requires cognitive flexibility, whereas digging deeper into ideas requires more synthesis and reasoning power. Personality becomes more central to the courage to explore ideas, requiring risk taking and openness to experience. The final stage, listening to one's inner voice, deals with clearly envisioning what you wish to accomplish and determining to overcome obstacles—again, personality characteristics.

There seems to be substantial evidence from literature of many cultures that people are most creative when they are motivated primarily by the interest, enjoyment, satisfaction, and challenge of the work itself (i.e., "intrinsic motivation"). When we come to those forces that inhibit such motivation, we come to the current emphasis on **high-stakes testing**, whose results can substantially change the future of a student. By forcing students to learn a cluster of facts to prepare for these tests, we deprive them of the search for new ideas and intellectual adventures leading to creativity.

Hennessey & Amabile (2010), in an extensive review of creativity literature, commented:

> One possibility is that with America's newfound emphasis on "high stakes testing" and other manifestations of the accountability movement has come a general de-emphasis on creative behavior in favor of the more easily quantified and assessed mastery of reading, writing, and arithmetic. (p. 587)

A similar finding was made in schools in China—specifically, that societal values and school pedagogic approaches impaired the creativity of students of that nation (Niu & Sternberg, 2003). So what are the positive environments that can enhance creativity? Renzulli (2002) has been well known for his three intersecting rings of productivity: superior ability, creativity, and task commitment. He went further with Operation Houndstooth, which asks the question, "What causes some people to mobilize their interpersonal, political, ethical, and moral realms of being in such ways that they place human concerns and the common good above materialism, ego enhancement, and self-indulgence?" (Renzulli & Reed, 2008). The article proposes that the following combination leads to intellectual productivity: optimism (positive feelings from hard work), courage (moral conviction), romance with a topic (passion), sensitivity to human concerns (empathy), physical/mental energy (curiosity), and sense of destiny (power to change). There is little doubt that such a combination should stir productivity. What remains is how educators can develop instruction that can enhance this collection of assets.

10-4 Identification of Students with Gifts and Talents

Before we can provide children who have SGT with special services to match their special needs, we have to find these children. Identification is not always an easy task. In every generation, many such children pass through school unidentified, their talents uncultivated (Johnsen, 2004).

Identifying these students requires an understanding of the requirements of the program for which they are chosen. If we want to choose a group of students for an advanced mathematics class, we would use a different approach than we would if we were looking for students with high aptitude for a creative writing program. Specific program needs and requirements shape the identification process (Coleman, 2012).

Any program for identifying children who have SGT in a school system should include both subjective and objective methods of evaluation. Classroom behavior, for example, can point out children's ability to organize and use materials and can reveal their potential for processing information, sometimes better than can a test. Products such as superior essays and term projects can be kept in a student portfolio and serve as an indication of special gifts.

Project U-STARS~PLUS (Using Science Talents and Abilities to Recognize Students, Promoting Learning for Under-represented Students) capitalizes on the teachers' knowledge of their students to help identify young children with outstanding potential (Coleman & Shah-Coltrane, 2011). The U-STARS approach relies on three key elements:

1. Teachers who know what to look for (how to recognize potential)
2. Teachers who know how to structure their classrooms so that children will be engaged
3. Teachers who know how to provide a psychologically safe environment in which students can show their best abilities (Coleman & Shah-Coltrane, 2010)

The structured observation approach used by U-STARS includes an observational note-taking system that gives teachers specific behaviors to look for. In this case, children to be observed would include those who learn easily, show advanced skills, display curiosity and creativity, have strong interests, show advanced reasoning and problem solving, display spatial abilities, are motivated, show social perceptiveness, and have leadership strengths. The basic belief underlying this approach and similar ones is that we must go beyond the use of IQ scores and standardized measures of achievement if we hope to identify "hidden giftedness."

In the visual and performing arts, talent usually is determined by the consensus of expert judges, often in an audition setting. Experts in the arts are not enthusiastic about tests of artistic ability or musical aptitude. They trust their own judgment more, although their judgment is susceptible to bias. Sometimes it is possible to judge the quality of a series of products or a portfolio of drawings or compositions that students produce over a period of time (Clark & Zimmerman, 1998).

10-4a Students with SGT Who Are Underachievers

One of the many myths surrounding children with SGT is the "cannonball" theory. The idea, simply put, is that such children can no more be stopped from achieving their potential than a cannonball, once fired, can be diverted from its path. Like most simplistic ideas about human beings, this one, too, is wrong. There is a subgroup of children referred to as **underachievers with SGT**, students whose academic performance consistently falls far short of expectations despite high cognitive abilities (e.g., a consistent C average or dropping out).

A substantial proportion of students never achieve the level of performance that their scores on intelligence and aptitude tests predict for them. In the Terman longitudinal study, researchers identified a group of 150 men who had not achieved to the level of their apparent ability and compared them with 150 men who had done well (Terman & Oden, 1947). In their self-ratings and in ratings by their wives and parents, four major characteristics separated the underachieving men from the achieving men: *greater feelings of inferiority, less self-confidence, less perseverance,* and *less of a sense of life goals.* More striking was an examination of teacher ratings that had been made on the men 20 years earlier, while they were in school. Even at that time, their teachers believed that the underachievers lacked self-confidence, foresight, and the desire to excel.

It is difficult to change the maladaptive behavior patterns of students who for 8 to 10 years have been developing precisely the wrong approach to academic stress or challenge. This goal of change requires great *intensity* of effort and *duration* of effort on the part of both the student and those trying to help that student change.

Bob Daemmrich/Alamy

High ability has been found in every ethnic and cultural group and so we need to search for it.

10-4b Culturally Diverse Students with SGT

A consensus is growing about what is needed to support students from different cultural environments to succeed in school. For many students and their families, such support would include a range of health and social services and teachers with broad training in special education methods and understanding of the child's cultural milieu (Callahan, 2007; Ford, 2002).

Just about every research project cites as positive forces in such families a home environment characterized by warmth and stability of mother-child interactions, opportunities for learning (reading books and being read to), and a neighborhood with play resources and security for children and youths (Ford, 2002). A strong partnership between school and families can encourage these favorable conditions for educational success (Coleman & Shah-Coltrane, 2010).

Kitano (2007) specifically urges "universal access to high-quality early childhood programs for those who face extreme poverty in the first four years of life" (p. 235). Such programs would include a multicultural curriculum, early literacy development, and support for creative thinking, as well as health and social services.

VanTassel-Baska (2004) proposed curricula that place emphasis on openness to experience and that allow creativity and fluency in thinking, opportunity to express ideas through the arts rather than verbally, preference for hands-on applications, and preference for oral expression. The problem-based learning (PBL) approach contains many of these characteristics and has been shown to be effective with low-income populations with SGT (Gallagher & Gallagher, 2013).

10-4c Children With Disabilities Who Have SGT (Twice Exceptional)

A student's inability to see, hear, or walk does not mean that he or she does not have special gifts and talents (Hua & Coleman, 2002). It only means that the child stands a good chance of having special talents overlooked. Coleman (2002) studied the coping strategies used by students who had both SGT and learning disabilities. She found that the students who had SGT and learning disabilities had constructive coping strategies, whereas the students with average ability and learning disabilities often displayed learned helplessness, escape/avoidance, and distancing.

Another condition in which giftedness and another exceptionality may be mixed is autism. Although the majority of children identified as autistic have average or below-average ability, a subset of children, sometimes those diagnosed with the autism spectrum disorder Asperger's syndrome, can be highly intelligent

(Attwood, 1998; Neihart, 2000; see also Chapter 5 in this volume). This high intelligence takes on a special flavor with such children, who can be encyclopedic in their knowledge but very poor in their social relationships. There are similar examples of students with SGT who also have vision impairment (such as Helen Keller), hearing loss (Beethoven), and orthopedic disabilities (Stephen Hawking) that need to be identified for a special education program.

10-5 Educational Responses for Students with Special Gifts and Talents

The planning for other fields of exceptional children has been focused on overcoming the areas of deficit or building on the remaining areas of strength. But children with SGT have already mastered the regular curricula, so what should our approach be?

What are our educational objectives for students with SGT?

- Master important conceptual systems that are at the level of their abilities in various content fields.
- Develop skills and strategies that enable them to become more independent and creative.
- Develop pleasure in and excitement about learning that will carry them through the routine that is an inevitable part of the learning process.

As with other exceptional children, we will find it necessary to make considerable adjustments to both the *organizational* and *instructional* components of education. Organizational changes ensure that students are in the best environment for learning advanced knowledge. Instructional changes help cultivate the inquiry strategies necessary to create and discover.

10-5a Organizational Structures to Support Students with Special Gifts and Talents

RtI Approaches for Students with Special Gifts and Talents

RtI

Universal Tier I for Students with SGT

Our first goal for students with SGT in Tier I is differentiating the curriculum. In differentiating curriculum for students with SGT, a teacher is faced with the problem of time, not too little time, which is the problem with other exceptionalities, but too much time because these students will finish the required work early and will be looking around for something to do.

Tier I is characterized by a high-quality curriculum for all learners, a Universal Design for Learning (UDL) approach, periodic screening and assessment to monitor a student's progress, and family engagement with school and classroom activities (Coleman, 2012).

We must realize that no matter how many interesting variations to the regular program we may suggest, we are still faced with data that suggest that such variations are rarely done in the general classroom, unless specific planning is done in advance of the session. Renzulli and Reis (1997) examined the work in general classrooms and found that rarely are differentiated experiences proposed. Similar results have been found by Subotnik et al. (2011). The instructional team should plan ahead for such assignments because it is too much to expect the general classroom teacher to come up with these UDL-type activities on the spur of the moment. A Summary of *UDL Supports for Students with SGT* can be accessed online.

TeachSource Digital Download

BOX 10.2 Types of Student Acceleration

- ***Early school admission***. The intellectually and socially mature child is allowed to enter kindergarten at a younger-than-normal age.
- ***Skipping grades***. The child can accelerate by completely eliminating one semester or grade in school. The primary drawback here is the potential for temporary adjustment problems for the student.
- ***Telescoping grades***. The child covers the standard material but in less time. For example, a three-year middle school program is taught over two years to an advanced group.
- ***Advanced placement***. The student takes courses for college credit while still in high school, shortening the college program.
- ***Dual enrollment in high school and college***. The student is enrolled in college while finishing high school.
- ***Early college admission***. An extraordinarily advanced student may enter college as young as 13 years of age.

Targeted Tier II for Students with SGT

The additional stimulation through Tier I activities often does not seem enough to meet the needs of many students with SGT, so they are placed in a more responsive setting. One of these strategies is to move them forward, to accelerate them, to find a more favorable setting for their intellect.

Tier II represents a major difference from the regular program, as recognition of the substantial knowledge and aptitude differences between some students with SGT and students in the average program. Tier II activities will often remove the student with SGT from the regular classroom for a considerable amount of time, and perhaps for all of the time.

Hands on activities help many chidlren realize their special talents.

Student Acceleration We can adapt the educational program by abandoning the traditional practice of moving from grade to grade and by varying the length of the educational program. Since more and more knowledge and skills must be acquired at the highest levels of the professions, students with SGT who are seeking advanced degrees or professional training in fields such as medicine can find themselves still in school at age 30 and beyond.

The process of student **acceleration**—passing students through the educational system as quickly as possible—is a clear educational objective for some students. Gallagher and Gallagher (1994) described six ways of accelerating students (see Box 10.2).

From early admission to school to early admission to college, research studies invariably report that children who have been accelerated, as a group, have adjusted as well as or better than children of similar ability who have not been accelerated (Colangelo, Assouline, & Gross, 2004). The major objection to the strategy is the fear that acceleration can displace individual children with SGT from their social and emotional peers, affecting their subsequent social adjustment. Box 10.3 outlines other concerns.

BOX 10.3 Ideas on Why Schools Hold Back America's Bright Students

- Schools' lack of familiarity with the research on acceleration
- A belief that children must be kept with their age peers
- A belief that acceleration "hurries" children out of childhood
- A concern that acceleration could hurt students socially
- Political concerns about "equality" for all
- The concern that other students will be offended

SOURCE: Colangelo, N., Assouline, S., & Gross, M. (2004). A nation deceived: How schools hold back America's brightest students. *The Templeton National Report on Acceleration*. Iowa City, IA: Belin-Blank International Center for Gifted Education.

TeachSource Video Connection

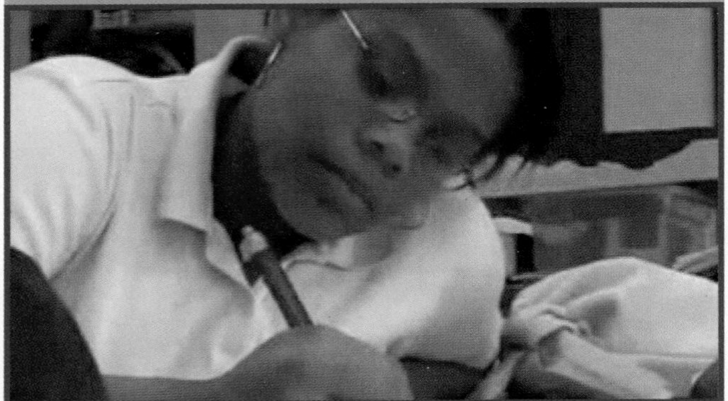

Watch the video "Middle School Science Instruction: Inquiry Learning." In this video you'll see how a middle school science teacher uses inquiry learning in teaching a lesson on the geology of the Grand Canyon. As you watch students construct knowledge through experimentation, you'll also hear the teacher's views on the benefits of inquiry learning, as well as the challenges it presents, such as extra planning and general "messiness." Why does the teacher feel that inquiry learning is beneficial? What might be some unique benefits or challenges in using this method with students with SGT? What are some ways that you could use inquiry learning in other subjects, such as English or mathematics?

Watch online

As more longitudinal studies are completed, it becomes possible to learn what actually happened to students who were accelerated, instead of what people hoped or feared would happen. Lubinski et al. (2001) conducted a ten-year follow-up of 320 students with profound gifts who scored high enough on the SAT to qualify as the top students among 10,000. Of these 320 students, 95 percent had taken advantage of various forms of acceleration (grade skipping, taking college courses while in high school, taking exams for college credit, entering college early, and so forth).

The perceptions of these students regarding their acceleration were highly favorable. They saw the procedures as an advantage in their academic progress and in maintaining their interest in learning. They found little or no effect of such acceleration on their social lives or peer relationships. By their early 20s, 23 had already attained PhDs, 9 had law degrees, and 7 were doctors of medicine. Another 150 or so of this sample continued to work toward advanced degrees. These results are even more positive than those of similar studies and clearly suggest that the fears of educators and parents that such acceleration would harm the students socially are largely unfounded (Colangelo et al., 2004).

Resource Rooms and Cluster Grouping Teachers can change the learning environment in many ways, but most of those ways are designed to bring children who have SGT together in small groups for instruction for a period of time and require collaborative teaching. The aim is threefold:

- To provide students with SGT with an opportunity to interact with one another and to learn with and be stimulated by their intellectual peers
- To reduce the range of abilities and performance within the classroom (past achievement, for example) to make it easier for the teacher to provide appropriate instruction matched to the student's needs
- To place students who have gifts with an instructor who has expertise in working with such students or in a relevant content field

Since changes in this learning environment affect the entire school system, they have received more attention at the school district level than have changes in skills and content, which remain primarily classroom issues.

Intensive Tier III for Students with SGT

Tier III takes the students with SGT into a totally new environment with special programming and staff.

Residential Schools Another type of educational setting for students with SGT is the **residential school** for science and math. Established in 10 states, these schools bring together highly talented students for their last two or three years of secondary school. Instead of floating through their last two years of high school, as many students with SGT do, students in these residential schools are given a rigorous introduction to higher-level thinking and study (Kolloff, 2003). The North Carolina School of Science and Math and the Illinois Math and Science Academy are two such schools.

Additional stimulation can be had in Governors Schools, a summer program of several weeks in many states that replaces the summer wasteland for intellectual interests with a program that may focus on self-understanding and special content not covered in secondary school.

Homeschooling One important educational phenomena is a steady interest in **homeschooling**, involving more than one million children who have been receiving their education at home (Kunzman, 2008). Although homeschooling originated with parents anxious to maintain a religious element in their children's education, it has also become a vehicle for many parents of students with SGT. Many of these parents have despaired of the public schools' ability to meet the needs of their exceptional children.

Such education has now become more feasible through the Internet. No longer is the school the gatekeeper or exclusive dispenser of knowledge. The access that the Internet provides opens wide the door to knowledge of all sorts.

There have been few serious efforts to evaluate the overall impact of homeschooling on students with SGT, but there have been favorable reports from parents seeking an educational alternative for a child with SGT. It has also caught the attention of educational administrators, who are aware of losing some of their better students to this alternative and who therefore seek ways to entice these children back into public school programs. A Summary of *RtI Approaches for Students with SGT* can be accessed online.

TeachSource Digital Download

10-5b Curriculum and Instruction for Students with Special Gifts and Talents

Once the organizational changes have been made, we face the problem of what content we will provide the students in these new settings. The emphasis here is on higher level thinking (see the IPM in Figure 10.1), processes that allow the students to problem-solve, find problems, be creative, and so on. But how do we differentiate the curriculum for students with SGT? Do we expect teachers to compose their own curricula? It is enough that they employ the special curriculum with grace and style, as a concert pianist would play music that they themselves had not composed. We should not expect individual teachers to design differentiated curricula, but they are capable of imaginative implementation of quality curricula that are available to them.

Advanced Placement and International Baccalaureate

Two approaches to systematic curriculum adaptations for students with SGT have been **Advanced Placement** (AP) courses and the International Baccalaureate (IB) program (Herzberg-Davis & Callahan, 2008). The AP program consists of more than thirty courses and exams offered by the College Board to provide the opportunity for high school students to take college-level courses while they are preparing to graduate. If the students score high enough on the exam for the course, they may earn credit with the college they choose to attend. Chances are that you took an AP course in high school, as over 1.2 million students took one in 2012 alone. An effort is now being made to ensure that as many students as possible have access to AP classes.

The **International Baccalaureate program** was designed to provide a rigorous pre-university course of study focusing on active learning, citizenship, internationalism, and respect for other cultures. IB begins as early as elementary school in some areas. A special Theory of Knowledge course is provided for all IB candidates, and each candidate must write an extended essay on an independent study topic, as well as report on a service activity he or she has performed. The informal reports from students and teachers have been favorable because the content is seen as challenging and relevant for students seeking higher education.

COMMON CORE STATE STANDARDS

Common Core State Standards (CCSS)

Some have suggested that the Common Core State Standards (CCSS) should provide the necessary challenging material for advanced students, but the creators of the CCSS themselves recognized that some students will finish early and will need additional tasks and assignments. One example of adapting the CCSS for advanced learners is provided in Table 10.2.

Table 10.2 shows examples of language arts expectations for typical learners and for advanced learners (VanTassel-Baska, 2013). Similar mathematics examples for advanced learners are available in a companion CCSS volume for mathematics (Johnson & Sheffield, 2013).

TABLE 10.2 Adapting CCSS for Advanced Learners: Example from ELA Standards for Speaking and Learning; Strand 1, Comprehension and Collaboration

Grade-Level Outcomes in Knowledge and Skills: Prepare for and participate effectively in a range of conversations and collaborations with diverse partners, building on others' ideas and expressing one's own clearly and persuasively.

Grade	Typical Learners	Advanced Learners
Grades 3-8 Engage effectively in a range of collaborative discussions (one-on-one, in groups, and teacher-led) with diverse partners on grade-level topics and texts, building on others' ideas and expressing their own clearly.	Students will participate in literature circles on grade-level topics.	Using Socratic seminars, advanced students will initiate and participate effectively in discussions on relevant real-world issues and reading key texts.
Grades 9-12 Initiate and participate effectively in a range of collaborative discussions (one-on-one, in groups, and teacher-led) with diverse partners on grades 9-10 (and 11-12) topics, texts, and issues, building on others' ideas and expressing their own clearly and persuasively.	Students will participate in face-to-face and virtual discussion groups on grade-level topics in language arts.	Advanced students will initiate virtual discussion groups on texts and topics of interest, posting and commenting regularly regarding text and ideas supported by textual evidence.

SOURCE: VanTassel-Baska, J. (Ed). (2013). Using the Common Core State Standards for English language arts with gifted and advanced learners. Waco, TX: Prufrock Press.

Perhaps the educator who has come closest to providing us with a useful approach to differentiating curriculum for students with SGT is Joyce VanTassel-Baska (2008). Her **integrated curriculum** model is composed of three interrelated dimensions that are responsive to the learner with special gifts and talents.

1. Emphasizing advanced content knowledge that frames disciplines of study
2. Providing higher order thinking and processing
3. Focusing learning experiences on major issues, themes, and ideas that define both real-world applications and theoretical modeling within and across areas of study (VanTassel-Baska, 2008).

It has been difficult and rare to design specific curricular content for students with SGT, because it takes a team of people, necessary funds and time, and is a multi-year project. Despite this, there have been some notable efforts: the Parallel Curriculum (Tomlinson et al.,2008); the Kaplan Grid (Kaplan, Purcell, Leppien, Tomlinson, & Burns, 2005); the Betts Autonomous Learner (Betts, 1985); and the Schoolwide Enrichment Model (Renzulli & Reis, 1997).

Curriculum Compacting

One strategy to help gifted students avoid the chronic boredom of having to "learn" things they already know is curriculum compacting. The basic principle of compacting is that if students already know something and have the basic skills to apply the knowledge, they should be allowed to move on to other areas of learning (Reis, 2008). The critical point of compacting is that students are allowed to show their knowledge when *they* are ready; they do not have to wait until the whole class is prepared for the assessment (Renzulli & Reis, 1997).

Once students have shown mastery of the basics, they can be released from further direct instruction, guided practice (class work), and independent practice (homework) on this set of knowledge and skills. Essentially, **curriculum compacting** allows students to "buy time" for other, more appropriate learning experiences. How can this time be used?

Problem-Based Learning

There are specific strategies to help students learn search techniques so that they themselves can gather information that will allow them to solve problems. The essence of **problem-based learning (PBL)** is as follows:

1. ***The students are presented with a problem in which the solution is not stated.*** For example, a student has suddenly become ill with a number of odd symptoms. The cause of this condition is not evident.
2. ***The students are made stakeholders in the problem.*** They are to play the role of medical detectives tracking down the diagnosis for the condition and must use a variety of search techniques, such as surfing the Internet, to arrive at an answer.
3. ***The instructor plays the role of metacognitive coach***, not information giver. The teacher may point out possible sources of information or ways of accessing various sources, perhaps even suggesting that students interview community medical personnel, but will not provide the answer.

Using a combination of small-group and individual work, the students try to arrive at the answer. (In the preceding problem, the students finally decided that the cause was the West Nile virus. They recommended controlling mosquitoes but not closing the school, as the disease is not contagious.)

Teachers receive special training for the role of coach in the PBL model. These PBL methods have been used to teach economics, social studies, language arts, science, and even medical school subjects. The observations from diverse PBL programs are remarkably similar: The students are energized by the nature of the

© iStockphoto/J-Elgaard

Problem based learning stirs the natural curiosity of children with SGT.

problems presented, play an active and enthusiastic role in seeking new knowledge to solve each problem, and report excitement and increased interest as a by-product of the PBL approach (Barrows, 1988; Doig & Werner, 2000; Gallagher & Stepien, 1996; Gallagher & Gallagher, 2013; Maxwell, Bellisimo, & Mergendoller, 2001).

One example of the use of all three levels of the RtI approach in education for gifted students is a problem-based learning unit on the Black Death (Gallagher & Gallagher, 2013). The process begins with the entire class of low-income sixth-grade students taking the roles of council members in a medieval Italian town who have heard that a terrible plague is coming.

The students' task is to determine how to protect their fellow citizens and what actions they need to take as a council. The students study in small groups, explore the Internet, and have discussions and sometimes debates about what should be done. From this Tier I whole-class exercise, a number of high-performing students were identified and placed in a special group that met three times a week (Tier II). They were given special lessons in self-assessment, discussed career goals, and were encouraged to believe in themselves and their special abilities (Gallagher, Cook, & Shoffner, 2003). Some of these students were then given individual tests and interviews to determine whether they qualified for the school program for students with SGT (Tier III).

RtI

Curriculum Example for Young Students with SGT

When many persons think of science, they think of large laboratories filled with sophisticated equipment and cannot imagine young children being involved. But science is really about careful observation, collecting data, and drawing inferences from that data; these activities are well within the range of children at an early age, especially children with SGT.

Take for example the material in Table 10.3 on weather, an activity that can easily be done with a young child and cooperating parent. Here the child is making observations, collecting data, and drawing inferences, activities well within her capabilities that teach the essence of science (Coleman & Shah-Coltrane, 2010).

Adapting to Cultural Differences

Once students with SGT from a variety of cultures are identified by any of a variety of methods, we must develop an educational plan to meet their special needs and circumstances. One objective is to encourage children's understanding of and respect for their own cultural backgrounds (Briggs, Reis, & Sullivan, 2008; Barbarin, 2002). Biographies and the works of noted writers or leaders from the particular cultural group are often the basis of special programs (Villegas & Lucas, 2002; Baldwin, 1987).

Ford (2007) is concerned about retaining African-American children in programs for students with SGT. Placing children in a special program does not guarantee that they will be happy to be there or will want to stay (Ford, Moore, & Milner, 2005). Ford (2002) and Ford and Grantham (2003) mention irrelevant curriculum; social, racial, and cultural backgrounds that are incompatible with those of the majority of the students; and even a lack of support from those parents who find themselves being torn between the culture of the school and the culture of the home as reasons for dropping out of a special program.

TABLE 10.3 Family Science: Weather Project

Day 1

1. Before you start, predict the weather for the week. Use today's weather to guide you. Record your predictions on your Observation Record.
2. On Day 1, pay close attention to the weather and the sky outside. After school, pick a weather symbol that best describes the weather you experienced this day. Circle the weather symbol for Day 1 on your Observation Record.
3. Notice the wind. How windy is it? Circle the set of words that best describes the wind for Day 1 on your Observation Record.
4. Notice the sky. Describe how the sky looked in the morning and now in the evening for Day 1 on your Observation Record.

Days 2–4

1. Repeat Steps 2–4 for the next 3 days.
2. Finish your Observation Record and discuss the Family Time Questions that follow.
3. Return your Observation Record and packet to school by the date due.

Family Time Questions

1. Did you have days when you could have used more than one symbol? Why do you think this happened?
2. How many days were windy? What kinds of weather did you have these days? How did the wind relate to the other weather?
3. Looking back at your morning sky drawings across the week, what was the same and what was different about the sky in the morning?
4. Looking back at your night sky drawings across the week, what was the same and what was different about the sky at night?

SOURCE: Coleman, M. R., & Shah-Coltrane, S. (2010). *U-STARS~PLUS Science & Literature Connections*. Arlington, VA: Council for Exceptional Children.

Table 10.4 provides brief descriptions of the diversity and range of interest encountered in developing special programming for talented students from low-income backgrounds. These programs range from kindergarten to secondary, from curriculum differentiation to out-of-school programs (Saturday and summer programs), to preparing for advanced placement programs. Despite the wide range of activities, each of these programs report good results from their efforts.

You will recall that we experienced a similar situation with autism spectrum disorders, where a wide range of program activities yield successful outcomes. We proposed at the time that as long as the program had two essential ingredients, *intensity* and *duration,* it seemed to get results. We seem to be seeing a similar situation here. It may be that the increased personal attention releases the human potential from students who, through a lack of opportunity, were not able to use the talents they have.

One of the major attempts to provide special intervention for minority students identified as gifted has been Project Excite (Olszewski-Kubilius, 2010). This was an attempt to provide a stimulating enrichment program to cohorts of 25 students, each identified by above-average achievement in math, science, and reading in third grade.

For the next six years, these children received a variety of special programming—from summer enrichment programs in math and science, to one-on-one tutoring, mentoring by college students, field trips, and family counseling—from the Center for Talent Development at Northwestern University.

TABLE 10.4 Programs That Support Low-Income, High-Ability Students

1. **Mentoring Mathematical Minds and Young Mathematicians (University of Connecticut)**

   Targets promising elementary students and encourages them to assume the role of mathematicians, conduct investigations, and create projects.

2. **The Middle Years Program (International Baccalaureate Program)**

   Helps students in grades 6–10 understand the connections between traditional subjects and the real world, to become reflective and critical thinkers. The program is designed to prepare the middle school student for advanced mathematics.

3. **Project Exile (Northwestern University)**

   Targets low-income students in Evanston, IL in grades 3–8 for participation in an out-of-school program. Includes summer programs and after-school classes, as well as individual counseling for students who have been identified as talented in mathematics. Program is a collaboration between the Evanston schools and Northwestern University.

4. **Project NEXUS: Linking Middle Schools with College Success (Maryland State Department of Education)**

   Conducted in nine high-poverty schools in Maryland, this program is aligned with later advanced placement programs. Special training in advanced placement strategies is given to teachers. The program includes visits to area colleges, career days, field trips, etc., to make up for experiences participating students are unlikely to have otherwise.

5. **Young Scholars Program (Fairfax Virginia Public School)**

   Designed to prepare promising K–2 students for advanced academic programs by fostering problem solving and reasoning at advanced levels. Students from diverse cultural backgrounds are identified by their teachers in K–2 and are then clustered with teachers who are trained in differentiated curriculum.

SOURCE: Olszewski-Kubilius, P., & Clarenbach, J. (2012). *Unlocking emergent talent: supporting high achievement of low-income, high-ability students.* Washington, D.C.: National Association for Gifted Children.

After six years with a cohort of 25 students each year, the tentative findings, through comparisons with other minority groups and interviews with students and families, were very promising. Table 10.5 shows some of the results of Project Excite, which focuses on achievement plus the important element of self-perception. That perception was shared with families and had other positive results.

If outside resources can be assembled to conduct such an out-of-school program, this approach could have promising potential for many other school systems.

Assistive Technology for Students with SGT

The rapid development of technology has opened many doors for gifted children and their teachers. From the computer there have emerged digital TV, smartphones, iPods, online courses, and virtual reality. Social media such as Facebook, YouTube, and wikis come as second nature to many students today. The student may spend as much as six hours a day with the communications media now available (Siegle & Mitchell, 2011).

If our goal is the stimulation of higher thought processes, this media provides us with many different opportunities. In particular, students with SGT who come from rural or small school districts with limited resources can now hook up with

TABLE 10.5 Tentative Results for Project Excite

Influence on Minority Students

- Viewed themselves as special, different, and gifted
- Had higher expectations for achievement
- Increased commitment to study
- Prioritized study over play
- Selected more rigorous coursework

Academic Influence

- Increased in content knowledge and skills
- Better preparation for next level of schooling

Affective Influence

- Increased confidence to succeed in challenging work and compete with nonminority peers

Adapted from Olszewski-Kubilius. (2010). Two perspectives on statistics in gifted education. In B. Thompson & R. Subotnik. *Methodologies for conducting research in giftedness*. Washington, D.C.: American Psychological Association.

simulations of history, medicine, science, and so on. They can learn decision making and problem solving through digital games like The Oregon Trail, where the student simulates a covered wagon trip across the country, meeting a variety of problems that they must solve. This can make it easier to individualize lessons for students with SGT.

There are online courses that could allow students with SGT to make up for deficiencies and shortcomings of their regular school offerings, particularly if their interests are in exotic fields or topics (Ng & Nicholas, 2007). There is evidence that students may perform better in online courses than face-to-face instruction (Means, Toyama, Murphy, Bakia, & Jones, 2009).

The downside to all of this activity is that teachers must become students also, so that they can encourage students with SGT to make maximum use of this cornucopia of media development. It is up to schools to provide opportunity for professional development so that the teacher can become knowledgeable about and comfortable with these innovations. Teachers must come to terms with the realization that they are no longer the exclusive gatekeeper of knowledge.

Effective Education Programs

An important question to raise in the education of gifted students—and in all education—is: Are the practices we are using beneficial, or do they just represent established practice?

Although a number of practices, such as problem solving, problem finding, and use of computers, can be used effectively with all students, their use can be especially relevant in the accelerated, high-level curriculum for students with SGT (Robinson, Shore, & Enersen, 2007).

A wake-up call to American educators came with the publication of the results of the Third International Mathematics and Science Study (TIMSS, 1998). This study, which involved about 15,000 schools around the world in tests of their students' mastery of mathematics and science at fourth-, eighth-, and twelfth-grade levels, revealed disturbing results for American students.

At fourth grade, American students appeared to be performing above average among the fourteen countries that participated in the TIMSS study. That result changed, however, at the middle school level, with American students falling

MORAL DILEMMA

What to Do with Postgraduate SGT?

Earlier in this chapter, we noted the economic threats posed by India and China and others, as well as the enormous number of engineers, scientists, and other highly educated persons that their education systems are turning out compared with the United States. We wonder why more of our bright students are getting off the education train before reaching the final station. The answer is right in front of us: time and money.

Whether they wish to excel in agriculture, economics, biology, or education, these students must delay the start of careers until age 25 or older and pay more money than they can afford as students. Who, if anyone, is responsible for doing something about this problem (if we agree that it is, indeed, a problem)? Is it up to individuals or their parents, or is it in society's best interest to provide resources to encourage these students with SGT to pursue the highest education goals possible? Should the rest of us be taxed so that a minority of students with SGT succeed and strengthen our society? The largest social experiment of this type was the GI Bill, which financed advanced education for soldiers returning from World War II. This policy was created to compensate soldiers for the sacrifices they made during the war, but it resulted in a major stimulus to society. Should we attempt something like this again? If so, what would be your justification?

below average in both subjects. The twelfth-grade results were even more devastating, with the American students at or near the bottom among the more than 20 countries with which they were compared.

A further bit of information came from the Program for International Studies (PISA), which measured the academic performance of 15-year-olds in mathematics (Schleicher, 2009). When PISA compared the percentage of students who performed at the two highest levels of math (those levels needed to solve complex problems), the United States had only 10 percent of its students performing at this level. We were, thus, ranked 25th in the world on this index.

10-6 Family and Lifespan Issues

10-6a Prolonged Schooling and Financial Considerations

The economic and vocational prospects for most individuals with SGT are bright. The vocational opportunities awaiting them are diverse, including the fields of medicine, law, business, politics, and science. Only in the arts, where a limited number of opportunities exist to earn a comfortable income, do people with SGT encounter major social and economic barriers to their ambitions.

The psychological problems that result from remaining dependent on others for financial support until the age of 30 or beyond remain unexplored. We need to consider these issues before we burden students with SGT with more schooling requirements intended to meet the demands of this rapidly changing world.

It is likely that most students with SGT will seek advanced education and preparation for professional careers. Two obstacles appear: the expense of advanced education, and the time that such an education takes. Pablo's parents, who wish for him to go to medical school, face expenses of up to a quarter of a million dollars over a five-year period when considering the combination of school, internships, and residency. Can Mr. and Mrs. Gomez, who have a modest family income, afford to encourage Pablo on this path? Even with scholarships and grants, Pablo is likely to leave school in serious debt.

In addition, the Gomez family has two other bright children in the public education system. Can they afford to encourage advanced education for them? This is not merely an issue for the Gomez family, but society at large. We continue to need highly trained scientists, economists, lawyers, engineers, and professors to operate a modern society. We don't want training for these professionals to be left solely to the wealthy who can afford it.

The time involved is also a factor. If Pablo follows the typical school trajectory, he will be 22 when he graduates from college, 26 when he finishes medical school, and nearly 30 when he is a licensed doctor. He will be deeply in debt and just beginning his career when others have already had years of experience. Zelda, discussed earlier, wants to be a professor—she will also be 30 when she finishes her Ph.D., with similar expenses to Pablo's. How can we as a society help Pablo and Zelda? Perhaps they can use acceleration, as noted in this chapter, to finish college and graduate school sooner. But what about the expense? These are real questions we have not faced as a society.

Summary

- We care about children with special gifts and talents (SGT) because we know they will become the leaders of tomorrow in science, arts, and business.
- Children who have special gifts and talents may show outstanding abilities in a variety of areas, including intellect, academic aptitude, creative thinking, leadership, and the visual and performing arts.
- Intellectual giftedness appears to be created by a strong combination of heredity and environment, with a close and continuing interaction between these two forces.
- Creativity depends on the individual's capacity for divergent thinking, a willingness to be different, strong motivation, and a favorable context.
- Longitudinal studies indicate that most children who are identified as having SGT are healthy and well adjusted and achieve well into adulthood. There are some exceptions, called *underachievers*.
- Some students with SGT may be underachievers due to personal characteristics (such as feelings of inferiority, low self-confidence, expectations of failure), whereas others may underachieve because of their resistance to traditional educational programs and practices.
- Ability grouping, combined with a differentiated program, has been demonstrated to be an effective strategy that results in improved performance by students who have SGT.
- Cognitive strategies—problem finding, problem solving, and creativity—are the focus of many special programs for students with SGT.
- Adaptations can be made in the Common Core State Standards for students with SGT.
- Acceleration, the more rapid movement of students with SGT through their long educational span, has shown positive results.
- Society's traditional gender roles may provide special obstacles for girls with SGT, limiting their willingness to explore the full range of their talents.
- Many students possess SGT that is "hidden" by differing cultural perspectives, linguistic backgrounds, and life experiences. A variety of tests, observations, and performance indicators are necessary to discover these students.
- Children with physical and sensory disabilities may have intellectual gifts (twice exceptional), but often their abilities are undiscovered because less has been expected of them.

Future Challenges

1. **Are there programs for young children who are gifted?**
   The early years are increasingly seen as fundamental to a developing intellect. Prekindergarten programs are blossoming across the country and will need to provide for their students with SGT who already can read and do basic arithmetic. This is an early challenge for educators to develop a differentiated curriculum for the preschool year.

2. **How can we ensure that gifted and talented students from culturally and linguistically diverse and/or economically disadvantaged families are recognized and served appropriately?**
   We continue to face the challenge of underrepresentation of some groups of children in our programs for students with SGT. Given the rapidly changing demographics across the country, this disproportionate representation will likely increase unless we take proactive steps to address it. We need to look to models that help teachers recognize and nurture potential, using structured observations of students engaged in meaningful and dynamic lessons.

3. **How can we help the public see the national need to educate students with SGT?**
   Professionals in this field of gifted education have had little impact when trying to communicate to the public about the key significance of these students to the nation's future well-being. How to communicate this idea?

4. **How can we provide programming that goes beyond CCSS for these students?**
   There is little doubt that these students are currently not being challenged to perform their best. We need innovative curriculum in various content fields to lay the groundwork for advanced performance. How can we convince higher education and financial sources such as foundations and state and federal governments to participate in such endeavors?

TeachSource Digital Download Access online

Key Terms

acceleration p. 333
advanced placement p. 335
correlated assets p. 322
creativity p. 328
curriculum compacting p. 337
high-stakes testing p. 329
homeschooling p. 335
integrated curriculum p. 337
International Baccalaureate program p. 336
multiple intelligences p. 320
perfectionism p. 327
problem-based learning (PBL) p. 337
prodigy p. 322
residential schools p. 335
talent development p. 320
underachievers with SGT p. 330

Resources

References of Special Interest

Colangelo, N., Assouline, S., & Gross, M. (Eds.). (2004). *A nation deceived: How schools hold back America's brightest students. The Templeton national report on acceleration.* Iowa City, IA: Belin-Blank International Center for Gifted Education. This report is a comprehensive compilation of the effects of educational acceleration on gifted students. Eleven specialists have written chapters reviewing research and practice.

Coleman, M.R., & Johnsen, S. (2013). *Implementing RtI with gifted students*. Waco, TX: Prufrock Press. This series of contributions from well-known professionals in the field discusses how the RtI service model fits into education for children with special gifts and talents. In particular, it describes how the tiered model of services can be utilized when providing special experiences for these students. Special attention is given to children from culturally diverse circumstances and twice-exceptional children (those with special gifts and talents and a disability).

Cross, T. (2013). *Suicide among gifted children and adolescents: Understanding the suicidal mind*. Waco, TX: Prufrock Press. The author presents a comprehensive view of one of the most frustrating issues facing educators, but one that is rarely covered in print. This book has information on the prime age for suicide attempts and the dynamics involved for gifted students. It also contains a number of useful and evidence-based suggestions for educators who are concerned with this problem.

Dixon, F., & Moon, S. (Eds.) (2006). *The handbook of secondary gifted education.* Waco, TX: Prufrock Press. A much-needed addition to the field of gifted education, this book is a series of 25 chapters presented on a largely neglected part of gifted education—secondary school. It covers such topics as secondary English for high-ability students; guiding gifted students toward science expertise; gender, adolescence, and giftedness; and development of visual arts talents in adolescence.

Johnson, S., & Sheffield, L. (Eds.) (2013). *Using the Common Core Standards for mathematics with gifted and advanced learners*. Waco, TX: Prufrock Press. A text that relates the Common Core State Standards to the special needs of gifted and talented students. This is important because the CCSS does not address the special needs of advanced learners directly, and many teachers are looking for guidance to make sure their advanced students are challenged by applications of these standards.

Karnes, F., & Bean, S. (2005). *Methods and materials for teaching the gifted* (2nd ed.). Waco, TX: Prufrock Press. This volume is devoted to updated strategies and resources for differentiating the instruction of learners who have SGT. The 22 chapters are organized into four sections: characteristics and needs of learners with gifts, instructional planning and evaluation, strategies for best practices, and supporting and enhancing gifted programs. The emphasis is on teaching strategies rather than the changes in content fields themselves.

Neville, C., Piechowski, M., & Tolan, S. (2013). *Off the charts: Asynchrony and the gifted child.* Unionville, NY Royal Fireworks Press. A collection of 19 chapters address the asynchrony of development in gifted children, with cognitive ability far in advance of social development. These differences create many family and educational problems and the authors have a variety of prescriptions for how to deal with them.

Plucker, J., & Callahan, C. (Eds.) (2008). *Critical issues and practices in gifted education: What the research says.* Waco, TX: Prufrock Press. This is a comprehensive research review of fifty subjects in gifted education that covers topics such as underachievers, gifted girls, suicide, and differentiated instruction. The chapters were prepared by some of the most noted authorities in this special field and form a baseline for discussions on these various topics.

Robinson, A., Shore, B., & Enerson, D. (2007). *Best practices in gifted education.* Waco, TX: Prufrock Press. This is an effort to bring together the evidence to support the various educational and personal attempts to improve the development of children who have SGT. Twenty-nine educational changes have been identified by the authors as significant; these are subdivided into suggestions for the home (developing specific talents), the classroom (inquiry-based learning and teaching), and school (acceleration). The reason for the limited set of practices is no doubt the lack of available funds for the research that would be necessary to meet the evidence-based criteria.

Subotnik, R., Olszewski-Kubilius, P., & Worrell, F. (2011). Rethinking giftedness and gifted education: A proposed direction forward based on psychological science. *Psychological Science in the Public Interest, 12*(1), 3–24. A good summary bringing the field of gifted education under review. It has a special interest in the "talent development" approach with different trajectories for different talents (verbal vs. music vs. math). It includes sections on barriers to developing giftedness and expected outcomes of gifted education.

Journals

Educational Leadership
www.ascd.org

Gifted Child Quarterly
www.nagc.org

Journal for the Education of the Gifted
www.prufrock.com
Journal for Secondary Gifted Education (now *Journal of Advanced Academics*)
http://www.jaa.uconn.edu/
Parenting for High Potential
www.nagc.org
Roeper Review
http://www.roeper.org/RoeperInstitute/index.aspx

Professional Organizations

National Association for Gifted Children **www.nagc.org**
The Association for the Gifted (TAG) **http://www.cectag.org/**

PART 3 Low-Incidence Exceptionalities

CHAPTER 11

Children Who Are Deaf or Hard of Hearing

Standards Addressed in This Chapter

All of the CEC Standards are addressed within this chapter. Please see the inside book covers for the complete list of the standards.

CEC

FOCUS QUESTIONS

11-1 How did the field of deaf education evolve, and what is the history of the debate between oral and manual communication?

11-2 What are some characteristics of children with hearing impairments, how are the terms *deaf* and *hard of hearing* defined, and why must we consider the degree, type, and age of onset of the hearing loss?

11-3 What are some causes of hearing loss, how are they detected, and why is early intervention so critical?

11-4 How do hearing losses affect a child's cognitive, academic, social, and language development, and what can be done to maximize a child's communication potential?

11-5 What is the Deaf culture, and why are bilingual and bicultural approaches to understanding the needs of individuals who are deaf and hard of hearing important?

11-6 What kinds of educational responses are needed for children with hearing loss?

11-7 Why are family involvement and transition planning so important for the child's communication?

The three chapters in Part 3 describe the educational needs of exceptional children who constitute less than 0.5 percent of the students in our schools. Special planning and individualized programming are important to support children who are deaf or hard of hearing, children with visual impairments, and children with physical or multiple and severe disabilities. In Chapters 11 through 13, we highlight how these exceptionalities affect students and discuss the supports and services needed to help students with these exceptionalities meet with school success.

Ellen B. Senisi/ The Image Works

Connecting with the world around us through our senses is important. We learn through what we see, touch, smell, taste, and hear, and when one of our senses is limited, our access to information can be reduced. According to the information processing model (IPM), *taking information in* is the first component of learning, and we take information in through our senses. Think of all the information you take in with your ears and all that you would miss if you could not hear. Listen for a moment to all of the sounds in your environment and think about all that you learn from them. Hearing individuals are surrounded by a sea of sounds and often take for granted the information gathered through listening to these sounds. For individuals who are deaf or hard of hearing, the world of sound is limited, and information that most people acquire through sound must be gained in other ways.

Building and maintaining strong connections with the world can be challenging when sensory input is reduced, and living without sensory input can feel isolating. Communication is critical to our sense of belonging; being able to exchange thoughts, feelings, and desires is key to establishing a bond with others. Belonging to a social group where you are accepted and understood is critical, and for many individuals who are deaf or hard of hearing, this is found within the Deaf community (the capitalized term *Deaf* is discussed later in the chapter). In this chapter we continue to explore the role of communication and language in learning and social relationships. We discuss the history of education for individuals who are deaf or hard of hearing, review definitions of what it means to have a hearing loss, and consider the supports and services that individuals and families need to help them thrive.

Marlee Matlin, a famous actress who is deaf, has led the way in advocating for individuals who are deaf and hard of hearing.

11-1 History of Education for Individuals Who Are Deaf or Hard of Hearing

Over the past three decades, we have seen a growing acceptance within the hearing society of individuals who are deaf or hard of hearing. This growing acceptance has come about in part because several individuals who are deaf or hard of hearing have come into prominence in their fields. Phyllis Frelich, an actor who is deaf, won a Tony award for her performance in the Broadway play *Children of a Lesser God*. Marlee Matlin, also deaf, received an Oscar for her performance in the motion picture based on the same play, and she starred in the television dramatic series *Reasonable Doubts* as a deaf lawyer. Miss America of 1995, Heather Whitestone McCallum, is deaf. Following in the athletic footsteps of Luther Taylor, who played baseball from 1900 to 1908, Kenny Walker played professional football in the 1990s and now coaches for the Iowa School for the Deaf. During the 2000 Olympics, Terrence Parkin, a swimmer who is deaf, won a silver medal. Today there are doctors, lawyers, directors of government agencies, and professionals in every walk of life who are deaf. The president of Gallaudet University, Dr. T. Alan Hurwitz, is deaf. There are many students who are deaf or hard of hearing in regular schools and more and more adults who are deaf or hard of hearing in the workplace. But there has not always been general acceptance by the hearing society of individuals who are deaf or hard of hearing.

The acceptance of individuals who are deaf or hard of hearing has greatly been assisted by government mandates, regulations, and continued advocacy for the rights of all people. Commissions established by Congress in 1986 and 1988 led to the establishment of the National Information Center on Deafness and the Helen

BOX 11.1 Synopsis of the Colorado Deaf Child's Bill of Rights (1996)

- Recognizes the unique needs of children with low-incidence disabilities. Identifies the specific educational needs of children who are deaf or hard of hearing.
- Requires the committee that prepares an individual educational program for a child who is deaf or hard of hearing to consider the child's specific communication needs, including the child's mode of communication; the availability of peers, adult models, and staff with whom the child can communicate; and the availability of appropriate educational services.
- Specifies reasons for which a child may not be denied education in a particular communication mode or language.
- Allows a child to receive education in multiple communication modes or languages.
- Requires that a child receive education in the communication mode or language that is deemed beneficial for the child.
- Clarifies that the committee does not have to ensure the availability of a specific number of peers, that the provisions of the act do not abrogate a parent's statutory rights to educational choice, and that no school district is required to expend additional resources or hire additional personnel to implement these requirements.

Keller National Center for Technical Assistance. Rules and regulations in 1990 that required statewide telephone relay systems helped ensure phone access for individuals with hearing impairments, and stipulations in 1993 that all television sets with screens 13 inches or larger sold in the United States must be equipped to receive captioned broadcasts have expanded media access. The Individuals with Disabilities Education Act (IDEA; Public Law 101-476), the Americans with Disabilities Act (PL 101-336), the Rehabilitation Act (PL 102-569), and other laws and regulations have increased public awareness of the talents and educational needs of persons who are deaf and hard of hearing. Some states, such as Colorado, have passed a Deaf Child's Bill of Rights to help ensure that children get the education they need. The key points of this important law are included in Box 11.1. Through legislation, court actions, and growing societal awareness, the world is becoming more accessible to individuals who are deaf or hard of hearing.

National Deaf Education Center **http://clerccenter.gallaudet.edu**

In spite of these gains, there are still challenges. Although many people with hearing impairments use a manual language called **American Sign Language (ASL)** that resembles spoken English, our speech-language–oriented society has not yet accepted ASL as a legitimate language. A lack of understanding can still cause barriers in the acceptance of individuals with differences. Since we are a speech-dominated society, some educators strongly advocate the use of oral-speech language for individuals who are deaf or hard of hearing. Others, however, advocate the use of sign language or some combination of these for a total communication approach.

The dispute over how to teach communication skills to a child with a hearing loss is not new; it began in Europe, with Samuel Heinicke in Germany stressing oralism (speech) and Abbé de l'Épée in France stressing manualism (gestures). An early conference held in Milan in 1880 stressed oralism and claimed that sign language impeded language development (Paul & Quigley, 1994). The debate was intense, with firm believers on both sides.

In the United States, the sign language approach was spearheaded by Thomas Hopkins Gallaudet, who, with Laurent Clerc, founded the first school for the deaf in Hartford, Connecticut, in 1817. Gallaudet College was founded in Washington, D.C., in 1884, and its patron, Abraham Lincoln, signed the school's charter. During the next one hundred years, from 1817 to 1917, schools for the deaf were founded in most of the states. The oral approach to instruction was advocated by Alexander Graham Bell, inventor of the telephone and audiometer, and the founder of the School of Vocal Physiology in 1872. Interestingly, both Gallaudet and Bell had mothers with severe hearing losses, and each man was firmly convinced of the correctness of his approach.

While best known as the inventor of the telephone, Alexander Graham Bell was also an advocate of the oral approach.

BOX 11.2 Sounds for Sammy

Sammy was born deaf. Because of infant hearing screening, this was detected shortly after his birth. Because Sammy has some residual hearing he was fitted with hearing aids by 3 months and he began to respond to the sounds around him. Sammy will need intense language interventions, focusing on interaction with his environment and the development of words and concepts. The family is working with an interdisciplinary team composed of an audiologist, a speech language therapist, and an early interventionist who is a specialist for children with hearing losses. The team has decided that a total communication approach using both oral and manual communication will be the best approach for Sammy. They are also aware that if his residual hearing does not seem to be sufficient for language development, a cochlear implant may be an option. The team has decided to reevaluate these decisions when Sammy is 9 months. The journey for Sammy and his parents has just begun and it will be a lifelong process of finding the right combination of supports and services to help Sammy develop to his fullest.

Not until the 1970s did Bob Holcomb (Gannon, 1981), a college graduate with a severe hearing loss, advocate the use of both systems and coin the term **total communication method** to describe this approach. In total communication, some type of manual communication is used simultaneously with speech. Because our hearing culture seems to prefer that people learn to speak, educators of students who have hearing losses may stress oral language within the total communication approach (Lynas, 2000). The most important thing, however, is to teach the child a communication system that the child can master, regardless of whether it is manual, oral, or a combination of both. The combination of manual and oral systems in a total communication approach is now being more widely recommended for those with hearing losses, regardless of whether the loss is moderate or severe (Moores, 2000). Today, total communications approaches can start at a very early age, as we see in Box 11.2, Sounds for Sammy.

As use of the total communication method increases, the recognition of American Sign Language as a legitimate language will become very important. Through this recognition, individuals whose primary language is ASL would receive protection and support services covered under the Bilingual Education Act as English-as-a-second-language users (Johnson & McIntosh, 2009; Simms & Thumann, 2007).

Recent technological and medical advances with hearing aids and cochlear implants have greatly increased the ability to capitalize on an individual's residual hearing and, through this, to expand his or her ability to communicate. We will learn more about these technological and medical advances later in the chapter. The impact of a hearing loss can vary widely depending on the degree of loss, the type of loss, and the age of onset at which the loss occurs.

11-2 Characteristics of Children and Definitions of Deaf/Hard of Hearing

There are many factors that influence the impact of a hearing loss. The individual patterns of children with hearing loss can vary widely, as we can see in the cases of three children, Kiesha, Carlos, and Raymond, who have hearing losses that will affect their learning and possibly also their social skills.

11-2a Meet Three Children Who Are Deaf or Hard of Hearing

Kiesha is hard of hearing. Carlos has a postlingual hearing loss, and his situation is complicated by the fact that his first language is Spanish. Raymond has prelingual deafness and moderate intellectual delays. The intraindividual differences among these children show the heterogeneous nature of children who have hearing losses.

Kiesha

Kiesha, who is 10 years old, has a moderate hearing loss of 50 decibels. (The **decibel (dB)**, a unit used to measure the intensity of a sound, will be explained more in the next section.) Kiesha's level of hearing loss means that without her hearing aids she will miss most normal conversations. Kiesha is of average height, slightly below average weight. Her motor coordination, cognitive abilities, and social maturity are on target for her age. Kiesha's language development, as might be expected, is slightly delayed. She has some difficulty with articulation, so she receives speech therapy. The language delays have affected Kiesha's reading and spelling skills, but her achievement in math is at her grade level (fifth).

Kiesha was first fitted with hearing aids when she was in preschool; as she has grown, she has received new hearing aids each year. Kiesha goes to the audiologist every year for a full evaluation, and the special education teacher and the speech-language pathologist work with her to make sure that her hearing aids are functioning well in the school environment. As a fifth grader, Kiesha receives support from the speech-language pathologist once a week, and she works with the special education teacher periodically when she needs some extra help with school tasks.

Even though Kiesha's development and educational achievement are close to those of her peers, she does need some special support from the classroom teacher. Her hearing aids and slight speech differences sometimes make her feel different from her friends, and this may become more of a problem as she moves into middle school. Kiesha's hearing also fluctuates somewhat when the weather changes or when she has a cold. Teachers who are not aware of this fluctuation may not realize that in some circumstances Kiesha may miss key information if she is not encouraged and supported to participate fully in the learning activity. Kiesha's information processing model, showing the areas that are impacted by her hearing loss, is shown in ▶ Figure 11.1.

Carlos

Carlos, who is now 11 years old, was born with normal hearing but suffered a severe hearing loss in both ears at age 4 due to an infection and high fever. His family moved from Mexico to the United States when he was 5, and his first hearing aids

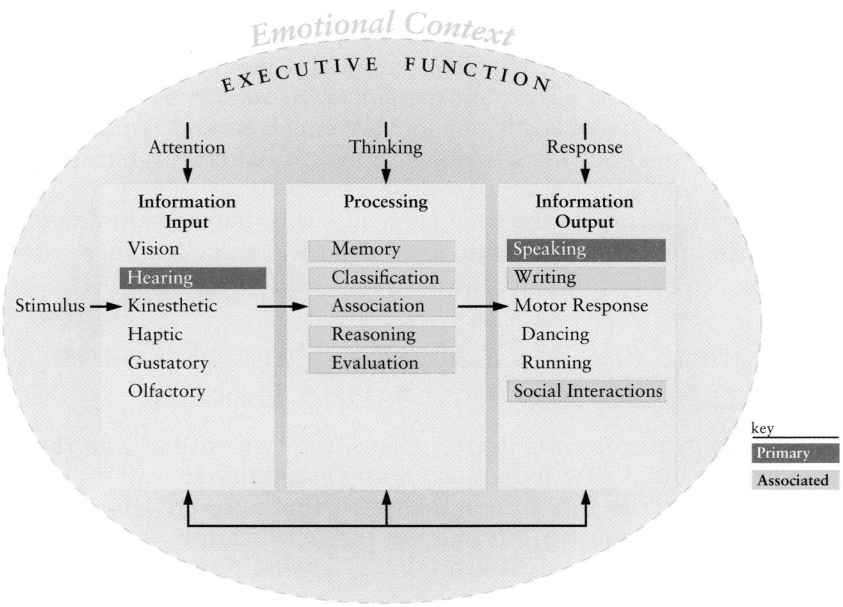

© Cengage Learning

▶ **Figure 11.1 Kiesha's Information Processing Model**

TeachSource Digital Download **Access online**

were fitted when he began kindergarten. Because he was already speaking when he lost his hearing, he is classified as having postlingual hearing loss. Carlos's needs are complicated by the fact that his first language is Spanish, and so, although his hearing loss is postlingual, he still has difficulties with English. Carlos's height and weight are typical for his age, and his motor coordination is above average. He is an intelligent young man, but because of his hearing challenges and his language differences his academic development has lagged behind. Because of his social maturity and excellent physical abilities, he is a leader on the playground, where the game of choice is soccer. The one area of academics in which he performs at grade level is mathematical computation.

On audiometric testing, Carlos showed a hearing loss of 75 decibels with the amplification provided by his hearing aids; this is a severe hearing loss. Since Carlos learned to talk before his loss of hearing, he is able to draw on his early language foundation for learning, and with hearing aids, speech therapy, and other special education services, he is moving ahead. For the first three years of schooling, Carlos attended a bilingual special education class for two hours each day. In this class he received academic support in both Spanish and English. He is now receiving weekly speech language support and special education services in reading. Carlos relies a good deal on his lipreading skills, and he sits at the front of the classroom, facing the teacher. He still needs extra help in developing his academic skills. The audiologist and speech-language pathologist have suggested that Carlos would be an ideal candidate for a cochlear implant. They are working to set up a meeting with his parents to share information on this option for Carlos (we will learn more about this later in the chapter).

Raymond

Raymond's hearing loss is profound, testing at a loss of more than 95 decibels. Raymond was born deaf; he has never heard a spoken word. In addition to deafness, Raymond is also intellectually and developmentally delayed. Although Raymond is 10 years old, due to his intellectual delays his mental age is estimated at around 4 years, and he has mild problems with physical coordination. Because of the severity of Raymond's hearing loss and the difficulties with learning that he encounters due to his cognitive delays, he is in a self-contained special class. Raymond's limited speech is difficult to understand, and he uses alternative communication picture boards to express his needs. In reading and other academic subjects, Raymond is several grades behind his age-mates.

Raymond's communication with his family and peers is limited; so are his sources of information and his social experiences. He often reacts to social situations in ways that are characteristic of a much younger child. Raymond will need intense support throughout his schooling and will need careful transition planning as he moves into adulthood.

These three students show the wide range of needs that are common for individuals with hearing losses. Each individual child will show a unique pattern of strengths and needs, and this pattern will change over time.

11-2b Definitions of Deafness, Hard of Hearing, and Central Auditory Processing Disorders

A hearing loss is defined by the degree of loss, the type of loss, and the age at which the loss occurred. The Individuals with Disabilities Education Act (IDEA, 2004) defines deafness as a hearing impairment that is severe enough that the child cannot process linguistic information through hearing, even when using amplification or hearing aids. This hearing loss adversely affects the child's educational performance. Being "hard of hearing" is defined as an impairment in hearing that may be permanent or fluctuating and that adversely affects a child's educational performance but that is *not* included under the definition of deafness. What we see in both definitions is that the hearing loss can adversely affect the child's education and that we must make special educational adaptations to support children with hearing losses.

In this chapter we use the term *deaf* to refer to a profound or complete inability to hear and the term *hard of hearing* to refer to all other categories of hearing loss. We also use a capital *D* when referring to the Deaf culture or community (discussed later in the chapter). On occasion, we also use the term *hearing losses* to describe these challenges. Because hearing losses can differ in degree, type, and age of onset, their impact on children can vary widely.

Spencer Grant/PhotoEdit

It is critical that all family members learn to communicate effectively with the child who is deaf or hard of hearing.

Degree of Hearing Loss

The severity of hearing losses is determined by the individual's reception of sound as measured in decibels (dB). A loss of between 16 and 25 dB is considered slight; increasing degrees of loss range from *mild* (26–40 dBs) to *moderate* (41–55 dBs) to *moderately severe* (56–70 dBs) to *severe* (71–90 dBs) and *profound* (more than 91 dBs) hearing loss or, to use a more common term, deafness (American Speech-Language-Hearing Association [ASHA], 2013b). Table 11.1 presents the range

TABLE 11.1 Level of Hearing Loss

Level of Hearing Loss (Measured in Decibels)	Description	Possible Causes	Sounds Heard
16–25 dB	Slight hearing loss	Otitis media, or fluid build up in the middle ear due to ear infections; damage to the ear through injury, illness, or noise exposure	Hears vowel sounds clearly; may miss unvoiced consonant sounds (*f, s, sh*)
26–40 dB	Mild hearing loss	Otitis media; prenatal exposure to infections (e.g., rubella, cytomegalovirus/CMV, herpes simplex virus); damage to the ear through illness, injury, or noise exposure	Hears only some louder-voiced speech sounds
41–55 dB	Moderate hearing loss	Chronic otitis media; middle ear anomalies; sensorineural damage; prenatal exposure to infections; genetic factors; and damage to the ear through illness, injury, or noise exposure	Misses most speech sounds at normal conversational level
56–70 dB	Moderately Severe hearing loss	Middle ear anomalies; sensorineural damage; prenatal exposure to infections; genetic factors; and damage to the ear through illness, injury, or noise exposure	Hears no speech sounds at normal conversational level
71–90 dB	Severe hearing loss	Same as moderately severe hearing loss	Hears no speech or other sounds
91 + dB	Profound hearing loss	Same as severe	Hears no Speech or other sounds

SOURCE: Adapted from the American Speech-Language-Hearing Association (ASHA) website, www.asha.org/public/hearing/Degree-of-Hearing-Loss/. Retrieved November 13, 2013.

of degrees of hearing impairments, their descriptive classification, and their possible causes. Individuals classified as hard of hearing may be able to hear and understand speech, or they can be helped to do so with hearing aids. Only a small percentage (less than 1 percent) of persons who are deaf are unable to hear speech under any conditions.

Types of Hearing Loss

The ear is a complicated structure (Figure 11.2), and it functions in a complex way. The outer ear is composed of the pinna, the temporal bone, and the auditory canal, or external auditory meatus. The middle ear is composed of the tympanic membrane, or **eardrum**, and the three ear bones: the malleus, the incus, and the stapes. The stapes lies next to the oval window, called the gateway to the inner ear. The inner ear contains the **cochlea**, which contains part of the hearing organs, the

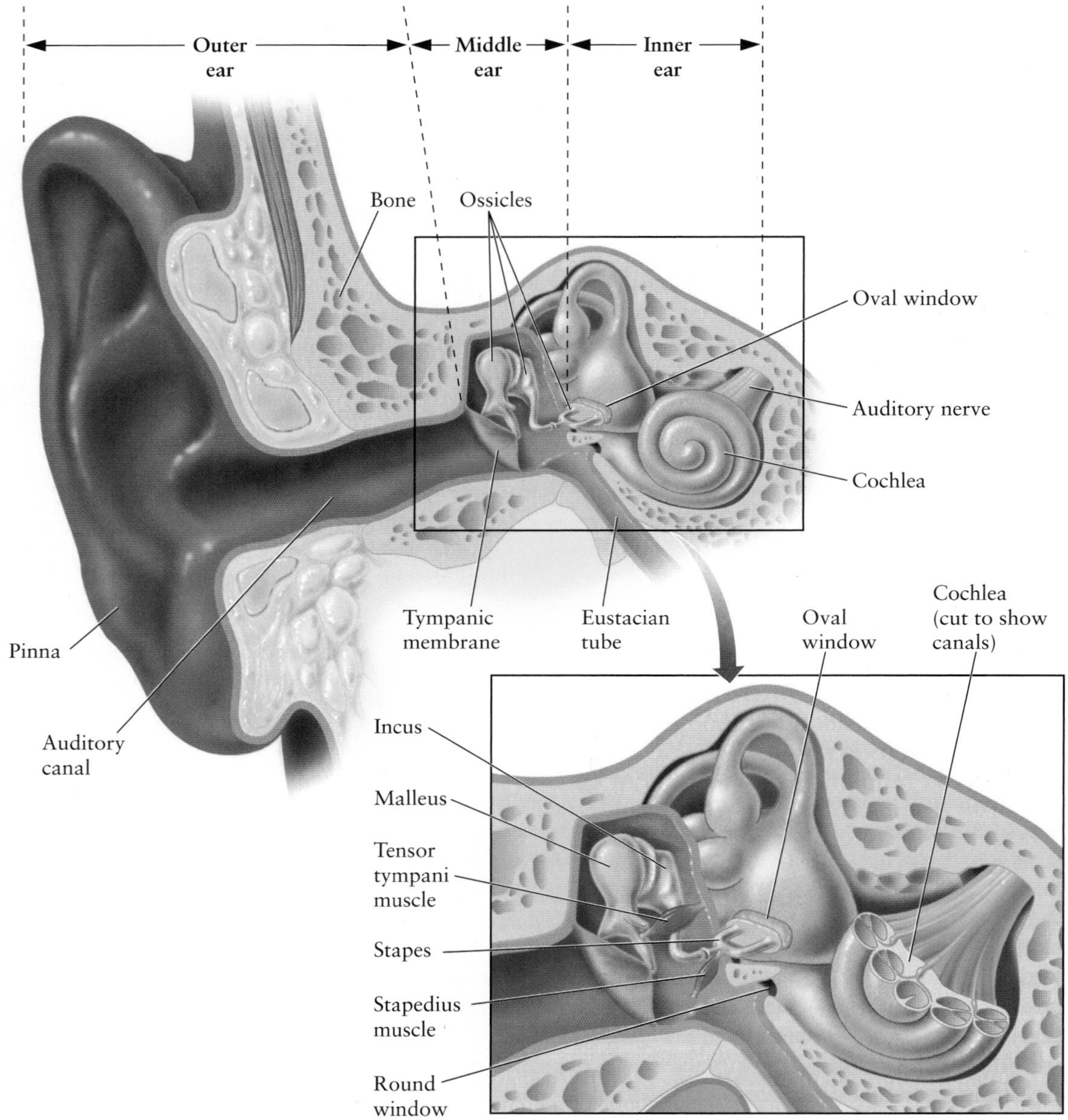

Figure 11.2 Anatomy and Structure of Ear

Source: Freberg, L. (2006). *Discovering Biological Psychology*, p. 392. Used by permission of Houghton Mifflin Harcourt Publishing Company.

vestibular apparatus, which includes the vestibule and three semicircular canals of the inner ear, and the **cochlear nerve**, or auditory nerve. Problems with hearing can be due to either the structure or the function of the ear. Hearing losses can be classified into four categories: *conductive losses, sensorineural losses, mixed hearing losses*, and *central auditory processing losses*. The first three types of hearing loss are considered to be due to problems with **auditory acuity**, or the ability to take in sounds and get these to the brain successfully. The fourth type of hearing loss is an **auditory processing** difficulty, which means that the individual can sense the sounds but has problems understanding them. Within the information processing model, the first three types of hearing loss are related to problems with input—getting the information to the brain—whereas the fourth type is due to difficulties in processing the input once it is received.

A **conductive hearing loss** occurs when something blocks the sound passing through the outer or middle ear (ASHA, 2013b). The blockage can be caused by wax, ear infections (otitis media), or any type of malformation of the ear canal. Conductive hearing losses make hearing faint sounds more difficult. This type of loss is usually temporary and can often be corrected by surgery or medication, but children will also need educational supports to help them with language development and may need speech-language support to help overcome articulation problems (ASHA, 2013b; Herter, Knightly, & Steinberg, 2002).

Sensorineural hearing losses are caused by damage to the inner ear (cochlea) or to the auditory nerve, particularly in the delicate sensory hairs of the inner ear or in the nerves that supply them. Sensorineural hearing losses affect both the ability to hear faint sounds *and* the ability to hear clearly, and this can make understanding speech sounds difficult. These hearing losses may be caused by genetic syndromes, diseases, injuries, or exposure to loud noise (Salvia, Ysseldyke, & Bolt, 2012). Hearing aids will likely be useful for the majority of individuals with sensorineural hearing loss, and cochlear implants can be considered for individuals with profound hearing loss in both ears who cannot benefit from hearing aids (ASHA, 2013b). Educational support and related speech-language services will be needed to help the child be able to achieve success.

Mixed hearing losses result from problems in the outer ear as well as in the middle or inner ear, combining both conductive and sensorineural difficulties (ASHA, 2013b). Persons with this type of loss may hear distorted sounds and have difficulty with sound levels. Depending on the specific site of the difficulty, a combination of medical treatment and amplification with hearing aids can be used to increase hearing. As with sensorineural hearing losses, some individuals may benefit from **cochlear implants** (a surgically implanted device that directly stimulates the auditory nerve), and all will need educational and related service supports.

In addition to the loss of hearing due to auditory acuity problems, an individual may have difficulties processing auditory information. *Central auditory processing* difficulties are considered a type of hearing loss because they limit the individual's ability to use auditory information (ASHA, 2005; Salvia et al., 2012). An individual with a **central auditory processing disorder (CAPD)** may have difficulties with sound localization, auditory discrimination, understanding speech sounds against a noisy background, auditory sequencing, memory, pattern recognition, sounding out words, and reading comprehension (ASHA, 2005; Salvia et al., 2012). Like individuals with other hearing losses, individuals with CAPDs will need the support of a multidisciplinary team to provide appropriate supports and services. We continue to discuss these supports and services later in this chapter.

Age of Onset of Hearing Loss

A hearing loss can be either **congenital**, meaning present at birth, or **acquired**, meaning that it has occurred in either childhood or adulthood. A hearing loss

TeachSource Video Connection

Watch the video "Amy: Accommodating a Gifted Student with Hearing and Visual Impairments in a Middle School Classroom." This video clip shows Amy in the classroom with her peers. Amy's teacher also discusses her experiences working with a student with hearing impairments. What are some of Amy's unique challenges discussed in the video? What additional strategies might help support Amy's learning?

Watch online

that occurs before the child's language has developed is a prelingual or **prelinguistic hearing loss**, and one that occurs after the child has acquired some speech and language is called a postlingual or **postlinguistic hearing loss**. The timing of an acquired hearing loss will have a critical impact on the child's oral language and speech. The timing of the hearing loss is critical because it shapes the child's early communication, language, and speech development. If the hearing loss occurs congenitally, the child will often have limited experience with the sounds of speech and will likely encounter greater difficulties understanding and producing speech. If the loss occurs before the child has acquired speech, the oral language delay is likely to be greater than it would be if the child had already developed a solid language and speech foundation. The stronger the child's speech and language foundation is prior to the loss of hearing, the more the child can draw on it to support his or her communication. For the child with prelingual deafness, the early introduction of sign language is critical to facilitating overall communication. The specific impact of any hearing loss will depend in part on how early the loss is detected, on whether the child is provided amplification or a cochlear implant, and on the supports and services the child and family receive.

11-2c Prevalence of Hearing Loss

An estimated 38 million persons in the United States, or 12 percent of the general population, have some degree of hearing loss (Center for Hearing and Communication, 2013). Of these, less than 1 percent are likely to be deaf. Hearing losses span the generations, affecting the following estimated numbers:

- 30–40% of people over age 65
- 14% of people ages 45–64
- 7% of people ages 29 to 40
- Approximately 3 million children and youths under the age of 18 (Better Hearing Institute, 2010; Center for Hearing and Communication, 2013)

An estimated 5 in 1,000 infants are born with serious to profound hearing losses. As infant screening increases, this number could prove to be a low estimate (Better Hearing Institute, 2010; Center for Hearing and Communication, 2013). During the 2003–4 school year, 73,421 students were listed as deaf or hard of hearing (U.S. Department of Education, 2009). Although students with hearing loss reportedly account for 1.3 percent of students with disabilities, this figure is likely to be a low estimate because many students with hearing losses have other disabilities as well (Jones, Jones, & Ewing, 2006).

The low incidence of students with profound hearing losses makes is challenging for districts to provide support that is intensive enough for the student to meet with success. Access to personnel with expertise in total communication needs, individuals who can manage the technology needs of the students, and teachers with experience working with students who are deaf may prove difficult in moderate and small districts.

11-3 Causes and Detection of Hearing Loss in Children and the Importance of Early Intervention

Understanding the causes of hearing losses and knowing how we can detect these allows us to begin interventions as early as possible to help the child meet with success. With hearing loss, as with all areas of disability, the earlier we start interventions the better the outcomes for the child.

11-3a Causes of Hearing Loss

Many factors may produce hearing loss in children. The causes are genetic, neurological, environmental or acquired, or of unknown origin (Herter, Knightly, & Steinberg, 2002).

Genetic Causes of Hearing Loss

Genetic factors are likely to be involved in more than half of all the incidents of **congenital hearing losses** (losses present at birth). The Joint Committee on Infant Hearing (JCIH; 2007) position paper states that there are nearly 600 syndromes and 125 genes associated with hearing that have been currently identified, and genetic research on deafness continues (Kurima et al., 2002). Genetically caused hearing losses are inherited from one or both of the parents and can be inherited from either a hearing parent or a nonhearing parent (ASHA, 2013b). Because many forms of deafness are at least partially related to genetic factors, it is now possible to test individuals for various genes associated with deafness (Sparrow, 2010). The use of genetic testing to help determine the probability of conceiving a child who is deaf has become quite controversial; members of the Deaf community are concerned that this information may perpetuate the deficit, or medical, view of deafness (Sparrow, 2010). Approximately 30 to 40 percent of children with hearing losses have associated disabilities that must be considered as part of their treatment (JCIH, 2007). Chapter 13 looks at the needs of children with multiple areas of disability, including children who are both deaf and blind.

Children with other genetically related disabilities may also have associated hearing problems. For example, children with Down syndrome (a genetic disorder associated with intellectual and developmental delays) often have narrow ear canals and are prone to middle-ear infections, which may cause hearing losses. Individuals with cleft palates (an opening in the lip and aboral ridge) also may have repeated middle-ear infections, which can result in conductive hearing losses (Herter et al., 2002).

Not all genetic hearing losses appear at birth. Babies born with perfectly normal hearing may lose their hearing in the early months or years as a result of hereditary factors (Herter et al., 2002). Teachers should be aware that a hearing loss can occur in a child who previously exhibited a normal range of hearing, so continued monitoring of students for signs of hearing loss is important.

Neurology and Brain Development Related to Children Who Are Deaf or Hard of Hearing

The brain is a complex organ that plays an essential role in all of our functions. Here is a simplified version of normal hearing: Sound comes in through the ear canal, vibrations move from the cochlea along the auditory nerve, and these vibrations are processed in the auditory cortex (within the left hemisphere) (Sakai, 2005). For young children, the sounds of most importance are related to language. So what happens when a child is deaf and the brain receives no input from sound?

Early work by Helen Neville and her colleagues (1997) using brain-imaging technology showed that for children born congenitally deaf, their "visual language," American Sign Language, is processed in the auditory cortex. Sakai (2005) had similar findings in a study of children whose first language was Japanese Sign Language. Other studies, however, found bilateral cortical activity (both hemispheres working) for processing both ASL and British Sign Language (BSL) (Sakai, 2005). The brain's plasticity, or ability to reorganize itself when needed, seems to be at work here (Pennington, 2009).

The result of studies done with children who have received cochlear implants show that the younger the children are when they receive the implants, the more benefit there is for speech and vocabulary outcomes (Connor, Craig, Raudenbush, Heavner, & Zwolan, 2006; Fagan & Pisoni, 2010; Geers, Tobey, Moog, & Brenner, 2008; Hayes, Geers, Treiman, & Moog, 2009). The critical age for the maximum benefit seems to be prior to 2.5 years. While cochlear implants have now been approved for infants (National Institute on Deafness and Other Communication Disorders [NIDCD], 2010), more research looking at the role of the brain in processing language (both oral and visual/manual) will help us understand these relationships better (Pennington, 2009).

Environmental Causes of Hearing Loss

Environmental causes include exposure to bacteria, viruses, toxins, and trauma, as well as infection during the course of pregnancy or in the birth process (Herter et al., 2002). The environmental effects that begin before birth are associated with illness or infections the mother may have had during pregnancy. For example, uncontrolled diabetes in the mother may cause a hearing loss in her child. A group of infections that affect the mother and that can also cause severe hearing losses in the fetus has been labeled **TORCHS** (de Jong et al., 2010) (see Table 11.2).

The most common cause of hearing loss for young children in their preschool years is otitis media. A middle-ear infection, very common in children of preschool age, **otitis media** can lead to hearing loss and language difficulties. Figure 11.2 (shown earlier), shows an area called the middle ear, where the malleus, the incus, and the stapes are located. When a child has otitis media, this area fills with a fluid that decreases the child's ability to hear. Depending on the frequency and severity of infections, the hearing loss may be mild or even moderate (ASHA, 2013b). Children are susceptible to ear infections because their Eustachian tubes are small and often more horizontal than those of adults, so fluids do not drain as effectively (ASHA, 2013b). Later in the chapter we look at specific strategies teachers can use to support children who may have hearing losses due to

TABLE 11.2 Maternal Infections That May Cause Hearing Loss to the Fetus: TORCHS

TO	Toxoplasmosis—a parasitic disease
R	Rubella (German measles)—mostly controlled within the United States by vaccines
C	Cytomegalovirus (CMV)—an infection in the mother's uterus which can go undiagnosed
HS	Herpes simplex virus—can cause neurological problems as well as deafness

otitis media ear infections. The most important thing is to detect the hearing loss as early as possible.

11-3b Assessing Hearing Loss in Children

Hearing losses can be detected at birth, and 43 states require a hearing screening for newborns (NIDCD, 2010). A Centers for Disease Control and Prevention report, based on data from 47 states and 3 territories, indicated that 97.4% of infants under the age of 1 month had been screened for hearing losses in 2007 (CDC, 2009b). Because 20 to 30 percent of hearing losses occur during early childhood, further screenings should be conducted at regular intervals. If a hearing loss is identified at birth, a comprehensive auditory evaluation can be conducted by 3 months of age, and the infant may be fitted with a hearing aid or may receive a cochlear implant. Early diagnosis can also alert the parents if the child is deaf and may need to learn sign language or an alternate communication system in order facilitate optimum development and to mitigate any developmental delays (Cruz et al., 2013). Testing for a hearing loss will take somewhat different forms depending on the age of the child.

Measuring a Hearing Loss

To assess hearing in an infant, we must first determine whether the ear is functioning appropriately and whether the brain is receiving the sound signal. Three methods for assessing hearing in infants are: **otoacoustic auditory emissions (OAE)**, **auditory brainstem response (ABR)**, and **auditory steady state response (ASSR)** (JCIH, 2007). While both OAE and ABR techniques measure the underlying physical activity for hearing, there are some differences between these approaches. ABR measurements are taken from surface electrodes that record the brain's activity in response to sounds delivered via an earphone. OAE is assessed by placing a small microphone in the child's ear. In the ear of a hearing child, when a click sound is played an echo is generated. This echo happens because as sounds move through the ear canal to the middle ear they stimulate thousands of hair cells, causing them to vibrate. The microphone placed in the child's ear makes it possible to receive and record this echo (Mauk & White, 1995). If no echo is received, further evaluation is indicated. The ASSR approach uses continuous stimuli to elicit a response and can provide frequency-specific auditory information that can be important if the child is being considered for a cochlear implant.

National Center for Hearing Assessment Management: **www.infanthearing.org**

A **bone-conductor test** can assess hearing in infants and preschool children younger than 3 years of age by measuring the movement of sound through the bone and the hearing system to the brain, bypassing the ear. The reception of this sound in the brain (auditory brainstem recognition) is recorded on a graph that charts the brain's response in vibrations (Salvia et al., 2012). By comparing the child's responses to the responses of a population of hearing persons, the audiologist can ascertain hearing abilities or losses. A bone-conductor test should *not* be done in a school setting because a special environment is needed.

Play audiometry can be used with very young children to assess their ability to hear. Tests are conducted in a pleasant environment with toys that move and make sounds. The toys are used to elicit responses, such as eye blinks and changes in respiration or heartbeat (slower heartbeats indicate attention).

In these types of tests, the child is brought into a room with his or her caregiver. An examiner distracts the child with an attractive toy. Sounds are piped into the room. A change in sound indicates that a curtain will be raised to reveal a more attractive toy. The child is not told that this will happen. After a few experiences of this, children without hearing losses hear the change of sound and turn to look at the hidden toy before the curtain is lifted to reveal it. If the child does not turn when the sound is changed, hearing losses are suspected (Herter et al., 2002).

The most frequently used hearing assessment is pure-tone audiometry. **Pure-tone audiometry** can be used with children about 3 years of age and older. The audiometer—an instrument for testing hearing acuity—presents pure tones (not speech) to the individual, who receives the tones in a headset (Salvia et al., 2012). The audiometer presents a range of sounds and measures the frequency (vibrations) and intensity (pitch) at which the individual is able to hear these sounds. The individual being tested responds to the sounds by raising a hand (or speaking into a microphone) if he or she can hear the tone. These responses are recorded on a graph called an *audiogram*. From an examination of the results, an audiologist can determine the degree and range of hearing loss.

11-3c The Importance of Early Intervention for Children with Hearing Losses

Early intervention is critical for children with hearing losses. The Joint Committee on Infant Hearing (2007) stated:

> Before newborn hearing screening was instituted universally, children with severe to profound hearing loss, on average, completed the twelfth grade with a third- to fourth-grade reading level and language levels of a 9- to 10-year-old.

The report further states that infants and children with mild to profound hearing loss who are identified in the first 6 months of life and are provided with immediate and appropriate intervention have significantly better outcomes in vocabulary development, receptive and expressive language, understanding of syntax, speech production, and social and emotional adjustment.

The impact and importance of early intervention for children with a hearing loss cannot be overstated. Early and intense intervention using a communication system that the child can master (Fitzpatrick, Crawford, Ni, & Durieux-Smith, 2011; Harrington, DesJardin, & Shea, 2010; National Association for the Deaf [NAD], 2010) is essential. Once a child's hearing loss has been detected, parents are faced with several decisions. Based on the type and severity of the hearing loss, parents must evaluate the use of amplification (hearing aids to maximize the child's residual hearing); communication systems (oral and/or manual); and the possibility of a cochlear implant (Duncan, 2009; Hardonk et al., 2011; JCIH, 2007; NIDCD, 2010). These decisions are not easy; there are pros and cons associated with each option. Because each child's situation is unique, professionals and parents must carefully review these pros and cons as they work to plan interventions that will be most successful for the child (Hardonk et al., 2011; NAD, 2010). During this decision-making process, parents may feel torn between the urgency of making a decision and starting the intervention and the need to think through the options so that they make the best decision (Duncan, 2009; Hardonk et al., 2011).

The following guidelines can help professionals provide appropriate support for parents during the decision-making process:

- Remember that parents of young children with hearing loss need time to deal with their feelings.
- Engage parents in discussing and determining their ambitions, aspirations, and desires for their child.
- Display clear, open, and harmonious beliefs, expectations, and assumptions.
- Provide parents with impartial, comprehensive, written, and spoken information presented free of jargon and in a judicious manner.
- Recognize common emotions, beliefs, and knowledge needed to make the decision-making process work (Duncan, 2009).

BOX 11.3

EXCEPTIONAL LIVES • EXCEPTIONAL STORIES

The Gift of Sight: A Story of Mathew

Mathew was traveling with his family—Mom, Dad, and elder brother, Michael. The tour took five days and circled Ireland with amazing views of the coastline, castles, and countryside! Sitting with his face pressed against the bus window—Mathew was taking it all in!

An interesting boy with a sparkle in his eye, Mathew communicated in many ways. Sign-langue with some speech and lip reading, lots of smiles, and a dramatic flair for the important information like battles on the castle parapets. He seemed curious about my camera and watched as I struggled to figure out how to use it. I handed it to him and we became instant friends.

Mathew had an eye for the shot. He framed the elements, he took multiple angles, and he often captured the spirit of his subject. His humor showed in his work. One series of photos showed the backsides of several beautiful horses. These were paired with photos taken while tailing members of our tour... the twinkle in his eye as he shared the pictures with me said it all!

After Mathew had taken several photos, he discovered the video function of the camera and began producing a mini-series. First, a restaurant walk through complete with a signed narrative about the food. Next, a castle walk-about with, of course, a battle scene. Finally, a general day on tour with the morning bus loading; people riding, sleeping, talking, and watching the scenery pass by; and the end of the day departure from the bus with happy, tired, tourists laden with small purchases acquired as reminders of the sights seen.

Mathew attended a school for the deaf where American Sign Language was the primary mode of communication. He had received a cochlear implant and was struggling to learn to use it and to incorporate speech. On the trip, he was wrestling to fit in with a hearing world; complicated communication challenges. With only a father who understood some sign language, surrounded by ambient noise that interfered with the sound quality of the implant, embedded in a group of adults who had limited patience to understand a boy's difficult speech, and only a few individuals who understood the importance of facing Mathew as they spoke (so he could read their lips)...communication did not seem to be worth his effort.

The photography seemed to help. Several people took an interest in his work. He share generously and often took their pictures in return for their interest. In this way, Mathew connected with many of the tour group members. He became the trips eyes—documenting all we saw.

On the last day, Mathew gave me back the camera and I promised to send him his work. We parted with a hug. While we have not been in touch for several years, my hope is that this charming, bright, energetic young boy has continued to use photography to communicate and connect. Mathew's gift is his sight... his photography captured and shared the essence of the world around him.

Early and intense communication with children, particularly in infancy and the preschool years, when the child's central nervous system is ready to learn language, is critical (Boons, et al., 2012; Cruz et al., 2012; Fitzpatrick et al., 2011). Adults must provide the language of the child, whether in manual or oral form, if the child is to learn to communicate. Box 11.3 reminds us that a child should be given multiple ways to communicate, including the arts!

11-4 Cognitive, Academic, Communication, and Social Development of Children with Hearing Loss

The development of each child will depend on the child's strengths and needs in combination with the supports of the family, the medical community, and the school. While we cannot predict any specific outcomes for individuals based on their hearing loss, we can look at overall patterns of development for cognitive abilities, academic achievement, language, and social adjustment.

11-4a Cognitive Development of Children with Hearing Losses

Children who are deaf or hard of hearing have the capacity for normal intelligence, and some may be intellectually gifted (Powers, 2011). However, because they cannot hear as well as children with normal hearing, they may experience developmental delays. Intelligence depends on the interaction between a person's innate capacity and his or her environmental experiences. As children with hearing losses mature, they will have different background experiences, communication histories, and access to information, and so they will need specialized instruction to reach the same cognitive and developmental milestones as children who can hear. A hearing loss may, however, be accompanied by disabilities that impact the child's cognitive abilities (Gallaudet Research Institute [GRI], 2008; Jones et al., 2006). An estimated 33 percent of students with hearing loss also have an additional area of disability (Jones et al., 2006). One area of special concern is children who are both deaf and blind. This is discussed in-depth in Chapter 12.

It can be difficult to determine the intellectual level of children with hearing losses in part because intelligence tests used to measure cognitive abilities are not designed for children with hearing losses. Orally (speech) administered intelligence tests that are heavily based on language often greatly underestimate the abilities of a child whose primary language is manual (Salvia et al., 2012). To assess children who are deaf or hard of hearing in written English is also problematic if the child's primary language is American Sign Language, because the vocabulary, syntax, and grammar of ASL are significantly different from those of English. A child whose first language is ASL should receive the same assessment accommodations that any child whose primary language is not English receives. This means that the assessment should be conducted in the child's primary language (ASL) and that the assessor should be bilingual and if possible bicultural (Johnson & McIntosh, 2009; Simms & Thumann, 2007). Furthermore, appropriate assessments must address both the child's access to the stimulus (spoken or printed words) and his or her ability to respond to the test prompts by either by speaking or writing (Salvia et al., 2012; Cawthon & Wurtz, 2008). When nonverbal tests are used with a sign language or manual communication system familiar to children, they often perform well within the normal range. The Universal Nonverbal Intelligence Test (UNIT) (Bracken & McCallum, 1998) is a highly recommended nonverbal assessment for students who are deaf (Maller, 2003). See ▶ Figure 11.3 for a sample item on the UNIT.

As part of the validation process of the UNIT, 106 students with hearing losses were assessed (Bracken & MaCallum, 1998). All of the students tested attended a special school for the deaf. When the outcomes for the students with hearing losses were compared with a demographically matched sample of hearing students, the mean differences in scores showed approximately one-third of a standard deviation lower for the students with deafness (Bracken & McCallum, 1998). These differences were considerably smaller than would be expected for a cognitive assessment if it depended heavily on the child's language. The smaller differences indicate that the UNIT is likely to be a better predictor of cognitive abilities for children with hearing losses. But caution is still warranted when using measures of cognitive abilities with students who are deaf, as these measures likely underestimate the students' potential (Maller, 2003).

One reason that we get a more accurate assessment of abilities with nonverbal assessments may be that these better capture the student's strengths. Hamilton (2011) found that students who were deaf showed strengths in visuospatial recall (that is, with items presented in visual format); imagery (such as the ability to create, maintain, and manipulate visual images); and dual encoding (using both speech and sign language). When specifically taught these

Figure 11.3 Sample of UNIT Assessment
In the UNIT assessment of analogic reasoning, children are asked to pick which of the pictures best fits in the empty box above.
From Universal Nonverbal Intelligence TestTM (UNIT)-Stimulus Book 1 (p 5), by B A Bracken & R S McCallum, 1998, Austin IX: PRO-ED Copyright 1998 by PRO-ED, Inc. Reprinted with Permission.

strategies students who were deaf also showed strengths in phonological encoding (using speech sounds) and rehearsal (repeating information to be recalled). Teachers may capitalize on these strengths to support the student's learning (Hamilton, 2011).

11-4b Academic Development in Reading for Children with Hearing Losses

Reading levels of children who are deaf or hard of hearing tend to be substantially lower than those of their hearing peers, but we may be closing this gap (Antia, 2007; Antia, Jones, Reed, & Kreimeyer, 2009; Luckner & Handley, 2008; McGough & Schirmer, 2005; Reed, Antia, & Kreimeyer, 2008; Schirmer & Schaffer, 2010; Trezek & Wang, 2006). Easterbrooks and Beal-Alvarez (2012) reviewed assessment data (grades 3, 5, and 8) from seven states and found that reading levels for many students who are deaf/hard of hearing have broken the perceived "glass-ceiling" of third- to fourth-grade level. Ensuring appropriate accommodations during large-scale assessments may help us get a more accurate picture of student achievements (Cawthon, Winton, Garberoglio, & Gobble, 2011).

New methods for reading instruction for students with hearing loss also hold great promise (Smith & Wang, 2010). Children who have not heard the sounds of the language will struggle to decode print if they are taught in the usual method of matching speech sounds (e.g., phonemes) to print. Since phonemic awareness, or the ability to use speech sounds, may be limited for children who are deaf or hard of hearing, alternative methods must be used to teach reading (Luckner & Handley, 2008; McGough & Schirmer, 2005; Schirmer & Schaffer, 2010; Smith & Wang, 2010 Trezek & Wang, 2006). If reading is taught visually or by a manual method (such as American Sign Language or finger spelling), children who are deaf or hard of hearing are able to learn how to read, write, and use appropriate language forms, such as past tense, questions, and logical propositions such as *if-then* and *either-or* (Smith & Wang, 2010; Trezek & Wang, 2006; Trezek, Wang, Woods, Gampp, & Paul, 2007).

Learning to read is more challenging for students who are deaf. Not surprisingly, students who are deaf use slightly different strategies than hearing students as they learn to read (Kyle & Harris, 2011). Following students (24 deaf and 23 hearing) for two years as they learned to read, Kyle and Harris (2011) found that early vocabulary, letter-sound knowledge, and speech-reading were key precursors for successful reading for the children who were deaf. Vocabulary is essential for reading and its development for children who are deaf must be explicit and intense (Luckner & Cooke, 2010). For students who can hear, many words are learned through incidental communication, but for students who are deaf, direct instruction of new words is critical (Luckner & Cooke, 2010).

Smith & Wang (2010) found that the use of "Visual Phonics" significantly increased phonological awareness for students who were deaf. Visual phonics is a multisensory tool that combines hand cues with written symbols that represent phonemes (speech sounds), allowing students who are deaf to manipulate phonemes without hearing the sound. The use of visual phonics to increase speech production and reading abilities for students who are deaf is a promising practice (Smith & Wang, 2010).

In addition, there is a movement to teach reading by the whole-word method. First, students learn to read words that stand for persons or things with which they are familiar; for example, *ball*. Then, after students have acquired a basic reading vocabulary, the teacher introduces phonics as a part of a continuing emphasis on teaching whole words (Hammil, 2004). For children who are deaf or hard of hearing, a picture of the object or person may accompany the presentation of the word, and a visual cue can be used for the word sounds (phonons). The child who can hear may have already made the association between the word and the object or person, but one cannot assume that the child who is deaf or hard of hearing has done so.

While there seems to be agreement that vocabulary and letter-sound knowledge are important for early reading, Miller et al. (2012) explored deficits in understanding **semantics**, or language meaning, as a possible cause for reading problems. More specifically, they examined children's understanding of structural language, using sentence comprehension tasks where students who were deaf were asked to identify "plausible" versus "nonplausible" sentences. A nonplausible sentence was one in which the structure did not make the meaning clear (e.g., the truck driver who hit the man was badly hurt). Researchers worked with 213 students who were deaf across four languages (Hebrew, Arabic, English, and German) and found similar deficits in understanding the importance of sentence structure to the comprehension of meaning. They conclude that access to language-rich environments, which intentionally promote awareness of sentence structure, are critical for students who are deaf (Miller et al., 2012).

A study compared methods for teaching reading to children who are deaf or hard of hearing with similar methods used to teach children who can hear (Luckner, Sebald, Cooney, Young, & Muir, 2005–2006). The study reviewed the National Reading Panel's recommendations for reading instruction (National Institute of Child Health and Human Development, 2000), and identified key areas of overlap in instructional practice. The promising elements of reading instruction identified in this study for children who are deaf or hard of hearing are given in Box 11.4 (Luckner et al., 2005/2006).

In summary, through improved teaching strategies, earlier intervention, new technology, and medical treatments (cochlear implants), children who are deaf or hard of hearing are making solid gains in learning to read. In spite of all we do know, however, there is still a critical need for additional research on instructional methods that work with children who are deaf (Luckner & Cooke, 2010; Luckner et al., 2005/2006).

BOX 11.4 Promising Elements of Reading Instruction for Children Who Are Deaf or Hard of Hearing

- Rehearsal of information
- Direct teaching of sight words and morphological rules (how sounds are combined to make words)
- Explicit vocabulary instruction and practice with short passages
- Use of high-interest reading materials
- Instruction in the grammatical principles of ASL and how these translate to written English
- Teacher-modeled discussions of stories and explicit instruction in reading comprehension strategies
- Interaction with text and peers in learning
- Reading to young children
- Use of captions
- Intensified instruction
- Use of word processing
- Use of simple stories and word recognition practice with young readers
- Use of general curriculum for reading reinforcement

SOURCE: Information was drawn from Luckner et al. (2005/2006). An examination of the evidence-based literacy research in deaf education. *American Annals of the Deaf, 150* (5), 443–456.

11-4c Impact of a Hearing Loss on Language, Speech, and Communication

During the first year of life, the *prelinguistic* period (meaning before or without speech), infants with hearing losses will exhibit the same behaviors as hearing infants: crying, making comfort sounds, and babbling to parents. In babbling, children produce their first sounds that resemble words (*baba, dada*), and the parents reinforce these sounds and transform them into words. What many parents do not realize is that these language behaviors are innately programmed and will appear whether infants can hear or not (Knight, 2003).

Infants who can hear typically produce their first word around 12 months of age. For the infant who is deaf, babbling does not develop into words. However, in a seminal study, Petitto and Marentette (1991) found that children with severe hearing losses gesture at about the same developmental age at which hearing children babble. They concluded that infants are innately predisposed to learn language and that they do so by stimulating the environment with babbling; if they cannot hear, they use babbling-like hand movements that are sign equivalents of speech sounds. These signs are not words, but they are similar to the babbling sounds. Parents who are deaf recognize these signs and begin teaching a manual form of communication; often this is American Sign Language. Each language, spoken or manual, proceeds in similar fashion. If the parents do not help the child form signs into a language, the child may develop her own sign system, called *home sign*.

Image Source/Corbis

Supporting enriched social interactions between students is an important step in developing social competence.

The innate language mechanism is so strong that children who hear will develop a spoken language and children who are deaf will develop a manual one. They will develop the language of their home. For the child who can hear, it will be whatever language is spoken in the home. For the child who is deaf, it will be the sign language (American Sign Language) taught in the home or another sign system (e.g., Signing Exact English or one developed by the child). One difficulty is that 90 percent of children who are deaf or hard of hearing are born into homes with hearing parents who do not recognize the child's early attempts at a manual communication system, so these attempts are not reinforced and the child's language development is delayed.

11-4d Social and Personal Adjustment of Children with Hearing Loss

Many youngsters who are deaf or hard of hearing will make friends with both their hearing and nonhearing peers. Luckner and Muir (2001) conducted interviews with twenty successful students who are deaf and who were receiving most of their education in general educational settings. They found that many of the students attributed their success to working hard, studying, paying attention, advocating for themselves, getting involved in sports, and *making friends*. Most students acknowledged the importance of their families and the help and support they received from teachers, interpreters, and note takers, but all of them spoke about the importance of their friends (Luckner & Muir, 2001). The students in this study had all done well and were recognized by their teachers as being successful, and forming friendships was part of this success. But friendships may be difficult for some children who are deaf or hard of hearing. A hearing loss often brings with it communication problems, and communication problems can contribute to social, emotional, and behavioral difficulties (NAD, 2010).

Lack of verbal language makes it difficult for children who are deaf to make friends with children who speak and do not sign. Several factors can improve the social adjustment of children who are deaf or hard of hearing (Luckner & Muir, 2001):

- Early identification and intervention that markedly improve the child's overall functioning and increase feelings of self-esteem
- Family support and acceptance of the child
- Sophisticated technological aids such as the Internet that provide access to information and social contacts
- Participation in extracurricular activities (sports, Scouts, service clubs)
- Skilled and caring professionals who work with the child and family.

Promoting Alternative Thinking Strategies (PATHS) is a curriculum designed to improve social competence and to reduce behavioral problems for children who are deaf. It teaches self-esteem and interpersonal competencies (Kam, Greenberg, & Kusche, 2004) and aims to assist students in achieving self-control, emotional understanding, and problem-solving skills (Greenberg & Kusche, 1998). The curriculum focuses on problem-solving techniques to resolve social problems and overcome frustrations. PATHS is useful from late preschool through sixth grade (Calderon & Greenberg, 2000).

Being able to communicate is an interactive process that enables persons with hearing loss to participate fully in their environment. Hearing is not the issue; communication is (Antia, Sabers, & Stinson, 2007). Recall that approximately 90 percent of the parents of children who are deaf or hard of hearing are not able to communicate fully with their children through speech. Therefore, parents will have to master a communication system that is appropriate for their child.

When expressing frustration over inadequate communication in their homes, five young adult deaf students mentioned family members with limited signing skills, attending gatherings with numerous untrained relatives, and watching television with family members who would summarize the program but not give the details (Bodner-Johnson & Sass-Lehrer, 2003). These students' main complaint was that communication issues prevented them from participating fully in family life. It is rare for all the hearing members of a family to learn a sign language. It is not surprising that some children with severe hearing losses prefer to be with children like themselves, with whom they can feel socially accepted and comfortable. This desire extends into adulthood and has led to the formation of the Deaf culture or community.

11-5 The Deaf Culture or Community and Bilingual Approaches to Deafness

The **Deaf community** exists as a separate cultural group within our society and has exhibited considerable cohesiveness for more than a century (MSM Productions, 2008). The community is a very diverse group whose membership is composed of people of many different religious, social, and ethnic backgrounds. The shared bonds, however, are similar values and traditions, a common language (ASL), and specific behavioral protocols that are known to and practiced by group members. Membership in the Deaf community is a part of an individual's identity, and allegiance to the group is often strong. Parents who are deaf often teach ASL to their children who are deaf, and many adults who are deaf learned ASL from their peers in residential schools, where they established close, long-lasting friendships (Stinson & Foster, 2000). When considering cochlear implantation for their child, parents who were deaf gave priority to Deaf identity, the use of sign language, and ethical issues related to the decision for their child (Hardonk et al., 2011).

The Deaf community has state and local networks, holds world games for the deaf, hosts a Deaf Miss America Pageant, publishes a newspaper, and produces other material. The community is strongly bonded, and many adults who are deaf in the United States move toward membership and involvement in it. The Deaf community has the status of a minority group within the mainstream culture. Its members are bilingual, using ASL (or another form of sign language) for communication with others and American English for reading and writing. They provide one another with a sense of belonging and pride, and they help one another overcome possible isolation from mainstream society. The Deaf community provides a sense of Deaf identity for its members. Deaf identity is not static; it is an ongoing quest for belonging and acceptance within the Deaf community while maintaining a voice within the hearing community (McIlroy & Storbeck, 2011). The use of a shared language, American Sign Language, is a key part of the identity within the Deaf community and is one of the reasons that bilingual-bicultural approaches to deafness are so important.

11-5a The Bilingual-Bicultural Approach to Deafness

The **bilingual-bicultural approach** asserts that persons who are deaf are bicultural in that they belong to the Deaf culture as well as to the broader culture of the society in which they live (NAD, 2010). Many are also bilingual because they use a sign language system (usually ASL) to communicate and use the spoken or written language of their culture (Crowe, McLeod, & Ching, 2012). In the United

BOX 11.5 African-American Hearing Parents with Deaf/Hard of Hearing Children

While African-American children make up 16% of all children with profound hearing loss, little attention has been given to cultural needs of these families in research and practice (Borum, 2012). The perspectives of African-American parents regarding choices for their children's language and communication pathways have largely been overlooked. Borum (2012) completed in-depth two-hour interviews with 14 African-American hearing parents (12 female, and 2 male) about communication and language decisions they had made for their child with hearing loss. Central themes that emerged for these parents included the importance of an oral tradition and the child's ability to participate in this, the need for the child to be able to talk with both hands and voice, the importance of written language and literacy, and the importance of maintaining a cultural identity as "Black" in addition to developing a Deaf identity. The families who participated in the interviews felt that their children would need to operate in a complex world where being deaf and Black was going to present challenges. They wanted their children to be prepared to navigate both hearing and Deaf cultures, and they wanted their children to be prepared to be successful within a hearing world. All the families wanted total communication approaches with both speech and manual communication (such as ASL, English Sing, Cued Speech, finger spelling) for their child. They also indicated that the use of gesturing, drawing, acting-it-out, and facial expressions were important for conveying the meanings of the spoken words. The rich cultural context and oral tradition was a key factor for the participating families, setting the stage for an emphasis on spoken language. Professionals working with African-American families need to understand the role of culture in the decisions that families make for their child (Borum, 2012).

States, the primary language is English, and Deaf individuals who speak a different first language would be considered trilingual if they use two oral and written languages in addition to ASL (Crowe et al., 2012; Easterbrooks, 1999; Moores, 2000). Individuals who use both ASL and Standard English often go back and forth between the two languages, *code switching*, depending on their communication demands (Andrews & Rusher, 2010). This code switching, in fact, facilitates the development of vocabulary in both languages.

Some specialists believe that children should be taught a sign language first and be introduced to oral language as a second language. Children with hearing losses who were taught in this manner would be considered bilingual, for example, using ASL as their first language and the written or oral form of English as their second language. The child's family cultural background must also be taken into account, as we see in Box 11.5, which presents information on African-American families with children who are deaf or hard of hearing.

Latino children who are deaf make up one of the fastest growing minorities in the U.S. school-age population (GRI, 2008). Think back to Carlos, one of the children we met at the beginning of the chapter. Carlos would be a trilingual child, with Spanish, ASL, and English. Clearly he needs support in all three languages to achieve success. Carlos is also a candidate for a cochlear implant, and his parents have decided to pursue this option in hopes that he will be better able to fit in with other children in his school and neighborhood community.

Knoors and Marschark (2012) call for a reevaluation of policies regarding the acquisition of spoken language for students who are deaf. They indicate that the policies should reflect the advancements that have been made in early hearing screening/intervention, digital hearing aids, and cochlear implants. This issue remains extremely sensitive, as Deaf identity is seen as a key part of self-acceptance for students who are deaf (McIlory & Storbeck, 2011). Gale (2010) also found that families whose child had cochlear implants still favored a bilingual approach to communication. A bilingual-bicultural approach for students who are deaf is likely to provide the support needed for students to meet with success both within their Deaf and hearing communities (Gale, 2010).

11-6 Educational Responses for Children Who Are Deaf or Hard of Hearing

Students who are deaf or hard of hearing, like most other populations of students with special needs, are a very heterogeneous population. Because of this, each child will need an individualized educational program (IEP) to specify supports and services needed. A continuum of services is also essential to address the range of strengths and needs of each student.

In 2007, 52 percent of these students were served primarily in regular classes (spending over 80 percent of their time in general education classrooms), 17.5 percent received services in both the resource room and general classroom, 17 percent received services primarily in special education classes (in general classroom < 40 percent of the time), and 14 percent attended separate environments or residential schools (U.S. Department of Education, 2009). Figure 11.4 shows the placements of children who are deaf and hard of hearing for their primary educational services.

Making sure that students who are deaf receive support that is both intense and sustained enough to make a difference is challenging given their low incidence in any given school district. Districts may face difficulty gathering the resources needed, hiring personnel with the appropriate expertise for teaching children who are deaf, securing and maintaining appropriate assistive technologies, and monitoring and adapting best instructional practices to meet student needs.

11-6a Organizational Structures and Supports for Students with Hearing Loss

The continuum of services needed to support students with hearing loss includes traditional schools as well as special programs and residential schools.

RtI Approaches for Students with Hearing Loss

RtI

Most students with hearing loss will require services provided within all three tiers of the response to intervention (RtI) model. Finding the optimal set of services for each child requires data showing the child's strengths and needs. Since

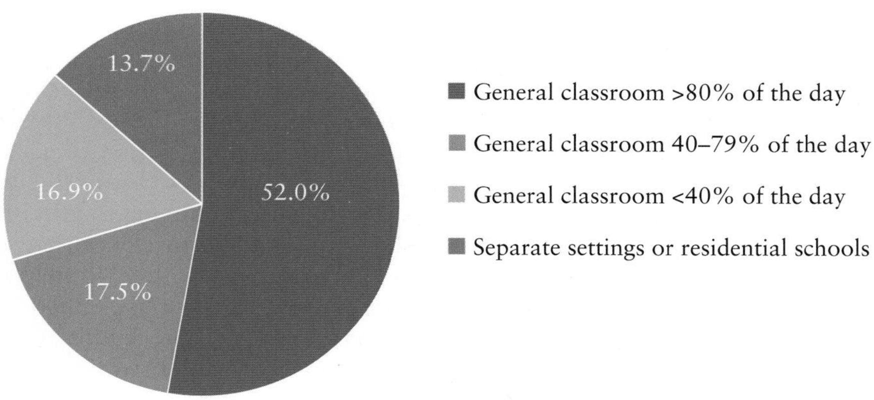

Figure 11.4 Educational Settings for Students Who Are Deaf or Hard of Hearing
Source: Data Accountability Center. (2011). *Part B Educational Environments 2011 [data file].* Retrieved from http://www.ideadata.org/PartBEnvironments.asp

the needs of children with hearing losses are dynamic and can change as they develop, assessment of these strengths and needs must be completed annually or possibly more frequently. Frequent assessments of strengths and needs are essential for several reasons including:

- The increasing educational and social demands placed on children as they grow up
- The changing physical structure of the ear and the need to make sure that amplification devices and other assistive technologies still fit and still work
- The rapid advancement of technology, with new options emerging at a quick rate
- The evolving needs of the child across the grade span

In addition to the need for formal assessments, the RtI approach hinges on collecting data that shows how each child is learning and monitoring the progress the child is making so that supports can be adjusted (Borders, Barnett, & Bauer, 2010). All of this data is used by the multidisciplinary team to plan for the child's strengths and needs (Cawthon, 2011).

The multidisciplinary team is critical in planning for children with hearing losses. This team usually includes an audiologist, a speech-language pathologist, and sign language interpreters, in addition to the child's teachers and parents and other professionals as needed. The audiologist is a critical member of the team, because he or she can assess the degree, type, and extent of the hearing loss and can help monitor the child's use of hearing aids and cochlear implant supports. The speech-language pathologist provides support for speech development and communication skills, and interpreters meet the child's communication needs within the classroom. The classroom teacher is responsible for the general education content, and the special education teacher (often an itinerant teacher for children who are deaf) works with the child on special needs (such as reading support using finger spelling and visual cues, use of picture boards for augmenting communication, intensive reinforcement of academic skills, and teaching strategies to help the child with academic and social tasks). The parents are critical team members, as they can both help the teachers understand the child's needs and work at home to support the child's development.

Universal Tier I Supports for Children with Hearing Loss

Like many children with a hearing loss, Kiesha, the child we met at the beginning of the chapter, is in a general education classroom for most of her day. Her fifth-grade classroom teacher, Ms. Langley, works to make sure that she is included in daily activities. Ms. Langley is also careful to check in with Kiesha periodically to make sure that she understands key information. The classroom library also has reading materials that are of high interest to all the students, and Ms. Langley is always on the lookout for readings on horses, fashion, and women's soccer, because these are Kiesha's favorites. The instructional strategies that she uses with Kiesha include more explicit instruction in vocabulary, additional hands-on materials for math and science, and word processing support for writing. Many of Ms. Langley's other students also benefit from these supports. One of the major differences for Kiesha is the periodic presence of the speech-language pathologist, Mr. Jackson. It is sometimes hard for Kiesha to participate in class discussions with all of the external noise and children talking over each other. To help with this problem, Mr. Jackson suggested a new procedure to the class, called "stop and think time," for some of the class discussions. Using this procedure, the class members must count to five before they raise their hands to answer a question, and during this time they must "stop and think." This has slowed down the discussions and allowed Kiesha to keep up and participate more. Interestingly enough, Ms. Langley has noticed that it has also increased the quality and length of the students' responses and has created time for a more reflective dialogue. Although the support of the speech-language pathologist is key to giving Kiesha strategies to help her understand what is happening in the classroom, he is not able to help in many informal situations, such as the playground or cafeteria when Kiesha is with her friends, so building Kiesha's own communication skills is also critical for her success (Stinson & Foster, 2000).

Kiesha is strong in math, and she often helps other students and leads the math talks for the class. This has built her confidence in speaking and has helped her with social relationships. Kiesha's parents know that reading is critical, and they work with her on special reading comprehension materials that Ms. Langley sends home. In addition to the Tier I supports, Kiesha also receives more intensive services at Tier II. A Summary of *UDL Supports for Students with Hearing Loss* can be accessed online..

TeachSource Digital Download

Targeted Tier II Supports for Children with Hearing Loss

The supports that a child receives at Tier II provide more intensive instruction in the academic areas and can also address special learning strategies or study skills. For Kiesha, Tier II activities include small group reviews with Ms. Langley to preview topics and skills that she plans to teach the following week or to review key things that have just been taught. Sometimes the special education teacher, Mrs. Cooke, works with small groups of children on study skills and organization strategies; Kiesha usually participates in these sessions. The guidance counselor also provides some Tier II supports in helping students become better self-advocates, and Kiesha has participated in several small-group sessions to learn and practice ways to help others understand and meet her needs.

Planning for the Tier II activities is usually collaborative. Ms. Langley often works with other members of the multidisciplinary team to determine the kinds of supports Kiesha needs. This collaboration is like a rhythmic dance, with different professionals taking the lead and others following, depending on the child's needs, but with everyone in tune and staying mindful of the importance of appropriate services to help the child be successful (Luckner & Muir, 2001). Even with extensive supports at Tier II, Kiesha, like most children who are deaf or hard of hearing, needs the individualized support of Tier III.

Intensive Tier III Supports for Children with Hearing Loss

The supports that children with hearing losses will receive at Tier III vary depending on their specific needs. Often support includes specific instruction on the use of hearing aids or cochlear implants. Instruction in speech reading and speech production is also important for many children. Specific instruction on communication skills and language development is often needed, though the specific form this takes will be determined by the child's needs. Examples of manual communication approaches, including American Sign Language, and Cued Speech, are given on the National Institute on Deafness and Other Communication Disorders website. Other forms of manual communication include Pidgin Sign English, Signing Exact English, and finger spelling.

Of these manual communication approaches, ASL is the only actual language with its own grammar and syntax. The others are manual coding approaches that use the structure of English, preserving its grammar and syntax. With greater emphasis on total communication, Tier III instruction is likely to focus on approaches that combine manual communication with oral methods.

ASL and Cued Speech:
http://www.nidcd.nih.gov/health/hearing/asl.asp

Kiesha's Tier III services include continued lessons in speech reading and communication strategies. Kiesha is given direct reading instruction using visual prompts and reading comprehension strategies (Schirmer & Schaffer, 2010). She also receives special instruction to help her in developing abstract language. This instruction includes a focus on multiple word meanings (mole as an animal, a skin blemish, and a spy collecting classified information), similes (*he has a head like a rock*), metaphors (*she is a moose*), onomatopoeia (the *whir* of the engine), idioms (*he pulled himself up by his bootstraps*), and inferences (*the inference taken from "the cold wind blew snow around the house"* is that it is winter). Explicit instruction that reinforces abstract language is often necessary for children with hearing losses to ensure that they do not miss critical nuances in communications by making literal interpretations of the message. The combined services in Tiers I, II, and III all help ensure that students have the supports they need to be successful.

Even with solid services provided across the tiers, a full continuum of services is needed to address the strengths and needs of students with hearing loss. These services must include special programs and a residential school for students who are deaf. A Summary of *RtI Approaches for Students with Hearing Loss* can be accessed online.

TeachSource Digital Download

Special Programs for Students with Hearing Loss

Because the needs of students with hearing loss can be quite demanding, the continuum of services must include special programs. Special programs for students who are deaf can extend and augment the services offered within the traditional school. These programs may include things like summer camps with an intense focus on the use of ASL for communication; Saturday or weekend programs for social gatherings and parent/family support networking; and special classes for reading or communications support. Because in many cases students who are deaf form a very small subset of students in any given school district, state and regional support may be needed to provide access to these special kinds of programs. In some cases residential schools for the deaf offer special programs for students who do not attend the school on a regular basis.

Residential Schools for the Deaf

The National Center for Education Statisics (2008) estimated that approximately 12.4 percent of deaf students in 2006 were educated primarily in residential schools. This means approximately 9,000 students attended residential schools for the deaf. Many factors have led to the shrinking attendance in residential schools. These include the increase in newborn screening programs and early intervention, decreasing incidence of severe to profound deafness, increasing numbers of children with cochlear implants, federal legislation directed at providing access to general education curriculum and setting, and the closing of state schools for the deaf (Luckner & Muir, 2001). Students who do attend residential schools tend to have more severe hearing losses, to come from lower income and lower socioeconomic status families, and to have poorer spoken-language skills. Also, a greater number of students have parents who are deaf or hard of hearing (Marschark et al., 2002). Although the trend is toward fewer students attending residential schools, these schools still provide an essential service for students who are deaf, and they must remain as part of the continuum of services available to meet students' needs.

11-6b Curriculum and Instruction for Students with Hearing Loss

Since some children will not have been identified before they enter school, one of the first responsibilities of the general classroom teacher is recognizing warning signs that a child might have a hearing problem.

The General Education Teacher's Role in Recognizing Hearing Problems

How does the classroom teacher identify a child with a possible hearing loss so the child can be referred for comprehensive examination? Indicators of a hearing loss can show up in several ways that allow teachers to recognize the potential

TABLE 11.3 Warning Signs for Potential Hearing Problems in Children

- ***Physical problems associated with the ears*** (earaches, discomfort in the ear or strange ringing or buzzing noises, discharge from the ears or excessively heavy waxy build up in the ear canal, pulling or scratching ear, frequent ear infections)
- ***Poor articulation of sounds when speaking*** (omits consonant sounds, difficulty with speech sounds)
- ***Extremely high volume for listening to audio materials*** (turning the sound up to a level that is uncomfortable for others)
- ***Cocking or turning the head to hear better*** ("cupping" of the ear with the hand to hear)
- ***Often requesting that audio information be repeated*** (misses auditory information the first time around or misinterprets oral information)
- ***Unresponsive or inattentive to normal voice*** (lack of attending in class may be a result of an inability to hear)
- ***Reluctance to participate in oral activities*** (if hearing is difficult, participation in discussions, debates, and other activities may be uncomfortable)

problem. A general education teacher can help identify a child with a possible hearing loss by observing his or her articulation, need for a higher volume of sounds, requests that information be repeated, and inattentiveness or unresponsiveness.

Table 11.3 lists specific student behaviors that can help teachers recognize potential problems with hearing.

Instructional Strategies for Accessing the Common Core State Standards for Children with Hearing Losses

COMMON CORE STATE STANDARDS

With most children who have hearing difficulties served in the general classroom for most of their day, it is essential that teachers incorporate strategies to help students be successful (Antia, 2007; Borders, Barnett, & Bauer, 2010; Luckner, 2006). The educational adaptations listed in Table 11.4 were developed to help children who have hearing loss gain access to the Common Core State Standards.

Luckner (2006) has outlined several strategies that can help students with hearing loss meet with success in a traditional classroom. He suggests that teachers structure the environment to facilitate communication by seating the student in a swivel chair close to the verbal interactions, minimizing background noise (using carpet, tennis balls on chair legs, acoustic tiles, and so forth), using amplification systems for primary speakers, and cueing the student when the primary speaker changes or an announcement comes in over the intercom. By intentionally modifying the environment teachers can increase academic engagement and decrease disruptive behaviors (Guardino & Antia, 2012). Luckner (2006) also recommends that teachers work to help hearing students understand hearing loss, learn some sign language, and adopt strategies that are helpful for students with hearing loss (face the students when talking, listen to them, and give them time to express themselves). With some intentional adaptations of the environment and support for social acceptance, students who are deaf or hard of hearing can be integrated into the general classroom. Making these kinds of small adjustments in the classroom environment can have a beneficial impact on the student. Students who are deaf and hard of hearing rated their quality of life significantly higher when they felt that their classroom participation was satisfying (Hintermair, 2011).

TABLE 11.4 Using Universal Design Principles to Give Students with Hearing Loss Access to the Common Core State Standards

Common Core Standard	Multiple Representations	Multiple Engagements	Multiple Assessments
Reading Standard Literacy, #9, Integration of knowledge and ideas, Grade 8 Analyze how a modern work of fiction draws on themes, patterns of events, or character types from myths, traditional stories, or religious works such as the Bible, including describing how the material is rendered new.	Advance organizers Text/Narrative Graphic organizers for compare and contrast Pictures Video with closed captions Dramatization with sign language Web-based text Story lines Short summaries of content (e.g., Cliff notes) Vocabulary builders Use picture or iconic prompts for material (e.g., an eye for narrative descriptions that promote visual images, and ear for words that evoke sounds)	Direct instruction on content, vocabulary, and strategies Reading text material with guided prompts for noting what you "see" and "hear" Guided reading for themes, patterns of events, and character types Watching dramatization or video (with closed caption) Discussions using appropriate support for participation Study buddy and note-taker support Debates Develop graphic organizers: compare/contrast Create visual representations of information or images Writing activities Prepare presentations (Powerpoint, etc.)	Written products (concept webs, note cards, and drafts) Oral presentations with visual support Pictures of images or photo essay Compare/Contrast Graphic organizers Documentary film showing differences modern depiction vs. myth, traditional, or religious origin Essay on the major themes, patterns of events, or character types portrayed and their antecedents in myth, traditional stories, or religious works Create a work of art sharing modern view of a traditional theme, event, or character.
Math Standard, #1, Know that there are numbers that are not rational and approximate them by rational numbers. Number Systems, Grade 8 Know that numbers that are not rational are called irrational. Understand informally that every number has a decimal expansion. For rational numbers, show that the decimal expansion repeats eventually and convert a decimal expansion which repeats eventually into a rational number.	Hands-on Materials Charts, Graphs, Pictures Drawings Real-world applications Highlighted problems (key words in color) Flash cards: Words to math symbol or operations Use sign language, lipreading, or amplification for communication Create problem-solving process guide/checklist	Direct Instruction on Concepts with meta-cognitive or "think-aloud" explanations of process Use hands-on manipulatives Create flash cards for formulas of area, surface area, and volume Draw pictures representing problems Use commercial software for practice Use calculators for checking Create word problems based on real-world data collection	Traditional written assessment of problem solving Student-developed word problems on concepts Drawings, Pictures, Charts, Graphs Math talks Students find real-world examples of rational and decimal numbers

TeachSource Digital Download Access online

11-6c Assistive and Instructional Technology for Students Who Are Deaf or Hard of Hearing

Assistive technology is the term for any equipment or product that assists the learner with special needs. Federal law requires that assistive technology be considered for every student with an identified disability (CEC, 2006).

Alerting devices and **alarm systems** have been developed for the deaf and hard of hearing that show flashing lights or use vibration. There are numerous devices of this kind, including alarm clocks, fire alerts, doorbell signals, phone signals, and baby-cry alarms.

Hearing aids provide essential amplification for many individuals who are deaf or hard of hearing. The technology of hearing aids has advanced rapidly, and today's aids are small, powerful, and have special features to help differentiate speech sounds from background noise. In addition to hearing aids, there are several devices that facilitate hearing. These include assistive listening devices (ALDs), which increase the volume of the voice received and reduce other sounds in the environment; induction loop devices, an audio loop system that surrounds a seating area connected to a microphone and amplifies the sound received by the hearing aid; frequency modulated (FM) systems, in which the teacher wears a microphone that sends a direct signal into the child's hearing aid; infrared devices, which transmit sound via invisible light waves; and vibrotactic aids, which transmit sound through vibrators worn on the skin. More information on all of these technologies can be found through the Better Hearing Institute and the American Speech-Language-Hearing Association (ASHA).

Cochlear implants involve a surgical procedure in which electrodes are inserted into the cochlea. A microphone worn behind the ear receives environmental sounds and sends them through the auditory system (NIDCD, 2010; Edwards & Tyskiewicz, 1999; Steinberg & Knightly, 1997). Cochlear implants bypass the damaged part of the ear and stimulate the hearing nerve. They do not restore hearing, but they do provide a sound system that can assist the user in understanding incoming auditory stimuli (Marschark et al., 2002). They appear to be effective over a longer period of use if used consistently. Recent research indicates that children who receive implants, particularly during the preschool years or earlier, develop vocabulary, speech, and reading at nearly normal rates and in sequences similar to those of children who are not deaf or hard of hearing (Boons et al., 2012; Deafness Research Foundation, 2000; Fagan & Pisoni, 2010; Hayes, Geers, Treiman, Moog, 2009; Marschark, Rhoten, & Fabich, 2007; Martindale, 2007; Serry & Blaney, 1999).

Although hearing aids simply amplify sounds, cochlear implants with twenty-two to twenty-four wires send sounds of different frequencies to the brain, thereby providing a direct connection between speech and sounds in the environment. Currently more than 41,000 people in the United States have received cochlear implants (over 25,000 are children), and the demand for implants is increasing by 20 percent each year (NIDCD, 2010). However, these implants cost over $40,000, with a follow-up expense of approximately $20,000 per year (ASHA, 2013b). Health insurance may cover these expenses depending on the person's health care plan and costs can be covered by Medicare and Medicaid for families that qualify (NIDCD, 2010). Once the cochlear implant is in place, this is just the beginning. Extensive therapy so the brain can learn how to interpret sounds is still needed (NIDCD, 2010). Parents of children who have received cochlear implants feel that their relatively high expectations for their child's outcomes have largely been met (Hyde, Punch, & Komesaroff, 2010). The Deaf community, however, has not fully accepted cochlear implants, and many deaf individuals feel that cochlear implants convey a negative impression of deafness (Sparrow, 2010).

Another type of assistive technology, **Visual Voice Tools**, provides a variety of visual displays, such as a balloon getting larger in proportion to the loudness of the speaker's voice. The program is designed to improve voicing, pitch, timing, and

Better Hearing Institute
www.betterhearing.org

American Speech-Language-Hearing Association
www.asha.org

Abledata Assistive Technology database
www.abledata.com

Cochlear Implant Association
www.clcl.org

Visual Voice Tools
web.riverdeep.net

Susie Fitzhugh

Assistive technology such as hearing aids and cochlear implants allow students to participate in the inclusive classroom.

sustained production. Several online dictionaries of line drawings of sign language also exist.

Speech-to-print systems reproduce the classroom dialogue on a computer screen. In some cases a captioner who is in the room types the dialogue as it occurs, but more frequently the computer is equipped with voice-activated software. These approaches have a dual advantage in that the student can read the discussion as it is taking place and can review it later in either a printout or electronic form (Stinson & Foster, 2000).

Telecommunications and media access have increased dramatically over the past few decades. **Telecommunications** refers to the transmission of signals over distance for the purpose of communications, such as television and radio. **Media access** refers to the availability of information that can be accessed and utilized by individuals with disabilities and includes captioned television. Captioned telephone relay services are available in forty-seven states, with a federal mandate being considered by the FCC; phones with text messaging and access to the Internet allow real-time communication; and the media industry increasingly uses captions for movies and productions. *The National Directory and Resource Guide for Telecommunications and Media Accessibility for People Who Are Deaf, Late-Deafened, Hard-of-Hearing, or Deaf-Blind* (2010), known colloquially as *The Blue Book*, provides up-to-date information on how to use these resources.

Telecommunications for the Deaf and Hard of Hearing, Inc.
http://tdiforaccess.org/

Instructional software programs are being developed at a rapid rate. High-speed computers make it possible to combine print, videos, sounds, and signs to help the student who is deaf or hard of hearing understand instruction. Multimedia programs are also available that contain video dictionaries of sign language (usually ASL). When users encounter an unfamiliar word, they highlight it and call up a video with a person signing the word. Applied computer technology has advanced to such an extent that special word processing systems can be used to translate written English into graphic finger spelling signed on the computer screen. The computer enables the student with severe hearing losses to practice both signed and written English. Speech recognition software converts speech to print and print to speech, allowing communication in a variety of settings. (Because advances in technology are so rapid, you may wish to locate more information by visiting the websites listed throughout the chapter.)

11-7 Family and Lifespan Issues

The family provides essential support for the child who is deaf or hard of hearing (Luckner & Muir, 2001). As members of the multidisciplinary team, the family helps shape the educational program for the child and reinforces the intervention in the home. Family-oriented approaches lead to better communication skills for children who are deaf or hard of hearing.

Focusing on the family system requires recognition of the family's strengths and respect for their values, beliefs, choices, and aspirations (Borum, 2012). It helps the family recognize the critical role that communication plays in the development of children who are deaf or severely hard of hearing. The child's development is facilitated when family members adopt interactive strategies to facilitate communication, encouraging the child to make requests, to respond, and to take the initiative. All these interactive patterns are important factors in effective learning, and they also stimulate the child to strengthen communication skills (Cruz et al., 2012; Bakar, Brown, & Remine, 2010).

When the parents of a child who is deaf are also deaf, they are likely to prefer having the child learn a sign or manual language, usually ASL, first. Children in this situation can learn a language early and may develop more quickly than children who are deaf and born to hearing parents, who may not recognize their child's needs for some time.

Most parents who can hear have little or no experience with deafness and may not know how to proceed with a child who is deaf. In many instances, they initially misperceive the condition, believing it to be an inability to speak rather than an inability to hear. The earlier the hearing problem is identified, the sooner appropriate support can be provided to the child and the family.

When early intervention for children who are deaf or hard of hearing begins in the home as soon as the child is identified and is continued in early intervention centers, the child experiences long-term positive gains (Gottardis, Nunes, & Lunt, 2011). The family, however, continues to play a key role as the child grows. Parents in a study completed by Luckner and Muir (2001) shared stories of moving to a specific location to access better services, driving long distances to get needed supports, learning sign language so they could communicate, securing technology and medical support for their child, and working to provide additional social opportunities for their child. Parents also help to ensure that their child's educational experiences are appropriate and meet his or her needs. Providing support for the family is essential, because the family is central to the child's success (Jackson, 2011). Parents of children with hearing loss indicated that contact with other parents of children with hearing loss, support for social and emotional needs, and help with educational advocacy were their primary needs (Jackson, 2011). McNee and Jackson (2012) also looked at the important role that grandparents play in supporting the family and helping the child. They conclude that grandparents can be key players in helping the family cope successfully with the needs of their child with hearing loss.

11-7a Transitions for Students Who Are Deaf or Hard of Hearing

Transition planning for students who are deaf and hard of hearing must begin in high school and should address the student's interests, strengths, and support needs. Identifying the postsecondary options for

MORAL DILEMMA

Students Who Are Deaf or Hard of Hearing

Family-centered intervention is critical to providing appropriate support for the child, and parents are key members of the multidisciplinary team. The involvement of the family is essential for children who are deaf or hard of hearing, because families support and reinforce early communication skills with the child.

Consider the following scenario: You are working with the parents of Tony, a preschool child who is deaf. Tony has been fitted with hearing aids, but even with amplification his residual hearing is very limited. The professionals on the team feel that he should receive a cochlear implant. Tony's mother is very worried about the risks of surgery and the fact that this would destroy any residual hearing Tony has, thus making later use of hearing aids impossible. She also feels strongly that they should accept Tony the way he is. You think that Tony's father is more open to the idea of the implant for Tony because he is worried about how his son will fit in to the hearing world.

How can you bridge the gap between the professionals and the parents? How can you support the mother and the father as they wrestle with this decision? What stress does the difference in beliefs place on the family? And how do you as a professional know when to push for what you feel the child needs, in spite of the stress this might cause, and when to back off?

Ellen Senisi/The Image Works

When children who are deaf and hard of hearing can communicate life is much easier!

each student early in high school is helpful as the student and family begin preparing for young adulthood. Students who are deaf or hard of hearing face the same question as hearing students: What do I want to do when I grow up? The role of the high school guidance counselor is to help the students explore their options and to help the families plan for these options. This exploration may include vocational school, job training, and college. For each option a close look at the student's interests and strengths is essential to see whether it is a good match. If college is the choice, and

TABLE 11.5 Questions to Ask Colleges About Supports and Services for Students Who Are Deaf or Hard of Hearing

Key Question	Related Questions
1. Who is eligible for support services?	What are the identification criteria? Are further diagnostic assessments required or available? What costs are associated with services? Are qualified personnel available who have experience working with students who are deaf or hard of hearing?
2. What academic supports are available for students who are deaf or hard of hearing?	Are qualified interpreters available who use the student's communication methods? Can the students have note takers, modified tests, learning strategies support, tutoring, writing labs, math labs, study sessions, computer support? Is financial assistance available to help cover costs of assistive technology that may be needed by the student?
3. What kinds of counseling supports are available?	Personal and social adjustment support? Self-advocacy? Career guidance?
4. What are the college's policies regarding academic issues?	Number of credit hours that count as full time Extended drop-and-add periods Taping classes and lectures Transferring credits from community colleges Auditing classes prior to enrollment for credit Substitution for foreign language (does ASL count?) Grade-point requirements for graduations Priority scheduling for students with special needs Selection of academic advisors Academic probation Office hours for faculty Teaching loads for faculty
5. What lifestyle modifications can be made?	Can students have access to study carrels equipped with their technology needs? Are health services appropriate? Is an audiologist available?
6. What extracurricular activities and social supports are available?	Is there a Deaf community network on campus? What religious affiliations are available and accessible? Are clubs, sports, and other campus activities accessible?

SOURCE: Adapted from M. R. Coleman (1994). Postsecondary educational decisions for gifted/learning disabled students. *Journal of Secondary Gifted Education*, *5*(3), 53–59. Waco, TX: Prufrock Press.

currently there are over 30,000 deaf students in U.S. colleges (Smith, 2010), the next step is to identify the school that best fits the student's needs. Although most colleges have support services for students with special needs, some are more comprehensive. Key questions that should be asked to help make the choice of a college are given in Table 11.5. Many of these questions would be helpful for any student with special needs, and you may want to adapt these as you think about the transition needs of students with disabilities discussed in the other chapters.

Summary

- Since the early 1800s the field of deaf education has been evolving through both legislation and the formation of schools and educational associations focused on teaching children who are deaf.
- Thomas Gallaudet and Alexander Graham Bell were early leaders of deaf education within the United States.
- A hearing loss is defined by the degree of loss, the type of loss, and the age at which the loss occurred. The impact of hearing loss also depends on these three factors.
- The Individuals with Disabilities Education Act (IDEA, 2004) defines deafness as a hearing impairment that is severe enough that the child cannot process linguistic information through hearing, even when using amplification or hearing aids.
- Individuals who are deaf or hard of hearing are a heterogeneous group with different strengths, interests, and needs; what they share is difficulty hearing.
- The ear is a complex organ, and problems with any part of the ear or the auditory nerve can result in hearing loss.
- Central auditory processing disorders (CAPD) are considered to be a hearing loss because they prevent individualS from making full use of the sounds in their environment.
- A prelingual hearing loss will likely have a greater impact on language development than a postlingual hearing loss.
- Hearing losses span all age groups, affecting approximately 3 million children and youths under the age of 18.
- There are both genetic and environmental causes of hearing loss. Otitis media is the most common cause of hearing loss in children.
- Early identification and intervention is essential to help children develop the communication skills that will be the foundation for their later success.
- A hearing loss does not affect a child's overall cognitive level; some children also have special gifts and talents, while others have developmental delays.
- Many students who are deaf and hard of hearing will need additional support for language development and academic success.
- Many individuals with hearing loss also have other exceptionalities.
- Students who are deaf or hard of hearing may need additional support for social adjustment.
- The Deaf culture or community provides its members a shared social identity with strong bonds.
- Members of the Deaf community are bilingual and use both ASL for communication with others and American English for reading and writing.
- Bilingual-bicultural approaches recognize the identities of individuals who are deaf or hard of hearing and acknowledge their membership in both Deaf and hearing communities.
- A multidisciplinary team is critical to the educational support of children who are deaf or hard of hearing, and an audiologist is a key member of this team.
- Total communication combines oral and manual methods to enhance the child's ability to communicate.

- Education services will likely be needed across all three tiers of intervention in the RtI model, and an IEP will need to be in place for many children.
- Technological advances have had a tremendous impact on the ability of individuals who are deaf or hard of hearing, allowing greater communication and access to information.
- Medical advances, especially cochlear implants, have dramatically changed the ability to hear speech sounds for many individuals who are deaf or hard of hearing.
- Family support is critical for the child's development.
- More and more students who are deaf or hard of hearing are attending college.

Future Challenges

1. **As hearing screening for infants increases, will we be able to provide adequate early intervention support for the children and their families?**
   Early intervention is key to the success of individuals who are deaf or hard of hearing. As infant screening programs increase, we are likely to see growing numbers of children and families who need early intervention. How can we ensure that the infrastructure of professionals and resources needed to provide early intervention supports and services is in place?
2. **How can we make sure that the needs of students who are deaf or hard of hearing and who are served in general education classrooms are met?**
   With the majority of students who are deaf or hard of hearing being placed in general education classrooms for part or most of the day, making sure that their needs are met is essential. How can we ensure that the multidisciplinary team includes an audiologist, that the interpreter has had experience working with children, and that teachers receive the support they need to be most effective with the child?
3. **How will the expanding use of cochlear implants affect individuals who are deaf or hard of hearing?**
   The demand for cochlear implants is growing each year, and implants are being used with more infants. Cochlear implants seem to have dramatically opened access to speech sounds for individuals who are deaf or hard of hearing. Preliminary research suggests that when cochlear implants are in place and are used, the language and academic trajectory for the child is significantly improved. Yet because this is still a relatively new technology, there are still questions. What impact will these changes have on the Deaf community? How will we ensure equitable access to this technology for children whose parents cannot afford the expensive procedures?

TeachSource Digital Download Access online

Key Terms

acquired hearing loss p. 357
alarm systems p. 377
alerting devices p. 377
American Sign Language p. 351
auditory acuity p. 357
auditory brainstem response (ABR) p. 361
auditory processing p. 357
auditory steady state response (ASSR) p. 361
bilingual-bicultural approach p. 369
bone-conductor test p. 361
central auditory processing disorder (CAPD) p. 357

cochlea p. 356
cochlear implant p. 357
cochlear nerve p. 357
congenital p. 357
conductive hearing loss p. 357
congenital hearing loss p. 359
Deaf community (culture) p. 359
decibel (dB) p. 353
eardrum p. 356
hearing aids p. 377
media access p. 378
mixed hearing loss p. 357
otitis media p. 360
otoacoustic auditory emissions (OAE) p. 361
play audiometry p. 361
postlinguistic hearing loss p. 358
prelinguistic hearing loss p. 358
pure-tone audiometry p. 361
semantics p. 366
sensorineural hearing loss p. 357
speech-to-print systems p. 378
telecommunications p. 378
TORCHS p. 360
total communication method p. 352
vestibular apparatus p. 357
Visual Voice Tools p. 377

Resources

References of Special Interest

Luckner, J. & Cooke, C. (2010). A summary of the vocabulary research with students who are deaf or hard of hearing. *American Annals of the Deaf, 155*(1), 1–67. Students who are deaf or hard of hearing tend to have smaller vocabularies than their hearing peers. It is important to address this gap, given that vocabulary is critical in communication, reading, thinking, and learning. In this literature review, the authors summarize research published in peer-reviewed journals between 1967 and 2008 and provide suggestions for future research.

Luckner, J., & Handley, M. C. (2008). A summary of reading comprehension research undertaken with students who are deaf or hard of hearing. *American Annals of the Deaf, 153*(1), 6–36. The purpose of this study is to identify, review, and summarize peer-reviewed research published in journals related to reading comprehension and school-age students who are deaf or hard of hearing. The study covers research spanning over 40 years.

Marschark, M., & Spencer, P. E. (Eds.) (2011). *Oxford handbook of deaf studies, language, and education* (2nd ed.). Oxford, UK: Oxford University Press. This comprehensive handbook gives a thorough overview of the history of deaf education, impact of schooling, and language acquisition for children with hearing loss. Included are specific examples and instructional ideas, as well as case studies and vignettes.

Moores, D. F., & Martin, D. S. (Eds.) (2006). *Deaf learners: Developments in curriculum and instruction.* Washington, D.C.: Gallaudet University Press. This book reviews the culture of deaf learners and how they should be included in mainstream classrooms. The authors incorporate standards from national associations, including NCTE and NCTM.

Journals

American Annals of the Deaf
http://gupress.gallaudet.edu/annals/
Communication Disorders Quarterly
http://cdq.sagepub.com
Journal of Deaf Studies and Deaf Education
http://jdsde.oxfordjournals.org

Journal of Speech, Language and Hearing Research (American Speech-Language-Hearing Association)
www.asha.org

The Volta Review
http://listeningandspokenlanguage.org/TheVoltaReview/

Professional Organizations

Alexander Graham Bell Association for the Deaf and Hard of Hearing
http://listeningandspokenlanguage.org/

Division for Communicative Disabilities and Deafness (DCDD) of the Council for Exceptional Children
http://education.gsu.edu/dcdd/

Gallaudet University
www.gallaudet.edu

National Association of the Deaf
www.nad.org

National Association of the Deaf Captioned Film/Video Program
http://www.dcmp.org/

National Technical Institute for the Deaf **http://www.ntid.rit.edu/**

Laurent Clerc National Deaf Education Center (formerly known as the National Information Center on Deafness, NICD)
http://www.gallaudet.edu/clerc_center.html

National Institute on Deafness and Other Communication Disorders
www.nidcd.nih.gov

PEPnet2
http://www.pepnet.org

Sorenson Communication
www.sorenson.com

Children with Visual Impairments

CHAPTER 12

Standards Addressed in This Chapter

All of the CEC Standards are addressed within this chapter. Please see the inside book covers for the complete list of the standards.

CEC

FOCUS QUESTIONS

12-1 How has the field of education for students with visual impairments (low vision and blindness) evolved?

12-2 What is the definition of "visual impairment" and how is it identified?

12-3 What are typical causes of visual impairments?

12-4 What are some general characteristics of children with visual impairments?

12-5 Why is early intervention so critical for children with visual impairments?

12-6 How can families support children with visual impairments?

12-7 What are some needs of culturally and/or linguistically diverse children with visual impairments?

12-8 What educational responses are needed to address the needs of students with visual impairments?

12-9 What challenges in transition to the adult world are faced by youths with visual impairments?

Sighted individuals tend to take vision for granted with little appreciation for all that they experience, engage in, and enjoy simply because they can see. For individuals with visual impairments, low vision and blindness, the world is experienced through the other senses; hearing, touching, smelling, and tasting all become primary avenues for understanding. Many individuals have visual problems that are correctable, but for 3 or 4 people in 10,000, their visual impairments are so severe that they cannot be ameliorated with glasses or contact lenses. These individuals have low vision or blindness. In this chapter, we discuss the special needs of children who are visually impaired and the educational adaptations needed to help them meet with success.

Brian Mitchell/Corbis

12-1 Brief History of the Field of Visual Impairments

Formal efforts in the United States to educate children with visual impairments began in Boston in 1829 with the establishment of the residential school now called the Perkins School for the Blind. Perhaps the most famous graduate of the Perkins school, Helen Keller, spent her life changing people's perceptions of what individuals who are blind can accomplish. In 1834, Louis Braille perfected his raised dots code of reading. Braille's system was inspired by Captain Charles Barbier's "night reading" system of coded messages impressed on thick paper that allowed soldiers to communicate through touch without using light or sound. Braille's raised dot reading system is still used today. In 1900, public school classes for children who were blind were organized in Chicago. Some thirteen years later, other classes for children with severe visual impairments were established in Boston and Cleveland. In the early 1900s, many students with blindness attended residential institutions, but as the century progressed, more and more students attended neighborhood schools.

With the passage of the Education for All Handicapped Children Act (PL 94-142) in 1975, access to public education for students with visual impairments increased and teacher preparation programs expanded. The development of assistive technologies also shaped instruction for students with blindness and low vision, giving them greater access to information and experiences for learning.

Before the implementation of the Individuals with Disabilities Education Act (IDEA) of 2004, children with multiple disabilities that included visual impairments were often refused education in schools for the blind and were placed in settings that focused on their other disabilities while ignoring their visual problems. Today, students with multiple disabilities constitute the majority of students with visual impairments, with estimates ranging from 50 to 75 percent of the total number of children with visual impairment. Chapter 13 addresses the needs of children with multiple areas of disability.

12-2 Definitions and Identification of Visual Impairments

Association for Education and Rehabilitation of the Blind and Visually Impaired
www.aerbvi.org

The legal definition of **blindness** sets a physical standard of sight at less than 20/200, meaning that one cannot see with vision correction at 20 feet what the typical person sees at 200 feet. A person with **low vision** would have, after correction, 20/70 to 20/200 vision. However, these definitions are not helpful for educational planning. As educators, we think of how a child can use sight for learning. Children with blindness cannot use vision for learning but may still be responsive to light and darkness and may have some visual imagery.

Children with low vision have difficulty accomplishing visual tasks, but they can learn through the visual sense using special technologies and teaching techniques. The major educational distinction is that children with blindness use their tactile or auditory senses as their primary learning channels, whereas children with low vision may, with aid, still use the visual sense as their major avenue for learning.

12-2a Identification and Assessment of Visual Impairments

Although most children with low vision and blindness are identified by parents and physicians long before they enter school, preschool vision screening, which

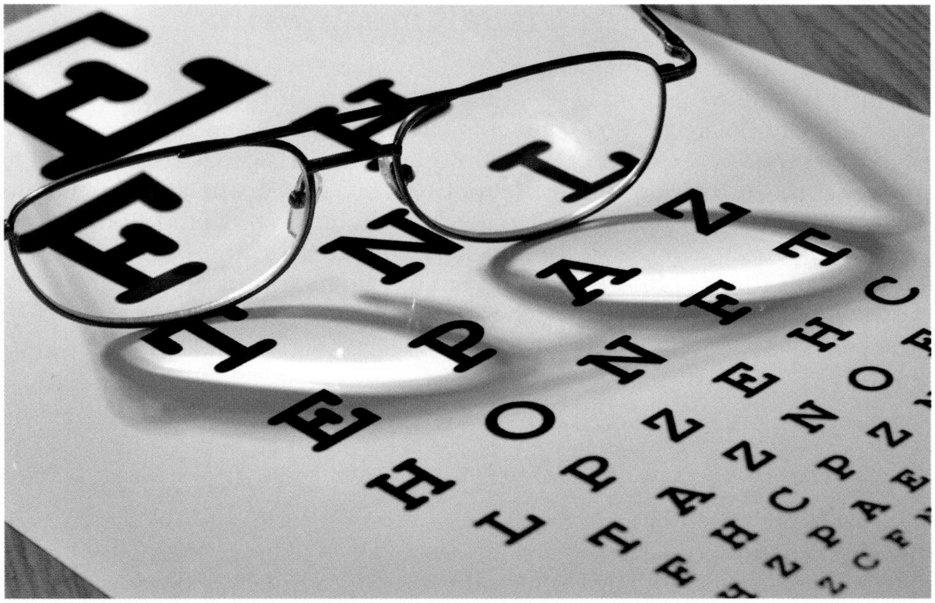

Figure 12.1 Near-Acuity Card

identifies children with moderate vision problems, is required by the majority of states. The standard school screening instrument for far-point visual acuity is the Snellen chart, which has rows of letters in gradually smaller sizes that children read at a distance of 20 feet. A variation of this for screening young children consists of capital *E*s pointing in different directions. The child is asked to indicate the direction in which the arms of the *E* are pointing. Near-point vision, used in reading and close tasks, can be screened using near-point cards like the ones shown in Figure 12.1. It is important to know what the student can read at near point, and the gradations of size here can give some understanding of the student's needs in responding to print. When potential problems with vision are found during screening, a full assessment is needed to identify the type and degree of the difficulty.

A comprehensive vision assessment includes an ophthalmological exam and an assessment of functional vision (Das, Spowart, Crossley, & Dutton, 2010). The ophthalmological exam looks at the structure of the eye, visual attention and fixation point (ability of the eye to focus), and visual acuity (both near and far point). This part of the assessment must be done by a qualified ophthalmologist. A functional assessment of vision is also important because this establishes the kinds of supports a child will need to be successful within different environments and with different tasks. The functional assessment may be done by a teacher of the visually impaired or an orientation and mobility specialist. Using a kit with a variety of visual prompts, the specialist determines the child's eye preference, visual field, ability to scan, and other aspects of vision that are needed in everyday activities.

A learning media assessment is also needed when the child reaches preschool age (around 3 years of age). This assessment helps determine how the child uses vision, touch, and hearing to take in and process information. If the child's preferred mode of learning is tactile, for example, and little vision is available, Braille may be considered the best mode of reading for the child (American Foundation for the Blind, 2013). Since many children with disabilities will also have visual impairments, a full vision assessment is recommended for all children with disabilities to establish their visual needs (Das et al., 2012).

12-2b Prevalence of Visual Impairments

Children with visual impairments qualify as having a low-incidence disability and make up a very small percentage, less than 1 percent, of the school population. There are approximately 26,000 students with low vision and blindness in the United States (National Center of Education Statistics, 2012), making it difficult to form classes for instruction in most school systems. In years past, most students with visual impairments were enrolled in state schools for the blind. Today, however, there is a strong effort to serve students in their local schools, and many residential schools for the blind are closing or changing their missions (Conference of Educational Administrators of Schools and Programs for the Deaf [CEASD]/ Council of Schools for the Blind [COSB], 2010).

12-3 Causes of Visual Impairments

A wide variety of conditions can cause serious visual impairments in children from birth to age 5. The potential causes include hereditary conditions, infectious diseases, cancer, injuries, premature birth, and various environmental conditions. In order of prevalence, the most common causes of **visual impairment** for children in the United States are as follows:

- Cortical visual impairment
- Retinopathy of prematurity
- Optic nerve hypoplasia
- Albinism
- Optic atrophy, and
- Congenital infection (Schwartz, 2010, p. 139).

The widely scattered prevalence of these conditions makes it difficult to assign percentages to particular causes.

One of these causes of visual impairment, **retinopathy of prematurity**, was formerly called *retrolental fibroplasia*. This genetic disorder was widely believed to be caused by the overadministration of oxygen to premature infants in an attempt to save the life of a child. However, the condition appears to be more complicated and seems to be associated with low birth weight as well.

12-3a Genetic Factors and Visual Impairment

Genetic causes of blindness are relatively rare. Vision impairments are often associated with **albinism**, the absence or lack of pigmentation resulting from and inheritance of recessive genes, a condition affecting approximately 1 in 20,000 individuals (Kong, Fry, Al-Samarraie, Gilbert, & Steinkuller, 2012). The visual problems associated with albinism include **nystagmus**, rapid irregular movements of the eye; **myopia**, **hyperopia**, and **astigmatisms**, refraction errors that create blurred vision; **amblyopia**, a decrease in acuity due to poor transmission of information to the brain; and **optic nerve hypoplasia**, the underdevelopment of the optic nerve. Treatment may include surgery to reduce eye movements, glasses to reduce the impact of glare and improve vision, and the use of large-print materials (Zimmerman & Zebehazy, 2011).

The actual cause of the disorder is not usually of primary interest to the teacher, who must deal with the functional consequences of the disorders; those functional consequences would seem to be similar from one condition to another. So whether the cause was an infection or a hereditary condition, the teacher faces similar instructional needs for students with visual impairments.

12-3b The Human Eye

Vision, or visual interpretation, is a function of the brain, experience, and adequacy of the eye, the sense organ that receives stimuli from the outside world. Faulty visual interpretation can result from a defect in the brain, inadequate experience, or a problem with the eye (sense organ).

The process of visual interpretation is as follows: Light enters the eye, focuses on the retina, and is transmitted along the optic nerve to the brain, where visual information is interpreted. The visual cortex, located at the back of the brain, is highly specialized to process static and moving visual objects and to recognize patterns. Two people with well-functioning sense organs can interpret the same visual experience differently, depending on their training and experience. Educators of children with visual impairments are concerned primarily with adapting instruction to limit the impact of the impairment. An in-depth description of how healthy eyes operate and a new technology, the "bionic eye," is accessible online.

TeachSource Digital Download

12-4 Characteristics of Children with Visual Impairments

While there is wide variation in the patterns of development of children with visual impairments, in some areas their development may progress at a slower pace than that of children without disabilities. With a rich physical environment and encouragement to take reasonable risks, parents can increase the adaptive skills of their children, helping them to master key developmental milestones.

The Office of Special Education Programs in the U.S. Department of Education funded a large longitudinal study of the development of young children with visual impairment (birth to 5 years) in seven sites around the country, project PRISM. This seminal study enabled the investigators to assemble data on a population of 202 youngsters receiving services for low vision and blindness. The study established baseline conclusions about visual acuity, behavior, temperament, and environment in an effort to discover differences between children with visual impairments and typically developing sighted children of similar ages. Project PRISM administered 2,446 standardized tests to the 202 children during the course of the project (Ferrell, Shaw, & Dietz, 1998). Some of the findings from this effort were as follows.

- Sixty percent of the PRISM children had additional disabilities, and two-thirds of these disabilities were considered severe.
- The leading diagnoses for the PRISM children were cortical visual impairment (21 percent), retinopathy of prematurity (19 percent), and optic nerve hypoplasia (17 percent).
- The majority of developmental milestones for the PRISM children were delayed in comparison with those of typical children; children with additional disabilities achieved these milestones later than children without these impairments.
- Measures of social maturity and cognitive development showed delays for the PRISM children.
- Measures of parental stress found more high scores among the parents of the PRISM children when compared to parents of typically developing children.

These findings underscore the importance of providing services to the child and family as early as possible and emphasize the need for special attention to children who have more than one area of disability.

The exposure to various environments can help ensure that children with low vision and blindness have opportunities to learn about the world around them. Box 12.1 shares a visit to the beach for Angela and her friend.

BOX 12.1 A Visit to the Beach for Angela, a Child Who Is Blind

uwe umstätter/ImageBroker/Glow Images

There are many ways that we can use our senses to experience the world around us.

Angela, a girl who is blind, is going to the beach for the first time with her best friend, Leta. Leta, who is sighted, is looking forward to introducing Angela to the joys of summer life at the beach, and she has described where they are going so that Angela has some preparation for what awaits her as she first sets foot on the beach. The girls anticipate eating a picnic lunch on the beach, having bought and prepared the food together and packed it in their ice chest. The two beachgoers have loaded the chest into the car and carried it from the car to the beach. Together, they have paused to pick up some sand and feel it sift through their fingers before they venture to the shore. Leta has pointed out to Angela how the sand becomes damper the closer they get to the water and Angela has picked up some more sand on her own to examine these changes in texture. She has helped spread the blanket on the sand, noticing how the wind makes it difficult to spread it flat. After listening to an explanation of why it is important to protect her skin from the sun, she is prepared to rub the parts she can reach with sunscreen and she asks Leta for help with the parts she cannot reach. Angela's attention to the sounds, smells, and tactile sensations at the beach give Leta another perspective on beach life and form an important part of the friends' conversation. With assistance, Angela has stashed her shoes in a bag on a particular corner of the blanket; Leta hopes she will remember where to retrieve them when it is time to put them on and go home.

The day has been rich in information and less scary than it might have been for Angela. Leta has answered questions and shown her, in small, understandable, and pleasant steps, how enjoyable and interesting the beach can be. Angela may not comprehend how huge the ocean looks or how beautiful the sky is that day, but she has had a better chance of relaxing in the sun, enjoying a swim, and feeling like one of the magicians who produced the lovely picnic at the beach.

SOURCE: Liefert, F. (2003). Introduction to visual impairment. In S. Goodman & S. Wittenstein (Eds.), *Collaborative assessment: Working with students who are blind or visually impaired, including those with additional disabilities* (pp. 1–22). New York: American Foundation for the Blind.

12-4a The Information Processing Model

Figure 12.2 shows the impact of low vision and blindness on the information processing model (IPM). What we can see is that the lack of vision impacts many other aspects of the system. In particular, the *cognitive* and *expressive* aspects of processing information are likely to be significantly impacted by a lack of visual input. Children with visual impairments may, for example, have limitations in understanding the three-dimensional world in which we live.

Like Angela at the beach, children with visual impairments have little grasp of the vastness of the ocean or space because it is vision that allows us to understand these concepts. Also, children with visual impairments often have limitations in navigating their living space and in traveling from one place to another. Just as for all children, the emotional context can either support learning and independence or it can create fear and **learned helplessness**, the feeling that no matter what I do I cannot control the outcome so I may as well just give up and passively accept whatever comes my way. The emotional context, if negative, impacts the child's ability to make use of the *executive function* to its fullest in making decisions and choices.

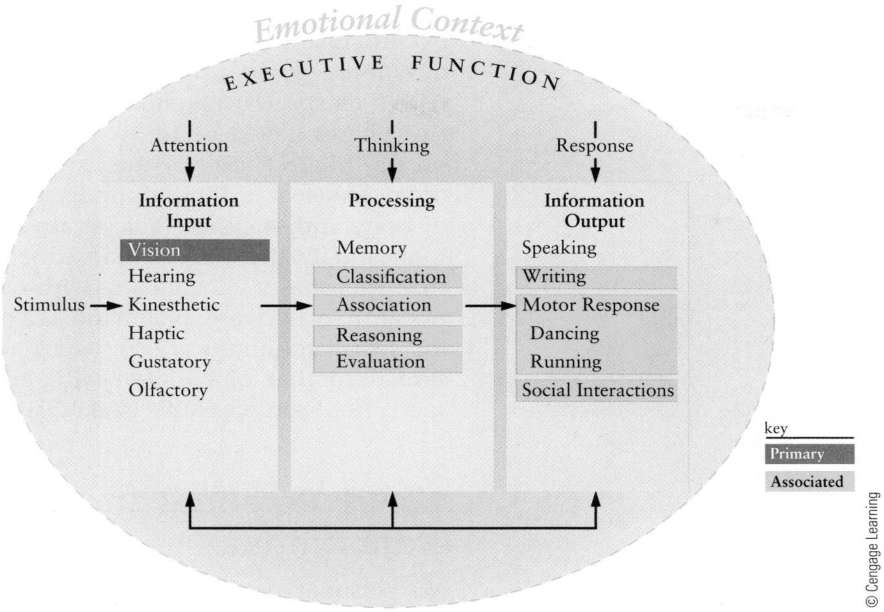

Figure 12.2 Information Processing Model for Students with Visual Impairments

TeachSource Digital Download Access online

12-4b Cognitive Development of Children with Visual Impairments

What we measure as intelligence in school-age children has been notably affected by their cumulative experiences in the early years of development. Lack of vision, then, is both a primary impairment and a condition that can hamper overall cognitive development. Without vision a child's ability to integrate the information gained in experiences is limited. Not being able to visually integrate information impacts the child's ability to use the thinking strategies of *association* and *classification* and also their ability to build an understanding of experiences through *reasoning* and *evaluation*. These limitations are especially notable when early intervention in the preschool years has not been provided. The verbal section of the Wechsler Intelligence Scale for Children (WISC) seems to provide the best measurement of intelligence for children with visual impairment.

12-4c Language Development for Children with Visual Impairments

Children with visual impairments acquire language in much the same way as sighted children, but the development of their language concepts is not supported by visual input. A sighted child develops the concept of a ball by seeing different balls; a child with blindness develops the same concept through tactile manipulation of different balls. Both are able to understand the word *ball*, and both are able to identify a ball.

Tadic, Pring, and Dale (2010), in their in-depth study of 26 children with visual impairments, found that despite some early delays and irregularities in vocabulary acquisition and semantics, structural language emerged without major concerns. However, pragmatic language, that used in social situations, was often more difficult for children with visual impairments. In social exchanges children

Dan Callister/Getty Images

World-class surfer Kip Jerger, lying down in water, leads by the hand as he teaches blind children surfing techniques in Manhattan Beach, California (July 17, 2000).

with visual impairments tended to ask extensive and sometimes inappropriate questions, lacked accompanying gestures with their speech, used imitative or repetitive phases, failed to adjust topics based on the interest level of the listener, and often showed a limited understanding of irony and sarcasm (Tadic et al., 2010). Interestingly, the study authors concluded that the ability of children with visual impairments to use pragmatic language for social communications seems to be similar to that of children with autism spectrum disorders (Tadic et al., 2010).

12-4d Personal and Social Adjustment

No personal or social problems *inevitably* follow from being visually impaired. However, the restricted mobility and consequent limited experiences of children who are visually impaired appear to cause, in some children, a state of passivity and dependency where social interactions may be limited (Levin & Rotheram-Fuller, 2011).

Jessup, Cornell, and Bundy (2010) studied the leisure habits of eight young people (ages 17–22) with blindness. The group's leisure activities included watching movies, sailing, skiing, rowing, reading, snorkeling, camping, and as the study was conducted in the United Kingdom, playing cricket. Through participation in leisure activities, these young people felt that they were able to make friends, develop positive self-identities, break through negative stereotypes of "blind people", have fun, stay fit, relieve stress, and feel accepted by others for who they are. The authors conclude that participation in leisure activities is central to the development of autonomy and resiliency for individuals with visual impairments.

This study indicates a need for continued implementation of programs designed to prepare students with visual impairments for a well-rounded adult life. The expanded core curriculum for students with visual impairments (discussed later in the chapter) includes leisure studies as a critical area of focus.

The story in Box 12.2 shows the importance of setting high expectations as a key part of developing both confidence and competence for students with visual impairments.

James Shaffer/PhotoEdi

Mobility is the number one element of independence for an individual with blindness.

12-5 Early Intervention for Children with Visual Impairments

It is especially important that the systematic education of children with visual impairment begin as early as possible. Sighted children

BOX 12.2 EXCEPTIONAL LIVES • EXCEPTIONAL STORIES

One Person's Reflections on the Consequences of Using a Unique Standard

I don't know when it began, this pervasive expectation that others would naturally give me a break because I am blind—probably as a very young child. I do remember in the first grade the teacher asked for volunteers to help me during recesses "so [I] wouldn't get hurt." I didn't need the help, but I have to admit I enjoyed the extra attention.

In fourth and fifth grades, the teachers let me complete only even-numbered problems in arithmetic homework while my classmates had to do them all. They told me that they were making this exception because I was blind and it took me longer to do my work. I had a teacher in seventh grade who required six book reports during the year for an A, but then turned to me and announced that four would be good enough for an A. Who was I to argue with such good fortune? Through high school, I guess I began to work the system to my advantage. I learned that if I looked uncomfortable, I wouldn't be called on in class; if I turned in partial work, I would often get full credit; if I happened to be late turning in assignments, it was OK because I was blind. Before long, I expected everyone to give me a break because of my blindness.

My first summer job after my junior year in high school really jolted me to reality. I was hired by a used car dealer to wash, wax, and vacuum six cars a day. At the end of the first week I questioned my paycheck—I thought they shortchanged me. My boss didn't pull any punches. "You serviced four cars a day this week, so I paid you for four cars a day. If and when you get up to speed and you finish six cars, I'll pay you what we agreed upon." I didn't argue—I knew he was right. I got myself organized, hustled a bit more, and put in some extra time that next week. I was proud to get my first paycheck on Friday; I knew I had earned it fair and square.

SOURCE: Reprinted from D. Tuttle & N. Tuttle, (2000). Psychosocial needs of children and youths. In M. C. Holbrook & A. J. Koenig (Eds.), *Foundations of education* (2nd ed.): *Vol. 1. History and theory of teaching children and youths with visual impairments* (p. 167). New York: AFB Press.

absorb a tremendous amount of information and experience from their environment in the ordinary course of events. We call this automatic absorption of information "incidental learning." For example, young children learn how to enter a group of children who are playing by watching others. No one explicitly teaches them the socially accepted skills needed to enter a group, and these skills may vary across cultural groups. Parents and teachers must, however, design experiences for children who are visually impaired to explicitly teach things that would be learned incidentally by sighted children (Celeste & Grum, 2010).

Many young children with a visual impairment are passive because they do not have a well-established motivation to move. For the sighted child, the environment is filled with visual stimulation: toys, enticing foods, bottles, people, colors, and shapes. The child has a natural impulse to move toward these elements. The child with a severe visual disability is not likely to be aware of these elements unless someone points them out. Other senses, such as sound and smell, must be used to entice the child. Interestingly, scent may come in to play for infants who are breastfeeding, helping them locate and orient to their mother for feeding.

An easily understood concept for the sighted child is **object permanence**. By the age of 6 or 7 months, sighted children realize that even when objects disappear from their visual field (mother left the room; the ball rolled under the couch), they still exist. This knowledge makes the world more orderly and predictable. And it makes sense to go after objects even if they are not in the line of sight. Object permanence is a more difficult concept for children with visual disabilities to understand. They need deliberate instruction and an organized environment

With appropriate support individuals with blindness can do many things.

before they can understand the concept that objects still exist even when they are not at hand.

The importance of starting education early for children with visual impairments was supported by a study showing that children with visual impairments are significantly delayed in their play skills, particularly symbolic play (Celeste & Grum, 2010). Because the children were functioning at expected developmental levels in other domains, such as receptive language, the study underlined the importance of helping them develop their play behavior. This is particularly important considering the heavy emphasis on play in most inclusive preschool settings and the role of play in developing social and academic skills (Celeste & Grum, 2010).

IDEA mandates services for infants and toddlers with disabilities and provides for earlier identification and earlier professional services for children with visual impairments. Early intervention should help reduce the number of secondary problems children with disabilities can experience.

12-6 The Role of the Family

Family members are the first teachers of a child with visual impairments. Parents and siblings are key to the development of the child's skills; this is one reason why legislation requires family involvement in the design and implementation of the Individual Family Service Plan (IFSP; Corn & Lusk, 2010).

Parenting a child with visual impairments offers some special challenges. Infants with visual impairments may be harder to console and less likely to calm themselves when distressed; they may show little interest in toys, use few facial expressions, may cry more often, and may use noncompliant posture (such as throwing their body back and waving their arms when being held) (Dote-Kwan & Chen, 2010). In addition, the infant's lack of sight may make bonding more difficult without eye-gazing contact between the parents and child. Families of young children with visual impairments will need help from an early intervention specialist to understand their child's temperament and the special skills that may be needed to help their child self-regulate and engage with social and physical environmental stimuli (Dote-Kwan & Chen, 2010).

Family members may also need to be reassured about the child's natural tendency toward exploring or taking risks. Parents are often overprotective of a child with visual impairments because of difficulties with mobility, but they can be reminded that children with typical vision often fall, twist ankles, and bruise as part of the experience of growing up.

Children with visual impairments gain confidence through exploring and gaining familiarity with their home and community. A parent's encouragement can coax an infant to turn toward a favorite toy or crawl into a new area (Fazzi & Naimy, 2010). Children with visual impairments also need to be part of the general family life, be given chores, and participate in family activities.

One of the major roles of families is advocacy for children with visual impairments; the National Agenda, discussed next, provides the platform for this work.

12-6a A National Agenda for Students with Visual Impairments

The national agenda for children with visual impairment was established in 1995 to help parents and professionals partner in advocating for services. The agenda was updated in 2005. Table 12.1 presents the agenda goals outlining best practices for children with visual impairments. For those programs that are *not* meeting

TABLE 12.1 National Agenda Goals for Children with Visual Impairments

1. **Early Referral.** Students and their families will be referred to an appropriate education program within 30 days of identification of a suspected visual impairment.
2. **Parent Participation.** Policies and procedures will be implemented to ensure the right of all parents to full participation and equal partnership in the education process.
3. **Professional Personnel.** Universities, with a minimum of one full-time faculty member in the area of visual impairment, will prepare a sufficient number of educators of students with visual impairments to meet personnel needs throughout the country.
4. **Case Loads**. Caseloads will be determined based on the assessed needs of students (rather than a set teacher-to-student ratio).
5. **Array of Services**. Local education programs will ensure that all students have access to a full array of placement options.
6. **Assessment**. All assessments and evaluations of students will be conducted by or in partnership with personnel having expertise in the education of students with visual impairments and their parents.
7. **Access to Instructional Materials**. Access to developmental and educational services will include an assurance that instructional materials are available to students in the appropriate media and at the same time as their sighted peers.
8. **Expanded Core Curriculum**. All educational goals and instruction will address the academic and expanded core curricula based on the assessed needs of each student with visual impairments.
9. **Transition.** Transition services will address developmental and educational needs (birth through high school) to assist students and their families in setting goals and implementing strategies throughout the life continuum commensurate with the student's aptitudes, interests, and abilities.
10. **Professional Development.** To improve student learning, service providers will engage in ongoing local, state, and national professional development

SOURCE: Corn, A. L., & Huebner, K. M. (Eds.). (2003). A report to the nation: The national agenda for the education of children and youth with visual impairments. New York, NY: American Foundation for the Blind.

these goals, it is a wake-up call that they are falling short of appropriate norms for good practice. The list itself can be a checklist for parents and others who want to make sure good practice is being adhered to.

12-7 Culturally and Linguistically Diverse Children with Visual Impairments

Just as the general public demographics in the United States are becoming more diverse, so are the demographics of students with visual impairments (Milian, 2013). The most recent, 2011, numbers from the Data Accountability Center (DAC, 2013) show that in the United States, students with visual impairments consist of 54 percent white, non-Hispanic; 23 percent Hispanic; 16 percent black, non-Hispanic; 4 percent Asian or Pacific Islanders; and 1percent American Indian and Alaskan Natives. In spite of the diversity of many students with visual impairments, the majority of educators working with these students are white females who likely have received little or no preparation in culturally responsive educational practices (Correa-Torres & Durando, 2012).

Correa-Torres and Durando (2012) surveyed over 204 educators (teachers, orientation and mobility specialists, administrators, and assistants) working with students with visual impairments who self-reported that they felt underprepared to meet the needs of their culturally diverse students. The participants identified six areas of professional development as being needed: culturally responsive teaching; resources to support culturally and linguistically diverse learners; information on how to work with culturally and linguistically families; information on working with interpreters; and additional practicum experiences with diverse children and families (Correa-Torres & Durando, 2012).

The respondents reported average caseloads of 19 students, with 7 of those students being from diverse backgrounds. Given that 58.8% of the participants also reported that they worked in suburban schools, the numbers of students from diverse families are likely higher in urban settings. The study concluded that in addition to the need for personnel preparation, attention should be given to recruiting more culturally diverse educators for students with visual impairments and to developing translators who can also serve as cultural brokers, helping educators and families build a greater understanding of each other (Correa-Torres & Durando, 2012).

12-8 Educational Responses for Students with Visual Impairments

The educational needs of students with visual impairments vary greatly depending on each student's level of functional vision (low vision or blindness), academic strengths and challenges, social and emotional needs, language and cultural background, and learning preferences. Because of these individual differences our educational responses must be tailored for each learner and the IEP (individualized education program) is used to plan for these responses. Figure 12.3 shows the educational setting currently used to address the needs of students with visual impairments.

More than half, 64 percent, of all students with visual impairments are primarily served within the general educational classroom for the majority of their day; an additional 13 percent spend one-third or more of their school day in the general education classroom. Twelve percent of students with visual impairments spend the majority of their school day in a setting other than the general education classroom, with 6 percent served in special schools and 4 percent attending residential schools.

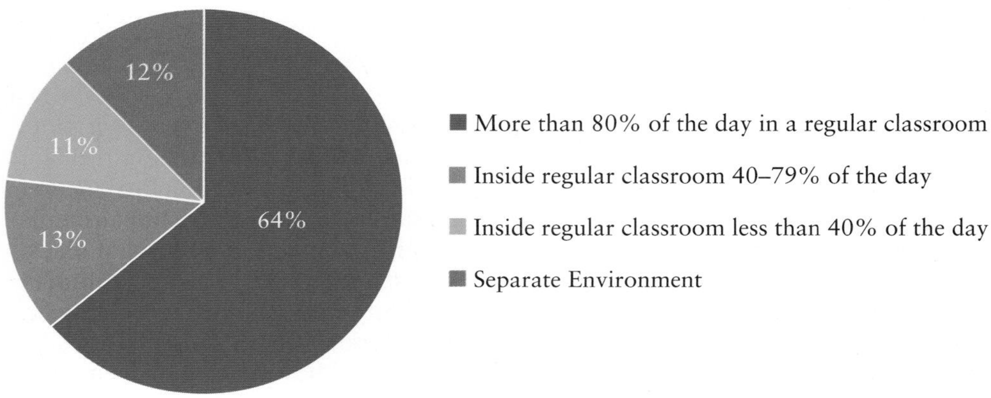

Figure 12.3 Educational Settings for Children with Visual Impairments
Source: Data Accountability Center. (2011). *Part B Educational Environments 2011* [data file]. Retrieved from http://www.ideadata.org/PartBEnvironments.asp

BOX 12.3 Jeanie and Wes

Jeanie, a second grader, entered the classroom and hung her pink baseball cap on the hook by the door. Her teacher of students with visual impairments, Ms. Carlyle, and her second-grade general education teacher, Ms. Burkette, had put up the hook so Jeanie would have a place to keep her cap and not have to hunt for it each time she went out. In preschool, Jeanie had usually crouched in the shade at recess before it was discovered that she has ocular albinism and photophobia. Jeanie's visual acuity is 20/200. She wears tinted eyeglasses; maybe when she was older she would wear contact lenses. With the tinted eyeglasses, indoor light almost never bothers her; but when outdoors, Jeanie really needs a cap with a visor as well. In the classroom, Jeanie sits at a desk in the front row, away from the windows. She reads regular second-grade books, sometimes propping them up on a reading stand, and occasionally using a handheld magnifier to view small print or the details of a picture. She was able to write using the same sort of pencil and paper as her classmates—and she could read what she had written, too.

Ms. Carlyle and Wes were practicing copying from the chalkboard with his handheld monocular. Wes has no trouble reading from the board with the device, but he habitually held the monocular in his right hand. The trouble was that Wes also writes with his right hand, so he had to lay down the monocular and pick up his pencil each time he was ready to write. It was an ineffective process, and Wes was having trouble keeping up when Mr. Taylor, the mathematics teacher, wrote a series of problems on the board. Ms. Carlyle had written several typical problems on the board, and Wes was experimenting with holding the monocular in his left hand while he copied part of a problem down with his right hand and then looking back at the board. This way, he does not have to put down either the monocular or the pencil. It is definitely a faster method, but Wes felt clumsy holding the monocular in his left hand. Ms. Carlyle told him that with practice, he might feel more comfortable and become more skilled in doing so.

SOURCE: Holbrook, M. C., & Koenig, A. J. (2000). *Foundations of education*. New York: AFB Press, pp. 464–465.

12-8a Organizational Structures to Support Students with Visual Impairments

A continuum of services options is vital to planning for the educational needs of students with visual impairments. These options range from within-school models, like RtI, to fulltime residential schools (Kamei-Hannan, Holbrook, & Ricci, 2012; CEASD/COSB, 2010).

RtI Approaches for Students with Visual Impairments

Schools with multi-tiered approaches, like RtI, are positioned well to address the needs of students with visual impairments if the levels of student needs can be matched with appropriate supports and services (Kamei-Hannan et al., 2012). Here is what this might look like for Jeanie and Wes, two students with low vision (see Box 12.3).

Universal Tier I for Students with Visual Impairments

Services are provided within the general education classroom by a teacher who is knowledgeable about students with visual impairments in collaboration with a specialist in visual impairments. The focus is access to the common core curriculum and full inclusion with same age peers. Universal design strategies are used to support learning, and intentional engagement strategies are used to facilitate social interactions. (Both of these are discussed fully later in the chapter.) Progress of student learning is monitored regularly so that supports and enhancements can be adjusted as needed. For Jeanie this means using tinted gels to cut down the glare on the computer, large print materials, and magnifiers as she completes her daily work. Wes, as noted above, uses a monocular to read from the board and is practicing his writing with this in hand. Wes also uses the computer with large print materials. A Summary of *UDL Supports for Students with Visual Impairments* can be accessed online.

TeachSource Digital Download

Targeted Tier II for students with Visual Impairments

In Tier II, students receive targeted support in their academic areas. These supports focus on areas where the learner needs more time for practice, additional direct instruction, or a modified teaching strategy to help them learn. With the help of the reading specialist, Jeanie is working on reading fluency using a computer-assisted program with enlarged font size that scrolls the words across the screen. Wes, who is an excellent reader, is working with math manipulatives that allow him to create three-dimensional graphs that represent the data he is collecting in his science experiment on weather. He is also learning to use raised line diagrams to help him display data. Their classroom teacher, Ms. Carlyle, oversees these activities in coordination with the reading specialist and the teacher of students with visual impairments (SVI).

Intensive Tier III for Students with Visual Impairments

Tier III, the most intensive support, is essential for children with low vision and blindness. The expanded core curriculum is often the focus of Tier III; the teacher of SVI takes the lead in these activities. For students with low vision like Jeanie and Wes, Tier III services may include specific instruction on technical assistance tools, self-advocacy coaching, and career and/or social skills counseling. Students with blindness may also need to learn Braille for reading and writing, and will need orientation and mobility training. The full expanded core curriculum needed for students with visual impairments is presented later in the chapter.

For the student with visual impairments to be successful in general educational settings using multitiered supports and services, the team approach is essential. The team includes the general education teacher, the teacher of students with visual impairments (SVI) and an orientation and mobility (O&M) specialist, in addition to others as necessary to address the strengths and challenges of the student. Ideally either the classroom teacher or the teacher of SVI, should take the role of case coordinator. This individual brings together all the information that relates to the child in a comprehensive assessment and leads a team of professionals who, with the parents, develop an IEP for the student. The IEP team relies on data about the student's strengths and needs to develop an optimal plan for instruction (Kamei-Hannan et al., 2012). A Summary of *RtI Approaches for Students with Visual Impairments* can be accessed online.

TeachSource Digital Download

Special Schools for Students Who Are Visually Impaired

Before the emphasis on the least restrictive environment and the inclusive classroom began in the 1980s, the education of children with visual impairments was often conducted in large residential state schools where students lived. There are still 51 residential schools in the United States and Canada (Council of Schools for the Blind [COSB], 2013). With the rapidly growing trend of educating students with low vision and blindness in the local schools, there is some question as to what will happen to the residential schools and the students who still need this level of support.

Special schools for students who are visually impaired are an essential part of the full continuum of services required by IDEA. Some students with visual impairments served in residential special schools may have additional areas of disability requiring more intense support. Others may need a curriculum that cannot be provided in the general education setting. The Texas School for the Blind and Visually Impaired, for example, is implementing a career education model that begins in the elementary school and continues through secondary school and beyond. At the elementary school level, the emphasis is on career awareness. Students may interview persons about their jobs and what they do to function in those jobs. At the middle school level, the emphasis is on career investigation. Students take a course in Introduction to Work and assess their own abilities, aptitudes, and interests. At the secondary school level, students focus on career preparation and career specialization, and the academic subjects are tailored to those objectives. This intensive focus on career development would be difficult to offer in a traditional neighborhood school.

Texas School for the Blind
http://www.tsbvi.edu/

There seem to be some specific benefits for children who attend special schools for visually impaired learners. One of these is access to assistive technology (Kelly, 2011). The use of assistive technology for learning and life skills has been shown to improve access to and success with the general curriculum (McDonnall, Cavenaugh, & Giesen, 2012) and to predict a better transition to effective post-secondary employment (McDonnall et al., 2012; Reed & Curtis, 2011; Kelly, 2011). In spite of the clear benefits that assistive technology offers students with visual impairments, Kelly (2011) found in a study analyzing Special Education Longitudinal Study (SEELS) data that less than half of the academically oriented students who needed assistive technology were receiving it. The study further showed that an average of only 36 percent of elementary and middle school students with visual impairments had the opportunity to use assistive technology. Students with visual impairments who attend special schools were, however, 1.8 times more likely to benefit from assistive technology for learning (Kelly, 2011). Because of the importance of assistive technology for accessing academic and life skills, students with visual impairments who are not receiving this support in their local school are placed at a distinct disadvantage (Kelly, 2011).

Special schools seem to offer another benefit for students with visual impairments: acceptance in a peer group and support for the formation of relationships. The importance of social identity and acceptance for students with visual impairments has been widely documented and will be discussed in more depth later in the chapter.

In addition to providing residential program options for students who need more intensive support and/or access to an appropriate curriculum, special schools are now playing a much broader role in supporting students, families, and educators (Sacks & Rothstein, 2010). Special schools are providing outreach services, offering information, conducting student assessments, and providing technical assistance to local schools (COSB, 2010).

They often provide an array of direct services for educators, families, and students with visually impairments who attend local schools (CEASD/COSB, 2010). The Council of Schools for the Blind lists the following services provided by special schools:

- Training and networking support for families
- Professional development opportunities for educators
- Summer programs and short courses for students focusing on areas of curriculum, assistive technology, and the expanded core curriculum
- Serving as a clearinghouse for instructional materials
- Developing specialized curricula and teaching practices
- Providing specialized and comprehensive assessments
- Assisting with research on students with low vision and blindness
- Offering Braille production for materials

In short, residential schools address children with diverse needs while playing a key role in the future education of children with visual impairments.

12-8b Curriculum and Instruction for Students with Visual Impairments

Lowenfeld (1973), a pioneer in educating children with visual impairments, proposed three general principles that are still important for adapting instruction for students with visual impairments:

1. ***Concrete experiences.*** Children with blindness and very low vision often learn primarily through hearing and touch. Working with concrete objects that they can feel and manipulate helps visually impaired children build an

understanding of the world. Through tactile observation of real objects in natural settings (or models, in the case of dangerous objects), students with visual impairments come to understand shape, size, weight, hardness, texture, pliability, and temperature.

2. ***Unifying experiences.*** Visual experience tends to unify knowledge, allowing us to process large amounts of information simultaneously. A sighted child who goes into a grocery store sees not only shelves and objects but also the relationships of shelves and objects in space, quickly understanding the various sections of the store and how they go together. Children with visual impairments cannot understand these relationships unless teachers allow them the *experience* of the grocery store. The experience must bring the "whole" into perspective, not only by giving students direct contact with objects, but also by explaining the relationships among the objects in the environment.

   Visual impairments can be isolating and may limit the individual's access to a variety of settings (Bell, 2012). Guiding children through space to help them understand large areas and expose them to different sizes, shapes, textures, and relationships of objects in the environment helps them generalize the common qualities of different objects and builds an awareness of spatial relationships.
3. ***Learning by doing.*** To learn about the environment, children with visual impairments must be motivated to explore that environment. An infant with blindness does not spontaneously reach out for an object unless that object attracts her attention through her other senses (touch, smell, hearing). Because of this it is critical to stimulate the children through sound, textures/touch, and smells, motivating them to explore and engage their environment.

The major considerations for successful instructional outcomes forstudents with visual impairments are the intensity and duration ofinterventions. To be effective, interventions must be significantly intenseand must be sustained over time.

COMMON CORE STATE STANDARDS

Access to the Common Core Standards: Universal Design for Learning

Mastery of the common core curriculum is important to the success of students with visual impairments. Academic accomplishments in math and reading are key predictors of life outcomes for students with low vision and blindness; because of this, it is essential that teachers ensure access to the curriculum and hold students with visual impairments to the same high standards as sighted peers (McDonnall, 2010). Mr. Jacob, teaches fifth grade and Halley, one of his students, is blind.

At the beginning of the year Mr. Jacob felt at a loss when trying to think about how to make sure that Halley was actively engaged with learning, but as the year progressed, Mr. Jacob's confidence (with the help and support of the teacher of SVI) increased and he grew excited about the unit he prepared to teach writing to the class. The unit focused on English Language Arts Writing Standard number 3:

> Write a narrative to develop real or imagined experiences or events using effective technique, descriptive details, and clear event sequences.

a. Orient the reader by establishing the situation and introducing a narrator and/or characters; organize an event sequence that unfolds naturally.
b. Use narrative techniques, such as dialogue, description, and pacing, to develop experiences and events or show the responses of characters to situations.
c. Use a variety of transitional words, phrases, and clauses to manage the sequence of events.
d. Use concrete words and phrases and sensory details to convey experiences and events precisely.
e. Provide a conclusion that follows from the narrative.

Mr. Jacob started the writing unit with a trip to a local bakery shop asking his students to document their trip with story strips. Working with their writing partners, the students filled in their story strips with pictures of each aspect of the trip. In addition to the sequence of events, he asked his students to pay particular attention to their sensory experiences during each part of the trip. He even gave them a template that asked them to note what they saw, heard, smelled, felt, and tasted. He told them that after the field trip they would work with their writing partner to describe the trip in an essay and that one of their essays will be published in the school newspaper!

Before the trip, Halley worked with her teacher of SVI to learn the basic layout of the bakery using a model. She had a chance to ask questions about the flow of the trip and to plan what she might need to bring. Halley decided to take a voice-activated recorder to keep her notes instead of her portable brailler (Braille writer) because she felt that the recorder would be easier to manage with her cane. She also decided to learn more about the bakery by visiting its website, which she did using her synthesized speech software to read her the content. She decided to print some of the information with her Braille output software so that she could have it on hand when she went to write her essay. The bakery website was pretty easy to navigate because the site creators had used the Web Accessibility guidelines as they designed the site. With her research done, Halley was excited about the trip.

Web Accessibility Guidelines
http://www.w3.org/WAI/eval/Overview.html

When the class returned they discussed the trip and created a word/phrase bank to capture their sensory experiences. The class was really impressed with Halley's descriptions of all that she had smelled, heard, touched, and tasted. The next day the students worked on their essays, receiving help and feedback from their writing partners. Halley did her essay outline in Braille but decided to dictate her essay using Dragon Speech, so that she could get a typed copy for her teacher. Her writing partner helped her make sure that no errors had crept into the essay because as Halley said, "sometimes Dragon Speech has a mind of its own!" Finally all the students read their essays to the class. Halley had printed hers in Braille, but had also memorized most of it. In her essay she concentrated on the sensory experiences and described these with such detail that, as one student said, "she makes me feel like I'm back there!" The class chose her essay for the school newspaper and sent a copy of it to the bakery thanking them for the great trip.

In order to master the curriculum, students with low vision and blindness must first gain access to it. When accessing the information is a struggle for students with visual impairments, more demand is placed on their information processing system, so they will have fewer cognitive resources available for problem solving or thinking about the information that makes learning challenging (Beal, Rosenblum, & Smith, 2011). **Universal Design for Learning (UDL)** can provide the scaffolding that gives students with visual impairments access to the content and assistive technology devices and tools that are part of UDL.

Halley accessed information about the bakery through the use of a tactile model, she used voice synthesizing software to learn more from the bakery website, and she used all her senses to directly experience the bakery during the trip. Halley also engaged with the information in multiple ways using all of her senses and interacting with both models and the actual bakery, as well as discussing the information with her classmates

TeachSource Video Connection

Watch the video "Amy: Accommodating A Gifted Student with Hearing and Visual Impairments in a Middle School Classroom." This video shows Amy, and how she is coping with visual and hearing impairments. After watching the Video Case, reflect on how Amy's strengths help her meet with success in the literature class. If you were part of Amy's multidisciplinary team, what suggestions would you make to further support her success? Amy is in middle school now; what additional challenges would you foresee for her in high school and how would you prepare her for these if you were her teacher?

Watch online

TABLE 12.2 Using Universal Design Principles for Accessing the Common Core State Standards

Common Core Standard	Multiple Representations	Multiple Engagements	Multiple Assessments
Reading Standard #4, Fluency, Grade 5 Read with sufficient accuracy and fluency to support comprehension. **a.** Read on-level text with purpose and understanding **b.** Read on-level prose and poetry orally with accuracy, appropriate rate, and expression on successive readings **c.** Use context to confirm or self-correct word recognition and understanding, rereading as necessary	*Low Vision:* Magnifiers Large print materials Computer screen Clean/bold print *Blindness:** Braille Audiobooks Voice synthesis Voiceactivated devices	*Low Vision:* Discussions/Talk High-interest readings Tell and write stories/poetry Focus on meaning Rhymes, chants, and songs Drama Choral reading Live reader *Blindness*: Braille writer Audiobooks Presentations Manipulatives (e.g., puppets to tell story)	*Low Vision & Blindness:* Story boards Oral presentations Reading journals Seminars Comprehension test Dramatizations Essays Discussions Interviews
Math Standard #1 Geometry, Grade 5 Use a pair of perpendicular number lines, called axes, to define a coordinate system, with the intersection of the lines (the origin) arranged to coincide with the 0 on each line and a given point in the plane located by using an ordered pair of numbers, called its coordinates. Understand that the first number indicates how far to travel from the origin in the direction of one axis, and the second number indicates how far to travel in the direction of the second axis, with the convention that the names of the two axes and the coordinates correspond (x-axis and x coordinate, y-axis and y-coordinate).	*Low Vision:* Magnifiers Large print materials Computer graphics Clean/bold print Raised-line diagrams Bold line drawings *Blindness*: Work with O&M specialist on spatial grids for room Three-dimensional model coordinate system	*Low Vision:* Chessboard math Graphing calculators Walk the room grids Ordered pairs games Different markers, colors, crayons, for drawing *Blindness*: Manipulatives for graphing O&M spatial grids Computer programs for graphing	*Low Vision:* Write word problems Tests of graphing Plot the points game *Blindness*: Assistive technology to access the assessments

*Note that strategies given for students with low vision should be used with students with blindness as appropriate.

TeachSource Digital Download Access online

COMMON CORE STATE STANDARDS

and peer editing partner. She used a voice-activated recorder, Dragon Speech, and Braille to capture and share her thoughts, and finally she presented her work in both written form and as a reading. Table 12.2 shows how UDL can help give students with low vision and blindness access to reading and math common core standards.

The use of universal design for learning is a starting place for giving students with visual impairments access to the core curriculum, but even more must be done to support success and independent life skills.

12-8c The Expanded Core Curriculum for Students with Visual Impairments

The **expanded core curriculum**, originally developed in 1996, identifies nine areas that students with visual impairments need to master. The expanded core does not replace the traditional academic areas and must be taught in addition to the core curriculum (Sacks & Rothstein, 2010). Because of the specialized nature of the expanded core it must be taught by a certified teacher of students with visual impairments and an orientation and mobility specialist. Table 12.3 shows the nine areas covered by the expanded core curriculum.

TABLE 12.3 Expanded Core Curriculum for Students with Low Vision and Blindness

1. Compensatory or Access Skills	• Concept development • Spatial understanding • Study and organization skills • Listening and speaking skills • Adaptations needed to access the general curriculum (e.g., Braille, large print, optical devices, tactile symbols, calendar systems, recorded materials)
2. Career Education	• Firsthand work experiences with jobs and roles in life • Mentor experiences • Exposure to career options
3. Independent Living Skills	• Personal hygiene • Food preparation • Financial management • Organizational skills
4. Orientation and Mobility (O&M)	• Understanding one's body in space • Planning trips to various environments • Navigating complex environments safely (e.g., crossing streets) • Accessing public transportation • Specific skills for independence (e.g., use of cane or dog)
5. Recreational and Leisure Skills	• Identifying areas of interest • Developing hobbies • Developing specific leisure skills (e.g., swimming, camping) • Becoming part of a group that enjoys the same leisure activity
6. Social Interaction Skills	• Gaze and focus when talking with others • Joining a group of peers • Asking someone out on a date • Establishing a social network • Sex education and body awareness
7. Self-Determination Skills	• Age-appropriate decision making • Evaluation of options • Making good choices • Self-advocacy skills

(Continued)

TABLE 12.3 Expanded Core Curriculum for Students with Low Vision and Blindness (*Continued*)

8. Use of Assistive Technology	• Ability to identify technologies that would be useful • Skills to use assistive technology for learning and life • Advocacy skills to get needed technology
9. Sensory Efficiency Skills	• Use of any remaining vision • Auditory learning (e.g., audiobooks) • Tactile learning (e.g., graphics, Braille) • Use of multiple senses for learning

TeachSource Digital Download Access online

Compensatory or Access Skills

Compensatory skills give students with visual impairments access to the general curriculum and foster autonomy in learning. Building on any residual vision the child has, strategies must be directly taught to facilitate access and enhance learning. For the child with visual impairments this means developing alternative methods for input using audio and tactile approaches.

Teaching Braille or Print

People with very low vision or blindness must develop a series of special communication skills, and using Braille may be a key for their success.

Braille is a system of touch reading developed in 1829 by Louis Braille, a Frenchman who was blind. The system uses embossed characters in different combinations of six dots arranged in a cell two dots wide and three dots high (see Figure 12.4). Users

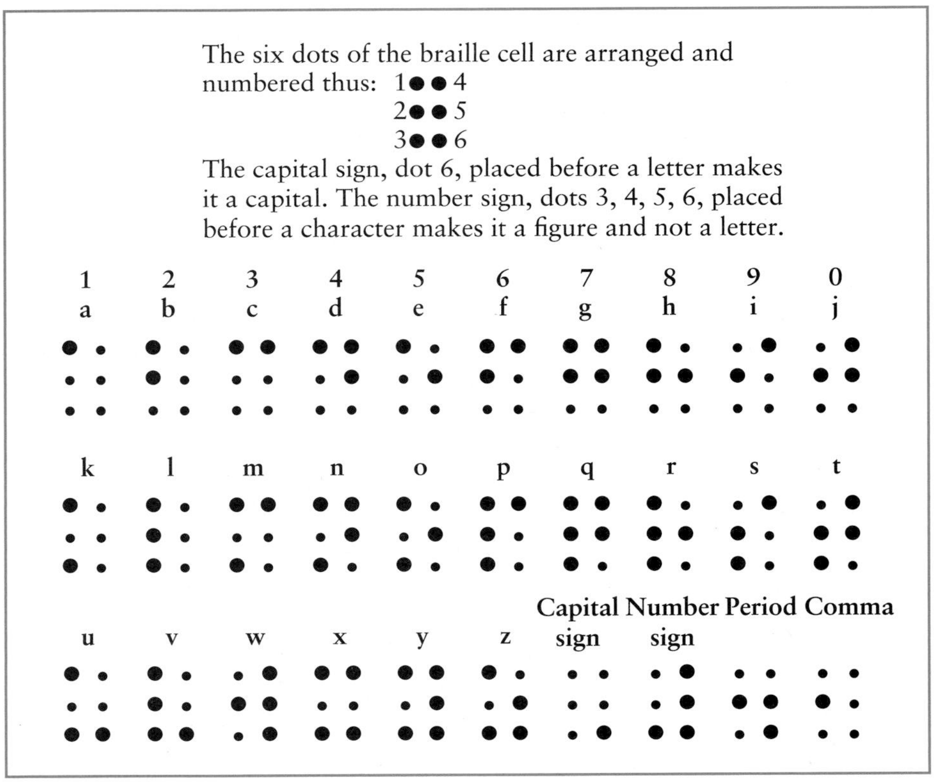

Figure 12.4 Braille Alphabet and Numerals

usually read with both hands—one leading, the other following. Advanced readers may use the second hand to orient themselves to the next line while reading the line above, and they may read as much as one-third of the lower line with the second hand. Punctuation, music, and mathematical and scientific notations are based on the same system.

One of the decisions faced by teachers and administrators is whether the child is capable of being a print reader or should be taught how to read Braille. This decision has long-term implications for the student. In many communities, itinerant teachers manage a growing caseload of children who are widely distributed across geographical areas, making it hard for teachers to have enough instructional time with each student. These teachers have less and less time to teach Braille and to transcribe print to Braille for their students. Without appropriate instruction it is difficult for students to become fluent Braille readers (Barclay, Herlich, & Sacks, 2010). It is very important for the school to provide sufficient time and practice so the children can master these crucial skills at a functional level.

Koenig and Holbrook (1995) identified characteristics of learners that can help teachers decide whether Braille, print, or a combination of both are best for the child; these guidelines are still used to help with decision making (see Table 12.4).

TABLE 12.4 Characteristics of Candidates for Print Reading and Braille Reading Programs

Characteristics of a Likely Print Reader	Characteristics of a Likely Braille Reader
Shows interest in pictures and demonstrates the ability to identify pictures or elements of pictures	Shows a preference for exploring the environment tactilely
Uses vision efficiently to complete tasks at near distances	Uses the tactile sense efficiently to identify small objects
Identifies his or her name in print or understands that print has meaning	Identifies his or her name in Braille or understands that Braille has meaning
Uses print to perform other prerequisite reading skills	Has an unstable eye condition or a poor prognosis for retaining the current level of vision in the near future
Has stable eye condition	Has a reduced or nonfunctional central field, to the extent that print reading is expected to be inefficient
Shows steady progress in learning to use vision as necessary to ensure efficient print reading	Shows steady progress in developing the tactile skills necessary for efficient Braille reading
Is free of additional disabilities that would interfere with progress in a developmental reading program in print	Is free of additional disabilities that would interfere with progress in a developmental reading program in Braille

SOURCE: Adapted from A. J. Koenig, & M. C. Holbrook, (1995). *Learning media assessment of students with visual impairments: A resource guide for teachers.* Austin, Texas: Texas School for the Blind and Visually Impaired.

In addition to using the best practices for teaching reading, Barclay et al. (2010) recommend the following six essential components of early Braille literacy instruction:

- Immersing the students in Braille
- Integrating listening, speaking, reading, and writing
- Focusing on meaning
- Modeling literacy behaviors
- Emphasizing process as well as product
- Encouraging students' participation in decision making (p. 745).

Whatever decisions are made regarding access to information needed for learning, students with visual impairments will need direct instruction on strategies, techniques, and tools to help them compensate for the loss of visual input. They also need access to appropriate materials, and this can be challenging (McDonnall et al., 2012). Reed & Curtis (2011) found that Braille transcripts were often not available, arrived too late to be of help, or were so poorly transcribed that they were of little use. Lack of access to materials and assistive technology may be the number one challenge faced by students with visual impairments (Zebehazy, Zigmond, & Zimmerman, 2012; Reed & Curtis, 2011).

Career Education

Meaningful and gainful employment for individuals with low vision, and especially for those with blindness, remains a challenge (Bell, 2012; Crudden, 2012). Traditional vocational education does not start early enough and the experiences are not intensive enough to provide adequate support for students with visual impairments (Sapp & Hatlen, 2010). Career education experiences for students who are visually impaired must begin in elementary school with age-appropriate chores and direct experiences to build career awareness (Crudden, 2012). Middle school students with visual impairments need continued career explorations through volunteer work and service learning projects, and high school students' career experiences should include part-time work for pay and mentored career opportunities (Crudden, 2012). Academic mastery (the common core curriculum) and competence in life skills (the expanded core curriculum) are both essential to successful employment (McDonnall, 2010). The Texas School for the Blind career curriculum described earlier is a good example of the intensity, direct instruction, and concrete experiences needed in career education for students with visual impairments.

Independent Living Skills

Sighted people take most of the skills needed for daily life for granted, but these can be challenging for individuals with visual impairments. Basic skills like cooking, choosing clothes that look good, and cleaning the house need to be directly taught with adequate hands-on experiences, so that these skills can be transferred to new situations. Developing appropriate independent living skills is essential to a satisfying and rewarding life for individuals with visual impairments (Sapp & Hatlen, 2010).

Orientation and Mobility (O&M) Skills

Being able to safely and independently navigate one's environment is a central aspect of autonomy and personal freedom; this can be one of the most challenging aspects of independence for students with blindness and very low vision. Simply defined, **orientation and mobility (O&M) training** involves developing an understanding of one's location in a given environment (orientation) coupled with the ability to physically move through that environment safely and independently (mobility) (Fazzi & Naimy, 2010). The goal of any mobility program is to bring individuals to their highest desired level of safe, independent travel.

O&M skills start with an understanding of one's body in space in relationship to other people and objects in the environment, and progress to independently navigating complex environments with safety. To do this individuals learn the floor plan for schools, home, and other buildings where they spend time. They also learn the routes to and from locations where they frequently travel, both walking and taking public transportation. To improve mobility, individuals with visual impairments use tools such as long canes, guide dogs, and sighted guides. Despite a variety of experiments with more sophisticated devices to aid in travel, the long white cane continues to be the instrument of choice for individuals with blindness (Pogrund & Fazzi, 2002). Because of the specialized nature of O&M skills, these must be taught by a certified O&M teacher (Sacks & Rothstein, 2010).

Recreational and Leisure Skills

Supporting individuals with visual impairments in developing age-appropriate recreation and leisure skills is not just a "nice" thing to do—it is essential to the individual's physical, mental, and emotional health (Jessup et al., 2010). Since low vision and especially blindness can be very isolating, direct and intentional introduction to and instruction in recreation and leisure activities is needed. Leisure and recreational experiences foster social relationships, build positive self-identities through developing competences, increase self-confidence, and develop a strong sense of pride when skills have been mastered (Jessup et al., 2010). One of the most powerful findings of a study on leisure activities was the debunking of negative stereotypes held by sighted people about what can be accomplished by individuals with low vision and blindness (Jessup et al., 2010)!

Many people find amazing the range of sports and leisure activities that students with visual impairments can participate in, given special instruction and aids. Such activities include bowling, bicycling, skiing, swimming, ice skating, and wrestling. In addition, card games and board games such as Scrabble and various arts and crafts are well within their capabilities when the materials are modified to accommodate visual impairments. It must be stressed, though, that special instruction is needed before the student with a visual impairment will feel comfortable and seek out such activities.

Social Interaction Skills

Social interaction skills are often learned through observation and are picked up by sighted individuals through incidental learning. For individuals with visual impairments, these same skills must be directly taught, coached, and practiced in a variety of settings beginning with young children in preschool (Celeste & Grum, 2010). Simply including students with visual impairments in the general classroom setting is not enough to ensure that meaningful social interactions will take place. Since few students in any given setting may have low vision and blindness, it can often be difficult to find peers who really understand each other. Coralyn's situation described in Box 12.4 helps us understand the dilemma a young girl with blindness faces with her sighted peers.

Mitch Wojnarowicz/The Image Works

Never underestimate what a child with visual impairments can do!

BOX 12.4 Coralyn's Story

Coralyn was socially isolated at school. She attributed this situation partly to being blind and partly to having different interests from those of her peers. "So you know, I didn't really care about fashion and makeup, which was quite a big deal in that age group. I was into music and opera, and no one else was into that at all." She tried to make friends, was criticized by school staff for not trying harder, and eventually gave up. When she began her music degree at the university, she found like-minded peers and "sort of suddenly managed to amass all these friends. I've never met so many people in one place who really don't have an issue with me being blind. I'm just 'normal' to them." When she joined a cricket team for individuals who are blind, she gained "a lot of confidence that I could get along with people who weren't music nerds." (Jessup et al., 2010, pp. 423–424).

The presence of accepting peer groups is one area where special schools can be helpful by bringing students together either through year-round or shorter term programming.

Self-Determination Skills

Self-determination is based on a combination of skills that promote self-regulation, goal-directed focus, and autonomy for the individual (Levin & Rotheram-Fuller, 2011). Self-knowledge and self-advocacy are key to self-determination for students with visual impairments. Guerette, Lewis, and Mattingly (2011) in a study of 51 students with low vision, found that while most of the students could describe their visual strengths and weaknesses, they had a limited understanding of the medical aspects of their impairments and so had difficulty communicating these to others. They recommend direct instruction about the specific causes of each condition and support for self-advocacy needed for success.

While there is clear agreement among professionals that self-determination skills are critical for students with low vision and blindness, these skills may be difficult to teach. Levin and Rotheram-Fuller (2011) looked at the effects of "Empowered Curriculum" for students with low vision and blindness and found that while students reported enjoying the lessons, only small gains were seen on measures of self-determination. The authors correctly conclude that while direct instruction of skills related to self-determination is critical, it is not by itself sufficient, and students must have many experiences that reinforce their autonomous decision making to strengthen these abilities.

Assistive Technology for Students with Visual Impairment and Blindness

Assistive technology gives students with visual impairments access to information, which is the first step to learning (Beal et al., 2011). The use of assistive technologies is a key predictor of the likelihood of paid employment for youths with visual impairments (Kelly, 2011).

IDEA mandates that assistive technology be "considered" when developing a student's IEP. The term "considered" has not been defined in detail. However, best practice indicates that consideration includes an evaluation of the student's assistive technology needs, the writing of goals and objectives related to assistive technology, and the acknowledgement of assistive technology as part of the expanded core curriculum for students with visual impairments (Presley, 2010, p. 607). Gaining access to assistive technologies can, however, be difficult, and parental advocacy plays a crucial role in this access (Kelly, 2011). Children with visual impairments whose parents attended *any* type of school-related meeting, special program, or family training were 1.4 times more likely to receive the assistive technology they needed (Kelly, 2011).

Often, the biggest stumbling block to using assistive technology is the child's reluctance. Many youngsters are self-conscious about devices that make them look "strange" or "weird." To overcome this self-consciousness, it is important to introduce these tools in a positive way (by playing games, for example) when the children are young and to allow classmates access to similar devices when needed so that the classroom is technology friendly.

There is a wide range of assistive technology devices to help children with visual impairments exchange information with sighted persons. A listing of some assistive technology devices for students with visual impairments can be found on the website for the text.

Robin Sachs/PhotoEdit

Assistive technology must be matched to the individual's needs and the demands of the enviroment.

While the benefits of assistive technology for students with visual impairments are clear, the disturbing reality is that less than half of the students who could benefit from this support receive it (Kelly, 2011). Kelly (2011) analyzed data from the two federal government longitudinal child outcomes surveys (SEELS and NLTS2) to identify what percentage of student with visual impairments who were academically oriented were using assistive technology. The high school students who were at or near grade level were the ones who used large print or Braille media and had access to assistive technologies; however, as noted above, less than half of the students in the study were using the assistive technology that they needed. Kelly concludes that part of the reason that students with visual impairments continue to fall further behind academically is that we do not provide them with the benefits of assistive technology to ensure that they have access to the information they need to learn.

Touch Graphics
http://www.touchgraphics.com/

Sensory Efficiency Skills

Information processing begins with input, or getting the information into the system, and this means using all the available senses as effectively as possible. Sensory efficiency begins with the use of any residual vision and includes the development of all the other senses to maximize input from and access to the environment. Students with visual impairments need a functional vision assessment (discussed earlier in the chapter) and direct instruction on the use of all their other senses. Many materials for students with visual impairments include tactile graphics, allowing students to access key information through touch. Students must be directly taught, however, to use these graphics in a deliberate, sequential manner so that the information makes sense (Hansen, Shute, & Landau, 2010). In addition to tactile information, auditory learning is critical for students with visual impairments.

Auditory and the Importance of Listening

Listening is the most important skill for learning through the auditory sense. This directed listening begins at birth when children turn their attention to speakers and listen to language that describes their environment. Directed listening continues in preschool, when young children listen to their classmates telling about experiences and describing favorite objects brought from home. Direct teaching of listening skills also occurs during orientation and mobility instruction, with auditory cues being used to orient to the environment for safe travel (Koenig & Holbrook, 2000).

As the child with visual impairments grows older, audio materials and books can become a favorite source of information and pleasure. Many users find that listening to information while simultaneously reading along in print or Braille allows them to cover the information faster and maintain better comprehension. Pairing the auditory with Braille or print is key, because listening alone does not help students develop or reinforce certain literacy skills. Because of this, students should not rely on auditory input as the only method of accessing information. The technology for accessing audio information is expanding at an exponential rate; with the passage of the 21st Century Communications and Video Accessibility Act (2010) requiring all smartphones, televisions, and modern communications technologies to be accessible to individuals with visual impairments and hearing loss, access will increase.

12-8d Individualized Education Programs

IEPs for children with visual impairment should include a variety of goals—some focusing on the effective use of the learning environment, some on instructional content, and some on skills that the student will need to perform effectively in the inclusive classroom. It will likely take a team of professionals to implement the goals.

Some sample IEP goals for such children are shown in Table 12.5. Note that Jerry has both academic and social goals in his IEP, reflecting the comprehensive goals of the program. The general education classroom teacher may need some help from an itinerant teacher to carry out these objectives successfully.

Teamwork is essential for implementing an IEP for students with visual impairments. In addition to the classroom teacher, teacher of SVI, and O&M specialist, the team may include other specialists as needed (e.g., gifted and talented, music, reading intervention). As always, parents and students are members of the team.

TABLE 12.5 Sample IEP Goals and Objectives for a Student Who Is Visually Impaired

Long-Term Goals	Short-Term Objectives
Jerry will use special devices and materials in order to perform at grade level in reading and mathematics.	**1.** Jerry will demonstrate effective use of various tools of magnification. **2.** Jerry will demonstrate effective keyboarding skills that allow him to do word processing. **3.** Jerry will score within one grade level of the class norm in academic achievement tests.
Jerry will establish effective social relationships with some of the nondisabled members of the class.	**1.** Jerry will join and participate in one of the clubs or organizations in the school that stresses social interactions. **2.** Jerry will work on class projects with other students as a contributing team member. **3.** In class parties, Jerry will join in the activities and interact with other class members.

SOURCE: Republished with permission of AFB Press, from *National agenda for the education of children and youths with visual disabilities, including those with multiple disabilities, revised.* A. Corn, P. Hatlen, K. M. Huebner, F. Ryan, and M. Siller, 2004, pp. 5–6. Permission conveyed through Copyright Clearance Center, Inc.

12-9 Transition to Independent Living and Work

Young adults with visual impairments face a number of challenges when transitioning from school to work. Low levels of employment for young adults with visual impairments have been well documened (Bell, 2012; Wolffe & Kelly, 2011). One of the challenges is with the system itself; navigating vocational rehabilitation and vocational educational supports can be difficult if agencies are not actively collaborating (Crudden, 2012). Transition service providers highlighted the need for increased interagency collaboration and greater communication with parents and students to promote successful transitions (Crudden, 2012).

McDonnall (2010) looked at factors that predict post high school employment for a sample of 140 individuals with visual impairments and found the following predictors: number of jobs held as a teenager, math and verbal achievement levels, early parental support, and self-reported health. Other factors that were important were the individual's use of assistive technology and levels of self-determination. She concluded that when students with visual impairments are not held to the same high academic standards as their sighted peers, lowered expectations lead to poor academic and employment outcomes. Supporting the development of independent living skills that lead to successful transitions is a major task of educators working with students with visual impairments. A synthesis of 15 studies found that effective transition programs include:

- Career awareness
- Job-seeking skills and placement assistance
- Social skills
- Career development activities
- Family support and involvement programs
- Work experiences (volunteer and service as well as paid)
- Independent living support, and
- Leisure skills (Cavenaugh & Giesen, 2010).

Wolffe and Kelly (2011), in their analysis of the National Longitudinal Transition Study number 2, which included 10,840 youths whose primary disability was low vision or blindness, further confirmed the importance of these aspects supporting successful transitions. They found a number of significant relationships between instruction in the core and expanded curriculum and positive outcomes such as employment, post-secondary training, and social engagement for students. Specifically, instruction in Braille, O&M, assistive technology, career counseling, job training, and academic achievements were found to relate to increased success with finding employment. The authors noted, however, that less than one-third of the visually impaired students had access to these kinds of volunteer and service opportunities. Assistive technology seemed to play a key role through social networking to increase invitations to activities with friends and establishing larger social networks for youth who had access to computers, Internet, e-mail, and chat rooms. This was an exciting finding, as social skills play a key role in work and life success (Celeste & Grum, 2010).

A mentoring program (Bell, 2012) in which 49 youth (ages 16–26) with blindness, from four states, were paired with successful adults with blindness showed positive results in career decision making and success. Bell (2012) found that after two years in the mentoring program, participating youth showed increases in social skills, an increased hopefulness about their lives, an improved attitude to their disability, and a more positive self-identity. Because the participants had an average age of 21, we do not yet know if the mentoring experiences will lead to successful lifelong careers. Bell concluded: "Mentoring is like planting a seed. We can provide the right conditions, ingredients, and environments for growth, but we cannot be certain that our efforts will be fruitful until the plant is fully grown." (2012, p. 177). Some special schools for students with visual impairments are offering a fifth year of high school, "the super senior year," focused on supporting transition (McDonnall, 2010).

Successful transitions to adult life and work depend on the cumulative efforts of teachers, families, and students working as a team (Crudden, 2012).

MORAL DILEMMA

To Braille or Not to Braille

Ruth, age 8, with very low vision, has been having trouble adjusting to her regular school program and has been referred to evaluation. After a comprehensive examination, the IEP committee has decided that Ruth needs to receive Braille training to aid her ability to master her lessons. Ruth, however, is seriously resisting such a move and is close to outright rebellion over the idea. The source of Ruth's concerns is clear. She is afraid that if other children see her using Braille, they will brand her as a "blind girl", and Ruth desperately wants to be like other children. After all, a number of the girls in her class wear glasses. Ruth would much prefer to continue to struggle with trying to decipher her lessons visually, even if she is unsuccessfully.

What should be the approach of the teacher in such a situation? What would you say to Ruth or to her classmates? Should her academic progress be bought at the price of social isolation?

Summary

- Children with visual impairments are classified into several ways. Educational classifications rest on the special adaptations necessary to help these children learn.
- Hereditary factors are one major cause of visual impairments in young children. Other causes are infectious diseases, injuries, and poisonings.
- A visual impairment can hamper the individual's understanding of the world, but such understanding can be enhanced through extending the experiential world of the child with visual impairments.
- Today most educators agree that the cumulative experiences of children as they develop affect intelligence. Youngsters with visual impairments lack the integrating experiences that come naturally to sighted children. The challenge for educators is to compensate for this lack of integration through special instructional programs.
- Early intervention for children with visual impairments is key, as many of these integrating experiences occur in early childhood. Early intervention provides children with visual impairments a foundation for their future educational and life experiences.
- Families play a key role in the ability of children with visual impairments to navigate the educational and social landscape.
- Just as diversity is increasing in the general U.S. population, so is it increasing among those with visual impairments. This highlights a need for culturally responsive practices and attentiveness to cultural difference in working with students with visual impairments.
- One of the important areas of curriculum adaptation is how to modify the standard core curriculum (e.g., math, language arts, social studies, science), including the Common Core State Standards, to take into account the special needs of children with visual impairments.
- Another major need is to implement the expanded core curriculum. That includes such items as orientation and mobility, independent living skills, uses of assistive technology, and so forth. Very specially trained personnel are needed for this expanded program.
- One of the by-products of restricted mobility and limited experience can be a passive orientation to life. Teachers play a critical role in helping students with visual impairments be active and independent.
- It is important for parents and teachers to help children with visual impairments develop their skills. It is equally important to let these children do things for themselves and to experience as much as possible the things that sighted children experience.
- Braille reading is slower than regular reading, a fact that can affect the academic performance of students with profound visual impairments.
- Orientation and mobility training are critically important parts of the curriculum for children with visual disabilities. Such services should be available in the public schools.

- Technology is improving the means of communication for those with visual impairments. It has also broadened their occupational choices. Keyboarding and word processing are particularly useful skills, along with access to necessary technology.

Future Challenges

1. **Will technology become more accessible for students with vision impairment?**
   Technology is wonderful—when it is accessible. The widespread distribution of assistive technology for those with visual impairments has been impeded by the cost of the equipment. How can we ensure access to appropriate technology for all students with visual impairments?
2. **Where will the specially trained teachers come from?**
   There has always been a thin supply of teachers with expertise in dealing with children with visual impairments. This situation has grown worse because of the many complications and multiple disabilities that are becoming the responsibility of the special education teacher. We are sure to face a major teacher shortage despite the financial help given by the Office of Special Education Programs in the U.S. Department of Education.
3. **How can we ensure that all students with blindness and low vision receive the instruction needed for success?**
   With low incidence of children with blindness and low vision and their wide distribution across geographic areas, it is challenging to provide instructional specialists (teachers of SVI and O&M) for each student who needs support. The intensity and duration of instruction determines the success of outcomes. This is particularly true in the expanded core curriculum areas. Current service delivery options for students with blindness and low vision may be spreading resources too thinly to have a significant impact on student success.

TeachSource Digital Download Access online

Key Terms

albinism p. 390
amblyopia p. 390
astigmatisms p. 390
blindness p. 388
Braille p. 407
expanded core curriculum p.405
hyperopia p. 390
learned helplessness p. 392
low vision p. 388
myopia p. 390
nystagmus p. 390
object permanence p. 395
optic nerve hypoplasia p. 390
orientation and mobility (O&M) training p. 408
retinopathy of prematurity p. 390
Universal Design for Learning (UDL) p. 403
visual impairment p. 390

Resources

References of Special Interest

Corn, A., & Erin, J. (Eds.). (2010). *Foundations of low vision: Clinical and functional perspectives* (2nd ed.) New York: American Foundation for the Blind. Division on Visual Impairments Quarterly: Special Issue on Diversity; Volume 58,

Number 2, 2013. This issue shares critical information on culturally and linguistically different children and the need for culturally responsive practices with assessment and family engagement. A valuable text covering the various challenges faced by children with low vision and their families. Special attention is directed to the various elements of assistive technology that can be of help. Educational adaptations to the core curriculum and the extended core curriculum are touched on, as well as the special additions necessary for children with multiple impairments.

Goodman, S., & Wittenstein, S. (Eds.). (2002). *Collaborative assessment.* New York: American Foundation for the Blind. The theme of this book is an appropriate assessment of children with visual impairments through a multidisciplinary team, each member bringing his or her own specialty to an overall collaborative assessment. Separate chapters are written by speech-language pathologists, psychologists, orientation and mobility specialists, and others. This professional collaboration is stressed not only in the initial planning for the child but also as continuing through the core curriculum.

Holbrook, M., & Koenig, A. (Eds.). (2000). *Foundations of education: Vol. I. History and theory of teaching children and youths with visual impairments* (2nd ed.). New York: American Foundation for the Blind. This volume, along with the companion Volume II, provides a solid basis for anyone interested in the education of children with visual impairments. The book focuses on the special developmental issues and problems that children with visual impairments face—challenges that require adaptations of the general education curriculum. Each chapter is prepared by a specialist on the topic.

Pogrund, R., & Fazzi, D. (2002). *Early focus: Working with children who are visually impaired and their families* (2nd ed.). New York: American Foundation for the Blind. This volume focuses its attention on young children, ages birth to 5, who are in need of early intervention and early education services. Educational vision specialists have been increasingly called upon to provide identification and services at an early age, because of the developmental importance of this age span. The eleven chapters, written by experts in the various developmental processes (e.g., cognition and language) explain how the family can be helpful in a team approach.

Silberman, R., Bruce, S., & Nelson, C. (2004). *Children with sensory impairments.* Baltimore, MD: Brookes. A thorough review of the challenge presented by children with visual impairments. Topics range from definitions to causation to the special techniques and technologies that can present a level playing field for these children in the public schools.

Spungin, S. (Ed.). *When you have a visually impaired child in your classroom: A guide for teachers.* New York: American Foundation for the Blind. A book filled with important ideas and techniques for teachers who have children with visual impairments in their classrooms. Covers the environmental changes that should be made, the curriculum adjustments to be introduced, and the technical tools that have to be included to meet the special needs of these students. Written by important veterans in this field.

Tuttle, D., & Tuttle, N. (2004). *Self-esteem and adjusting with blindness: The process of responding to life's demands* (3rd ed.). Springfield, IL: Charles C. Thomas. A book that focuses on the personal and social adjustment of children with visual impairment. A good review of what is known up until the present time.

Journals

Journal of Special Education Technology
http://www.tamcec.org/jset/

Journal of Visual Impairment and Blindness
www.afb.org/jvib.asp

Professional Organizations

American Foundation for the Blind **www.afb.org/afb**

Association for Education and Rehabilitation of the Blind and Visually Impaired **www.aerbvi.org**

Division on Visual Impairment of the Council for Exceptional Children **www.cec.sped.org**

National Association for Parents of the Visually Impaired, Inc. **www.napvi.org**

Lighthouse International **www.lighthouse.org**

New YORK city

CHAPTER 13

Children with Physical Disabilities, Health Impairments, and Multiple Disabilities

Standards Addressed in This Chapter

All of the CEC Standards are addressed in this chapter. Please see the inside book covers for the complete list of the standards.

CEC

FOCUS QUESTIONS

13-1 What are some of the historical events that contributed to disability awareness and legislation?

13-2 What are some characteristics of children with physical disabilities, health impairments, and multiple disabilities?

13-3 How are physical disabilities, health impairments, and multiple disabilities defined and what are the prevalences of these?

13-4 What challenges are associated with the assessment of children with physical disabilities?

13-5 What educational responses are needed for students with physical, health, and multiple impairments at each intervention tier?

13-6 What special issues face the families of children with physical disabilities, health impairments, and multiple disabilities across their life span?

Philosophers and theologians have debated for millennia about what makes us who we are—what makes us human. We have bodies, minds, and hearts, and many religions believe that we have souls, or spirits. None of these things alone is "us," but they combine to make us both amazingly unique and simultaneously just like everyone else. Often we are distracted by external things. We are judgmental about appearances, and we are fearful, dismissive, or just uncomfortable when the appearance of another is different from our own. We may

Realistic Reflections/Getty Images

experience this uneasiness with others of different races or cultures, and we may experience it with others who have physical disabilities. These outer differences, however, are like the waves on the ocean: They can sometimes look blue, sometimes green; they distract us with their constant motion; but they are not the ocean itself. The ocean consists of deep currents that flow with a steady power that can be felt but not easily seen. Just like the waves, the surface differences we see in the appearances of others may mask the deeper humanity that we all share. In this final chapter, we reflect on how the deep currents of humanity can allow us to connect with others in spite of our surface differences.

We explore the impact that physical disabilities, chronic health problems, and multiple disabilities can have on a child's life and look at how we can address the educational needs of these children and their families. The physical, health, and psychosocial needs will be uniquely individual for each child. Meeting these needs, however, requires that a comprehensive infrastructure be in place to support the child and family. Nowhere is the need for a multidisciplinary team more evident than in the identification of and planning for children with the complex needs discussed in this chapter. Working together, the multidisciplinary team provides that support network to help the child meet with success. In this chapter you will need to draw on all that you have learned thus far as you think about how the unique and complex needs of children with physical disabilities, health impairments, and multiple disabilities can be met.

13-1 History of Special Education for Children with Physical Disabilities, Health Impairments, and Multiple Disabilities

The first major legislative response to individuals with physical disabilities was passed in 1917 to help meet the vocational needs of World War I veterans with disabilities (Best, Heller, & Bigge, 2010). President Franklin Delano Roosevelt is credited with advancing the cause of individuals with disabilities through his New Deal; the 1935 Social Security Act provided funds for vocational rehabilitation, retirement support, and insurance benefits (Best et al., 2010). World War II veterans with disabilities added another powerful voice for physical access to jobs for individuals with disabilities. The civil rights movement served as a model for the disabilities rights movement, and the 1968 Architectural Barriers Act laid the groundwork for later accessibility legislation. The laws, however, are a means and not an end. They provide a platform that guides practice and allows us to advocate for needed supports and services. Laws in and of themselves do not, however, prevent prejudice, ignorance, or malice—they only mitigate it. People with physical disabilities may still face intentional and unintentional discrimination from other people and from the "system." Fear, ignorance, lack of experience, and inflexibility are the most common causes of discrimination, but with mandatory accessibility and expectations for inclusion, we are moving toward full participation for individuals with disabilities within all aspects of life.

Three key areas in which we have made substantial progress in supporting full participation for individuals with physical disabilities are *universal access, medical interventions* and *technology*. Greater accessibility for individuals with disabilities has been the goal of universal design. Universal designs and modifications like curb cuts, accessible bathrooms, wheelchair ramps, and elevators all help individuals gain mobility and offer accessibility for wheelchair-mobile individuals in most public settings. Private businesses are also encouraged to ensure accessibility for all individuals.

Advances in medicine have led to lifesaving interventions for children with physical disabilities and health impairments. As medical interventions have improved, the life expectancy for preterm infants has increased, and the overall life expectancy for children with severe disabilities has been extended. Improved medical interventions are also increasing the survival rate for soldiers who have been wounded in battle and who, like the returning veterans from previous wars, often have disabilities. Medical supports also can enhance the quality of life and prevent secondary complications. Newly developed prostheses can help individuals who have lost limbs regain functioning, new blood sugar monitors can maintain a continuous check to help regulate diabetes, improvements in surgical procedures for infants allow doctors to repair heart defects, and new treatments for cancer have led to nearly 80 percent survival rates for children (Landier, 2007).

The third area in which we have seen dramatic advances that affect the lives of individuals with disabilities is technology. Through technology we can now greatly increase mobility, communication, and independent functioning for individuals with disabilities. Later in this chapter, we look at the role of assistive technologies in supporting autonomous living for individuals with disabilities.

13-2 Characteristics of Children with Physical Disabilities, Health Impairments, or Multiple Disabilities

The following profiles describe two fifth-grade children, Pam and Henry. Both children have special needs, but each is unique in terms of individual developmental profile. Pam and Henry both have *cerebral palsy*, but as you will see Henry has multiple disabilities that are more severe.

Pam: Pam is a happy young girl who is slightly built and small for her age. She has spastic cerebral palsy (CP). Her CP is hemiplegic; it affects her ability to control the right side of her body. She uses a wheelchair with special supports to help her sit and move. Although Pam's motor control on her right side is severely affected by the CP, her cognitive and academic abilities are not affected; in fact, Pam is intellectually gifted, and her academic achievements are above grade level. She is an especially good speller and is always chosen first for class spelling bees. She has won the districtwide spelling bee twice.

Pam seems to make friends easily, and other students enjoy helping her get around. She is usually at the center of things in the lunchroom but sometimes feels left out when it comes to recess and physical education. Pam spends most of her day in the general education fifth-grade class, but because of her unique needs she also receives supplemental services. Twice a week she receives services for students with gifts and talents, and twice a week she receives services for students with disabilities. In her gifted education services, she participates in seminar discussions of advanced books and works on an independent project studying robotics. She is very interested in how robotics can be used to help people accomplish things that they cannot physically do. In her special education services she works on mobility, has occupational and physical therapies, and gets specific support for such things as self-advocacy and the use of assistive technology. Even with her special services, which take her out of the general education class for as much as four hours a week, Pam is doing well academically, but her teachers must be

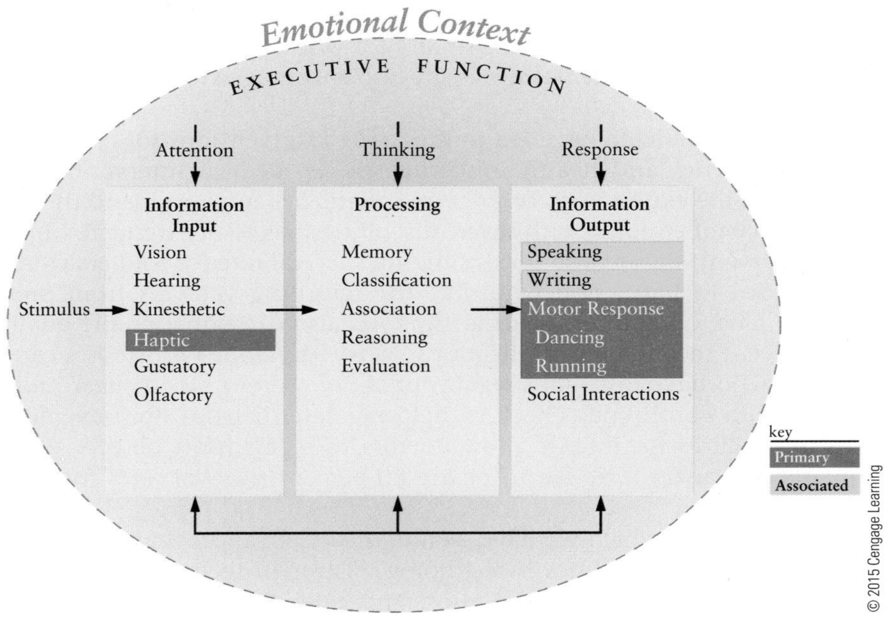

Figure 13.1 Pam's Information Processing Model

TeachSource Digital Download Access online

attentive to her fatigue level and responsive to her physical and emotional needs. The information processing model in Figure 13.1 shows the impact for Pam.

Henry: Henry, like Pam, has spastic cerebral palsy, but he has quadriplegia, meaning that all four limbs and his torso are affected, making his motor control very limited. Henry also has speech difficulties and severe intellectual delays. Because his needs are intense and complex, Henry attends a special self-contained class all day. His related services are integrated into his day, and he receives occupational therapy, speech-language therapy, and physical therapy weekly. The goals for Henry are more functional than academic, and his teachers are working to help him with basic communication skills. Henry uses a touch Dynavox (for digital speech) that is configured for each portion of his day to help him make choices and express his wants. The Dynavox shows pictures and icons and produces digitalized speech when the picture is touched. Because he has the most control over his neck muscles, Henry uses a head stick to point to the picture of his choice. When he arrives at school he chooses whether he wants to start his day with a story or with music; Henry must point to a picture of either a book or a CD player. His teachers have added a second level of choice that requires him to select the specific music or story he would like to hear. At lunch Henry can choose from pictures that show his menu options, and throughout the day he can select some of his learning activities. Because of his cognitive level, Henry is still learning to communicate simple, direct needs and wants. Making choices is key to developing Henry's ability to communicate and to supporting his development of self-determination. At home his parents use a similar system to reinforce and extend his communication.

Henry's teachers work to help him initiate activities and ask for things that he wants. Recently they have begun using a self-activating system that allows Henry to start his morning activities on his own by selecting and turning on the recordings. His teachers prompt him to start but wait for him to actually select the program. Some days this works smoothly, but on other days Henry stubbornly waits for his teachers to help him. Building autonomy in daily routines can be a slow process, and it is sometimes very hard for Henry's parents and teachers to allow him to do things for himself that they could do more quickly and easily. The reward for their patience, however, is seeing the pleasure in Henry's eyes when he does accomplish something on his own.

13-3 Definitions of Physical Disabilities, Health Impairments, and Multiple Disabilities

As we look at definitions of the disability areas addressed in this chapter, we first turn to the Individuals with Disabilities Act (IDEA) of 2004, but because the law includes only some of the areas we are addressing, we augment these definitions. IDEA 2004 specifically includes children with *orthopedic impairments, traumatic brain injury* (TBI), *deafblindness*, multiple disabilities, and *other health impairments* within its definitions (Council for Exceptional Children, 2006). Table 13.1 gives the legal definitions for each of these areas.

TABLE 13.1 Federal Definitions for Areas That Include Physical Disabilities, Multiple Disabilities, and Other Health Impairments

Disability Area	Definition from IDEA 2004
Orthopedic impairments	A severe orthopedic impairment that adversely affects a child's educational performance (e.g., cerebral palsy, amputations, and fractures or burns that cause contractures)
Traumatic brain injury	An acquired injury caused by an external physical force, resulting in total or partial functional disability and/or psychosocial impairment that requires special educational services
Deafblindness	Concomitant hearing and visual impairments, the combination of which causes severe communication, developmental, and other educational needs that require special services
Multiple disabilities	Concomitant impairments (such as intellectual and developmental disabilities–blindness or intellectual and developmental disabilities–orthopedic impairment) that result in severe educational needs that require special services
Other health impairments	Limited strength, vitality, or alertness, including heightened alertness to environmental stimuli, that are due to chronic or acute health problems such as asthma, attention deficit disorders, diabetes, epilepsy, cystic fibrosis, heart conditions, hemophilia, lead poisoning, leukemia, nephritis, ulcerative colitis and Crohn's disease, rheumatic fever, sickle cell anemia, or Tourette syndrome and that require special educational services

SOURCE: Material was drawn from the Council for Exceptional Children (2006). *Council for Exceptional Children policy and advocacy services: Understanding IDEA 2004 regulations*. Arlington, VA: Council for Exceptional Children.

TeachSource Digital Download Access online

TABLE 13.2 List of Physical Disabilities

Neuromotor impairments

Cerebral palsy (CP)—a disorder of movement and posture caused by damage to the motor control centers of the brain

Neural tube defects—occur when the neural tube surrounding the spine is exposed to the amniotic fluid during gestation (e.g., spina bifida)

Seizure disorders—caused by abnormal electrical discharge within the brain that disrupts the brain's normal functioning, may be symptomatic of an underlining problem (e.g., juvenile myoclonic epilepsy)

Traumatic brain injury (TBI)—such as severe head injury, the most common acquired disorder within TBI (more than two million each year within the United States)

Degenerative diseases

Muscular dystrophy—an inherited, progressive disorder that affects movement and function of the muscles (e.g., Duchenne muscular dystrophy)

Orthopedic and musculoskeletal disorders

Juvenile arthritis—onset before age 16, causing swelling, stiffness, effusion, pain, and tenderness in the joints; can lead to joint deformities, limited use of hands, and mobility problems.

Spinal curvatures—problems with the function of curvature of the spine include scoliosis in which the spine forms a "c" or "s" when viewed from behind.

TeachSource Digital Download Access online

13-3a Physical Disabilities

Understanding the physical disabilities that can affect a child can be difficult because of the wide variety of problems that can exist. Children with physical disabilities will require direct special education support, and thus it is important that teachers have a basic understanding of these conditions. Here we address some of the physical disabilities that are most likely to affect children. Additional information on less common physical disabilities can be accessed online. Table 13.2 gives a list and brief description of some of the areas of physical disability, including cerebral palsy (CP), neural tube defects; seizure disorders, traumatic brain injury (TBI), muscular dystrophy, juvenile arthritis, and spinal curvatures.

TeachSource Digital Download

Three areas are discussed more fully below to help teachers understand the impact a physical disability can have on a child's life and ability to learn.

Cerebral Palsy

Cerebral palsy (CP) refers to a disorder of movement and posture caused by damage to the motor control centers of the brain (Liptak, 2002; Pellegrino, 2002). *Cerebral* refers to the brain and *palsy* to disorders of movement (March of Dimes, 2010). The damage that results in cerebral palsy can occur before birth, during the birth process, or after birth from an accident or injury (e.g., a blow to the head, lack of oxygen). The condition affects muscle tone (the degree of tension in the muscles), interferes with voluntary movement and full control of the muscles, and delays gross and fine motor development.

United Cerebral Palsy Association
www.ucp.org

There are four major classifications of CP: **spastic**, **dyskinetic**, **ataxic**, and **mixed**. Children can have one or a combination of types of cerebral palsy. The form and degree of physical involvement vary from child to child, as do the affected areas of the body (Best et al., 2010). Figure 13.2 shows the brain areas involved and the regions of the body that will be affected for each type of CP.

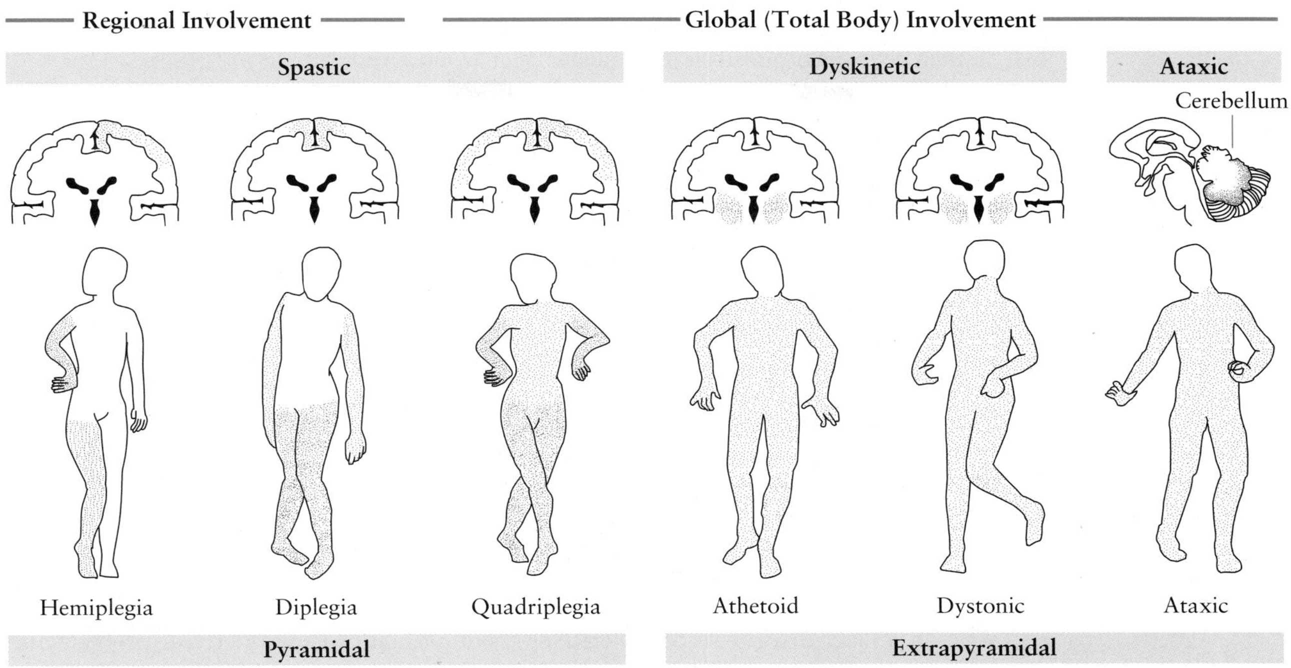

Figure 13.2 Regions of the Brain and Body Affected by Various Forms of Cerebral Palsy
Source: Dorman, J. P., & Pellegrino, L. (1998). *Caring for children with cerebral palsy: A team approach.* Baltimore, MD: Paul H. Brookes, p. 12. Reprinted by permission of the author Mark L. Batshaw.

Some children with CP are **hemiplegic**; just one side of the body (either left arm and left leg or right arm and right leg) is affected. Others are **diplegic**; the whole body is involved, but the legs are more severely involved than the arms. Still others are **quadriplegic**; involvement is equally distributed throughout the body.

Additional problems that can be associated with cerebral palsy include learning disabilities, intellectual and developmental disabilities, seizures, speech impairments, eating problems, sensory impairments, and joint and bone malformations such as spinal curvatures and contractures (permanently fixed, tight muscles and joints). Although CP can bring with it concomitant problems with vision, hearing, speech, and cognition, it is essential to remember that many individuals with CP have normal intelligence and that some, like Pam, are gifted and talented (Best et al., 2010). An individual's cognitive abilities can *never* be assumed by looking at the severity of the physically disabling condition; and as we discuss later in the chapter, cognitive abilities can be hard to assess in the presence of physical disabilities (Best et al., 2010).

Neurology and Brain Development: What We Know about Cerebral Palsy

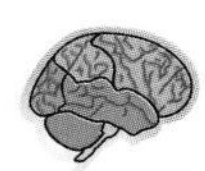

Cerebral palsy literally means brain weakness or problems with bodily positioning and movement. CP can result from damage to any part of the brain and can be either mild or severe depending on the extent of the damage.

The largest part of the brain is the cerebrum, which accounts for about 85 percent of the brain's weight. The cerebrum helps us reason. The right side seems to be more involved with abstract things like music and spatial abilities, while the left side may be more analytical and language oriented. The left side of the brain controls the right side of the body, so damage to different parts of the cerebrum will impact the child's functioning and body lateralization.

The cerebellum controls coordination and how muscles work together for movement and balance. The brain stem controls involuntary muscles that keep the body going without having to "think" (breathing, digesting food, heart beating). The brain stem also is the part of the brain that sorts out all the messages sent between the brain and nervous system. Emotional regulation seems to be located in the amygdala cells (an almond-shaped cluster of cells) on either side of the brain.

Think back to Pam and Henry—the two children you met early in the chapter. Each has CP, but the degree and type of impact are very different. See if you can determine, by looking at the type and extent of abilities and functions, which areas of the brain are damaged for Pam and for Henry.

Seizure Disorders

A seizure is caused by abnormal electrical discharge within the brain that disrupts the brain's normal functioning. Seizures can be general, in which the individual often loses consciousness, or partial, in which the individual maintains awareness of the environment (Porter & Kaplan, 2012). The intensity of the seizure varies from mild to severe and may include muscle contractions, purposeless movement, vocalizations, urinary and fecal incontinence, and frothing at the mouth. Most seizures will end spontaneously within a few minutes, but they will leave the individual disoriented and sleepy, with a headache and sore muscles. Absence seizures (formally called *petit mal*) may last only 10 to 30 seconds, during which time the child's eyelids may flutter and the child appears to be "spaced out." If not treated, these seizures can occur several times a day and cause the child to miss much of what is happening in the classroom.

A **seizure disorder** is considered to be symptomatic of an underlying problem and requires a full medical evaluation, including EEG and a possible MRI and CAT scan of the brain. With school-age children, the major cause of seizures is likely to be **juvenile myoclonic epilepsy**, a form of epilepsy that starts in childhood or adolescence. There are an estimated two million children and adolescents with seizure disorders in the United States (Porter & Kaplan, 2012). Most seizure disorders respond well to medical treatment (either medication or surgery). All teachers should be aware of how to respond to the immediate needs of a child during a seizure. The *Merck Manual for Neurological Disorders* (Porter & Kaplan, 2012) recommends the following:

> During a seizure, injury should be prevented by loosening clothing around the neck and placing a pillow under the head. Attempting to protect the tongue is futile and likely to damage the patient's teeth or the rescuer's fingers. The patient should be rolled onto his or her side to prevent aspiration.

With appropriate support, children with cerebral palsy can participate fully in life.

fatihhoca/Vetta/Getty Images

Once the child awakes from the seizure, teachers must provide immediate comfort and security to ensure that the child has time to rest and recover both physically and emotionally. The child may feel embarrassed and will need reassurance that things are back to normal. For children with known seizure disorders, teachers should plan ahead with the parents to have clean clothes available at school and contact information for immediate notification if the child has had a seizure. If the seizure is prolonged, lasting more than 5 minutes, or if seizures are occurring repeatedly, medical help should be sought. Parents and the child should also help decide what information should be shared ahead of time with classmates who may witness a seizure. Students who have witnessed the seizure must also be comforted and must be given appropriate information regarding the seizure. It is not unusual for children to worry that they might "catch" the disorder and to react by either withdrawing from or teasing the child. Negative reactions can usually be prevented if the teacher has prepared the students and takes time to help them process their feelings, but teachers must in all cases intervene when children are behaving in a hurtful manner to each other.

Epilepsy Foundation of America
www.epilepsyfoundation.org

Traumatic Brain Injury

Severe head injury is the most common acquired disorder in the category of traumatic brain injury (TBI) (Michaud, Semel-Concepcíon, Duhaime, & Lazar, 2002). With more than two million brain injuries occurring annually within the United States, it is also the most common cause of accidental death and disabilities (Porter & Kaplan, 2012). Injuries may be either closed (i.e., covered by flesh) or open, and the trauma caused to the brain can be mild or severe. Severe injuries may result in learning disabilities, attention-deficit disorders, personality changes, cerebral palsy, or other physical disabilities, but traumatic brain injury is considered a separate category of disability. TBI can result in cognitive, social, and language deficits as well (Pershelli, 2007). Individual cases of TBI may vary in terms of the severity of injury, manifestations of disability, and potential for recovery (Carter & Spencer, 2007; Keyser-Marcus et al., 2002).

Brain Injury Association, Inc.
www.biausa.org

13-3b Major Health Impairments

When children are dealing with serious health problems, their life and education will be impacted. The support needed for each child will depend on the range and severity of the problem. In this section we discuss some of the major health issues that children face (see Table 13.3). Additional information on less common health challenges can be accessed online. Medical experts take the lead on diagnosis and planning medical interventions, while the general education teacher takes responsibility for needed daily supports and for knowing the appropriate protocols for initial response in an emergency. Children with health concerns may also need some support from the special education teacher as well, and this support may be consultative in nature.

TeachSource Digital Download

Some specific challenges are discussed below, along with general ideas that teachers can implement for children with health impairments.

Asthma

Asthma, an immune system–allergy disease, is a condition affecting an individual's breathing due to bronchial swelling. It usually has three features: the lungs are swollen, breathing is difficult, and the airways react negatively to a variety of environmental triggers (such as dust, smoke, cold air, mold, and exercise). Asthma may also cause acute constriction of the bronchial tubes (CDC, 2009a). Asthma affects about 23 million Americans (7 million under 18 years of age) and accounts for between 3,000 and 4,000 deaths each year (CDC, 2009a). Asthma is

TABLE 13.3 List of Health Impairments

Major health impairments

Juvenile diabetes: a disorder in which the blood sugar is abnormally high because the body does not produce enough Insulin (Type 1) or the body is insensitive to insulin (Type 2)

Asthmal an immune system-allergy disease affecting breathing

Cardiac conditions: heart defects that may impact physical well-being (e.g., murmurs, rapid heartbeat)

Blood disorders and hemophilia: a hereditary bleeding disorder caused by clotting factor deficiency

Cancer: most common forms in children include leukemia, lymphoma, and brain tumors

Cystic fibrosis: an inherited disease that affects breathing and digestion, with secretions of mucus and other thick fluids clogging the lungs and ducts connecting the pancreas with the small intestines

Sickle cell anemia: a form of anemia caused by a mutation in the gene that tells the body to make hemoglobin A (the red iron-rich compound in blood); symptoms include stroke, speech difficulties, seizures, painful joints, vision problems, fatigue, fever, and infections

Congenital diseases

Acquired Immune Deficiency Syndrome/Human Immunodeficiency Virus: when HIV enters the blood stream the body reacts with antibodies to fight the infection, the presence of these antibodies means the individual is "HIV positive." A person can be HIV positive without developing AIDS for many years, but they will still be able to infect others.

TORCHS: infectious congenital diseases that include toxoplasmosis, rubella, cytomegalovirus infections, and herpes simplex infections

Acquired Diseases

Hepatitis B, meningitis, encephalitis, and other conditions

TeachSource Digital Download Access online

Merck Childhood Asthma Network
www.mcanonline.org

the leading cause of hospitalization for children and the number one cause of elementary school absenteeism (Porter & Kaplan, 2012). In children, the condition varies from mild to severe.

"Back to school" time often coincides with more asthma attacks for children with an increased exposure to common triggers like dust, molds, cleaning products, exercise, and viral infections (Porter & Kaplan, 2012). An asthma attack includes tightness in the chest, shortness of breath, coughing, wheezing, and an inability to continue with normal activities; an acute attack may include blueness of lips and fingertips (National Institutes of Health [NIH], 2007). All asthma attacks require an immediate response to ensure that the child is safe and can breathe freely. Each child with asthma should have an action plan that specifies the steps that must be taken if the child has an asthma attack at school. This plan should include typical triggers for the child; what medications or inhalers are needed, what dosages are prescribed, whether or not the child can self-medicate, and where medicines are located. The teacher(s) and the school nurse should have copies of this plan and all school staff should be prepared to assist in the advent of an attack. The action plan should also give names and contact information in case of an emergency (NIH, 2007).

Cancer

Cancer, a malignant abnormal growth or tumor, is rare in children, with fewer than 11,000 cases in children in the United States each year (Porter & Kaplan, 2012). The most common forms of cancer in children are leukemia (33 percent), brain tumors (21 percent), and lymphoma (8 percent). In contrast to cancers in adults, cancers in children are much more curable. Nearly 80 percent of children with cancer will survive at least five years, and many researchers now consider childhood cancer to be a chronic illness (Landier, 2007). However, in spite of optimal treatments, approximately 1,500 children ages 0 to 14 years with cancer will die each year (Porter & Kaplan, 2012). Medical treatments for children with cancer include a combination of chemotherapy, radiation, surgery, and medications. Because children are still growing, the side effects of these treatments may differ from those in adults; for example, an arm that receives radiation therapy may not reach its full growth (Porter & Kaplan, 2012). Long-term impacts of the treatments may also include such things as infertility, poor overall growth, damage to the heart, and secondary cancers (Porter & Kaplan, 2012). Treatments for children with cancer must be overseen by specialists with expertise in childhood cancers.

The impact of cancer on the family and child can be overwhelming. In addition to anguish and worry for the child's well-being, the family is often faced with an intense medical regimen that requires full-time management, leaving little time for siblings, work, or "normal" activities. Meeting the needs of the child and family can be more stressful if the treatment center is located far from the family's home. The family and child will need as much support as possible to cope with these difficulties. Children who are attending school will need academic support, emotional support, and health support to help them cope successfully.

American Cancer Society
www.cancer.org

Sickle Cell Anemia

Sickle cell anemia is a form of anemia caused by a mutation in the gene that tells the body to make hemoglobin A, which allows red blood cells to carry oxygen to all parts of your body. Sickle cell is most common among African Americans and individuals of Middle Eastern and Indian ancestry. The symptoms of sickle cell anemia include stroke, speech difficulties, seizures, painful joints and extremities, vision problems, fatigue, fever, and infection.

Treatment for sickle cell anemia includes pain relievers, antibiotics, blood transfusions, and in some cases therapeutic oxygen. Most children with sickle cell anemia can continue to function well in school, but teachers must help them avoid trauma, extreme temperatures, and dehydration.

Sickle Cell Disease
Association of America
www.sicklecelldisease.org/

HIV/AIDS

Acquired immune deficiency syndrome (AIDS) is a breakdown of the body's immune system caused by the **human immunodeficiency virus (HIV)**. When HIV enters the bloodstream, the body reacts with antibodies to fight the infection; it is the presence of these antibodies in the blood that leads to the diagnosis of "HIV positive." A person can carry HIV and can infect others for ten or more years without developing AIDS. People with AIDS are more susceptible to certain diseases and cancers because their immune systems are compromised. Ninety percent of AIDS cases in children are the result of the virus being transmitted from the infected mother during pregnancy, the birth process, or breastfeeding (Rutstein, Conlon, & Batshaw, 1997). Because many women do not know that they are infected with HIV, the Centers for Disease Control and Prevention (CDC) recommends HIV screening for all pregnant women. HIV is now being treated before birth with some success, and the number of babies born with HIV in the United States has dropped from a high of about 1,650 in 1991 to an estimated 100 to 200 in 2010 (CDC, 2013).

1. Use of gloves when dealing with any body fluids (for example, blood, urine, fecal material, vomit) produced by a child. This protects the teacher from contamination and also reduces the risk of spreading an infection to the child if the teacher is in direct contact with an open wound. Teachers should practice "gloving," which is the safe way to don and remove gloves.
2. Proper hand washing when accidents occur that involve bodily fluids. Any areas of contact with the biohazard (the contaminated bodily fluids) should be washed immediately because some pathogens can enter the body even through skin that is chapped but not broken. If no direct contact occurs with the biohazard, hand washing should occur after taking care of the child or cleaning the site of contamination. Hand washing should be completed even when gloves have been worn. All surface areas should be scrubbed with soap for between 10 and 30 seconds and rinsed in warm water. Drying hands with paper towels or air driers is recommended.
3. Cleanup procedures for biohazards should follow a protocol using appropriate disinfectants and placing all clean-up materials in a biohazard waste disposal container. Gloves should be worn during cleanup, and hands must be thoroughly washed after cleanup.

Figure 13.3 Minimum Universal Precautions for Classroom Teachers
Adapted from Siegel, J. D., Rhinehart, E., Jackson, M., Chiarello, L., & the Healthcare Infection Control Practices Advisory Committee. (2007). Guideline for isolation precautions: Preventing transmission of infectious agents in healthcare settings, http://www.cdc.gov/ncidod/dhqp/pdf/isolation2007.pdf

With early diagnosis and medical treatment, approximately 80 percent of infants born with HIV in the United States are still living at age 5 (NIH, 2008), with the average survival rate for children born with HIV being 9.4 years (Franks, Miller, Wolff, & Landry, 2004). This means that increasing numbers of HIV-infected children are attending preschool and elementary school. AIDS is a serious concern in our society, and communities are still formulating policies on how to work with infants and children who have the infection. The likelihood of a child with HIV infecting others during normal classroom activities is low, but all teachers should still use the **universal precautions** (Edens, Murdick, & Gartin, 2003; Franks et al., 2004, Siegel, Rhinehart, Jackson, Chiarello, & the Healthcare Infection Control Practices Advisory Committee, 2007) listed in Figure 13.3.

CDC National Prevention Information Network (HIV and AIDS)
www.cdcnpin.org

Because there is no way of knowing for sure which children may be HIV positive, *universal precautions should be used with all children in all classrooms.*

Acquired Diseases

Children who become seriously ill may require regular medication or other medical treatment. Some serious or chronic illnesses, such as chronic Lyme disease, encephalitis, and meningitis, will require a prolonged hospital stay for the child. If this is the case, everything should be done to continue the child's educational support in the hospital. Many large children's hospitals have educational programs. Ideally the educational support received in the hospital should be coordinated with the child's school to facilitate reentry for the child when he or she is able to attend school again. Teachers working with these children should be knowledgeable about medical procedures needed at school, limitations on activities, and emergency procedures that may be necessary if problems arise (Best et al., 2010).

Figure 13.4 lists these procedures and recommendations.

Teachers must be alert to signs of fatigue or pain and to the vitality needs of their students. Parents and teachers must also watch for indications of depression and should plan ahead for emotional and social support (Key et al., 2001). It is important for all members of the child's environment (e.g., medical personnel,

Teachers with a student who has serious health problems should:

1. Learn about the child's health diagnosis and the impact this may have on learning, social development, emotional well-being, and physical needs for support.
2. Learn about the medical treatments the child is receiving and what impact these may have on learning, social development, emotional well-being, and physical needs for support.
3. Plan for any specific medication or medical needs that may need attention during the school day (e.g., use of an inhaler for breathing or an EpiPen for allergies).
4. Develop a plan, with the child and the child's family, to share information about the health issues with others (including peers).
5. Learn about the other support systems the child has and how you can coordinate with them when needed (i.e., family, counselors, nurses, etc.).
6. Be prepared for extensive absences while the child receives needed medical treatments, and have a plan in place for helping the child make up work by targeting only critical work for completion.
7. Learn about specific limitations and needs so that you can modify the environment and/or activities for the child (e.g., remove sharp items that may cause bleeding, limit contact sports, keep the child hydrated, remove food allergens).
8. Be prepared to recognize signs of an emerging health-related difficulty (i.e., fatigue, faintness, stress, flushing, etc.) and know how to support the child.
9. Be prepared for medical emergencies and have a response plan in place.
10. Learn about the child's interest and strengths so that these are nurtured and supported as well.

Figure 13.4 Teacher and School Roles in Supporting Children with Serious Health Needs

TeachSource Digital Download Access online

therapists, parents, teachers) to prepare a detailed plan once the child is ready to enter or reenter the school environment following an illness or chronic condition. This plan should provide a detailed description of all aspects of the child's day, including what exercise is recommended, periods of rest and quiet times, and ways of encouraging a positive self-concept (Mukherjee, Lightfoot, & Sloper, 2000; Prevatt, Heffer, & Lowe, 2000). Because wellness-illness is a continuum and health needs can fluctuate, these plans must be individualized and reviewed when circumstances change.

In addition to the plans for individual children, a comprehensive district plan should also be developed that includes policies at the school and district levels that address provision of services, provision of emergency care, steps for supporting the child in school, and guidelines for related service personnel.

13-3c Severe and Multiple Disabilities

In addition to the definitions of physical disabilities and health impairments presented earlier, The National Dissemination Center for Children with Disabilities (NICHCY; formerly known as the National Information Center for Handicapped Children and Youth) has defined what it means to have a severe disability. The NICHCY definition, by and large, addresses children who have

Tony Freeman/PhotoEdit

Children form friendships as they work and learn together.

multiple disabilities, but it also includes those whose primary area of disability creates extreme limitations in life functioning. NICHCY defines severely disabled individuals as those

> who require extensive ongoing support in more than one major life activity in order to participate in integrated community settings and enjoy the quality of life available to people with fewer or no disabilities. (NICHCY, 2004).

Any definition of individuals with multiple or severe disabilities must be broad, because it includes a very heterogeneous population: for example, persons with psychiatric disorders, deafblindness, and combinations of health, motor, or cognitive impairments (Best et al., 2010; Bruce, 2011).

Deafblindness

Although the term "deafblind" seems to imply a complete loss of vision and hearing, it actually includes children with a range of vision and hearing losses (Malloy, 2009).

Because of the range of sensory abilities for children who are deafblind (sometimes written "deaf-blind"), it is essential that the multidisciplinary planning team carefully assess the child's vision and hearing to determine how to support the maximum use of the child's sensory input for learning (Janssen, Riksen-Walraven, Van Dijk, Huisman, & Ruijssenaars, 2012; Riggio, 2009). Many children who are deafblind have other disabilities, including 66 percent with cognitive disabilities; 57 percent with physical disabilities; 38 percent with complex health needs; 9 percent with behavior challenges; and 30 percent with other complications (Malloy, 2009). But, deafblindness is not always associated with other disabilities; more than half of the deafblind population have Usher syndrome, which is an inherited condition. Individuals with **Usher syndrome** have progressive sensorimotor deafness, retinitis pigmentosa (vision loss), and central nervous system problems (Batshaw, 2002).

Helen Keller National Center
www.helenkeller.org/national

The National Consortium on Deaf-Blindness estimated that there were 9,387 individuals from birth to age 21 with deafblindness in 2008 (NCDB, 2012). Because of the intensity of their needs, most children who are deafblind are served in separate settings. Figure 13.5 shows the educational placements for children who are deafblind.

Helen Keller, the most famous deafblind individual, is reported to have said that being blind isolates you from things, while being deaf isolates you from people. This double isolation can make it challenging for individuals to learn (Riggio, 2009; Anthony, 2009). It takes a great deal of time, patience, empathy, and repetition to establish the first word (usually a sign) with the child who is

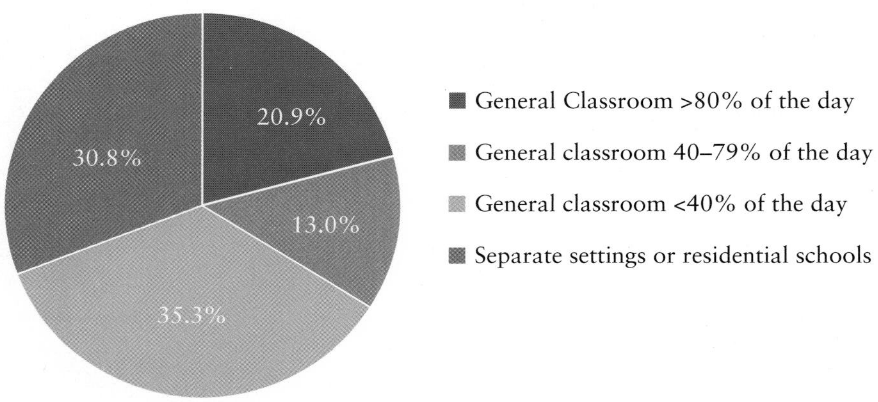

Figure 13.5 Educational Settings for Students with Deaf-Blindness
Source: Data Accountability Center. (2009). *Part B Educational Environments 2009 [data file].* Retrieved from http://www.ideadata.org/PartBEnvironments.asp

deafblind. The goal is to connect a movement made by the child to a sign. The learning process often begins with the names of parents (*mama, papa*) or a toy or activity the child likes (*swing,* for example).

If the child is blind, the sign is taught by placing both hands on the child and encouraging the child to respond. Bear in mind that children who can see and hear do not speak until they have heard thousands of words. Children with deafblindness need similar multiple experiences with the activity and the corresponding sign (McKenzie, 2009; Miles & Riggio, 1999). The use of interactive partners helps establish turn-taking needed for reciprocal communications (e.g., the partner initiates a message, a second partner responds, and the conversation continues) (Janssen et al., 2012). Communication is central to overcoming barriers to involvement for individuals who are deafblind.

Bruce and Parker (2012) worked with six young adults who are deafblind on advocacy and civic engagement. The young adults designed a series of study questions to learn more about how to influence policy makers and they applied their knowledge with visits to legislators. Kevin, one of the participants, defined advocacy as "standing up for what you believe," and Diana, a second participant, added that advocacy is "everything that you need to do to explain to someone when they say 'no' to something" (Bruce and Parker, 2012, p. 20). Kristie reflected that "being deafblind isn't something that has to stop us from doing what we want. Having deafblind mentors who hold respectable jobs in their field also shows us that if they can do it, so can we." (Bruce and Parker, 2012, p. 21). Resources for working with individuals who are deafblind can be found in the *American Annals of the Deaf* journal at Project Muse.

American Annals of the Deaf
http://muse.jhu.edu/journals/american_annals_of_the_deaf/

13-3d Prevalence of Physical Disabilities, Health Impairments, and Multiple Disabilities in Children

The U.S. Department of Education (2009) reports that in the 2007 the number of individuals ages 6 through 21 receiving special education services was 6,007,832. Table 13.4 shows the distributions within this category for orthopedic impairments, deafblindness, traumatic brain injuries, multiple disabilities, and other health impairments.

TABLE 13.4 Disability Distribution for Children Ages 6–21 Who Receive Special Education and Related Services, Fall 2007*

Area of Disability	Percentage of Special Education	Numbers of Children*
Orthopedic impairments	1%	60,078
Deafblind	<.01%	601
Traumatic brain injury	0.4%	24,473
Multiple disabilities	2.2%	132,172
Other health impairments	10.5%	630,822

*Numbers are based on the total population of 6,007,832 children ages 6–21 reported as receiving special education and related services in the fall of 2007.

SOURCE: U.S. Department of Education (2009). *Thirty-first annual report to Congress: Implementation of the Individuals with Disabilities Act.* Washington, D.C.: Office of Special Education Programs.

13-3e Genetic Factors and Disabilities

Many disabilities are caused by genetic differences that include mutations, damage, and general anomalies. Genetics-related disabilities can be inherited or they can be specific to the individual who is impacted. In this chapter we look at several disability and health areas that have their origins in genetic differences, including muscular dystrophies, sickle cell anemia, hemophilia and blood-related diseases, cystic fibrosis, and juvenile diabetes. One area of emerging research to address some genetic defects is **gene replacement therapy** (Smith, Bainbridge, & Ali, 2009), where the defective genetic material is replaced and corrected. There are two approaches being developed. The first is **germ line therapy**, in which sperm or egg cells are modified by introducing functional genes ("Gene therapy," 2010). The genetic change is then integrated into the genome and is passed to future generations. The second type of therapy is **somatic gene therapy**, in which the therapeutic genes are transferred into the somatic cells and only impact the patient ("Gene therapy," 2010). Current studies are underway to use gene replacement therapies for spinal muscular atrophies (University of Sheffield, 2010), muscular dystrophies, metabolic liver disease (Hoglund, 1999), sickle cell disease and other blood disorders (Townes, 2008), and retinal degeneration (Smith, Bainbridge, & Ali, 2009). While the results for genetic replacement therapies are promising, the techniques are not without controversy. The ethical implications of genetic replacement include concerns about bioengineering, the use of genetics to alter the natural course of human development and the use of genetic replacement technology to create "smart" biological weapons that could target groups based on their genetic makeup. These ethical issues will need to be explored as research on gene replacement continues.

13-4 Assessment of Children with Physical Disabilities, Health Impairments, and Multiple Disabilities

The initial assessment of children with physical disabilities and health impairments is primarily the responsibility of pediatricians; neurologists, who specialize in conditions and diseases of the brain, spinal cord, and nervous system; orthopedists and orthopedic surgeons, who are concerned with muscle function and conditions of the joints and bones; and doctors who specialize in childhood diseases. Other specialists involved in identification include physical therapists, speech-language pathologists, and occupational therapists.

The identification process involves a comprehensive medical evaluation, which includes a medical and developmental history (illnesses, medical history of family members, problems during pregnancy and labor, and developmental progress), a physical examination, and laboratory tests or other special procedures needed for accurate diagnosis. When the child enters preschool or kindergarten, a comprehensive educational assessment must be completed.

13-4a Educational Assessments for Children with Physical or Multiple Disabilities

IDEA requires that assessments be timely, comprehensive, and multidisciplinary (CEC, 2006). The greater the impact of the disability, the more challenging it can be to assess the child's abilities. Federal regulations about assessing or evaluating the skills of individuals with multiple or severe disabilities are, however, quite clear: The evaluation must be appropriate to the needs of the individual and the family, and it must take into account the child's culture and primary language. There is currently a movement for the development of "universally designed assessments" that would give all students access to the information This would benefit individuals with all kinds of differences in abilities, language, and areas of challenge (Salvia, Ysseldyke, & Bolt, 2012). Currently, a computer-based instrument designed to facilitate comprehension of spoken language in young children with cerebral palsy is now being field-tested (Geytenbeek, Heim, Vermeulen, & Oostrom, 2010). As more test designers work toward incorporating universal design features in their assessments, it will likely become easier to assess children with disabilities. Until then, however, educational assessment of children who have physical disabilities remains a complex and challenging task. These challenges involve both the administration of the assessment and the interpretation of the assessment results.

The specific accommodations needed for each student should be listed in the student's individualized education program (IEP) and should be available for all the assessments that the student takes. A small percent of children's needs go beyond just appropriate modifications during assessments, and these children will need alternate assessment based on alternative achievement standards (Kleinert, Browder, & Towles-Reeves, 2009). Standard assessments, even with accommodations, are not appropriate for children with significant cognitive disabilities that prevent them from reaching grade-level standards even with high-quality instruction (IDEA, 2004). For this small group of children (approximately 1 percent of all students) alternative assessments, aligned with the standards, must be designed (Kearns, Towles-Reeves, Kleinert, Kleinert, Thomas, 2011). The specific nature of the alternative assessment must be determined by the student's IEP team, directed by their state guidelines (Kleinert et al., 2009; Wehmeyer, 2011).

In addition to administering assessments so that children with disabilities can take them, we also must be careful how we interpret the results of these assessments. Interpreting the results of assessments of children who have physical and/or multiple or severe disabilities presents very specific challenges. The primary difficulty is with **norm-referenced tests**. These are tests that are "standardized" on groups of children in order to allow us to compare an individual child's score with the typical score for other children in his or her age group. The difficulty with the use of norm-referenced tests for children with disabilities is that the group of children we are using as the comparison base (the norm group) rarely includes other children who have disabilities, and so drawing conclusions about the child with disabilities in comparison with this group can lead to faulty assumptions.

The main thing to remember when interpreting test results for a child with significant areas of disabilities is to use caution! Tests cannot capture all of the areas of strength that the child has, they may underpredict their abilities, and they may overestimate their areas of limitation. When trying to get a full picture of the strengths and challenges of a child with significant areas of impact, multiple types of information must be gathered from multiple sources. We must include direct observations in a variety of contexts (home, classroom, playground, work setting), work samples showing the child's strength areas and challenges, and interviews with the child, family members, teachers, medical personnel, and caregivers. All of this information must be used by the multidisciplinary team to design supports and services that will maximize the child's chances of success.

13-5 Educational Responses for Children with Physical Disabilities, Health Impairments, and Multiple or Severe Disabilities

The range and nature of the educational needs of the children discussed in this chapter are wide and varied. Strategies to address these needs include the use of a multidisciplinary team for planning and implementation, access to appropriate technologies to support independence, and educational interventions that respond to both strengths and challenges.

13-5a Organizational Structures to Support Children with Physical Disabilities, Health Impairments, and Multiple or Severe Disabilities

A full continuum of services is needed to support students with physical, health, and multiple or severe disabilities. This continuum includes classroom services in both general special education as well as special programs and residential schools.

RtI

RtI Approaches for Students with Physical and Health Impairments, and Multiple or Severe Disabilities

When supports and services are provided within a multitier system, students with physical disabilities, health impairments, and multiple or severe disabilities will need all three tiers of the response to intervention (RtI) model. The development of an IEP is critical to guiding the instructional modification and a transition plan is critical to ensuring that the transition needs of the student have been addressed.

Universal Tier I for Students with Physical Disabilities, Health Impairments, and Multiple or Severe Disabilities

Pam, the fifth-grade student we met at the beginning of the chapter, spends most of her day in the general classroom receiving solid instructional support in the common core state standards (CCSS). Pam's classroom has been redesigned for accessibility and she can maneuver her wheelchair with ease to reach all the things she needs. Pam uses a computer with special software to help her read and write, and her classmates assist her with physical tasks like cutting or doing science labs. Pam also assists her classmates as a math tutor. While Pam does well in the general classroom, she has also received services that required collaboration among her teachers (Tier II). A Summary of *UDL Supports for Students with Health Impairments and Physical, Multiple, or Severe Disabilities* can be accessed online.

TeachSource Digital Download

Targeted Tier II for Students with Physical Disabilities, Health Impairments, and Multiple or Severe Disabilities

For Pam, Tier II supports focused on self-advocacy and general career planning were taught by the guidance counselor. Pam participated in a small group to explore careers through job shadowing. She was able to learn more about becoming an engineer to design robots! Pam also receives Tier II enrichment in reading.

Intensive Tier III for Students with Physical Disabilities, Health Impairments, and Multiple or Severe Disabilities

Pam also received intervention support at the Tier III level, with special education and physical and occupational therapy, and she will soon begin transition planning. Pam also works on her independent research project on robots as part of her Tier III support.

What we see from Pam's example is that RtI is not a linear set of services by which a student begins in Tier I, moves to Tier II, and finally is served in Tier III. All three levels of services are often needed by the same child for different aspects of their supports and enhancements. The conception of the three tiers helps teachers and service providers determine the level of the child's needs and organize their responses to meet these needs. Again, remember that the greater the strengths and needs of the child, the more intensive the services must be.

Henry, the second child discussed in the chapter, has multiple and complex needs and requires more intense services to meet these needs. Henry spends most of his day in the special education class, where intensive supports can be provided to him on an individualized basis. His related services and therapies are integrated into his day. Although Henry spends much of his day within the special education classroom, on Wednesdays he attends music with Pam's general education class. Henry also has a group of fifth-grade "buddies" who read with him each afternoon.

A Summary of *RtI Approaches for Students with Health Impairments and Physical, Multiple, or Severe Disabilities* can be accessed online.

TeachSource Digital Download

Inclusion in General Education for Students with Physical, Health-Related, and Multiple or Severe Disabilities

A substantial body of research conducted over many years has established the following benefits of inclusion of students with physical, multiple, and health-related disabilities in public schools and community settings:

- Children with disabilities have shown greater academic gains (Drasgow, Wolery, Halle, Hajiaghamohseni, 2011; Wehmeyer & Schwartz, 1998; Wehmeyer, 2011; Zang, Katsiyannis, & Kortering, 2007).
- Positive changes have been reported in the attitudes of nondisabled individuals toward their peers with severe disabilities at various age levels (Drasgow et al., 2011; Grenot-Scheyer, 1994; Ryndak & Alper, 2003; Voeltz, 1980).
- Inclusion has led to improvements in the social and communication skills of children with severe disabilities (Drasgow et al., 2011; Jackson, Ryndak, & Billingsley, 2000; Jenkins, Speltz, & Odom, 1985; McDonnell, 2011; Newton, Horner, Ard, LeBaron, & Sapperton, 1994; Wehmeyer, 2011).
- Inclusion has improved interaction between students with severe disabilities and their nondisabled age-mates (Downing & Eichinger, 2003; Drasgow et al., 2011; Roberts, Burchinal, & Bailey, 1994; Wehmeyer, 2011).
- Inclusion facilitates adjustment to community settings as students transition into adulthood (Drasgow et al., 2011; Hasazi, Gordon, & Roe, 1985; Helmstetter, Peck, & Giangreco, 1994; McDonnell, 2011).

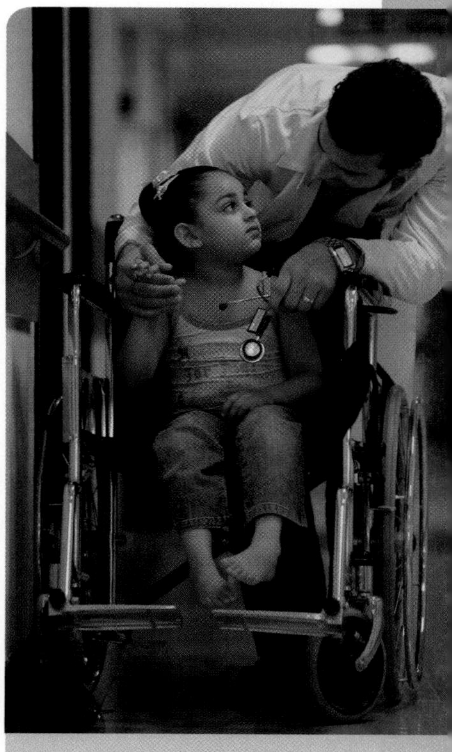
Hemant Mehta/Getty Images

It takes a multi-disciplinary team to plan for the needs of students.

Full and meaningful inclusion, however, does not happen simply by placing children with disabilities in the same room with their nondisabled peers (Drasgow et al., 2011; Division for Early Childhood and National Association for the Education of Young Children [DEC/NAEYC], 2009; Schwartz, 2000). Teachers must specifically and intentionally plan for full inclusion and must be prepared to help develop a sense of belonging for each student (Solish, Perry, & Minnes, 2010). Three aspects of full and meaningful inclusion are access, participation, and supports (DEC/NAEYC, 2009). But creating the environment for full inclusion and belonging can be challenging for children with multiple and/or severe disabilities (Solish et al., 2010). Guralnick and colleagues (2009) found that while mothers believed that social networks were important for their child with intellectual and developmental disabilities, actually establishing these networks was difficult. Parents and teachers must intentionally structure activities to facilitating belonging and the formation of relationships that can develop into friendships (Schwartz, 2000; Solish et al., 2010). Also, inclusion must go beyond the social benefits; to be of most value it must facilitate the student's academic success.

A picture is worth a thousand words . . . see the joy in learning with friends!

Brian Mitchell/Corbis

13-5b Curriculum and Instruction for Children with Physical, Multiple, or Severe Disabilities

Access to the common core state standards is critical for students with physical, multiple, or severe disabilities, and this requires careful planning. For children with physical disabilities, an expanded core curriculum must also include motor skills; children with cognitive challenges will need functional skills for daily living (Best et al., 2010).

Access to the Common Core State Standards for Students with Physical Disabilities, Health Impairments, and Multiple or Severe Disabilities

Students with significant cognitive disabilities will likely have IEPs that include alternative curriculum standards and focus on functional applications of reading and math. These alternate standards must be aligned with grade-level standards but may differ in complexity and difficulty (Wehmeyer, 2011). The IEPs should also include strategies to document the students' success and progress in reaching these modified standards (Drasgow et al., 2011; Wehmeyer, 2011). If accommodations such as augmentative communication or assistive technologies are used during instruction, these must also be used during assessments (Kearns et al., 2011).

Student with physical disabilities who do not have significant cognitive delays will still need support (modified physical interactions with materials, assistive technologies, or communication boards with vocabulary, for instance) to access the CCSS. Teachers must plan these in advance of their lessons. While the IEP team must select the specific support for each child, Table 13.5 shares general UDL ideas for supporting students with physical disabilities in accessing the CCSS.

TABLE 13.5 Using Universal Design Principles to Give Students with Physical Disabilities Access to the Common Core State Standards

Common Core Standard	Multiple Representations	Multiple Engagements	Multiple Assessments
Speaking and Listening, #1, Comprehension and Collaboration, Grade 8 Engage effectively in a range of collaborative discussions (one-on-one, in groups, and teacher-led) with diverse partners on grade *8 topics, texts, and issues*, building on others' ideas and expressing their own clearly.	Advance organizers for discussions Graphic organizers for compare and contrast of ideas to be discussed Pictures Video of material for discussion Web-based text with large font Short summaries of content (Cliff notes) Vocabulary builders Use picture or iconic prompts for ideas and present these on augmentative communication devices	Direct instruction on participation, Guidelines and strategies Use appropriate alternative and augmentative communication supports Practice with listening skills (help classmates learn to listen) Guided discussion of topics, texts, and issues Watching dramatization or video related to discussion information Discussions using appropriate support for participation Discussion buddy to practice with Develop graphic organizers to capture thoughts prior to discussion Create visual representations of information Writing activities Prepare presentations (e.g., PowerPoint)	Written products (concept webs, note cards, and drafts) Oral presentations with visual support Pictures of images or photo essay of ideas shared Compare/Contrast Graphic organizers Essay reflecting your ideas and building on at least one idea shared by another student Create a work of art sharing multiple ideas expressed during the discussion
Math Standard, #9, Solve real-world and mathematical problems involving volume of cylinders, cones, and spheres, Grade 8 Know the formulas for the volumes of cones, cylinders, and spheres and use them to solve real-world and mathematical problems	Hands-on materials adapted for use given the physical constraints of student Charts, Graphs, Pictures Drawings of shapes Identify shapes in real-world settings Highlighted problems (key words in color) Flash cards for formulas Create problem-solving process guide/checklist	Direct instruction on concepts with real-world experiences Use appropriate alternative and augmentative communication supports Use hands-on manipulatives that have been adapted for student Work with study buddy to measure and record physical properties of real-world examples Create flash cards for formulas of volumes Draw pictures representing problems Use commercial software for practice Use calculators for checking Create word problems based on real-world data collection	Traditional written assessment of problem solving Student-developed word problems on concepts Drawings, Pictures, Charts, Graphs Math talks Students find real-world examples of cones, cylinders, and spheres and give volumes for these

TeachSource Digital Download Access online

Systematic activity-based instruction can be used to teach many skills in the context in which they will be used and give the student additional practice (Saunders, Bethune, Spooner, & Browder, 2013). Basic academic skills can be embedded in the skill training. For example, Colin, a young man with cerebral palsy and mild intellectual delays, is being taught how to buy food in the cafeteria. He learns how to maneuver his wheelchair into the line, survey the food, make a selection and take it to the cashier, pay for it, and count his change. Reading the name of the food and its price, knowing whether he has enough money to pay for it, and determining whether the change is correct all involve basic academic skills (Hunt, Soto, Maier, & Doering, 2003). For many students with physical, multiple, and/or severe disabilities an expanded core curriculum is needed.

Expanded Core Curriculum for Students with Physical, Health-Related, and Multiple or Severe Disabilities

Whatever the age of the students or the severity of their disabilities, we must provide them with an **expanded core curriculum** that is functional and as age-appropriate as possible. This expanded core includes both motor skills and functional life skills.

Motor Skills and Mobility

Motor skills and mobility constitute a critical area of skill development for children with physical disabilities. These skills are necessary to maintain upright postures (sitting, standing), to perform functional movements (reaching, grasping), and to move around in the environment. The programming priorities for motor skill development should include developing functional movements and postures that are needed to perform classroom and school activities. Appropriate positioning techniques include developing the following:

- Sufficient head and trunk control to maintain an upright sitting posture in order to perform needed activities throughout the school day (attending and listening, writing, using a computer or communication device, eating)
- Arm movements and fine motor skills for performance of needed activities throughout the school day (holding a pencil and paper to write, holding a book and turning pages, using keyboards or switches to access a computer or communication device)
- Standing and balance for assisted ambulation (using braces and crutches)
- Skills needed to maneuver a wheelchair in the classroom and throughout the school environment (using arms to propel, learning to use an electric wheelchair with a joystick or other control, turning corners and entering doorways, negotiating ramps and curbs, and crossing streets)

Physical and occupational therapists assume the primary responsibility for setting goals in motor development and mobility. They must work closely with teachers, other professionals, and parents, however, for the child to meet these goals. Teachers should become familiar with the basic working components of mobility equipment (wheelchairs, braces, crutches, walkers) and report needed repairs or adjustments to the child's therapist. Therapists should provide teachers and others with information related to the child's physical condition, limitations, and abilities.

American Physical Therapy Association
www.apta.org

Increasingly, children with cerebral palsy are involved in motor skill activities under the guidance of a physical therapist. These activities include swimming, dance, martial arts, horseback riding, and other real-life experiences. The activities prevent atrophy of damaged muscles. The vast majority of children with disabilities that are not severe will spend part or most of their days in the general education classroom.

Functional Skills for Individuals with Physical and Multiple or Severe Disabilities
Functional skills can be used immediately by the student, are necessary in everyday settings, and increase the student's independence to some extent. Folding a sheet of paper in half is not a functional skill; folding clothes is (Campbell, 2000; Kaiser, 2000). Teaching functional skills that students will use in daily living is an important part of the curriculum, because this helps build autonomy for the student.

For individuals with intellectual delays, we need to teach **age-appropriate** skills that match the student's chronological age, not his or her mental age. A 16-year-old boy who has severe disabilities is taught how to engage in activities similar to those that his nondisabled age-mates participate in. Skills appropriate for a 16-year-old, for example, may include eating in a restaurant, using a neighborhood health club, or operating a television set or using a cell phone. If the skills are not age-appropriate, they are not as likely to be functional. Moreover, age-appropriate skills give students with severe disabilities a measure of social acceptance. Table 13.6 shows age-appropriate life skills for students across the grade levels.

13-5c Assistive Technology for Students with Physical Disabilities, Health Impairments, and Multiple Disabilities

The child with multiple challenges may have diverse technology needs, including instructional technology, **assistive technology (AT)**, and technology related to augmentative communication (Mechling & Bishop, 2011).

TABLE 13.6 Life Skills across the Grades

Student	Domestic	Community	Leisure	Vocational
Tim (elementary age)	Picking up toys Washing dishes Making bed Dressing Practicing eating skills & toileting skills Sorting clothes	Eating meals in a restaurant Using restroom in a local restaurant Putting trash into container Choosing correct change to ride city bus Giving the clerk money Recognizing pedestrian safety signs Participating in local scout troop	Climbing on swing set Playing board games Tumbling activities Riding bicycles Playing with age-appropriate toys	Clearing the table after a meal Returning toys to appropriate storage Cleaning the room Working on a task (for 15–30 minutes) Following two- to four-step instructions Answering phone Taking messages to people
Mary (junior high age)	Washing clothes Preparing simple meals Keeping bedroom clean Yard work Making grocery lists Purchasing items from a list Vacuuming and dusting living room	Crossing streets safely Purchasing items from store Purchasing a meal at a restaurant Using local transportation system Participating in local scout troop Going to a neighbor's house for lunch on Saturday	Playing volleyball Taking aerobics classes Playing checkers Playing miniature golf Attending high school or local basketball games Swimming Attending craft class	Waxing floors Cleaning windows Filling lawn mower with gas Working for 1–2 hours at a job Following a job sequence

(Continued)

TABLE 13.6 Life Skills across the Grades (*Continued*)

Sandy (high school age)	Cleaning all rooms in place of residence Developing a weekly budget Cooking meals Operating thermostat Doing yard work Maintaining personal needs Caring for and maintaining clothing	Utilizing bus system Depositing checks into bank account Using community stores, restaurants, health facilities (e.g., physician, pharmacist)	Jogging, Archery, Boating Watching college basketball games Playing video games Playing card games Attending athletic club or community center class Gardening Going on a vacation or trip	Performing required janitorial duties at business Performing house-keeping duties at hotel Performing groundskeeping duties Performing food service at cafeteria Performing photocopying at bank Performing food-stocking duties

The first step in providing AT is determining what kinds of supports are needed. Table 13.7 is a checklist that can be used to help assess the child's needs for AT.

Selecting the appropriate technology is just the first step. Once this has been done, the child will need direct instruction with the technology and time to practice with it (Watson, Ito, Smith, & Anderson, 2010). He or she may need emotional support while learning how to manage this new aspect of life. The most important factor in the successful use of the AT device is not which device is selected but how the teacher adapts it for the students (Sze, 2009). The sustained use of any AT device depends on how well it matches the student's capabilities and limitations; how easy it is to use; and how appropriate it is for the individual based on gender, age, and personal preferences (Sze, 2009). AT is designed to help the individual gain autonomy, and this is especially true for technologies that help the individual communicate.

Augmentative Communication

Students with physical disabilities who cannot acquire understandable speech or legible writing skills must be provided with **augmentative communication**, or nontraditional methods of communication that may include the use of assistive technology devices (Ogletree, Bruce, Finch, Fahey, & McLean, 2011; Okolo, 2006). Some children with cerebral palsy, for example, have severe impairment of the oral muscles used in speech and limited fine motor abilities that hamper their writing skills. Muscular dystrophy or arthritis can leave children so weak that they tire easily when writing.

Teachers and parents should work closely with speech therapists in selecting, designing, and implementing augmented and alternative communication devices for children with physical disabilities (Pickl, 2011). The success of augmentative communication approaches depends on the sustained support given to the child. Effective stakeholders must ensure open communicative environments with appropriate support and resources to allow for successful communication (Ogletree et al., 2010; Pickl, 2011). Direct instruction in listening skills for those who will be communicating with the student is a key part of creating an open communicative environment (Hustad, Dardis, Kramper, 2011). Listeners can learn to use context clues, word sounds, and active listening skills

TABLE 13.7 Matching Assistive Technology to a Disability Area

Type of Disability	Objectives/Tasks	Devices	Applications
Cognitive learning	Reading	Electronic reading machine	WYNN
	Language arts	Portable reading pens	L&H
	Writing	Portable hand-held dictionaries	Kurzweil 3000
	Note taking	Instructional software	Quicktionary Reading
	Mathematics	Instructional software	Pen Scan-a-Word
	Auditory memory	Word cueing and prediction programs	Speaking Language Master
	Reading	Speech synthesis software	The American Heritage Dictionary
		Speech recognition software	My Reading Coach
		Spelling, grammar, and style checkers	Simon Sounds It Out
		Portable keyboards	Co:Writer
		Instructional software	Write:Outloud
		Talking calculators	IntelliTalk II
		Portable prompting devices	DragonDictate
		Video magnifiers	ViaVoice
		Scanner/OCR systems	Write This Way
		Braille translation software	Alphasmart 2000
			Math for Everyday Living Math Sequence
			Radio Shack Talking Calculator
			Mobile Digital Recorder
			Aladdin Pro+ Magnicam
			Reading Edge
			Duxbury Braille Translator MegaDots

SOURCE: Sze, S. (2009). The effects of assistive technology on students with disabilities. *Journal of Educational Technology Systems, 37*(4), 419–429, Table 1.

to support communication with students who have challenges with spoken expression (Hustad et al., 2011). The most important aspects of communication of any kind are showing interest in what is being said and listening patiently to understand the message.

Speech: Boards and Electronic Devices

The most common augmented and alternative methods for speech are communication boards and electronic devices with synthesized speech output. Henry, you may recall, used a Dynavox to select his daily activities. Some key points pertaining to the use of speech technologies are:

- Most children use the board or electronic device by pointing with a finger or fist to a word or symbol.
- Children who are not able to point accurately can use a handheld pointer, a head-mounted wand, a mouthstick, or a laser pointer.
- Youngsters with limited use of their hands may use their eyes instead, visually focusing on the intended word or letter.

A single switch may be necessary for students who have limited or no use of their hands. The type of switch depends on the child's movement abilities. Numerous commercial switches are available, and many can be made at home.

TeachSource Video Connection

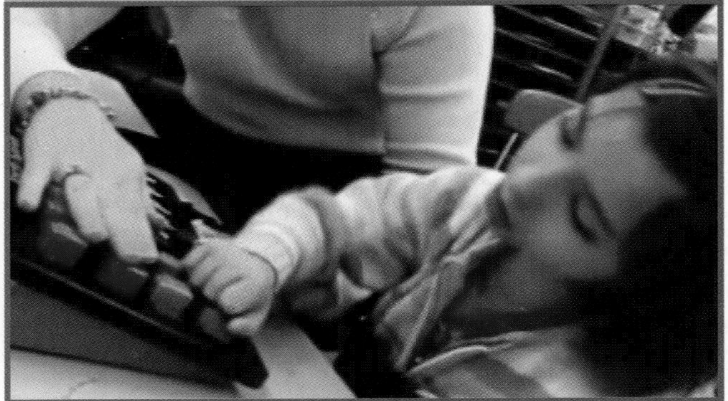

Watch the video "Assistive Technology in the Inclusive Classroom: Best Practices." In this video, you will meet Jamie, a kindergarten child with cerebral palsy. Jamie is an active member of Mr. Byers's classroom, and she participates with her classmates in all of the learning activities. As you watch this video, reflect on how assistive technologies help Jamie communicate and on the ways her teacher (Mr. Byers) and the inclusion specialist (Ms. Woodruff) work together to make sure that Jamie is learning.

Watch online

A switch is used with devices that light each possible selection on the board by rows, then by columns. When the correct row is lit and the child presses the switch a second time, the correct sentence, phrase, word, or letter is "spoken." Although this method is slower than accessing the device by pointing or using a keyboard, it can accommodate students with severe physical impairments. Many electronic communication devices can be connected to a computer for word processing or computer-assisted instruction (Ashton, 2006).

Supplemental boards or overlays for electronic devices may be needed for academic content areas. For example, a mathematics board contains numbers, mathematics symbols, and words related to current classroom instruction. Other subject boards reflect the content and vocabulary of the specific academic subject (science, social studies, history). These boards should be revised or replaced as classroom content changes throughout the school year. Without augmented communication support, many students might be denied placement in a less-restrictive environment (resource room or general education classroom) because of their lack of spoken language.

Writing Aids and Systems

A variety of **writing aids** and augmented and alternative systems are available for written communication. Students with physical disabilities that cause muscle weakness, involuntary movements, and poor coordination of the fingers and hands may require a writing aid or an alternative system to complete written assignments in school and at home in a neat and timely manner. Some specific aids to help a child with writing include:

- Hand splints to aid in grasping a crayon or pencil
- Special pencil holders
- Slant board to support forearms
- Clipboard, heavy weight, or masking tape to secure paper while writing
- Wide-lined paper (Bigge & Best, 2000)

Computers provide another alternative means of written communication. Word-processing software can be used to complete written assignments. Keyguards are available for most types of computer keyboards. For students who cannot use a standard keyboard because they lack fine motor skills, expanded keyboards with large keys are easier to use. A student with muscular dystrophy might use a miniature keyboard if he or she lacks the range of motion in the arms required to use a standard keyboard yet has good finger movement within a limited range. Alternative keyboards are placed directly on the student's lap, desk, or lap tray for easy access.

13-5d Enhancing Self-Determination and Autonomy

The first steps toward autonomy are self-awareness and self-determination (Field & Hoffman, 2007). Henry, the fifth-grade student we met at the beginning of the chapter, is sometimes resistant to doing things without help. Henry's teachers and parents, you recall, are working hard to teach him how to choose what he wants and to eventually self-initiate his morning routine. This may seem like a small thing, but it leads to life skills and habits that will be essential as he grows to adulthood.

Being able to take care of themselves is of critical importance for children with physical disabilities. Self-care skills include eating, toileting, dressing, bathing, and grooming. Students with severe physical involvement may require physical assistance in eating or may have to be fed. Some children need assistive devices or physical help perform many of these tasks; for example, utensils with built-up or larger handles, special plates and cups, or nonskid mats to stabilize the child's plate. The goal is to provide tools and support to help the student become as independent as possible.

13-6 Family and Lifespan Issues

Parents are the child's first teachers, first advocates, and first caregivers. They provide the support needed to help the multidisciplinary team understand their child and often spend hours securing appropriate supports to meet their child's needs (Horn & Kang, 2012). As the child grows, these needs will change, and parents need to be prepared for lifelong issues that they and their child may face. Table 13.8 offers an overview of some of these issues.

Children with multiple or severe disabilities need early intervention so that the parents can provide appropriate and consistent care (Bruce, 2011). Parents and

TABLE 13.8 Possible Issues Encountered by Parents at Each Stage of Their Child's Life

Early Childhood, Ages 0–5	Obtaining an accurate diagnosis Informing siblings and relatives Locating services Seeking to find meaning in the exceptionality Clarifying a personal ideology to guide decisions Addressing issues of stigma Identifying positive contributions of exceptionality Setting great expectations
Elementary School, Ages 6–12	Establishing routines to carry out family functions Adjusting emotionally to educational implications Clarifying issues of mainstreaming vs. special class placement Participating in IEP conferences Locating community resources Arranging for extracurricular activities
Adolescence, Ages 12–21	Adjusting emotionally to possible chronicity of exceptionality Identifying issues of emerging sexuality Addressing possible peer isolation and rejection Planning for career/vocational development Arranging for leisure time activities Dealing with physical and emotional changes of puberty Planning for postsecondary education
Adulthood, Ages 21 On	Planning for possible need for guardianship Addressing the need for appropriate adult residence Adjusting emotionally to any adult implications of dependency Addressing the need for socialization opportunities outside the family Initiating career choice or vocational program

SOURCE: From A. P. Turnbull, H. R. Turnbull, E. Erwin, L. Soodak, & Shogren, K. *Families, professionals, and exceptionality: Positive outcomes through partnership and trust* (6th ed.). (Upper Saddle River, NJ: Prentice Hall, 2010).

BOX 13.2 EXCEPTIONAL LIVES • EXCEPTIONAL STORIES

Counting on Me

I've always believed life to be a continual learning process. January 23, 1998, my greatest lesson began with the birth of my daughter, Isabel Soledad. Isabel was born in Germany two weeks postterm via emergency cesarean, weighing only five pounds. She had to be revived. No one knew and no one was prepared, least of all me. It was later determined that Isabel has a chromosomal disorder, a unique genetic rearrangement, never before documented (a partial trisomy 22 and a partial trisomy 7)—and so it began.

Motherhood can be an overwhelming experience itself, but when a grave disappointment for the dreams you so carefully envisioned is suddenly replaced with a lifelong responsibility to a difficult unknown, it's like being hit over the head with a hammer. Once your head stops spinning and the realization sets in, you focus on what you can control and move on. There is no time for mourning.

Courtesy of Author

Isabel and Crystal have learned to count on each other.

The first year was the most frightening. In my case, there was no information, no research, no data, no studies. Even still, I sought second and third opinions. I conducted my own research online and in libraries and medical universities around the world. I have refused to accept anything less than the best I can provide for my daughter; and because of this, I have excused many professionals from my child's care over the years whenever I have felt that her best interests were not on their forefront.

Isabel's condition is responsible for a wide range of developmental delays. She has received physical, occupational, and speech therapies from a very early age. Although I was warned that my child would never walk, most frequently I am continually given the frustrating prognosis of "wait and see." I view this as a mixed blessing. There are no other children like Isabel to compare missed milestones with, and, therefore, no predetermined shortcomings.

By the time Isabel was 18 months old, her amazing little spirit had emerged in full. Many of my fears had subsided and much of my faith was restored; however, a new challenge arose to the occasion when I returned to the U.S. as a single parent.

Encountering the System

Becoming established into the system was relatively easy through Wake County's Early Intervention Services, which, in turn, led me to Community Partnerships, Inc., and Smart Start. These exceptional organizations helped provide funding for child care, special equipment, as well as additional therapies which

therapists need to help children with severe disabilities recognize that they are persons in an environment and that they can influence their environment (Horn & Kang, 2012). The adults need to teach the children to turn outward—from their internal world to the external world of the environment and other people for stimulation. If they do not, children with multiple or severe disabilities tend to respond to internal rather than external stimuli and to use their genetic capacity for curiosity to explore by manipulating their internal world through body movements. As with many areas of disabilities, early intervention can both mediate the impact of the disability and prevent secondary problems from emerging (Bruce, 2011).

All of the definitions presented earlier help us understand the broad categories that are addressed by physical disabilities, health impairments, and multiple or severe disabilities, but we must remember that the specific needs of children within each category will be unique. On one blog, Ellen Seidman chronicles the

BOX 13.2 EXCEPTIONAL LIVES • EXCEPTIONAL STORIES

Counting on Me (*Continued*)

insurance would not cover. Eventually we also received a CAP-C slot, which provides respite care and Medicaid. Once my daughter turned 3, however, the bulk of support and assistance (which had been such a godsend) ended abruptly. In its place a different system arose, with lots of paperwork, policies, red tape, and many, many closed doors.

Frustration and disappointment landed me on the doorstep of The Arc of Wake County, where I met one of the most remarkable and passionate human beings I have ever known, Ms. Lynn Schwartz, family resource coordinator and guardianship specialist. For years now, she has been at my side through hours of individualized education program (IEP) meetings with the school board, as our advocate and our dear friend. Sometimes, that makes all the difference.

Through the unending trials and transitions, I quickly learned to lean on those I could count on and cut the losses from those I could not. I called upon friends when I needed support and reassurance. I called upon family when I needed a break. I called upon caseworkers when I ran out of ideas, and in the midst of desperation, I have even enlisted the aid of politicians and local news media. I have built my own vast invaluable support network.

No doubt, over the years, my heroes have had many faces—countless doctors, nurses, caseworkers, therapists, advocates, teachers, counselors, mothers, friends, and family. I could not have survived with less; however, my greatest debt of gratitude I owe to my daughter; she is my strength, my angel, and the most extraordinary teacher I have ever known.

Currently, Isabel is 5 years old, but developmentally she functions mentally and physically at a 2-year-old level (and yes, we are now in the terrible 2's!). She does not walk independently nor does she speak; we communicate primarily through ASL (American Sign Language), as this is far more efficient than mind reading. She has made incredible progress and every day is a celebration.

Changing Horizons

Isabel is beginning public school this fall (a terrifying experience for me). When we went to meet her new teacher, Isabel quickly extinguished my fears of my precious little one being trampled by some mean old fifth grader when she proudly tore off down the halls with her walker, running over toes and taking no prisoners! She has no idea that she is any different than anyone else. ... I think this is going to be a good year!

Because of Isabel, I am more patient, more persistent, and more understanding than I ever imagined possible. I am more educated and knowledgeable in matters of health, humanity, and humility. I have learned more about government systems, care, and resources (or lack of) than I ever cared to. I have learned how to ask for help when I cannot do it alone, and I have learned how to ask again. I have found that there are small groups of wonderful people out there who do care and want to help. I've learned about Medicaid and IEPs (having once been accused of being a lobbyist!). I have mastered the art of effective letter writing for my causes. I know how to smile proudly at the weak-minded apologies of those who see my life as misfortune. Because of Isabel, I am a passionate advocate, a loving mother, and a better human being because I have learned the hard way how to laugh, how to cry, and how to keep going—all because there is a strong, beautiful, and determined little person who believes in me and who calls me "mama." For Isabel, I have learned to count on me.

SOURCE: Crystal de la Cruz, Counting on me, *All Together Now!* 9(3), 2003. Reprinted by permission of Partnerships for Inclusion.

joys and challenges of raising her young son Max, who has CP. In Box 13.2, one mother shares some of the unique joys and challenges in raising her daughter, who has a rare genetic disorder.

Love that Max: Special Needs Blog
www.lovethatmax.com

13-6a Culturally Responsive Practices

The areas of race, culture, language, and disabilities all combine when we look at special education practices and equitable support for children with exceptionalities (Klingner, Blanchett, & Harry, 2007, Pickl, 2011). Culturally responsive communication and support are critical to building the partnerships with families that help children be successful (Nehring, 2007; Pickl, 2011). Cultural sensitivity includes a focus on the family's strengths and a valuing of the family's input into goal setting for their child (Nehring, 2007). Children who use augmentative communication face unique challenges when the languages spoken at home

© iStockphoto.com/ktaylorg

Family support is key to the wellbeing of all children.

and school are different (Pickl, 2011). For these children, communication support must be carefully coordinated between teachers and families, allowing the child to function in a multilingual world (Pickl, 2011).

Klingner and her colleagues (2009) offer ten suggestions for working with students of color with disabilities and their families:

1. Recognize the effect of race, culture, language, and social class issues on families' access to relevant special education services.
2. Acknowledge that special education and related services provisions are based on White, middle-class, English-speaking cultural norms and values and may not reflect the child and family's culture.
3. Communicate with students and families in their native language.
4. Communicate using lay and cultural terminology and avoid overreliance on professional jargon.
5. When meeting families, ask about their hopes and dreams for their child and recognize that these may be different from those typical of mainstream culture (but are just as valid).
6. Make sure print material is prepared in the native language.
7. Be familiar with and acknowledge within-group difference.
8. Whenever possible, provide services to ethnically, culturally, and linguistically diverse families within the context of relevant community or cultural centers.
9. Involve individuals of color in the development of appropriate IEPs and IFSPs.

13-6b Transition for Students with Multiple and/or Severe Disabilities

Table 13.9 lists ten things that can help prepare adolescents with disabilities for their transition to adulthood (Cobb, 2004).

For all individuals with disabilities, the transition from school to work and independent living presents a range of challenges, such as obtaining a driver to take them to and from work, remodeling an apartment so that all appliances can be reached from a wheelchair, or having a live-in aide with special knowledge of how to deal with various kinds of equipment. The focus of this transition should move beyond the individual's limitations to include a recognition of the individual's skills and strengths so that independence and self-fulfillment are enhanced. Growing up means becoming as autonomous as possible in all environments, self-regulation, self-evaluation, self-confidence, and finding ways to reach desired goals (Cobb, 2004).

Many students with physical disabilities will indeed go on to colleges and universities. A review of the transition planning for selecting a college in Chapter 11 may be useful in thinking about what this transition may require for individuals with physical disabilities. In this chapter, we focus on the transition to independent living and work.

To be able to accomplish the transition, the individual needs to be taught to move from high school vocational skills development to the community setting

TABLE 13.9 Top Ten Things to Think About in the Transition to Adulthood

1. Know your disability.	How does it affect you, your learning, and your activities, and how have you learned to manage it?
2. Know your needs.	What will be required of you in the new setting(s) and what will you need to be successful?
3. Weigh your options.	Gather information and seek advice from others, but most important, look at what you want out of life and set your goals accordingly.
4. Plan for "gatekeepers" (for example, college entrance exams, job-related exams).	Plan early for any known gatekeepers that you will need to negotiate in order to reach your goals.
5. Document your disability and your abilities.	Create a portfolio that documents your disability and your accomplishments.
6. Advocate for yourself.	Your ability to advocate for yourself is critical to your success. Know the laws and requirements and how to ask for what you need and deserve.
7. Use all services available to you.	Find and use *all* possible supports (such as vocational rehabilitation, student support services, special financial aid support, and community-based services).
8. Plan for independence in your living space.	Review your needs and plan ahead for appropriate supports, modifications, and accessibility to your new home, work, and/or learning environments.
9. Learn to manage your time.	Know what you must do, what you should do, and what you want to do, and plan twice as much time as you think you need!
10. Remember that making mistakes is *not* the end of the world.	Everyone struggles with change. Learning as you go is natural and will help you in the future.

Adapted from J. Cobb (2004). *Top ten things to think about as you prepare for your transition into adulthood.* Washington, D.C.: GW Heath Resource Center.

in which the work is to take place. This requires a **transition coordinator**, who plans for and assists in the transition (Bellamy, Rhodes, Mank, & Albin, 1988; Falvey, Coot, Bishop, & Grenot-Scheyer, 1989; Kochhar-Bryant, 2007; O'Neill, Gothelf, Cohen, Lehman, & Woolf, 1991).

Institute for Community Inclusion **www.communityinclusion.org**

An individual transition plan (ITP) is required for each student with disabilities (Bruce, 2011). The ITP requires a great deal of information from the school, the individual, the parents, and the community. Questions to be answered by the ITP include the following:

- What will the student need to learn before leaving school?
- Where will the person live as an adult?
- What activities will replace school for recreation?
- How will this individual support himself or herself?
- What will he or she do in leisure time?
- How will this person travel using community transportation?
- How will he or she gain access to medical care?
- What will be the relationship with his or her family?

MORAL DILEMMA

Gene Replacement Therapies

Current studies are underway to use gene replacement therapies for spinal muscular atrophies, muscular dystrophies, metabolic liver disease, sickle cell disease and other blood disorders, and retinal degeneration. While the results for genetic replacement therapies are promising, the techniques are not without controversy. The ethical implications of genetic replacement include concerns about bioengineering, the use of genetics to alter the natural course of human development and the use of genetic replacement technology to create "smart" biological weapons that could target groups based on their genetic makeup.

Because of your interest in children with special needs, you have been asked to provide a policy brief on the use of gene replacement for your state senators who are trying to decide if they should vote for additional research funding. What should you say... do the potential benefits for individuals outweigh the possible harm?

Naturally, every person with multiple or severe disabilities is unique and will need individualized planning. Advice, support, and guidance can be found through a state's center for independent living and center for vocational research. The coordinator must have the skill to develop a plan for each person. The teacher or coordinator collects information on the individual to find the most suitable community site, conduct a task analysis of what will be required at that work site, and then initiate a prescriptive program to meet these demands. The coordinator will try to match the individual to activities on the basis of the person's preferences. Key to the successful transition are services provided by vocational rehabilitation services within each state.

Transition planning can address: postsecondary programs, on-the-job education, internships and apprenticeships, adult education, trade school, and technical schools, as well as college and career education, depending on the individual's needs for support (NICHCY, 2000).

13-6c Honoring the Family's Journey: Coping with Chronic Sorrow

Each family will respond to their child's challenges in its own way; there is no "right" way. Some families will be strengthened and will find deeper meaning through the lessons learned because of their child's disabilities, other families will experience a sense of chronic sorrow. Perhaps most families experience both a sense of deeper meaning and feelings of chronic sorrow. **Chronic sorrow** is the presence of recurring intense feelings of grief sometimes experienced by parents of children with disabilities. It is a normal grief response to a "living loss"; filling the emotional chasm between "what is" and "what should have been". While chronic sorrow is not debilitating, its periodic surfacing brings with it a deep sense of sadness. Learning to accept and cope with this is part of the family's journey. Learning to support families in this journey is the responsibility of each professional.

ILRU Directory of State Centers for Independent Living
www.ilru.org/html/publications/directory/

Summary

- The history of services for children with physical disabilities, health impairments, and multiple disabilities shows an evolution from isolation toward meaningful inclusion with the support of a multidisciplinary team.
- Legislation supports and protects the rights of individuals with disabilities and requires accessibility to allow participation in social, educational, recreational, and vocational activities.
- Children with physical disabilities, health impairments, and multiple disabilities are a heterogeneous group, and each child will have unique physical, health, educational, and psychosocial needs.
- Advances in medical technologies continue to extend the life expectancy and enhance the quality of life for individuals with physical disabilities and health impairments.
- Federal definitions for each area of exceptionality have been given in IDEA, but each child's specific combination of strengths and areas of need must be taken into consideration in educational planning.

- The 2009 data from the U.S Department of Education indicates that just under 4 percent of students receiving special education have been identified with orthopedic impairments, deafblindness, traumatic brain injuries, or multiple disabilities, and that another 8.4 percent have been identified as other health impaired.
- Assistive technologies, including augmentative communication devices, help individuals gain independence.
- Universally designed assessment may someday help us get fair and accurate information regarding children's abilities and needs, but until then assessments are likely to underpredict children's capabilities.
- Children with physical disabilities will likely need an expanded core curriculum that includes functional and life skills, and they will likely need services at all three tiers of intervention (RtI).
- Families of children with physical disabilities, health impairments, and multiple disabilities face special challenges and may need intensive and ongoing support.
- Planning for transitions to adulthood must begin early and will require careful consideration of the student's strengths and needs.

Future Challenges

1. **How will we ensure that supports are available for the increasing numbers of adults with complex needs?**
   As medical advances help to extend the lives of individuals with severe disabilities and complex health needs, more individuals are living longer with more debilitating conditions. Currently, vocational rehabilitation services can work with only a fraction of the individuals who need support, and long-term care options for individuals with severe disabilities are often not available. How will we provide appropriate supports to ensure quality of life for these individuals?

2. **As assistive technologies are developed, how can we make sure that all children who need them have access to them and that they are supported by experts who can fix them when they malfunction?**
   The benefits of assistive technology are so great that they can mean the difference between dependence and independence for individuals with physical disabilities, but assistive technologies can be expensive. How can we make sure that cost is not a barrier to access for children who need the new technologies? How can we also ensure that support services include a person who can fix the technology when it breaks?

3. **How can we enhance meaningful collaboration that is transdisciplinary in nature?**
   The numbers of people needed on the multidisciplinary team to meet the needs of individuals with physical disabilities, health impairments, and multiple disabilities are substantial. These teams require individuals with expertise in health, education, social services, and technology. How can we enhance collaboration that moves from being cross-disciplinary to transdisciplinary in nature, in which professionals engage in meaningful collaboration?

TeachSource Digital Download Access online

Key Terms

acquired immune deficiency syndrome (AIDS) p. 429
age-appropriate p. 441
assistive technology (AT) p. 441
asthma p. 427
augmentative communication p. 441
cancer p. 429
cerebral palsy (CP) p. 424
chronic sorrow p. 450
diplegic p. 425
expanded core curriculum p. 440
functional skills p. 441
gene replacement therapy p. 434
germ line therapy p. 434
hemiplegic p. 425
human immunodeficiency virus (HIV) p. 429
juvenile arthritis p. 424
juvenile myoclonic epilepsy p. 426
mixed p. 424
motor skills and mobility p. 440
muscular dystrophy p. 424
neural tube defects p. 424
norm-referenced tests p. 435
quadriplegic p. 425
seizure disorder p. 426
seizure disorders p. 424
sickle cell anemia p. 429
somatic gene therapy p. 434
spastic, dyskinetic, ataxic p. 424
spinal curvatures p. 424
transition coordinator p. 449
traumatic brain injury (TBI) p. 424
universal precautions p. 430
Usher syndrome p. 432
writing aids p. 444

Resources

References of Special Interest

Best, S., Heller, K., & Bigge, J. (2010). *Teaching individuals with physical or multiple disabilities* (6th ed.). Upper Saddle River, NJ: Pearson. A recent edition of a comprehensive work that discusses educational and treatment issues. Practical suggestions and the names of vendors specializing in assistive technology are provided.

Kauffman, J. M., & Hallahan, D. P. (2011). *Handbook of special education.* New York, NY: Routledge. This book provides a comprehensive account of the field of special education in the United States today. The 57 chapters are written by a range of experts in the field and offer implications for both research and practice. In particular, see the chapters by Drasgow, Wolery, Halle, and Hajiaghamosheni, "Systematic instruction of students with severe disabilities," and Wehmeyer, "Access to general education curriculum for students with significant cognitive disabilities."

Snell, M., & Brown, F. (2005). *Instruction of students with severe disabilities* (6th ed.). Baltimore: Brookes. Twenty leaders in the field discuss in twelve chapters issues of teaching, policy, integration, research, and suggestions for practice. This book presents current thinking on persons with multiple or severe disabilities.

Journals

Journal of Applied Behavior Analysis
http://seab.envmed.rochester.edu/jaba/

Journal of the American Physical Therapy Association
www.ptjournal.org

Physical and Occupational Therapy in Pediatrics
http://informahealthcare.com/journal/pop

Research and Practice for Persons with Severe Disabilities (formerly *Journal of the Association for Persons with Severe Handicaps)*
http://www.researchgate.net/journal/1540-7969_Research_and_Practice_for_Persons_with_Severe_Disabilities

Professional Organizations

The Association for Persons with Severe Disabilities (TASH) **www.tash.org**

Division for Physical and Health Disabilities (DPHD)/ Council for Exceptional Children (CEC) **http://web.utk.edu/~dphmd/**

Epilepsy Foundation of America (EFA) **www.epilepsyfoundation.org**

March of Dimes Birth Defects Foundation **www.modimes.org**

National Consortium on Deafblindness **http://nationaldb.org/**

National Rehabilitation Information Center **www.naric.com**

United Cerebral Palsy Association, Inc.**www.ucp.org**

Glossary

acceleration An intervention for students with special gifts and talents by which the school moves the student through the system more rapidly.
acquired hearing loss A hearing loss that has occurred in either childhood or adulthood.
acquired immune deficiency syndrome (AIDS) A breakdown of the body's immune system, allowing the body to become vulnerable to a host of fatal infections that it normally is able to ward off.
adaptation Changes in the student program that take into account the special needs of children with exceptionalities to help them meet with success.
advanced placement A series of advanced courses designed for secondary students to earn college credit while still in high school. Student performance is monitored by the College Entrance Examination Board.
age-appropriate Skills that match a student's chronological age, as opposed to his or her mental age.
alarm systems (alerting devices) Devices and systems for the deaf and hard of hearing that use flashing lights or vibration to provide notification of events that hearing people detect through sound, such as a baby crying, fire alarm, or alarm clock.
albinism The absence of pigmentation resulting from an inheritance of recessive genes (affecting approximately 1 in 20,000 individuals); can lead to problems with vision.
amblyopia A decrease in visual acuity due to poor transmission, through the optic nerve, of information to the brain (sometimes called "lazy-eye" affects 1–5% of the population).
American Recovery and Reinvestment Act Federal legislation passed in 2009 to stimulate economic recovery, including large one-time grants for early intervention services.
American Sign Language (ASL) A manual language used by many people with hearing impairments, considered to be a full language, just as spoken English is.
Americans with Disabilities Act Passed in 1990, this civil rights legislation prohibits discrimination based on disability. This law led to greater access to public transportation, commercial facilities, and telecommunications for individuals with disabilities. The law was further amended in 2008 to give broader protections for workers with disabilities.
antecedent behaviors Behaviors which precede a student crisis, which may lead to greater understanding of the student behavior.
anticipatory anxiety A fear and undermining of self-confidence caused by past experiences of failure and frustration, which can sabotage success with new experiences.
Apgar test A screening test administered to an infant at one minute and five minutes after birth.
applied behavior analysis (ABA) A learning approach that is based on individual analysis of a student's functioning and relies on the learning of behaviors to remediate learning problems.
articulation The movement of the mouth and tongue that shapes sound into speech.
articulation disorder Difficulty forming and stringing sounds together, usually characterized by substituting one sound for another (*wabbit* for *rabbit*), omitting a sound (*han* for *hand*), or distorting a sound (*ship* for *sip*).
Asperger's syndrome A form of autism that features the usual social and behavior problems, but where the cognitive abilities may be average or above.
assessment A process for identifying a child's strengths and weaknesses; it involves five steps: screening, diagnosis, classification, placement, and monitoring or discharge.
assistive technology (AT) Tools that enhance the functioning of persons with disabilities.
asthma A respiratory condition that results in difficulty breathing or coughing.
astigmatism A refraction error that creates blurred vision.
ataxic cerebral palsy A condition in which voluntary movement involving balance is abnormal.
attention deficit hyperactivity disorder (ADHD) A disorder that causes children to have difficulty settling down to do a particular task, especially desk work.
audition Thought transformed into words and received by a listener through hearing.
auditory acuity The ability to take in sounds and get them to the brain successfully.
auditory brainstem response (ABR) A neurological hearing test for infants which is used to determine whether the ear is functioning appropriately and the brain is receiving the sound signal.
auditory perception One's ability to process information from different sources, including hearing speech against background noise, sound discriminations, and sound recognition.
auditory processing The brain's ability to recognize and interpret sounds.
auditory steady state response (ASSR) A hearing evaluation that uses continuous stimuli to elicit a response

and can provide frequency-specific auditory information.

augmentative communication Nontraditional methods of communication, including the use of assistive technology devices, for children with physical and other disabilities who cannot acquire understandable speech or legible writing skills.

augmented and alternative communication A variety of assistive technologies that help an individual communicate. These range from sophisticated voice synthesizers to relatively simple story boards with pictures that indicate words and actions.

authentic assessment Measuring a child's ability by means of an in-class assignment.

behavior contract A written document signed by student and teacher in which there is an agreement that the student will change his or her behavior. There will be rewards for carrying out the contract and consequences for breaking the contract.

behavior disorder A condition in which a student consistently violates social and school rules and disrupts the classroom and requires educational action to meet with success.

behavior intervention plan (BIP) Similar to the individualized education program (IEP), in which a team of professionals, in collaboration with the family and student, lay out a plan to counteract unacceptable behavior and develop positive behaviors for a student who has been excluded for disciplinary reasons.

behavioral support plan A plan of services devised by teachers and parents to give support to children trying to overcome challenging behavior. This plan focuses on antecedents to the difficult behavior, what the actual behavior is, and the consequence of the behaviors in order to provide the child with support.

bilingual-bicultural approach Cultural viewpoint that persons who are deaf are bicultural because they belong to both the Deaf culture and the society in which they live. Many who are deaf are also bilingual because they use both a sign language system (usually ASL) and the spoken or written language of their culture, such as English.

blended practices Practices that bridge the gap between special and general education by creating one comprehensive approach for teaching young children with and without disabilities.

blind/blindness Sight ability less than 20/200. Children who are blind cannot use vision for learning, but may still be responsive to light and darkness and may have some visual imagery.

bone-conductor test A test used to assess hearing in children under age 3 by bypassing the ear and measuring the movement of sound through the bone and the hearing system to the brain.

Braille A system using embossed characters in different combinations of six dots arranged in a cell that allows people with profound visual impairments to read by touch as well as to write by using special aids.

bullying A display of interpersonal violence in which the bully asserts power through some form of aggression and the victim experiences distress and the loss of power, resulting in an unequal relationship.

cancer A malignant abnormal growth or tumor. Rare in children, the most common forms are leukemia, lymphoma, or a brain tumor.

central auditory processing disorder (CAPD) Disorder characterized by difficulties with sound localization, auditory discrimination, understanding speech sounds against a noisy background, auditory sequencing, memory, pattern recognition, sounding out words, and reading comprehension.

central auditory processing loss Hearing difficulty that limits the individual's ability to process and use auditory information.

central processing Classification of a stimulus through the use of memory, reasoning, and evaluation; the second step in the information-processing model.

cerebral palsy A condition caused by damage to the motor control centers of the brain before birth, during the birth process, or after birth.

Child Find Public awareness activities, screening, and evaluation designed to locate, identify, and refer as early as possible all young children with disabilities and their families who are in need of Early Intervention Program (Part C) or Preschool Special Education (Part B/619) services of the Individuals with Disabilities Education Act (IDEA).

child with exceptionalities A child who differs from the norm in mental characteristics, sensory abilities, communication abilities, social behavior, or physical characteristics to the extent that special education services are required for the child to develop to maximum capacity.

chronic sorrow The presence of a deep sense of grief experienced as a "living loss" by some parents of children with disabilities.

class action suit A legal case in which the results of the suit apply to an entire class of people, not just the immediate persons involved in the case. A parent suing for the rights of her child with autism can reaffirm rights that apply to all children with autism.

cleft palate A congenital abnormality that occurs when the roof of the mouth has not joined completely during prenatal development.

cochlea Part of the inner ear that contains part of the hearing organs.

cochlear implant A small electronic device that can be surgically implanted into the ear of a person who is profoundly deaf or severely hard-of-hearing to provide a sense of sound. It consists of a microphone, a speech processor, a transmitter and receiver/stimulator, and an electrode array.

cochlear nerve Bundle of nerve fibers that carries hearing information from the cochlea to the brain (also known as the *auditory nerve*).

coercive family system The use of physical or psychological force for imposing will within a family.

cognitive strategy approach A family of strategies that help individuals gain greater awareness of and responsibility for their actions.
collaborative problem solving Working with a multidisciplinary team of individuals and parents to design services that address the student's needs.
Common Core State Standards (CCSS) These curriculum standards were developed at the request of the National Governors Association and the Council of Chief State School Officers to provide a single set of standards for children throughout the United States. The standards address learning in reading/language arts/English and mathematics in grades K-12.
communication The exchange of thoughts, information, feelings, or ideas.
communication disorders Impairments in articulation, fluency, voice, or language.
comorbidity The coexistence of conditions that can make diagnosis and treatment more complex (e.g., ADHD and anxiety disorders).
comprehensive treatment models A group of interventions that address the core symptoms of autism spectrum disorders and are presented over a period of time (a year or more) with intensive treatment. Examples include the UCLA Young Autism Program and TEACCH.
conceptual skills One area used to define the presence of intellectual and developmental disabilities, this includes the individual's ability to use language and literacy, and understand concepts such as money and time.
conductive hearing loss Hearing loss caused by something (wax, ear infections [otitis media], or any type of malformation of the ear canal) blocking the sound that passes through the outer or middle ear, which makes hearing faint sounds more difficult.
congenital hearing loss Losses present at birth.
contextual Teaching that embeds key information to be learned within a rich and meaningful sequence of experiences that activate the students' prior knowledge and anchor new learning.
cooperative learning A set of instructional strategies that emphasize the use of groups for teaching students techniques of problem solving and working constructively with others.
correlated assets Conditions linked favorably with one another, such as high IQ scores with personality.
correlated constraints Conditions that tend to appear with one another and perform on another condition. For example, good academic performance and the presence of supportive adults tend to operate as a brake on aggression.
co-teaching When two (or more) teachers work collaboratively to share expertise, combine resources, and create optimal learning experiences for their students. Co-teachers are mutually responsible for the outcomes of the students; they jointly plan and carry out instruction (e.g., a general education content specialist co-teaches with a special educator to meet the needs of their class).
creativity Mental process by which individuals create new ideas and products or recombine existing ideas and products in a fashion that is novel to them.
culture The attitudes, values, customs, and language that form an identifiable pattern or heritage.
curriculum compacting Content modification that allows students who are gifted to move ahead. It consists of three steps: finding out what the students know, arranging to teach the remaining concepts or skills, and providing a different set of experiences to enrich or advance the students.
Deaf community (culture) This community exists as a separate cultural group of diverse individuals who share the bonds of a common language, specific behavioral protocols, and traditions (e.g., world games, newspapers, advocacy activities) established over many years of membership. Individuals often feel a strong allegiance and identity with the Deaf community.
deafblindness The condition of little or no useful sight and little or no useful hearing, the combination of which causes severe communication, developmental, and other educational needs that require special services.
decibel (dB) Unit used to measure the intensity of a sound.
developmental delays Each state defines what constitutes a "developmental delay" across five domains: cognitive, communicative, social-emotional, motor, and adaptive development. Based on the state's definition, children with developmental delays and their families qualify for early intervention supports and services.
developmental disabilities Mental retardation and related conditions (e.g., cerebral palsy) that create a substantial delay in the child's development and require intervention from many professional disciplines.
developmental profile A chart presenting the intraindividual differences in development for a particular student.
developmentally appropriate practice (DAP) Curriculum practices that match the level of development of the child and are presented in ways that children learn, such as in play.
dialect A variant in pronunciation and syntax of a spoken language.
differentiated instruction Refers to the changes in teacher strategies and curriculum made necessary by the characteristics of the exceptional child.
diplegic A form of cerebral palsy affecting the whole body, where the legs are often more impacted than the arms.
Down syndrome A chromosomal abnormality that leads to mild or moderate intellectual and developmental disabilities and, at times, a variety of hearing, skeletal, and heart problems.
dysgraphia Brain dysfunction or disease that causes an inability to write, or to write legibly.

dyskinetic cerebral palsy A condition characterized by tonal abnormalities that involves the entire body and muscle tone that changes constantly.

dyslexia A severe reading disability involving difficulties in understanding the relationship between sounds and letters.

dysphonia A disorder in voice quality.

eardrum A thin layer of skin at the end of the external ear canal.

early intervention Systematic efforts designed to prevent deficits or to improve an existing disability in children between birth and age 5.

ecological model A view of exceptionality that examines the individual in complex interaction with environmental forces and believes that exceptionalities should be remediated by modifying elements in the environment to allow more constructive interactions between the individual and the environment.

ecology of the child Those forces surrounding and impacting on the child from family, culture, peers, physical setting, etc.

educational infrastructure The capacity to support organizational change through personnel preparation, research, technical assistance, and policy.

embedded instruction The use of a child's daily activities to teach and reinforce key skills, allowing teachers to use typical classroom routines to strengthen and reinforce learning.

emotional disorder The internalization of difficulties and challenges, which can lead to stress, depression, and anxiety that interfere with life.

encephalitis An inflammation of the brain, usually refers to brain inflammation caused by a virus. It is a rare disease that only occurs in approximately 0.5 per 100,000 individuals—most commonly in children, the elderly, and people with weakened immune systems (i.e., those with HIV/AIDS or cancer).

episodic memory One's ability to recall whole scenes or episodes from one's past, often brought on by smells.

evidence-based interventions Intervention strategies that research has demonstrated to be effective.

evidence-based practice Practices that have shown effectiveness based on research, practitioner's wisdom, and family values.

executive function The hypothesized decision-making element that controls reception, central processing, and expression.

executive processing The monitoring or decision-making component of the Information Processing Model, sometimes referred to as "metacognitive processing."

expanded core curriculum A plan of study which includes functional and life skills as well as academic skills.

explicit teaching Instruction that involves using language that is both precise and concise, giving clear examples of what is to be learned, and providing schema that show the organization of ideas to be learned.

expressive language The ability to produce a message to send; typically involves speaking and writing.

family-centered intervention (model, approach) Empowering families to take a lead role with professionals in determining what is best for their child. This is done through support that focuses on the strengths of the child and family. The family is directly involved in decision making, planning, and implementing interventions for their child.

fetal alcohol spectrum disorder Defects in a child as a result of the mother's heavy use of alcohol during her pregnancy; fetal alcohol syndrome is the most serious type.

fidelity of implementation The degree to which a program, curriculum, or intervention is used as it was intended or designed to be used. This is also known as the integrity of implementation.

fluency/fluency disorder The flow of speech and difficulties with producing smooth speech.

focused intervention practice An intervention which is short term with specific goals (e.g., reduce an undesirable behavior).

fragile X syndrome (FXS) A restriction at the end of the X chromosome that may result in mental retardation or learning disabilities.

free and appropriate public education (FAPE) The courts have affirmed that children with exceptionalities are guaranteed the right to an education provided by the state that is suitable to their needs.

functional behavioral assessment (FBA) Valuations of behavior that define a behavior, explain why this behavior occurs, describe where and when the behavior is present, and demonstrate how the behavior impacts the child and his or her surroundings. The premise is that there is a rational purpose for every behavior and that it is necessary to understand why and how negative or destructive behaviors are triggered in order to reduce them.

functional skills Skills that can be used immediately by the student, are necessary in everyday settings, and increase to some extent the student's independence (e.g., folding clothes).

gene replacement therapy A method by which defective or damaged genetic material is replaced and corrected.

gene-environment interaction A description of how certain conditions are caused by both genetics and environment. Neuroscience has shown us that almost all behavioral traits emerge from complex interactions among multiple genes and environments; thus, we cannot say that genes cause depression or ADHD, rather the complex mix of environments and multiple genes can result in some unfavorable outcomes.

generalization The ability to transfer a skill or strategy to a new or different context, content area, or situation (e.g., the student learns to order and pay for his lunch at school and can use these skills in a public restaurant; a student learns to outline a chapter in social studies and can use this strategy in science; a student learns to introduce herself to new members of the class and shows that she is able to do this at the community center as well).

genetic counseling A source of information for parents about the likelihood of their having a child with genetically based disabilities.

germ line therapy A method by which sperm or egg cells are modified by introducing functional genes.

hearing aids Small electronic devices that provide sound amplification for individuals who are deaf and hard of hearing.

heightened sensitivity Oversensitivity to sensory input, including lights, sounds, smells, and tastes.

hemiplegic A form of cerebral palsy where just one side of the body (both arm and leg) are affected.

high-incidence disabilities The disabilities that are most prevalent in the United States, composing at least 1 percent of the school population.

high-stakes testing Any examination whose results can substantially change the future of a student, such as course failure or admittance to college.

homeschooling Educating at home. The home-schooling movement involves over a million U.S. parents who have chosen to educate their children at home rather than send them to schools. This movement began as a response to parental concerns about appropriate religious instruction, but today many parents homeschool because they feel their child's needs cannot be met within the traditional school setting.

human immunodeficiency virus (HIV) A virus that breaks down the body's immune system, causing AIDS.

hyperopia Vision problem, commonly known as "farsightedness," that creates blurred vision and difficulty focusing on near objects.

hypersensitivity A shared characteristic of persons with autism spectrum disorders in which they cannot modulate sounds or other stimuli.

hypertext software A computer program that aids reading by providing definitions, pronunciations, and other supplemental materials.

hypertonia Having abnormally high muscle tone characterized by rigidity or spasticity; can be treated through physical therapy.

incidental learning Learning that occurs when the information is not being explicitly taught (e.g., the social norm of standing 2–3 feet away from individuals we do not know well is "learned" but not usually explicitly taught). For students with disabilities explicit teaching may be needed for skills that are usually learned incidentally.

inclusion The process of bringing children with exceptionalities into the regular classroom.

individualized education program (IEP) A program written for every student receiving special education; it describes the child's current performance and goals for the school year, the particular special education services to be delivered, and the procedures by which outcomes are to be evaluated.

individualized family service plan (IFSP) An intervention program for young children and their families that identifies their needs and sets forth a program to meet those needs.

Individuals with Disabilities Education Act (IDEA) The law originally passed in 1975 as PL 94-142 and reauthorized in 2004, addressing the school's responsibility to children with exceptionalities in the classroom.

information processing model (IPM) A model that describes learning as a series of components that involve sensory stimulation/input, processing/thinking, and output, or the sharing of what has been learned.

instructional technology A growing field of study that uses technology as a means to solve educational challenges, both in the classroom and in distance learning environments.

integrated curriculum Curriculum that incorporates advanced content, higher order thinking, and experiences build around major themes, problems, or real world applications.

intellectual and developmental disabilities (IDD) Significant delay in intellectual development and adaptive behvior, formerly known as *mental retardation*.

interindividual difference A substantial difference among people along key dimensions of development.

International Baccalaureate program A program that provides a rigorous course of study with active learning, citizenship, internationalism, and respect for other cultures.

intervening hierarchy A model for organizing intervention strategies from least to most intensive. The model has three or more tiers; Tier I is a high-quality general learning environment, and the additional tiers provide more help for students whose needs require more intensive supports.

intraindividual difference A major variation in the abilities or development of a single child.

juvenile myoclonic epilepsy A disease that causes seizures in school-age children.

language A code whereby ideas about the world are represented through a conventional system of arbitrary signals for communication.

language content The meaning of words and sentences. Also called *semantics*.

language disorders The impairment or deviant development of comprehension or use (or both) of a spoken, written, or other symbol system.

language form The sounds, words, and grammar that underlie a language to create its individual form, or structure; includes phonology, morphology, and syntax.

language function The use of language within a given society and a specific context.

language pragmatics The ways that language is used to communicate appropriately within a variety of contexts.

learned helplessness The belief that nothing one does can prevent negative things from happening.

learning disability An identified area of disability that impacts the individual's ability to learn. This may impact any learning area including reading, spelling, mathematics, writing, and/or social skills. Individuals often need additional support to meet with success in school.

learning environment This may be the classroom, but may also include the home, neighborhood, community, and any other setting where structured learning is taking place.

least restrictive environment The educational setting in which a child with special needs can learn that is as close as possible to the general education classroom.

long-term memory A way of storing information in the brain for future retrieval.

low vision Visual acuity of 20/70 to 20/200. Students with low vision can still benefit from visual learning through the use of various technologies to enhance their sight.

low-incidence disabilities The disabilities that comprise less than 1 percent of the school population in the United States.

media access Availability of information that can be accessed and utilized by individuals with disabilities, including captioned television.

medical model A view of exceptionality that implies a physical condition or disease within the patient.

memory The process by which information is encoded, stored, and retrieved for use (includes working, short-term, and long-term).

mental retardation A term formerly used for children with intellectual and developmental disabilities. Refers to children who are developmentally delayed and who need special education services to meet with success.

metacognition The ability to think about one's own thinking and monitor its effectiveness.

metacognitive approach Helping students understand how to "think about their thinking" as they work to solve problems, activate or select strategies to use, and anchor learning in their memory.

mirror neurons Cells in the nervous system that allow the individual to imitate others' speech and actions. Apparently not fully functional in children with autism.

mixed cerebral palsy A condition with a combination of spastic, dyskinetic, and ataxic cerebral palsy that impacts each child differently, but affects balance and coordination for almost all children.

mixed hearing loss Hearing loss resulting from problems in the outer ear, as well as in the middle or inner ear.

morphology The rules that address how words are formed and their structure.

motor memory The ability to program one's body movements to learn patterns and retain them for future use.

motor skills and mobility Skills that are necessary to maintain upright postures (sitting, standing), to perform functional movements (reaching, grasping), and to move around in the environment.

multidisciplinary team A group of professionals who work together to help plan and carry out intervention or treatment for children with disabilities to help them achieve their full potential.

multiple disabilities A combination of impairments, such as deafblindness or intellectual delays-orthopedic impairment, that results in severe educational needs that require special services.

multi-modal support The use of a variety of instructional approaches including tactile, auditory, kinesthetic, and/or visual strategies.

multiple intelligences A theory associated with Howard Gardner that proposes nine separate intelligences instead of one general intelligence.

Multi-Tiered Systems of Support Models, like RtI, that provide supports across levels of service, varying in intensity.

myopia A vision problem, commonly known as "nearsightedness" with blurring or difficulty focusing on distant objects.

natural environments Settings that are typical for children with and without disabilities; including the home, neighborhood, community setting and place of worship.

neurotransmitters Chemicals that transmit signals across the synaptic cleft between neurons, allowing information exchange throughout the nervous system.

No Child Left Behind (NCLB) Federal legislation designed to aid children who have fallen behind their grade level in performance, including children with disabilities.

norm-referenced tests Standardized assessments used to compare an individual child's score with the typical score for other children in his or her age group.

nystagmus Rapid and irregular involuntary movements of the eye that cause difficulty focusing.

object permanence The understanding that objects which are not in the visual field still exist.

optic nerve hypoplasia Underdevelopment of the optic nerve, often associated with other developmental delays.

orientation and mobility (O&M) training Teaching a person with visual loss or with blindness how to move through space.

orthopedic impairment A severe injury or disorder of the skeletal system and surrounding muscles, joints, and ligaments that adversely affects a child's educational performance (such as cerebral palsy, amputations, or fractures or burns that cause a distortion of the scar tissue or joints).

otitis media Middle-ear infection that can lead to hearing loss.

otoacoustic auditory emissions (OAE) A technique for measuring hearing ability by placing a small microphone in a child's ear and testing for the child's ability to hear the echo produced by the stimulation of hair cells in the ear.

peer tutoring An instructional strategy in which a child with disability is paired with a student who has been coached by the teacher to provide specific help (e.g., reading to each other).

Perfectionism Thoughts and behaviors that lead to the setting of high standards and that, if taken too far, can cause failure avoidance and emotional stress.

performance assessment A measure of the application of knowledge.

pervasive developmental disorders not otherwise specified (PDDNOS) These are autistic-like conditions that do not fulfill all of the diagnostic characteristics for autism, but show strong resemblance in terms of social and communication problems. Increasingly referred to as autistic spectrum disorders, reflecting the variations found in these conditions.

phenotype The composition of an organism's observable characteristics resulting from the interaction of the genes and the environmental influences (e.g., our skin color and our weight are part of our phenotype).

phenylketonuria (PKU) A single-gene defect that can produce severe retardation because of the body's inability to break down phenylalanine, which when accumulated at high levels in the brain results in severe damage; can be controlled by a diet restricting phenylalanine.

phonation The production of sound by the vibration of the vocal cords.

phonology The science of speech sounds and the rules that govern how these sounds combine to form words and to convey meaning.

PL 88-164 Refers to federal legislation authorizing funds for personnel preparation. It was the first of many legislative efforts to meet the needs of children with disabilities.

PL 94-142 The original law, passed in 1975, that became IDEA (originally known as Education for All Handicapped Children Act).

PL 99-457 Extends previous legislation to include children with disabilities from birth on instead of just school-age children. The title of the basic act was changed to Individuals with Disability Education Act (IDEA).

play audiometry Hearing tests for young children conducted in a pleasant environment using toys that move and make sounds to elicit responses such as eye blinks and changes in respiration or heartbeat (slower heartbeats indicate attention).

positive behavior interventions and supports (PBIS) An approach to intervention based on behavior science principles and meant to replace punitive measures for behavior control. It includes functional assessments, positive interventions, and evaluative measures to assess progress.

postlinguistic hearing loss The loss of hearing after spontaneous speech and language have developed.

practical skills Life skills needed to be successful in real-world settings (e.g., counting money, making a sandwich, riding the bus); these may be part of the student's IEP.

prelinguistic hearing loss The loss of hearing before speech and language have developed; referred to as *deafness*.

prereferral committee or team Professionals who support the teacher in planning interventions for the student prior to referral for special education, to see if referral is still needed after additional support is given for the student's success.

problem-based learning (PBL) A problem that encourages the student to define the issue, organize the components, and then solve the problem.

prodigy A child who has shown extraordinary development in his or her early years of development and is capable of adult behavior while still very young, such as chess playing, musical composition, or poetry writing.

progress monitoring Using data (such as test results or performance on screening measures) on student's achievement, performance, and other needs to monitor progress, guide decision making, and plan for future needs.

proprioceptive An awareness of where one's body is in relation to the space around it.

psychotropic Affecting the neurosystem.

pure-tone audiometry The most frequently used method for assessing hearing in which an audiometer presents pure tones of varying frequency and intensity to an individual wearing a headset.

quadriplegic A form of cerebral palsy where the impact is equally spread throughout the body.

receptive language The ability to take in a message and understand it (that is, listening with understanding to oral language or reading written language with comprehension).

reciprocal teaching A technique in which small groups of students and teachers take turns leading a discussion.

related services Support services that are required to assist the child in benefiting from special education.

relationship-focused intervention (RF) Intervention that helps parents develop responsive interactions with their children, building on the social nurturing between the parents and the child. This approach was first developed to support parents of children who have autism.

replacement behaviors Positive behaviors for children with behavior disorders, such as asking for permission to talk, that are designed to replace unacceptable behavior. This practice is based on the principle that the child often has no acceptable behaviors in his repertoire and is in trouble as a consequence.

residential schools Schools where students live as well as attend classes. Some residential programs are year-round, whereas others include a range of schedules (e.g., school year only, weekdays only). Students with sensory, multiple, or severe disabilities may be able to receive more intensive supports within a residential school than they could get from a traditional school program.

resonation The process that gives the voice its special characteristics.

respiration Breathing; the process that generates the energy that produces sound.

respite care Short-term care provided to give major caregivers a break from their caregiving responsibilities.

Response to Intervention (RTI) A multilevel approach to helping children face difficulties in school. Proposes a range of interventions from general classroom to special education.

retinopathy of prematurity A disease of the retina in which a mass of scar tissue forms in back of the lens of the eye. Both eyes are usually affected, and it occurs chiefly in infants born prematurely who receive excessive oxygen.

Rett syndrome A condition included within autism spectrum disorders because its symptoms resemble autism. It is a progressive neurological disorder in which individuals reveal a loss of muscle functions, hand flapping, and autistic behavior. Symptoms appear in children 6 to 18 months, and educational treatment is similar to treatment for autism.

rubella German measles, which in the first three months of pregnancy can cause visual impairment, hearing impairment, intellectual and developmental disabilities, and birth defects in the fetus.

scaffolding A strategy in which a teacher models the expected behavior and guides the learning of the student.

schoolwide behavior supports An attempt to use behavior principles to create an emotionally healthy school environment. This would include rules for behavior and guidelines for punishment. The goal is to bring to the entire school population the positive behavior supports usually given to specific students.

Section 504 A section of the Rehabilitation Act of 1973 that requires a plan for support outlining the accommodations and interventions needed to help the student who has a condition that substantially limits a major life activity succeed in school.

seizure disorder A condition characterized by multiple seizures (i.e., abnormal electrical discharge within the brain that disrupts the brain's normal functioning). This is considered to be symptomatic of an underlying problem that requires a full medical evaluation.

self-determination The ability to set personal goals and to take appropriate actions to achieve them.

self-evaluation Students are asked to compare their current behavior with some criterion (e.g., paying attention in class) and adjust accordingly.

self-instructional training A series of instructions designed to help the students plan for themselves to engage in problem solving or managing anger or resisting peer pressure.

self-management Having children with disabilities make decisions and be responsible for their lives. Many intervention programs are designed to help students attain this responsibility gradually.

self-monitoring or self-regulatory skill An individual's ability to continuously adapt thoughts, speech, and actions to accomplish goals and adapt to the environment.

self-reinforcement Reward of a token or tally after meeting some performance standard (i.e., reducing aggressive outbursts); tokens are turned in for some privileges in the classroom, such as doing puzzles.

semantic memory Stores concepts, words, symbols, and generalizations; most often used in school.

semantics The meaning of words or the content of the message, which must be interpreted within the context of the communication.

sensorineural hearing loss Hearing loss caused by damage to the inner ear (cochlea) or to the auditory nerve, particularly in the delicate sensory hairs of the inner ear or in the nerves that supply them. These losses affect both the ability to hear faint sounds and the ability to hear clearly, making understanding speech sounds difficult.

sensory integration The ability to use two or more senses simultaneously and smoothly.

sensory memory The ability to accommodate a large amount of information for a short period of time (2-3 seconds), which allows us to take in information and interpret what we are seeing, hearing, tasting, smelling, etc.

short-term memory Temporarily storing information while simultaneously completing tasks; involves strategies for consciously storing information, such as rehearsal.

sickle cell anemia A form of anemia caused by a mutation in the gene that tells the body to make hemoglobin A (the red, iron-rich compound), which allows red blood cells to carry oxygen to all parts of your body. The symptoms include stroke, speech difficulties, seizures, painful joints and extremities, vision problems, fatigue, fever, and infection.

slope of improvement A visual graph depicting the change in a student's rate and level of growth on skills.

social skills One area used to identify children with intellectual and development disabilities; include things such as interpersonal abilities, gullibility/naiveté, social problem solving, and following rules.

somatic gene therapy A method by which therapeutic genes are transferred into somatic cells and therefore only impact the patient, not future generations.

spastic cerebral palsy A form of cerebral palsy marked by tight muscles and stiff movements.

speech The systematic oral production of words of a given language.

speech disorders Disorders of articulation, voice, or fluency.

speech-to-print systems Computer programs that reproduce the classroom dialogue on a computer screen, either through typing captions or voice-activated software.

spinal curvatures Curvatures in the spine that deviate from the spine's "normal" shape and may cause difficulties for the individual.

standard protocol A prescribed manner of conducting interventions. It may include a specified lesson or series of steps.

strategic teaching Using mnemonics, organizational strategies, and specific approaches that facilitate memory; making connections across information being learned; and the ability to apply information within new contexts in order to instruct students.

stuttering A speech disorder of fluency.
support services Services provided to help a student meet with success.
support teacher A teacher who provides direct assistance to the student with disabilities and to their teacher within the regular classroom setting. This support may include assistance with behavior management, focused work with learning activities, therapeutic tutorials, and general assistance with classroom needs to allow the regular classroom teacher time to work with the student with disabilities.
supralinguistics The sophisticated analysis of meaning when the literal meaning of the word or phrase is *not* the intended meaning.
syntax The rules that guide how words are combined to form sentences and the relationships of components within the sentence.
tactile defensiveness Oversensitivity to touch that causes discomfort.
talent development A term used to describe the special educational strategies used with children with special gifts and talents. Some use it to replace the term "education of gifted students."
task analysis A process of breaking a large and complex task into manageable pieces so that these can be accomplished in sequence.
team approach A collaborative approach that builds partnerships across professionals and with families to combine the expertise needed to help the student meet with success.
telecommunications The transmission of signals over distance for the purpose of communication, such as television and telephone.
teratogen A substance ingested by the mother that can damage the growth and development of the fetus.
Theory of Mind A condition where children are unable to put themselves in the place of others in order to understand what they are feeling or thinking. This inability leads to predictable social problems.
tiered assignment Assignment of greater or lesser difficulty to students to match their level of possible attainment. In this way, all students can be involved in the same problem but at levels that match their capabilities.
TORCHS A group of infections that affect the mother and that can also cause severe hearing losses in the fetus: toxoplasmosis (*TO*), rubella (*R*; German measles), cytomegalovirus (*C*; CMV), and herpes simplex virus (*HS*).
total communication method A method of teaching deaf students that combines finger spelling, signs, speech reading, speech, and auditory amplification. Also called *combined method* and *simultaneous method.*
transactional theory Describes child development as an ongoing series of reciprocal relationships between the child and her or his environment.
transition coordinator The individual who plans for and assists a student with disabilities in the transition from school to work.
transition planning The process of planning to support students moving to post-secondary settings (e.g., jobs, college, assisted living) through goal setting, support, and resource identification.
traumatic brain injury (TBI) An injury of the brain caused by an external physical force, resulting in total or partial functional disability and/or psychosocial impairment that requires special educational services.
twice-exceptional Presence of both giftedness and an area of disability.
underachievers with SGT Students with special gifts and talents whose academic performance consistently falls far short of expectations despite high cognitive abilities.
unexplained underachievement A learning problem that does not have a neurological base but which is characterized by performance below expected levels.
Universal Design for Learning (UDL) A variety of strategies that give all students access to the curriculum. These strategies include the use of technology to reduce the impact of sensory and learning disabilities, the incorporation of flexible entry points to allow students to begin work at a level appropriate to their needs, and the use of multiple instructional approaches to respond to different student learning needs and styles.
universal group behavior support A schoolwide strategy setting rules and standards for expected behavior in cafeterias, hallways, etc., to improve student behavior in the schools.
universal precautions Methods for reducing the spread of germs and infections (such as AIDS), including proper handwashing routines, use of gloves to clean up bodily fluids, and following biohazard cleanup protocols.
Usher syndrome A progressive degeneration of vision and hearing occurring some years after birth.
vestibular apparatus The vestibule and three semicircular canals of the inner ear. These structures work with the brain to sense, maintain, and regain balance and to perceive one's body orientation relative to the earth.
visual impairment Any form of visual loss. These visual difficulties can be very moderate (such as the need for glasses) or a complete loss of vision.
visual perception One's ability to process information from figure-ground input (seeing an object against the background), closure (completion of a figure), and spatial relationships.
Visual Voice Tools Computer software designed to improve voicing, pitch, timing, and sustained production of users with hearing loss.
voice The intonation and quality of the production of words, such as pitch, loudness, and resonance.
voice disorder A variation from accepted norms in voice quality, pitch, or loudness.
wraparound approach An approach to interventions tailored to children with disabilities and their families that offers full support from multiple perspectives across the community. The support may include counseling, educational assistance, medical services, and assistance from social services. The purpose is to provide a full-support network to help the child and family move toward success.
writing aids Augmented and alternative systems that are available for written communication.

References

Agran, M., & Wehmeyer, M. (2005). *Teaching problem solving to students with mental retardation*. Boston, MA: Pearson/Merrill/Prentice.

Albinism. (2010, July). In *Wikipedia, The Free Encyclopedia*. Retrieved July 2010, from http://en.wikipedia.org/w/index.php?title=Albinism&oldid=388946528.

American Association on Intellectual and Developmental Disabilities (AAIDD), 2013. Definition of Intellectual Disability. Retrieved from http://www.aaidd.org/content_100.cfm?navID=21

American Foundation for the Blind. (2013). Braille: An overview. Retrieved from http://www.familyconnect.org/parentsite.asp?SectionID=72&DocumentID=4018

American Psychiatric Association. (2000). *Diagnostic and statistical manual of mental disorders*. (4th ed., p. 92). Washington, D.C.: Author.

American Psychiatric Association. (2013a). *Diagnostic and Statistical Manual of Mental Disorders* (5th ed.). Arlington, VA: Author.

American Psychiatric Association. (2013b). *DSM-5 Attention Deficit/Hyperactivity Disorder Fact Sheet*. Arlington, VA: Author.

American Speech-Language-Hearing Association. (2005). *(Central) auditory processing disorders: The role of the audiologist* (Position statement). Retrieved from www.asha.org/policy

American Speech-Language-Hearing Association. (2008). *The prevalence and incidence of hearing loss in children*. Retrieved from www.asha.org/public/hearing/disorders/children.htm.

American Speech-Language-Hearing-Association. (2010). *Stuttering*. Retrieved from www.asha.org/public/speech/disorders/stuttering.htm

American Speech-Language-Hearing Association. (2013a). How does your child hear and talk? Retrieved from http://www.asha.org/public/speech/development/chart.htm

American Speech-Language-Hearing Association. (2013b). Degree of hearing loss. Retrieved from http://www.asha.org/public/hearing/Degree-of-Hearing-Loss/

Anastasiow, N., & Nucci, C. (1994). Social, historical, and theoretical foundations of early childhood special education and early intervention. In P. Safford (Ed.), *Early childhood special education: Vol. 5. Yearbook in early childhood education*, (pp. 7–25). New York, NY: Teachers College Press.

Anastasiow, N. J. (1982). *The adolescent parent*. Baltimore, MD: Brookes.

Anastasiow, N. J. (1996). Psychobiological theory of affect and self-development. In S. Harel & J. Shonkoff (Eds.), *Early childhood intervention* (pp. 111–112). Jerusalem, Israel: JDC-Brookdale Institute.

Anastasiow, N. J., Frankenberg, W., & Fandall, A. (1982). *Identifying the developmentally delayed child*. Baltimore, MD: University Park Press.

Anastopoulos, A. D., Smith, T. F., Garrett, M. E., Morrissey-Kane, E., Schatz, N. K., Sommer, J. L., ... Ashley-Koch, A. (2011). Self-regulation of emotion, functional impairment, and comorbidity among children with AD/HD. *Journal of Attention Disorders, 15*(7), 583–592.

Anderson, C., Shibuya, A., Ihori, N., Swing, E., Bushman, B., Sakamoto, A., Rothstein, H., & Saleem, M. (2010). Violent video game effects on aggression, empathy, and prosocial behavior in Eastern and Western countries: A meta-analytic review. *Psychological Bulletin, 136*(2), 151–173.

Andrews, J. F. & Rusher, M. (2010). Codeswitching techniques: Evidence-based practices for the ASL/English bilingual classroom. *American Annals for the Deaf, 155*(4), 407–424.

Anthony, T. (2009). Deafblindness: One TVI's story. *DVI Quarterly, 54*(3), 16–17.

Antia, S. D., Jones, P. B., Reed, S., & Kreimeyer, K. H. (2009). Academic status and progress of deaf and hard-of-hearing students in general education classrooms. *Journal of Deaf Studies and Deaf Education, 14*(3), 293–313.

Antia, S. D., Sabers, D. L., & Stinson, M. S. (2007). Validity and reliability of the classroom participation questionnaire with deaf and hard of hearing students in public schools. *Journal of Deaf Studies and Deaf Education, 12*(2), 158–171.

Antia, S. (2007, February 19). *Teachers College Record*. Retrieved from http://www.tcrecord.org.

Ashton, T. M. (2006). Assistive technology centers: Getting technology into the hands of users. *Journal of Special Education Technology, 21*(4), 55–57.

Attwood, T. (1998). *Asperger's syndrome: A guide for parents and professionals*. Philadelphia: Kingsley.

Bailey, D., Raspa, M., Humphreys, B., & Sam, A. (2011). Promoting family outcomes in early intervention. In J. Kauffman & D. Hallahan (Eds.), *Handbook of Special Education* (pp. 668–684). New York, NY: Routledge.

Bailey, D. B., Raspa, M., & Fox, L. (2012). What is the future of family outcomes and family-centered services? *Topics in Early Childhood Special Education, 31*(4), 216–223.

Bailey, U. L., Lorch, E. P., Milich, R., & Churnigo, R. (2009). Developmental changes in attention and comprehension among children with attention deficit hyperactivity disorder. *Child Development, 80*(6), 1842–1855

Bakar, Z. A., Brown, P. M., & Remine, M. D. (2010). Sensitivity in interactions between hearing mothers and their toddlers with hearing loss: The effect of cochlear implantation. *Deafness & Education International, 12*(1), 2–15.

Balcazar, F. E., Taylor-Ritzler, T., Dimpfl, S., Portillo-Peña, N., Guzman, A., Schiff, R., & Murvay, M. (2012). Improving the transition outcomes of low-income minority youth with disabilities. *Exceptionality, 20*(2), 114–132.

Baldwin, A. (1987). Undiscovered diamonds. *Journal for the Education of the Gifted, 10*(4), 271–286.

Bambara, L., & Knoster, T. (2005). Designing positive behavior support plans. In M. Wehmeyer & M. Agran (Eds.), *Mental retardation and intellectual disabilities: Teaching students using innovative and research-based strategies*. Boston, MA: Merrill/Prentice Hall.

Bambara, L. M., & Koger, F. (2005). Opportunities for daily choicemaking. In M. Wehmeyer & M. Agran (Eds.), *Mental retardation and intellectual disabilities: Teaching students using innovative and research-based strategies* (pp. 213–233). Boston: Pearson.

Bank, P. (2010). Brief overview of common psychotropic medications: A practical guide from a clinical viewpoint. University of Michigan. Retrieved from www.ssw.umich.edu/.../Brief_Overview_of_Common_Psychotropic_Medications.pdf

Banks, J.A., (2012). Assessment in special and inclusive education. In J.A. Banks (Ed.). *Encyclopedia of diversity in education*. Thousand Oaks, CA: Sage.

Banks, R., Milagros, R., & Roof, V. (2003). Discovering family ancestry, priorities and resources: Sensitive family information gathering. *Young Exceptional Children, 6*(3), 11–19.

Barac, R., & Bialystok, E. (2012). Bilingual effects on cognitive and linguistic development: Role of language, cultural background, and education. *Child Development, 83*(2), 413–422.

Barbarin, O. A. (2002). Culture and ethnicity in social, emotional and academic development. *The Kauffman Early Education Exchange, 1*(1), 45–61.

Barclay, L., Herlich, S. L., & Sacks, S. Z. (2010). Effective teaching strategies: Case studies from the Alphabetic Braille and Contracted Braille Study. *Journal of Visual Impairment & Blindness, 104*(12), 753–764.

Barnard-Brak, L., Sulak, T. N., & Fearon, D. D. (2011). Coexisting disorders and academic achievement among children with ADHD. *Journal of Attention Disorders, 15*(6), 506–515.

Barnett, D. W., Elliott, N., Wolsing, L., Bunger, C. E., Haski, H., McKissick, C., & Vander Meer, C. D. (2006). Response to intervention for children with extremely challenging behaviors: What it might look like. *School Psychology Review, 35*(4), 568–582.

Barnett, W. S., Carolan, M. E., Fitzgerald, J., & Squires, J. H. (2012). The state of preschool 2012: State preschool yearbook (Executive Summary). New Brunswick, NJ: National Institute for Early Education Research.

Baron-Cohen, S., Cox, A., Baird, G., Sweettenham, J., Nightingale, N., Morgan, K., Drew, A., & Charman, T. (1996). Psychological markers in the detection of autism in infancy in a large population. *British Journal of Psychiatry, 168,* 1–6.

Barrows, H. (1988). *The tutorial process.* Carbondale: Southern Illinois School of Medicine.

Barth, R., & Haskins, R. (2009). Will parent training reduce abuse, enhance development, and save money? Let's find out. (Policy brief: *The Future of Children*) Princeton, NJ.

Basch, C. E. (2011). Inattention and hyperactivity and the achievement gap among urban minority youth. *Journal of School Health, 81*(10), 641–649.

Basu, S., Salisbury, C. L., & Thorkildsen, T. A. (2010). Measuring collaborative consultation practices in natural environments. *Journal of Early Intervention, 32*(2), 127–150.

Bateman, B. D., & Linden, M. A. (2006). *Better IEPs: How to develop legally correct and educationally useful programs* (4th ed.). Champaign, IL: Research Press.

Bates, E., Reilly, J., Wulfeck, B., Dronkers, N., Opie, M., Fenson, J., Kriz, S., ... Herbst, K. (2001). Differential effects of unilateral lesions on language production in children and adults. *Brain and Language, 79,* 223–265.

Batshaw, M. (Ed.). (2002). *Children with disabilities* (5th ed.). Baltimore, MD: Brookes.

Baum, S. M., & Owen, S. V. (2004). *To be gifted and learning disabled.* Mansfield Center, CT: Creative Learning Press.

Bausch, M. E., Ault, M. J., & Hasselbring, T. S. (2006). *Assistive technology planner: From IEP consideration to classroom implementation.* Lexington, KY: National Assistive Technology Research Institute.

Beal, C. R., Rosenblum, P., & Smith, D. W. (2011). A pilot study of a self-voicing computer program for prealgebra math problems. *Journal of Visual Impairments & Blindness, 105,* 157–169.

Beauchaine, T., Neuhaus, E., Brenner, S., & Gatzke-Kopp, L. (2008). Ten good reasons to consider biological processes in prevention and intervention research. *Development and Psychopathology, 20,* 745–774.

Beghetto, R. (2008). Creativity enhancement. In J. Plucker & C. Callahan (Eds.), *Critical issues and practices in gifted education* (pp. 139–154). Waco, TX: Prufrock Press.

Beirne-Smith, M., Ittenbach, J., & Patton, J. R. (2001). *Mental retardation: An introduction to intellectual disability* (6th ed.). Upper Saddle River, NJ: Prentice Hall.

Bell, E. C. (2012). Mentoring transition-age youth with blindness. *The Journal of Special Education, 46*(3), 170–179.

Bellamy, G., Rhodes, L., Mank, D., & Albin, J. (1988). *Supportive employment.* Baltimore, MD: Brookes.

Bergeron, R., & Floyd, R. (2006). Broad cognitive abilities of children with mental retardation: An analysis of group and individual profiles. *American Journal on Mental Retardation, 111*(6), 417–432.

Berkeley, S., Scruggs, T. E., & Mastropieri, M. A. (2010). Reading comprehension instruction for students with learning disabilities, 1995–2006: A meta-analysis. *Remedial and Special Education, 31*(6), 423–436.

Berninger, V. W., & Amtmann, D. (2003). Preventing written expression disabilities through early and continuing assessment and intervention for handwriting and/or spelling problems: Research into practice. In H. L. Swanson, K. R. Harris, & S. Graham (Eds.), *Handbook of learning disabilities* (pp. 345–363). New York, NY: Guilford Press.

Best, S., Heller, K., & Bigge, J. (2010). *Teaching individuals with physical or multiple disabilities* (6th ed.). Upper Saddle River, NJ: Merrill-Prentice.

Best, S. J., Heller, K. W., & Bigge, J. L. (2005). *Teaching individuals with physical, health, and multiple disabilities* (5th ed.). Upper Saddle River, NJ: Merrill-Prentice Hall.

Bettelheim, B. (1978). *A home for the heart.* New York, NY: Alfred A. Knopf.

Better Hearing Institute (2010). *Better Hearing Institute: Advocates for America's Ears.* Retrieved from: http://www.betterhearing.org/.

Betts, G. T. (1985). *Autonomous learner model for the gifted and talented.* Greeley, CO: ALPS.

Bialystok, E., & Viswanathan, M. (2009). Components of executive control with advantages for bilingual children in two cultures. *Cognition, 112*(3), 494–500.

Biederman, J., Petty, C. R., Evans, M., Small, J., & Faraone, S. V. (2010). How persistent is ADHD? A controlled 10-year follow-up study of boys with ADHD. *Psychiatry Research, 177,* 299–304.

Bigge, J. L., & Best, L. (2000). *Teaching individuals with physical and multiple disabilities.* Upper Saddle River, NJ: Merrill.

Bishop, V. E. (2004). *Teaching visually impaired children.* Springfield, IL: C.C. Thomas.

Blacher, J., & Hatton, C. (2007). Families in context: Influences on coping and adaptation. In S. Odom, R. Horner, M. Snell, & J. Blacher (Eds.), *Handbook of Developmental Disabilities.* New York, NY: The Guilford Press.

Blackorby, J., & Wagner, M. (1996). Longitudinal outcomes of youth with disabilities. *Exceptional Children, 62*(5), 399–413.

Blumberg, S. J., Bramlett, M. D., Kogan, M. D., Schieve, L. A., Jones, J. R., & Lu, M. C. (2013). Changes in prevalence of parent-reported autism spectrum disorder in school-aged US children: 2007 to 2011–2012. *National Health Statistics Reports, 65,* 1–11.

Bodner-Johnson, B., & Sass-Lehrer, M. (2003). *The young deaf or hard of hearing child: A family-centered approach to early education.* Baltimore, MA: Brookes.

Boons, T., Brokx, J. P., Dhooge, I., Frijns, J. H., Peeraer, L., Vermeulen, A., . . . Van Wieringen, A. (2012). Predictors of spoken language development following pediatric cochlear implantation. *Ear and Hearing, 33*(5), 617–639.

Booster, G. D., DuPaul, G. J., Eiraldi, R., & Power, T. J. (2012). Functional impairments in children with ADHD: Unique effects of age and comorbid status. *Journal of Attention Disorders, 16*(3), 179–189.

Borders, C. M., Barnett, D., & Bauer, A. M. (2010). How are they really doing? Observation of inclusionary classroom participation for children with mild-to-moderate deafness. *Journal of Deaf Studies and Deaf Education, 15*(4), 348–357.

Borum, V. (2012). Perceptions of communication choice and usage among African American hearing parents: Afrocentric cultural implications for African American deaf and hard of hearing children. *American Annals of the Deaf, 157*(1), 7–15.

Botuck, S., & Winsberg, B. (1991). Effects of respite on mothers of school-age and adult children with severe disabilities. *Mental Retardation, 29*(1), 43–47.

Boyd, B. A., Odom, S. L., Humphreys, B. P., & Sam, A. (2010). Infants and toddlers with autism spectrum disorders: Early diagnosis and early intervention. *Journal of Early Intervention, 32*(2), 75–98.

Bracken, B., & McCallum, R. (1998). *UNIT: Universal nonverbal intelligence test (examiner's manual).* Itasca, IL: Riverside Publishing Co.

Brice, A. E., Carson, C. K., & O'Brien, J. D. (2009). Spanish-English articulation and phonology of 4- and 5-year-old preschool children. *Communication Disorders Quarterly, 31*(1), 3–14.

Brice, A. E., Miller, K. J., & Brice, R. G. (2006). Language in the English as a second language and general education classrooms: A tutorial. *Communication Disorders Quarterly, 27*(4), 240–247.

Brice, R. G., & Brice, A. E. (2009). Investigation of phonemic awareness and phonic skills in Spanish-English bilingual and English-speaking kindergarten students. *Communication Disorders Quarterly, 30*(4), 208–225.

Briggs, C. J., Reis, S. M., & Sullivan, E. E. (2008). A national view of promising programs and practices for culturally, linguistically, and ethnically diverse gifted and talented students. *Gifted Child Quarterly, 52*(2), 131–145.

Brinton, B., & Fujiki, M. (2006). Social intervention for children with language impairment: Factors affecting efficacy. *Communication Disorders Quarterly, 28*(1), 39–41.

Bronfenbrenner, U. (1989). Ecological systems theory. In R. Vasta (Ed.), *Annals of Child Development, 6*, (pp. 187–249). London: Jessica Kingsley.

Brown, C. W., Olson, H. C., & Croninger, R. G. (2010). Maternal alcohol consumption during pregnancy and infant social, mental, and motor development. *Journal of Early Intervention, 32*(2), 110–126.

Brown, W. H., Odom, S. L., & Conroy, M. A. (2001). An intervention hierarchy for promoting preschool children's peer interactions in natural environments. *Topics in Early Childhood Special Education, 21*, 162–175.

Brown, W. H., & Conroy, M. A. (2011). Social-emotional competence in young children with developmental delays: Our reflection and vision for the future. *Journal of Early Intervention, 33*, 310–320.

Bruce, S. M., & Parker, A. T. (2012). Young deafblind adults in action: Becoming self-determined change agents through advocacy. *American Annals of the Deaf, 157*(1), 16–26.

Bruder, M., & Dunst, C. (2000). Expanding learning opportunities for infants and toddlers in natural environments. *Zero to Three, 20*(3), 34–36.

Bruer, J. (2010). *Preparing the next generation of STEM innovators: Identifying and developing our nation's human capital.* Washington, D.C.: National Science Foundation.

Bryant, D., & Maxwell, D. (1999). The environment and mental retardation. *International Review of Psychology, 11*, 56–67.

Buck, G., Polloway, E., Smith-Thomas, A., & Cook, K. (2003). Prereferral intervention process: A survey of state practices. *Exceptional Children, 69*(3), 349–360.

Bunce, D. (2003). Children with culturally diverse backgrounds. In L. McCormick, D. F. Loeb, & R. L. Schiefelbusch (Eds.), *Supporting children with communication difficulties in inclusive settings* (pp. 367–407). Boston, MA: Allyn & Bacon.

Burchinal, M., Peisner-Feinberg, E., Pianta, R., & Howes, C. (2002). Development of academic skills from preschool through second grade: Family and classroom predictors of developmental trajectories. *Journal of School Psychology, 40*(5), 415–436.

Burchinal, M., Roberts, J., Riggins, R., Zeisel, S., Neebar, E., & Bryant, D. (2000). Relating quality of center-based child care to early cognitive and language development. *Child Development, 71*(2), 339–357.

Bush, T. W., & Reschly, A. L. (2007). Progress monitoring in reading. *Assessment for Effective Intervention, 32*(4), 223–230.

Bussing, R., Mason, D. M., Bell, L., Porter, P., & Garvan, C. (2010). Adolescent outcomes of childhood attention-deficit/hyperactivity disorder in a diverse community sample. *Journal of the American Academy of Child & Adolescent Psychiatry, 49*(6), 595–605.

Bussing, R., Porter, P., Zima, B. T., Mason, D., Garvan, C., & Reid, R. (2012). Academic outcome trajectories of students with ADHD: Does exceptional education status matter? *Journal of Emotional and Behavioral Disorders, 20*(3), 131–143.

Butter, E. M., Mulick, J. A., & Metz, B. (2006). Eight case reports of learning recovery in children with pervasive developmental disorders after early intervention. *Behavioral Interventions, 21*(4), 227–243.

Cabell, S. Q., Justice, L. M., Konold, T. R., & McGinty, A. S. (2010). Profiles of emergent literacy skills among preschool children who are at risk for academic difficulties. *Early Childhood Research Quarterly, 26*, 1–14.

Cairns, R. B. (1983). The emergence of developmental psychology. In W. Kessen (Ed.), *Handbook of child psychology: Vol. 1* (4th ed., pp. 41–102). New York, NY: Wiley.

Calderon, R., & Greenberg, M. (2000). Challenge to parents and professionals in promoting socio-emotional development. In P. Spencer, C. Ertling, & M. Marschark (Eds.), *The deaf child in the family and at school* (pp. 275–291). Mahwah, NJ: Erlbaum.

Callahan, C. M. (2007). Identifying gifted students from underrepresented populations. *Theory into practice, 44*, 98–104.

Campbell, F. A., Pugnello, E. P., Burchinal, M., Kainz, K., Pan, Y., Wasik, B. H., . . Ramey, C. (2012). Adult outcomes as a function of an early childhood educational program: An Abecedarian project follow-up. *Developmental Psychology, 48*(4), 1033–1043.

Campbell, F., Pungello, E., Keyserling, R., & Steen, R. (2012, October). *Does Enhancement of Academic Skills in Childhood Also Enhance Adult Health Status?* Presentation to the Summit on the Science of Eliminating Heath Disparities, National Harbor, MD.

Campbell, F. A., & Ramey, C. T. (1995). Cognitive and school outcomes for high-risk African-American students at middle adolescence: Positive effects of early intervention. *American Educational Research Journal, 32*(4), 743–772.

Campbell, F. A., Ramey, C. T., Pungello, E. P., Sparling, J. J., & Miller-Johnson, S. (2002). Early childhood education: Young adult outcomes from the Abecedarian Project. *Applied Developmental Science, 6*(1), 42–57.

Campbell, P. (2000). Promoting participation in natural environments by accommodating motor disabilities. In M. Snell & F. Brown (Eds.), *Instruction of students with severe disabilities* (5th ed., pp. 291–330). Upper Saddle River, NJ: Merrill.

Campbell, P., Milbourne, S., Dugan, L., & Wilcox, M. (2006). A review of evidence on practices for teaching young children to use assistive technology devices. *Topics in Early Childhood Special Education, 26*(1), 3–17.

Campbell, P. H., & Sawyer, B. (2007). Supporting learning opportunities in natural settings through participation-based services. *Journal of Early Intervention, 29*(4), 287–305.

Campbell, P. H., Sawyer, B., & Muhlenhaupt, M. (2009). The meaning of natural environments for parents and professionals. *Infants & Young Children, 22*(4), 264–278.

Campos, J. J., Frankel, C. B., & Camaras, L. (2004). On the nature of emotion regulation. *Child Development*, 75(2), 377–394.

Carlson, E., Klein, S., Schroll, K., & Wittig, S. (2002). Study of personnel needs in special education (SPeNSE). Gainesville, FL: University of Florida.

Carta, J. J., & Kong, N. Y. (2007). Trends and issues in interventions for preschoolers with developmental disabilities. In S. L. Odom, R. H. Horner, M. E. Snell, & J. Blacher (Eds.), *Handbook of developmental disabilities* (pp. 181–198). New York, NY: Guilford Press.

Carter, B. B., & Spencer, V. G. (2007). Another beautiful mind: A case study of the recovery of an adolescent male from a TBI. *Physical Disabilities: Education and Related Services, 25*(2), 33–58.

Cartledge, G. (2011). Introduction to the special issue: Cultural diversity and special education. *Exceptionality, 19,* 137–139.

Casey, A. M., & McWilliam, R. (2008). Graphical feedback to increase teachers' use of incidental teaching. *Journal of Early Intervention, 30*(3), 251–268.

Casey, A. M., & McWilliam, R. A. (2007). The STARE: The Scale for Teachers' Assessment of Routines Engagement. *Young Exceptional Children, 11*(1), 1–15.

Castellani, J., & Warger, C. (Eds.). (2009). *Accommodating students with disabilities: Instructional and assistive technology tools that work!* Reston, VA: Exceptional Innovations, INC.

Castellanos, F, Lee, P., Sharp, W., Jeffries, N., Greenstein, D., Clasen, L., ... Rapaport, J. (2002). Developmental trajectories of brain volume abnormalities in children and adolescents with attention-deficit/hyperactivity disorder. *JAMA, 288*(14), 1740–1748.

Castro, D., Garcia, E., & Markos, A. (2013). *Dual language learners: Research informing policy.* Chapel Hill: The University of North Carolina, Frank Porter Graham Child Development Institute, Center for Early Care and Education-Dual Language Learners.

Cavenaugh, B., & Giesen, J. M. (2010). A systematic review of transition interventions affecting the employability of youths with visual impairments. *Journal of Visual Impairment & Blindness, 106*, 400–413.

Cawley, J., Hayden, S., Cade, E., & Baker-Kroczynski, S. (2002). Including students with disabilities into the general education science classroom. *Exceptional Children, 68,* 423–436.

Cawthon, S. W. (2011). Education of deaf and hard of hearing students and accountability reform: Issues for the future. *American Annals of the Deaf, 156*(4), 424–430.

Cawthon, S. W., Winton, S. M., Garberoglio, C. L., & Gobble, M. E. (2011). The effects of American Sign Language as an assessment accommodation for students who are deaf or hard-of-hearing. *Journal of Deaf Studies and Deaf Education, 16*(2), 198–211.

Cawthon, S. W., & Wurtz, K. A. (2008). Alternate assessment use with students who are deaf or hard of hearing: An exploratory mixed-methods analysis of portfolio, checklists, and out-of-level test formats. *Journal of Deaf Studies and Deaf Education,* Advance Access 7/23/2008.

Celeste, M., & Grum, D.K. (2010). Social integration of children with visual impairment: A developmental model. *Elementary Education Online, 9*(1), 11–22.

Centers for Disease Control and Prevention. (2009). FastStats: Asthma. Retrieved from http://www.cdc.gov/nchs/fastats/asthma.htm

Centers for Disease Control and Prevention (CDC, 2009b). EHDI Hearing Screening and Follow-up Survey. Retrieved from http://www.cdc.gov/ncbddd/hearingloss/ehdi-data2009.html

Centers for Disease Control and Prevention. (2010). *Vital and Health Statistics*. Washington, D.C.: Author.

Centers for Disease Control and Prevention, (2012). Summary Health Statistics for U.S. Children: National Health Interview Survey, 2011, Series 10, Number 254.

Centers for Disease Control and Prevention. (2013). HIV among pregnant women, infants, and children: Fact sheet. Atlanta, GA: U.S. Department of Health and Human Services, Division of HIV/AIDS Prevention, National Center for HIV/AIDS.

Center for Hearing and Communication (2013). Facts about hearing loss. Retrieved from http://www.chchearing.org/about-hearing-loss/facts-about-hearing-loss

Center on the Developing Child. (2013). The science of early childhood development [Issue brief]. Cambridge, MA: Author.

Center on the Social and Emotional Foundations for Early Learning (2010a). Research synthesis: Infant mental health and early care and education providers [Web report]. Vanderbilt University. Retrieved from http://csefel.vanderbilt.edu/documents/rs_infant_mental_health.pdf

Center on the Social and Emotional Foundations for Early Learning (2010b). Research synthesis: Early childhood mental health consultation [Web report].Vanderbilt University. Retrieved from http://csefel.vanderbilt.edu/documents/rs_ecmhc.pdf

Chandrasekaran, B., Hornickel, J., Skoe, E., Nicol, T., & Kraus, N. (2009). Context-dependent encoding in the human auditory brainstem relates to hearing speech in noise: Implications for developmental dyslexia. *Neuron, 64*, 311–319.

Charach, A., Yeung, E., Climans, T., & Lillie, E. (2011). Childhood attention-deficit/hyperactivity disorder and future substance use disorders: Comparative meta-analyses. *Journal of the American Academy of Child & Adolescent Psychiatry, 50*(1), 9–21.

Children and Adults with Attention-Deficit/Hyperactivity Disorder (CHADD). (2003). What we know #15: Social skills in adults with AD/HD. Landover, MD: National Resource Center on AD/HD.

Children and Adults with Attention-Deficit/Hyperactivity Disorder (CHADD). (2004). What we know #7: Psychosocial treatment for children and adolescents with AD/HD. Landover, MD: National Resource Center on AD/HD.

Children and Adults with Attention-Deficit/Hyperactivity Disorder (CHADD). (2008). What we know #20B: AD/HD and teens: Information for parents. Landover, MD: National Resource Center on AD/HD.

Chomsky, N. (1965). *Aspects of the theory of syntax*. Cambridge, MA: MIT Press.

Christle, C. A., & Yell, M. L. (2010). Individualized education programs: Legal requirements and research findings. *Exceptionality: A Special Education Journal, 18*(3), 109–123.

Christensen, L., Lazarus, S., Crone, M., & Thurlow, M. (2008). 2007 State policies on assessment participation and accommodations for students with disabilities (Synthesis Report 69). Minneapolis, MN: University of Minnesota, National Center for Educational Outcomes.

Clark, G., & Zimmerman, E. (1998). Nurturing the arts in programs for gifted and talented students. *Phi Delta Kappan, 79,* 746–751.

Cobb, J. (2004). *Top ten things to think about as you prepare for your transition to adulthood.* Washington, D.C.: G. W. Heath Resource Center.

Colangelo, N., Assouline, S., & Gross, M. (2004). *A nation deceived: How schools hold back America's brightest students. The Templeton national report on acceleration.* Iowa City, IA: Bolen and Blank International Center for Gifted Education.

Coleman, L. (2002). A shock to study. *Journal of Secondary Gifted Education, 14,* 39–52.

Coleman, L., & Cross, T. (2001). *Being gifted in school: An introduction to development, guidance, and teaching.* Waco, TX: Prufrock Press.

Coleman, L. (2005). Nurturing talent in high school: Life in the fast lane. New York, NY: Teachers College Press.

Coleman, M. R. (1994). Postsecondary educational decisions for gifted/learning disabled students. *Journal of Secondary Gifted Education, 5*(3), 53–59.

Coleman, M. R. (2005). Academic strategies that work for gifted students with learning disabilities. *Teaching Exceptional Children, 38*(1), 28–32.

Coleman, M. R. (2011). The importance of starting early. *Perspectives on Language and Literacy*, Summer, 9–11.

Coleman, M. R. (2013). Response to intervention (RtI) approaches to identification practices within gifted education. In C. Callahan & H. Hertberg-Davis (Eds.) *Fundamentals of Gifted Education Considering Multiple Perspectives* (Chapter 16; pp 152–158). New York, NY: Routledge Press.

Coleman, M. R., Buysse, V., & Neitzel, J. (2006a). *Recognition and response: An early intervening system for young children at risk for learning disabilities.* Chapel Hill, NC: University of North Carolina at Chapel Hill, FPG Child Development Institute.

Coleman, M. R., Buysse, V., & Neitzel, J. (2006b). Establishing the evidence base for an emerging early childhood practice: Recognition and response. In V. Buysse & P. W. Wesley (Eds.), *Evidence-based practice in the early childhood field* (pp. 195–225). Washington, D.C.: Zero to Three Press.

Coleman, M. R., Gallagher, J. J., & Job, J. (2012). Developing and sustaining professionalism within gifted education. *Gifted Child Today, 35*(1), 27–36.

Coleman, M. R., Gillis, M., & West. T. (2011). The Early learning observation and rating scale (ELORS): Honoring parental and teacher concerns. *Perspectives on Language and Literacy, 37*(3), 35–37.

Coleman, M. R., & Hughes, C. (2009). Meeting the needs of gifted students within an RTI framework. *Gifted Child Today, 32*(3), 15–17.

Coleman, M. R., Roth, F., & West, T. (2009). *Roadmap to pre-K RTI: Applying response to intervention in preschool settings.* New York, NY: National Center for Learning Disabilities.

Coleman, M. R., & Shah-Coltrane, S. (2010). *U-STARS~PLUS Science & Literature Connections.* Arlington, VA: Council for Exceptional Children.

Coleman, M. R., & Shah-Coltrane, S. (2011). Remembering the importance of potential: Tiers 1 and 2. In M. Coleman & S. Johnsen (Eds.). *RtI for gifted students: A CEC-TAG educational resource* (pp. 43–61). Waco, TX: Prufrock Press.

Coleman, M. R., West, T., & Gillis, M. (2010). *Early learning observation and rating scales (ELORS): Teacher-individual child form.* New York: National Center for Learning Disabilities.

Coles, E. K., Slavec, J., Bernstein, M., & Baroni, E. (2012). Exploring the gender gap in referrals for children with ADHD and other disruptive behavior disorders. *Journal of Attention Disorders, 16*(2), 101–108.

Committee on Prospering in the Global Economy of the 21st Century (2007). *Rising above the gathering storm: Energizing and employing America for a brighter economic future.* Washington, D.C.: The National Academies Press.

Compton, D. L., Fuchs, D., Fuchs, L. S., & Bryant, J. D. (2006). Selecting at-risk readers in first grade for early intervention: A two-year longitudinal study of decision rules and procedures. *Journal of Educational Psychology, 98*, 394–409.

Conference of Educational Administrators of Schools and Programs for the Deaf (CEASD)/Council of Schools for the Blind (COSB). (2010). Joint statement on schools for the deaf and schools for the blind. Retrieved from http://www.csb-cde.ca.gov/joint_statement.html

Conners, C. K. (2008). *Conners-3 teacher assessment report.* North Tonawanda, NY: Multi-Health Systems, Inc.

Conners, C. K. (2013). CPT-II V.5. North Tonawanda, NY: Multi-Health Systems. Retrieved from http://www.mhs.com/product.aspx?gr=cli&prod=cptii5&id=overview

Connor, C., Craig, H., Raudenbush, S., Heavner, K., & Zwolan, T. (2006). The age at which young deaf children receive cochlear implants and their vocabulary and speech-production growth: Is there an added value for early implantation? *Ear & Hearing, 27*(6), 628–643.

Cook, C., Dart, E., Collins, T., Restori, A., Daikos, C., & Delport, J. (2012). Preliminary study of the confined, collateral, and combined effects of reading and nehavioral interventions: evidence for a transactional relationship. *Behavioral Disorders, 38*(1), 38–56.

Cope, N., Harold, D., Hill, G., Moskvina, V., Stevenson, J., Holmans, P., et al. (2005). Strong evidence that KIAA0319 on chromosome 6p is a susceptibility gene for developmental dyslexia. *The American Journal of Human Genetics, 76*(4), 581–591.

Corn, A. L., & Lusk, K. E. (2010). Perspectives on low vision. In A. Corn & J. Erin (Eds.) *Foundations of low vision: Clinical and functional perspectives* (2nd ed., pp. 3–34). New York, NY: American Foundation for the Blind.

Correa-Torres, S. M., & Durando, J. (2012). Perceived training needs of teachers of students with visual impairments who work with students from culturally and linguistically diverse backgrounds. *Journal of Visual Impairment & Blindness, 105*, 521–532.

Corso, R., Santos, R., & Roof, V. (2002). Honoring diversity in early childhood educational material. *Teaching Exceptional Children, 34*(3), 30–37.

Cortese, S., Kelly, C., Chabernaud, C., Proal, E., Di Martino, A., Milham, M. P., & Castellanos, X. (2012). Toward systems of neuroscience of ADHD: A meta-analysis of 55 fMRI studies. *The American Journal of Psychiatry, 169*, 1038–1055.

Cortiella, C. (2009). *The State of Learning Disabilities.* New York, NY: National Center for Learning Disabilities.

Cortiella, C., & Burnette, J. (2009). *Challenging change: How schools and districts are improving the performance of special education students.* New York, NY: The National Center for Learning Disabilities.

Cosmos, C. (2001). Abuse of children with disabilities. In *Today* (pp. 1–15). Arlington, VA: Council for Exceptional Children.

Coufal, K. (Ed.). (2007). Letter from the editor. *Communication Disorders Quarterly, 28*(3), 133–134.

Council for Exceptional Children. (2003). *What every special educator must know: The international standards for the preparation and certification of special education teachers.* Arlington, VA: Author.

Council for Exceptional Children. (2006). *Council for Exceptional Children policy and advocacy services: Understanding IDEA 2004 regulations.* Arlington, VA: Author.

Council for Exceptional Children. (2007). *Understanding IDEA 2004: Frequently asked questions*. Arlington, VA: Author.

Council for Exceptional Children. (2010). *Positive behavior interventions & supports*. Arlington, VA: CEC.

Council of Schools for the Blind. (2013). Current members. Retrieved from http://www.cosb1.org/membership/members

Cowley, G. (2000). Understanding autism. *Newsweek*, July 31, 2000; 136(5):46–54.

Cox, M., & Paley, B. (1997). Families as systems. *Annual Review of Psychology, 48*, 243–267.

Crews, S., Bender, H., Gresham, F.M., Kern, L., Vanderwood, M., & Cook, C.R. (2007). Risk and protective factors of emotional and/or behavioral disorders in children and adolescents: A "mega"-analytic synthesis. *Behavioral Disorders,* 32(2), 64–77.

Cross, T. (2013). *Suicide among gifted children and adolescents: Understanding the suicidal mind*. Waco, TX: Prufrock Press.

Cross, T., Cassady, J., & Miller, K. (2006). Suicide ideation and personality characteristics among gifted adolescents. *Gifted Child Quarterly, 50, 295–306.*

Crowe, K., McLeod, S., & Ching, T. Y. (2012). The cultural and linguistic diversity of 3-year-old children with hearing loss. *Journal of Deaf Studies and Deaf Education, 17*(4), 421–438.

Crudden, A. (2012). Transition to employment: Components for success. *Journal of Visual Impairment & Blindness, 106*(7), 389–399.

Cruickshank, N. M., Bentzen, F. A., Ratzenburg, F. H., & Tannhauser, M. T. (1961). *A teaching method of brain-injured and hyperactive children*. Syracuse, NY: Syracuse University Press.

Cruz, I., Quittner, A. L., Maker, C., Desjardin, J. L., CDaCI Investigative Team, (2012). Identification of effective strategies to promote language in deaf children with cochlear implants. *Child Development 84*(2), 543–59.

Cryer, D., & Clifford, R. (Eds.). (2003). *Early childhood education and care in the U.S.A*. Baltimore, MD: Brookes.

Cuenca-Sanchez, Y., Mastropieri, M., Scruggs, TY., & Kidd,J. (2012) Teaching students with emotional and behavioral disorders to self-advocate through persuasive writing. *Exceptionality 20*, 71–93.

Cullinan, D. (2004). Classification and definition of emotional and behavioral disorders. In R. Rutherford, M. Quinn, & S. Mathur (Eds.), *Handbook of research in emotional and behavior disorders* (pp. 32–53). New York, NY: Guilford Press.

DaDeppo, L. M. W. (2009). Integration factors related to the academic success and intent to persist of college students with learning disabilities. *Learning Disabilities Research & Practice, 24*(3), 122–131.

Danckaerts, M., Sonuga-Barke, E. J. S., Babaschewski, T., Buitelaar, J., Dopfner, M., Hollis, C., . . . Coghill, D. (2010). The quality of life of children with attention deficit/hyperactivity disorder: A systematic review. *European Child and Adolescent Psychiatry, 19*, 83–105.

Das, M., Spowart, K., Crossley, S., & Dutton, G. N. (2010). Evidence that children with special needs all require visual assessment. *Archives of Disease in Childhood, 95*(11), 888–892.

Data Accountability Center. (2013). *Part B child count (2011)* [data set]. Retrieved from https://www.ideadata.org/arc_toc13.asp#partbLRE

Dautenhahn, K., & Billard, A. (2002). Games children with autism can play with Robota, a humanoid robotic doll. In S. Keates, P. M. Langdon, P. J. Clarkson, & P. Robinson (Eds.) *Universal access and assistive technology* (pp. 179–190). London, England: Springer-Verlag.

Davis, A., Kruczek, T., & McIntosh, D. (2006). Understanding and treating psychopathology in schools: Introduction to the special issue. *Psychology in the Schools, 43*(4).

Deault, L. C. (2010). A systematic review of parenting in relation to the development of comorbidities and functional impairments in children with attention-deficit/hyperactivity disorder (ADHD). *Child Psychiatry and Human Development, 41*, 168–192.

de Graaf, I., Speetjens, P., Smit, F., de Wolff, M., & Tavecchio, L. (2008). Effectiveness of the triple P positive parenting program on behavioral problems in children: A meta-analysis. *Behavior Modification, 32,* 714–735.

de Jong, E. P., Lopriore, E., Vossen, A., Steggerda, S. J., Te Pas, A. B., Kroes, A., & Walther, F. J. (2010). Is routine TORCH screening warranted in neonates with lenticulostriate vasculopathy? *Neonatology, 97*, 274–278.

Deafness Research Foundation. (2000). *Research News, 1*(1).

Delgado, C. (2009). Fourth grade outcomes of children with a preschool history of developmental disability. *Education and Training in Developmental Disabilities, 44*(4), 573–579.

Dell, A., Newton, D., & Petroff, J. (2008). *Assistive technology in the classroom: Enhancing the school experiences of students with disabilities.* Columbus, OH: Pearson Merrill Prentice Hall.

Deshler, D. D., Robinson, S., & Mellard, D. F. (2009). Instructional principles for optimizing outcomes for adolescents with learning disabilities. In G. D. Siderides & T. A. Citro (Eds.), *Classroom strategies for struggling learners* (pp. 173–189). Weston, MA: Learning Disabilities Association Worldwide.

Deshler, D., Schumaker, J., Lenz, B., Bulgren, J., Hock, M., Knight, J., & Ehren, B. (2001). Ensuring content-area learning by secondary students with learning disabilities. *Learning Disabilities Research and Practice, 16*(2), 96–108.

DiCarlo, C., & Vagianos, L. (2009). Using child preferences to increase play across interest centers in inclusive early childhood classrooms. *Young Exceptional Children, 12*(4), 31–39.

Division for Early Childhood / National Association for the Education of Young Children. (2009). *Early childhood inclusion: A joint position statement of the Division for Early Childhood (DEC) and the National Association for the Education of Young Children (NAEYC)*. Chapel Hill, NC: The University of North Carolina, FPG Child Development Institute. Retrieved from http://npdci.fpg.unc.edu/resources/articles/Early_Childhood_Inclusion

Division for Early Childhood of the Council for Exceptional Children, National Association for the Education of Young Children, & National Head Start Association(2013). *Frameworks for Response to Intervention in Early Childhood: Description and Implications*. Missoula, MT and Washington, D.C.: Author. Retrieved from http://www.naeyc.org/content/frameworks-response-intervention

Division for Learning Disabilities. (2007). *Thinking about response to intervention and learning disabilities: A teacher's guide*. Arlington, VA: Author.

Dixon, F., & Moon, S. (2006). (Eds.). *The Handbook of Secondary Gifted Education*. Waco: TX. Prufrock Press, Inc.

Doig, K., & Werner, E. (2000). The marriage of a traditional lecture-based curriculum and problem-based learning: Are the offspring vigorous? *Medical Teacher, 22*, 173–178.

Dong, W. K., & Greenough, W. T. (2004). Plasticity of non-neuronal brain tissue: Roles in developmental disorders. *Mental Retardation and Developmental Disabilities Research Reviews, 10*(2), 85–90.

Donovan, M., & Cross, C. (2002). *Minority students in special and gifted education*. Washington, D.C.: National Academy Press.

Dorman, J. P., & Pellegrino, L. (1998). *Caring for children with cerebral palsy: A team approach*. Baltimore, MD: Brookes.

Dote-Kwan, J., & Chen, D. (2010). Temperament and young children with visual impairments: Perceptions of

Anglo and Latino parents. *Journal of Visual Impairment & Blindness, 104*(9), 542–553.

Downing, J., & Eichinger, J. (2003). Creating learning opportunities for students with severe disabilities in inclusive classrooms. *Teaching Exceptional Children, 36*(1), 26–31.

Drahota, A., Wood, J. J., Sze, K. M., & Van Dyke, M. (2011). Effects of cognitive behavioral therapy on daily living skills in children with high-functioning autism and concurrent anxiety disorders. *Journal of Autism and Developmental Disorders, 41,* 257–265.

Drasgow, E., Wolery, M., Halle, J., & Hajiaghamohseni, Z. (2011). Systematic instruction of students with severe disabilities. In J. M. Kauffman & D. P. Hallahan (Eds.), *Handbook of special education* (pp. 516–531). New York, NY: Routledge.

Duchan, J. F. (2008). *Getting here: A short history of speech pathology in America.* Retrieved from http://www.acsu.buffalo.edu/~duchan/history.html

Duncan, J. (2009). Parental readiness for cochlear implant decision-making. *Cochlear Implants International, 10*(S1), 38–42.

Dunlap, G., & Carr, E. (2007). Positive behavior support and developmental disabilities: A summary and analysis of research. In S. Odom, B. Horner, M. Snell, & J. Blacher (Eds.), *Handbook of developmental disabilities* (pp. 469–482). New York, NY: Guilford Press.

Dunlap, G., Strain, P., Fox, L., Carta, J., Conroy, M., Smith, B., ... Sowell, C. (2006). Preventing and intervention with young children's challenging behavior: Perspectives regarding current knowledge. *Behavioral Disorders, 32*(1), 29–45.

Dunst, C. J. (2007). Early intervention for infants and toddlers with developmental disabilities. In S. L. Odom, R. H. Horner, M. E. Snell, & J. Blacher (Eds.), *Handbook of developmental disabilities* (pp. 161–180). New York, NY: Guilford Press.

Dunst, C. J. (2012). Parapatric speciation in the evolution of early intervention for infants and toddlers with disabilities and their families. *Topics in Early Childhood Special Education, 31,* 208–215.

Durkin, K., Fraser, J., & Conti-Ramsden, G. (2012). School-age prework experiences of young people with a history of specific language impairment. *The Journal of Special Education, 45,* 242–255.

Durston, S. (2010). Imaging genetics in ADHD. *NeuroImage, 53,* 832–838.

Early Childhood Technical Assistance Center. 2013. Retrieved from http://www.ectacenter.org/

Dworzynski, K., Remington, A., Rijsdijk, F., Howell, P., & Plomin, R. (2007). Genetic etiology in cases of recovered and persistent stuttering in an unselected, longitudinal sample of young twins. *American Journal of Speech-Language Pathology, 16,* 169–178.

Early, D. M., Maxwell, K. L., Burchinal, M., Alva, S., Bender, R. H., Bryant, D., . . . Zill, N. (2007). Teachers' education, classroom quality, and young children's academic skills: Results from seven studies of preschool programs. *Child Development, 78*(2), 558–580.

Easterbrooks, S. (1999). Improving practice for students with hearing impairments. *Exceptional Children, 65*(4), 537–554.

Easterbrooks, S. R., & Beal-Alvarez, J. S. (2012). States' reading outcomes of students who are d/deaf and hard of hearing. *American Annals of the Deaf, 157*(1), 27–40.

Eber, L., & Keenan, C. (2004). Collaboration with other agencies: Wraparound and systems of care for children and youth with EBD. In R. Rutherford, M. Quinn, & S. Mathur (Eds.), *Handbook of research in emotional and behavioral disorders* (p. 502). New York, NY: Guilford Press.

Eber, L., Sugai, G., Smith, C., & Scott, T. (2002). Wraparound and positive behavioral interventions and supports in the schools. *Journal of Emotional and Behavioral Disorders, 10*(3), 171.

Eckenrode, L., Fennell, P., & Hearsey, K. (2007). *Tasks galore for the real world.* Chapel Hill, NC: Tasks Galore.

Edens, R. M., Murdick, N. L., & Gartin, B. C. (2003). Preventing infection in the classroom: The use of universal precautions. *Teaching Exceptional Children, 35*(4), 62–66.

Education for All Handicapped Children Act, Pub. L. 94–142 (1975).

Edwards, J., & Tyskiewicz, E. (1999). Cochlear implants. In J. Stokes (Ed.), *The hearing impaired infant: The first eighteen months* (pp. 129–162). London, England: Whurr. (Distributed by Paul H. Brookes)

Edyburn, D. L. (2006). Assistive technology and mild disabilities. *Special Education Technology Practice, 8*(4), 18–28.

Egger, H. L., & Angold, A. (2006). Common emotional and behavioral disorders in preschool children: presentation, nosology, and epidemiology. *Journal of Child Psychiatry, 47*(3/4), 313–337.

Eichenwald, E., & Stark, A. (2008). Management and outcomes of very low birth weight. *New England Journal of Medicine, 358,* 1700–1711.

Ellis, E., Farmer, T., & Newman, J. (2005). Big ideas about teaching big ideas. *Teaching Exceptional Children, 38*(1), 34–40.

Erwin, E., & Brown, F. (2003). A contextual framework for understanding self-determination in early childhood environment. *Infants and Young Children, 16*(4), 1.

Fabiano, G. A., Vujnovic, R. K., Pelham, W. E., Waschbusch, D. A., Massetti, G. M., Pariseau, M.E., . . . Volker, M. (2010). Enhancing the effectivenss of special education programming for children with attention deficit hyperactivity disorder using a daily report card. *School Psychology Review, 39*(2), 219–239.

Fagan, M. K., & Pisoni, D. B. (2010). Hearing experience and receptive vocabulary development in deaf children with cochlear implants. *Journal of Deaf Studies and Deaf Education, 15*(2), 149–161.

Faggella-Luby, M., & Deshler, D. D. (2008). Reading comprehension in adolescents with LD: What we know, what we need to know. *Learning Disability Research and Practice, 23*(2), 70–78.

Falvey, M. A., Coot, J., Bishop, K. D., & Grenot-Scheyer, M. (1989). Educational and curricular adaptations. In S. Stainback, W. Stainback, & M. Forest (Eds.), *Educating all students in the mainstream of regular education.* Baltimore, MD: Brookes.

Fantuzzo, J. W., Gadsden, V. L., & McDermott, P. A. (2010). An integrated curriculum to improve mathematics, language, and literacy for Head Start children. *American Educational Research Journal, 48*(3), 763–793.

Farber, B. (1959). The effects of severely retarded children on the family system. *Monographs for the Society for Research in Child Development, 24* (2, Serial No. 71).

Farmer, T., Farmer, E., Estell, D., & Hutchins, B. (2007). The developmental dynamics of aggression and the prevention of school violence. *Journal of Emotional and Behavioral Disorders, 15*(4), 197–208.

Fazzi, D. L., & Naimy, B. J. (2010). Orientation and mobility services for children and youths with low vision. In A. Corn & J. Erin (Eds.) *Foundations of low vision: Clinical and functional perspectives* (2nd ed., pp. 655–727). New York, NY: American Foundation for the Blind.

Ferguson, C. (2013). Violent video games and the Supreme Court: Lessons for the scientific community in the wake of Brown v. Entertainment Merchants Association. *American Psychologist, 68*(2), 57–74.

Ferrell, K., Shaw, A., & Dietz, S. (1998). *Project PRISM: A longitudinal study of developmental patterns of children who are visually impaired.* Greeley: University of Northern Colorado, Division of Special Education.

Fey, M., Windsor, J., & Warren, S. (Eds.). (1995). *Language intervention: Preschool through elementary years.* Baltimore, MD: Brookes.

Field, S., & Hoffman, A. (2007). Self-determination in secondary transition assessment. *Assessment for Effective Intervention, 32*(3), 181–190.

Field, T. (1989). Interaction coaching for high risk infants and their parents. *Prevention in Human Services, 1,* 8–54.

Firth, N., Greaves, D., & Frydenberg, E. (2010). Coping styles and strategies: A comparison of adolescent students with and without learning disabilities. *Journal of Learning Disabilities, 43*(1), 77–85.

Fischbach, G. D. & Lord, C. (2010). The Simons Simplex collection: A resource for identification of autism genetic risk factors. *Neuron, 68,* 192–195.

Fitzpatrick, E. M., Crawford, L., Ni, A., & Durieux-Smith, A. (2011). A descriptive analysis of language and speech skills in 4- to 5-yr-old children with hearing loss. *Ear and Hearing, 32*(5), 605–616.

Flavell, J., & Miller, P. (1998). Social cognition. In W. Damon (Ed.), *Handbook of child psychology: Vol. 2. Cognition, perception and language* (5th ed., pp. 851–898). New York, NY: Wiley.

Fleming, J. L., Sawyer, L. B., & Campbell, P. H. (2011). Early intervention providers' perspectives about implementing participation-based practices. *Topics in Early Childhood Special Education, 30,* 233–244.

Fletcher, J. M., Denton, C., & Francis, D. J. (2005). Validity of alternative approaches for the identification of learning disabilities: Operationalizing unexpected underachievement. *Journal of Learning Disabilities, 38,* 545–552.

Flowers, A., & McDougle, L. (2010). In search of an ADHD screening tool for African American children. *Journal of the National Medical Association, 102*(5), 372–374.

Flynn, J. (1999). Searching for justice: The discovery of IQ gains over time. *American Psychologist, 54*(1), 5–20.

Fombonne, E. (2003). The prevalence of autism. *Journal of the American Medical Association, 289,* 97–89.

Ford, D. (2008) Culturally different students in special education: Lookinf backward to move foreward. *Exceptional Children 4,* 78–88.

Ford, D. Y. (2002). Racial identity among gifted African American students. In M. Neihart, S. Reis, N. Robinson, & S. Moon (Eds.), *The social and emotional development of gifted children: What do we know?* (pp. 155–164). Waco, TX: Prufrock Press.

Ford, D. Y., & Grantham, T. C. (2003). Providing access for culturally diverse gifted students: From deficit to dynamic thinking. *Theory Into Practice, 42*(3), 217–225.

Ford, D. Y. (2002). Racial identity among gifted African American students. In M. Neihart, S. Reis, N. Robinson, & S. Moon (Eds.), *The social and emotional development of gifted children: What do we know?* (pp. 155–164). Waco, TX: Prufrock Press.

Ford, D. Y., & Grantham, T. C. (2003). Providing access for culturally diverse gifted students: From deficit to dynamic thinking. *Theory Into Practice, 42*(3), 217–225.

Ford, D. Y., Moore, J. L. III., & Milner, H. R. (2005). Beyond colorblindness: A model of culture with implications for gifted education. *Roeper Review, 27*(2), 97–103.

Forgatch, M., Patterson, G., Degarmo, D., & Beldavs Z. (2009). Testing the Oregon delinquency model with 9-year follow-up of the Oregon divorce study. *Developmental Psychopathology, 21*(2): 637–660.

Foshay, J. D., & Ludlow, B. L. (2005). Implementing computer-mediated instructional supports. In M. Wehmeyer & M. Agran (Eds.), *Mental retardation and intellectual disabilities: Teaching students using innovative and research-based strategies.* Boston: Merrill/Prentice Hall.

Fossett, B., & Mirenda, P. (2007). Augmentative and alternative communication. In S. Odom, B. Horner, M. Snell, & J. Blacher (Eds.), *Handbook of developmental disabilities* (pp. 330–348). New York, NY: Guilford Press.

Fowler, A. (1998). Language in mental retardation: Associations with and dissociations from general cognition. In J. Burack, R. Hodapp, & E. Zigler (Eds.), *Handbook of mental retardation and development* (pp. 290–333). New York, NY: Cambridge University Press.

Fowler, M. (2010). Increasing on-task performance for students with ADHD. *New Jersey Education Association Review, 83,* 8–10.

Fowler, S. A., Ostrosky, M. M., & Yates, T. J. (2007). Teaching and learning in the early years. In L. Florian (Ed.), *The Sage handbook of special education* (pp. 349–359). Thousand Oaks, CA: Sage.

Fox, L., Carta, J., Strain, P., Dunlap, G., & Hemmeter, M. L. (2010). Response to intervention and the pyramid model. *Infants and Young Children, 23*(1), 3–13.

Fox, L., Dunlap, G., Hemmeter, M. L., Joseph, G., & Strain, P. (2003). The teaching pyramid: A model for supporting social competence and preventing challenging behavior in young children. *Young Children, 58*(4), 48–52.

Fox, J., & Gable, R. A. (2004). Functional behavioral assessment. In R. Rutherford, M. Quinn, & S. Mathur (Eds.), *Handbook of Research in Emotional and Behavioral Disorders* (pp. 143–162). New York: Guilford.

Fox, L., Hemmeter, M. L., Snyder, P., Perez Binder, D., Clarke, S. (2011). Coaching early childhood special educators to implement a comprehensive model for promoting youg children's social competence. Topics in Early Childhood, 31(3), 178–192.

Franks, B. A., Miller, M. D., Wolff, E. J., & Landry, K. (2004). HIV/AIDS and the teachers of young children. *Early Child Development and Care, 174*(3), 229–241.

Freberg, L. A. (2006). *Discovering biological psychology.* Boston, MA: Houghton Mifflin.

Frey, J. R., & Kaiser, A. P. (2011). The use of play expansions to increase the diversity and complexity of object play in young children with disabilities. *Topics in Early Childhood Special Education, 31,* 99–111.

Frick, P. J., & Nigg, J. T. (2012). Current issues in the diagnosis of attention-deficit hyperactivity disorder, oppositional defiant disorder, and conduct disorder. *Annual Review of Clinical Psychology, 8,* 77–107.

Friend, A. C., Summers, J. A., & Turnbull, A. P. (2009). Impacts of family support in early childhood intervention research. *Education and Training in Developmental Disabilities, 44*(4), 453–470.

Frodl, T., & Skokauskas, N. (2012). Meta-analysis of structural MRI studies in children and adults with attention deficit hyperactivity disorder indicates treatment effects. *Acta Psychiatrica Scandinavica, 125,* 114–126.

Fuchs, D., & Fuchs, L. S. (2006). Introduction to response to intervention: What, why, and how valid is it? *Reading Research Quarterly, 41*(1), 93–98.

Fuchs, D., Fuchs, L. S., Mathes, P. G., Lipsey, M. L., & Roberts, P. H. (2002). Is "learning disabilities" just a fancy term for low achievement? A meta-analysis of reading differences between low achievers with and without the label. In R. Bradley, L. Danielson, & D. Hallahan (Eds.), *Identification of learning disabilities* (pp. 737–762). Mahwah, NJ: Erlbaum.

Fuchs, D., Mock, D., Morgan, P. L., & Young, C. L. (2003). Responsiveness-to-intervention: Definitions, evidence, and implications for the learning disabilities construct. *Learning Disabilities Research and Practice, 18*(3), 157–171.

Fuchs, L. S., & Fuchs, D. (2007). A model for implementing responsiveness to intervention. *Teaching Exceptional Children, 39*(5), 14–20.

Fuchs, L. S., Fuchs, D., Prentice, K., Hamlett, C. L., Finelli, R., Courey, S. J. (2004). Enhancing mathematical problem solving among third-grade students with schema-based instruction. *Journal of Educational Psychology, 96*, 635–647.

Gage, N. A., Lewis, T. J., and Stichter, J. P. (2012). Functional behavioral assessment-based interventions for students with or at risk for emotional and/or behavioral disorders in school: A hierarchical linear modeling meta-analysis. *Behavioral Disorders, 37*, 55–77.

Gale, E. (2010). Exploring perspectives on cochlear implants and language acquisition with deaf community. *Journal of Deaf Studies and Deaf Education, 16*(1).

Gallagher, J. (1972). The special education contract for mildly handicapped children. *Exceptional Children, 38*, 527–535.

Gallagher, J. (2000). The beginnings of federal help for young children with disabilities. *Topics in Early Childhood Special Education* (pp. 3–6). Austin, TX: PRO-ED.

Gallagher, J. (2002). Interventions and children with special needs. In A. Cranston-Gingus & E. Taylor, *Rethinking professional issues in special education* (pp. 43–68). Westport, CT: Ablex.

Gallagher, J. (2006). *Driving change in special education.* Baltimore, MD: Brookes.

Gallagher, J., & Clifford, R. (2000). The missing support infrastructure in early childhood. *Early Childhood Research and Practice, 2*(1), 1–24.

Gallagher, J., & Gallagher, S. (1994). *Teaching the gifted child* (4th ed.). Boston, MA: Allyn & Bacon.

Gallagher, J. J., Cook, E., & Shoffner, M. (2003). *Project insight II: Program evaluation.* Chapel Hill, NC: Frank Porter Graham Child Development Institute.

Gallagher, P., & Lambert, R. (2006). Classroom quality, concentration of children with special needs, and child outcomes in Head Start. *Exceptional Children, 73*(1), 31–52.

Gallagher, P., Powell, T., & Rhodes, C. (2006). *Brothers and sisters: A special part of exceptional families*. Baltimore, MD: Paul H. Brookes.

Gallagher, S. & Gallagher, J. (2013). Using problem based learning to explore unseen academic potential . *Interdisciplinary Journal of Problem Based Learning 7*(1), 112–131.

Gallagher, S., & Stepien, W. (1996). Content acquisition in problem based learning: Depth versus breadth in American studies. *Journal for the Education of the Gifted, 19*, 257–275.

Gallaudet Research Institute (November 2008). *Regional and national summary report of data from the 2007–2008 annual survey of deaf and hard of hearing children and youth.* Washington, D.C.: GRI, Gallaudet University.

Gannon, J. (1981). *Deaf heritage: A narrative history of deaf America.* Silver Spring, MD: National Association of the Deaf.

Garcia, S. B., Ortiz, A. A., & Sorrells, A. M. (2012). Intersectionality as a framework for research and practice in special education. *Multiple Voices for Ethnically Diverse Exceptional Learners, 13*(1), 1–3.

Gardner, D. (1983). A nation at risk: The imperative for education reform. Washington, D.C.: U.S. Department of Education.

Geers, A., Tobey, E., Moog, J., & Brenner, C. (2008). Long-term outcomes of cochlear implantation in the preschool years: From elementary grades to high school. *International Journal of Audiology, 47*, S21–S30.

Gene therapy. (2010). In *Wikipedia, the free encyclopedia.* Retrieved from en.wikipedia.org/wiki/Gene_therapy

Gerber, M. M., Jimenez, T., Leafstedt, J., Villaruz, J., Richards, C., & English, J. (2004). English reading effects of small-group intensive intervention in Spanish for K-1 English learners. *Learning Disabilities Research and Practice, 19*, 239–251.

Gerdes, A. C., Haack, L. M., & Schneider, B. W. (2012). Parental functioning in families of children with ADHD: Evidence for behavioral parent training and importance of clinically meaningful change. *Journal of Attention Disorders, 16*(2), 147–156.

Gerdes, A. C., Lawton, K. E., Haack, L. M., & Dieguez Hurtado, G. (2013). Assessing ADHD in Latino families: Evidence for moving beyond symptomatology. *Journal of Attention Disorders, 17*(2), 128–140.

Gersten, R., Chard, D. J., Jayanthi, M., Baker, S. K., Morphy, P., & Flojo, J. (2009). Mathematics instruction for students with learning disabilities: A meta-analysis of instructional components. *Review of Educational Research, 79*(3), 1202–1242.

Gersten, R., Compton, D., Connor, C. M., Dimino, J., Santoro, L., Linan-Thompson, S., & Tilly, W. D. (2008). *Assisting students struggling with reading: Response to Intervention and multi-tier intervention for reading in the primary grades. A practice guide.* (NCEE 2009–4045). Washington, D.C.: National Center for Education Evaluation and Regional Assistance, Institute of Education Sciences, U.S. Department of Education. Retrieved from http://ies.ed.gov/ncee/wwc/publications/practiceguides/.

Gersten, R. & Edybum, D. (2007). Enhancing the evidence base of special education technology research. *Journal of Special Education Technology, 23*(3), 3–18.

Geytenbeek, J. J., Heim, M. M., Vermeulen, R. J., & Oostrom, K. J. (2010). Assessing comprehension of spoken language in nonspeaking children with cerebral palsy: Application of a newly developed computer-based instrument. *Augmentative and Alternative Communication, 26*(2), 97–107.

Gillis, M. (2011). Promoting success: Early indicators of learning disabilities in preschool children. *Perspectives on Language and Literacy, 37*(3), 29–31.

Gillis, M., West, T., & Coleman, M. R. (2010a). *Early learning observation & rating scale: Development manual.* New York: National Center for Learning Disabilities.

Gillis, M., West, T., & Coleman, M. R. (2010b). *Early learning observation & rating scale: Teacher's guide.* New York: National Center for Learning Disabilities.

Gildroy, P., & Deshler, D. D. (2008). Effective learning strategy instruction. In R. Morris & N. Mather (Eds.), *Evidence-based practices for students with learning and behavioral challenges* (pp. 288–301). London, England: Routledge.

Girolametto, L., & Weitzman, E. (2007). Promoting peer interaction skills: Professional development for early childhood educators and preschool teachers. *Topics in Language Disorders, 27*(2), 93–110.

Given, B. (2002). *Teaching to the brain's natural learning systems.* Alexandria, VA: Association for Supervision and Curriculum Development.

Goh, A. E. & Bambara, L. M. (2010). Individualized positive behavior support in school settings: A meta-analysis. *Remedial and Special Education, 33*(5), 271–286.

Goldstein, B., & Iglesias, A. (2001). The effect on phonological analysis: Evidence from Spanish-speaking children. *American Journal of Speech-Language Pathology, 10*(1), 394–406.

Goldstein, H., Schneider, N., & Thiemann, K. (2007). Peer-mediated social communication intervention: When clinical expertise informs treatment development and evaluation. *Topics in Language Disorders, 27*(2), 182–199.

Goldstein, K. (1936). The modification of behavior consequent to cerebral lesions. *Psychiatric Quarterly, 10*, 586–610.

Goldstein, K. (1939). *The organism.* New York, NY: American Book Co.

Goodman, S., & Wittenstein, S. (Eds.). (2002). *Collaborative assessment.* New York, NY: American Foundation for the Blind.

Gottardis, L., Nunes, T., & Lunt, I. (2011). A synthesis of research on deaf and hearing children's mathematical achievement. *Deafness & Education International, 13*(3), 131–150.

Gottlieb, G. (1997). *Synthesizing nature-nurture: Prenatal roots of instinctive behavior.* Mahwah, NJ: Erlbaum.

Graham, S., & Harris, K.R. (2009). Almost 30 years of writing research: Making sense of it all with *The Wrath of Khan. Learning Disabilities Research & Practice, 24*(2), 58–68.

Grandin, T. (2011). *The Way I See It.* (2nd ed.) Arlington TX Future Horisons.

Greenberg, M., & Kusche, C. (1998). Preventive intervention for school-age deaf children: The PATHS curriculum. *Journal of Deaf Studies and Deaf Education, 3*(1), 49–63.

Greenspan, S. (2006). Functional concepts in mental retardation: Finding the natural essence of an artificial category. *Exceptionality, 14,* 205–224.

Greenspan, S., & Switzky, H. (2006). *Forty-four years of AAMR Manuals.* Washington, D.C.: American Association on Mental Retardation.

Greenspan, S., & Wieder, S. (2006). *Engaging autism: Using the floor-time approach to help.* Cambridge, MA: DaCapo Press.

Grenot-Scheyer, M. (1994). The nature of interactions between students with severe disabilities and their friends and acquaintances without disabilities. *Journal of the Association for Persons with Severe Handicaps, 19,* 253–262.

Gresham, F. (1998). Social skills training: Should we raze, remodel or rebuild? *Behavior Disorders, 24*(1), 19–25.

Gresham, F. (2007). Response to intervention and emotional and behavioral disorders. *Assessment for Effective Intervention, 32*(4), 214–222.

Gresham, F., Beebe-Frankenberger, M., & Macmillan, D. (1999). A selective review of treatments for children with autism: Description and methodological considerations. *School Psychology Review, 28*(44), 559–575.

Gresham, F., Van, M., & Cook, C. (2006). Social skills training for teaching replacement behaviors: Remediating acquisition deficits in at-risk students. *Behavioral Disorders, 31*(4), 363–377.

Gresham, F. M., & Kern, L. (2004). Internalizing behavior problems in children and adolescents. In R. Rutherford, M. Quinn, & S. Mathur (Eds.), *Handbook of research in emotional and behavioral disorders.* New York, NY: Guilford Press.

Grisham-Brown, J., Hemmeter, M. L., & Pretti-Frontczak, K. (2005). *Blended practices for teaching young children in inclusive settings.* Baltimore, MD: Brookes.

Guardino, C., & Antia, S. D. (2012). Modifying the classroom environment to increase engagement and decrease disruption with students who are deaf or hard of hearing. *Journal of Deaf Studies and Deaf Education, 17*(4), 518–533.

Guardino, C.M., Buddin, R., Pham, C., & Cho, M. (2010). Demographic factors associated with the early identification of children with special needs. *Topics in Early Childhood Education, 30,* 162–175.

Guerette, A.R., Lewis, S., & Mattingly, C. (2011). Students with low vision describe their visual impairments and visual functioning. *Journal of Visual Impairment & Blindness, 105,* 287–298.

Guiberson, M. (2009). Hispanic representation in special education: Patterns and implications. *Preventing School Failure: Alternative Education for Children and Youth, 53*(3), 167–176.

Guiberson, M. M., Barrett, K. C., Jancosek, E. G., & Itano, C. Y. (2006). Language maintenance and loss in preschool-age children of Mexican immigrants: Longitudinal study. *Communication Disorders Quarterly, 28*(1), 4–17.

Guralnick, M. (1997). *The effectiveness of early intervention.* Baltimore, MD: Brookes.

Guralnick, M. (1998). Effectiveness of early intervention: A developmental perspective. *American Journal of Mental Retardation, 102*(4), 319–345.

Guralnick, M., Hammond, M., Connor, R., & Neville, B. (2006). Stability, change, and correlates of the peer relationships of young children with mild developmental delays. *Child Development, 77*(2), 312–324.

Guralnick, M. J. (Ed.). (2005). *The developmental systems approach to early intervention.* Baltimore, MD: Brookes.

Guralnick, M. J., Conner, R. T., & Johnson, L. C. (2009). Home-based peer social networks of young children with Down syndrome: A developmental perspective. *American Journal on Intellectual and Developmental Disabilities, 114*(5), 340–355.

Hall, L. J. (2009). *Autism spectrum disorders: From theory to practice.* Columbus, OH: Merrill Publishing Co.

Hallahan, D. P., & Mock, D. R. (2003). A brief history of the field of learning disabilities. In H. L. Swanson, K. R. Harris, & S. Graham (Eds.), *Handbook of learning disabilities* (pp. 16–29). New York, NY: Guilford Press.

Hallam, R.A., Rous, B., Grove, J., & LoBianco, T. (2009). Level and intensity of early intervention services for infants and toddlers with disabilities: The impact of child, family, system, and community-level factors on service provision. *Journal of Early Intervention, 31,* 179–196.

Hamilton, H. (2011). Memory skills of deaf learners: Implications and applications. *American Annals of the Deaf, 156*(4), 402–423.

Hammil, D. (2004). What we know about correlates of reading. *Exceptional Children, 70*(4), 453–468.

Hanks, J., & Velaski, A. (2003). A cooperative collaboration between speech-language pathology and deaf education. *Teaching Exceptional Children, 36*(4), 58–63.

Hansen, E. G., Shute, V. J., & Landau, S. (2010). An assessment-for-learning system in mathematics for individuals with visual impairments. *Journal of Visual Impairments & Blindness, 104,* 275–286.

Hardonk, S., Daniels, S., Desnerck, G., Loots, G., Van Hove, G., Van Kerschaver, E., . . . Louckx, F. (2011). Deaf parents and pediatric cochlear implantation: An exploration of the decision-making process. *American Annals of the Deaf, 156*(3), 290–304.

Harms, T., & Clifford, R. (1980). *Infant/toddler environmental rating scales.* New York, NY: Teachers College Press.

Harms, T., Cryer, D., & Clifford, R. M. (1990). *Infant/toddler environment rating scale.* New York, NY: Teachers College Press.

Harrington, M., DesJardin, J. L., & Shea, L. C. (2010). Relationships between early child factors and school readiness skills in young children with hearing loss. *Communication Disorders Quarterly, 32*(1), 50–62.

Harry, B. (2007). The disproportionate placement of ethnic minorities in special education. In L. Florian (Ed.), *The Sage handbook of special education* (pp. 67–84). New York, NY: Sage Publications.

Harry, B., & Klingner, J. (2006). *Why are so many minority students in special education? Understanding race and disability in schools.* New York, NY: Teachers College Press.

Hart, J. (2009). Strategies for culturally and linguistically diverse students with special needs. *Preventing School Failure, 53*(3), 197–208.

Hart, K. C., Massette, G. M., Fabiano, G. A., Pariseau, M. E., & Pelham, W. E. (2011). Impact of group size on classroom on-task behavior and work productivity in children with ADHD. *Journal of Emotional and Behavioral Disorders, 19*(1), 55–64.

Hart, S. L., & Banda, D. R. (2010). Picture Exchange Communication System with individuals with developmental disabilities: A meta-analysis of single subject studies. *Remedial and Special Education, 31*(6), 476–488.

Hasazi, S., Gordon, L., & Roe, C. (1985). Factors associated with the employment status of handicapped youth exiting high school from 1979 to 1983. *Exceptional Children, 51,* 455–465.

Haskins, R. (2007). Fighting poverty through incentives and work mandates for young men. *The Future of Children* [Policy brief] (pp. 1–7). Princeton, NJ: Brookings Institution Press.

Hasselbring, T. (2001). A possible future of special education technology. *Journal of Special Education Technology, 16*(4), 19–26.

Hayes, H., Geers, A. E., Treiman, R., & Moog, J. S. (2009). Receptive vocabulary development in deaf children with cochlear implants: Achievement in an intensive auditory-oral education setting. *Ear & Hearing, 30*(1), 128–135.

Haywood, H. (2006). Broader perspectives on mental retardation. In H. Switzky & S. Greenspan (Eds.), *What is mental retardation?* Washington, D.C.: American Association forMental Retardation, (pp. xv–xx).

Hebbeler, K., Spiker, D., & Kahn, L. (2012). Individuals with Disabilities Education Act's early childhood programs: Powerful vision and pesky details. *Topics in Early Childhood Special Education, 31*(4), 199–207.

Hebbler, K., Spiker, D., Bailey, D., Scarborough, A., Mallik, S., Simeonsson, R., ... Nelson, L. (2007). *Early intervention for infants and toddlers with disabilities and their families: Participants, services and outcomes: Final report of the National Early Intervention Longitudinal Study (NEILS).* Menlo Park, CA: Stanford Research Institute. Retrieved from http://www.sri.com/neils/

Helmstetter, E., Peck, C., & Giangreco, M. (1994). Outcomes of interaction with peers of moderate and severe disabilities: A statewide survey of high school students. *Journal of the Association for Persons with Severe Handicaps, 19*(4), 260–276.

Hemmeter, M. L., Fox, L., Jack, S., & Broyles, L. (2007). A program-wide model of positive behavior support in early childhood settings. *Journal of Early Intervention, 29*(4), 337–355.

Henderson, K., Klein, S., & Gonzalez, P. (2005). Teachers of children with emotional disturbance: A national look at preparation, teaching conditions, and practices. *Behavioral Disorders, 31*(1), 6–17.

Hennessey, B., & Annabele, T. (2010). Creativity. *Annual Review of Psychology, 61,* 569–598.

Henningsson, G., Kuehn, D. P., Sell, D., Sweeney, T., Trost-Cardamone, J. E., Whitehill, T. L., & Speech Parameters Group. (2008). Universal parameters for reporting speech outcomes in individuals with cleft palate. *Cleft Palate 45*(1), 1–17.

Herter, G., Knightly, C., & Steinberg, A. (2002). Hearing: Sound and silences. In M. Batshaw (Ed.), *Children with disabilities* (5th ed., pp. 193–228). Baltimore, MD: Brookes.

Herzberg-Davis, H. & Callahan, C. (2008). Advanced placement and international baccalaureate programs. In J. Plucker & C. Callahan (Eds.). *Critical Issues and Practices in Gifted Education: What the Research Says* (31–34). Waco, TX: Prufrock Press.

Hibbard, R. A., Desch, L. W., & The Committee on Child Abuse and Neglect and Council on Children with Disabilities. (2007). Maltreatment of children with disabilities. *Pediatrics, 119,* 1018–1026.

Hidi, S., & Ainley, M. (2008). Interest and self-regulation: Relationships between two variables that influence learning. In D. Schunk & B. J. Zimmerman (Eds) *Motivation and self-regulated learning: theory, research, and applications* (p. 77–109). New York/London: Lawrence Erlbaum Associates, Inc.

Hintermair, M. (2011). Health-related quality of life and classroom participation of deaf and hard-of-hearing students in general schools. *Journal of Deaf Studies and Deaf Education, 16*(2), 254–271.

Hitchcock, C., Meyer, A., Rose, D., & Jackson, R. (2002). Providing new access to the general curriculum: Universal design for learning. *Teaching Exceptional Children, 32,* 8–17.

Hoeft, F., Hernandez, A., McMillon, G., Taylor-Hill, H., Martindale, J., Meyler, A., ... Gabrieli, J. D. (2006). Neural basis of dyslexia: A comparison between dyslexic and nondyslexic children equated for reading ability. *The Journal of Neuroscience, 26*(42), 10700–10708.

Hoff, E. (2004). Progress, but not a full solution to the logical problem of language acquisition. *Journal of Child Language, 31,* 923–926.

Hoff, E. (2009). *Language development* (4th ed.). Belmont, CA: Wadsworth Cengage Learning.

Hoff, E., and Elledge, C. (2005). Bilingualism as one of many environmental variables that affect language development. In J. Cohen, K. T. McAlister, K. (Eds.), *Proceedings of the 4th International Symposium on Bilingualism* (pp. 1034–1040). Sommerville, MD: Cascadilla Press.

Hoglund, T. (1999). Time magazine covers gene therapy. Retrieved from www.mdsupport.org/library/jgenether.html

Hojnoski, R., Caskie, G., Gischlar, K., Key, J., Barry, A., & Hughes, C. (2009). Data display preference, acceptability, and accuracy among urban Head Start teachers. *Journal of Early Intervention, 32*(1), 38–53.

Hojnoski, R., Gischlar, K., & Missall, K. (2009). Improving child outcomes with data-based decision making graphing data. *Young Exceptional Children, 12*(4) 15–30.

Holahan, C., & Sears, R. (1995). *The gifted group in later maturity.* Stanford, CA: Stanford University Press.

Holbrook, M. C., & Koenig, A. J. (2000). *Foundations of education.* New York, NY: AFB Press.

Holt, L. L. (2005). Temporally nonadjacent non-linguistic sounds affect speech categorization. *Psychological Science*, 16, 305–312.

Horn, E., & Kang, J. (2012). Supporting young children with multiple disabilities: What do we know and what do we still need to learn? *Topics in Early Childhood Special Education, 31*(4), 241–248.

Horner, R., Sugai, G., Swolenski, K., Eber, L., Nakasoto, J., Todd, A., & Zsperanzay, J. (2009). A randomized, wait-list controlled effectiveness trial assessing school-wide positive behavior support in elementary schools. *Journal of Positive Behavior Interventions. 11,* 133–145.

Horowitz, S., & Stecker, D. (2010). *Checklist for Learning Disabilities.* New York, NY: National Center for Learning Disabilities.

Hua, C. B., & Coleman, M. R. (2002). Preparing twice exceptional students for adult lives: A critical need. *Understanding Our Gifted 14*(2), 17–19.

Hughes-Lynch, C. (2010). *Children with high-functioning autism: A parent's guide.* Waco, TX: Prufrock Press.

Human Genome Project (2013). Retrieved from http://www.ornl.gov/sci/techresources/Human_Genome/home.shtml#index

Hunt, J. M. (1961). *Intelligence and experience.* New York, NY: Ronald Press.

Hunt, P., & McDonnell, J. (2007). Inclusive education. In S. Odom, B. Horner, M. Snell, & J. Blacher (Eds.), *Handbook of developmental disabilities* (pp. 269–291). New York, NY: Guilford Press.

Hunt, P., Soto, G., Maier, J., & Doering, K. (2003). Collaborative teaming to support students at risk and students with severe disabilities in general education classrooms. *Exceptional Children, 69*(3), 315–332.

Hustad, K. C., Dardis, C. M. , Kramper, A. J. (2011). Use of listening strategies for the speech of individuals with dysarthria and cerebral palsy. *Augmentative and Alternative Communication. March, 27*(1), 5–15.

Hwa-Froelich, D., Kasambira, D. C., & Moleski, A. M. (2007). Communicative functions of African American Head Start children. *Communication Disorders* Quarterly, *28*(2), 77–91.

Hyde, M., Punch, R., & Komesaroff, L. (2010). A comparison of the anticipated benefits and received outcomes of pediatric cochlear implantation: Parental perspectives. *American Annals of the Deaf, 155*(3), 322–338.

Hynd, G. (1992). Neurological aspects of dyslexia. *Journal of Learning Disabilities, 25*, 100–113.

Hyter, Y. D. (2007). Pragmatic language assessment: A pragmatics-as-social-practice model. *Topics in Language Disorders, 27*(2), 128–145.

Immordino-Yang, M.H., & Damasio, A. (2007). We feel, therefore we learn: The relevance of affective and social neuroscience to education. *Mind, Brain, and Education, 1*(1), 3–10.

Individuals with Disabilities Education Improvement Act of 2004, PL 108–446, U. S. Department of Education, Washington, D.C.

International Dyslexia Association. (2013). Frequently asked questions about dyslexia. Retrieved from http://www.interdys.org/FAQ.htm.

Jackson, C. W. (2011). Family supports and resources for parents of children who are deaf or hard of hearing. *American Annals of the Deaf, 156*(4), 343–362.

Jackson, L., Ryndak, D. L., & Billingsley, F. (2000). Useful practices in inclusive education: A preliminary view of what experts in moderate to severe disabilities are saying. *Journal of the Association for Persons with Severe Handicaps, 25*(3), 129–141.

Janssen, M. J., Riksen-Walraven, J. M., Van Dijk, J. P., Huisman, M., & Ruijssenaars, W. A. (2012). Enhancing sustained interaction between children with congenital deaf-blindness and their educators. *Journal of Visual Impairment & Blindness, 106*(3), 177–183.

Jenkins, J., & O'Connor, R. (2002). Identification and intervention for young children with reading/learning disabilities. In R. Bradley, L. Danielson, & D. Hallahan (Eds.), *Identification of learning disabilities: Research to practice* (pp. 99–172). Mahwah, NJ: Erlbaum.

Jenkins, J., Speltz, M., & Odom, S. (1985). Integrating normal and handicapped preschoolers: Effects on child development and social interaction. *Exceptional Children, 52*(1), 7–17.

Jensen, E. P. (2008). A fresh look at brain-based education. *Phi Delta Kappan, 89*(6), 408–417.

Jessup, G. M., Cornell, E., & Bundy, A. C. (2010). The treasure in leisure activities: Fostering resilience in young people who are blind. *Journal of Visual Impairment & Blindness, 104*, 419–430.

Johnsen, S. K. (Ed.). (2004). *Identifying gifted students: A practical guide.* Waco, TX: Prufrock Press and Texas Association for the Gifted and Talented.

Johnson, J. R., & McIntosh, A. S. (2009). Toward a cultural perspective and understanding of the disability and deaf experience in special and multicultural education. *Remedial and Special Education, 30*(2), 67–83.

Johnson, S., & Sheffield, L. (Eds.) (2013). *Using the Common Core Standards for mathematics with gifted and advanced learners*. Waco, TX: Prufrock Press.

Joint Committee on Infant Hearing. (2007). *Year 2007 position statement: Principles and guidelines for early hearing detection and intervention.* Available from www.asha.org/policy

Jones, T. W, Jones, J. K., & Ewing, K. M. (2006). Students with multiple disabilities. In D. F. Moore and D. S. Martin (Eds.), *Deaf learners: Developments in curriculum and instruction.* (pp. 127–143). Washington, D.C.: Gallaudet University Press.

Jung, L. A., & Guskey, T. R. (2010). Grading exceptional learners. *Educational Leadership, 67*(5), 31–35.

Jusczyk, E. W. (1997). *The discovery of spoken language.* Cambridge, MA: MIT Press.

Just, M., & Varma, S. (2007). The organization of thinking: What functional brain imaging reveals about the neuroarchitecture of complex cognition. *Cognitive, Affective, and Behavioral Neuroscience, 1*(3), 153–191.

Justice, L., Mashburn, A. J., Hamre, B. K., & Pianta, R. C. (2008). Quality of language and literacy instruction in preschool classrooms serving at-risk pupils. *Early Childhood Research Quarterly, 23*, 51–68.

Kaiser, A. (2000). Teaching functional communication skills. In M. Snell & F. Brown (Eds.), *Instruction of students with severe disabilities* (5th ed., pp. 453–492). Upper Saddle River, NJ: Merrill.

Kam, C. M., Greenberg, M., & Kusche, C. (2004). Sustained effects of the PATHS curriculum on the social and psychological adjustment of children in social and psychological adjustment of children in special education. *Journal of Emotional & Behavioral Disorders, 12*(2), 66–78.

Kame'enui, E. J. (2007). A new paradigm: Responsiveness to intervention. *Teaching Exceptional Children, 39*(5), 6–7.

Kamei-Hannan, C., Holbrook, M. C., & Ricci, L. A. (2012). Applying a response-to-intervention model to literacy instruction for students who are blind or have low vision. *Journal of Visual Impairment & Blindness, 106*, 69–80.

Kanne, S. M., & Mazurek, M. O. (2011). Aggression in children and adolescents with ASD: Prevalence and risk factors. *Journal of Autism and Developmental Disorders, 41*, 926–937.

Kanner, L. (1943). Autistic disturbance of affective contact. *Nervous Child, 2*, 217–250.

Kaplan, S. Purcell, J., Leppien, J., Tomlinson, C., & Burns, D. (2005). *Parallel Curriculum in the Classroom. Book 1*. London: Sage.

Kasari, C., & Bauminger, N. (1998). Social and emotional development in children with mental retardation. In J. Burack, R. Hodapp, & E. Zigler (Eds.), *Handbook of mental retardation and development* (pp. 411–433). New York, NY: Cambridge University Press.

Kasprzak, C., Hurth, J., Rooney, R., Goode, S. E., Danaher, J.C., …Cates, D. (2012). States' accountability and progress in serving young children with disabilities. *Topics in Early Childhood Special Education, 32*, 151–163.

Kauffman Early Education Exchange (2002, Summer). Set for success: Building a strong foundation for school readiness based on the social-emotional development of young children. Kansas City, MO: The Ewing Marion Kauffman Foundation.

Kauffman, J., Brigham, F., & Mock, D. (2004). Historical to contemporary perspectives of the field of behavior disorders. In R. Rutherford, M. Quinn, & S. Mathur (Eds.), *Handbook of research in emotional and behavioral disorders* (pp. 15–31). New York, NY: Guilford Press.

Kavale, K., Mathur, S., & Mostert, M. (2004). Social skills training and teaching social behavior to students with emotional and behavioral disorders. In R. Rutherford, M. Quinn, & S. Mathur (Eds.), *Handbook of research in emotional and behavioral disorders* (pp. 446–461). New York, NY: Guilford Press.

Kavale, K. A., & Forness, S. R. (1999). Interference, inhibition, and learning disability: A commentary on Dempster and Corkill. *Educational Psychology Review, 11*(2), 97–104.

Kavale, K. A., Holdnack, J. A., & Mostert, M. P. (2005). Responsiveness to intervention and the identification of specific learning disability: A critique and alternative proposal. *Learning Disability Quarterly, 28*(1), 2–16.

Kavale, K. A., Spaulding, L. S., & Beam, A. P. (2009). A time to define: Making the specific learning disability definition prescribe specific learning disability. *Learning Disability Quarterly*, 32(1), 39–48.

Kearns, J. F., Towles-Reeves, E., Kleinert, H. L., Kleinert, J. O. R., & Thomas, M. K. K. (2011). Characteristics of and implications for students participating in alternate assessments based on alternate academic achievement standards. *The Journal of Special Education, 45*(1), 3–14.

Kelly, S.M. (2011). The use of assistive technology by high school students with visual impairments: A second look at the current problem. *Journal of Visual Impairment & Blindness, 105*, 235–239.

Kent, K. M, Pelham Jr., W. E., Molina, B. S. G., Sibley, M. H., Waschbusch, D. A., Yu, J., . . . Karch, K. M. (2011). The academic experience of male high school students with ADHD. *Journal of Abnormal Child Psychology, 39*, 451–462.

Kerr, B. A., & Cohn, S. J. (2001). *Smart boys: Talent, manhood, and the search for meaning*. Scottsdale, AZ: Great Potential.

Kerr, M., & Nelson, C. (2002). *Addressing behavior problems* (4th ed.). Upper Saddle River, NJ: Prentice Hall.

Key, J. D., Brown, R. T., Marsh, L. D., Spratt, E. G., & Recknor, J. C. (2001). Depressive symptoms in adolescents with a chronic illness. *Children's Health Care, 30*(4), 283–292.

Keyser-Marcus, L., Briel, L., Sherron-Targett, P., Yasuda, S., Johnson, S., & Wehman, P. (2002). Enhancing the schooling of students with traumatic brain injury. *Teaching Exceptional Children, 34*(4), 62–67.

King-Sears, M., & Carpenter, C. (2005). Teaching self-management to elementary students with developmental disabilities. In M. Wehmeyer & M. Agran (Eds.), *Mental retardation and intellectual disabilities: Teaching students using innovative and research-based strategies*. Boston, MA: Merrill/Prentice Hall.

Kirby, J. R., Silvestri, R., Allingham, B. H., Parrila, R., & LaFave, C. B. (2008). Learning strategies and study approaches of postsecondary students with dyslexia. *Journal of Learning Disabilities, 41*(1), 85–96.

Kirk, S. (1950). A project for pre-school mentally handicapped children. *American Journal of Mental Deficiency, 55*, 305–310.

Kitano, M. (2007). Gifted girls. In J. Plucker & C. Callahan (Eds.) *Critical issues and practices in gifted education* (pp. 225–240). Waco, TX: Prufrock Press.

Kleeck, A., & Schuele, C. M. (2010). Historical perspectives on literacy in early childhood. *American Journal of Speech-Language Pathology, 19*, 341–355.

Klingner, J., Blanchett, W., & Harry, B. (2007). Race, culture, and developmental disabilities. In S. Odom, B. Horner, M. Snell, & J. Blacher (Eds.), *Handbook of developmental disabilities* (pp. 55–76). New York, NY: Guilford Press.

Klingner, J. K. (2009). *RTI in Culturally and Linguistically Diverse Schools* (5 Blog Postings). Council for Exceptional Children (Cec.Sped.org)

Klingner, J., & Harry, B. (2006). The special education referral and decision-making process for English language learners. *Teachers College Record, 108*, 1–20.

Knight, M. (2003). A natural history of language. *Contemporary Psychology, 48*(3), 306–308.

Knoors, H., & Marschark, M. (2012). Language planning for the 21st century: Revisiting bilingual language policy for deaf children. *Journal of Deaf Studies and Deaf Education, 17*(3), 291–305.

Kochhar-Bryant, C. A. (2007). The summary of performance as transition "passport" to employment and independent living. *Assessment for Effective Intervention, 32*(3), 160–170.

Koegel, R. L., & Koegel, L. K. (2007). *Pivotal response treatments for autism: communication, social & academic development*. Baltimore MD: Paul H. Brookes.

Koenig, A., & Holbrook, M. (2000). Literacy skills. In A. Koenig & M. Holbrook (Eds.), *Foundations of education: Vol. II. Instructional strategies for teaching children and youths with visual impairments* (2nd ed., pp. 264–329). New York, NY: Foundation for the Blind Press.

Koenig, A., & Rex, E. (1996). Instruction of literacy skills to children and youths with low vision. In A. Corn & A. Koenig (Eds.), *Foundations of low vision: Clinical and functional perspectives* (pp. 280–305). New York, NY: American Foundation for the Blind.

Koenig, A. J., & Holbrook, M. C. (1995). *Learning media assessment of students with visual impairments: A resource guide for teachers*. Austin, Texas: Texas School for the Blind and Visually Impaired.

Kolloff, P. (2003). State supported residential high schools. In N. Colangelo & C. Davis (Eds.), *Handbook of gifted education* (pp. 219–228). Boston, MA: Allyn & Bacon.

Kolvin, I., Miller, F.J., Scott, D.M., Gatzanis, S.R., & Fleeting, M. (1990). *Continuities of depravation. The Newcastle 1,000 family study.*(1990) Aldershot, England.

Kong, L., Fry, M., Al-Samarraie, M., Gilbert, C., & Steinkuller, P. G. (2012). An update on progress and the changing epidemiology of causes of childhood blindness worldwide. *Journal of American Association for Pediatric Ophthalmology and Strabismus, 16*(6), 501–507.

Konidaris, J. (1997). A sibling's perspective on autism. In D. Cohen & F. Volkman (Eds.), *Handbook of autism and pervasive developmental disorders* (2nd ed., pp. 1021–1031). New York, NY: Wiley.

Konrad, K., & Eickhoff, S. B. (2010). Is the ADHD brain wired differently? A review on structural and functional connectivity in attention deficit hyperactivity disorder. *Human Brain Mapping, 31*, 904–916.

Kortering, L. J., Braziel, P. M., & Tomkins, J. R. (2002). The challenge of school completion among youths with behavioral disorders: Another side of the story. *Behavioral Disorders, 27*, 142–154.

Kosine, N. R. (2007). Preparing students with learning disabilities for postsecondary education: What the research literature tells us about transition programs. *Journal of Special Education Leadership, 20*(2), 93–104.

Krauss, M. W., Seltzer, M. M., Gordon, R., & Friedman, D. H. (1996). Binding ties: The roles of adult siblings of persons with mental retardation. *Mental Retardation, 34*, 83–93.

Kravets, M. (2006). Hidden disabilities: Another diverse population [Electronic version]. *Journal of College Admission, 190*, 18–25.

Kunzman, R. (2008). Homeschooling. In J. Plucker & C. Callahan (Eds.). *Critical Issues and Practices in Gifted Education: What the Research Says* (155–166). Waco, TX: Prufrock Press.

Kurima, K., Peters, L., Yang, Y., Riazuddin, S., Ahmet, Z., Naz, S., ... Griffith, A. (2002). Dominant and recessive deafness caused by mutations of a novel gene, TMC1, required for cochlear hair-cell function. *Nature Genetics, 30*, 277–284.

Kyle, F. E., & Harris, M. (2011). Longitudinal patterns of emerging literacy in beginning deaf and hearing readers. *Journal of Deaf Studies and Deaf Education, 16*(3), 289–304.

Lacava, P. G., Golan, O., Baron-Cohen, S., & Myles, B. S. (2007). Using assistive technology to teach emotion recognition to students with Asperger syndrome. *Remedial and Special Education, 28*(3), 174–181.

Lahey, M., & Bloom, L. (1988). *Language disorders and language development*. Columbus, OH: Merrill.

Lambek, R., Tannock, R., Dalsgaard, S., Trillingsgaard, A., Damm, D., & Thomsen, P. H. (2011). Validating neuropsychological subtypes of ADHD: How do children with and without an executive function deficit differ? *The Journal of Child Psychology and Psychiatry, 51*(8), 895–904.

Landier, W. (2007). *Establishing and enhancing services for childhood cancer survivors: Long-term follow-up program resource guide*. Monrovia, CA: Children's Oncology Group.

Landmark, L.J. & Zhang, D. (2013). Compliance and practices in transition planning: A review of individualized education program documents. *Remedial and Special Education, 34*(2), 113–125.

Lansing, A. E., Max, J. E., Delis, D. C., Fox, P. T., Lancaster, J., Manes, F. F., & Schatz, A. (2004). Verbal learning and memory after childhood stroke. *Journal of the International Neuropsychological Society, 10*, 742–752.

Larson, K., Russ, S. A., Kahn, R. S., & Halfon, N. (2011). Patterns of comorbidity, functioning, and service use for US children with ADHD, 2007. *Pediatrics, 127*, 462–470.

Lazarus, S., Thurlow, M., Lail, K., & Christensen, L. (2009). A longitudinal analysis of state accommodation policies. *Journal of Special Education, 43*(2), 67–80.

Lee, A. S. Y., Law, J., & Gibbon, F. E. (2009). Electropalatography for articulation disorders associated with cleft palate (review). *The Cochrane Library, 4*, 1–23.

Lee, V., & Burkam, D. (2002). *Inequality at the starting gate: Social background differences in achievement as children begin school.* Washington, D.C.: Economic Policy Institute.

Leech, E. R. B., & Cress, C. J. (2011). Indirect facilitation of speech in a late talking child by prompted production of picture symbols or signs. *Augmentative and Alternative Communication, 27*, 40–52.

Leffert, J., Siperstein, G., & Millikan, E. (2000). Understanding social adaptation in children with mental retardation. *Exceptional Children, 66*(4), 530–545.

Lemons, C. J., & Fuchs, D. (2010). Phonological awareness of children with Down syndrome: Its role in learning to read and the effectiveness of related intervention. *Research in Developmental Disabilities, 31*, 316–330.

Lerner, L., & Johns, B. (2012). *Learning disabilities and related mild disabilities: Teaching strategies and new directions* (12th ed.). Belmont, CA: Wadsworth Cengage Learning.

Levin, D. S., & Rotheram-Fuller, E. (2011). Evaluating the empowered curriculum for adolescents with visual impairments. *Journal of Visual Impairment & Blindness, 105*, 350–360.

Levine, M. (2003). *The myth of laziness.* New York, NY: Simon & Schuster.

Levine, M. (2005). *Ready or not, here life comes.* New York, NY: Simon & Schuster.

Levine, M. (2006, Summer). The NBO promotes family-centered care in early intervention. *Ab Initio.* Retrieved from www.brazelton-institute.com/abinitio2006summer/art3.html

Lewis, M. D., & Stieben, J. (2004). Emotion regulation in the brain: conceptual issues and directions for developmental research. *Child Development, 75*(2), 371–376.

Lewis, T., Hudson, S., Richter, M., & Johnson, N. (2004). Scientifically supported practices in emotional and behavioral disorders: A proposed approach and brief review of current practices. *Behavioral Disorders, 29*(3), 247–259.

Lewis, T., Lewis-Palmer, T., Newcomer, L., & Stichter, J. (2004). Applied behavior analysis and the education and treatment of students with emotional and behavioral disorders. In R. Rutherford, M. Quinn, & S. Mathur (Eds.), *Handbook of research in emotional and behavior disorders* (pp. 523–545). New York, NY: The Guilford Press.

Lewis, T.J., Jones, S.E.L., Horner, R.H., & Sugai, G. (2010). School-wide positive behavior support and students with emotional/behavioral disorders: Implications for prevention, identification and intervention. *Exceptionality: A Special Educational Journal, 18*(2), 82–93.

Liefert, F. (2003). Introduction to visual impairment. In S. Goodman & S. Wittenstein (Eds.), *Collaborative assessment* (pp. 1–22). New York, NY: American Foundation for the Blind.

Lifter, K., Mason, E. J., & Barton, E. E. (2011). Children's play: Where we have been and where we could go. *Journal of Early Intervention, 33*(4), 281–297.

Liptak, G. (2002). Neural tube defects. In M. Batshaw (Ed.), *Children with disabilities* (5th ed., pp. 467–492). Baltimore, MD: Brookes.

Lo, Y. Y., Mustian, A. L., Brophy, A., & White, R. B. (2011). Peer-mediated social skill instruction for African American males with or at risk for mild disabilities. *Exceptionality, 19*(3), 191–209.

Loeber, R., & Farrington, D. (Eds.). (1998). *Serious and violent juvenile offenders: Risk factors and successful interventions.* London, England: Sage.

Loncke, F. T. (2011). Communication disorders. In J. M. Kauffman & D. P. Hallahan (Eds.), *Handbook of special education* (pp. 221–232). Florence, KY: Routledge.

Lord, C. (1995). Follow-up of two-year-olds referred for possible autism. *Journal of Child Psychology and Psychiatry, 36*, 1365–1382.

Lord, C. (2001). *Children with autism.* Washington, D.C.: National Academy of Sciences.

Lord, C., & Risi, S. (2000). Diagnosis of autism spectrum disorders in young children. In A. Wetherby, & B. Prizant (Eds.), *Autism spectrum disorders* (pp. 11–30). Baltimore, MD: Brookes.

Lovaas, O. J. (1993). The development of a treatment project for developmentally disabled and autistic children. *Journal of Applied Behavior Analyses, 26*(4), 617–630.

Lowenfeld, B. (Ed.). (1973). *The visually handicapped child in school.* New York, NY: Day.

Lubinski, D. (2009). Cognitive epidemiology: With emphasis on untangling cognitive ability and socioeconomic status. *Intelligence, 37*, 625–633.

Lubinski, D., & Benbow, C. P. (2006). Study of mathematically precocious youth after 35 years: Uncovering antecedents for the development of math-science expertise. *Perspectives in Psychological Science, 1*, 316–345.

Lubinski, D., Benbow, C. P., Webb, R. M., & Bleske-Rechek, A. (2006). Tracking exceptional human capital over two decades. *Psychological Science, 27*, 194–199.

Lubinski, D., Webb, R. M., Morelock, M. J., & Benbow, C. P. (2001). Top 1 in 10,000: A 10-year follow-up of the profoundly gifted. *Journal of Applied Psychology, 86*, 718–729.

Luby, J. L., Heffelfinger, A., Mrakotsky, C., Brown, K., Hessler, M., Wallis, J., & Spitznagel, E. (2003). The Clinical Picture of Depression in Preschool Children. *Journal of the American Academy of Child Adolescent Psychiatry, 42*(3): 340–348.

Luckner, J., & Cooke, C. (2010). A summary of the vocabulary research with students who are deaf or hard of hearing. *American Annals of the Deaf, 155*(1), 1–67.

Luckner, J., & Handley, C. M. (2008). A summary of the reading comprehension research undertaken with students who are deaf or hard of hearing. *American Annals of the Deaf, 153*(1), 6–36.

Luckner, J. L. (2006). Evidence-based practices with students who are deaf. *Communication Disorders Quarterly, 28*(1), 49–52.

Luckner, J. L., & Muir, S. (2001). Successful students who are deaf in general education settings [Electronic version]. *American Annals of the Deaf, 146*(5), 435–446.

Luckner, J. L., Sebald, A. M., Cooney, J., Young, J., & Muir, S. G. (2005–2006). An examination of the evidence-based literacy research in deaf education [Electronic version]. *American Annals of the Deaf, 150*(5), 443–456.

Lundy, B. (2003). Father and mother-infant face-to-face interactions: Differences in mind-related comments and infant attachment? *Infant Behavior and Development, 26*, 200–212.

Luze, G., & Hughes, K. (2008). Using individual growth and development indicators to assess child and program outcomes. *Young Exceptional Children, 12*(1), 31–41.

Lynas, W. (2000). Communication options. In J. Stokes (Ed.), *The hearing impaired infant: The first eighteen months* (pp. 98–128). London, England: Whurr. (Distributed by Paul H. Brookes)

Lyon, G. R. (1995). Toward a definition of dyslexia. *Annals of Dyslexia, 45*, 3–27.

Lytle, R., & Rovins, N. (1997). Reforming deaf education. *American Annals of the Deaf, 142*(1), 7–15. MA: Pearson. p. 516.

Maccini, P., Mulcahy, C. A., & Wilson, M. G. (2007). A follow-up of mathematics interventions for secondary students with learning disabilities. *Learning Disabilities Practice, 22*(1), 58–75.

MacMillan, D., Siperstein, G., & Heffert, J. (2006). *Children with mild mental retardation: A challenge for classification practices—Revised.* Washington, D.C.: American Association on Mental Retardation.

Maguire, M. J., Hirsh-Pasek, K., Golinkoff, R. M., Imai, M., Haryu, E., Vanegas, S., ... Sanchez-Davis, B. (2010). A developmental shift from similar to language-specific strategies in verb acquisition: A comparison of English, Spanish, and Japanese. *Cognition, 114*, 299–319.

Mahoney, G., & Perales, F. (2003). Using relationship-focused intervention to enhance the social-emotional functioning of young children with autism spectrum disorders. *TECSE, 23*, 74–86.

Mainzer, R. W., Deschler, D., Coleman, M. R., Kozleski, E., & Rodriguez-Walling, M. (2003). To ensure the learning of every child with a disability: Report to the Council of Exceptional Children. *Exceptional Children, 35*, 1–12.

Maisog, J. M., Einbinder, E. R., Flowers, D. L., Turkeltaub, P.E., & Eden, G.F. (2008). A meta-analysis of functional neuroimaging studies of dyslexia. *Annals of the New York Academy of Sciences, 1145*, 237–259.

Maller, S. J. (2003). Intellectual assessment of deaf people: A critical review of core concepts and issues. In M. Marschark & P. Spencer (Eds.). *Oxford handbook of deaf studies, language and education.* (pp. 451–463). New York: Oxford University Press.

Malloy, P. (2009). Who are children who are deaf-blind? *Division on Visual Impairments Quarterly*, 54(3), 5–7.

Mandell, D. S., Ittenbach, R. F., Levy, S. E., & Pinto-Martin, J. A. (2007). Disparities in diagnoses received prior to a diagnosis of autism spectrum disorder. *Journal of Autism and Developmental Disorders, 37*, 1795–1802.

Mandell, D. S., Listerund, J., Levy, S. E., & Pinto-Martin, J. A. (2002). Race differences in the age at diagnosis among Medicaid-eligible children with autism. *Journal of the American Academy of Child and Adolescent Psychiatry, 41*(12), 1447–1453.

March of Dimes. (2010). *Birth defects and genetic conditions.* Retrieved from www.marchofdimes.com/pnhec/4439.asp

March of Dimes. (2013). Birth defects. Retrieved from http://www.marchofdimes.com/baby/chromosomal-conditions.aspx

Marland, S. (1972). *Education of the gifted and talented.* Report to the Congress of the United States by the U.S. Commissioner of Education Washington, D.C.: U.S. Government Printing Office.

Marschark, M., Lang, H., & Albertini, J. (2002). *Educating deaf students.* New York, NY: Oxford University Press.

Marschark, M., Rhoten, C., & Fabich, M. (2007). Effects of cochlear implants on children's reading and academic achievement. *Journal of Deaf Studies and Deaf Education, 12*(3), 269–282.

Martindale, M. (2007). Children with significant hearing loss: Learning to listen, talk, and read: Evidence-based best practices. *Communication Disorders Quarterly, 28*(2), 73–76.

Mattison, R. (2004). Psychiatric and psychological assessment of emotional and behavior disorders during school mental health consultation. In R. Rutherford, M. Quinn, & D. Mathur (Eds.) *Handbook of research in emotional and behavior disorders.* New York, NY: The Guilford Press, 163–180.

Mauk, G., & White, K. (1995). Giving children a sound beginning: The promise of universal hearing screening. *Volta Review, 97*(1), 5–32.

Maxwell, N. L., Bellisimo, Y., & Mergendoller, J. (2001). Problem-based learning: Modifying the medical school model for teaching high school economics. *Social Studies, 92*, 73–78.

McCabe, A., & Champion, T. B. (2010). A matter of vocabulary II: Low-income African American children's performance on the Expressive Vocabulary Test. *Communication Disorders Quarterly, 31*(3), 162–169.

McCandliss, B., & Noble, K. (2003). The development of reading impairment: A cognitive neuroscience model. *Mental Retardation and Developmental Disabilities Research Reviews, 9*, 196–205.

McCarthy, M. (1994). Inclusion and the law: Recent judicial decisions. *Phi Delta Kappa Research Bulletin,* No. 13.

McCathren, R., Yoder, P., & Warren, S. (1995). The role of directives in early language intervention. *Journal of Early Intervention, 19*(2), 91–101.

McCombs, K., & Moore, D. (2002). Substance abuse prevention and intervention for students with disabilities: A call to educators. *ERIC Digest,* E627.

McConnell, S. (2000). *Interventions to facilitate social interaction for young children with autism: Review of available research and recommendations for educational intervention* [Paper prepared for National Research Council of the National Academy of Sciences]. Minneapolis, MN: University of Minnesota.

McDonnall, M. C. (2010). Factors predicting post-high school employment for young adults with visual impairments. *Rehabilitation Counseling Bulletin*, 54(1), 36–45.

McDonnall, M. C., Cavenaugh, B. S., & Giesen, J. M. (2012). The relationship between parental involvement and mathematics achievement for students with visual impairments. *The Journal of Special Education, 45*(4), 204–215.

McDonnell, J. (2011). Instructional contexts. In J. M. Kauffman & D. P. Hallahan (Eds.), *Handbook of special education* (pp. 532–543). New York, NY: Routledge.

McGee, G., Feldman, R., & Morrier, M. (1997). Benchmarks of social treatment for children with autism. *Journal of Autism and Developmental Disorders, 27*, 353–364.

McGough, S. M., & Schirmer, B. R. (2005). Teaching reading to children who are deaf: Do the conclusions of the National Reading Panel apply? [Electronic version]. *Review of Educational Research, 75*(1), 83–117.

McGuffin, P., Riley, B., & Plomin, R. (2001). Toward behavioral genomics. *Science, 291*, 1232–1249.

McIlroy, G., & Storbeck, C. (2011). Development of deaf identity: An ethnographic study. *Journal of Deaf Studies and Deaf Education, 16*(4), 494–511.

McKenzie, A. R. (2009). Emergent literacy supports for students who are deaf-blind or have visual and multiple impairments: A multiple-case study. *Journal of Visual Impairment & Blindness, 103*(5), 291–302.

McLaughlin, J., & Lewis, R. (2001). *Assessing students with special needs* (5th ed.). Upper Saddle River, NJ: Prentice-Hall.

McLaughlin, M. J. (2012, September/October). Access for all: Six principles for principals to consider in implementing CCSS for students with disabilities. *Principal,* 22–26.

McLesky, J. and Waldron, N. (2011). Educational programs for elementary students with learning disabilities: Can they be both effective and inclusive? *Learning Disabilities Research and Practice, 26*, 48–57.

McNamara, J. K., & Willoughby, T. (2010). A longitudinal study of risk-taking behavior in adolescents with learning disabilities. *Learning Disabilities: Research & Practice, 25*(1), 11–24.

McNee, C. M., & Jackson, C. W. (2012). The experiences and involvement of grandparents in hearing detection and intervention. *Topics in Early Childhood Special Education, 32*(2), 122–128.

McNulty, R. J., & Gloeckler, L. C. (2011). Fewer, clearer, higher common core state standards: Implications for students receiving special education services. Retrieved from http://www.leadered.com/pdf/Special%20Ed%20&%20CCSS%20white%20paper.pdf

McWilliam, R. A., & Casey, A. M. (2008). *Engagement of every child in the preschool classroom.* Baltimore, MD: Brookes.

Means, B., Toyama, Y., Murphy, R., Bakia, M., & Jones, K. (2009). *Evaluation of evidence-based practices in online learning: A meta-analysis and review of online learning studies.* Washington, D.C.: U.S. Department of Education.

Mechling, L. C., & Bishop, V. A. (2011). Assessment of computer-based preferences of students with profound multiple disabilities. *The Journal of Special Education, 45*(1), 15–27.

Merikangas, K. R., He, J-P., Brody, D., Fisher, P. W., Bourdon, K., & Koretz, D. S. (2010). Prevalence and treatment of mental disorders among US children in the 2001–2004 NHANES. *Pediatrics, 125*(10), 75–81.

Mesibov, G. (2006). A tribute to Eric Schopler. Journal of Autism and Developmental Disorders. 36(8), 967–970.

Mesibov, G. (2009). *TEACCH programming.* Chapel Hill, NC: University of North Carolina at Chapel Hill.

Mesibov, G. B., Shea, V., Schopler, E., Adams, L., Burgess, S., Chapman, S. M., . . . Van Bourgondien, M. E. (2005). *The TEACCH approach to autism spectrum disorders.* New York, NY: Kluwer Academic/Plenum.

Meyer, D., & Vadasy, P., (2007). *Sibshops: Workshops for siblings of children with special needs.* Baltimore, MD: Paul H. Brookes.

Michaud, L., Semel-Concepcíon, J., Duhaime, A., & Lazar, M. (2002). Traumatic brain injury. In M. Batshaw (Ed.), *Children with disabilities* (5th ed., pp. 525–546). Baltimore, MD: Brookes.

Miles, B., & Riggio, M. (1999). *Remarkable conversations: A guide to developing meaningful communication with children and young adults who are deafblind.* Watertown, MA: Perkins School for the Blind.

Milian, M. (2013). Emergent Bilinguals with Visual Impariments: Guidlines for Instruction. *DVI Quarterly, 58* (2).

Miller, C. J., Sanchez, J., & Hynd, G. W. (2003). Neurological correlates of reading disabilities. In H. L. Swanson, K. R. Harris, & S. Graham (Eds.), *Handbook of learning disabilities* (pp. 242–255). New York, NY: Guilford Press.

Miller, P., Kargin, T., Guldenoglu, B., Rathmann, C., Kubus, O., Hauser, P., & Spurgeon, E. (2012). Factors distinguishing skilled and less skilled deaf readers: Evidence from four orthographies. *Journal of Deaf Studies and Deaf Education, 17*(4), 439–462.

Mistrett, S., Ruffino, A., Lane, S., Robinson, L., Reed, P., & Milbourne, S. (2006). *Technology supports for young children* [TAM Technology Fan]. Arlington, VA: Technology and Media Division (TAM).

Montague, M., Enders, C., & Castor, M. (2005). *A longitudinal study of students at risk for learning behavior and emotional disorders.* Paper presented at the American Educational Researchers Association. Montreal, Canada.

Montessori, M. (1912). *The Montessori method.* New York, NY: Frederick A. Stokes.

Montgomery, J. K. (2006). Your competitive edge: The art of interpersonal communication. *Communication Disorders Quarterly, 28*(1), 56–58.

Moore, D., Cheng, Y., McGrath, P., & Powell, N. (2005). Collaborative virtual environment technology for people with autism. *Focus on Autism and Other Developmental Disabilities, 20*(4), 231–243.

Moores, D. (1996). *Educating the deaf: Psychology, principles, and practices* (4th ed.). Boston, MA: Houghton Mifflin.

Moores, D. (2000). *Educating the deaf: Psychology, principles, and practices* (5th ed.). Boston, MA: Houghton Mifflin.

More, C. M., & Travers, J. C. (2013). What's app with that? Selecting educational apps for young children with disabilities. *Young Exceptional Children, 16,* 15–32.

Morgan, P. L., Farkas, G., Hillemeier, M. M., & Maczuga, S. (2012). Minority children disproportionately represented in early intervention and early childhood special education? *Educational Researcher, 41,* 339–351.

Morrier, M. J., & Gallagher, P. A. (2012). Racial disparities in preschool special education eligibility in five southern states. *Journal of Special Education, 46,* 152–169.

Morrison, R., Sainato, D., Benchaaban, D., & Endo, S. (2002). Increasing play skills of children with autism using activity schedules and correspondence training. *Journal of Early Intervention, 25,* 58–72.

Mostofsky, S. H., Reiss, A. L., Lockhart, P., & Denckla, M. B. (2010). Evaluation of cerebellar size in attention-deficit hyperactivity disorder. *Journal of Child Neurology, 13,* 434–439.

MSM Productions (2008). What is deaf culture? Retrieved from http://www.deafculture.com/.

Mukherjee, S., Lightfoot, J., & Sloper, P. (2000). The inclusion of pupils with a chronic health condition in mainstream school: What does it mean for teachers? *Educational Research, 42*(1), 59–72.

Muratori, M., Stanley, J., Ng, L., Ng, J., Gross, M., Tao, T. & Tao B. (2006). Insights from SMPY's greatest child prodigies: Drs. Terrence (Terry) Tao and Lenhard (Lenny) Ng reflect on their talent development. *Gifted Child Quarterly, 50*(4), 307–324.

National Academies of Sciences. (2006). *Rising Above the Gathering Storm.* Washington, D.C.: National Academies Press.

National Academy of Sciences. (2007). *Rising Above the Gathering Storm.* Washington, D.C.: National Academies Press.

National Association for the Deaf. (2010). *Position statement on early hearing detection and intervention.* Retrieved from www.nad.org/issues/early-intervention/position-statement-early-hearing-detection-and-intervention

National Association for the Education of Young Children. (2009). *Developmentally appropriate practice in early childhood programs serving children from birth through age 8* [Position statement]. Washington, D.C.: Author.

National Association of State Directors of Special Education. (2005). *Response to intervention: Policy considerations and implementations.* Alexandria, VA: Author.

National Center for Education Statistics. (2012). Digest of education statistics, 2011 (NCES 2012–001). U.S. Department of Education. Retrieved from http://nces.ed.gov/fastfacts/display.asp?id=64

National Information Center on Children and Youth with Disabilities. (2000). *Severe and/or multiple disabilities.* (Available from NICHCY, P.O. Box 1492, Washington, D.C., 20013).

National Information Center on Children and Youth with Disabilities. (2004). *Severe and/or multiple disabilities.*

National Information Center on Deafness. (1999). Deafness: A fact sheet. (Available from NICD, Gallaudet University, 800 Florida Ave., N.E., Washington, D.C. 20002–3695.)

National Institute of Child Health and Human Development. (2000). *Report of the National Reading Panel. Teaching children to read: An evidence-based assessment of the scientific research literature on reading and its implications for reading instruction* (NIH Publication No. 00–4769). Washington, D.C.: U.S. Government Printing Office.

National Institute of Mental Health. (2008). *Attention Deficit Hyperactivity Disorder (ADHD)*. Bethesda, MD: Author.

National Institute on Deafness and Other Communication Disorders. (2010). *Hearing loss in children: Delayed speech and language*. (Available from NIDCD Information Clearinghouse, National Institute of Health, One Communication Avenue, Bethesda, MD 20892–3456.)

National Institute of Mental Health. (2001). *Blueprint for change: Research on child and adolescent mental health*. Rockville, MD: Author.

National Institute of Mental Health. (2010). Treatment of children with mental illness. U.S. Departmentt of Health and Human Services. Retrieved from www.nimh.nih.gov/health

National Institutes of Health. (2007). Expert panel report 3: Guidelines for the diagnosis and management of asthma—Full Report 2007. Retrieved from http://www.nhlbi.nih.gov/guidelines/asthma/asthgdln.pdf

National Institutes of Health, National Institute of Allergy and Infectious Disease (2008). *HIV infection in infants and children*. Washington, D.C.: Author.

The National Joint Council on Learning Disabilities (2006). *Learning Disabilities and Young Children: Identification and Intervention* (Report). Arlington, VA: Author.

National Organization on Fetal Alcohol Syndrome. (2004). What teachers need to know about FASD. Washington, D.C.: National Organization on Fetal Alcohol Syndrome.

National Research Council. (2002). *Minority students in special and gifted education*. Washington, D.C.: National Academy Press.

National School Safety Center. (2002). *Understanding, preventing and responding to school bullying*. Westlake Village, CA: Author.

National Standards Project. (2009). Randolph, MA: National Autism Center.

National Suicide Prevention Lifeline. 1-800-273-8255. Washington, D.C.: U.S. Department of Health and Human Services.

Neale, B. M., Medland, S. E., Ripke, S., Asherson, P., Franke, B., Lesch, K-P., ... Nelson, S. (2010). Meta-analysis of genome-wide association studies of attention-deficit/hyperactivity disorder. *Journal of the American Academy of Child & Adolescent Psychiatry, 49*(9), 884–897.

Nehring, W. M. (2007). Cultural considerations for children with intellectual and developmental disabilities. *Journal of Pediatric Nursing, 22*(2), 93–102.

Neihart, M. (2000). Gifted children with Asperger's syndrome. *Gifted Child Quarterly, 44*, 222–230.

Neihart, M., Reis, S., Robinson, N., & Moon, S. (Eds.). (2002). *The social and emotional development of gifted children: What do we know?* Waco, TX: Prufrock Press.

Neitzel, J. (2011). Current research on early intervening services for young children at risk for learning disabilities. *Perspectives on Language and Literacy, 37*(3), 13–14.

Nelson, C., & Huefner, D. (2003). Young children with autism: Judicial responses to the Lovaas and discrete trial training debates. *Journal of Early Intervention, 26*, 1–19.

Nelson, J., Crabtree, M., Marchand-Martella, N., & Martella, R. (1998). Teaching good behavior in the whole school. *Teaching Exceptional Children, 30*(4), 4–9.

Neville, H. J., Coffey, S. A., Lawson, D. S., Fischer, A., Emmorey, K., & Bellugi, U. (1997). Neural systems mediating American Sign Language: Effects of sensory experience and age of acquisition. *Brain and Language, 57*(3), 285–308.

Newman, L., Wagner, M., Cameto, R., & Knokey, A. (2009). The post-high school outcomes of youth with disabilities up to 4 years after high school. A report from the National Longitudinal Transition Study-2 (NLTS2)(NCSER 2009-3017). Washington, D.C.: U.S. Government Printing Office.

Newman, S. (2008). Neural bases of giftedness. In J. Plucker & C. Callahan (Eds.). *Critical Issues and Practices in Gifted Education: What the Research Says* (469–478). Waco, TX: Prufrock Press.

Newschaffer, C. J., Croen, L. A., Daniels, J., Giarelli, E., Grether, J. K., Levy, S., . . . Windham, G. (2007). The epidemiology of autism spectrum disorders. *Annual Review of Public Health, 28*, 235–258.

Newton, J., Horner, R., Ard, W., LeBaron, N., & Sapperton, G. (1994). Social aspects and social relationship of individuals with disability. *Mental Retardation, 32*(5), 393–402.

Ng, W., & Nicholas, H. (2007). Technology and independent learning. *Roeper Review, 29*(3), 190–196.

Nigg, J. T., Tannock, R., & Rohde, L. A. (2010). What is to be the fate of ADHD subtypes? An introduction to the special section on research on the ADHD subtypes and implications of the DSM-V. *Journal of Clinical Child & Adolescent Psychology, 39*(6), 723–725.

Niu, W. & Sternberg, R. J. (2003). Societal and school influences on student creativity: The case of China. *Psychology in the Schools, 40*(1), 103–114.

Noonan, M. J., & McCormick, L. (2006). *Young children with disabilities in natural environments: Methods and procedures*. Baltimore, MD: Brookes.

Nugent, J. K., & Blanchard, Y. (2006). Newborn behavior and development: Implications for health care professionals. In J. F. Travers & K. Theis (Eds.), *The handbook of human development for health care professionals* (pp. 79–94). Boston, MA: Jones & Bartlett.

Nugent, J. K., Blanchard, Y., & Stewart, J. S. (2007). Supporting parents of premature infants: An infant focused family-centered approach. In D. Brodsky & M. A. Ouellette (Eds.), *Primary care of the premature infant*. New York, NY: Elsevier.

Nugent, J. K., Keefer, C. H., Minear, S., Johnson, L. C., & Blanchard, Y. (2007). *Understanding newborn behavior and early relationships: The Newborn Behavioral Observations (NBO) system handbook*. Baltimore, MD: Brookes.

O'Neill, J., Gothelf, C., Cohen, S., Lehman, L., & Woolf, S. (1991). *A curricular approach to support the transition to adulthood of adolescents with visual or dual sensory impairments and cognitive disabilities*. Albany, NY: New York State Education Department, Office of Special Education and Rehabilitation Services.

Odom, S., Horner, R., Snell, & Blacher, J. (2007). Postschool and adult issues. *Handbook of developmental disabilities*. New York, NY: Guilford Press.

Odom, S. L., Boyd, B. A., Hall, L. J., & Hume, K. (2010). Evaluation of comprehensive treatment models for individuals with autism spectrum disorders. *Journal of Autism and Developmental Disorders, 40*, 425–436.

Odom, S. L., Buysse, V., & Soukukou, E. (2011). Inclusion for young children with disabilities: A quarter century of research perspectives. *Journal of Early Intervention, 33*, 344–356.

Odom, S., Hume, K., Boyd, B., & Stabel, A. (2012). Moving beyond the intensive behavior treatment versus eclectic dichotomy: Evidence-based and individualized programs for learners with ASD. *Behavior Modification, 36(3)*, 270–297.

Odom, S. L., Horner, R. H., Snell, M. E., & Blacher, J. (Eds.). (2007). *Handbook of developmental disabilities*. New York NY: Guilford Press.

Odom, S. L., Rogers, S., McDougle, C. J., Hume, K., & McGee, G. (2007). Early intervention for children with autism spectrum disorder. In S. L. Odom, R. H. Horner, M. E. Snell, & J. Blacher (Eds.), *Handbook of developmental disabilities* (pp. 199–223). New York, NY: Guilford Press.

Office of Special Education Programs. (2003). *Twenty-fourth annual report to Congress*. Washington, D.C.: Author.

Office of Special Education Programs (OSEP). (2005). *Twenty-fourth annual report to Congress*. Washington, D.C.: U.S. Department of Education.

Office of Special Education Programs (OSEP). (2011). *Thirtieth annual report to Congress on the implementation of IDEA*. Washington, D.C.: U.S. Department of Education.

Ogletree, B. T., Bruce, S. M., Finch, A., Fahey, R., & McLean, L. (2011). Recommended communication-based interventions for individuals with severe intellectual disabilities. *Communication Disorders Quarterly, 32*(3), 164–175.

Okolo, C. M. (2006). Content-area applications. *Journal of Special Education Technology, 21*(4), 58–61.

Olley, J. (1999). Curriculum for students with autism. *School Psychology Review, 28*(4), 595–604.

Olmsted, M. G., Bailey, D. B., Raspa, M., Nelson, R. E., Robinson, N. D., Simpson, M. E., & Guillen, C. (2010). Outcomes reported by Spanish-speaking families in early intervention. *Topics in Early Childhood Special Education, 30*, 46–55.

Olswang, L. B., Coggins, T. E., & Svensson, L. (2007). Assessing social communication in the classroom: Observing manner and duration of performance. *Topics in Language Disorders, 27*(2), 111–127.

Olszewski-Kubilius, P. (2010). Two perspectives on statistics in gifted education. In B. Thompson & R. Subotnik (Eds.). *Methodologies for Conducting Research on Giftedness*. Washington, D.C.: American Psychological Association.

Ornstein, P., Schaaf, J., Hooper, S., Hatton, D., Mirrett, P., & Bailey, D. B. (2008). Memory skills of boys with Fragile X syndrome. *American Journal on Mental Retardation, 113*(6), 453–465.

Ortiz, A. (2001). English language learners with special needs: Effective instructional strategies. = Retrieved from http://www.cal.org/resources/digest/digest_pdfs/0108-ortiz.pdf

OSEP. (2009). Parent training and information centers and community parent resource centers. Washington, D.C.: U.S. Department of Education Office of Special Education Programs.

Osher, D., Cartledge, G., Oswald, D., Sutherland, K., Artiles, A., & Coutinho, M. (2004). Issues of cultural and linguistic competency and disproportionate representation. In R. Rutherford, M. Quinn, & S. Mather (Eds.), *Handbook of research in behavioral disorders*. New York, NY: Guilford Press.

Paracchini, S., Scerri, T., & Monaco, A.P. (2007). The genetic lexicon of dyslexia. *Annual Review of Genomics and Human Genetics, 8*, 57–79.

Parette, H., & Petch-Hogan, B. (2000). Approaching families. *Teaching Exceptional Children, 33*(2), 4–10.

Park, J., Hoffman, L., Marquis, J., Turnbull, A. P., Poston, D., Mannan, H., ... Nelson, L. L. (2003). Toward assessing family outcomes of service delivery: Validation of family quality of life scale survey. *Journal of Intellectual Disability Research, 47*(4/5), 367–384.

Pastor, P. N., & Reuben, C. A. (2005). Racial and ethnic differences in ADHD and LD in young school-age children: Parental reports in the National Health Interview Survey. *Public Health Reports, 120*, 383–392.

Patterson, D., & Spence, J.C. (1921). The after-effects of epidemic encephalitis in children. *The Lancet, 2*, 491–493.

Paul, P., & Quigley, S. (1994). *Education and deafness*. White Plains, NY: Longman.

Pellegrino, L. (2002). Cerebral palsy. In M. Batshaw (Ed.), *Children with disabilities* (5th ed., pp. 443–466). Baltimore, MD: Brookes.

Pennington, B. F. (2009). How neuropsychology informs our understanding of developmental disorders. *Journal of Child Psychology and Psychiatry, 50*(1–2), 72–78.

Pershelli, A. (2007). Memory strategies to use with students following traumatic brain injury. *Physical Disabilities: Education and Related Services, 26*(1), 31–46.

Petitto, L., & Marentette, P. (1991). Babbling in the manual mode: Evidence for the ontogeny of language. *Science, 251*, 1493–1495.

Pianta, P., Howes, C., Burchinal, M., Bryant, D., Clifford, R., Early, D., & Barbarin, O. (2005). Features of pre-kindergarten programs, classrooms, and teachers: Do they predict observed classroom quality and child-teacher interactions? *Applied Developmental Science, 9*(3), 144–159.

Pianta, R. C. (2007). Early education in transition. In R. C. Pianta, M. J. Cox, & K. L. Snow (Eds.), *School readiness and the transition to kindergarten in the era of accountability*. Baltimore, MD: Brookes.

Pianta, R. C., Cox, M. J., & Snow, K. L. (2007). *School readiness and the transition to kindergarten in the era of accountability*. Baltimore, MD: Brookes.

Pierangelo, R., & Giuliani, G. (2006). *Learning disabilities: A practical approach to foundations, assessment, diagnosis, and teaching*. Boston, MA: Pearson Education.

Pickl, G. (2011). Communication intervention in children with severe disabilities and multilingual backgrounds: Perceptions of pedagogues and parents. *Augmentative and Alternative Communication, 27*(4), 229–244.

Planty, M., Hussar, W., Snyder, T., Kena, G., KewalRamani, A., Kemp, J., ... Dinkes, R. (2009). *The Condition of Education 2009 (NCES 2009-081)*. Washington, D.C.: National Center for Education Statistics, Institute of Education Sciences, U.S. Department of Education.

Plomin, R., Defries, J., Craig I., & McGuffin, P. (2003). *Behavioral genetics in the postgenomic era*. Washington, D.C.: American Psychological Association.

Plomin, R., & Petrill, S. (1997). Genetics and intelligence: What's new? *Intelligence, 24*(1), 53–77.

Plucker, J., & Callahan, C. (Eds.). (2008). *Critical issues and practices in gifted education*. Waco, TX: Prufrock Publishers.

Pogrund, R., & Fazzi, D. (Eds.). (2002). *Early focus: Working with young blind and visually impaired children and their families* (2nd ed.). New York, NY: American Foundation for the Blind.

Polloway, E., Patton, J., & Nelson, M. (2011). Intellectual and developmental disabilities. In J. Kauffman & D. Hallahan (Eds.), *Handbook of special education* (pp. 175–186). New York, NY: Routledge.

Polsgrove, L., & Smith, S. (2004). Informal practice in teaching self-control to children with emotional and behavior disorders. In R. Rutherford, M. Quinn, & S. Mathur (Eds.), *Handbook of research in emotional and behavior disorders* (pp. 399–425). New York, NY: Guilford Press.

Porter, R. S., & Kaplan, J. L. (2012). *The Merck manual for health care professionals*. Retrieved from http://www.merckmanuals.com/professional/index.html

Povenmire-Kirk, T. C., Lindstrom, L., & Bullis, M. (2010). De escuela a la vida adulta/from school to adult life: Transition needs for Latino youth with disabilities and their families. *Career Development for Exceptional Individuals, 33*(1), 41–51.

Powers, K. M., Gil-Kashiwabara, E., Geenen, S. J., Powers, L. E., Balandran, J., & Palmer, C. (2005). Mandates and effective transition planning practices reflected in IEPs. *Career Development for Exceptional Individuals, 28*(1), 47–59.

Powers, S. (2011). Learning from success: High achieving deaf students. *Deafness and Education International, 13*, 92–109.

President's Commission on Excellence in Special Education. (2002). *A new era: Revitalizing special education for children and their families.* Retrieved from www.ed.gov/inits/commissions boards/whspecialeducation /index.html

Presley, I. (2010). The impact of assistive technology: Assessment and instruction for children and youths with low vision. In A. Corn & J. Erin, *Foundations of low vision: Clinical and functional perspectives* (2nd ed., pp. 589–654). New York, NY: American Foundation for the Blind.

Prevatt, F. A., Heffer, R. W., & Lowe, T. A. (2000). A review of school reintegration programs for children with pediatric cancers. *Journal of School Psychology, 38*(5), 447–467.

Priester, G. H., & Goorhuis-Brouwer, S. M. (2008). Speech and language development in toddlers with and without cleft palate. *International Journal of Pediatric Otorhinolaryngology, 72,* 801–806.

Pullen, P. C., Lane, H. B., Ashworth, K. E., & Lovelace, S. P. (2012). Learning disabilities. In D. P. Hallahan & J. M. Kauffman (Eds.), *Handbook of Special Education* (pp. 187–197). New York, NY: Routledge.

Quesenberry, A., Ostrosky, M. M., & Corso, R. (2007). Skilled and knowledgeable caregivers: The role of fathers in supporting young children's development. *Young Exceptional Children, 10*(4), 11–19.

Qui, M., Ye, Z., Li, Q., Lui, G., Xie, B., & Wang, J. (2011). Changes of brain structure and function in ADHD children. *Brain Topography, 24,* 243–252.

Ramos, V., & Gardner, H. (2003). Multiple intelligences: A perspective on gifted. In N. Colangelo & G. Davis (Eds.), *Handbook of gifted education* (pp. 100–112).Boston, MA: Allyn & Bacon.

Ramtekkar, U. P., Reiersen, A. M., Todorv, A. A., & Todd, R. D. (2010). Sex and age differences in attention-deficit/hyperactivity disorder symptoms and diagnoses: Implications for DSM-V and ICD-11. *Journal of the American Academy of Child & Adolescent Psychiatry, 49*(3), 217–228.

Reed, M., & Curtis, K. (2011). High school teachers' perspectives on supporting students with visual impairments toward higher education: Access, barriers, and success. *Journal of Visual Impairment & Blindness, 105,* 548–559.

Reed, S., Anita, S. D., & Kreimeyer, K. H. (2008). Academic status of deaf and hard-of-hearing students in public schools: Student, home, and service facilitators and detractors. *Journal of Deaf Studies and Deaf Education, 13*(4), 485–502.

Reichow, B. (2012). Overview of meta-analyses on early intensive behavioral intervention for young children with autism spectrum disorders. *Journal of Autism and Developmental Disorders, 42,* 512–520.

Reichow, B. & Volkmar, F. R. (2010). Social skills interventions for individuals with autism: Evaluation for evidence-based practices within a best evidence synthesis framework. *Journal of Autism and Developmental Disorders, 40,* 149–166.

Reis, D. (2003). Child effects in family systems. In A. C. Crocker & A. Booth (Eds.), *Child influence on family dynamics* (pp. 1–23). Mahwah, NJ: Erlbaum.

Reis, S. (2008). Talented readers. In J. Plucker & C. Callahan (Eds.), *Critical issues and practices in gifted education* (pp. 655–668). Waco, TX: Prufrock Press.

Reis, S. M. (2003). Gifted girls, twenty-five years later: Hopes realized and new challenges found. *Roeper Review, 25,* 154–157.

Renzulli, J. S. (2002). Expanding the conception of giftedness to include co-cognitive traits and to promote social capital. *Phi Delta Kappan, 84*(1), 33–58.

Renzulli, J. S. & Reed, R. E. (2008). Intelligences outside the normal curve: Co-cognitive traits that contribute to giftedness. In J. Plucker & C. Callahan (Eds.). *Critical Issues and Practices in Gifted Education: What the Research Says* (303–319). Waco, TX: Prufrock Press.

Renzulli, J. S. & Reis, S. M. (1997). *The schoolwide enrichment model: A how-to guide for educational excellence* (2nd ed.). Mansfield Center, CT: Creative Learning Press, Inc.

Reynolds, C.R., & Shaywitz, S.E. (2009). Response to intervention: Prevention and remediation, perhaps, diagnosis, no. *Child Development Perspectives, 3*(1), 44–47.

Riggio, M. (2009). Deafblindness: Educational service guidelines. *DVI Quarterly, 54*(3), 13–14.

Ritzman, M. J., Sanger, D., & Coufal, K. L. (2006). A case study of a collaborative speech-language pathologist. *Communication Disorders Quarterly, 27*(4), 221–231.

Roberts, J., Burchinal, M., & Bailey, D. (1994). Communication among preschoolers with and without disabilities in same-age and mixed-age classes. *American Journal of Mental Retardation, 99*(3), 231–249.

Robinson, A., Shore, B., & Enersen, D. (2007). *Best practices in gifted education.* Waco, TX: Prufrock Press.

Roeper, A. (2003). The young gifted girl: A contemporary view. *Roeper Review, 25,* 151–153.

Rooney, K. J. (2011). Attention-deficit/hyperactivity disorder. In J. M. Kauffman & D. P. Hallahan (Eds.), *Handbook of special education* (pp. 198–208). New York, NY: Routledge.

Rose, D., & Meyer, A. (2002). *Teaching every student in the digital age.* Alexandria, VA: Association for Curriculum Development.

Rosenkoetter, S. E., Hains, A. H., & Fowler, S. A. (1994). *Bridging early services for children with special needs and their families: A practical guide for transition planning.* Baltimore, MD: Brookes.

Ross, P. (Ed.). (1993). *National excellence.* Washington, D.C.: U.S. Department of Education.

Roth, F., Troia, G., Worthington, C., & Handy, D. (2006). Promoting awareness of sounds in speech: A follow-up report of an early intervention program for children with speech and language impairments. *Learning Disabilities Quarterly, 29,* 67–88.

Rourke, B. P. (1994). Neuropsychological assessment of children with learning disabilities. In G. Lyon (Ed.), *Frames of reference for the assessment of learning disabilities* (pp. 475–514). Baltimore, MD: Brookes.

Rous, B., Hallam, R., McCormick, K., & Cox, M. (2010). Practices that support the transition to public preschool programs: Results from a national survey. *Early Childhood Research Quarterly, 25,* 7–32.

Rous, B., Myers, C. T., & Stricklin, S. B. (2007). Strategies for supporting transitions of young children with special needs and their families. *Journal of Early Intervention, 30*(1), 1–18.

Rous, B. S., & Hallam, R. A. (2006). *Tools for transition in early childhood: A step by step guide for agencies, teachers and families.* Baltimore, MD: Brookes.

Russell, M., Hoffman, T., & Higgins, J. (2009). NimbleTools: A universally designed test delivery system. *Teaching Exceptional Children, 42*(2), 6–12.

Rutstein, R., Conlon, C., & Batshaw, M. L. (1997). HIV and AIDS. In M. L. Batshaw (Ed.), *Children with disabilities* (pp. 163–181). Baltimore, MD: Brookes.

Rutter, M. (1996). Autism research: Prospects and priorities. *Journal of Autism and Developmental Disorders, 26,* 257–275.

Rutter, M. (2000). Resilience reconsidered: Conceptual considerations, empirical findings,and policy implications. In J. P. Shonkoff & S. J. Meisels (Eds.), *Handbook of early childhood intervention* (2nd ed., pp. 651–682). New York, NY: Cambridge University Press.

Rutter, M. (2003). Commentary: Causal processes leading to antisocial behavior. *Developmental Psychology, 39,* 372–378.

Rutter, M., (2007). *Genes and behaviors: Nature and nurture interplay explained.* Malden, MA: Blackwell Publishing.

Rylance, B. J. (1997). Predictors of high school graduation or dropping out for youths with severe emotional disturbance. *Behavioral Disorders, 23,* 5–18.

Ryndak, D., & Alper, S. (2003). *Curriculum and instruction for students with significant disabilities in inclusive settings* (2nd ed.). Boston, MA: Allyn & Bacon.

Rydell, A-M. (2010). Family factors and children's disruptive behavior: An investigation of links between demographic characteristics, negative life events and symptoms of ODD and ADHD. *Social Psychiatry and Psychiatric Epidemiology, 45,* 233–244.

Sacks, S. Z., & Rothstein, S.M. (2010). The expanded core curriculum and the reauthorization of IDEA: Reality or rhetoric? *Journal of Visual Impairment & Blindness, 104,* 781–782.

Saenz, T. I., & Felix, D. M. (2006). English-speaking Latino parents' literacy practices in Southern California. *Communication Disorders Quarterly, 28*(2), 93–106.

Sakai, K. L. (2005). Language acquisition and brain development. *Science, 310,* 815–819.

Sallows, G. O., & Graupner, T. D. (2005). Intensive behavioral treatment for children with autism: Four-year outcome and predictors. *American Journal on Mental Retardation, 110*(6), 417–438.

Salvia, J., Ysseldyke, J. E., & Bolt, S. (2007). *Assessment in special and inclusive education* (10th ed.). Boston, MA: Houghton Mifflin.

Salvia, J., Ysseldyke, J., & Bolt, S. (2010). Assessment in special and inclusive education (11th ed.). Boston, MA: Wadsworth Publishing.

Salvia, J. S., Ysseldyke, J. E, & Bolt, S. (2012). *Assessment in special and inclusive education* (12th ed.). Boston, MA: Cengage Learning.

Sameroff, A. (1990). Neo-environmental perspectives on developmental theory. In R. Hodapp, J. Burack, & E. Zigler (Eds.), *Issues in the developmental approach to mental retardation.* New York, NY: Cambridge University Press.

Sameroff, A., Seifer, R., Baldwin, A., & Baldwin, C. (1993). Stability of intelligence from preschool to adolescence: The influence of social and family risk factors. *Child Development, 64*(1), 80–97.

Sandall, S., Hemmeter, M. L., Smith, B. J., & McLean, M. E. (2005). *DEC recommended practices: A comprehensive guide for practical application in early intervention/early childhood special education.* Missoula, MT: Division for Early Childhood.

Sandman, C. A., & Kemp, A. S. (2007). Neuroscience of developmental disabilities. In S. L. Odom, R. H. Horner, M. E. Snell, & J. Blacher (Eds.), *Handbook of developmental disabilities* (pp. 129–157). New York, NY: Guilford Press.

Sanger, D. Mohling, S., & Stremlau, A. (2012). Speech-language pathologists' opinions on Response to Intervention. *Communication Disorders Quarterly, 34,* 1–16.

Sapp, W., & Hatlen, P. (2010). The expanded core curriculum: Where we have been, where we are going, and how we can get there. *Journal of Visual Impairment & Blindness, 104,* 338–348.

Saunders, A. F., Bethune, K. S., Spooner, F., & Browder, D. M. (2013). Solving the common core equation: Teaching mathematics CCSS to students with moderate and severe disabilities. *Teaching Exceptional Children, 45*(3), 24–33.

Schaeffer, C., Petras, H., Ialongo, N., Poduska, J., & Kellam, S. (2003). Modeling growth in boys' aggressive behavior across elementary school: Links to later criminal involvement, conduct disorder, and antisocial personality disorder. *Developmental Psychology, 39,* 1020–1035.

Shaffer, D. & Kipp, K. (2010). *Developmental Psychology* (8th Ed.). Belmont, CA: Wadsworth, Cengage Learning.

Schalock, R., (Chair). (2010) *Intellectual disability: Definition, classification, and systems of support* (11th ed.). Washington, D.C.: American Association on Intellectual and Developmental Disabilities.

Scherer, N. J., D'Antonio, L. L., & McGahey, H. (2008). Early intervention for speech impairment in children with cleft palate. *Cleft Palate-Craniofacial Journal, 45*(1), 1–31.

Scherer, N. J., Williams, A. L., & Proctor-Williams, K. (2008). Early and later vocalization skills in children with and without cleft palate. *International Journal of Pediatric Otorhinolaryngology, 72,* 827–840.

Scheuermann, A. M., Deshler, D. D., & Schumaker, J. B. (2009). The effects of the explicit inquiry routine on the performance of students with learning disabilities on one-variable equations. *Learning Disability Quarterly, 32,* 103–120.

Schirmer, B. R., & Schaffer, L. (2010). Guiding reading approach: Teaching reading to students who are deaf and others who struggle. *Teaching Exceptional Children, 42*(5), 52–58.

Schleicher, A. (2009). Securing quality and equity in education: Lessons from PISA. *Prospects, 39*(3), 251–263.

Schonberg, R. (2013). Birth defects and prenatal diagnoses. In M. L. Batshaw, N. Roizen, & G. R Lotrecchiano (Eds.), *Children with disabilities* (7th ed., pp. 47–60). Baltimore, MD: Brookes.

Schopler, E., Mesibov, G., & Hearsey, K. (1995). Structured teaching in the TEACCH system. In E. Schopler & G. Mesibov (Eds.), *Learning and cognition in autism* (pp. 243–268). New York, NY: Plenum Press.

Schumaker, J. B., & Deshler, D. D. (2010). Using a tiered intervention model in secondary schools to improve academic outcomes in subject-area courses. In M. R. Shinn & H. M. Walker (Eds.), *Intervention for achievement and behavior problems in a three-tier model including RTI.* Bethesda, MD: National Association of School Psychologists.

Schwartz, I. (2000). Standing on the shoulders of giants: Looking ahead to facilitating membership and relationships for children with disabilities. *Topics in Early Childhood Special Education, 20*(2), 123–128.

Schwartz, I. S., & Sandall, S. R. (2010). Is autism the disability that breaks Part C? A commentary on "Infants and toddlers with Autism Spectrum Disorder: early identification and early intervention," by Boyd, Odom, Humphreys, and Sam. *Journal of Early Intervention, 32*(2) 105–109.

Schwartz, T. L. (2010). Causes of visual impairments: Pathology and its implications. In A. Corn & J. Erin (Eds.), *Foundations of low vision: Clinical and functional perspectives* (2nd ed., pp. 137–191). New York, NY: American Foundation for the Blind.

Schweinhart, L. J., Montie, J., Xiang, Z., Barnett, W. S., Belfield, C. R., & Nores, M. (2005). *Lifetime effects: The High/Scope Perry Preschool study through age 40* [Monograph of the High/Scope Educational Research Foundation, No. 14]. Ypsilanti, MI: High/Scope Press.

Sciberras, E., Efron, D., & Iser, A. (2011). The child's experience of ADHD. *Journal of Attention Disorders, 15*(4), 321–327.

Seida, J., Ospona, M., Karkhaneh, M., Hartling, L., Smith, V., & Clark, B. (2009). Systematic reviews of psychosocial interventions for autism: An umbrella review. *Developmental Medicine & Child Neurology, 51,* 95–104.

Seligman, M. E. P. (1991). *Learned optimism.* New York, NY: Knopf.

Senhoff, D., & Lignugaris-Kraft, B. (2007). A review of the effects of peer tutoring on students with mild disabilities in secondary settings. *Exceptional Children, 74,* 8–31.

Serry, T., & Blaney, P. (1999). A four-year investigation into phonetic inventory development in young cochlear implant users. *Journal of Speech, Language, and Hearing Research, 42*(1), 887–899.

Shattell, M. M., Bartlett, R., & Rowe, T. (2008). "I have always felt different": The experience of attention-deficit/hyperactivity disorder in childhood. *Journal of Pediatric Nursing, 23*(1), 49–57.

Shaw, P., Gilliam, M., Liverpool, M., Weddle, C., Malek, M., Sharp, W., . . . Giedd, J. (2011). Cortical development in typically developing children with symptoms of hyperactivity and impulsivity: Support for a dimensional view of attention deficit hyperactivity disorder. *American Journal of Psychiatry, 168*(2), 143–151.

Shaywitz, S. E., & Shaywitz, B. A. (2008). Paying attention to reading: The neurobiology of reading and dyslexia. *Development and Psychopathology, 20,* 1329–1349.

Sheffield, K., & Waller, R. J. (2010). A review of single-case studies utilizing self-monitoring interventions to reduce problem classroom behaviors. *Beyond Behavior, 19*(2), 7–13.

Shonkoff, J. P., & Phillips, D. A. (2000). *From neurons to neighborhoods: The science of early childhood development.* Washington, D.C.: National Academies Press.

Shumate, L., Campbell-Whatley, G.D., & Lo, Y. (2012). Infusing culturally responsive instruction to improve mathematics performance of Latino students with specific disabilities. *Exceptionality, 20*(1), 39–57.

Sibling Support Project. (2010). Bellevue, WA: A Kindering Center Program.

Siegel, J. D., Rhinehart, E., Jackson, M., Chiarello, L., & the Healthcare Infection Control Practices Advisory Committee. (2007). Guideline for isolation precautions: Preventing transmission of infectious agents in healthcare settings. Retrieved from http://www.cdc.gov/ncidod/dhqp/pdf/isolation2007.pdf

Siegle, D., & Mitchell, M. S. (2011). Learning from and learning with technology. In J. VanTassel-Baska & C. A. Little (Eds.), *Content-based curriculum for high-ability learners* (2nd ed., pp. 347–373). Waco, TX: Prufrock Press.

Silver, L. B. (2010). Is your child's learning disability the only problem? You should know about other related disorders. Learning Disabilities Association of America. Retrieved April 15, 2010, from http://www.ldanatl.org/aboutld/parents/ld_basics/comorbidity.asp.

Simms, L., & Thumann, H. (2007). In search of a new, linguistically and culturally sensitive paradigm in deaf education. *American Annals of the Deaf, 152*(3), 302–311.

Simonoff, E., Bolton, P., & Rutter, M. (1998). Genetic perspectives on mental retardation. In J. Burack, R. Hodapp, & E. Zigler (Eds.), *Handbook of mental retardation and development* (pp. 41–79). New York, NY: Cambridge University Press.

Simonsen, B., Shaw, S., Faggella-Luby, M., Sugai, G., Coyne, M. D., Rhein, B., ... Alfano, M. (2008). A schoolwide model for service delivery. *Remedial and Special Education, 31*(1).

Simpson, L. A., & Oh, K. (2013). Using circle time books to increase participation in the morning circle routine. *Teaching Exceptional Children, 45,* 30–36.

Singer, G. H. S., Maul, C., Wang, M., & Ethridge, B. L. (2011). Resilience in families of children with disabilities: Risk and protective factors. In J. M. Kauffman & D. P. Hallahan (Eds.), *Handbook of special education* (pp. 654–667). New York, NY: Routledge.

Skeels, H. M. (1966). Adult status of children with contrasting early life experiences. *Monographs of the Society for Research in Child Development, 31*(Serial No. 105).

Skeels, H. M., & Dye, H. (1939). A study of the effects of differential stimulation on mentally retarded children. *Proceedings and Addresses of the American Association on Mental Deficiency 44,* 114–136.

Skinner, D. G., Correa, V., Skinner, M., & Bailey, D. B. (2001). Role of religion in the lives of Latino families of young children with developmental delays. *American Journal on Mental Retardation, 106*(4), 297–313.

Slobin, D. (2006). Imitation and grammatical development in children. In A. Bundura (Ed.), *Psychological modeling: Conflicting theories* (p. 166). New Brunswick, NJ: Transaction Publishers.

Smith, A. (2005). *The brain's behind it: New knowledge about the brain and learning.* Norwalk, CT: Crown House.

Smith, A. J., Bainbridge, J. W. & Ali, R. R. (2009). Prospects for retinal gene replacement therapy. *Trends in Genetics, 25*(4), 156–165.

Smith, A., & Wang, Y. (2010). The impact of Visual Phonics on the phonological awareness and speech production of a student who is deaf: A case study. *American Annals of the Deaf, 155*(2), 124–130.

Smith, K. (2010). RTI/NTID's center on access technology: Helping deaf students succeed in college. Retrieved from http://nysstlc.syr.edu/Newsletter/researchspotlight/NTIDCAT/default.aspx.

Snell, M., & Voorhees, M. (2006). On being labeled with mental retardation. In H. Switzky & S. Greenspan (Eds.), *What is mental retardation?* Washington, D.C.: American Association on Mental Retardation.

Snell, M. E., Luckasson, R., Borthwick-Duffy, S. A., Bradley, V., Butinx, W. H. E., Coulter, D. L., ...Yeager, M. (2009). The characteristics and needs of people with intellectual disabilities who have higher IQs. *Intellectual and Developmental Disabilities, 47,* 220–233.

Solish, A., Perry, A., & Minnes, P. (2010). Participation of children with and without disabilities in social, recreational, and leisure activities. *Journal of Applied Research in Intellectual Disabilities, 23,* 226–236.

Solomon-Rice, P. & Soto, G. (2011). Co-construction as a facilitative factor in supporting the personal narratives of children who use augmentative and alternative communication. *Communication Disorders Quarterly, 32,* 70–82.

Sopko, K., & Reder, N. (2007). *Public and parent reporting requirements: NCLB and IDEA regulations.* Alexandria, VA: National Association of State Directors of Special Education.

Sopko, K. M. (2009). Early childhood mental health services: Four case studies. *inForum In Depth Policy Analysis.* Alexandria, VA: NASDSE.

Sousa, D. (2011). *How the brain learns: A classroom teacher's guide* (4th ed.). Thousand Oaks, CA: Corwin.

Southern California Comprehensive Assistance Center. (2005). Six research based guiding principles serving the needs of English learners in preschool "school readiness" programs. Paper developed by a Working Group from Eight County Offices of Education.

Sparling, J. (2007). *Creative curriculum learning games: 12–24 months.* St. Paul, MN: Red Leaf Press.

Sparrow, R. (2010). Implants and ethnocide: Learning from the cochlear implant controversy. *Disability & Society, 25*(4), 455–466.

Sparrow, S., Cichetti, D., & Balla, D. (2006). Vineland adaptive behavior scales (2nd ed.) (Vineland-II). San Antonio, TX: Pearson.

Spear-Swerling, L. (2006). Learning disabilities in English language learners. *LD Online.* Retrieved 4/17/10 from www.ldonline.org/article/learning_disabilities_in_English_language_learners.htm

Spinath, F., Harlaar, N., Ronald, A., & Plomin, R. (2004). Substantial genetic influence on mild mental impairment in early childhood. *American Journal of Mental Retardation, 109,* 34–43.

Spitz, H. (2006). How we eradicated familial (hereditary) mental retardation-updated. In H. Switzky & S. Greenspan (Eds.), *What is mental retardation?* (pp. 81–92). Washington, D.C.: American Association for Mental Retardation.

Sprague, J., & Walker, H. (2000). Early identification and invention for youth with antisocial and violent behavior. *Exceptional Children, 66*(3), 367–379.

Spungin, S. (Ed.). (2002). *When you have a visually impaired child in your classroom: A guide for teachers.* New York, NY: American Foundation for the Blind.

Squires, J., & Bricker, D. (2007). *An activity-based approach to developing young children's social emotional competence.* Baltimore, MD: Brookes.

Stancliffe, R., & Lakin, C. (2007). Independent living. In S. Odom, R. Horner, M. Snell, & J. Blacher. Handbook of Developmental Disabilities. New York, NY: The Guilford Press, p. 429–448.

Stang, K., Carter, K., Lane, K. L., & Pierson, M. (2009). Perspectives of general and special educators on fostering self-determination in elementary and middle school. *Journal of Special Education, 43*(4), 94–106.

Steinberg, A., & Knightly, C. (1997). Hearing: Sounds and silences. In M. L. Batshaw (Ed.), *Children with disabilities* (pp. 241–274). Baltimore, MD: Brookes.

Sternberg, R. J. (2008). The answer depends on the question: A reply to Eric Jensen. *Phi Delta Kappan, 89*(6), 418–420.

Sternberg, R. J., & Grigorenko, E. L. (2002). The theory of successful intelligence as a basis for gifted education. *Gifted Child Quarterly, 46*(4), 265–277.

Stinson, M., & Foster, S. (2000). Socialization of deaf children and youths in school. In P. Spencer, C. Ertling, & M. Marschark (Eds.), *The deaf child in the family and at school* (pp. 191–209). Mahwah, NJ: Erlbaum.

Stone, W., Lee, E., Ashford, L., Brissie, J., Hepburn, S., Coonrod, E., & Bahr, H. (1999). Can autism be diagnosed accurately in children under 3 years? *Journal of Child Psychology and Psychiatry, 40*, 219–226.

Stone, W., Ousley, O., & Littleford, C. (1997). Motor imitation in young children with autism: What's the object? *Journal of Abnormal Child Psychology, 25*(6), 475–483.

Strain, P., Kohler, F., & Goldstein, H. (1996). Learning experiences, an alternative program: Peer-mediated interventions for young children with autism. In E. Hibbs & P. Jensen (Eds.), *Psychosocial treatments for child and adolescent disorders: Empirically based strategies for clinical practice* (pp. 573–586). Washington, D.C.: American Psychological Association.

Strand, S., Drury, I., & Smith, P. (2006). Sex differences in cognitive abilities test scores: A UK national picture. *British Journal of Educational Psychology, 76*, 463–480.

Strauss, A. A., & Lehtinen, L. E. (1947). *Psychopathology and education of the brain-injured child.* New York, NY: Grune and Stratton.

Stremel, K., & Campbell, P. H. (2007). Implementation of early intervention within natural environments. *Early Childhood Services, 1*(2), 83–105.

Subcommittee on Attention/Hyperactivity Disorder, Steering Committee on Quality Improvement and Management. (2011). ADHD: Clinical practice guideline for the diagnosis, evaluation, and treatment of attention-deficit/hyperactivity disorder in children and adolescents. *Pediatrics, 128*(5), 1–16.

Subotnik, R., Kassan, L., Summers, E., & Wasser, A. (1993). *Genius revisited: High IQ children grown up.* Norwood, NJ: Ablex.

Subotnik, R., Olszewski-Kubilius, P., & Worrell, F. (2011). Rethinking giftedness and gifted education: A proposed direction forward based on psychological science. *Psychological Science in the Public Interest, 12*(1), 3–24.

Sugai, G., & Horner, R. (2006). A promising approach for expanding and sustaining the implementation of schoolwide positive behavior support. *School Psychology Review, 35*, 245–259.

Sullivan, A.L. (2011). Disproportionality in special education identification and placement of English language learners. *Exceptional Children, 77*(3), 317–334.

Swanson, H. L., & Sáez, L. (2003). Memory difficulties in children and adults with learning disabilities. In H. L. Swanson, K. R. Harris, & S. Graham (Eds.), *Handbook of learning disabilities* (pp. 182–198). New York, NY: Guilford Press.

Swanson, H. L, Zheng, X., & Jerman, O. (2009). Working memory, short-term memory, and reading disabilities: A selective meta-analysis of the literature. *Journal of Learning Disabilities, 42*(3), 260–287.

Switzky, H., & Greenspan, S. (2006). Lessons from the Atkins Decision for the next *AAMR Manual*. In H. Switzky & S. Greenspan (Eds.), *What is mental retardation?* Washington, D.C.: American Association on Mental Retardation.

Sze, S. (2009). The effects of assistive technology on students with disabilities. *Journal of Educational Technology Systems*, 37(4), 419–429.

Tadic, V., Pring, L. & Dale, N. (2010). Are language and social communication intact in children with congenital visual impairment at school age? *Journal of Child Psychology and Psychiatry, 51*(6), 696–705.

Tannenbaum, A. (2000). A history of giftedness in school and society. In K. Heller, R. Subotnik, & R. Sternberg (Eds.), *International handbook of giftedness and talent.* New York, NY: Elsever.

Tannock, R. (2013). Rethinking ADHD and LD in *DSM-5*: Proposed changes in diagnostic criteria. *Journal of Learning Disabilities, 46*(1), 5–25.

Tartaglia, N. R., Hansen, R. L., & Hagerman, R. J. (2007). Advances in genetics. In S. L. Odom, R. H. Horner, M. E. Snell, & J. Blacher (Eds.), *Handbook of developmental disabilities* (pp. 98–128). New York, NY: Guilford Press.

Taylor, B., Miller, E., Lingam, R., Andrews, N., Simmons, A., & Stowe, J. (2002). Measles, mumps, and rubella vaccination and bowel problems or developmental regression in children with autism: Population study. *British Medical Journal, 324*, 393–396.

Taylor, S. J. (2007). Editor's note. *Intellectual and Developmental Disabilities, 45*(1), ii.

Telecommunications for the Deaf and Hard of Hearing, Inc. (TDI). (2010). *TDI national directory & resource guide.* Silver Spring, MD: Author.

Terman, L., & Oden, M. (1947). *The gifted child grows up: Twenty-five-year follow-up of a superior group* (Vol. 4). Stanford, CA: Stanford University Press.

The National Consortium on Deaf-Blindness (2012). The 2011 national child count of children and youth who are deaf-blind. Monmouth, OR: The National Consortium on Deaf-Blindness, Teaching Research Division. Retrieved from http://www.nationaldb.org/documents/products/2007-Census-Tables.pdf

Third International Mathematics and Science Study. (1998). Washington, D.C.: U.S. Department of Education.

Thompson, J. R., Wehmeyer, M. L., & Hughes, C. (2010). Mind the gap! Implications of a person-environment fit model of intellectual disability for students, educators, and schools. *Exceptionality, 18*(4), 168–181.

Thompson, R. A., & Raikes, H. A. (2007). Early socioemotional development and the roots of school readiness. In J. Knitzer, R. Kaufmann, & D. Perry (Eds.), *Early childhood mental health.* Baltimore, MD: Paul H. Brookes Publishing Co, pp. 13–35.

Thompson, T. (2005). Paul E. Meehl and B. F. Skinner: Autotaxia, autotype and autism. *Behavioral Philosophy, 33*, 101–131.

Timler, G. R., Vogler-Elias, D., & McGill, K. F. (2007). Strategies for promoting generalization of social communication skills in preschoolers and school-aged children. *Topics in Language Disorders, 27*(2), 167–181.

Tomlinson, C. (2008). Differentiated instruction. In J. Plucker & C. Callahan (Eds.), *Critical issues and practices in gifted education* (pp. 167–178). Waco, TX: Prufrock Press.

Torgeson, J. K. (2009). The response to intervention instructional model: Some outcomes from a large-scale implementation in reading first schools. *Child Development Perspectives, 3*, 38–40.

Towles-Reeves, E., Kleinert, H., & Muhomba, M. (2009). Alternate assessment: Have we learned anything new? *Exceptional Children, 75*, 233–252.

Townes, T. M. (2008). Gene replacement therapy for sickle cell disease and other blood disorders. In *Hematology*. Retrieved from asheducationbook.hematologylibrary.org

Treffinger, D., Young, G., Selby, E., & Shepardson, C. (2002). *Assessing creativity: A guide for educators*. Storrs, CT: National Research Center on the Gifted and Talented.

Trends in International Math and Science Study – (TIMSS) (1998). Washington, D.C.: National Center for Educational Statistics.

Trezek, B. J., & Wang, Y. (2006). Implications of utilizing a phonics-based reading curriculum with children who are deaf or hard of hearing. *Journal of Deaf Studies and Deaf Education, 11*(2), 202–213.

Trezek, B. J., Wang, Y., Woods, D. G., Gampp, T. L., & Paul, P. V. (2007). Using visual phonics to supplement beginning reading instruction for students who are deaf or hard of hearing. *Journal of Deaf Studies and Deaf Education, 12*(3), 373–384.

Trivette, C. M., & Dunst, C. (2010). Evaluating family-based practices: Parenting experiences scale. *Young Exceptional Children, 7*(3), 12–19.

Turnbull, A., & Turnbull, H. (2002). From the old to the new paradigm of disabilities and families. In J. Paul, C. Lavely, A. Cranston-Gingras, & E. Taylor (Eds.), *Rethinking professional issues in special education* (pp. 83–118). Westbrook, CT: Ablex.

Turnbull, A., Zuna, N., Turnbull, H., Poston, D., & Summers, J. (2007). Families as partners in educational decision making: Current implementation and future directions. In S. Odom, B. Horner, M. Snell, & J. Blacher (Eds.), *Handbook of developmental disabilities* (pp. 570–590). New York, NY: Guilford Press.

Turnbull, A. P., Turbiville, V. & Turnbull, H. R. (2000). Evolution of family-professional partnership models: Collective empowerment as the model for the early 21st century. In S. J. Meisels & J. P. Shonkoff (Eds.), *Handbook of Early Intervention* (pp. 630–650). New York: Cambridge University Press.

Turnbull, A. P., & Turnbull, H. R. (1997). *Families, professionals, and exceptionality: A special partnership* (3rd ed.). Upper Saddle River, NJ: Merrill.

Turnbull, A. P., & Turnbull, H. R. (2004). *Individuals with Disabilities Education Act: Resources for Educators*. Paper presented at the Conference on Equity, Community, and Social Justice for Urban Students. New York, NY.

Turnbull, A. P., & Turnbull, H. R. (2006). *Families, professionals and exceptionality: A special partnership*. Upper Saddle River, NJ: Pearson/Merrill-Prentice Hall.

Turnbull, H., Stowe, M., Turnbull, A., & Schrandt, M. (2007). Public policy and developmental disabilities: A 35-year retrospective and a 5-year prospective based on the core concepts of disability policy. In S. Odom, B. Horner, M. Snell, & J. Blacher (Eds.), *Handbook of developmental disabilities* (pp. 15–34). New York, NY: Guilford Press.

Tuttle, D., & Tuttle, N. (2000). Psychosocial needs of children and youths. In M. C. Holbrook & A. J. Koenig (Eds.), *Foundations of education: Vol. 1. History and theory of teaching children and youths with visual impairments* (2nd ed., p. 167). New York, NY: AFB Press.

Tuttle, D., & Tuttle, N. (2004). *Self-esteem and adjusting with blindness: The process of responding to life's demands* (3rd ed.). Springfield, IL: Charles C. Thomas.

Twachtman-Cullen, D. (2000). Moveable children with autism spectrum disorders. In A. Wetherby & B. Prizant (Eds.), *Autism spectrum disorders: A transactional developmental perspective* (pp. 225–250). Baltimore, MD: Brookes.

Unger, D., Tressell, P., Jones, C. W., & Park, E. (2004). Involvement of low-income single caregivers in child-focused early intervention services: Implications for caregiver-child interaction. *Family Relations, 53*(2), 210–218.

University of Sheffield. (2010, June 10). Novel gene replacement therapy holds promise for spinal muscular atrophy. Retrieved from http://www.news-medical.net/news/20100610/Novel-gene-replacement-therapy-holds-promise-for-Spinal-Muscular-Atrophy.aspx.

U.S. Department of Education, National Center for Education Statistics. (2009). *Indicators of school crime and safety: 2009*. Washington, D.C.: U.S. Government Printing Office.

U.S. Department of Education, National Center for Education Statistics. (2009). *The condition of education 2004* (NCES 2004–077). Washington, D.C.: U.S. Government Printing Office.

U.S. Department of Education, Office of Special Education Programs (2004). *Individuals with Disabilities Education Improvement Act of 2004*. Washington, D.C.

U.S. Department of Education, Office of Special Education Programs. (2008a). *Identifying and treating attention deficit hyperactivity disorder: A resource for school and home*. Washington, D.C.: Author.

U.S. Department of Education, Office of Special Education Programs. (2008b). *Teaching children with attention deficit hyperactivity disorder: Instructional strategies and practices*. Washington, D.C.: Author.

U.S. Department of Education, Office of Special Education Programs, Data Analysis System (DANS). (2011). Children with disabilities receiving special education under part B of the Individuals with Disabilities Education Act. Washington, D.C.: Author.

U.S. Department of Education, Office of Special Education Programs. (2013). *Child find*. Retrieved from http://www.childfindidea.org/

U.S. Department of Health and Human Services, Administration for Children and Families, Administration on Children, Youth and Families, Children's Bureau. (2006). *Child Maltreatment 2004. Retrieved from http://www.acf.hhs.gov/programs/cb/pubs/cm04*

U.S. Department of Health and Human Services, Administration for Children and Families, Administration on Children, Youth and Families, Children's Bureau. (2012). *Child Maltreatment 2011*. Available from http://www.acf.hhs.gov/programs/cb/research-data-technology/statistics-research/child-maltreatment.

Valdez, K., Williamson, C., & Wagner, M. (1990). *The national longitudinal study of special education students. Statistical almanac: Vol. 3. Youth categorized as emotionally disturbed*. Menlo Park, CA: SRI International.

VanDerHeyden, A. M., & Snyder, P. (2006). Integrating frameworks from early childhood intervention and school psychology to accelerate growth for all young children. *School Psychology Review, 35*, 519–534.

Van Tassel-Baska, J. (Ed.). (2004). *Curriculum of gifted and talented students*. Thousand Oaks, CA: Corwin Press.

Van Tassel-Baska, J. (2008). *Alternative Assessment with Gifted and Talented Students*. Waco: TX: Prufrock Press.

VanTassel-Baska, J. (Ed). (2013). *Using the Common Core State Standards for English language arts with gifted and advanced learners*. Waco, TX: Prufrock Press.

Vaughn, S., & Fuchs, L. (2003). Redefining learning disabilities as inadequate response to instruction: The promise and potential problem. *Learning Disabilities Research and Practice, 18*(3), 137–146.

Vellutino, F. R., Scanlon, D. M., Sipay, E. R., Small, S. G., Pratt, A., Chen, R., et al. (1996). Cognitive profiles of difficult-to-remediate and readily remediated poor readers: Early intervention as a vehicle for distinguishing between cognitive and experiential deficits as basic cause of specific reading disability. *Journal of Educational Psychology, 88*(4), 601–638.

Verret, C., Gauy, M-C., Berthiaume, C., Gardiner, P., & Beliveau, L. (2012). A physical activity program improves behavior and cognitive functions in children with ADHD: An exploratory study. *Journal of Attention Disorders, 16*(1), 71–80.

Villegas, A. M., & Lucas, T. (2002). Preparing culturally responsive teachers: Rethinking the curriculum. *Journal of Teacher Education, 53*, 20–32.

Vincent, C. G., Swain-Bradway, J., Tobin, T. J., & May, S. (2011). Disciplinary referrals for culturally and linguistically diverse students with and without disabilities: Patterns resulting from school-wide positive behavior support. *Exceptionality, 19*(3), 175–190.

Voeltz, L. (1980). Children's attitudes toward handicapped peers. *American Journal of Mental Deficiency, 84*, 455–464.

Volkmar, F., Paul, R., Klin, A., & Cohen, D. (2007). *Handbook of autism and pervasive developmental disabilities* (3rd ed). New York, NY: Wiley.

Wallace, T., Anderson A., Bartholomay, T., & Hupp, S. (2002). An ecobehavioral examination of high school classrooms that include students with disabilities. *Exceptional Children, 68*, 345–360.

Ward, D. (2008). The aetiology and treatment of developmental stammering in childhood. *Archives of Disease in Childhood, 93*, 68–71.

Ward, L., & McCune, S. (2002). The first weeks of life. In M. Batshaw (Ed.), *Children with disabilities* (5th ed., pp. 69–84). Baltimore, MD: Brookes.

Watson, A. H., Ito, M., Smith, R. O., & Anderson, L. T. (2010). Effort of assistive technology in a public school setting. *American Journal of Occupational Therapy, 64*(1), 18–29.

Webb, J., Gore, J., Amend, E., & DeVries, A. (2007). *A parent's guide to gifted children*. Scottsdale, AZ: Great Potential Press.

Wehmeier, P. M., Schacht, A., & Barkley, R. A. (2010). Social and emotional impairment in children and adolescents with ADHD and the impact on quality of life. *Journal of Adolescent Health, 46*, 209–217.

Wehmeyer, M. (2006). Self-determination and individuals with severe disabilities: Reexamining meanings and interpretations. *Research and Practice in Severe Disabilities, 30*, 113–120.

Wehmeyer, M. L. (2011). Assessment and intervention in self-determination. *Advances in Learning and Behavioral Disabilities, 24*, 213–249.

Wehmeyer, M., & Schwartz, M. (1998). The relationship between self-determination and quality of life. *Education and Training in Mental Retardation and Developmental Disabilities, 33*, 3–12.

Weisz, J. (1999). Cognitive performance and learned helplessness in mentally retarded persons. In E. Zigler & D. Bennett-Gates (Eds.), *Personality development in individuals with mental retardation* (pp. 17–46). New York, NY: Cambridge University Press.

Werner, E. E. (2000). Protective factors and individual resilience. In J. P. Shonkoff & S. J. Meisels (Eds.), *Handbook of early childhood intervention* (2nd ed., pp. 115–132). New York, NY: Cambridge University Press.

Werner, E. E., & Smith, R. S. (1992). *Overcoming the odds: High risk children from birth to adulthood*. Ithaca, NY: Cornell University Press.

Werner, E. E., & Smith, R. S. (2001). *Journeys from childhood to midlife: Risk, resilience,and recovery*. Ithaca, NY: Cornell University Press.

Wery, J., & Nietfeld, J. (2010). Supporting self-regulated learning with exceptional children. *Teaching Exceptional Children, 42*(4), 70–78.

West, T. (2011). RTI approaches to early intervening supports. *Perspectives on Language and Literacy, 37*(3), 17–20.

Whitten, E., Esteves, K., & Woodrow, A. (2009). *RTI success: Proven tools and strategies for schools and classrooms*. Minneapolis, MN: Free Spirit Book Publishing.

Wickenden, M. (2011). Talking to teenagers: Using anthropological methods to explore identity and the lifeworlds of young people who use AAC. *Communication Disorders Quarterly, 32*, 151–163.

Wiener, N. (1953). *Exprodigy: My childhood and youth*. New York, NY: Simon and Schuster.

Wilcox, M. J., Gray, S. I., Guimond, A. B., & Lafferty, A. E. (2011). Efficacy on the TELL language and literacy curriculum for preschoolers with developmental speech and/or language impairment. *Early Childhood Research Quarterly, 26*, 278–294.

Willingham, D. (2008). When and how neuroscience applies to education. *Phi Delta Kappan, 89*(6), 421–423.

Willis, J. (2008). Building a bridge from neuroscience to the classroom. *Phi Delta Kappan, 89*(6), 424–427.

Winerman, L. (2005). The mind's mirror. *Monitor on Psychology, 36*(9), 1–5.

Wolgemuth, J. R., Cobb, R. B., & Alwell, M. (2008). The effects of mnemonic interventions on academic outcomes for youth with disabilities: A systematic review. *Learning Disabilities Research & Practice, 23*(1), 1–10.

Wong, B. (Ed.). (2004). *Learning about learning disabilities* (3rd ed.). New York, NY: Academic Press.

Wood, L., Lasker, J., Siegel-Causey, E., Beukelman, D., & Ball, L. (1998). An input framework for augmentative and alternative communication. *Augmentative and Alternative Communication, 14*, 261–267.

Workgroup on Principles and Practices in Natural Environments, OSEP TA Community of Practice: Part C Settings. (2008, March). *Seven key principles: Looks like / doesn't look like*. Retrieved from http://www.ectacenter.org/~pdfs/topics/families/Principles_LooksLike_DoesntLookLike3_11_08.pdf

Xu, Y. (2008). Developing meaningful IFSP outcomes through a family-centered approach: The ABCX model. *Young Exceptional Children, 12*(1), 2–19.

Yamaki, K., & Fugiura, G. (2002). Employment and income status of adults with developmental disabilities living in the community. *Mental Retardation, 40*(2), 132–144.

Yell, M., Katsiyannis, A., and Bradley, M. (2011). The Individuals with Disabilities Education Act: The evaluation of special education law. In J. M. Kauffman & D. P. Hallahan (Eds.), *Handbook of special education*. New York, NY: Routledge.

Yirmiya, N., Erel, O., Shaked, M., & Solomonica-Levi, D. (1998). Meta-analysis comparing theory of mind abilities of individuals with autism, individuals with mental retardation, and normally developing individuals. *Psychological Bulletin, 124*, 283–307.

Zablocki, M. & Krezminen, M. P. (2013). Drop-out predictors among students with high-incidence disabilities: A national longitudinal and transitional study 2 analysis. *Journal of Disability Policy Studies, 24*(1), 53–64.

Zang, D., Katsiyannis, A., & Kortering, L. J. (2007). Performance on exit exams by students with disabilities: A four-year analysis. *Career Development for Exceptional Individuals, 30*(1), 48–57.

Zebehazy, K. T., Zigmond, N., & Zimmerman, G. J. (2012). Performance measurement and accommodation: Students with visual impairments on Pennsylvania's Alternate Assessment. *Journal of Visual Impairment & Blindness, 106*, 17–30.

Zeitlin, S., & Williamson, G. (1994). *Coping in young children*. Baltimore, MD: Brookes.

Zero to Three. (2009). *Early Childhood Mental Health.* Retrieved from www.zerotothree.org/site/PageServer?pagename=key_mental_health

Zigler, E., Finn-Stevenson, M., & Hall, N. (2003). *The first three years and beyond: Brain development and social policy*. New Haven, CT: Yale University Press.

Zigler, E., & Styfco, S. (2004). Head Start's national reporting system: A work in progress. *Pediatrics, 114*, 858–859.

Zigmond, N., Kloo, A., & Volonino, V. (2009). What, where, how? Special education in the climate of full inclusion. *Exceptionality, 17*, 189–204.

Zimmerman, B. J., & Schunk, D. H. (2008). Motivation: An essential dimension of self-regulated learning. In D. Schunk & B. J. Zimmerman (Eds) *Motivation and self-regulated learning: Theory, research, and applications* (pp. 1–30). New York/London: Lawrence Erlbaum Associates.

Zimmerman, G. J., & Zebehazy, K. T. (2011). Blindness and low vision. In J. M. Kauffman & D. P. Hallahan (Eds.), *Handbook of special education* (pp. 247–261). New York: Routledge.

Zirkel, P.A. (2013). The Hale position for a "third method" for specific learning disabilities identification: A legal analysis. *Learning Disability Quarterly, 36*, 93–96.

Subject Index

Name Index

Standard 6 Professional Learning and Ethical Practice

Beginning special education professionals use foundational knowledge of the field and professional Ethical Principles and Practice Standards to inform special education practice, to engage in lifelong learning, and to advance the profession.

6.1 Beginning special education professionals use professional Ethical Principles and Professional Practice Standards to guide their practice.

6.2 Beginning special education professionals understand how foundational knowledge and current issues influence professional practice.

6.3 Beginning special education professionals understand that diversity is a part of families, cultures, and schools, and that complex human issues can interact with the delivery of special education services.

6.4 Beginning special education professionals understand the significance of lifelong learning and participate in professional activities and learning communities.

6.5 Beginning special education professionals advance the profession by engaging in activities such as advocacy and mentoring.

6.6 Beginning special education professionals provide guidance and direction to paraeducators, tutors, and volunteers.

Standard 7 Collaboration

Beginning special education professionals collaborate with families, other educators, related service providers, individuals with exceptionalities, and personnel from community agencies in culturally responsive ways to address the needs of individuals with exceptionalities across a range of learning experiences.

7.1 Beginning special education professionals use the theory and elements of effective collaboration.

7.2 Beginning special education professionals serve as a collaborative resource to colleagues.

7.3 Beginning special education professionals use collaboration to promote the well-being of individuals with exceptionalities across a wide range of settings and collaborators.

Source: National Council for the Accreditation of Teacher Education (2012). Washington, DC: Author. Retrieved from http://www.cec.sped.org/Standards/Special-Educator-Professional-Preparation/CEC-Initial-and-Advanced-Preparation-Standards